Pitt Latin American Series

The Constitution of
TYRANNY

Regimes of Exception in
SPANISH AMERICA

Brian Loveman

UNIVERSITY OF PITTSBURGH PRESS

Pittsburgh and London

Published by the University of Pittsburgh Press, Pittsburgh, Pa., 15260
Copyright © 1993, University of Pittsburgh Press
All rights reserved
Manufactured in the United States of America
Printed on acid-free paper

Library of Congress Cataloging-in-Publication Data

Loveman, Brian.
    The constitution of tyranny : regimes of exception in Spanish
America / Brian Loveman.
        p.   cm. — (Pitt Latin American series)
    Includes bibliographical references and index.
    ISBN 0-8229-3766-2 (alk. paper)
    ISBN 0-8229-5536-9 (pbk.)
    1. Latin America—Constitutional history.   2. Latin America—
Politics and government—19th century.   3. Executive power—Latin
America—History—19th century.   4. Civil-military relations—Latin
America—History—19th century.   5. Latin America—Armed Forces—
Political activity—History—19th century.   I. Title.   II. Series.
JL952.L68   1993
351.003'22'09809034—dc20   93-28177
                                                                    CIP

A CIP catalogue record for this book is available from the British Library.
Eurospan, London

The accumulation of all powers, legislative, executive, and judiciary, in the same hands, whether of one, a few, or many, and whether hereditary, self-appointed, or elective, may justly be pronounced the very definition of tyranny.   —*James Madison*

But where the peril is of such proportions that the machinery of the law is an actual obstacle in dealing with it, then a single ruler must be appointed who can reduce all law to silence and temporarily suspend the sovereign authority. In a case of this kind the general will is not in doubt, and it is obvious that the People's first concern must be to see that the State shall not perish.   —*J. J. Rousseau*

Now in a well-ordered republic it should never be necessary to resort to extra-constitutional measures; for although they may for the time be beneficial, yet the precedent is pernicious, for if the practice is once established of disregarding the laws for good objects, they will in a little while be disregarded under that pretext for evil purposes. Thus no republic will ever be perfect if she has not by law provided for everything, having a remedy for every emergency, and fixed rules for applying it.
                                                           —*Machiavelli*

Contents

Acknowledgments

MY INTEREST IN SPANISH AMERICAN POLITICS OWES MUCH TO JAMES Scobie, a brilliant and exacting historian whose memory and rigorous standards are a constant inspiration. Over twenty-five years ago Vincent Ostrom inspired a concern for the importance of the rule of law, constitutions, and constitutional choice that frames *The Constitution of Tyranny.*

Generous colleagues have read part or all of this manuscript and made numerous suggestions for its improvement. They include Paul Drake, Iván Jaksić, David Bushnell, Judy Ewell, Thomas Davies, Paul Vanderwood, Gonzalo Palacios, Mark Burkholder, Lars Schoultz, Eric Van Young, Phil Flemion, Augusto Varas, David Rock, Mathew McCubbins, Peter Gourevitch, and Vincent Ostrom. None of them except Iván Jaksić is responsible for any errors of fact or interpretation that remain.

Heidi Beirich provided invaluable research assistance and critical comments, prepared the tables, and shared a sense of humor that more than once salvaged an otherwise abominable day. Karolyn Schwind proofread the manuscript, adding more to its final form than is customary in such a tedious assignment.

A special thanks goes to Elizabeth Cullen for the most wonderful, creative, supportive, and witty editing and critical review— mixed with an insatiable resolve to delete extra words (or the wrong ones)—I have ever encountered. She was unable to overcome entirely my bad habits, inconsistency, and profane affinity for gastronomical and theatrical metaphors, but readers owe her an unpayable debt (as do I) for whatever clarity, shortening of sentences, and extirpation of metaphoric (and other) excesses that she imposed on the lengthy manuscript.

ix

Part 1

Introduction

THIS IS A BOOK ABOUT LATIN AMERICAN POLITICS AND CONSTITU-
tions in the nineteenth century. It is also a book about the importance of symbols, the reality of fiction, and the durability of political
beliefs, institutions, and practices.

In the late eighteenth century, two great political revolutions
against absolute monarchy and colonialism marked the beginning
of a new era. In the former British colonies that became the United
States of America, and also in France, the new era was demarcated
and consecrated by constitutions that sought to limit government
authority. The hegemony of governments legitimated by divine
right, claiming absolutist power to achieve the "common good," had
ended. A new political religion, liberalism, claimed legitimacy in
"natural rights" and "the people"; it elaborated its claims in political
constitutions.

Constitutions are legal charters that specify the formula for
government of a polity. They are also secular sacraments, philosophical proclamations, moral commitments, and the result of compromise, violence, and war. Since the independence of the Anglo-
American colonies from Britain and since the French Revolution
political elites in Europe and the Americas sought legitimacy for
governments by claiming adherence to constitutional principles.
These included popular sovereignty and guarantees of civil rights
and liberties such as freedom of assembly, speech, association, religion, and the press.

In the name of popular sovereignty and in "defense of the constitutional order," however, governments in Europe and the Americas sought to legitimate barbaric repression of adversaries, to
justify the unjustifiable, and to legalize slavery, slaughter, and
mayhem.[1] Constitutions replaced religious principles, faith, and di-

3

vine right as the foundations of politics in the Occident. They often proved equally useful in sanctifying intolerance.

Constitutions also provided, in a few instances, legitimacy and design for limited government, expansion of human liberty, and the possibility of a society in which citizens, in the words of Alexis de Tocqueville, "would feel an equal love and respect for the laws of which they consider themselves the authors; in which the authority of government would be respected as necessary, and not divine."[2]

In Latin America this has rarely occurred. When the independence movements of the early nineteenth century overturned the divinely inspired law of the Spanish kings, the liberal principles of France, Britain, and the United States usually failed as replacements. From 1811, Spanish American constitutions claimed liberal inspiration, but they usually established Catholicism as the state religion, and freedom of public worship for non-Catholics was not common. The press laws of the early nineteenth century significantly restricted freedom of the press, allowing a priori or a posteriori censorship. They also prescribed severe penalties for offending the church and inciting public disorder or subversion.

The enumeration of civil liberties and rights was routinely accompanied, in constitutions, legislation, and decrees, by provisions for their suspension or restriction in times of political crisis. Penal codes and state security decrees detailed numerous political crimes, including offending the honor of government and military officials, and subjected civilians to military tribunals. Sometimes this entailed summary execution for threatening internal order or for high treason (*lesa nación*).

In the first seventy or more years after independence, Spanish Americans wrote constitutions proclaiming popular sovereignty while military officers, brigands, would-be national saviors, and aristocrats sought to impose order on peoples tormented by despotism, instability, and misery. Called caudillos, these personalistic leaders of small military bands or national armies came and went in Mexico, Central America, the Caribbean, and South America.[3]

The caudillos claimed to be liberals or conservatives, federalists or centralists, anticlericals or clericals, glorifying with high-sounding principles the quest for power and dominance. Cynicism and opportunism prevailed. In the words of a priest in Gabriel García Marquez's novel *One Hundred Years of Solitude:* "This is silly; the defenders of the faith of Christ destroy the church and the Masons order it rebuilt." Caudillos battled for power, but they never seemed able to pacify the former Spanish colonies, to overcome the class and racial inequities that had evolved since 1492, to consolidate a political order with (returning to Tocqueville) "every individual in possession of rights which he is sure to retain."

Why dream that such a political order would emerge in Spanish America? Why impose upon these new nations the burden of securing rights and liberties rarely enjoyed? One good reason is that this was the dream, the promise, the passion, and the rhetoric of Spanish American political elites in the nineteenth century. They shared this dream with North American and European liberals, even when they meant it to apply, like their European and North American counterparts, only to the affluent, the educated, the male, and the noncolored.

At first civil liberties and rights, protection of property, and limits on government authority were matters of intraelite concern. As Domingo Faustino Sarmiento, the great liberal educator, philosopher, and president (1868–1874) of Argentina put it: "The constitution of the popular masses is the ordinary law, the judges, the security police. It is the educated classes who need a Constitution that assures their liberty of action and thought."[4] With time, however, the scope of the dream expanded to include most or all of the population: extending the dream—that is, democratizing society and politics—remains the declared goal of Latin American political leaders in the twentieth century.

Spanish Americans proclaimed these dreams from the moment of independence. Even those nineteenth-century caudillos who had no attachment to constitutional principles felt compelled to prepare new charters or review old ones—"succession constitutions"—to justify their caprice and legitimate their personalist rule.

The constitutions they wrote both reflect the dream of liberty and contain its negation. Many Latin American leaders recognized the socioeconomic and institutional obstacles to constitutional democracy. They sought to overcome them and failed. These obstacles included racial and class antagonisms, great inequalities of wealth and income, concentration of land and power in the hands of a small ruling elite, the vestiges of the monarchical tradition and the powers of king, viceroy, captain-general, and intendant appropriated by Latin American presidents, and the quasi-autonomy and privileges of the Catholic church and military. They also came to include in their constitutions provisions for suspension, denial, suppression, and evasion of those rights and liberties that each individual is "sure to retain."

Latin American constitutions almost always included provisions for "emergency powers," or "extraordinary powers" (*facultades extraordinarias*), to be used in times of internal strife or external threat. These powers might be exercised by presidents, military officers, police, and even judges. They might be conferred by legislatures, councils of ministers, and presidents when "the fatherland is in danger," when there is "internal commotion" (*conmoción interna*), or when the government "is threatened by sedition or rebellion." Under these conditions, the constitutions provided for *regimes of exception*; normal constitutional protections were suspended, rights and liberties were temporarily voided, and the government's authority was greatly expanded.

Much of Latin America experienced unremitting rebellion and civil war in the nineteenth century. Appeal to extraordinary powers became a habit. Regimes of exception sometimes permitted constitutional dictatorship. Even when strict interpretation of the constitution might argue against exercising such powers, the lines between constitutional dictatorship and usurpation were fuzzy. In practice, liberalism and authoritarianism merged; dictators and constitutional presidents executed opponents, sent adversaries into exile, censored the press, jailed and abused authors and publishers, and confiscated property—in short, ruled their nations with virtually absolute authority. They usually did this, however, in accord with the constitutions that purportedly guaranteed civil liberties, civil rights, and popular sovereignty.

Military force made authoritarian liberalism possible. The privileges and immunities (*fueros*) carried over from the colonial era often exempted military officers from civilian courts; control of military garrisons and armories was the difference between presidents and corpses. Here too, constitutions played an important role. The constitutions of independent Spanish America charged the military with protecting the political system, conserving internal order, defending the government against internal subversion, and maintaining law and order. In effect, the military became a fourth branch of government, with constitutionally defined status and a political mission. With some exceptions, the military retained the colonial *fueros* and expanded tremendously its political role. Almost any coup, any barracks revolt, or any local uprising could be justified as an effort to preserve the constitution or restore constitutional government purportedly threatened by government abuses. Latin American constitutions invited, indeed demanded, military participation in politics.

Authoritarian government, military rule, intolerance, and violence all found constitutional rationale. Admittedly, some dictators and caudillos mocked the constitutions, but most claimed to defend them against the enemies of liberty, law, and order. By the end of the nineteenth century, no Spanish American nation lacked a history of revolts, civil war, and military participation in politics, or a legal foundation for constitutional dictatorship.

Clauses in constitutions providing for regimes of exception did not cause violence and dictatorship. Nor did militarism originate in the nineteenth-century charters. Moreover, Spanish Americans shared the burden of regional, ethnic, and racial conflicts, civil war, and the struggle to establish legitimate political institutions with most of western Europe and the United States in the nineteenth century. While this study focuses on the constitutional experiments of Spain's former colonies, parallel studies of Spain, France, Italy, Germany, Portugal, and the United States would find regimes of exception, methods of repressing ethnic and religious minorities, political opposition to rising labor movements, and claims of defending the constitutional order. Just as the modes of political, racial, ethnic, and class repression adopted by the United States and European nations in the nineteenth century have shaped twentieth-century development—indeed, have reemerged ferociously in the 1980s and 1990s—so the political solutions of Spanish America in the nineteenth century molded twentieth-century patterns of civil-military relations and political tyranny from Mexico to the Strait of Magellan.

This applies especially to constitutional regimes of exception, to criminalizing certain types of political opposition as threats to internal security of the state, and to the central role of the armed forces in politics. Incorporating provisions for regimes of exception into the legal and political culture of Spanish America made them invisible yet hegemonic premises of political life. By custom, by law, by practice, and by reaffirmation, intolerance, inquisitorial suppression of opposition, constitutional dictatorship, and militarism became everyday ingredients of Latin American politics. Constitutional debates, reforms, and litigation strengthened the underlying premises that regimes of exception were the building blocks of constitutional government, the necessary counterpart of civil liberties and rights if order were to be maintained.

A number of shared socioeconomic circumstances reinforced these underlying premises in the nineteenth century: the vulnerability of Spanish American economies to international economic cycles, slavery and neofeudal conditions in much of the countryside, and the multifaceted impact of increased urbanization and of technological revolutions in transportation, communication, and industry. Despite these similarities, differences among the Spanish American nations in socioeconomic structure, race relations, elite cohesiveness, and the evolution of political parties, labor movements, and government institutions contributed to the variations in the design and use of regimes of exception and to distinctive political roles of the armed forces. Important differences in civil-military relations and political development occurred, for example, between Costa Rica and most of Central America and between Chile and Colombia and the rest of South America. Notwithstanding these differences, however, universal reliance on constitutional regimes of exception provided a common foundation for Spanish American politics.

Nineteenth-century political history gave way to World War I, the Great Depression of the 1930s, World War II, and the cold war. Press laws now focused on "communist" literature and repression of so-called subversives or Marxist revolutionaries instead of liberals, conservatives, or socialists. Repression of opponents from the "political class" expanded to deal with new political enemies and threats to "internal security." The labor movement, political parties, and opposition social movements replaced the personalist or clerical and anticlerical factions of the nineteenth century.

The constitutional foundations for repression, exile, trial of civilians in military courts, newspaper closures, dissolution of Congress, and internal war—albeit updated somewhat with new laws for protecting the internal security of the state—were the legacy of the liberals and conservatives of the nineteenth century. The extraordinary powers extended to presidents, the state of siege or state of assembly imposed to smash the so-called threats to state security, the exemptions of military personnel from punishment for "abuses" (torture, murder, rape) that occurred in internal war or internal commotion—or their protection from prosecution by civilian courts by virtue of their *fueros*—all stemmed from constitutional and legal development in the nineteenth century.

Detailed narration of such constitutional development is risky. Paragraphs describing constitutional provisions, amendments, derogations, and reforms may lull the reader into a drowsy indifference. Even the accompanying political history, the struggles for power, the clash of principles, and the meanness and brutality of nineteenth-century politics in Spanish America seem hardly enough to sustain attention to the numbing succession of constitutional clauses reciting provisions for regimes of exception and conferring a political role on the armed forces.

Although I have tried, I do not know how to overcome this problem entirely, except to say that the clauses I discussed, or those like them, are the constitutional foundation for tyranny almost everywhere in Latin America today—even where elected civilian governments rather than personalist dictators or military juntas preside, as occurred generally in the 1980s and early 1990s.

In the last decade of the twentieth century, regimes of exception, the relative autonomy and constitutional mission of the military, and an associated political culture of intolerance represent entrenched challenges to democratization and pervasive threats to effective exercise of civil liberties and rights. The constitutional foundations of nineteenth-century authoritarian liberalism, modified only slightly, persist; the salvational mission of the armed forces, the draconian codes of military justice applied to civilians who "threaten national security," the lack of autonomy of the judiciary, and the fragility of civil liberties and rights (*garantías*) impede real democratization in Latin America.

No elections, no delicately orchestrated set of presidential musical chairs, and no transitions from authoritarian to elected governments will succeed in consolidating constitutional democracy without drastic reform of these constitutional foundations of tyranny bequeathed by liberals and conservatives in the nineteenth century and reaffirmed by social democrats, corporatists, Christian democrats, and revolutionaries in the twentieth.

It is time to investigate the origins of these constitutional foundations of tyranny. It is also time to reassess the rationale for and consequences of such provisions. And it is time to overcome the legacy of imperial Spain, the French Revolution, the Spanish liberals of the nineteenth century, and the authoritarian liberalism of Latin America. The following chapters may contribute to the first two of these objectives; political leaders and social movements in Latin America will have to do the rest.

1

Constitutional Government and Regimes of Exception

CONFRONTED WITH PROTESTS AND STREET DEMONSTRATIONS BY THE urban poor, merchants and industrialists fear for the future. Rural turmoil disconcerts landowners fearful of peasant demands for land or the unionization of agricultural workers. Rising prices, declines in real wages, and a devalued currency contribute to heightened social tensions.

The worsening economic conditions are accompanied by political polarization. Relations between government supporters and opponents deteriorate; social conviviality disappears. Anger, frustration, impatience, acrimonious name-calling, and escalating threats destroy the veneer of civility. Government authority and the customary compliance with social norms is lost. Diffuse clamor for change and peaceful protests give way to demonstrations and disorder. Frustration culminates in violence. Looters vandalize shops, hurling insults and rocks at police. Public and private vehicles are attacked and destroyed. Wall slogans call for justice but also, ominously, for the restoration of law and order. Anger at government failure to resolve the economic and political crises destroys any disposition to tolerance.

The inability of political leaders to dissuade crowds from disorderly conduct or to persuade the powerful and wealthy to make concessions that might restore tranquility, even if temporarily, appears to leave repression as the only recourse. By government order, by default, or against the will of the administration, the police and the military quell the civil disturbances.

The corpses of unlucky civilians, strikers, and protesters litter the streets. Dazed wounded flee. Police and combat-outfitted troops kick and curse cowering prisoners sprawled on the pavement, loading them onto open trucks and paddy wagons. Some prisoners never reach their destination; they resist, they fail to resist, they are killed "attempting to escape."

But most of the disheveled captives arrive at impromptu detention centers for processing and interrogation. In some cases the government ferrets out the "leaders" of the disturbances to prevent further troubles or to mete out exemplary punishment. Simultaneously, palliative measures such as price controls, retraction of unpopular policies, rollbacks of price increases for public transportation or bread, and emergency distribution of food may be introduced to quell the unrest.

Perhaps the government or armed forces act under the authority of the ancient doctrine of civil necessity ("salus publica suprema lex," public safety, the supreme law) or, as in the British tradition, according to common-law precepts regarding the obligation of the forces of order and private citizens to assist in repressing civil disorders. Based on the premise that the state "must have every facility and the widest latitude in defending itself against destruction," repressive actions by government officials violate the rights and liberties enjoyed by citizens in "normal" times. These repressive measures are justified only "in order to preserve the society" that guarantees the rights and liberties now suspended temporarily.[1] As soon as the threat to society and public order is eliminated—that is, the rioters dispersed, the looting stopped, the political or military danger overcome—government authorities are again liable for their actions under customary or common law.

Since the American and French revolutions in the late eighteenth century, government emergency powers, including repression of disturbances or threats to public order, have been justified by activating previously contemplated constitutional provisions and statutes. In accord with the constitution, all or part of existing constitutional procedures and individual guarantees are suspended. At the same time, government authority is enhanced and often redistributed, for example, from legislative to executive officials or from civilian to military authorities. This creates a regime of exception, a legal and political order for times of crisis.

A regime of exception goes beyond the routine political repression associated with the British common law on seditious libel or the 1798 United States Sedition Law that punished public criticism of government officials or policy as a crime.[2] It also goes beyond the typical European and Latin American penal codes of the nineteenth century that outlawed a priori various forms of religious expression, political doctrines, and political behavior, including party and union organization, while also restricting press freedom. Whether in response to economic or political crisis or a natural disaster, a regime of exception enhances or reassigns normal government authority while curtailing temporarily certain civil liberties and rights. In some instances it entirely suspends constitutional guarantees and procedures during the emergency.

Perhaps the best-known regime of exception clause in the twentieth century is Article 48 of the German Weimar Constitution—a provision often cited as a juridical foundation for the Nazi dictatorship that emerged in the early 1930s. Like many regime of exception clauses in nineteenth- and twentieth-century constitutions, Article 48 contained vague references to "disturbance" or "endangerment" of "public safety or order" as justification for suspension of constitutional guarantees and subordination of civilian authority to military authority. Like other provisions for regimes of exception, Article 48 gave to the executive broad and ill-defined authority to "take the measures necessary" to defend public order while militarizing implementation of public policy. It read, in part:

> If the public safety and order in the German Reich are seriously disturbed or endangered, the President of the Reich may take the measures necessary to the restoration of the public safety and order, and may if necessary intervene with the armed forces. To this end he may temporarily suspend in whole or in part the fundamental rights established in Articles 114 [inviolability of persons], 115 [inviolability of domicile], 117 [secrecy of communications], 118 [freedom of opinion and expression thereof], 123 [freedom of assembly], 124 [freedom of association], and 153 [inviolability of property]. . . . A national law shall prescribe the details.[3]

When the regime of exception is initiated by the executive or legislative authorities of the existing government, according to established laws and customs, there is little need for extrinsic legitimation of the emergency measures—beyond the existence in fact of the emergency. In the face of disorder or violence, or the threat of such, the government decrees partial or complete suspension of constitutional rights and liberties. This may be followed by the imposition of a juridically defined regime of exception such as state of siege or state of emergency.

Such an event, common in Latin American politics, might be justified as follows:

> This year, unlike any other in our recent history, produced grave breakdowns of public order, and the impact of the extremist violence brought grief and sorrow to many Salvadoran families. Agents of authority—judges, mayors, teachers, congressmen, and citizens from the most diverse sectors of the nation—fell victims at the hands of criminals.
>
> . . . Thus it was in the face of increased violence and disorder that we made use of the resource which the basic law of the republic provides—the suspension of constitutional guarantees—a situation we feel obligated to extend in view of the fact that the conditions which prompted its implementation still exist.[4]

When, rather than being decreed by the existing government, the regime of exception supplants the existing government or a new leadership asserts its claim to authority in the midst of the crisis, the new rulers typically issue proclamations justifying their actions. These declarations are at least partially intended to convince the population that the actions taken were necessary to salvage a desperate situation and are legal—that is, in accord with the contingencies specified in the existing constitutional and legislative texts concerning public authority in times of emergency. The declaration of the military junta that ousted Chilean President Salvador Allende in 1973 is illustrative:

> The Allende government has exceeded the bounds of legitimacy by violating the fundamental rights of liberty, of speech, and of education; the right to congregate, to strike, and to petition; the right to own property and, in general, the right to a worthy and stable existence. . . . The government has placed itself outside the law on multiple occasions; . . . the supreme authority has deliberately exceeded its attributes . . . gravely compromising the rights and liberties of all; . . . anarchy, stifling of liberties, moral and economic chaos . . . have led the country to ruin. . . .
>
> For the foregoing reasons the armed forces have taken upon themselves the moral duty, which the country imposes

upon them, of deposing the government, which, although legitimate in the early exercise of power, has since fallen into flagrant illegitimacy.[5]

In both the case of a temporary suspension of citizen rights and that of a declaration of a more comprehensive regime of exception, society is juridically in an emergency. In the face of a natural disaster or the threat of social and political breakdown, it mobilizes to meet the challenge. In the latter case, society is officially at war with its internal enemies, under siege, or in a state of emergency. Its actual existence or fundamental values and institutions are declared at risk. Those who speak for it claim the historical right of necessity, of social self-defense, the right to protect the established order against its adversaries and their collaborators. This right may mean defending the government against it opponents, or it may mean overturning the incumbent government, which has supposedly exceeded or failed to exert its authority and thereby undermined the legitimate institutional order.

Emergency conditions may require rapid, forceful, and effective response. Ordinary government procedures and capabilities may be insufficient to meet the crisis. Perhaps customary emergency measures consistent with traditional authority suffice. If not, perhaps new laws or decrees might be needed to provide a rationale for present action.

The need for special rules of government behavior in times of crisis is recognized in the Anglo-American legal tradition as well as in European systems. Through diffusion of these political traditions to colonies in Africa, Asia, and Latin America, regimes of exception made their appearance in the constitutions of new nations in the nineteenth and twentieth centuries.

A historical landmark in emergency legislation was the British Riot Act of 1714. Passed in response to the threat of violence by supporters of the Stuarts against the new Hanover monarchy, it authorized the forces of order to disperse, after proper warning, any group of twelve or more persons "riotously assembled." If, after an hour, the group failed to disperse, the army and any other subjects might be called upon to assist. Once called upon, the army and private citizens were immune from criminal or civil sanction for injuring or killing rioters.

This latter stipulation is critical, for it protects government officials from sanction for actions committed during the emergency. Under the special conditions mentioned—in this case, "reading the

Riot Act" and waiting an hour—government officials and their private collaborators were liberated from normal common-law restraints. They need show neither that the force used to stop felonious behavior was necessary, and no more than necessary, nor that all ordinary skill and caution were exercised so as to do no more harm than could be reasonable avoided.[6] Under the provisions of the Riot Act a felony had been committed by those who failed to disperse, thereby justifying whatever action was being taken by the forces of order.

> Our Sovereign Lord the king chargeth and commandeth all persons being assembled, immediately to disperse themselves, and peaceably to depart to their habitations, or to their lawfull business, upon the pains contained in the Act made in the first year of King George the First, for preventing tumults and riotous assemblies. God save the King.
> . . . And if any of the persons so unlawfully assembled happen to be killed, maimed or hurt in the dispersing, seizing or apprehending, or endeavouring to disperse, seize or apprehend them, by reason of their resisting, the justices constables shall be fully indemnified for any such killing or hurting.

Once riots, public disorder, social protests, or other menaces to law and order become likely, even if infrequent, procedures for managing such situations become a public concern. In the case of the Riot Act, it was decided to go beyond the previous periodic suspensions of habeas corpus by parliament and to indemnify, a priori, supporters of government authority against excesses prohibited by common law.

Although prototypical of one sort of narrow emergency legislation, the Riot Act did not suspend citizens' rights or liberties nor alter the fundamental distribution of political authority. Likewise, it did not modify the political regime. For example, it did not shift legislative authority from Parliament to the Crown nor did it assign broad emergency powers to the executive. It did not assign political prerogatives to military institutions or subject civilians to military law and tribunals, nor did it delegate political authority to special commissions or executive officers. It merely shielded officials from liability for repression under special conditions.

In this sense the Riot Act was consistent with the trend of English constitutional evolution toward: (1) absolute sovereignty of Parliament; (2) legitimacy of parliamentary acts suspending privileges or rights of subjects (for example, suspension of habeas corpus in 1689, 1696, and later in 1716, 1744, 1745, 1777–1779, and 1794–1801); and (3) retroactive "amnesty" for officials through periodic indemnity bills.[7]

Under the special conditions of the English unwritten constitution, however, only specific liberties or rights were suspended, pursuant to parliamentary legislation. This did not involve establishment of an extraconstitutional or alternative regime of exception precisely because Parliament was always authorized to legislate on matters of immediate or long-term concern—without limitation as to the scope of legitimate action. If emergency conditions required, whether due to threats to public health and safety or national security, Parliament could and did suspend or modify civil liberties and civil rights or alter routine government procedures.

In contrast, the written constitutions of the new liberal regimes that replaced the nineteenth-century European monarchies in North America and the former colonies of Spain and Portugal in Central and South America sought to limit government authority and guarantee specified liberties and rights to citizens. Simultaneously, recognition that government might need additional authority under emergency conditions made constitution writers hesitant to make citizen rights and liberties unconditional. Thus, provisions for regimes of exception appeared in almost all constitutional charters to anticipate the special conditions of natural disaster, rebellion, subversion, and war. Where such special conditions require action not constitutionally authorized without recourse to emergency powers or, at the least, the declaration that some sort of emergency or crisis exists, the regime of exception allows temporary reorganization or redefinition of government authority and procedures for the explicit purpose of dealing with emergency conditions.

In some cases, regimes of exception are extremely limited with respect to which rights or liberties may be suspended or to the scope of emergency powers assigned to government officials. In the Constitution implemented in the United States of America in 1789, for example, the only explicit regime of exception clause declared: "The privilege of the Writ of Habeas Corpus shall not be suspended unless when in Cases of Rebellion or Invasion the public Safety may require it" (Art. 1, Sec. 8).[8]

In other political systems, regimes of exception may allow the government almost unlimited authority while the emergency persists. The revolutionary constitution of France in the early nineteenth century permitted the Senate to declare departments (administrative jurisdictions) outside the protection of the constitution and to void judicial decisions when they "threatened the security of the State" (Art. 55, Senate Consulto, May 18, 1802). Under these provisions, any constitutional guarantee of civil rights and civil liberties might be suspended for "reasons of state."[9]

Implementation of a regime of exception may involve a variety of actions, including

1. suspension of specified civil liberties or civil rights, for example, freedom of speech, assembly, or association, for (a) the duration of the crisis or (b) a particular period of time (sometimes renewable), within part or all of the national territory;
2. declaration of a constitutionally stipulated regime of exception (for example, a state of siege, state of internal commotion, state of internal war, or state of danger) with (or without) delineation of the extent and duration of emergency powers either in the constitution itself or in supplementary "organic laws" or "constitutional acts";[10]
3. blanket suspension of the rule (*imperio*) of the constitution with virtually unlimited dictatorial powers exercised by legislative, executive, or perhaps military authorities;
4. delegation of extraordinary powers to government authorities (for example, assignment by the legislature of authority to the executive to rule by decree, suspend civil liberties and rights, impose special taxes or forced loans, or even exercise the full sovereign power) for either a specified period or for the duration;
5. declaration of martial law.

This last action may provide for direct legislation and enforcement by military authorities as well as subjection of civilians to military law and tribunals. Variations and combinations of these five general types of regimes of exception form the legal basis of modern authoritarian government and constitutional dictatorship. They provide the cornerstone for the constitution of tyranny.

Examples of all of these approaches may be found in nineteenth-century Europe and Latin America, as illustrated in the chapters that follow. The last four alternatives, potentially permitting temporary civilian or military "constitutional dictatorship," date at least from the time of Roman dictatorship, a constitutional delegation of absolute authority to a "dictatura rei gerundae causa" (dictatorship for getting things done) or to a "dictatura seditionis sedanae et rei gerundae causa" (dictatorship for suppressing civil insurrection).

The Romans conferred these emergency powers upon dictators for limited periods of time (not exceeding six months). The dictator could not initiate the state of emergency but rather was charged by the legitimate government with emergency powers and could not legally alter the existing constitutional order—only defend it. Eventually, of course, certain Roman dictators violated these limitations. Sulla used the dictatorship to introduce a new constitution and remained well beyond the customary six months (ca. 84 B.C.). Caesar made the dictatorship a more permanent form of political rule (ca. 49–44 B.C.), and his grandnephew, Octavian, presided over the transition from republic to empire (after 31 B.C.).[11]

The juridical questions raised by regimes of exception such as the Roman dictatorship are irrelevant in an absolute monarchy, British-type parliamentary system, or totalitarian regime. If the sovereign power recognizes no limits to its authority, more or less in the fashion of Hobbes's *Leviathan,* then emergency powers are not necessary.[12] Only the formal existence of constitutional regimes, with limited and enumerated powers and correlative rights and liberties of citizens (called *garantías individuales* in most nineteenth-century Spanish American constitutions), poses the dilemma of elaborating and implementing special regimes for emergency conditions.

This is the case whether sovereign authority supposedly resides in the people, the Crown, or Parliament or is delegated to a designated personification of the nation such as an emperor or president. It also holds where exercise of sovereign authority is divided among branches of government and among concurrent, overlapping, or self-contained units of government within nations, as in federal and confederal regimes. Unless government authority is explicitly limited in scope, it matters little whether its structure is centralized or decentralized, unitary or federal. Formal regimes of exception are required only when constitutionally defined and enumerated authority is insufficient, or believed to be insufficient, to deal effectively with special circumstances, from natural disasters to epidemics, civil disturbances, and war.[13]

Foresight in constitution making and legislation, as in the Roman case, provides a constitutional and statutory foundation for public response to emergency conditions, whether from natural catastrophe, war, economic crisis, or social disorder. Formal declaration of a state of constitutional exception or application of emergency legislation to create a temporary constitutional dictatorship legitimizes the actions that follow. Public officials and those following their directive may then do legally what under other conditions is illegal or unthinkable.

Thus, the British Riot Act of 1714 was a very limited departure from normal police procedures; but nonetheless it increased official discretion and put citizens at risk. Unlike later, more comprehensive versions, it did not provide any expansion of legislative or judicial authority to the civilian government or to military officers charged with overcoming the threat to public order. It did not create a comprehensive regime of exception but only circumstantial immunity for police or other repressive forces in confronting a material emergency. In contrast, the Roman dictatorship and later versions of emergency government established an alternative political regime with greatly enhanced policy-making and enforcement powers.

From the time of the first republican constitutions in the United States and France, regimes of exception were used to confront opponents of liberalism, advocates of monarchist restoration, and political movements that challenged the new institutional order. Preservation of the basic principles of liberalism, however interpreted in the United States, France, Spain, and later in Latin America, seemed to require temporary suspension of civil liberties and civil rights when so-called subversive elements threatened public safety, internal order, or the security of the state. Almost always the justification for imposition of regimes of exception referred to threats to national security. For example, Article 306 of Spain's first liberal constitution, the 1812 Cádiz Constitution, allowed suspension of prohibitions on search and seizure within domiciles (*allanamiento*) when required by order or state security ("buen orden y seguridad del Estado").

Frequently, at least in the last two centuries in Europe and the last one in Africa and Latin America, the juridical nomenclature that formalizes emergency powers under crisis conditions has been *state of siege, state of internal war, state of emergency,* or *state of internal commotion.* However, this has been far from universal, and an impressive diversity of usage of refinement in the range of emergency powers has occurred.

Whatever the precise nomenclature, imposing a regime of exception involves invoking a previously anticipated constitutional response to a perceived crisis. Under these conditions, some or all civil liberties and civil rights may be restricted or suspended. In addition, ordinary government procedures for legislation, administration, and judicial decision making may be replaced temporarily with special methods for making and implementing public policy. These special methods may range from unrestrained constitutional dictatorship by chief executives, emergency juntas, legislatures, or military officers, to carefully detailed and limited powers, for a stipulated period, to confront the crisis.

It is difficult to isolate the unique historical referent for the modern constitutional regime of exception. Nevertheless, the emergency measures and constitutional provisions emerging from the French Revolution are certainly the benchmark for nineteenth- and twentieth-century constitutional practice in Europe, Latin America, and other excolonial regions.[14]

From 1791 to 1797, during the course of revolutionary strife, international threats, and civil war, French constitutional and statutory initiatives gradually consolidated the modern legal concept of the state of siege (*état de siège*) as a juridical regime of exception. On July 10, 1791, a law of the convention defined three classifications for fortified cities and military posts: state of peace, state of war, and state of siege. In this legislation, the state of siege referred not to a legal concept but to a material state in which enemy forces interrupted communications at a distance of approximately 3,500 meters from a military post or fortified city. The existence of a state of siege justified subordinating civilians to military authority and implementing a repressive administration for the duration. In contrast, a state of war had to be declared by the legislature or, when the legislature was not in session, by the monarch, inasmuch as a state of war was defined politically rather than by material conditions.

From the time of this legislation until 1797, periodic emergency decrees accompanied France's revolutionary turmoil. The constitution adopted in 1795 by the Revolutionary Directorate included provisions allowing the government to arrest persons "conspiring against the internal or external security of the state" (Art. 145). In August 1797, with the occupation of Paris, a law extended authority to the directorate "to place a commune in a state of siege" by decree. At this moment, the *state of siege* passed from a description of a material state that implied politico-legal consequences to that of a special juridical regime applicable to cities and towns as well as military posts. This special juridical regime implied authority to (1) suspend individual rights and liberties, (2) exercise emergency legislative or executive powers, and (3) submit civilians to military jurisdiction. Although the later diffusion of *state of siege* or its equivalent as a regime of exception did not always entail all of these broad departures from constitutional routine, the principle of declaring the legal existence of a regime of exception passed into European constitutionalism.

In 1799, the French added the concept of "état de troubles civils." This law allowed the state to take family members of ex-nobles and emigrés as hostages and to punish them for the "crimes" of their relatives. Although there is academic debate as to whether this "state of civil troubles" was to be understood as a material condition or a juridical fiction declared by the authorities, the idea of civil troubles was later referred to as *public disorder, public disturbance, internal commotion,* or other such legal terminology in Europe and Spanish America. By 1800, the French constitution allowed for suspension of civil liberties and rights in the places, and for the time, determined by law "when the security of the state required" or when parliament was in recess.[15]

In November 1811, Napoleon further consolidated the institution of juridical states of emergency with a decree based on the legislation of the revolutionary period. This decree again referred to three possible states in which a military post or town could find itself—peace, war, or siege. The state of war and state of siege were determined by imperial decree or materially—for example, by actual siege, unauthorized assembly, or sedition. This Napoleonic reform of the 1790s legislation submitted all civilians to military jurisdiction in the territory affected by the declaration of a state of siege.

Finally, the Acte Additionnel of 1815 adopted the terminology *état de siège* to describe the general regime of exception that would permit suspension of stipulated rights (for example, freedom of assembly, speech, and the right to be tried in an ordinary civil court). What in the Constitution of 1799 had been called "suspension of the imperium of the constitution" had become by 1815 "state of siege."

Later diffusion of this principle did not always mean adoption of the same terminology, but the notion that the modern state had to avail itself of special, constitutionally prescribed emergency powers spread through Europe, Latin America and, in the twentieth century, to other former colonies.[16] The Acte Additionnel that incorporated the *état de siège* into the 1815 Constitution required that parliament initiate the state of siege. In Europe and elsewhere this precedent was sometimes followed and other times modified to allow for determination of the existence of emergencies and initiation of regimes of exception by the executive rather than by the legislative authority.

Generally, a regime of exception thus legitimizes the drastic measures adopted to meet natural or man-made threats to the existing political and social order. However, it does not necessarily legitimize all measures or extend immunity to government officials for every action carried out to meet the emergency conditions. Nor is it always certain that the legally declared emergency that justifies invoking the exceptional regime corresponds to a verifiable emergency. Thus, government lawlessness may also occur under regimes of exception, not merely in the sense of abusing authority or violating citizen rights and liberty but in the sense of unconstitutional actions, that is, executive, legislative, or judicial behavior that exceeds constitutional authorization for the regime of exception.

In practice, considerable variation developed in nineteenth-century Europe regarding the characteristics of regimes of exception and the extent of the liability of government officials for actions carried out under emergency powers. In the English common law tradition, the judiciary would determine whether the government had proceeded lawfully after the fact. However, as mentioned above, legislation such as the British Riot Act and periodic indemnity bills could limit judicial review as well as the liability of officials for government lawlessness. In this sense, parliament could legalize illegality post hoc.

European traditions left either executive or legislative authorities, or both, with the responsibility for determining the lawfulness of official behavior. In either case, these eventualities raise the subsequent political issue of punishment for tyranny and despotism as well as the question of remedy or compensation for victims— though the French tradition of official immunity for actions taken for "reasons of state" severely limited citizen remedies and official liability. The Spanish Constitution of 1812 offered an intermediate, though contradictory, solution, which made the king immune from any liability for his actions (Art. 168) but held ministers or lesser officials personally responsible for violating the constitution, even if so ordered by the king (Art. 226).[17]

These fundamental constitutional and political dilemmas of the post-1800 regimes in Europe and North America were complicated by rising nationalism, lingering regionalism, and profound socioeconomic changes. Agrarian transformation, technological change, urbanization, and industrialization induced new types of conflict. The growing complexity of nineteenth- and twentieth-century nations, with the accompanying intensification of class cleavages, induced sometimes violent conflicts over control of resources and shares of the growing economic surplus. The newly emerging working classes, technicians, entrepreneurs, and professionals viewed government and politics as a key to social and economic opportunities. Erosion of traditional values and patterns of social deference also contributed to new types of social and political conflict. More traditional sources of political unrest, such as demands for regional autonomy and religious, ethnic, and linguistic differences, also continued to produce tension even as the underlying principles of liberalism continued to be challenged by monarchists and clerical opponents.

Under these conditions the spontaneous outbursts such as food riots, protests against government policies, and ethnic violence of preindustrial Europe gave way to organized resistance against existing social conditions and institutional patterns. Such resistance included the challenges of labor organization, political party activity, the press, and antigovernment literature, theater, and art. In the face of such challenges and, sometimes, armed resistance, governments resorted to repressive violence and regimes of exception.[18] Likewise, efforts to initiate revolutionary or restorationist political experiments by capturing the state apparatus and directing dramatic changes from the top down used the legal device of exceptional regimes in Europe as well as in Latin America, Asia, and Africa. For example, in imperial Germany the *kriegszustand,* or state of war, served the same purpose as the French state of siege. Article 68 of the imperial constitution stated: "The Kaiser can, if the public safety in the federal territory is threatened, declare the state of war in any part thereof. Until the enactment of an imperial statute regulating the conditions, the form of the proclamation and the effects of such a declaration, the provisions applying thereto shall be those of the Prussian statute of June 4, 1851."

Since no federal statute was ever enacted, the kaiser acted more or less in accord with the Prussian law of 1851. This law suspended most basic constitutional rights, subjected civilians to military courts, and transferred important aspects of government authority from civilian to military authority. Unlike its French and Spanish counterparts, this German "state of war" clause was rarely invoked in the nineteenth century but served as a legal antecedent of Article

48 of the Weimar Constitution.[19] In contrast, the basic regime of exception clauses in Latin American constitutions were repeatedly invoked throughout the nineteenth century, as the following chapters detail.

The law of necessity and the right of social self-defense frequently have degenerated into savage repression against the so-called enemies of society. Rousseau's observation in the *Social Contract* that "it is impossible to live in peace with those whom we believe to be damned"[20] has been translated into brutality and persecution in the name of defending the state or society, whether revolutionary or counterrevolutionary, against its enemies.

This dilemma prevailed prior to the appearance of modern constitutional government after the French and American revolutions. However, the innovation of constitutional and limited government introduced the philosophical and political quandary of defending liberalism and republican institutions against monarchical restoration or other antiliberal subversion without abandoning civil liberties and rights. Provisions for regimes of exception were the common, if double-edged, solution to this dilemma. In more than a few instances, the repression instituted under regimes of exception lasted years or decades.

But not always. Regimes of constitutional exception have frequently served their intended purposes, eventually returning society to normal constitutional government: preventing social dissolution, limiting panic, and controlling violence in the face of natural disaster, epidemic disease, or episodic social upheavals such as riots, rebellions, or insurrections. Regimes of exception also allow for mobilizing needed resources and controlling civilian populations during wartime in a way not ordinarily permitted by limited representative government. Some modern constitutions provide explicitly for separate regimes of exception in the event of economic emergency.[21]

Regimes of exception, therefore, entail a fundamental political challenge to constitutional government. Their existence represents the risk of falling into authoritarianism in the name of defending the constitutional order that is purportedly under siege. Yet, despite the risk, they have been widely adopted, even where they are not clearly defined in constitutional texts.[22] Emergencies or crises sometimes require extraordinary measures to avoid disaster. For example, control of epidemics or response to natural disaster or war may require limits on individual behavior or violation of property rights unacceptable under normal conditions. Recognition of this possibility provides the rationale for constitutional regimes of exception and, inherently, for their potential abuse.

There is, therefore, a potential constitutional foundation of tyranny in most modern constitutions. Or, in Rousseau's terminology, there exist the dual threats of tyranny (usurpation of authority in the name of defending authority) and despotism (usurpation of authority and the constitution of new authority) in all so-called free societies.[23]

With this in mind, the present study begins with a survey of the historical circumstances giving rise to the constitutionalization of regimes of exception in Western Europe and North America and the transfer of these institutions to Latin America in the nineteenth century.[24] In Latin America, as in Africa and parts of Asia, efforts to create constitutional regimes of exception have been translated into institutions and political practices similar to, yet significantly distinct from, their European counterparts. Great variety also developed in regimes of exception among the Latin American nations.

The precise political significance and juridical interpretation of regimes of exception, the extent and consequences of their application, and the manner of the restoration of normal government are related both to international and regional constitutional development and to idiosyncratic socioeconomic, cultural, and political attributes of individual nations. Similarly, the nature of the emergency conditions confronted, in both subjective terms (the perceived character of the emergency by diverse groups and interests in the society) and more objective terms (the more measurable and concrete impacts of the emergency, for example, deaths from epidemics, the extent of economic crisis indicated by price fluctuations or food shortages, or the severity of rioting and looting) influences both the propensity to initiate regimes of exception and the manner of their implementation. Similarities exist, but the same words and similar constitutional provisions mean different things in different places and at different times in the same place. Despite this diversity, the use of regimes of exception becomes addicting. In most of Spanish America it became routine.

However diverse the subjective or objective character of the circumstances occasioning regimes of exception, a common implication is the enhanced significance and visibility of the organized forces of coercion—typically, the police and armed forces. Regimes of exception magnify the political authority and power of the police, military, and quasi-military forces. Frequently, political authority, or much of it, passes by law or slips by default from the control of civilian officials to military leaders.

This consequence of regimes of exception makes the relationship between professional military and police forces and the constituted authorities before, in the initiation of, and during the administration of regimes of exception a critical constitutional and political concern. The conditions for lifting states of constitutional exception and restoring the status quo ante are also of immense importance.

In eighteenth-century Spain, for example, officers called *capitán general* (a government office rather than a military rank) acting as administrators in each of the provinces routinely served as the chief civilian bureaucrat, president of the high courts (*audiencias*), and chief military authority. In times of emergency or social protest, the *capitán general* declared the equivalent of a state of siege and took over all civil authority. After 1784, these officials had jurisdiction over banditry and political suspects. Moreover, they administered public works projects, enforced quarantines, and supervised tax collections. In addition, military officers enjoyed the *fuero militar,* which included permanent military courts with exclusive jurisdiction over criminal and civil cases involving selected military personnel. This left privileged military personnel beyond the grasp of civil courts for almost all types of litigation or criminal procedures.

The adaptation of the French intendant system by the Bourbons in Spain after 1718 had also involved meshing military and civilian jurisdictions. Meeting some internal resistance, the administrative reform was suspended in 1721 but reestablished in 1749. *Intendentes* were responsible for administration, economic affairs, law enforcement, military conscription, supply, and troop payment within their territorial jurisdiction.

Spain extended this system to its American colonies, beginning with Cuba in 1764, Venezuela in 1776, and Rio de la Plata in 1782. In part to overcome the corruption and inefficiency of the governors, *corregidores,* and *alcaldes mayores* who administered the smaller local jurisdictions, the *intendentes* reinforced the fusion of civil and military authority.[25] During the same years, expansion of regular army units and colonial militia occurred in response to European threats and Indian revolts in parts of the empire. This extended military *fueros* to colonial militia personnel and greatly increased the previously quite limited military presence in most Spanish colonies. For example, between 1760 and 1800 regular army forces more than tripled in Mexico and Peru.

With this tradition of a militarized internal administration and special privileges for military personnel, the role of the military institutions in Spain, and later in Latin America, came to differ significantly from their French, German, or Italian counterparts.[26] The denomination of certain colonial administrative jurisdictions as *capitanía general,* beginning in the sixteenth century, implied an even more permanent overlapping of civil and military authority in Spain's American territories. Tensions among military, ecclesiastical, and civil jurisdictions permeated Spanish imperial administration; certain antecedents of nineteenth- and twentieth-century civil-military conflicts in Spanish America appeared in the last half-century of colonial rule.[27] This would make the constitutional role of the military in independent Spanish America a central issue in politics and constitutional design.

In practice, constitutional and legislative guidelines for military participation in regimes of exception must be understood in terms of more general patterns of civil-military relations from nation to nation. Police and military institutions are key elements in all political systems. Even in societies with high degrees of internal consensus regarding the legitimacy of existing political institutions, the need for external defense and for suppressing occasional disorders or protests necessitates maintaining some organized military or paramilitary forces. In some cases, constitutions themselves establish military institutions as an integral part of the political order. This became common practice in Latin America in the nineteenth century. Most constitutions specifically established some sort of armed forces and even assigned them the constitutional role of defending the institutional order, upholding the laws, and defending the constitution. In other cases, legislative or executive officials are vested with exclusive or overlapping authority to create, staff, budget for, manage, and deploy military and police forces. Therefore, the critical issue of the relative autonomy and the scope of the role of the armed forces may have both constitutional and politico-historical origins.[28]

Like any organized group within the state and society, with the important difference of their relative monopoly over heavy armaments and war-making capability, police and military personnel always participate in political life. They are naturally concerned with the constitutional framework, statutory definitions, and administrative regulations that affect their professional mission. They also seek to influence the amount of resources available for their institutions, their career opportunities, their status within society, and their relationships with other components of the government. Likewise, military personnel have opinions concerning the social, economic, and political issues of the day and may be involved in the larger conflicts of society both as individuals and as members of ethnic, religious, professional, or other groups. Personal ambitions and intraorganizational differences may also influence political participation by military and police personnel.

These realities offer the prospect for both concerted political action by military professionals in some instances and divisions among military professionals in others. Variations in the type, extent, overtness, and consequences of military and police political participation occur within and among nations over time. Such variations naturally become more critical in times of emergency or crisis—but they routinely influence political life in all political systems.

Thus, in marked contrast to the Spanish practices previously described, British law established relatively firm civilian control over military institutions by the late seventeenth century. It subjected military officers to the jurisdiction of civil courts for all but violations of military law and introduced severe penalties for mutiny or rebellion. Consistent with the basic principle of British law that soldiers were not exempt from the ordinary liabilities of citizenship, the first Mutiny Act of 1689 declared:

> Whereas no man may be forejudged of life or limb or subjected to any kind of punishment by martial law, or in any other manner than by the judgement of his peers, and according to the known and established laws of this realm; yet, nevertheless, it [is] requisite for retaining such forces as are, or shall be, raised during this exigence of affairs, in their duty an exact discipline be observed; and that soldiers who shall mutiny or stir up sedition, or shall desert their majesties' service, be brought to a more exemplary and speedy punishment than the usual forms of law will allow.

Subsequent army acts essentially repeated this British solution to the threat of military coup d'état. Commenting on this solution, Dicey indicates that the key elements are that (1) soldiers and officers are subject to all the duties and liabilities of ordinary citizens, (2) "Nothing in this Act contained . . . shall extend or be construed to exempt any officer or soldier whatsoever from the ordinary process of law," (3) in all conflicts of jurisdiction between a military and a civil court, the authority of the civil court prevails, and (4) when a soldier is charged with a crime, obedience to superior orders is not itself a defense. Specifically, "a soldier cannot any more than a civilian avoid responsibility for breach of law by pleading that he broke the law in *bona fide* obedience to the orders (say) of the commander-in-chief."[29]

Inasmuch as most modern political systems assume that the source of ultimate political authority (sovereignty) resides in the people—however that authority is manifested in particular political institutions—police and military participation in politics is theoretically subject to the control of the incumbent government.[30] The relationship of military forces and police to government authority is usually specified in constitutional and statutory mandates. However, emergency conditions or internal disorders present particularly difficult moments for civilian-military relations, especially when the fundamental legitimacy of the government or of the constitutional order itself is called into question.

Neither constitutions nor legislation can prevent usurpation of authority, expansion of the relative autonomy, or excesses in carrying out repression by the armed forces of a society.[31] Nevertheless, constitutional and legislative definitions of regimes of exception are to some extent both determinants and products of the historical patterns of civil-military relations and also of the nature of military participation in exceptional regimes. In this sense, constitutional and legislative enactments may affect the propensity for such regimes to be instituted, the character of policy making and administration under such regimes, the duration of such regimes, and the likelihood that the status quo ante will be restored to the fullest extent possible on lifting the state of constitutional exception. These enactments also may influence the role of police and military forces both in initiating and in managing or controlling government policy and administration during the regime of exception.

These issues are nowhere more salient than in Latin America. High levels of participation by Latin American military officers and institutions in the political life of the republics of the region are an obvious historical reality.[32] From the time of the independence movements of the early nineteenth century to the present, generals, colonels, and even sergeants have draped themselves in presidential sashes as they proclaimed themselves protectors of the common good and saviors of their nations. Rarely have these military presidents and their entourage lacked civilian support. Frequently, the military-civilian coalitions of the nineteenth and especially the twentieth century have come to power under the authority of emergency provisions of Latin American constitutions and supplementary legislation.

The emergencies and disorders of the nineteenth century in Europe and Latin America gave way to the class antagonisms and ideological struggles of the twentieth century. More complete integration of Latin American nations into the international economy intensified these trends, as did the conflicts of international politics after World War I. In these circumstances, the character and practical evolution of diverse regimes of exception became increasingly significant in the political life of Latin America.

Dictatorships alternated periodically with elected civilian governments from the early nineteenth century to the present. Latin American leaders and intellectuals observing political change in the region came to expect cycles of "democratic" and authoritarian governments. These cycles corresponded roughly with global economic and political changes and with regional diffusion of current political trends (either of democracy or dictatorship). Yet the fundamental institutional basis for regimes of exception, usually elaborated in the first decades after independence, nearly always survived.[33]

Latin American socioeconomic and political institutions, with variations from country to country, originated in the Iberian peninsula and borrowed heavily from eighteenth- and nineteenth-century Western Europe—especially England, France, and Spain. Some Latin American leaders also deliberately copied institutions of the newly independent United States of America, while others detested and rebelled against them.[34]

Chapter 2 focuses on the domestic and international factors shaping the evolution of the regimes of exception in Latin America, with special attention to Iberian sources of Spanish American constitutionalism, law, and public administration. This analysis anticipates discussion of the institutional alternatives debated, adopted, amended, and rejected in Spanish America in efforts to establish political systems that achieved the elusive goals of legitimacy, liberty, and order in the years following independence.

2

Iberian Origins of Spanish American Regimes of Exception and Civil-Military Relations

ADVENTUROUS SPANISH CONQUISTADORES, IN PARTNERSHIP WITH THE Crown of Castile, created a vast colonial empire in the Western Hemisphere after Columbus's first voyage in 1492. As Romans (200 B.C.) and then North African Muslims (A.D. 711) had conquered and transformed Spain, the Iberians would now conquer and transfigure America. They subjugated native American peoples, spread the Christian gospel, built new towns and cities, and administered a hierarchically stratified society for more than three centuries. The new civilization they created would meld Roman, North African, Iberian, and Amerindian cultures and institutions.[1]

Ferdinand and Isabella, monarchs of several Spanish kingdoms, based their claims to these colonies on papal decrees and treaties dating from the 1470s.[2] In May 1493 Pope Alexander VI declared it "well pleasing to the Divine Majesty and cherished of our heart . . . that the health of souls be cared for and that barbarous nations be overthrown and brought to the faith itself." Recognizing the "recovery of the Kingdom of Granada from the yoke of Saracens" in 1492, also the year of Christopher Columbus's first expedition to the West Indies, the Pope granted to his "very dear son in Christ, Ferdinand, King, and our very dear daughter in Christ, Isabella, Queen of Castile, Aragon, Sicily and Granada" the territories discovered by their emissaries:

by the authority of Almighty God conferred upon us in blessed Peter and the vicarship of Jesus Christ, which we hold on earth, do by tenor of these presents, should any of said islands have been found by your envoys and captains, give, grant, and assign to you and your heirs and successors, kings of Castile and León, forever, together with all their dominions, cities, camps, places and villages, and all rights, jurisdictions, and appurtenances, all islands and mainlands found and to be found, discovered and to be discovered [here follows geographical demarcation of the empire]. . . . With the proviso however that none of the islands and mainlands, found and to be found, discovered and to be discovered, beyond that said line towards the west and south, be in the actual possession of any Christian king or prince up to the birthday of our Lord Jesus Christ just past from which the present year one thousand four hundred and ninety-three begins.

By this authority and the Treaty of Tordesillas in 1494, which revised the demarcation of territory between Spain and Portugal, Ferdinand and Isabella sent priests, soldiers, and settlers to conquer *Las Indias,* the name given to the Caribbean, Central America, South America, and parts of Asia.

Before Columbus's second voyage in 1493, the king and queen issued instructions concerning the conversion of native peoples to Catholicism and the treatment of these peoples by the Spanish. Thereafter, royal officials issued decrees regulating Indian life, labor, and relations with the colonial administration. From the instructions of 1501 issued to Nicolás de Ovando, governor of Hispaniola (1502–1509), regarding the need to convert "the Indians to our Holy Catholic faith," the Spanish combined religious imperialism with economic exploitation of the colonies. Thus, Ovando's instructions also included the charge: "In order to secure gold and to do the other tasks that we are ordering done it will be necessary to employ the service of Indians; you are to compel them to work in the affairs of our service."

Twenty years after Columbus's initial voyage the Crown issued the Laws of Burgos, the first legal code to govern colonial society. These laws focused on Indian-Spanish relations; they reflected disdain for Indians, "who were prone to idleness and vice," but also a paternalistic effort to protect them from abuses. For example, colonists and royal officials were prohibited from sending Indian women more than four months pregnant to work in the mines.

Eventually, Spanish colonial administration regulated almost all aspects of daily life for the colonized, colonizers, imported African slaves, and their offspring.[3] A Council of the Indies, established in 1524, oversaw government and administration of the colonies. This council combined legislative, administrative, judicial, religious, and military authority. The Crown initially divided its American possessions into two viceroyalties. New Spain, established in 1535, included the territory from Mexico to the border of Panama, and some Caribbean islands. Peru, created in 1542 with its capital at Lima, included most of South America.[4] These largest units were subdivided into *audiencias*, and these into lesser jurisdictions such as *corregimientos*, *alcaldías mayores*, and *gobernaciones*. The smallest administrative units were municipalities, typically consisting of a city or town and the surrounding countryside.

The legitimacy of the empire resided in the merger of religious and secular authority in the monarchy and the colonial regime. Disobedience to authority offended both God and king; heresy and political dissent were practically indistinguishable. The Office of the Holy Inquisition was to maintain the purity of the faith and protect the realm against those who "seek to pervert or tempt believers from our Holy Catholic Faith . . . communicate false opinions or heresies, or distribute heretical books." To achieve this, the Tribunal of the Inquisition, authorized for the Americas after 1569, censored written and oral communication, scrutinized public and private behavior, and "punished and extirpated" deviance.[5]

To administer the colonies, the king assigned extensive authority to each viceroy and his subordinates. The authority of the viceroys, which evolved through royal decrees and instructions, was modeled in some ways on the Aragonese system used also in Catalonia and Valencia. Responsible for maintenance of public order, general administration, fiscal policy, tax collection, public works, and defense against European and native attacks, the viceroy was, effectively, a vice king.

The viceroy also served as captain-general of the territory, thereby unifying military and civilian authority, and as president of the *audiencia* (the royal court) in the capital of the viceregal administration, for example, Mexico City or Lima. Charged with carrying out the sentences of the Inquisition and given the power to banish delinquents or undesirables from his jurisdiction, the law also required the viceroy to punish "public sins" ("Que los Vireyes y

Justicias hagan castigar los pecados públicos"). The viceroy and his subordinates were ordered to "punish blasphemers, witches [*hechiceros*], procurers [*alcahuetes*], adulterers [*amancebados*] and authors of other public sins, that might cause scandal."[6] Captains-general and presidents exercised considerable autonomy, fusing military and civil authority in their jurisdictions and frequently communicating directly with the Crown.

The Spanish empire was governed by decree without any parliamentary or representative institutions. A compilation of these decrees, *cédulas,* and ordinances was published in 1681 as the *Recopilación de Leyes de los Reynos de las Indias.* Subsequent additions to this compendium constituted the basic law of the colonies but never a systematized legal code. Thus, colonial law and administrative regulations accrued over the centuries through royal orders and instructions. Since the Crown avoided transplanting the limited vestige of representative institutions in Spain—the *cortes*—to the colonies, it prevented development of countervailing power to royal authority. There were no medieval privileges to defend, no towns or cities that had exacted concessions from the Crown in previous centuries, no historical pacts with nobles or other social estates that constrained, even symbolically, the exercise of royal authority. Spanish America never experienced the juridical fragmentation of political authority typical of feudal Europe. All rights and privileges depended upon royal concessions in a centralized patrimonial empire.

Although the power of the Council of the Indies was reduced after 1714 with the appointment of a Minister of Marine and the Indies, and further reforms in this system were introduced by the Bourbon monarchs in the last half of the eighteenth century to streamline administration and reallocate authority within the imperial bureaucracy, the fundamental character of policy making and administration remained unaltered. In Spain, too, Bourbon rule perpetuated the basic assumptions, even as the centralized administration expanded the role of the military in provincial administration and criminal justice and carried out public works programs and fiscal reforms.[7]

Food riots and widespread disorders in 1766 convinced Charles III of the need to further involve the military in internal administration.[8] Revised military *ordenanzas* (1768) and a 1774 decree (*pragmática*) regarding the control of tumults (*asonadas*) provided the precedent and language for military involvement in maintaining internal order, which would be emulated in Spanish

America and Spain itself into the late twentieth century. In addition
to expanding military authority over protesters (*reos y autores de
bullicio*), the 1774 *pragmática* outlawed distributing and affixing
posters in public places. Moreover, persons who copied, read, or lis-
tened to seditious material (*papeles sediciosos*) and failed to report
this promptly to local authorities would be considered accomplices
to sedition.

By the late eighteenth century, internal administration in Spain
depended upon provincial captains-general and a network of military governors and lesser officers in the small towns. With the exception of the chief civilian officials' (*intendentes*) control over fiscal
affairs, civilians were subordinate to the captains-general. Well before the French Revolution, Spanish captains-general could rule
their provinces under emergency powers during *estados de guerra*,
applying military law against rebels and "bandits."[9] (Later, political
opponents and guerrilla fighters would be labeled "bandits" in
Spanish American nations, thereby subjecting them to military law
and *consejos de guerra*. The authority of Spanish captains-general
would be incorporated into the regulations for provincial administration in many Spanish American nations, as would their broad
discretion in dealing with "rebels" and "threats to the security of the
state.") In the words of E. Christiansen, "the soldier-administrator
thus occupied in fact as well as in form the leading position in provincial society, and his privileges, coveted by every officer, reflected
glory on the profession as a whole."[10]

Monarchical Spain also created an authoritarian political regime in Spanish America but without the inconveniences to centralized and uniform royal authority of medieval *cortes*, regional
kingdoms with their customary privileges and other historical im-
pediments to absolutism. Dominated by European-born Spaniards,
(*peninsulares*) and American-born "Europeans" (*criollos*), the colonial
empire provided mineral treasures, new agricultural commodities,
and raw materials for European markets. Envied by her European
allies and adversaries alike, the empire also offered economic and
military targets for Spain's enemies and for pirates. Despite the
challenges of European powers and the revolutionary movements
in North America and Europe in the late eighteenth century, Spain
entered the nineteenth century with its American empire intact. It
also resisted and diluted the influence of revolutionary and liberal
principles in Spain itself, though the inept reign of Charles IV
(1788–1808) and the unpopular ministry of Manuel Godoy (1792–
1808) eroded the authority of the Spanish monarchy.

Even a long litany of colonial laments against Spanish rule, from dissatisfaction with economic and trade policies to social and economic discrimination against *criollo* subjects, failed to engender movements that seriously threatened Spanish control of its American colonies.[11] Neither the gradual penetration of eighteenth-century philosophical trends nor the upheavals of the French and American revolutions provided sufficient momentum to precipitate rebellion by the small minority of Spanish American colonials who dreamed of independence.[12] Events in Europe rather than in the Western Hemisphere precipitated the dissolution of the empire in Spanish America. Spain's alliance with Napoleonic France, orchestrated by Manuel Godoy, the most important policy maker in Spain from the mid-1790s, allowed French troops to invade Portugal through Spanish territory. Napoleon decided to occupy Spain and make it a satellite state. Mobs at Aranjuez in March 1808 protested the French invasion, the deteriorating economic conditions, and the rumor that Godoy had persuaded the king to sail for America (as the Portuguese monarchs had gone to Brazil).

The tumult in Aranjuez led Charles IV to dismiss Godoy and, the next day, to abdicate in favor of his son, Ferdinand VII. Napoleon refused to recognize Ferdinand, his father reconsidered the abdication, and both went at Napoleon's invitation to Bayonne in France. Rather than mediate the dynastic squabble, Napoleon obtained the abdication of Ferdinand, then of Charles again, in his own favor. He then named his brother, Joseph Bonaparte, king of Spain.

These events produced rebellion in Spain, ostensibly in the name of King Ferdinand VII. On May 2, 1808, prior to the abdications, mobs in Madrid had attacked French troops; later in May, violent demonstrations occurred in other regions of the country. While the internal resistance maintained the facade of loyalty to Ferdinand VII (the so-called mask of Ferdinand), the "internal collapse" of the Spanish monarchy, "which was divided between King and heir, centralists and regional oligarchs," eventually brought the army to the fore as the new arbiter of Spanish politics.[13]

THE CONSTITUTION OF BAYONNE, JULY 1808

Attempting to legitimize the new political regime, Napoleon used a group of Spanish clerics, nobles, and other elites to adopt Spain's first constitution, a purportedly liberal one. Despite Napoleon's attacks on the church elsewhere, the Bayonne Constitution made

Catholicism the religion of the king and declared that no other religion would be permitted (Art. 1). At the same time, the unified crown of the Spanish provinces and the American territories was given to Joseph Bonaparte and his direct male descendants, perpetually excluding female heirs. If Joseph failed to produce male heirs, the crown would return to Napoleon, "emperor of the French and king of the Italians," and his male descendants. Seeking support from Spanish aristocrats, the constitution even recognized existing titles of nobility.

Though this constitution established a parliament (*cortes*), the king and an appointed council of state retained most of the political initiative and effective political power. The *cortes* was to be convened by the king, at least every three years, and could be dissolved by him. It was to meet in closed sessions, and votes were to be neither made public nor published. All judges and officials of the public administration were to be named by the king. In short, the constitution provided a juridical facade for Napoleonic domination of Spain.

Although the Bayonne Constitution was never effectively implemented in Spain, like subsequent liberal constitutions in Spain and Spanish America it enumerated the rights and liberties guaranteed to citizens, including the inviolability of domicile and prohibitions against arrest without warrant, detention in private jails, and torture (Arts. 126–31). It also specified the conditions under which the *cortes* could "suspend the rule [*imperio*] of the constitution," thereby introducing into the Spanish constitutional tradition the basic elements of regimes of exception.

At the king's request, the Senate (composed of twenty-four lifetime appointees of the king) could suspend the constitution "in case of an armed uprising, or disquiet [*inquietudes*] that threaten the security of the State" within a territory and for a specified period of time. In urgent cases, again at the king's request, the Senate could "take whatever other extraordinary measures [were] required to conserve public security" (Art. 38). Moreover, if the government had information that a "conspiracy against the State" was being plotted, the minister of police could "order the appearance and detention of those identified as authors and accomplices" of the conspiracy (Art. 134). Imposed though it was, the first constitutional instrument of liberalism in Spain established a precedent for regimes of exception for future Spanish charters.

Most Spaniards rejected the Bayonne Constitution, both because it was identified with the French intervention and because it appealed neither to Spanish monarchists nor to the fundamental aspirations of Spanish liberals. During the next five years, civil war in Spain, guerrilla resistance against the French, and clerical opposition to the abolition of the Inquisition, among other things, made the Bayonne document a dead letter. However, the French effort to pacify Spanish America by giving the colonies representation in the *cortes* (Art. 92) and by making colonials equal citizens of the Spanish realm and subject to the same laws, privileges, and rights as Iberian Spaniards, frontally challenged the old imperial order.

For Spanish America, the Bayonne Constitution offered the end of colonial status as the price of support for Napoleon against Ferdinand VII and the Spanish resistance. Few took the bait. Still, the idea of representation in the *cortes* and the end of discriminatory treatment by authorities in Spain was attractive to Spanish Americans. When Spanish and English forces later sought colonial support in efforts to expel the French from the Iberian peninsula, the Central Junta and the constituent *cortes* called to create a new Spanish regime could hardly offer less than had the French.

Certain liberals in Spain who expected a progressive era to sweep away the institutional and cultural baggage of an archaic social order had initially welcomed the French intervention. So did some monarchists and mercantile, agrarian, military, and bureaucratic interests who preferred the order of Bonapartist administration to the threat of republican anarchy.[14] However, Napoleon's anticlerical image and the threat to the residual corporate privileges (*fueros*) of towns, regional-ethnic enclaves (for example, the Basque provinces and Catalonia), military and ecclesiastical orders, and occupational groups produced an unlikely alliance against the invaders. Spanish nationalism, though still more constrained by regionalism then in certain other parts of Europe, also provoked resistance. Finally, loyalty to the Crown and to the church inspired intense emotional rejection of the French occupation.

In 1809, the Central Junta, which resisted the French in the king's name, proclaimed that the colonial subjects were colonists no more but the equal of Iberian Spaniards: "Your destinies no longer depend on ministers or viceroys or governors, they are in your hands."[15] Juntas created in the colonies, parallel to the Central Junta and provincial juntas in Spain, took broad political and military initiatives, ostensibly in the name of Ferdinand VII, but thereby weakened the authority of Iberian government over the colonies. While the legal fiction of loyalty was maintained, the *criollo* elite enjoyed the greater autonomy permitted by events in Spain.

For the minority of colonials intent on independence, these developments represented the initial, if highly ambiguous, steps toward their objective.

Besieged by French troops and Spanish collaborationists, the Central Junta fled from Seville to Cádiz. In 1810 it convoked a national *cortes* and then resigned, leaving power with a makeshift, five-man regency. Debates within the *cortes* that began meeting in September 1810 reflected the multiple divisions within Spanish society and the fundamental political questions confronting the Spanish polity after 1808. Could the king, without the consent of the nation, transfer the crown and its patrimony to another sovereign (Joseph Bonaparte)? Did such a a transfer violate the mythical social contract and require (or allow) a new contract founded upon the ancient rights and privileges (*fueros*) of Spanish kingdoms, localities, and estates?

Conservatives and moderates tended to favor this latter interpretation, which would preserve the monarchy and Spanish legal codes in a new constitution, legitimated by reference to largely mythical medieval origins of political authority. This alternative would also conserve the central role of the church in Spanish life. In contrast, some liberals and republicans insisted upon the sovereign rights of the people, in the tradition of the French Revolution of 1789; they desired a constitution that would establish the foundations of a new political order.

THE CONSTITUTION OF 1812

In 1810 the *cortes* named a commission to write a constitution for Spain. After extensive debate of drafts, the new constitution was promulgated in March 1812.[16] Political expediency led the *cortes* to adopt a constitutional hybrid. With representatives from the provinces of Spain and most of the Spanish American colonies, the *cortes* enacted Spain's first constitutional monarchy and its first formal departure from patrimonial absolutism. The Cádiz Constitution, or Constitution of 1812, was modeled partly on France's 1791 Constitution. However, the debates in the *cortes* symbolically recalled the ancient privileges and immunities of regions and social groups in medieval Spain, though radical liberals (*exaltados*) among the representatives derided this source of constitutional legitimacy. Ultimately, the constitution was a testament to the contradictions between republican-liberal principles and the persistence of the monarchy, especially in traditional and Catholic Spain.

By making "all free men born in the dominions of Spain" citizens and by declaring that "the nation of Spain is independent and free, and is not, nor can it ever be, the patrimony of any family or person," the Cádiz Constitution served both as a political instrument against the French usurpation and as a foundation for an emergent constitutional monarchy (Arts. 1–4). The constitution proclaimed that "sovereignty resides essentially in the nation, and therefore the right to establish its fundamental laws pertains exclusively to [the nation]" (Art. 3). The constitution assigned to the *cortes,* in representation of the nation, the authority for "proposing, and decreeing the laws, and interpreting them and derogating them, if necessary" (Art. 131). However, the power of making the laws "resides in the *cortes* with the king" (Art. 14), language reminiscent more of British than French constitutional monarchy.

With the *cortes* central to the new political order, the constitution also created a centralized, hierarchical, administrative regime that eliminated archaic medieval privileges as well as the institutions of local political initiative. An attack both on the ancien régime and the threat of democratic or populist political movements, the Constitution of 1812 limited political participation in the elections of deputies to the unicameral *cortes.* Members were selected through a system of limited male suffrage (with property, occupational, and literacy requirements) and indirect elections.

The monarch became a limited ruler with restricted suspensive veto over the *cortes*'s legislation. The king's veto could delay promulgation of laws for a year at a time, for up to three years, without the possibility of legislative override (Arts. 144–49). The constitution also declared that "the person of the king is sacred and inviolable, the king is not responsible" (liable for his actions) (Art. 108). The king would be treated as "His Catholic Majesty" and have exclusive authority for executing the law. This authority "extends to all matters directed to conservation of internal public order and the external security of the State, in conformity with the Constitution and the laws" (Arts. 169–70).

Although Article 172 limited the king's powers, the constitution designated him as the commander of all armies and navies, with the power to name general officers and to deploy the armed forces as required (Art. 171). Further, the ratification of all colonial legislation (dating back to the still-recognized *Recopilación de Leyes de los Reynos de las Indias,* 1681), insofar as it did not conflict with the Cádiz document, reinforced the broad executive authority of administrators, the commingling of civil and military offices, and sweeping government power in times of emergency.

To prevent the king from usurping legislative authority, the constitution prohibited him from suspending legislative sessions or dissolving the *cortes*. Any person who advised the king to do so, or assisted such efforts, would be declared a traitor and prosecuted as such (Art. 172). Cognizant of the immediate political crisis, the authors of the constitution prohibited the king from leaving Spain or abdicating without permission of the *cortes*. (The provision against leaving the country without permission was later widely applied to presidents in the constitutions of Spanish American nations in the nineteenth century, as were other provisions related to executive authority and civil-military relations.)

Whereas the constitution maintained the monopoly of the Catholic religion, a year later the *cortes* abolished the Inquisition, confirming an 1808 order of the Bonapartists. It also charged the *cortes* with protecting political liberty and freedom of the press, an obvious attack on the political functions of the Inquisition in the ancien régime. In short, the Cádiz Constitution sought to transform the fundamental political formula of Spain, if less radically than in France in the early 1790s.

A fundamental dilemma of the Spanish *cortes* in elaborating a charter for a constitutional monarchy, a dilemma shared by other European legislators after the Napoleonic revolution, concerned the scope of executive authority in the new regime. This dilemma, solved in the United States with the unique presidency of the 1787 Constitution, combined with the elaboration of enumerated powers, a bill of rights and, ultimately, judicial review, was resolved in Spain with a peculiar constitutional monarch. The king remained responsible for keeping internal order, was commander of the armed forces, and would be "His Catholic Majesty." The *cortes* had the authority to legislate, alter the constitution, implement regimes of exception when necessary, and regulate the internal affairs of the military. This was a radical departure from the past absolutist royal authority and also from future liberal constitutions that would restore certain emergency powers to the executive. It provided, however, no direct checks on the king's executive actions; he was not criminally or civilly liable for breaches of the constitution or the law.

In the 1812 charter, the *cortes*, rather than the executive, was authorized to suspend certain civil liberties and rights, in all or part of the nation, "in extraordinary circumstances required by security of the State" (Art. 308). The *cortes* also could determine when protection against search and seizure in private domiciles might be removed "for good order or security of the State" (Art. 305). In effect, the *cortes* sought to maintain "the mask of Ferdinand VII" at the same time that the legislators claimed to act as sovereign representatives of the Spanish people and to limit royal authority. The contradiction in this was well illustrated when the *cortes* imprisoned Bishop Pedro Quevedo for refusing to take an oath of loyalty to the *cortes* without the qualification that such an oath did not infringe on the king's ultimate authority.[17] The *cortes* released the bishop when he agreed to take the unqualified oath, but it did not resolve the basic constitutional contradictions.[18]

The Cádiz Constitution also challenged traditional civil-military relations. Military officers exercised considerable civil authority as provincial administrators in eighteenth-century Spain, including the use of extensive emergency powers when deemed necessary. The officers who governed the thirteen local capitals and the lieutenants responsible for smaller towns formed the nucleus of public administration. Military officers routinely made political and social decisions, from price control of basic consumer goods to managing the effects of unemployment, housing shortages, and public health problems.

The new constitution declared that "there shall be a permanent national military and naval force, for the external defense of the State and for the conservation of internal order" (Art. 356). It also provided that "military schools be established for education and instruction for the different branches of the army and navy" (Art. 359). The constitution defined the political mission of the armed forces as "conservation of internal order." The oath taken by military personnel to "defend [*guardar*] the constitution presumed a legitimate, constitutionally prescribed role for the military in Spanish politics. By constitutional prescription, the military and its mission to conserve internal order became fundamental pillars of the new political system. In this sense, the military could not intervene in politics; it was defined as a critical component of the political order. Although the *cortes* had authority to determine the size and budget of the armed forces, the constitution consecrated a place for the military in the political system. (This constitutional role of the armed forces would be a common feature of Spanish American constitutions after the colonies achieved independence.)

If the Cádiz Constitution guaranteed a political role for the Spanish military, it also threatened certain entrenched patterns of civil-military relations. Designation of *jefes superiores* as chief administrative officers in each province, and *jefes políticos* at the local level, potentially challenged the customary role of military officers in internal administration (Arts. 309, 324). Likewise, the duty to preserve the constitution and to be loyal to the king (Art. 374) departed from the army's customary oath of allegiance to the Crown rather than to the nation and its institutions. Further innovations appeared in the *cortes's* authority to establish through regulations (*ordenanzas*) all matters "relating to internal discipline, promotions, salaries, administration, and all else corresponding to the good formation of the army and navy" (Art. 359).

These provisions, among others, portended drastic changes in civil-military relations in Spain, particularly since the military typically accounted for 50 percent of the national budget, had been accountable only to the king and its own military courts, and was accustomed to special privileges and exemptions from civil jurisdiction and certain taxes. As late as 1793, Charles IV decreed that military courts had "exclusive and absolute jurisdiction over all criminal and civil cases in which members of my army are cited . . . excepting only entail cases [*mayorazgo*] . . . and the partition of inheritances."[19] The challenges of these traditional military privileges created controversy in Spain and the new nations in Spanish America throughout the nineteenth century.

The Cádiz Constitution also provided for national militias in each province, regulated by their own *ordenanzas.* The king could call upon these forces in "cases of necessity" for service only within their home province—unless the *cortes* authorized their deployment elsewhere (Arts. 362–65). In part, these provisions acknowledged the central role of the local guerrilla bands bleeding the French occupying army, which caused the Duke of Wellington to remark that "the more ground the French hold, the weaker they will be at any point."[20] It also recognized the need for military reserves in the provinces to confront local riots or political uprisings. However, in internal disputes provincial militias tended to weaken the power of the Crown and the army while reinforcing Spanish regionalism and political bossism (caudillismo) in the provinces. This effect would also influence politics in Central and South America, where elements of the 1812 Constitution became part of national charters in the next decade.

The constitutional monarchy defined in the 1812 Constitution provided conceptual and juridical antecedents for executive institutions and civil-military relations in parts of Spanish America after independence. In particular, the powers extended to the monarch, the powers shared between monarch and *cortes,* the role assigned to the military in the Cádiz Constitution, and the broad definition of emergency powers all found their expression, to some extent, in later Spanish American documents. The conflict over how to assign authority for the adoption and implementation of emergency measures and the installation of regimes of exception—in the executive or legislative branches—also became a legacy of the Cádiz debates.

RESISTANCE AND RESTORATION OF FERDINAND VII

Fighting on behalf of the imprisoned monarch, Spanish guerrillas, irregulars, and elements of the old royal army as well as British troops challenged the French invasion. This resistance, combined with Napoleon's losses in other European military adventures, eventually ended the French occupation of Spain. Napoleon moved his best troops from Spain to central Europe in 1813; in June, after the British forces defeated the French at Vitoria, Joseph Bonaparte returned to France. In December 1813, Napoleon imposed a treaty of alliance against the British on Ferdinand VII, and the king returned to Spain.

During the years of French occupation, severe strains developed in Spanish civil-military relations, as the Central Junta (though it included three general officers) and provincial juntas offended officers with their interference in military policy, promotions, and tactics. Claiming that the army officers "embodied the general will of the nation, perverted by a selfish clique of unpopular politicians," conservative military leaders determined to save the nation from both the French and the revolutionary threat of the radical liberals (*exaltados*).[21] Bemoaning the civilian failure to supply adequately the troops and its disposition to blame defeats and policy failures on the military, the military elite viewed the juntas and then the *cortes* with disdain and mistrust. They also feared the growing liberal influence within the army and the political divisions this created within the military.

With the withdrawal of the French armies and Spanish collaborators, General Francisco Javier Elío, who had served in the *banda oriental* (later Uruguay) and resisted the independence movements in Buenos Aires after 1810 (see chapter 7),

> bade Ferdinand welcome and handed him the baton which he
> had received from "the nation represented in Cortes" as token

of his command. Ferdinand, who was probably still undecided whether or not he should swear allegiance to the Constitution, demurred, but Elío insisted: "Grasp it, Sire! If your Majesty grasp it but a single moment, it will acquire new virtue, new power."

The King did so and handed the thing back; the General, who had saluted the constitutional monarch, then kissed the hand of a master. In a month the *Cortes* had been dissolved, the Constitution abrogated, and the Liberals proscribed.[22]

To the dismay of Spanish liberals, and with the support of conservative deputies in the *cortes*, Ferdinand VII denounced the Constitution of 1812 and rejected the principle of constitutional monarchy shortly after his return. On May 14, 1814, his Decree of Valencia restored the absolutist monarchy and rejected the actions of the *cortes* "as if they had never occurred" ("como si no hubiesen pasado jamás"). The king also decreed that any person who dared to uphold the Cádiz Constitution was "guilty of '*lèse-majesté*,' and I sentence him to death, whether he does this by his actions or his writings or by what he says, inciting or in any way exhorting and persuading others to keep and observe the said Constitution."[23]

What the king could not undo or control were the numerous changes that had occurred within the Spanish military: the tripling of men under arms, demands for further professionalization of the military career and for additional resources, requests for new educational opportunities and sinecures. The army had become a hothouse of political intrigue and a source of political power. Its commanders, acting as political warlords or de facto viceroys, had become arbiters of provincial and national politics.

From the time of the Restoration in 1814, persecution of liberal leaders, journalists, and military officers had embittered the king's adversaries. Dismissal, assignment to undesirable posts, and the repression of liberal military officers by the king's conservative war minister, General Francisco Eguia, further politicized the armed forces. General Eguia also sought to destroy the military reforms introduced between 1808 and 1814, from petty liberalizations regarding dress and grooming to improved pay and pension programs and the military academy. These counterreforms angered enlisted personnel and some officers, thereby further undermining military unity.[24]

A series of unsuccessful military mutinies (1814–1820), originating in discontent among officers and noncoms who had fought against the French as loyalists, foreshadowed civil-military dilemmas in Spain for the rest of the nineteenth century.[25] The first of these *pronunciamientos*, or army-led political uprisings, occurred in 1814 when guerrilla chief Francisco Epoz y Mina was transferred to Pamplona. Epoz y Mina had expected a more important post in recognition of his successes in the war against the French. Though earlier not openly associated with liberal political convictions, his revolt made him the first of the liberal caudillos to demand the restoration of the 1812 Constitution.

Factors beyond the obstinacy and reactionary vision of Ferdinand VII and his advisers induced similar mutinies in the next five years. These included the inability of the regular forces to absorb permanently the thousands of guerrillas and officers inherited from the war against the French; animosities between guerrilla and regular officers; intergenerational cleavages within the army, particularly between professionals and the old aristocratic officers; the penetration into the army of several thousand officers influenced by Masonry (and efforts by military commissions to purge this liberal threat to the military); the lack of political sensitivity by the government and its failure to recognize the danger of slighting the military leaders who made restoration possible.

These factors, as well as the general lack of political consensus in Spain and the ungovernability from Madrid of the still militarized provinces, inhibited Ferdinand VII's endeavor to reestablish the hegemony of the ancien régime.[26] It also hampered the politico-military struggle to reaffirm the empire in the Western Hemisphere.[27] Indeed, discontent within the army that was amassed in Andalusia to reinforce the Spanish military in America precipitated a liberal *pronunciamiento* in 1820.[28] Under the pressure of the military *pronunciamiento* led by Colonel (self-promoted to General) Rafael del Riego, Ferdinand VII convoked the *cortes* and swore allegiance to the Cádiz Constitution.[29] With this ironic impetus and the erosion of absolutist legitimacy, the army came to occupy a central role in Spanish politics.

The liberals, now in tenuous political control, attempted to meet the often conflicting demands of various elements within the military in order to consolidate the new government. A "Constituent Law of the Army" (1821) mandated establishment of military schools for each service branch, reform of conscription procedures, shorter tours of duty (from eight years to five), benefits for retired and disabled personnel and their dependents, and maintenance of the *fuero militar*.[30] Overall, the new law promised more resources, patronage, and privileges than the nation could afford. Liberal officers occupied ministries; nepotism, cronyism, and favoritism permeated the armed forces. These political, professional, and personal antagonisms divided the military and repeatedly asserted themselves from 1823 until the late nineteenth century. Politically committed and ambitious military officers understood only too well the political foundations of career advancement and national power for themselves and their institutions and therefore sought to control the state that dispensed these opportunities.

In their efforts to prevent a counterrevolutionary movement, liberals in 1820 also provided the Spanish government and future Spanish American republican governments with a classic model for civil-military coups d'état "in the name of the people" or "the nation":

> The *pronunciamiento* was the instrument of liberal revolution in the nineteenth century ... an officer revolt, justified by a crude political theory which made the officer corps the ultimate repository of a general will. When that will was vitiated either by the monarch's evil counsellors or, as the later theoreticians of military indiscipline were to maintain, by the corrupt operation of Parliamentary institutions run by a clique of 'anti-national' politicians, then it could be salvaged by the heroic gesture of a general or the conspiracy of an officer's mess.[31]

Seeking to defend liberal principles and the constitutional order, the liberals provided model legislation for regimes of exception and the subordination of civilian to military authority in times of crisis. The Spanish liberals, fearing the restoration of absolute monarchy, promulgated the foundations for constitutional dictatorship.

THE CADIZ CONSTITUTION AND THE LAW OF APRIL 17

In 1821, the liberal *cortes* adopted Spain's first republican legislation to protect the "security of the state," that is, to repress opponents of the 1812 Constitution. As in France (see chapter 1), the Spanish equivalent of state of siege legislation was the work of liberals intent on defending the new order against the forces of reaction. Known as the Law of April 17, this new legislation (theoretically adopted in conformity with Article 286 of the Constitution of 1812, which called for the *cortes* to legislate concerning the administration of criminal justice) defined as criminals those who conspired against the observance of the constitution or against the internal or external security of the state "or against the sacred and inviolable person of the constitutional King" (Art. 1). Article 2 made violators subject to military law, under the jurisdiction of *consejos de guerra,* supposedly in a manner consistent with eighteenth-century royal ordinances. Article 3 placed under military jurisdiction any person who resisted government forces. Resistance, according to Article 4, included any conspiratorial behavior after the government had ordered the termination of such activity. Violators included those who were "found meeting with the subversives (*facciosos*), even if unarmed; those apprehended by the forces of order after meeting with the subversives; those who having been with the subversives, are in hiding, [or] out of their homes with arms."

This legal device, a cynical analogue to "reading the Riot Act" in England (see chapter 1), made political opposition a crime and subjected these "criminals" to military law and repression.[32] Article 288 of the Constitution of 1812 further declared that "if there is resistance [to arrest] or if flight [*la fuga*] is feared, force may be used to secure [*asegurar*] the person." The Cádiz Constitution thus presaged the justification for the deaths of numerous victims in Spain and Spanish America "shot while seeking to escape" during the next century.

Determination of when to apply the Law of April 17 was also left to military officers charged with provincial administration. This further militarization of Spanish politics and judicial administration mocked the liberal pretense of guaranteeing civil liberties through the Constitution of 1812. Thereafter, an evolving constitutional monarchy would have recourse to the legislation introduced by liberals, and other antisubversive legislation, to protect the security of the state. Indeed, after 1834, the captains-general periodically met disturbances with state of siege decrees that, ipso facto, imposed martial law without any formal restraint on military authorities. The military commander was authorized "to take all measures he believes convenient to achieve the objectives assigned to him" ("tomar las medidas que crea convenientes para conseguir el objeto que se le ha encomendado").[33]

RESTORATION II: 1823–1833

By 1823, conservative forces assisted by French troops and the Holy Alliance again prevailed in Spain. Spanish liberalism represented a fundamental challenge to the monarchies of Europe; the destruction of the liberal regime and the restoration of absolutism in Spain became a principal foreign policy objective of the European monarchies. The spread of liberal subversion threatened revolution; dynastic loyalties, ideological concordance, and the requirements of European *real politique* resulted in a return of French troops to Spain, justified by the Treaty of Verona signed in 1822 by representatives of Austria, France, Prussia, and Russia:

> The great powers who are signatories to this treaty, fully convinced that a system of representational government is as incompatible with the principle of monarchy as is the idea of sovereignty of the people with the principle of divine right, formally undertake to use all the means at their disposal to destroy the representational system of government in every European state in which it now exists and to prevent its introduction into those countries where it is now unknown.
>
> As there can be no doubt that the freedom of the press is the most powerful single weapon in the armoury of those who pretend to defend the rights of the people in their struggle against their kings, the great powers who are signatories to this treaty promise to take every measure to suppress it, not only in their own states but also in every other European country.
>
> . . . Since the state of affairs in Spain and Portugal at the present time brings together all the unfortunate circumstances which are referred to in this treaty, entrusting to France the task of reforming them, assures her of their support in that form which will least compromise her with their own peoples and with the French people—that is, in the form of an annual subsidy of twenty million francs each, effective from the day of ratification of this treaty and valid for as long as the war shall last.[34]

This international commitment to suppress the spread of liberalism through military intervention and support for Ferdinand VII proved to be inadequate. It would be impossible to contain ideological diffusion with occupation armies and local civil-military allies. Although Ferdinand VII reasserted his authority in 1823 at the point of French bayonets and with the support of Spanish royalists and elements of civil society more fearful of disorder and attacks on property than of authoritarian government, underlying social and political changes precluded the complete restoration of the ancien régime. The king and his government survived until 1833, but the *cortes* and the military maintained the political roles carved out from 1812 to 1814 and from 1820 to 1823.

Ironically, though Ferdinand VII heavily indebted Spain by compensating the Holy Alliance for its intervention, to protect French bankers the French government prevented the king from voiding the debt contracted by the liberal government.[35] The absolutist era had ended, even though the monarchy, landowners, provincial and local officials, and even certain social elites—for a variety of contradictory reasons—sought to limit the institutionalization of liberal doctrine and practices. Spanish politics entered a period of bastardized constitutional monarchy, military political dominance, and regional conflicts that bled the country without respite. After the initial purges (*purificaciones*) eliminating liberals from the public administration and the armed forces, and after the repression of the military commissions, Ferdinand's policies became more pragmatic—though he never overcame his hatred for the leadership of the 1812 *cortes* or the 1820 liberal *pronunciamiento*. Indeed, when Riego was executed just after the 1823 Restoration, the king began a decree with "so that even the remotest idea that sovereignty resides in other than my royal person shall forever disappear from Spanish soil."[36]

By 1826–1827, nevertheless, dissatisfied with Ferdinand VII's apparent concessions to liberals, radical royalists revolted, proposing Carlos, the king's brother, as an alternative sovereign. Suppressed by force, the uprising evidenced the intense cleavages within the royalist and monarchical factions of Spain. This left the army, or temporarily dominant factions of the army, as the arbiter of Spanish politics. Ferdinand VII's death in 1833 precipitated decades of recurrent dynastic wars. The labyrinth of Spanish politics became more complex as monarchists supporting different royal lineages slaughtered one another while liberals and moderates sought to consolidate the constitutional monarchy or to destroy it to create a nonmonarchical republic.

Throughout this period, civilian politicians wooed the military elite to their respective causes; ultimately, military officers occupied the most important ministries in the most conservative or most liberal governments. In 1841, "liberal" General Espartero even served as regent, after forcing the queen regent into exile.[37] Military officers had become the leading political figures in a Spain afflicted by episodic civil war and political strife. Even before Spain suffered this fate, indeed by the time Ferdinand VII defeated the liberals in 1823, most of the American colonies were lost. Resignation to this reality came only later in the nineteenth century, and the final demise of Spanish imperial glory occurred with the loss of Cuba, Puerto Rico, and the Philippines in 1898.[38]

SPANISH AMERICAN INDEPENDENCE

Napoleon's invasion of the Iberian peninsula in 1807–1808 and the imposition of his brother, Joseph Bonaparte, upon the Spanish throne provoked a political crisis in Spanish America analogous to the political breakdown that occurred in Spain. This crisis induced the birth of independent Spanish American nations.[39]

In Spanish America, as in Spain, resistance to the French-imposed administration degenerated into civil war. Royalists, conservatives, liberals, and republicans, along with opportunists, visionaries, and nationalists, fought for over fifteen years before most of Latin America's present nations emerged independent. Influenced by changing military capabilities and the vicissitudes of internal politics in Spain and by international intrigues involving European and North American policies toward Spain's rebellious colonies, Spanish American independence movements exhibited many of the same internal contradictions as the war of independence waged by Spaniards against the Bonapartist regime. The politico-military struggle left death and destruction throughout the Western Hemisphere—without forging unified nations or consensus on the nature of the political order to replace the Spanish imperial regime.

For Spanish America, the Cádiz Constitution and the *cortes's* decree abolishing the Council of the Indies (the monarchy's principal administrative instrument for governing the colonies, though much of its previous authority had shifted to the secretary of state for the Indies) presented myriad opportunities and profound dilemmas. By 1812, only Venezuelans had declared independence from Spain (1811), though ambiguous declarations of both separation and loyalty to the king occurred in Upper Peru (Bolivia) and Quito (1809) and in Colombia, Buenos Aires, and Chile (1810). Thus, the new political institutions adopted in Spain might have wrested from the potential independence coalition those colonials desiring reforms within a restored Bourbon regime, such as the political moderates looking for new economic and political opportunities without a definitive break from Spain.

Yet the Cádiz Constitution offended both unrequited conservative monarchists who opposed constitutional constraints on traditional absolutist authority and the small radicalized minority already determined to achieve independence. With the restoration of Ferdinand VII in Spain and the arrival of new expeditionary forces to reconquer the colonies, theory gave way to the reality of repression of liberals and supporters of local autonomy. As the facade of authority in the name of the king was removed, opposing forces drew clearer battle lines in the colonies. After 1815, conditions in much of Spanish America were catastrophic: war, civil war, rebellion, disorder, banditry, fragmentation, and disillusionment. Old colonial subdivisions became the fiefdoms of competing warlords or regional leaders (caudillos), who proclaimed themselves liberals or conservatives but always depended upon military forces to secure their autonomy or to negotiate temporary stalemates.

From 1810 to 1820, the intensity of conflict and the commitment of *criollo* elites to independence varied greatly from colony to colony. The ebb and flow of combat resulted in victories both for royalists and independence armies; political events in Spain from 1820 to 1823 and the erosion of Spanish military morale and determination allowed rebel victories, tipping the scales toward independence. With the second restoration of Ferdinand VII in 1823, the king sought the support of the French and other European monarchies to reimpose imperial rule in the colonies; French, British, and U.S. policies, including the Monroe Doctrine proclaimed in 1823, foreclosed international support for Spanish reconquest. In December 1824, at the Battle of Ayacucho, Peru, independence forces defeated the royalist army. A last-gasp invasion sent from Cuba to Veracruz, Mexico, in 1829 ended serious Spanish efforts to reconquer the American colonies.

The newly independent nations of Latin America faced practically insurmountable social and economic problems in their first quarter century. Fifteen years of war had destroyed much economic infrastructure, discouraged private investment, and disrupted the economy, particularly in the traditional mainstays of agriculture and mining. The elimination or disorganization of the professional bureaucracy made tax administration and revenue collection uncertain; military expenditures absorbed large shares of national budgets.

Social tensions compounded economic problems. Class and racial stratification persisted, with Indian, black, and *casta* (mixtures of blacks, Indians, and Europeans) occupying the base of a rigid social hierarchy. Predominantly rural and poor, dominated by owners of large rural estates and mines, the majority of Latin Americans gained little or nothing from political independence. Yet military caudillos and independence leaders made political promises that teased the underclasses with the possibilities of a better life.

Political independence brought the obvious problems of organizing national government institutions in the midst of civil strife and economic stagnation. Spanish colonial rule had left very limited models for representative government (elections to the Central Junta and *cortes* from 1809 to 1813) and no institutions for popular participation in policy making. It also left no conception of limited government—except perhaps the constitutional monarchy briefly experienced with the Constitution of 1812. The new nations nevertheless declared themselves republics and wrote and rewrote constitutions guaranteeing the rights and liberties of the American Constitution, the French Revolution, and the Cádiz Constitution.[40] Political elites declared themselves centralists or federalists, liberals or conservatives, clericals or anticlericals—and by the 1840s, some even proclaimed the ideals of socialism sweeping Europe.

With few exceptions (Chile after 1833 is the most frequently mentioned), political and economic instability persisted long after independence as the military and civilian caudillos of the independence struggle battled one another for national and regional hegemony. Consolidation of permanent national government institutions occurred nowhere in Latin America before the 1860s and, in many cases, not until much later in the nineteenth or early twentieth century. This meant that all constitution writers, conservative or liberal, federalist or unitarian, anticipated the possibility of disorder and violence—and the requisite authority for its suppression. In some cases, this anticipation manifested itself in vague assignments of authority to the executive to maintain peace and internal order. In other cases, it resulted in more explicit designs for constitutional regimes of exception.

Leaders of the new nations replaced the preindependence legitimacy of the imperial system with the extremely fragile authority of republican constitutions proclaiming lofty principles unintelligible to most of the population. In practice, political conflict, except in the event of episodic riots or protests characteristic of the ancien régime, occurred among a minuscule political class. Typically, control over the armed forces, political assassination, or victory in civil war determined who governed or who attempted to govern. During the first decades after independence, politics were extremely exclusionary and nonparticipatory. Rather than elections, popular participation meant serving as soldiers, fighting as rebels or guerrillas,

or pillaging as bandits—much as in Spain after 1808. In these cir-˙
cumstances, the reestablishment of political order had priority. Like
the French after the revolution of 1789 and the Spanish after the
liberal Constitution of 1812 (and emulating also the enumerated
powers of the congress and president of the United States), Latin
American elites incorporated provisions for strong executives and
for regimes of exception, or both, into almost all of their many constitutions. The well-known Peruvian scholar, José Pareja Paz-
Soldán, suggested that the president in Latin American
constitutions "was a natural heir of the viceroys" and, citing
nineteenth-century Venezuelan president Carlos Soublette, that
"Venezuelans could not convince themselves that the President of
the Republic was not a *capitán general.*"[41]

Perhaps the constitutional king of the 1812 Cádiz Constitution
was also an appropriate comparison. Many early Latin American
constitutions defined executive authority quite similarly to Article
170 of the Cádiz document: "The power [*potestad*] to execute the
laws resides exclusively in the King, and his authority extends to all
matters directed to the conservation of internal public order and
the external security of the State, in conformity with the Constitution and the laws." As in Europe, and especially in Spain, republicans in Spanish America faced the challenge of those still favoring
monarchy. Beyond this fundamental cleavage, centralists were opposed by supporters of federalism or confederal regimes. Conflicts
over the basic political formula and structure of government over-
lapped ideological, religious, and personalist differences. The character of church-state relations, the extent of political participation
(property and racial qualifications for voting and office holding),
the abolition of slavery, and a number of other issues remained un-
resolved. The new nations experimented with radical confederal
and federal schemes, more moderate centralist-republican institutions, and the quasi-monarchical constitutions with life-tenure presidents and three-house legislatures suggested by Simón Bolívar in
1826 (adopted in Bolivia and with modifications elsewhere).[42]

Whichever was adopted, the reality of almost perpetual strife,
antagonistic personalist factions, and overlapping civilian-military
jurisdictions conflicted dramatically with the republican institutions and the separation of powers proclaimed by the new constitutions. A vast gap between political theory and practice meant that
cynicism and frustration permeated Spanish American politics.
Force rather than law, or law interpreted through the prism of
force, came to dominate the region. The wars of independence and

the subsequent civil and international wars had militarized Latin American governments (and budgets). Understandably, the role of the military also received considerable attention in the nineteenth-century constitutions. Spanish customs and traditions (including the *fuero militar*) and the French revolutionary tradition exercised significant influence. Apparently, the role of the Spanish military on the peninsula from 1812 to 1823 also impressed Spanish American constitution writers with the desirability of limiting the deliberative and political role of the armed forces.

Most of the new constitutions attempted to forbid military participation in politics, to assign budgetary and force-level authority to legislative (and occasionally executive) officials, and to reserve decisions over promotions, military education, and deployment to civilian authorities. Contradictions between these provisions and political necessity, along with the variety of regimes of exception included in the new constitutions, often made civilian control over the military illusory. Torn between the requirements of order and stability, the legacy of the Spanish colonial regime (and its Spanish liberal opponents), and the ideals of French, British, and North American liberalism, Spanish American political elites sought constitutional foundations for their newly won political liberty. Usually, however, as in Spain, the constitutions of nineteenth-century Spanish America contained the juridical foundations for constitutional dictatorship.

Part 2

Introduction

THE 1820 MILITARY UPRISING IN SPAIN AND THE TEMPORARY REAF-
firmation of the Cádiz Constitution precipitated the final struggle
for independence in most of Spanish America. The bastions of
royal authority—Lima, Mexico City, Guatemala—succumbed to
military force and to the erosion of Spanish political credibility. In
much of the region, particularly in Mexico and Central America,
conservative and clerical reaction to the policies of Spanish liberals
proved decisive, though in other regions independence had long
since been declared and a number of constitutional experiments
undertaken.

Whatever the idiosyncratic character of local independence movements,[1] several issues dominated the debates over new political systems for the emergent nations. The first of these was the basic form
of government and source of sovereign power. Although proponents of constitutional monarchism surfaced everywhere, republican constitutions were ultimately adopted almost without
exception—even where, as in Bolivia, Peru, and later Guatemala,
presidents-for-life were briefly introduced as republican surrogates
for constitutional monarchs. In Mexico and Central America, a
short-lived empire (1821–1823) followed independence; only in
Brazil did monarchy survive in South America until late in the
nineteenth century.[2]

In sharing the dramatic and destabilizing change from divine-
right monarchy to republics based on popular sovereignty, Spanish
Americans faced the unique legacy of Iberian colonialism. Bereft
of national identity, representative political institutions, and autonomous local government, they also inherited class- and caste-
stratified societies that belied proclamations of liberty and equality

59

as first principles. After centuries of religious intolerance and inquisitorial persecution of dissidents, the Spanish Americans faced even more imposing obstacles to creating viable republican institutions than did either the Europeans who shed monarchy or the U.S. citizens after separating from the British. Almost every facet of the Spanish American past conflicted with the premises of liberalism, republicanism, and limited government.

A second issue was the desirability of centralist as opposed to federalist regimes. In contrast to the North American case that certain political leaders sought to emulate, Spanish America lacked any strong institutional foundations for federalism, although the Cádiz Constitution of 1812 had encouraged provincial and elected local councils (*diputaciones provinciales* and *ayuntamientos*) in some parts of the American colonies. Perhaps more importantly, geographical isolation, regional jealousies and animosities, intermittent warfare, and personal ambitions made federalism—understood as relative autonomy for local and regional elites—attractive. The attractiveness of federalism for some intellectuals and regional caudillos conflicted directly with the colonies' tradition of centralized, bureaucratic organization and the pervasiveness of broad executive authority and patrimonial rule. It also seemed to ignore the urgency of establishing effective national regimes to fill the void left by the expulsion of Spanish authority.

Third, the new nations or confederations had to define the relative political weight of legislative and executive institutions, just as the *cortes* at Cádiz had been forced to define the character of a constitutional monarchy and its relationship to the legislative and judicial authorities. Solutions ranged from the equivalent of constitutional monarchs to emasculated presidents of fragile confederations.

Particular issues of grave concern included the authority and manner of the election of legislators and the executive and control by the legislature over budgets, taxes, and appointments to the judiciary and the public administration. Extensively debated were the role and control of the military, militia, and police, and the types and manner of implementation of regimes of exception. A number of other constitutional issues also received nearly universal attention, including the role of the Catholic church and the persistence of ecclesiastical *fueros;* the maintenance of entail and primogeniture, noble titles, and other vestiges of Spanish social rank and status; and the role of the state in economic regulation and enterprise. This last issue was frequently expressed in debates on internal taxes and export and import duties, and over the desirability of state monopolies on certain areas of commerce or production, such as tobacco, alcoholic beverages, or mineral products.

Republican institutions took diverse forms in nineteenth-century Spanish America. Most were undergirded by Rousseau's revolutionary doctrine of popular sovereignty moderated by Montesquieu's conception of power divided among executive, legislative, and judicial branches.[3] The Inquisition had declared these contributions of revolutionary French literature to be seditious and contrary to state security. Often they had been smuggled into the colonies in religious articles that were immune from customs inspection. Now they were mixed with adaptations from British, U.S., Spanish, and other continental constitutions. In most cases Spanish colonial legislation was also retained, usually preceded by the caveat "insofar as it does not conflict with the present constitution." With time, the Spanish Americans also borrowed from one another, did considerable comparative analysis of their own constitutional experiments, and debated the merits of numerous institutional designs. By the time Uruguay adopted its first constitution in 1830, for example, delegates to the constitutional convention borrowed directly and liberally from earlier charters in the Rio de la Plata, Venezuela, Colombia, and Chile, as well as from Spain, France, and the United States.[4]

At times this borrowing was useful. At other times it produced indigestible constitutional stews, spiced with clauses lifted verbatim and inappropriately from Europe or from other Spanish American nations. Both conscious, careful choice among alternative constitutional designs and thoughtless plagiarism from other charters characterized constitution making in Spanish America. Frequently, these lifted clauses became customary, associated as they were with the essence of republican institutions. Such clauses, once adopted, had a life of their own, surviving revolutions, coups, and subsequent constitutional reforms without debate. This occurred, for example, with the ubiquitous iteration of life, liberty, security, and property as main objectives of government. It also occurred with the proscription on military participation in politics that Venezuelans (1811, 1819) and then other Spanish Americans lifted from the 1791 French Constitution (Title IV, Art. 12): "the armed forces are essentially obedient, no armed force may deliberate." This French restriction—the military was not to enact laws, policies, and regulations for governing society (*deliberer*), but to act (*agir*) subject to civil authority—became commonplace in nineteenth-century Spanish American constitutions. It remains so, as do other such lifted constitutional clauses, in the twentieth century.

In practice, political and military reality often diverged radically from constitutional precepts. Force of arms, personalist alliances, and regional caudillos dominated the first half century in almost all of independent Spanish America. The significance of the various constitutions, which were adopted, modified, rejected, readopted, and discarded, lies not in the relationship between constitutional form and reality but rather in the unceasing efforts of political elites to resolve political and socioeconomic crises with new or revised constitutions. Indeed, the first half century of postindependence politics in Latin America demonstrated an almost puzzling insistence on seeking constitutional solutions to insoluble political and economic problems. This was complicated by a pervasive longevity of Spanish attitudes toward authority, religion, dissidence, and the need for order combined with the authoritarian liberalism of French revolutionaries.

Political disorder and instability in Spanish America led some of the leaders of the independence movements to despair. Antonio José de Sucre, who introduced a number of drastic liberal reforms in Bolivia (1825–1828), including the confiscation of church properties and the nationalization of tithe collection, the temporary abolition of the sales tax (*alcabala*), the elimination of state monopolies, and the nationalization of abandoned mines, lamented in a letter to Simón Bolívar: "Our political edifices are constructed on sand; as strong as we make the walls, as much adornment as we provide them, we cannot overcome the defect of the foundation."[5] In 1830, after Sucre's assassination in southern Colombia and only a month before his own death, Bolívar declared: "America is ungovernable. Those who serve the revolution plough the sea. The only thing to do in America is emigrate."[6]

The historical record confirmed Bolívar's despair. Paz Soldán, writing on constitutional development in Peru over a century later, commented: "The Republic of Peru has lived making and unmaking constitutions."[7] Heraclio Bonilla, commenting on two of Peru's nineteenth-century constitutions (1856, 1860), suggested that they "are notable for their total lack of relevance to the economic and social realities of mid-nineteenth century Peru and provide interesting reading only insofar as they illustrate an enormous gap which existed between the educated elite and the nation as a whole."[8]

Similar judgments apply to most of the constitutions of the new Spanish American nations in the half century after independence. Yet certain components of these constitutions became accepted elements of Latin American constitutional formulas and political traditions. The cumulative politico-cultural synthesis of making and unmaking constitutions created a legacy of institutions and political practices that seemed, after more than a century, natural, correct, and necessary. If no particular constitution or political regime gained overwhelming acceptance, certain constitutional precepts and phraseology, along with distinctive patterns of governance and regime succession, evolved by accretion and by practice as national and regional systems of political life.

The iteration and reiteration of philosophical premises, constitutional phrases, and governmental structures and processes copied from the American Revolution of 1776, the French Revolution of 1789, and the Spanish Constitution of 1812—and the reactions to these struggles as well as to the internal civil strife suffered in Spanish America after 1810—created a diverse, but widely shared, Spanish American political culture. Central to this political culture was a lack of consensus regarding the legitimacy of any particular political regime and a tendency for violence to determine the timing and character of government succession. Also widely shared was a nasty mixture of Spanish and liberal intolerance for so-called enemies of the state, factions, and subversives. Opponents were dangerous enemies and critics were heretics who threatened the revealed truth of the new order—and the government in power.

But if state terror eradicated adversaries and violence ended governments and installed new ones—rather than the elections indicated by all but a few of the early constitutions—even the most brutal, lawless caudillos sought legitimation for their repression or their insurgency in new constitutions or constitutional reforms. Constituent assemblies met often, exercised routine legislative functions as well as framing scores of constitutions, and frequently appointed the caudillo of the moment as constitutional president. Many Spanish American dictators disparaged philosophical principles and constitutional debates; very few cared to rule without the facade of constitutional legitimacy.

These circumstances, combined with the symbolic (therefore, real) importance of form and procedure, made provisions within the Spanish American constitutions for regimes of exception, extraordinary emergency powers, and civil-military relations of great concern. Dictators and presidents wanted legal cover for the exercise of power; elites wishing to limit executive authority and arbitrary government action sought constitutional restrictions on emergency powers. With military force the key to the survival of any government, the constitutional role and privileges assigned to the armed forces concerned all political leaders.

Spanish Americans harbored no fantasy that constitutional prohibitions on military intervention guaranteed civilian control of the military, nor that lack of carefully defined emergency authority for the executive and the legislature prevented the exercise of dictatorial powers. Likewise, strict separation of powers, restrictions on the delegation of legislative authority, and even explicit prohibitions on the suspension of constitutionally sacred individual liberties did not guarantee that any of these liberal innovations prevailed. Indeed, the Mexican case (described in chapter 3) is a blatant example of unconstitutional practice dominating constitutional principles. Legislative authorities, presidents, and military officers flagrantly violated constitutional law.

Even in these early constitutions, however, certain alternative approaches to constitutional regimes of exception developed, along with different patterns of civil-military relations. For example, political elites debated eliminating military *fueros* and the constitutional definition of the role of the military as an essential component of the state structure versus leaving the definition of the role of the military to legislative or executive policy. In all the cases studied, however, regimes of exception were integrated as essential components into nineteenth-century constitutions. In over 80 percent of the constitutions promulgated, Spanish American constituents also opted for the constitutional definition of the role of the armed forces.

By the mid-nineteenth century there was no Spanish American nation without some sort of provision for regime(s) of exception woven into its constitutional fabric.

The chapters that follow describe the evolution of regimes of exception and civil-military relations in nineteenth-century Mexico, Central America, northern South America, Peru and Bolivia, Rio de la Plata (Argentina, Paraguay, Uruguay), Chile, and the Dominican Republic. In each case, the development of regimes of exception and the constitutional role of the armed forces is related to internal political development and to the diffusion from Mexico to Patagonia of a particular Spanish American model for constitutional design and politics. This design had at its core a reliance on regimes of exception, an ample constitutional role for the armed forces, and institutionalized political intolerance.

Anticipating the summary of findings reported in chapter 10, each country case study concludes with a brief sketch of the nation's twentieth-century regimes of exception and constitutional provisions for the armed forces in politics. For all the nations studied, the regimes of exception current in the 1990s are clearly linked to constitutional choices made before 1900, just as the pervasive influence of the armed forces in politics is grounded in constitutional and statutory enactments of the nineteenth century.

3

Regimes of Exception in Mexico

IN THE EARLY NINETEENTH CENTURY, MEXICO ACCOUNTED FOR OVER two-thirds of Spain's colonial revenues and remained Spain's most important American possession. Dominated politically and, to a lesser extent, economically by a small elite of less than 20,000 *peninsulares* (in a population of more than 6 million), Mexican colonial society epitomized the race and class stratification generated by Spanish imperialism and by serious *criollo* resentment of *peninsular* privilege.

After 1804, shifting Spanish alliances and wars in Europe placed increasing tax burdens on Mexican colonials. Rising tensions and minor conspiracies from the 1790s onward made Spanish elites uneasy, but it was the potentially destabilizing effects of French intervention in Spain and the ambiguity of Spanish junta politics after 1808 that moved conservative interests to political action in Mexico. As early as 1808, when word reached Mexico of the French invasion of Spain and the abdication of Ferdinand VII, peninsular Spaniards, church leaders, and conservative military-bureaucratic elites effected a quasi-coup against the viceroy, whom they viewed as too concessionary to *criollo* interests. This development encouraged autonomist sentiments, if not desires for independence.[1] The conservative *golpistas* sent the viceroy back to Spain.

Poor economic conditions in Mexico coincided with the political crisis in Spain. In particular, inflation and food shortages (especially corn) occasioned in part by drought (1809–1810) induced social unrest and suffering in the towns and the countryside.[2] Combined with the political conspiracies of Mexican liberals and royalists, both dissatisfied by the impact of events in Spain on Mexico, the economic crisis provoked violent confrontations and drastic counterrevolutionary measures.[3] The pillage, massacre, and devastation wrought by the forces of early independence leaders Miguel Hidalgo and José María Morelos warned *peninsulares* and wealthy *criollos* that an independence movement threatened social revolution. The memory of the looting and atrocities of Hidalgo's "army" at Guanajuato in September 1810 provided ample rationale for preferring restoration of order to "liberty."[4] Largely for that reason, liberal and anti-Spanish independence forces in Mexico failed to construct a social base for the political consolidation of a new regime. Independence resulted only when Spanish liberals, temporarily successful in resurrecting the Constitution of Cádiz in Spain (1820–1823), threatened the church, the military, and royalist interests in Mexico, in addition to reasserting the colonial status of Mexicans.[5]

The ineffectual and counterproductive policies of Spain's liberal government toward Mexico, including the elimination of military *fueros*, forged an unlikely and ultimately unsustainable politico-military alliance of Mexican traditionalists and liberal military leaders. This coalition proclaimed an ambiguous independence for a new Mexican Empire in 1821. Independence came to Mexico after much bloodshed and the suffocation of racial and social challenges to *criollo* dominance. Political leadership devolved on military officers who quit or betrayed the royal army, on ex-royal officials, and on the conservative clergy.[6] Thus Mexican independence would be uniquely conservative, resulting in the coronation of the ex-commander of the royal army as emperor rather than in the establishment of republican institutions. Nowhere else did this occur in Spanish America.

Late in 1820, the viceroy of Mexico had appointed Colonel Agustín de Iturbide to command an army charged with defeating the remaining rebel forces led by Vicente Guerrero. Iturbide had led troops against the early independence movements of the wayward priests, Miguel Hidalgo and (after Hidalgo's execution) José María Morelos. The 1810–1815 Hidalgo-Morelos movement had achieved initial military successes but could not mold a broad social base capable of resisting the absolutist restoration of 1814. Fearful of the populist, even revolutionary, proclamations of Hidalgo and Morelos,[7] many moderate *criollos*, military officers, bureaucrats, and educated colonials preferred reincorporation into the Spanish orbit, albeit with reforms, to the radical challenge of independence and social revolution. Morelos's execution after military defeat in 1815 appeared to signal the end of the independence movement. For the next five years intermittent guerrilla warfare persisted, but the royalist forces were so confident that Viceroy Juan Ruiz de Apodaca assured King Ferdinand VII that Mexico did not require military reinforcements. He sought to cement the military victory with pardons for rebels willing to turn in their weapons.[8]

In the meantime, however, Iturbide had waged a fierce counterinsurgency campaign against the rebels, arresting their family members, relocating the population in "protected villages," and profiteering from the military campaigns. For this reason, the first Mexican constitution, the Decreto Constitucional Para la Libertad de la America Mexicana (Apatzingán, 1814) "is little more than historical memorabilia."[9] Adopted by a constituent assembly on the run from Spanish military forces after fleeing from Chilpancingo, where most of the constitution was debated, to Apatzingán, this document reflected efforts by Mexican liberals to adapt the Spanish 1812 Constitution to local conditions. In this sense, it is the first liberal constitution of Mexico, later incorporated into the official national history as a cornerstone of Mexican independence and nationalism. It is, therefore, of interest in the analysis of the evolution of Mexican political institutions.

THE APATZINGÁN CONSTITUTION

The Apatzingán Constitution merits discussion as a juridical foundation of Mexican liberalism. Like its Spanish analogue, the Cádiz Constitution, the first liberal constitution of Mexico declared in its first article that the apostolic Roman Catholic religion "is the only one that may be professed."[10] Following this reassurance to clerical interests and the social conservatism of elite Mexican colonials, the constitution then announced that the people had the inalienable right to establish the government of its choice and to alter, modify, and abolish it when the people's felicity required (Arts. 3–4). In short, French and North American ideas of sovereignty had replaced the more moderate language of the 1812 Spanish *cortes.*

This revolutionary declaration was reinforced by defining any "threat against the sovereignty of the people" as the crime of high treason (*lesa nación*) (Art. 10). Following the common post-Montesquieu conception, sovereignty was defined as making, executing, and applying or interpreting laws corresponding to legislative, executive, and judicial authorities. Significantly, the constitution clearly provided that these three functions "shall not be exercised by the same person, nor by the same entity" (Arts. 11–12). This last provision restricted delegation of extraordinary powers to the executive, whether these extraordinary powers were legislative or judicial. This made certain types of regimes of exception unconstitutional, though Mexican legislators directly violated these constitutional precepts from 1824 to 1843. Citizenship was lost for the crimes of *lesa nación*, heresy, and apostasy, giving government officials adequate authority to deal with "subversives" (Art. 15).

The four basic purposes of government dear to early nineteenth-century liberals—equality, security, property, and liberty—were declared "the only purpose of political association" (Art. 24). With this in mind, the constituents incorporated into the constitution a list of personal rights and liberties—press, speech, petition of government officials, commerce, and the protection of private property (Arts. 24–40)—guaranteed under the rubric of the four basic purposes of government.

Like the Cádiz document, the Apatzingán Constitution gave dominant power to the newly created legislature. This included control over the size, budget, and internal regulations of the armed forces and militia. A curiosity rarely imitated in Spanish America, the executive branch consisted of a troika, with members alternating as president in an order determined by lot. To further limit executive authority and the possibility of one-man dictatorship, the constitution prohibited an individual's reelection for three years after acting as president.

Despite this intent to limit presidential authority, vague language reminiscent of the Cádiz Constitution authorized the "Supreme Government" to organize the armies and national militias, devise plans of operation, deploy the armed forces, and "to take whatever measures deemed appropriate, whether to assure internal tranquility of the State, or to provide for its external defense, without necessity of prior notification of Congress, to which notification shall be given at the opportune moment" (Art. 160). Article 160 extended such broad authority to the government "to assure the internal tranquility of the State" that other regime of exception provisions seemed superfluous.

As occurred frequently in postindependence Spanish America, the constitution also made the old royal *ordenanzas* the basis for military operations, including, thereby, the *fueros* and military discretion in times of emergency or of "resistance" to legitimate public authority (Art. 171). Further, the constitution incorporated all existing Spanish legislation, except that derogated or in conflict with the new constitution (Art. 211).

In synthesis, the Apatzingán Constitution, like its Spanish predecessor of 1812, sought to make compatible "sovereignty of the people," civil liberties, protection of property, and the reaffirmation of the key pillars of the ancien régime: church and military privilege and the accumulated decrees and regulations of three centuries of Spanish rule. Without explicitly emulating French state of siege legislation or the Cádiz Constitution, the document's vague emergency powers to protect internal security and defend against external aggression offered the possibility of sweeping executive initiatives ("take whatever measures deemed appropriate") to achieve security. This authority was similar to that of the Spanish king in the 1812 Constitution but was not restricted by a critical limitation on executive authority present in the Spanish charter: "the authority of the king extends to whatever means [*a todo cuanto conduce*] appropriate to achieve conservation of internal order, and external security of the State, in conformity with the Constitution and the laws" (Art. 197). The Mexican charter of 1814 lacked this last qualification.

If the Apatzingán Constitution contained many of the internal contradictions characteristic of Spanish liberalism, failure to implement it due to the royalist defeat of the Morelos-led forces distinguished the first constitution of Mexican liberals from the Cádiz Constitution of their Spanish counterparts. In Mexico, as in Spain, however, the struggle between liberals and conservatives, monarchists and republicans, and clericals and anticlericals would prevent a national political consensus for over a century and push military caudillos to the forefront of national politics. Indeed, the perpetual focus on constitutional issues in Mexico produced innumerable "plans" (the Mexican version of Spanish *pronunciamientos*) by civil-military coalitions headed by caudillos supporting or opposing centralism/federalism, republicanism/monarchy, or military-clerical *fueros*/equality before the law.

The first of these caudillos to head the Mexican nation would be a royalist officer, Augustín de Iturbide, who had not only opposed the early independence movements but directed harsh counterinsurgency measures against the rebels. Iturbide would establish an independent Mexican Empire as a counterrevolutionary response to Spanish liberalism. If the conquest of Mexico by Hernán Cortés was achieved with the assistance of the supposed treason of his Indian concubine, Malinche, the birth of an independent Mexico was also the result of treason. This time the betrayal was by officials of the royal army, the royal bureaucracy, the clergy, and a few liberals and guerrilla forces allied in the Army of the Three Guarantees. This unlikely union overcame a monarchy subverted from within by Spanish liberals and their military collaborators.

THE ARMY OF THE THREE GUARANTEES AND
THE MEXICAN EMPIRE

Ordered to crush the rebel forces, Iturbide instead negotiated an agreement with their leader, Vicente Guerrero, and announced the Plan de Iguala. This plan called for the organization of Mexico as a constitutional monarchy with the crown offered to Ferdinand VII or some other European prince, the exclusive monopoly of the Roman Catholic religion and perpetuation of the *fueros* and authority of the church, and the equal treatment of *criollos* and *peninsulares.* Iturbide and Guerrero merged their forces into the Army of the Three Guarantees and pledged to implement these three principles. Despite the inherent contradictions of an alliance of vagabonds, bandits, Masons, liberals, monarchists, peninsular merchants, high clergy, and former royalists, the appeal of unity and an end to strife gave Iturbide a brief political opportunity, which he exercised. In August 1821, without significant further military action, the new captain-general, Juan de O'Donojú, signed the Treaty of Córdoba (later rejected by the Spanish government). This treaty declared in its first two articles that "this America [Mexico] will be considered an independent and sovereign nation and will be called the Mexican Empire" and that Ferdinand VII or, in the event of his refusal, his brother Carlos or other royal alternatives, would rule the new empire.[11]

In the interim, the treaty provided for a provisional junta, which included the captain-general, to govern in accord with Spanish law and the Plan de Iguala. The junta elected Iturbide president. He then assumed power as emperor, and Mexico, with most of Central America (see chapter 4), would be spared republican institutions until after 1823. Iturbide's short-lived empire, replete with coronation, royal family, and all the fanfare of European monarchy, crowned Mexico's independence, proclaimed September 28, 1821, with an abbreviated monarchical charter: the Reglamento Provisional Político del Imperio Mexicano. This document, necessary as a basis for "administration, order, and internal and external security of the State" until a political constitution could be adopted, left in place all Spanish legislation adopted before February 24, 1821, not in conflict with the present (1822) document.[12] In addition, it provided for a system of internal administration dependent upon provincial "jefes superiores políticos" like those in Spain's 1812 charter but combined military and civil authority "during the present threat by external enemies" (Art. 46). It allowed the *jefe po-*

lítico to arrest persons suspected of "conspiracy against the state" (Art. 51).

With a long list of other broad discretionary powers (Art. 54), the Reglamento Provisional also enumerated most of the rights and liberties associated with the liberal doctrines—as well as specific conditions under which these rights could be suspended or modified (Arts. 10, 17). It also gave the emperor almost unlimited power to organize and deploy armed forces to "defend internal and external security" (Art. 19). The charter also formally established censorship under ecclesiastical and civil jurisdictions, a return to pre-1812 government and church regulation of the press, publishing, and public expression.

Importantly, the charter restored military and ecclesiastical *fueros*, the elimination of which had helped to cement the temporary alliance of the military, church, and anti-Spanish elements that had won independence (Art. 59). The clergy and military, however, lost these privileges in cases of *lesa majestad*—conspiracy against the fatherland or the established government. Finally, the authority of the emperor included most of the powers vested in the Spanish monarchy in the Cádiz Constitution regarding the deployment of military force, the obligation to "conserve internal order and external security," and extensive emergency powers in cases of "internal convulsion" (Art. 31).

Limitations on the emperor's authority paralleled, in many ways, those on the Spanish monarch after 1812, including prohibitions on leaving the country without congressional permission. (This prohibition was included in all of Mexico's subsequent constitutions, and many of the constitutions in the rest of Spanish America, to prevent repetition of the imprisonment and abdication of the executive as had occurred with the Spanish monarchs in Napoleonic France.) Likewise, the emperor could not "deprive anyone of his liberty . . . unless the welfare and security of the State require their arrest." If detained, they were to be brought before a judge within fifteen days (Art. 30).

Although this Reglamento Provisional Político del Imperio Mexicano endured briefly, it incorporated most of the elements characteristic of the French and Spanish regimes of exception: suspension of constitutional guarantees and broad executive authority to deal with political crisis or threats to state security. Thus, both Mexican liberals (in 1814) and conservatives and monarchists (in 1822) incorporated into their first constitutional documents provisions for suspending constitutional guarantees and for emergency powers for the executive-military authorities in times of crisis. Both also confirmed the special role and privileges of military institutions, including the *fueros.* Neither, however, provided for state of siege or complete suspension of the *imperio* of the constitution. This would not occur in Mexico until 1843.[13]

Iturbide's empire proved illusory. He could not maintain the coalition that obtained military victory, despite repression of opponents, dissolution of the legislature, suppression of critical newspapers, and a series of populist measures such as the reduction of sales and liquor taxes and the distribution of government concessions. Lack of revenues merely exacerbated the political and military crisis. There were too many officers, not enough discipline, and few resources to maintain the forces accumulated during the years of war, a situation somewhat reminiscent of the plight of Ferdinand VII in Spain from 1814 to 1820.

More military caudillo than royal emperor, Iturbide lost control of his throne and his army when one of the most colorful politico-military figures in Mexican history, Antonio López de Santa Anna, pronounced against him in Vera Cruz. Santa Anna, like Iturbide, was a former royalist army officer. He had served as aide-de-camp to the viceroy in Mexico City. Replicating Iturbide's own betrayal of the Spanish viceroy, Santa Anna joined forces with General José Antonio Echávarri, the commander of the imperial forces. Recognizing the impossibility of victory, Iturbide abdicated the throne in March 1823 and went into European exile. Unwisely, he returned to Mexico briefly in 1824, ostensibly to defend his homeland against a new effort at Spanish reconquest. The Mexican Congress refused Iturbide's offer of services and decreed that upon his return he would be executed as a traitor. Two days after touching Mexican soil, Agustín I died by firing squad in the small town of Padilla.

A military junta assumed power upon Iturbide's departure in 1823. After months of debate the new constituent assembly, which began sessions in November 1823, adopted a federalist constitution. Two members of the 1823 military junta were selected as president and vice president of the new republic, Guadalupe Victoria and Nicolás Bravo, respectively.

During the next thirty years incessant internal strife and intrigue, punctuated by military interventions by General Santa Anna, drained Mexican resources. Foreign loans and attempted reforms failed to alleviate the fiscal crisis. Still another former Mexican president, Vicente Guerrero (1829), died by firing squad (1831). Thereupon followed a parade of abbreviated presidencies as Mexico confronted a Spanish invasion (1829), the loss of Texas

(1836), and a French incursion (the Pastry War of 1838). Between the years 1833 to 1855, the presidency of Mexico changed hands thirty-six times, with Santa Anna its occupant on eleven different occasions. To 1851, presidents held military rank in all but three years.[14] The country "constantly teetered between simple chaos and unmitigated anarchy."[15] Bandits, brigands, and guerrillas lived off the disorder; politicians debated whether Mexico should be a federal or centralist republic as regional power brokers and armies defied rule from the capital.

Two constitutions promulgated during these years of political violence and instability, the Federal Constitution of 1824 and the centralist constitution of 1836 (or the Constitution of Seven Laws), served as the fundamental law of Mexico in this period. Based upon conflicting organizational principles, both constitutions, nevertheless, provided for broad emergency powers for government officials, privileged roles for the armed forces, and a shared underlying commitment to the maintenance of order through the repression of regime opponents. The adaptation of Spanish colonial traditions and the institutions of the Constitution of Cádiz had firmly established the foundations of constitutional dictatorship in Mexico by the mid-nineteenth century.

THE FEDERAL CONSTITUTION OF 1824

Responding to the recent experience of empire and the dictatorial suppression of political liberties and opposition activities by Iturbide, and influenced by the U.S. Constitution, the constituents of 1823–1824 designed a highly decentralized federal system. The federal constitution not only conflicted with the traditional centralism of the colonial order but also sought to adapt the executive and legislative powers to the liberal vision of Spain's 1812 charter. Opponents to federalism insisted that emulating the United States was a mistake, that Mexicans had no experience with republican and federal institutions, that artificial divisions were not analogous to the separate colonies in North America with their own legislatures, and that "to federalize ourselves, now united, is to divide ourselves and bring upon us the very evils they sought to remedy with their federation."[16] Advocates of a centralist system feared that federalism would bring further fragmentation, regional political bossism (caudillismo), and civil war.

At the national level, the constitution concentrated authority in Congress and severely limited executive authority. The president, elected indirectly by the states, was left with control over the armed forces (though he could not command them directly without congressional permission) to provide internal security and national defense. He could order the arrest of persons if required for the welfare and security of the federation, but they had to be brought before a magistrate within forty-eight hours (Arts. 110–12). In the Cádiz tradition, the 1824 Constitution prohibited the president from leaving the country during his tenure without congressional permission. It also forbade executive interference in national elections. Even the familiar obligation to conserve internal order and provide for national security was assigned by the constitutional assembly to the legislature instead of the president (Art. 49, Secs. I, II).

Whereas the executive authority was drastically curtailed, the prerogatives of the church and military institutions were reaffirmed. The liberals did not confuse the federal cause with anticlericalism or an attack on the military. The 1824 Constitution guaranteed the military and ecclesiastical *fueros* and traditional Spanish privileges to these key interest groups. Unlike the liberal Spanish Constitution of 1812, however, the Mexican 1824 Constitution did not define the role of the armed forces in Mexican politics and society—leaving that matter to the customs of imperial Spain. The Congress was also to protect a free press and assure that "its free exercise shall never be suspended nor abolished in any state or territory of the federation" (Art. 50, Sec. III).

Ambiguity in defining congressional authority in Article 49 led to important political conflicts. It also resulted in grants of emergency powers to executives despite the lack of clear constitutional specification of authority for such delegation. Article 49 read: "The Laws and decrees that emanate from the Congress will have as their object: I. Sustain national independence and provide for the conservation and security of the nation in its external relations; II. Conserve the federal union, and peace and public order within the federation." Under the cover of this clause, in August 1829 the Mexican legislature gave the president emergency powers when threatened by a Spanish invasion and internal strife. The Congress authorized the president "to adopt whatever measures necessary for the conservation of independence, the federal system and public tranquility." This precedent would be followed periodically in the nineteenth century, despite objections by opponents of delegating such powers to the president.

That the language of this decree so closely resembled the enumerated powers of Congress might generously allow the conclusion that the legislature acted within its constitutional authority. Yet when displeased with abusive executive actions under this delegated authority, Congress declared invalid a number of presidential actions. Nonetheless, the basic principle seemed entrenched; Congress again gave extraordinary powers to the president in order to deal with internal strife, first on October 8, 1832, and then again in 1833 and 1834.

Writing in the 1960s, the eminent Mexican constitutional authority, Ignacio Burgoa, rigorously denounced these legislative actions as "in open contradiction with the principle of separation of powers consecrated in . . . the Constitution of 1824" and therefore in flagrant violation of the constitution.[17] The lack of any explicit provision for emergency powers or for the delegation of legislative authority to the executive, and the specific prohibition on suspension of freedom of the press, support Burgoa's assessment. Mexican congressmen, however, found in the 1824 document sufficient latitude (and obviously seemed to find sufficient necessity in circumstances) to incorporate a regime of exception into the political system of the new republic. This would prevail when conservatives overturned the liberal experiment and implemented a more centralist regime after 1836.

THE CONSTITUTION OF 1836

From 1829 to 1843, Mexican politics consisted of "a theater in which the people were spectators . . . watching over changing scenes and different characters occupy the presidency."[18] Factional, personal, and ideological conflicts permeated everyday political life. For example, in the administration of President Valentín Gómez Farías (1833–1834), liberal efforts to eliminate clerical and military *fueros*, abolish the mandatory tithe, secularize education, and assert government control over internal church administration, in addition to reducing the size of the army, precipitated a conservative uprising under the banner *Religión y Fueros*. As would become characteristic of General Santa Anna's colorful career, the erstwhile liberal who had defeated Iturbide and saved his nation from the Spanish invasion in 1829 now headed the conservative reaction.

Victorious in the uprising against his former vice president, Gómez Farías, Santa Anna called for the Congress to modify the 1824 Constitution and replace the federal charter with a centralist document. Lacking constitutional authority to act as a constituent body, the Congress nevertheless managed to shroud its seemingly illegal constitutional revision in the wrappings of parliamentary gauze—in effect, a sort of parliamentary coup d'état. Henceforth, many liberals and federalists would argue that the 1824 Constitution never ceased to govern Mexico (until 1857), and politics from 1836 to 1857 frequently focused upon the issue of restoration of the 1824 charter.

The 1836 Constitution consisted of seven constitutional laws, preceded by a decree (October 23, 1835) that transformed the federal republic into a centralist regime on the old Spanish model, with governors of departments (instead of states) appointed by and directly responsible to the national executive. The first of the seven constitutional laws consisted of a list of the obligations and rights of Mexican citizens, typical of Spanish American constitutions since 1812. As with the liberal constitutions of Spain in 1812 and Mexico in 1814 and 1824, Catholicism was enshrined as the official religion, but now Mexicans were constitutionally obligated "to profess the religion of the fatherland" (Art. 3, Sec. I).

A unique feature of the 1836 charter, elaborated in the second of the constitutional laws, was the supreme conservatory power ("supremo poder conservador"), which the constituents added to the traditional executive, legislative, and judicial branches. This supreme authority, composed of five individuals serving rotating terms and selected in a complex process originating at the departmental level, could declare congressional legislation unconstitutional, declare executive actions and Supreme Court decisions null and void, suspend Congress for up to two months, approve or disapprove constitutional reforms, and command absolute obedience, inasmuch as "formal disobedience would be taken as the crime of high treason" (Art. 15).

Whereas the supreme conservatory power had ultimate review authority, the Congress retained most of the powers associated with the Spanish *cortes* and the 1824 Constitution in Mexico. However, Article 45 (Sec. V) prohibited the suspension or deprivation of the rights and liberties enumerated in the first constitutional law. Article 45 (Sec. VI) further prohibited concentration of executive and legislative authority in the same hands, whether of Congress or the executive, through self-assignment or delegation of extraordinary powers. This prohibition responded directly to the several occasions on which Congress, acting under the vague language in the 1824 Constitution, had delegated extraordinary powers to the executive.

The president kept control of the armed forces and their "deployment in order to provide for internal security and external defense." In the now customary fashion, the president could also order the detention of "suspicious" individuals when "public welfare and security" required—with the limitation that they be brought before a magistrate within there days (Art. 18, Sec. II). Significantly, the fifth constitutional law of 1836 reaffirmed ecclesiastical and military *fueros* (Art. 30) and also the *ley fuga*, in the Spanish liberal tradition (Art. 42). This meant that force could be used against those fleeing or "resisting authority."

The proclamation of the 1836 Constitution induced a number of rebellions throughout Mexico. Separatist factions in Texas and Yucatán justified autonomist movements by reference to the unconstitutional derogation of the 1824 federal system and its replacement with the 1836 centralist regime. Amid tumult, revolts, a brief war with France (in which Santa Anna again defended Mexican honor at Vera Cruz), and demands to restore the 1824 charter, Santa Anna orchestrated a new constituent Congress, in blatant violation of the 1836 document. A special congressional committee once again set about to elaborate a new constitution, under the aegis of "General Antonio López de Santa Anna, *benemérito* of the Fatherland and provisional president of Mexico."[19]

BASES DE ORGANIZACION POLITICA, 1843

After two years of debating and reviewing several draft constitutions, in June 1843 the Bases de Organización Política de la República de Mexico replaced the 1836 Constitution.[20] These drafts contained language defining the constitutional role of the military for the first time in Mexican institutional development. The first 1842 draft declared that "the primary purpose of the armed forces is the conservation of internal order in the republic" (Art. 154). The second proposal contained a more extensive role for the armed forces (Arts. 75–76; Art. 81, Sec. IV), including assisting the executive in restoring order and maintaining the constitution. This official recognition of the central role of the military, particularly given the permanent state of internal war, was also reflected in the national budget. Military expenditures in 1842 accounted for almost 75 percent of the budget; the army spent more than double the income of the government, with the balance borrowed at high interest rates from loan sharks (*agiotistas*).

While maintaining the centralist system, the *Bases* eliminated the supreme conservatory power and provided for the more traditional tripartite separation of powers into legislative, executive, and judicial branches. Military and ecclesiastical *fueros* were maintained (Art. 9, Sec. VIII). Few politicians dared risk the enmity of the military, and the defeat of the liberals temporarily ended any effort to eliminate the privileges of the church. The *Bases* also introduced for the first time in Mexican constitutional law explicit provisions for regimes of exception. The legislature was authorized, by a two-thirds vote, to (1) expand (*ampliar*) executive authority under the terms of Article 198 (see below) in the cases of foreign invasion or sedition "too grave for ordinary measures to repress" (Art. 65, Sec. XVIII) and (2) suspend or diminish civil rights or liberties (*garantías individuales*) under the terms of Article 198 (Art. 67, Sec. IV).

The president, in turn, charged with maintaining internal order and tranquility and external security (Art. 85), was constitutionally immune from criminal or civil prosecution for a year after his term of office, except in the case of treason against national independence or the established form of government (Art. 90). As in Mexico's earlier constitutions, the president could act directly as commander of the armed forces on the battlefield only with legislative permission and by temporarily giving up presidential authority (previously to vice presidents; in 1843, to a council of state; and later to a person elected by the Senate).

The key article of the constitution regarding regimes of exception authorized both the suspension of *garantías individuales* and, less clearly, the delegation of legislative authority to the president. Article 198 read: "If in extraordinary circumstances national security requires, either in all the Republic or part thereof the suspension of the formalities prescribed in these bases, [*bases constitucionales*], for the apprehension and detention of criminals [*delincuentes*], Congress may declared such [suspension] for a stipulated period." Inasmuch as Article 65 (Sec. XVIII) ambiguously authorized Congress to expand the authority of the executive (subject to the conditions of Article 198) to deal with "sedition," the 1843 document potentially introduced the constitutional foundations for several distinctive regimes of exception. Interestingly, in contrast to the two constitutional drafts discussed in 1842, no constitutional definition of the role of the armed forces appeared in the 1843 document. Only later would the Mexican military—which retained its *fueros* in 1843—receive constitutional authority for its internal security role.

Another year of chaos followed the adoption of the 1843 document. Santa Anna again left the presidency when faced with the military and political machinations of his opponents. By 1845 another plan was proclaimed by an ambitious general-politician who contemplated a return to Iturbide's *Plan de Iguala* (constitutional monarchy with a European prince). Further political schemes brought Santa Anna back from Cuban exile in 1846, in time to declare his support for a return to the 1824 Constitution and to lead Mexican forces against the United States invasion. In May 1847, another "extraordinary constituent congress" adopted the Constituent and Reform Act, which, among other reforms, eliminated the office of vice president (since vice presidents had so many times led coups against presidents) and reestablished the 1824 Constitution as "the only political constitution of the Republic."

In the midst of war against the United States and attempts to recover Texas, the Mexican government also sought to reorganize the armed forces. A legislative definition of the role of the military appeared in the Ley Orgánica de la Guerra Nacional, which subjected all males aged eighteen to fifty-five years to conscription into a force that would "defend the independence of the nation, sustain its institutions, conserve public tranquility, and enforce the laws and respect for the authorities [of the nation]."[21] Henceforth, internal security as well as national defense would be a constitutional mission of the Mexican armed forces.

Confusion continued into the 1850s, with General Santa Anna opportunistically returning to the political scene under a variety of banners. Meanwhile, the constitutional debate over regimes of exception and emergency powers surfaced repeatedly. Congress dramatically denied the request for extraordinary powers by President/General Mariano Arista in 1852; faced with military uprisings (after attempting to reduce the size of the army) and with regional rebellions, Arista resigned. Improvised elections gave the presidency and dictatorial powers to Santa Anna, who governed without a constitution for a year and even considered the idea of bringing a Spanish prince to Mexico. In the interim, a decree of 1853, titled "Bases Para la Administración de la República Hasta la Promulgación de la Constitución," served as a "constitution," while still another "constituent" Congress worked on a new document.

The 1853 decree declared the federal and state legislatures in recess and reinstituted a centralized administrative system in which Santa Anna exercised almost unlimited power. In July, Santa Anna suppressed the use of the term *state* and eased the country back toward a centralist order.[22] His dictatorship lasted until 1855, when a new plan, which joined liberal exiles, anticlerical forces, and regional rebel armies—the Plan de Ayutla (proclaimed in 1854)—succeeded in ousting the many-times president for the last time. When

Santa Anna left the presidency in 1855, the new government included the most famous liberal leaders in nineteenth-century Mexico: Ignacio Comonfort, Melchor Ocampo, Miguel Lerdo de Tejada, and Benito Juárez.[23]

The Plan de Ayutla conferred broad powers (*amplias facultades*) on the interim president and promised the army, called "the bulwark of order and social guarantees," that the interim government would "conserve it [the army] and attend to its needs" (Arts. 3, 6). Victory against Santa Anna was followed by the proclamation in 1855 of the Estatuto Orgánico Provisional de la República Mexicana. This statute, an amalgamation of the 1824 and 1843 charters, served as an interim constitution until another constituent assembly worked through a new draft constitution. It conditioned the exercise of free speech on "not perturbing public order" (Art. 35) and gave the president broad discretionary authority "when necessary to . . . sustain the established order or to conserve public tranquility." These powers included the authority to suspend the *garantías individuales* (Art. 82).

However, the first reform law issued by the new government (Ley Juárez) abolished the ecclesiastical and military *fueros*, prompting vociferous protests that splintered the new coalition. This was followed by legislation requiring the church and civil corporate entities, including the traditional *ejidos* (villages), to divest themselves of most real estate, including communal farmland; wresting control over the registry of births, marriages, and deaths from the church; and regulating fees charged by the church for administering the sacraments. Conflict over these measures continued, but in 1857 "the single most important document and symbol of reform in Mexico in the middle of the nineteenth century . . . the Constitution of 1857" incorporated these reforms and consolidated, at least formally, the federalist regime in Mexican politics.[24]

THE CONSTITUTION OF 1857

The 1857 Constitution is traditionally viewed as the victory of Mexican liberals over conservative and clerical opponents, of federalism over centralism, and as the institutionalization of the bill of rights contained in the first section of the document (De los derechos del hombre—the first twenty-nine articles of the constitution). A more skeptical assessment emerges from Richard Sinkin's analysis of the votes taken in the constitutional assembly: "Fear of anarchy pervaded the debates."[25]

The constitution incorporated the reform laws and restored the federal regime. The federal government acquired significantly enhanced authority in relations with the states compared with the 1824 charter and a unicameral assembly replaced the bicameral legislature of 1824, although reforms in the 1870s would restore the bicameral legislature. Most importantly, the 1857 Constitution adopted the definitive language on Mexico's constitutional regimes of exception, later copied precisely into the 1917 Constitution (even to the extent of retaining its numerical identity after the Revolution). Article 29 stipulated:

> In the case of invasion, grave perturbation of public peace, or other [circumstances] which place society at great danger or conflict, only the President of the Republic, with agreement by the ministers and approval of the congress of the Union, and, when the congress is in recess, of the permanent deputation [of the Congress], may suspend the guarantees granted in this Constitution, with the exception of those that protect human life; but this must be done for a limited period of time, according to general dispositions, and not limited to a specific individual.
>
> If the suspension takes place with congress in session it shall concede the authority deemed necessary for the executive to confront the situation. If it takes place while congress is in recess, the permanent deputation shall convoke the congress without delay to obtain its approval.

Despite the broad language of Article 29 ("concede the authority deemed necessary"), Article 50 of the 1857 Constitution reiterated the ban on joining "two or more of the Supreme powers of the federation" or depositing the legislative power "in the hands of an individual." Borrowing from the U.S. Constitution, however, it also gave Congress the authority to "despatch all laws necessary and proper" to carry out its constitutional authority and the authority "conceded by this Constitution to the powers of the union" (Art. 72, Sec. XXX).

The liberals thus had confirmed two main types of regime of exception: concession of extraordinary powers to the executive and suspension of specified garantías. Inasmuch as the president was to use the armed forces to maintain internal security and external defense (Art. 85), the legislature arguably could "concede the authority deemed necessary" to the president for this purpose. While constitutional ambiguity existed regarding delegation of "emergency powers," from 1857 until the overthrow of Porfirio Díaz in 1910 Congress gave extraordinary powers to the executive on a number of occasions. No doubt prevailed regarding the constitutional authority to suspend some or all constitutional *garantías* in cases of "invasion," "perturbation of public peace," or other circumstances involving "great danger or conflict"—as determined by the president and approved by Congress.

At the same time that concern for law and order and political stability consolidated provisions for regimes of exception in the 1857 Constitution, the liberal-dominated constituent body again sought to establish civil control over the military institutions and to abolish military *fueros*. Article 122 prohibited military authorities, in times of peace, from exercising any civil authority, and Article 13 abolished the *fueros*, limiting the authority of military courts to cases involving military discipline. Again the army was offended by the liberals and again a liberal constitution ignored or rejected the constitutional status of the armed forces.

A final "self-protection" clause (Art. 128) stipulated that the constitution would not lose its legal force, even if a rebellion temporarily established a contrary government, and that upon its reaffirmation those responsible "shall be brought to trial in accord with the laws of [this] constitution." Opponents of the constitution wasted little time making this constitutional prophecy a reality. Three years of vicious fighting and atrocities followed (the War of Reform). Ousted from Mexico City, the liberals made Vera Cruz, the source of government revenues from customs receipts, their headquarters. Three years later they marched victoriously back into the valley of Mexico to retake the capital.

Elected president in 1861, Benito Juárez reaffirmed the 1857 Constitution, attempted reconciliation with his opponents, and faced the impossible task of economic reconstruction. He also created a rural police force, the *Rurales*, in May 1861, attempting to convert former bandits, guerrillas, and peasants into a national public security force. By the mid-1870s the *Rurales* would become prominent symbols of national authority in the festering conflicts among local, regional, and national caudillos.

Meanwhile, to confront the immediate economic crisis, Juárez suspended payment on the foreign debt. This provided a pretext for Emperor Napoleon III of France, with the initial collaboration of the English and Spanish governments, to occupy Mexico's coast and administer the customs receipts. The English and Spanish withdrew, unwilling to support the more ambitious imperial plans of the French, who, after a year of military struggle, occupied Mexico City. Congress granted extraordinary powers to Juárez to continue the resistance, but clerical and monarchical forces welcomed the French, who established a new Mexican Empire headed by Austrian Archduke Ferdinand Maximilian of Hapsburg. Like Napoleon before him and many Latin American caudillos to follow, the archduke insisted on a plebiscite (albeit administered by the French occupation forces) to legitimize the new monarchy.

Emperor Maximilian, however, proved too liberal for his conservative Mexican supporters, and his fiscal policies required forced loans from the church to pay for the occupation army and the costs of the imperial life-style. Meanwhile, Juárez and his supporters engaged in guerrilla warfare, with bases and financial support in Texas and El Paso del Norte (present-day Ciudad Juárez). In 1865, the emperor decreed the death penalty for all rebels apprehended with firearms. With the end of the Civil War in the United States, substantial arms shipments reached the *Juaristas.* This contributed to Napoleon's decision to withdraw French troops in 1866. Without the occupying army Maximilian could not sustain the empire. Defeated militarily, the emperor surrendered and was tried by court martial. He shared the fate of the last Mexican emperor, Iturbide, and of several presidents: death by firing squad.

While of little durable significance, the empire of 1862–1867 produced its own constitution and added its own provisions for emergency powers and regimes of exception to the Mexican political experience. By the mid-nineteenth century, the notion of constitutional monarchy implied enumerated civil liberties and rights for citizens, even in the case of an empire imposed by foreign troops. In April 1865, therefore, Maximilian had promulgated the Estatuto Provisional del Imperio Mexicano. Sovereignty was vested in the emperor, who exercised it through his ministry of nine cabinet members. Territorial administration was assigned to military commanders or *jefes políticos,* and for the first time in Mexico, provision was made for states of siege (Art. 48). Articles 58–77 of this curious statute granted *garantías individuales* in the now customary liberal constitutional tradition, subject to discretionary application when citizens were apprehended for "crimes against the State or perturbation of public order" (Art. 61). In a clause similar to that of the 1857 Constitution, the Estatuto provided that "only by decree of the emperor or by Imperial Commissioners, when required for conservation of peace and public order, may some of these *garantiás* be temporarily suspended" (Art. 77).

Monarchists, conservatives, and liberal Mexicans had achieved at least one fundamental agreement: Mexico could not be governed unless civil rights and liberties could be suspended when circumstances required. Presidents needed extraordinary powers to conserve public order and internal security. Constitutional regimes of exception would be essential components of any Mexican political system.

With the French removed and Maximilian executed, Benito Juárez reassumed the presidency, only to be frustrated by fragmentation within the liberal coalition and opposition from his old conservative and clerical nemeses. Juárez pushed forward his plans for constitutional amendments in 1867 "utilizing the extraordinary powers with which I have been invested."[26] Reelected president in 1867, Juárez attempted to introduce a range of liberal socioeconomic reforms. He also drastically reduced the size of the army while expanding the role of the *Rurales* in efforts to control banditry and restore order in the countryside. The liberal government also encouraged completion of the Mexico City–Vera Cruz railway and many other projects. It continued to face opposition from conservative forces, the church, and dissidents within its own ranks.

To deal with incessant minor rebellions and banditry, Juárez urged Congress to suspend the constitutional *garantías* of "bandits." Congress initially refused. As elsewhere in Spanish America and Spain, military jurisdiction over bandits under the criminal codes lent itself to political repression. When disorder and brigandage persisted Congress finally approved the president's request but not without acrimonious debate. Extensions of the suspension of *garantías* for "bandits and kidnappers" into the 1870s allowed the *Rurales* to execute supposed bandits on the spot and not infrequently to make use of the *ley fuga* against "resisters." Liberal policymakers judged that maintaining law and order, not to mention controlling political opponents, required exercising "special" constitutional powers.[27]

Juárez's decision to seek reelection in 1871 split the Liberal party severely. The old issue of *continuismo* generated opposition to another term for the incumbent. When the Congress selected Juárez from among the three leading contenders, military leader Porfirio Díaz pronounced against the government. The government invoked its emergency powers and the federal army defeated

Díaz's forces. However, the president's fatal heart attack in July 1872 reopened the Pandora's box of government succession. In the elections that followed, former Supreme Court Chief Justice and interim President Lerdo de Tejada triumphed. Since Porfirio Díaz's *pronunciamiento* had been based on opposition to *continuismo,* Díaz offered little objection to the newly elected president. When Lerdo de Tejada sought reelection four years later, however, Díaz carried out a successful coup in the name of "effective suffrage and no reelection."

For the next thirty-five years, the regimes of exception of the 1857 Constitution would stand Mexico's constitutional dictator in good stead.[28] Having changed the limitations on presidential reelection and the manner of his selection by Congress (1887, 1890, 1904), Díaz used the 1857 charter to make himself constitutional dictator. Broad executive powers and the conjoining of civil and military authority to deal with "perturbation of public peace" formed the legal foundations of dictatorship. Regimes of exception woven into the constitutional fabric of the nation in the first half century of Mexican independence served Díaz admirably. The liberal victory of 1857 bequeathed permanent language and authority for constitutional regimes of exception that buttressed the dictatorship from 1884 to 1910.

Díaz's dictatorship was sustained by the resources of a growing export economy and the president's skillful mixture of repression with the co-optation of local and regional caudillos. Yet, even impressive economic growth and increased political centralization never permitted Díaz to suppress entirely localism, brigandage, and resistance to the hegemony of the national government. The country's endemic banditry, *caciquismo,* racial rebellions, and agrarian conflicts marred the mythical tranquility and order of the Porfirian peace.

The president consciously used the expansive powers of the liberal constitution to justify his repressive measures, deploying the *Rurales* and sometimes the army to hammer bandits, political opponents, and the rising labor movement. As in Uruguay, Chile, and Argentina, by the first decade of the twentieth century political repression in Mexico frequently no longer targeted its traditional political opposition, whether conservative or liberal, and instead focused on anarchists, socialists, nascent labor movements (miners; textile, port, and railroad workers; other proletarians), and peasant villagers demanding the restoration of traditional rights and land lost to the liberal onslaught.[29]

In 1910 the aged president was forced from office by a new generation of liberals spouting his own original slogan: Effective suffrage and No Reelection. After seven years of revolution, a new constitution overturned the bastions of power and property in Mexico: the Church, the *hacendados,* the military, the *Rurales,* and foreign investors. One thing did not change, however. The revolutionaries, like their monarchist, conservative, and liberal predecessors, used the military and police to impose their will; they required regimes of exception to govern the country. As a foundation for their new order, they found the provisions adopted in 1857 quite suitable.

The first president of the Mexican Revolution, Francisco Madero, requested in December 1911 that Congress suspend constitutional *garantías* of bandits; military tribunals and summary execution would be used to wipe out insurgency and brigandage.[30] In 1913, the government proposed the expansion of the *Rurales* to a corps of 13,000, compared to the 2,000–2,400 historian Paul Vanderwood estimated in Díaz's force.[31] After Madero's assassination and several years of civil war, the revolution adopted a Press Law (1916) that banned "malicious expressions intended to induce hatred of the authorities, the army, the national guard, or the fundamental institutions of the country," and a new constitution. Again the tradition of regimes of exception prevailed. Article 29 of the 1917 Constitution read:

> In the case of invasion, grave perturbation of public peace or other [cases] that put society in conflict or grave danger, only the President of the Mexican Republic, in accord with the Council of Ministers and with approval of the Congress of the Union, or if in recess, of the Permanent Commission, may suspend in all the country, or specified parts thereof, those *garantías* that are an obstacle to rapidly and easily confronting the situation.

To meet such contingencies, the constitution also gave the president authority "to use the permanent armed forces . . . to [ensure] the internal and external security of the state" (Art. 89, Sec. VI). Article 49 removed the ambiguity concerning extraordinary powers in the 1857 charter:

> The Supreme Power of the Federation is divided into Legislative, Executive and Judicial [*branches*].

Two or more of these powers may not be joined in one person, or corporation, nor may the legislative power be deposited in an individual, except in the case of [conceding] extraordinary powers to the Executive of the Union, in accord with Article 29. In no other case except that referred to in the second paragraph of Article 131 [raise, decrease, eliminate export and import taxes], shall extraordinary powers be conferred for legislative purposes.

Days after the promulgation of the constitution, President Venustiano Carranza requested extraordinary powers from the legislature. Congress obliged. From 1920 to 1938, much of Mexico's most important legislation and the creation of government agencies resulted from presidential decrees using extraordinary powers. According to William Stokes, this included the creation of the industrial relations system, regulation of the church, the civil, commerical, agrarian, fiscal, tax, and penal codes, the Organic Law of Federal Justice, and the Property Nationalization Law. Presidential legislation using decree powers transformed Mexican property law, reformed the public health system, and implemented sweeping economic changes. Extraordinary powers were the ordinary instruments of government.[32]

This practice remained unmodified until 1938, when President Lázaro Cárdenas supported a reform to limit violations of the principle of separation of powers. In the congressional debates Cárdenas informed the Congress: "It has been an inveterate practice for the President of the Republic to request from congress the concession of extraordinary powers to legislate on certain matters. . . . The administration over which I preside believes that the indefinite continuation of this practice lamentably lessens the role of the legislative power."[33] The reform deleted any reference to Article 131 (export and import taxes) and stipulated that extraordinary powers could be conferred on the president only in accord with Article 29, that is, to confront invasion, grave perturbation of public peace, or "other [cases] that put society in conflict or great danger."[34]

After 1940, the development of Mexico's unique dominant one-party political system strengthened presidentialism. Amendments to the penal code during World War II created the crime of "social dissolution" and subjected those who "meet with a group of three or more individuals to discuss ideas or programs that tend to disturb public order or affect Mexican sovereignty" with from two to twelve years in prison (Arts. 145, 145b). Intended to combat Nazi wartime activities, this provision was used repeatedly against political dissidents after the war. Constitutional Articles 29 and 89 (para. VI) continued to provide ample legal foundations for repressing worker protests and peasant land occupations, for imprisoning political opponents, for cajoling and censoring the media, and for suppressing rural and urban guerrilla movements in the 1960s and 1970s. They also gave the government the necessary authority to order troops to kill protesting students in 1968 at Tlatelolco in Mexico City just prior to the opening of the Olympic games.

A month earlier, in his state of the union address, President Gustavo Díaz Ordaz declared that he would "exercise, whenever strictly necessary, the powers vested in me by Article 89, Paragraph VI, to maintain . . . internal security and defend the country from external threats."[35] According to the president, communists and other subversives had infiltrated the student movement, threatening the sovereignty and security of the Mexican nation. This necessitated exceptional measures, deployment of the armed forces, and repression of the subversive threat. Díaz Ordaz, like Juárez, Madero, and Porfirio Díaz, resorted to regimes of exception and military force to repress dissent, to defeat the "enemies of Mexico" (and the incumbent government).

Into the 1990s, these provisions for regimes of exception and national security remained in place. Eighty years after the beginning of a revolution that claimed more than a million victims, provisions for suspension of constitutional *garantías* and concession of extraordinary powers to the president of Mexico were virtually the same as those of 1857.[36] The revolution transformed the country's social and economic structure, imposed Latin America's first constitution to legalize unions and agrarian reform, gave birth to the most successful ruling party (the Partido Revolucionario Institucional, or PRI) in Spanish America—and retained the country's nineteenth-century foundations of constitutional dictatorship. In this regard, the Mexican Revolution would be emulated by revolutionaries in Bolivia (see chapter 6), Guatemala, and Nicaragua (see chapter 4) later in the twentieth century.[37]

4

Regimes of Exception in Central America

IN 1786, SPANISH ADMINISTRATIVE REFORMS DIVIDED THE OLD KING-dom of Guatemala into four *intendencias:* El Salvador, Honduras, Nicaragua, and Chiapas. Guatemala remained under the direct administration of the president-captain-general and was the seat of the *audiencia*. This administrative reform and the new economic policies of the last decades of the eighteenth century intensified existent regional jealousies and competition. Political reforms implemented in Central America after the adoption of the 1812 Cádiz Constitution further encouraged tendencies toward local identity and regional fragmentation.[1] These developments exacerbated rivalries among the major towns and administrative centers in each of the Central American states after 1824, thereby debilitating efforts at regional and national union. Afflicted by an economic crisis different in origin but similar in impact to that of Mexico in the first decade of the nineteenth century, Central American colonials also faced higher taxes, demands for military contributions, and trade disruptions as a result of conflicts on the peninsula and in Mexico. These conditions provoked limited protests and political dissension but no widespread social movements or serious challenges to imperial rule.

Captain-general José de Bustamante de Guerra (1811–1818) managed the political and economic challenges relatively successfully. After the restoration of Ferdinand VII in 1814, he purged backers of the liberal regime and sought to protect traditional Spanish mercantile interests against supporters of freer trade and local economic autonomy. Following his removal in 1818, an elderly military officer, Carlos Urrutia y Montoya, replaced Bustamante. Urrutia loosened colonial controls and seemed amenable to reaffirming the 1812 Constitution following the 1820 Spanish military revolt of Riego. In March 1821, an infirm Urrutia delegated his authority to Gabino Gaínza, an army inspector recently arrived from Chile.

In the meantime, regional authorities in Chiapas and Yucatán moved toward independence or association with the Iturbide movement in Mexico, conditioned upon respect for the Cádiz Constitution. A government decision in Madrid to allow provincial deputations and elections in the *intendencias* further confused the isthmian situation. Faced with internal political intrigues and threats from Mexican Emperor Iturbide to invade the isthmus, Gaínza announced the adhesion of Central America to Mexico in 1822. Briefly, and only after the repression of opposition forces in El Salvador, the provinces of Central America were integrated into the Mexican Empire. The demise of the Mexican Empire in 1823 (see chapter 3) brought the second and definitive declaration of Central American independence.[2] Nowhere in Spanish America did colonials fight and suffer less to achieve independence than in Central America.

In July 1823, the national constituent assembly convened in Guatemala City, acting both as an ordinary legislature of the United Provinces of Central America and as a constituent assembly.[3] Confronted by regional and autonomist movements, the assembly issued a number of decrees and declarations, anticipating the federal constitution promulgated in late 1824, the first of several efforts to unite Central America during the nineteenth and twentieth centuries. This first effort at Central American union never overcame endemic civil and regional war, economic fragility, and the fundamental inability to fashion an effective federal regime. Nevertheless, the federal union survived until 1838, and the Federal Constitution of 1824 established important precedents for subsequent political institutions in Central America.[4]

THE FEDERAL CONSTITUTION OF CENTRAL AMERICA, 1824

The Federal Constitution of 1824 was a short-term victory for liberals over the conservatives, clericals, and traditionalists of Central American society. Inspired by the Cádiz Constitution, Mexican liberalism, and the U.S. Constitution, it emphasized legislative control of the executive and broad discretion for state governments. This was modeled on the U.S. Constitution's "reservation to the states" of all powers not delegated to the federal government (Art. 10). Legislative dominance and discretion for the states was incorporated into individual state constitutions in the mid-1820s.

The framers of the federal constitution duly proclaimed the four basic purposes of governments according to nineteenth-century Spanish American liberals: to guarantee liberty, equality, security, and property (Art. 2). However, the carefully enumerated "garantías de la libertad individual" (Arts. 152–74) were selectively subject to suspension through legislative and executive action, thereby creating regimes of exception from the inception of constitutional government for the region. For example, the 1824 Constitution prohibited the death penalty, "except for those crimes which directly threaten public order" (Art. 152).

A unicameral congress was charged with "devising the laws," raising and maintaining the army and navy, devising military regulations, and authorizing the executive authority to employ the state militias when the execution of the law required or it was necessary "to contain insurrections or repel invasions" (Art. 69, Secs. 1–4). The legislature could also "concede extraordinary powers to the Executive, expressly detailed and for a determined period of time, in the case of war against national independence" (Art. 69, Sec. 5). In turn, the president of the federation could unilaterally deploy the armed forces to repel invasions or contain insurrections but could not, as in Mexico, directly command the armed forces without the approval of the Senate and temporary delegation of his duties to the vice president. This provision would be reiterated in many of the Central American state and national constitutions from the mid-1820s into the 1880s.

The constitution specified that no law of Congress or of the state assemblies could "violate the individual *garantías*," but Article 176 of the constitution allowed basic civil rights and liberties to be suspended in "the case of tumult, rebellion, or armed attack against the constituted authorities." In these circumstances the government could (1) confiscate weapons (the constitution guaranteed the right to keep and bear arms), (2) suspend the right of peaceful assembly, (3) suspend the need for search warrants to enter domiciles, (4) suspend the privacy of correspondence, (5) detain or incarcerate suspects without normal constitutional protections, and (6) create special commissions or tribunals to prosecute "stipulated crimes" or to judge certain citizens or residents. The language of this article ("the government may not, except in the case of tumult, rebellion, or armed attack against the constituted authorities") made even more explicit than in other liberal constitutions of the era the fact that exceptional regimes superseded normal constitutional provisions.

Each of the states of the new federation adopted constitutions with certain idiosyncrasies derived from local history or from the relationship of the state and its internal politics to the federal regime. These state constitutions became the foundation of constitutional development for the future Central American republics. They also served as basic constitutional frameworks, after the dissolution of the federal union in 1838, until new national constitutions could be elaborated. Thus, the Guatemalan Constitution of 1825 declared the state of Guatemala "sovereign, independent and free in its internal administration," limited in its rights by "the pact of union celebrated by the free states of Central America in the Federal Constitution of 22 November, 1824" (Arts. 3, 4).[5] In contrast, El Salvador, from the outset a source of autonomist movements and military insurrections against the Guatemalan authorities, declared in its first state constitution that "the State is and will always be free and independent of Spain and Mexico and of any other foreign power or government, and will never be the patrimony of any family or person" before acknowledging that "it will be one of the federated States of the Republic of Central America" (Arts. 1, 2).

In regard to constitutional regimes of exception, the state constitutions also exhibited a certain individuality. The Guatemalan state charter (1825), much like the Federal Constitution of 1824, allowed the state assembly to "concede to the executive extraordinary powers, expressly detailed and for a limited period, in the case of insurrection or sudden invasion" (Art. 14). The Guatemalan document added insurrection to the case of invasion, tying executive emergency powers to internal order and security. However, unlike the federal charter of Central America or the Mexican Federal Constitution of 1824, the Guatemalan state constitution contained an important definition of the role of the armed forces in the political system: "to defend the State from external enemies, to provide for the general defense of the Republic, and to assure, within the State, order and implementation of the law" (Art. 238). Constitutional treatment of the armed forces also specified, in the language common to Spanish American documents, that the armed forces were not to deliberate on political matters or petition the government:

"La fuerza pública es esencialmente obediente;ningún cuerpo armado podrá deliberar; ningún cuerpo, ni fracción alguna de la fuerza pública del Estado puede hacer peticiones a las autoridades con las armas en la mano" (Art. 239). The Guatemalan state constitution also declared that the "security police" could only be subject to civilian authority (Art. 17). Though *policía de seguridad* cannot be translated as secret police or political police, the constitution did reflect a concern for civilian rather than military control over the coercive power of the government. While the federal constitution did not address civil-military relations in such modern terms, Guatemala's state constitution anticipated the central dilemma of Guatemalan and Central American politics in the future.

In contrast, the sketchier constitution of the state of El Salvador (June 1824), which actually preceded the federal constitution, provided for no explicit regime of exception, allowed limited executive authority in deploying troops to cases of "sudden invasion" but not insurrection (Art. 40, Sec. 4), and offered no constitutional definition of the role of the armed forces.[6] It did, however, reaffirm customary Spanish legislation insofar as it did not contradict the federal and state constitutions, and readopted the *ley fuga:* "Cuando hubiere resistencia a la expresada orden, o se temiere la fuga, podrá usarse de la fuerza para asegurar a la persona" (Art. 64).

In Honduras, too, the state constitution (1825) was brief and provided for no explicit regime of exception beyond Article 176 of the federal constitution. It also failed to offer any constitutional definition of the role of the armed forces.[7] *Ley fuga* was, however, constitutionally reaffirmed and traditional Spanish laws and dispositions, insofar as they did not conflict with the federal or state constitutions, were constitutionally acknowledged to have the full force of law (Art. 97).

Further south, the state constitutions of Nicaragua and Costa Rica also offered variety in regard to regimes of exception and civil-military relations.[8] The Nicaraguan state constitution, adopted in April 1826, shared almost the same language as that of Guatemala regarding civilian control over the *policía de seguridad,* and borrowing from Article 176 of the federal constitution but without a separate constitutional article, it authorized the suspension of the right to bear arms and the right of peaceful assembly "in the case of tumult, rebellion, or armed attacks on the constituted authorities" (Art. 14, 15). The Nicaraguan assembly was likewise authorized to: "concede [to the executive] extraordinary powers, expressly detailed, and for a specified period, in the cases of insurrection or sudden invasion" (Art. 81, Sec. 13).[9] This generic language authorizing the concession of extraordinary powers paralleled like clauses in South America and the Caribbean. However, executive authority in Nicaragua was greater and more discretionary regarding the armed forces and maintenance of internal order than in either Guatemala or El Salvador. The executive was authorized to "direct the armed forces, call out the militia in cases of insurrection or sudden invasion, [this authority in El Salvador had been limited to cases of invasion, not insurrection] and make full use of these forces." When exercising this authority, the constitution required the president to immediately inform the assembly or, if it were in recess, the council (a body of representatives of each departmental jurisdiction), which would inform the federal congress. In "grave or urgent cases," the president could order the arrest and interrogation of persons, if required for the welfare and security of the State, so long as within three days the suspects were brought before a judge (Arts. 5, 6).

Departing from the Guatemalan and Salvadoran state constitutions, the Nicaraguan document permitted special tribunals or commissions in cases of "tumult, rebellion, or armed attack on the constituted authority," making possible the application of military or special law to opponents of the government (Art. 116). The church and military *fueros* also continued in effect (Art. 118), and in a vague article in the section "The Rights and Duties of the State," the armed forces (*fuerza pública*) were charged with "common security" and warned that "the functionary who abuses this charge commits a grave crime" (Art. 9). As in Guatemala, the *policía de seguridad* were assigned to civilian authorities (Art. 9). In language practically identical to the Guatemalan state constitution, that of Nicaragua provided for the death penalty in cases of "crimes that directly threaten public order," although, in the tradition of the Cádiz Constitution, torture, whippings, and cruel punishment were prohibited (Arts. 123, 124).

In Costa Rica, geographically isolated from both the Mexican and Guatemalan centers of authority, autonomist sentiment produced two provisional constitutions between 1821 and 1824. The first, the Interim Fundamental Social Pact, or Pact of Concorde (1821), combined a declaration of independence with a provisional constitution.[10] Based on the Cádiz Constitution and written at a time when it was unclear whether Costa Rica would be annexed to Mexico, a Central American federation, or even Colombia, this document is precious in Costa Rican history but of little precedent for the political organization of the country. The same is true for the First Political Statute of the Province of Costa Rica (March 1823) and the Second Political Statute of the Province of Costa Rica (May 1823). Both conformed more closely to traditional Spanish law than to the constitution that followed after 1824.

In January 1825, Costa Rica adopted a state constitution within the framework of the Central American Federation. From the beginning, Costa Rican distinctiveness was evident, with the constitution recognizing "the moral right of resistance against oppression" as a basic human right as well as "a right of citizens" (Art. 9). The constitution also created a "Conservatory Authority" (*Poder Conservador*) with the power to review all legislation, decrees, or resolutions and to deny promulgation if they "violated the constitution in all or in part, or were opposed to the general welfare of the State" (Art. 72). A two-thirds vote in the congress could override the veto of the conservatory authority, but from the 1820s concern for limits on government authority appear more clearly in Costa Rica than in any of the other Central American states.

Further illustrating this pattern was the abolition of military *fueros* (Art. 97); strict limitations on imprisonment without a court order (Art. 101), though this protection could be suspended for specified periods by Congress if required by "security of the State" (Art. 108); and rejection of the traditional meaning of *ley fuga* (Art. 102). The reason for these early differences in constitutional development between Costa Rica and the other Central American states remains to be determined. However, evidence that geographical and social cohesion of the landed elite contributed to the evolution of a distinctive Costa Rican political system has a parallel in Chile from the 1830s.

In some respects, however, language associating Costa Rica with the federation recalled clauses in the other Central American constitutions (for example, "free and independent of Spain and Mexico, and all other foreign powers or governments," and "never the patrimony of any family or person" [Art. 12]). Likewise, the executive power was charged with "conserving order, tranquility and the security of the State," deploying the army and militia in the case of invasion (but never without notifying and obtaining the permission of the Congress or the council), and ordering the arrest of persons when "public tranquility is threatened" (such persons must be brought before a judge within forty-eight hours) (Art. 82).

Given the apparent concern with limitations on government authority and the effort to protect civil rights and liberties in Costa

Rica's 1825 state constitution, it is surprising that the president also was authorized "in extraordinary circumstances in which the State is threatened with some risk, to act as he deems most convenient to save it from same" (Art. 82, Sec. 13). This is perhaps the broadest and vaguest allocation of executive authority "in extraordinary circumstances" found in any of the Central American state constitutions in the mid-1820s. (It would have analogues in Chile [1828], Uruguay [1830], and the Dominican Republic [1844].) Thus Costa Rica did not avoid the internal contradictions and confusion apparent in applying liberal principles to constitution making in the new nations of Spanish America. Indeed, these broad executive powers reappeared in Costa Rican constitutions from 1849 into the 1870s.

Despite the variety of these documents, all of the state constitutions within the Central American federation provided for some sort of regime of exception, whether through

1. suspension of certain constitutional rights or liberties by legislative or executive action;
2. concession of extraordinary powers to the executive when required for state security or to restore public order;
3. vague executive authority to take "appropriate" measures to conserve or restore order;
4. subjecting civilians to the authority of military tribunals (or other "special commissions") according to military law;
5. application of Article 69 (Sec. 5) of the federal constitution (concession of extraordinary powers to the federal president);
6. application of Article 176 of the federal constitution (suspension of certain *garantías*) in the case of "tumult, rebellion or armed attack against the constituted authorities."

These constitutional provisions would not prevent the next fifteen years of intermittent war among and within the states. Incessant internal strife and regional war further convinced Central Americans of the inevitable necessity for constitutional regimes of exception. Liberals attacked conservatives, clericals attacked anticlericals, liberal clergy joined liberal caudillos against conservative clergy and conservative caudillos. Personalist rivalries among regional military leaders, insincerely proclaiming liberal or conservative programs and prone to harsh repressive measures to assure their own domination, left Central America in a shambles.[11] The violence of the independence struggles that Central America had avoided from 1810 to 1823 would now afflict the region as the individual states rejected federation, moved toward nationhood, and were submerged by civil war.

REFORM OF THE FEDERAL CONSTITUTION, 1835

Liberals in each state generally supported their counterparts on the isthmus with some success until the mid-1830s. Conferring extraordinary powers on the state governments to repress conservative opponents after 1829, federation president Francisco Morazán still failed to establish peace and order. When his elected successor, José del Valle, died before taking office, Congress reelected Morazán. Revolts against Morazán and the liberal program, especially in Guatemala and El Salvador, presaged the end of the Central American federation. After 1835 conservatives gained ground on the isthmus, under the tutelage of Guatemalan caudillo Rafael Carrera. A last effort to reform the federal constitution in 1835 failed to stop the bloodshed or mend the union and changed little the legislative and executive authority to suspend the *garantías* in times of emergency or to implement broader regimes of exception.[12] Indeed, the language remained almost identical, except that the president was now authorized to "convoke the congress in extraordinary session when the republic was threatened with invasion or when public order was disturbed in a considerable part of the republic . . . or in any other extraordinary circumstances" (Art. 119).

Responding to the previous decade of violence and warfare, the framers added five articles to the constitution (Arts. 152–56) designed to prevent anyone from "assuming supreme power of the republic by other than constitutional means." The constitution stated that officials of any state who took power by force would not be recognized by federal authorities. The reformed constitution also affirmed that "sovereignty resides only in the nation; the right of insurrection belongs only to the people of the entire republic, and not any of its parts" (Art. 155). Three years later only the parts remained. The federal congress, assembled in San Salvador, declared that "the states are free to constitute themselves as they deem convenient, conserving the republican, popular, and representative form of government, with separation of powers."

A devastating cholera epidemic (1837–1838), which conservative caudillos and local priests blamed on the liberals and on the government's poisoning of water supplies, contributed to a rural-conservative upsurge of protest and violence. Revolts and civil war culminated in 1838 with the secession of Nicaragua, Honduras, and Costa Rica.

So ended the federal experiment, though the dream of Central American union endured. Several years more of fratricidal wars between federal forces headed by Francisco Morazán and conservative-autonomist forces led by Guatemalan Rafael Carrera ended in 1842 with Morazán's execution. The execution symbolized the death of the federation.

CONSTITUTIONAL DEVELOPMENT AFTER 1838

With the victory of Carrera and the imposition of conservative leaders in most of the five Central American states, the sovereign and independent nations adopted national constitutions to confirm their autonomous status: Nicaragua (1838), Honduras (1839), El Salvador (1841), Costa Rica (1844), and Guatemala (1851). Independence, however, would end neither civil war nor the dream of union. Both would necessitate continuous concern with "tumult, rebellion, insurrection and invasion" and require constitutional regimes of exception to deal with such circumstances. Out of these conditions evolved the language and institutions of constitutional dictatorship in Central America. By the middle to late nineteenth century, each Central American nation had adopted particular but generally comparable constitutional provisions for regimes of exception that would survive well into the twentieth century.

Economic fragility, regional conflicts, and the political failure of the Central American federation gave way to five small struggling nations, each with its own dilemmas yet intertwined in the web of isthmian machinations concerned with reunification. With international and domestic wars practically one and the same, the political identities of the individual states nevertheless took shape based on unique social and economic structures and home-crafted political institutions.[13]

In each of these emergent nations, periodic constituent assemblies debated the limits on executive authority and the advisability of centralist versus federal regimes. Often merely a pretext for extending presidential terms, eliminating bans on reelection, or obtaining temporary dictatorial powers to confront internal opposition, these assemblies nevertheless gave a veneer of legitimacy to incumbent or incoming governments. By the 1880s, these debates and political conflicts had established constitutional provisions for regimes of exception everywhere in the region. Everywhere, the principles of constitutional dictatorship found practitioners ready to avail themselves of extraordinary powers, to suspend constitutions, and to govern with predominant reliance on military force.

Guatemala

Civil wars in Central America left liberals in control of the federation and the state of Guatemala by 1830. Central American liberals, influenced by the North American experiment and by European intellectuals such as Jeremy Bentham and Alexis de Toqueville, frontally attacked the old order. One of the founders of the federation, José del Valle, wrote to Jeremy Bentham that one pressing need of the new republic was to eliminate the old Spanish codes, to create new ones, worthy of the leading lights of this century who have perfected jurisprudence.[14] Bentham agreed with del Valle, recommending that the Central Americans adopt the legal code developed by Edward Livingston (1764–1836) for Louisiana. This included jury trials, elected sheriffs, and a number of innovations that were inappropriate for Guatemala in the 1820s, a country of 500,000 people, the majority of whom were non-Spanish-speaking Indians farming communal land in isolated villages.

To implement their reforms, the liberals relied upon British loans obtained at outrageous discounts and submerged the isthmus in bloody, destructive warfare. They encouraged foreign colonization, favored British mining, lumbering, and commercial ventures, and angered domestic economic interests as well as the church. From 1826 and 1829, conservatives held control of the federation and of Guatemala City, but after three years of warfare the liberals, led by Honduran Francisco Morazán, again dominated the federation. In 1829 the liberals used the regime of exception clause in the federal constitution, allowing state governments to imprison, exile, or repress political opponents. The Morazán government also adopted more drastic anticlerical legislation than anywhere else in Spanish America. It sent the archbishop of Guatemala into exile, abolished the clerical *fueros,* confiscated the property of religious orders, made tithes voluntary, permitted civil marriage, and even legalized divorce. These radical measures could not be sustained for long in the Central America of the 1830s; under pressure, Morazán moved the federal capital to El Salvador and the isthmian conflict worsened.

In Guatemala, Governor Manuel Gálvez (1831–1838) introduced a broad program of liberal reforms that included the privatization of public and communal lands, attacks on the church, export promotion, the liberalization of trade, and the adoption of laws borrowed from the Livingston Codes in Louisiana. During-Gálvez's tenure, Guatemala enacted a penal code (Código de Procedimientos Criminales, 1835) that guaranteed habeas corpus, outlawed torture, and introduced the right of *socorro,* an antecedent to the later celebrated Mexican writ of *amparo* (Art. 74).

Despite apparently progressive legal measures, Gálvez's economic program incited intense resistance. Indian anger at the concessions granted to foreigners, the appropriation of communal lands, and the reimposition of head taxes (though theoretically also applicable to non-Indians) induced rebellions. Combined with the church's spiritual and ideological influence in the countryside, the government's misguided economic policies undermined its support and efficacy. Further, in order to build the jails required by the Livingston Codes, the government used forced Indian labor, which was exacted by the generals responsible for administering the four *comandancias* into which the state was divided. Gálvez and the liberals had militarized the internal administration of the state; they sought to impose their reforms at the point of bayonets, administering Guatemala through military officers under an almost permanent regime of exception.

A cholera epidemic in 1837 provided an opportunity for opponents to take advantage of the disaffection of the population. Priests declared the plague to be divine retribution for the government's attack on the church and religion; they also spread rumors that the liberals had poisoned the water supply, despite government warnings and efforts at vaccination. Amid the panic of the epidemic and a rural rebellion led by Rafael Carrera, Gálvez resigned in favor of the lieutenant governor. Carrera's peasant army occupied Guatemala City in late January 1838; the federation had practically dissolved with the secession of several states. Carrera's rallying cry included abolition of the Livingston Codes, return of the archbishop and religious orders, elimination of the head tax, and amnesty for those exiled by the liberals. By 1840, the political will and military successes of Rafael Carrera dominated national politics.

Rising from pig herder to commander in chief of the Guatemalan military, Carrera epitomized the conservative reaction against liberal reformers. He restored the privileges of the church and consolidated the central role of the military, exercising political dominance for years as commander in chief of the armed forces rather than as president. Carrera rejected the dominant role of foreign investors, free trade, educational and judicial reforms, and the liberal spirit of the early days of Central American independence.

Guatemala adopted no new constitution until 1851, being governed instead by several decrees issued by a constituent assembly in 1839: Decree 65, constituting the executive authority; Decree 73, constituting the judicial authorities; and Decree 76, setting forth the rights of the state and its inhabitants. No legislative authority beyond the constituent assembly existed until adoption of the 1851 Constitution.

The decree constituting the executive authority (December 3, 1839) vested power in a "president of the state of Guatemala" until such time as the constitution [under consideration] is promulgated" (Art. 1). The president enjoyed comprehensive authority, naming all government officials and all military officers up to the rank of colonel as well as devising and enforcing the laws. The decree also charged the president with maintaining public order, raising and organizing military forces, and using these forces as deemed necessary to overcome insurrections and stifle conspiracies. This authority included ordering the arrest and interrogation of suspects— with the limitation of their appearance before a magistrate within three days. The president also was to protect the Roman Catholic church, the established church of the nation, and its ministers.

On December 14, 1839, president Mariano Rivera Paz issued the decree "On the Rights of the State and Its Inhabitants." Unlike the liberal constitutions adopted during this period in other parts of Spanish America, this decree defined the limits of popular sovereignty rather than the limits on government authority. Popular sovereignty could not exceed "the principles of reason, . . . the common good, conservation of good customs, repression of vices, punishment of crimes" (Art. 6). The people, in the plenitude of its sovereignty, have "only the power to do what is just and convenient for the good of all" (Art. 7).

Despite reverting to Ibero-Catholic traditions, the decree listed a number of rights and liberties incorporated by Spanish liberals, after 1812, into Spanish and Spanish American constitutions. These included the abolition of slavery and torture, the right to bear arms, freedom of expression and the press (subject to "repression of abuses" of this freedom), privacy of mail, and freedom from unreasonable search and seizure within the domicile. No explicit regime of exception permitted suspending these rights and liberties, beyond the presidential authority to "stifle conspiracies" and put down insurrections (Art. 16).

The decree of December 16, 1839, set out a plan for a national system of courts and judicial procedures but in no way inhibited the president's role as the dominant legal force in the country. In practice, control of the military was obviously the key to political domination. This tentative, preconstitutional legal order survived until 1851, when Rafael Carrera consolidated his de facto control with a new constitution.

The Constitution of 1851   In July 1844, the constituent assembly enacted Decree 27, authorizing the government to provide for national security and defense without considering the restrictions previously imposed by the federal constitution. After the failure of a Central American conference on reunification, Guatemala declared its independence in March 1847, based upon an earlier assembly decree (1833) that, in the event of failure of the federal pact, Guatemala would be "considered organized preexistent to the Pact [of federal union]."[15]

During the next three years, civil war, accompanied by presidential musical chairs, the brief exile of Carrera (1847–1848), and partisan debates in the assembly left Guatemala a political quagmire. Carrera's return in 1849, followed by two more years of war, consolidated the conservative victory. It also allowed, finally, the adoption of a national constitution.

The Constitution of 1851 was brief and highly authoritarian. It concentrated authority in the executive branch. The legislature was to meet in ordinary session from November 25 until January 31 (Art. 11). When the legislature was not in session, the president could suspend operation of the laws and, "in urgent cases," proclaim "decrees with the force of law," pledge the credit of the nation in obtaining foreign loans, and ratify treaties. The president was responsible for organizing, deploying, and commanding the armed forces in accord with the decree (left in force) of November 29, 1839 (Art. 8). In short, the Guatemalan Constitution of 1851 placed few limits on executive authority and extended little power to Congress. It included no articles construed as a bill of rights or list of *garantías* typical of Spanish American constitutions after 1812. Instead, Article 3 of the 1851 document specifically incorporated Decree 76 (December 5, 1839). This decree did enumerate basic civil rights and liberties, including "perpetual abolition of torture" (Art. 14), abolition of slavery, the right of petition, freedom of the press and association, and most of the commonly proclaimed principles of liberalism. These rights and liberties could be suspended under the president's authority to suspend the laws or to proclaim decree-laws "in urgent cases" (Art. 7, Sec. 4).

The following year, however, the assembly approved an interpretive law modifying the decree of December 5, 1839. The "Ley Reglamentaria Adicional a la de 5 de Diciembre de 1839" provided limited rights for the accused in criminal cases but specifically reaffirmed *ley fuga* and allowed the death penalty for "crimes that threaten the public order" and those punishable by death according to military law (Arts. 18–24).

By 1855, the legislature had amended the constitution to allow a life presidency for Rafael Carrera and to make him immune from liability for any presidential actions. This provision paralleled that of the 1812 constitutional monarchy of Spain and the presidential regimes of Bolivia and Peru (1826) in constitutions influenced by Simón Bolívar (see chapter 6). Ministers were liable for their actions, but the president, even when ordering ministers to perform illegal acts (if such were possible, since Carrera could suspend the law or decree new laws), remained beyond the law. The reforms also gave the president exclusive authority to propose new laws, to name ministers without legislative approval, and to suspend or postpone legislative sessions by notification (subject to approval of his council of state). Carrera had made himself the constitutional dictator of Guatemala.[16]

Although Carrera died in 1865, the constitutional framework he imposed, with the elimination of the life presidency, survived until 1879. Personal and factional conflicts over succession eventually produced victory for the self-named "liberal" forces in Guatemala and most of Central America in the 1870s. In Guatemala, the liberal victory would produce a new constitution (1879) and the twelve-year rule of Justo Rufino Barrios (1873–1885).

The Constitution of 1879 Adoption of a new constitution in 1879 climaxed a liberal attack on Carrera's conservative successors and almost eight years of intermittent constitutional debates. This attack had begun in 1871 with an invasion from Mexico by a group of exiled liberals armed with U.S. Civil War surplus Remington rifles. Led by Miguel García Granados and Justo Rufino Barrios, the invaders overcame the government quickly, occupying Guatemala

City three months after entering the country. Support by liberal forces in Mexico made the victory easier; a liberal wave then swept across El Salvador and Honduras.

In 1873, the relative moderation of Granados's presidency gave way to the liberal dictatorship of Barrios, who was ratified by a constituent assembly in 1876 and by popular vote (the electorate amounted to some 40,000) in 1880. The Barrios administration implemented a raft of anticlerical, secularizing legislation as well as economic modernization through expanded contacts with foreign investors, appropriation of lands owned by Indian communities, and the incorporation of Guatemala more fully into the international commodity trade. Barrios's rejection of continuation of Spanish institutions and laws led to promulgation of new civil, penal, and military codes as well as a new constitution in 1879.

On September 11, 1876, the constituent assembly convoked by Barrios opened debate. Concluding that the country had not yet achieved the necessary stability to enact a constitution, it passed a budget and a decree giving Barrios "supreme and unrestricted power" for four years. After consolidating his government, Barrios called a new constituent assembly in November 1878, noting that "dictatorship is not in accord with republican principles, and if I accepted it, it was due to the difficult conditions in which the country found itself . . . until the State could devise, through its legitimate representatives, a fundamental law."[17] The delegates debated a draft in November and approved the constitution in December 1879. With reforms, it would endure until 1944.

The 1879 Constitution conferred the full range of liberal *garantías* on the citizens of Guatemala (Arts. 16–39), added habeas corpus to the traditional list, and charged the government with assuring liberty, equality, security, and property to its citizens (Art. 16). It also included several extremely flexible regimes of constitutional exception at the discretion of either legislative or executive authorities. The Congress could "concede extraordinary powers to the executive whenever the needs or interests of the Republic require, specifying in the decree to this effect what extraordinary powers are conferred" (Art. 54, Sec. 12). The president, in turn, and on his own initiative, could suspend the *garantías*, with agreement by the council of ministers, when public order so requires (Arts. 18, 39). (This clause imitated similar provisions in Chile, 1833, the Dominican Republican, 1844, and Venezuela, 1857.) In addition, the constitution allowed the president to raise and deploy military forces "to impede or put down insurrections" (Art. 13).

Reforms in 1885 restricted presidential emergency powers after Barrios's death, but these were restored in further reforms in 1887 that provided for conceding extraordinary powers to the president "when the interest or necessity of the Republic demand, determining in the decree [of extraordinary powers] which powers [to concede]" (Art. 8, Sec. 12). The reforms also allowed temporary "suspension of the constitution" (Transitory Art. 4) while the 1887 reforms were debated. Modifications in 1897 and 1903 (Art. 1) reconfirmed the basic elements of regimes of exception and extended the presidential term to six years.

After Barrios's death in 1885 in battle at Chalchuapa, El Salvador, in his quest to reunite Central America, he was succeeded by Alejandro M. Sinibaldi, who had the distinction of serving the shortest term in Guatemalan history: four days. The assembly then named Manuel Lisandro Barillas as provisional president, followed by his formal appointment to a six-year term. Barillas failed to be reelected and spent much of the rest of his life, which ended in assassination on a Mexican streetcar in 1907, plotting his return to power. Barillas's successor, Barrios's nephew José María Reina Barrios, completed one term but despaired of reelection. When the legislature refused to extend his term, he illegally dissolved the Congress in 1898, defeated the revolt of General Próspero Morales, and initiated a regime of terror against the opposition. Assassination on the street in Guatemala City in February 1898 ended his brief dictatorship.

Reina Barrios was legally succeeded by his minister and first designate, Manuel Estrada Cabrera, who maintained himself in office with fraudulent elections every six years and with resources from foreign investors, an export boom, and a network of paid informers and political thugs. Like Porfirio Díaz in Mexico, Estrada Cabrera believed in so-called modernization and development, using an expanded military to impose order, enforce land thefts from the Indian communities to the benefit of local landowners and foreign firms such as the United Fruit Company, and impose labor discipline on the Indian population. The military also managed elections, made easier by the fact that all citizens between the ages of twenty and sixty were considered soldiers. A compliant legislature conceded to Estrada Cabrera extraordinary powers when the "interest or necessity of the Republic demanded." Even Estrada Cabrera preferred constitutional dictatorship, if he could avail himself of it.

Estrada Cabrera was ousted, finally, in 1920, when his supporters joined with the opposition in the Congress to declare that the president was suffering from a "mental disturbance." The president threatened to impose a state of siege (no provision for state of siege existed in the constitution, though the reforms of 1887 allowed legislative delegation of extraordinary powers) but was not supported by his cabinet. Only after the United States discreetly informed prominent Guatemalans that it would not object to a new government, and after more than a week of street fighting in Guatemala City that left hundreds dead, was Estrada Cabrera ousted.

Constitutional reforms in 1921 to legitimate Estrada Cabrera's successors added new regimes of exception with a more complex presidential authority to suspend constitutional *garantías* for thirty days, renewable for a month at a time, "in the case of invasion or grave perturbation of peace" (Art. 39). Reforms in 1927 added "epidemics and any other grave calamity" to the conditions justifying suspension of *garantías.* They also provided for state of siege, with civilian authority subordinated to the military commanders (Art. 39). Small revisions in Article 39 were made again in 1935 but without modifying the essential regimes of exception in Guatemala: state of siege, concession of extraordinary powers to the executive, suspension of constitutional *garantías,* and in extreme cases, martial law.

The basic authority of the president to exercise extraordinary powers, and of either legislative or executive authorities to suspend all or certain civil liberties and rights, was firmly embedded in Guatemalan constitutional practice by the mid-1880s. The liberal Barrios, like the conservative Carrera, helped to confirm the practice of constitutional dictatorship. Under Barrios's rule the principles of liberal dictatorship contained in the 1879 Constitution were entrenched. So, too, was the prominent role of the armed forces in Guatemalan politics—the mainstay of Barrios's regime. These foundations of constitutional dictatorship and the central role of the military in Guatemalan politics endured, with modifications, from 1887 to 1935. Not even the abortive social revolution from 1944 to 1954, codified in the 1945 Constitution, significantly affected this juridical tradition. The revolutionaries, as in Mexico, virtually maintained the same language regarding suspension of *garantías* as the liberals, conservatives, and military presidents after 1851. Article 138 of the 1945 Constitution provided that,

in the case of invasion of the national territory, grave perturbation of peace, epidemic or other general calamity, the President of the Republic, in accord with the Council of Ministers, by means of a decree, may restrict the exercise of the *garantías* mentioned in Article 54 of this Constitution [freedom of assembly, association, privacy of the mails and personal papers, press, prohibitions on search and seizure in domiciles, arrest without warrant, habeas corpus (after forty-eight hours *incomunicado*)]. . . .

Congress shall be convened to approve, modify or reject this decree within three days. . . . This restriction on *garantías* may not exceed thirty days each time it is decreed. . . . After thirty days the *garantías* shall automatically be in force unless there is another decree restricting them. . . .

During the restriction, the Law of Public Order [an organic law regulating internal security and the effects of suspension of *garantías*] shall apply in the affected territory.

U.S. intervention to overthrow the Guatemalan government in 1954 inaugurated a sequence of military governments from 1954 into the 1980s (with a brief civilian interlude from 1966 to 1969). These governments, fighting an almost endemic insurgency, found ample precedent and authority for constitutional dictatorship and even martial law. This tradition legitimated the repression of insurgency in the 1960s and the "salvation of the fatherland" by military dictators and their civilian allies into the 1980s.

Transition to civilian government in the mid-1980s failed to erode the constitution of tyranny. A new constitution adopted in 1985 allowed suspension of civil liberties and rights in the case of invasion, grave perturbation of the public peace, activities against the security of the state, and public calamity. It also included various regimes of exception (state of prevention, state of alarm, state of public calamity, state of siege, and state of war) echoing the 1879 Constitution's concern for public order, while giving the president authority to decree whatever measures might be necessary (*dictar las disposiciones que sean necesarias*) to deal with emergencies or public calamity (Arts. 139, 182 [f]). As in the past, the armed forces were assigned the constitutional mission of maintaining internal and external security, as well as the honor, sovereignty, and independence of the nation (Arts. 249–50). As Guatemala entered the 1990s, regimes of exception and a predominant role for the military pervaded politics as they had from the nation's birth—whether that was in 1838 with the demise of the federation, with its declaration as a republic in 1847, or with its adoption of the first national constitution in 1851.

El Salvador

Regional, economic, and personal conflicts made El Salvador the most important rival of Guatemala within the Central American federal union.[18] When antifederal sentiment prevailed in Guatemala in the 1830s, the federal capital was removed from Guatemala to El Salvador. Federal presidents and military commanders based in El Salvador battled both local politicos and troops and antifederal forces from Guatemala and elsewhere.

When the federal Congress, meeting in San Salvador in May 1838, authorized the states to constitute themselves as they deemed convenient, first Nicaragua and then the other members of the federation declared their independence in 1838 and 1839. El Salvador, however, remained until 1841 part of a federation that had effectively dissolved. Francisco Morazán, president of the federation, *general en jefe* of El Salvador, antagonist of the Guatemalan caudillo Carrera, and a key actor in Central American politics from the late 1820s, rejected the political consequences of dissolution. Morazán invaded Guatemala and sent troops against Honduras and Nicaragua. Meanwhile, a devastating earthquake destroyed San Salvador in 1839, occasioning the transfer of the capital to Cojutepeque. Eventually defeated, Morazán sailed to exile in Peru, returned to Central America, and died at the hands of a firing squad in Costa Rica in 1842 on the anniversary of Central American independence.[19]

In the course of El Salvador's political and constitutional development as one center of the battles between federal and state authorities and between liberals and conservatives in the region, the practices of delegating legislative authority to state presidents and of exercising extraordinary powers by the executive became common. At the same time, important political groups in El Salvador opposed the reestablishment of certain pre-1812 Spanish institutions and the dominance of the church—the apparent objectives of the conservative forces headed by Carrera. Therefore, a marked contrast was found in the postfederal regimes of Guatemala and El Salvador in the 1840s.

The Constitution of 1841   In February 1841, the constituent assembly of El Salvador proclaimed a new constitution for the independent nation. The framers of the constitution incorporated, by reference, Spanish colonial law not in conflict with the new norms, sections of the 1812 Cádiz Constitution, parts of the 1824 Federal

Constitution (including Article 176, the basic regime of exception clause, discussed previously), and a number of constitutional laws predating the 1841 Constitution. As the last bastion of the federal union, the Salvadoran constitution proclaimed El Salvador an autonomous state. Not until 1859 did this designation change to "independent republic." The 1841 Constitution, though amended several times in the following two decades, served as the basic charter of the country until 1864.[20]

Due to the extraconstitutional provisions appended in 1841, the Salvadoran regime represented a complex amalgam of liberal innovations and traditional Iberian authoritarianism. It combined resplendent civil rights and liberties conditioned by broad executive and legislative authority to restrict, suspend, and eliminate these same rights and liberties. Seemingly incompatible provisions simultaneously served as the country's fundamental law.

Unique constitutional stipulations anticipated basic political conflicts in the century to follow: (1) unconstitutional seizure of power by force or popular uprising was defined as criminal usurpation, (2) all acts of such a government were declared null and void as soon as the constitutional order was restored (Art. 69), (3) all government actions taken as a result of pressure by military forces or under threat of popular tumult were declared, in advance, unlawful and null and void (Art. 70), (4) the military was prohibited from requisitioning or taking other action to supply itself without the formal orders of civilian authorities (Art. 71), (5) the military forces were declared "essentially obedient" and prohibited from "deliberating," and (6) active-duty officers were forbidden from serving in the Congress (Art. 72). (This last provision emulated Uruguay's 1830 Constitution and would be adopted elsewhere in Central America.)

The constitution also denied military courts jurisdiction over civilians and the application to them of military law (Art. 78). Likewise, special commissions and tribunals were forbidden (Art. 80). Finally, the legislative and executive authorities were forbidden from restricting, altering, or violating the enumerated *garantías.*

All these provisions distinguished the Salvadoran regime from the conservative, authoritarian system adopted in Guatemala in 1851. But the president had extensive powers in El Salvador also. He was charged with "maintaining peace and internal tranquility, raising the armed forces necessary to defend the nation from invasion or to contain insurrections, and convoking the congress in emergency session if invasion or public disorder threatened the nation." Shortly after adoption of the constitution, Article 78 was suspended in order to deal with rebel forces—and then reestablished in a decree (July 29, 1842) declaring "the referred-to article is reestablished in full force, therefore halting the trial of civilians by military tribunals."[21]

Thus the Salvadoran Constitution of 1841 allowed action, by virtue of Article 176 of the Federal Constitution of 1824, to suspend specified civil rights and liberties and to try civilians by special commissions" in the case of tumult, rebellion, or armed attacks on the constituted authorities." With this authority, Carrera's ally, Francisco Malespín, governed El Salvador until his assassination in 1846. Indeed, Malespín exercised more influence as commander in chief of the armed forces than as president. From 1840 until his assumption of presidential power in 1844, Malespín used the armed forces to determine the outcome of internal politics, suspended (illegally) Article 78 of the 1841 Constitution, which prohibited trial of civilians by military courts, and made the presidency "a nominal and decorative [office] with highly restricted power."[22]

Even Malespín's election as president violated the constitution, which prohibited active-duty officers from serving as president. Malespín thus initiated the political dominance of the military in Salvadoran politics. His efforts at alliance with antiliberal forces in Nicaragua and Honduras resulted in disaster both for the cause of union and for El Salvador. Partly as a response to Malespín's cruelty in the Nicaraguan campaign, the bishop of San Salvador excommunicated him in 1845. However, in the military campaign Malespín almost conformed with constitutional law—leaving the presidency in the hands of the vice president in order to serve as commander in chief (Art. 45, Sec. 9).

Thereafter, almost continual civil war between liberal and conservative caudillos, influenced by the intermittent interventions of Carrera from Guatemala, made Salvadoran politics deadly serious. One of El Salvador's great national heroes and the champion of Central American liberalism, General Gerardo Barrios, was credited with founding the modern Salvadoran military as he resisted Carrera's power (1858–1865) in what was ultimately a losing cause. Eventually Carrera was victorious. Two years prior to his own death, and having defeated El Salvador's General Barrios, he was able to impose conservative Francisco Dueñas upon El Salvador (1863–1871). Under Dueñas's aegis, a more frankly conservative constitution was adopted in 1864—a constitution that for the first time explicitly incorporated provisions for a state of siege.

The Constitution of 1864   The victory of Carrera's conservative allies in El Salvador brought several innovations to the new constitution. First, the president became commander in chief and captain-general of the armed forces (Art. 34), no longer needing the approval of the legislature to take command of the military. Second, he was authorized to "decree extraordinary measures" when raising forces to repel invasions and contain rebellions (Art. 35, Sec. 11), thereby considerably expanding the authority conveyed in a similar clause of the 1841 charter. This gave the Salvadoran president powers closer to the ample authority of Carrera under Guatemala's 1851 Constitution.

Third, the 1864 Constitution provided for "declaration of a state of siege" in conditions and with effects "to be determined by law" (Art. 63). This provision, a sweeping regime of exception clause, allowed for a future law to suspend, limit, or otherwise modify any of the rights and liberties listed in the constitution.

Fourth, Title 16 (Art. 58–63) specifically defined the role of the armed forces in El Salvador to include responsibility for "the maintenance of internal order and execution of the laws." Though Articles 61 and 62 prohibited political deliberation by the armed forces and subjected the military to "the constituted authorities," they also reaffirmed military *fueros*. From 1864, the Salvadoran military never lost its pivotal role in the country's political system.

Preserving the usurpation and sedition clauses of the 1841 Constitution, the 1864 document also considerably expanded executive authority and confirmed the central role of the military in national politics. Even the provision (Art. 101) prohibiting the three branches of government from restricting, altering, or violating any of the *garantías* (Art. 76–100) was conditioned by the extraordinary powers of the executive in cases of "invasions" or "rebellions" and the "to-be-elaborated-by-law" provisions of legislation regulating the conditions under which a state of siege would prevail. The 1864 Constitution presaged modern Salvadoran politics with its militarization of politics and government by regime of exception.

All subsequent nineteenth-century constitutions in El Salvador (1871, 1872, 1880, 1883, 1885 [unpromulgated], 1886) contained provisions allowing for declarations of state of siege, with increasing latitude for presidential and legislative imposition of regimes of exception. In addition, the clause from the 1841 Constitution carried over to 1864, which prohibited the restriction, alteration, or violation of civil liberties and rights by government officials, was modified. In 1883 the constitution permitted the enunciated *garantías* to be suspended when "foreign invasion or internal commotion" made such suspension necessary in order to defend the nation and conserve or restore order (Art. 35). Either the legislature or, when not in session, the executive could declare that such circumstances existed.

In the constitutions of 1885 and 1886, this clause would be conditioned by the extent to which a state of siege law suspended basic rights and liberties. The State of Siege Law adopted in 1886 made the crimes of "treason, sedition, and rebellion" subject to military courts, as well as crimes "against peace, independence, state sovereignty, and the rights of persons." Under the state of siege legislation, the basic *garantías* regarding assembly, association, press, speech, inviolability of correspondence, and freedom of movement could all be suspended until the president determined that "the circumstances that occasioned its implementation have been eliminated." Thus El Salvador expanded the scope of constitutional dictatorship and the role of the military in politics at a time when reforms in Argentina, Chile, and even Venezuela moved in the opposite direction. A weak legislature and lack of an authentic political party system allowed executive and military institutions to prevail.

Article 39 of the unpromulgated 1885 Constitution had stated: "The State of Siege Law will determine which [constitutional *garantías*] may be suspended and the cases in which this suspension may occur." In 1886 this exact language was retained in Article 39 of the constitution that took effect—and remained operative until 1939.

The constitutional mission of the armed forces in the 1864 Constitution—"to defend the country against external enemies and assure internal order and enforcement of the law"—was also expanded in the next two decades. In contrast, the prohibition on deliberation—"The armed forces are essentially obedient. No armed group may deliberate"—was weakened. In the unpromulgated Constitution of 1885 this was changed to read: "may not deliberate on military matters" (*en asuntos del servicio militar*). This precise language became law in 1886 (Art. 132), remained in effect until 1939 (Art. 167), was reinstituted exactly in the 1945 Constitution (Art. 143), and was modified slightly in the constitution of 1950. The qualifier, "en asuntos del servicio militar," made this clause much weaker than in most of Spanish America; the Salvadoran military had achieved constitutional liberation from the prohibition on deliberation common in Spanish American constitutions since Venezuela's 1811 emulation of the 1791 French restriction on the military.

In the 1872 Constitution and thereafter, an expanded definition of the role of the armed forces included the duty to "maintain intact the integrity of the national territory, conserve and defend national autonomy, enforce the law and maintain public order, and see to the enforcement of constitutional *garantías*" (1883, Art. 120). This language was retained in the constitutions of 1885, 1886, 1939, 1944 (reforms), and 1945.

Thus, by 1864 and, in more definitive terms, by 1886, the juridical foundations of Salvadoran regimes of exception, civil-military relations, and the constitution of tyranny were well established. As in Mexico, the precise language of twentieth-century regimes of exception had been incorporated into Salvadoran constitutional life by conservatives and liberals in the nineteenth century. The military became a constitutional branch of government; it was an essential component of the political system.

This remained true into the 1970s. In the 1970s and 1980s El Salvador was bloodied by guerrilla warfare and vicious counterinsurgency campaigns that devastated the country. These campaigns continued into the early 1990s. Despite numerous constitutional reforms and amendments, the government always retained the power to suspend *garantías*, declare a state of siege, rule by decree, and subject civilians to military jurisdiction. For example, the 1962 Constitution provided that, once the *garantías* had been suspended in accord with Article 175, military tribunals would hear cases involving treason, espionage, rebellion, sedition, and "other crimes against peace or independence of the State or against human rights." Moreover, when the *garantías* were restored, the military tribunals retained jurisdiction over pending cases (Arts. 175–78).

A new constitution promulgated in 1983 reaffirmed the armed forces's custodianship over the nation, their mission as guarantors of peace, tranquility, internal security, and the constitutional regime (Arts. 211–13). As in 1864, and thereafter, emergencies such as "serious disturbance of the public order," rebellion, and "general disaster" justified suspension of civil liberties and rights, as well as media censorship and declaration of state of siege (Arts. 29, 131).

El Salvador's nineteenth-century constitutional evolution had provided strong bases for constitutional dictatorship and the militarization of politics. This legacy still dominated the country without respite in the 1990s, even as guerrillas and a civilian government negotiated a tenuous cease-fire in a civil war two decades long.

Honduras

Beset by historical conflicts between its two major towns, Comayagua and Tegucigalpa, Honduras served repeatedly as a battleground for federal and antifederal forces as well as for armies of competing local caudillos. The separation of Honduras from the Central American union in 1838 was followed shortly by the defeat of a combined Honduran-Nicaraguan army by Morazán in El Salvador (1840).[23] The defeated army was commanded by General Francisco Ferrera, who had been elected president under the new 1839 Constitution and had become an ally of Carrera, despite his earlier service under Morazán. Ferrera's government strongly supported the role of the church, reestablished tithes, and ordered compliance with the traditional laws of Spain (Siete Partidas, Ordenanzas de Minería y Militares) when they did not conflict with post-1840 legislation. After a second term as president (1843–1845), Ferrera continued as the power behind the throne in the positions of ministers of defense and commander in chief of the armed forces. Throughout this period, Honduran forces battled internal adversaries and armies from Nicaragua, El Salvador, and Guatemala.

Caudillismo at its worst characterized Honduran politics into the 1870s, with British territorial and economic claims and U.S. diplomatic intervention adding complications. By one account, between 1821 and 1876, eighty-five different presidents and interim presidents attempted to govern the country.[24] The alternation of executives sympathetic to Salvadoran liberals or Guatemalan conservatives kept Honduras in constant strife. Endemic warfare and violence inflicted suffering on the population and hindered economic development in this poorest of Central American nations.

Perhaps the worst excesses occurred under the presidency of General José María Medina, imposed upon Honduras by Carrera in 1863. Medina hung captured adversaries in the forests of Olancho, decorating the trees for miles with his victims. Although Medina's excesses drew attention, atrocities characterized most of the perpetual civil and international warfare affecting Honduras during this period.[25]

Six nineteenth-century constitutions provided the institutional stage for the Honduran theater of caudillismo. Each proclaimed liberal principles and civil liberties—property, security, equality, and liberty—while also providing the juridical foundations for constitutional regimes of exception.

The Constitutions of 1839 and 1848   The Honduran 1839 Constitution incorporated all laws enacted since the 1825 state constitution not in conflict with the new charter (Art. 129). Unlike most other constitutions of this period, the president was not named as commander in chief of the armed forces (instead, the minister of war was) and was not vested with inherent emergency powers. Even the Congress had few emergency powers, limited in "the case of tumult, rebellion, and armed attack" to (1) disarming those who illegally maintain firearms; (2) impeding the right of assembly, the object of which is pleasure, political discussion, or consideration of the conduct of public officials; and (3) ignoring customary legal formalities in carrying out the search and seizure of domiciles (Art. 124). No other provisions allowed suspension or violation of the *garantías* (Art. 109–23). Indeed, clear prohibitions existed on suspension of freedom of the press, petition, speech, and publication. Torture was outlawed (Art. 123).

In these respects, Honduras adopted a moderate liberal constitutional document with no distinct definition of the role of military institutions and reiterating civilian control of the security police (Art. 112). Perhaps most surprising was the freedom of conscience and religion (even though the Roman apostolic faith was made the state religion) adopted in Article 16, which stands in contrast to most of Central and South America during this era. In practice, however, under virtually continuous wartime conditions, the old Spanish laws of war prevailed and the commander in chief of the armed forces became the most important political figure in the country. Until 1848, this meant General Francisco Ferrera.

Pressure to reform the 1839 Constitution came from conservatives unhappy with the freedom of conscience clause and from the newly elected president, Juan Fernández Lindo (1847–1852), who preferred longer presidential terms (four years instead of two) and the possibility of reelection. Having served as Agustín de Iturbide's intendant for the province of Honduras under the Mexican empire, as president of the constituent assembly that proclaimed the 1839 charter, and even, briefly, as provisional president of El Salvador, the new president had conservative credentials and political ambition. He flamboyantly declared war against the United States to support Mexico during the U.S. invasion of that country. Despite his conservatism and affinity for Iberian institutions, President Fernández Lindo opposed the Guatemalan caudillo Rafael Carrera and sought the union of Honduras with El Salvador. Appropriately inconsistent, given the disarray of Central America, his new constitution, proclaimed in 1848, nevertheless altered in certain important aspects the juridical foundations of Honduran politics.

First, public exercise of all but the Catholic religion was prohibited (Art. 16), although others would be tolerated if they did not seek to replace Catholicism or upset public order. Second, a bicameral legislature replaced the unicameral chamber of 1839, with a Senate whose membership was limited to substantial property owners. The legislature could not concede extraordinary authority to the executive nor expand the authority set out in the constitution (in contrast to Art. 24, Sec. 9, of the 1839 document).

Nevertheless, executive authority was greater than it had been in the 1839 charter. The president was now commander in chief of the armed forces, eliminating the potential for an alliance between the minister of war and the vice president or some other caudillo, which had frequently led to rebellion. The constitution also gave extensive emergency powers to the executive. In order "to repel invasions or contain insurrections" or "to conserve internal order," the president could raise the necessary armed forces and deploy them as required. In the case of threats to the public order or invasion, the president could also impose forced loans or new taxes, subject to legislative approval (Art. 46).

A long list of civil rights and liberties complemented a clause that defined the assumption of power, other than as provided by the constitution, as criminal usurpation (Art. 95). The constitution also declared null all laws, decrees, or resolutions adopted as a result of pressure by military forces or in cases of tumult (Art. 96) and prohibited political deliberation by the military. Active-duty officers were forbidden to stand for election to Congress or the presidency (Arts. 97, 98).

Significantly, the constitution prohibited in all circumstances trials of civilians by military courts and the application of military law or punishments ("penas y castigos prescritos por las ordenanzas del ejército") to civilians (Art. 105). Finally, a clause similar to Article 93 of the Salvadoran Constitution of 1841 (and retained into the 1880s) declared: "Neither the legislative power, nor the executive, nor any tribunal or authority may restrict, alter or violate any of the enunciated *garantías:* any authority or power that infringes [the *garantías*] will be individually responsible for the damage incurred . . .

and guilty of usurpation" (Art. 113). Efforts to institute these idealistic principles failed when faced with the reality of isthmian civil wars. In the main, Honduras served as a battleground for competing caudillos of neighboring Guatemala and Nicaragua who used internal aspirants to power for their own ends.

The Constitution of 1865   From 1848 until 1865, the rule of war governed Honduras more often than the rule of law. Occupation of the presidency by Carrera's ally, General José María Medina, led in 1865 to the replacement of the 1848 document with a charter more in line with those of other Central American countries. This included the broadening of executive emergency powers and the constitutionalization of the political role of the military.

1. The legislature could now concede extraordinary authority to the president (Art. 25) as well as a number of routine legislative functions, including the authority to issue decree laws (Arts. 25, 26).
2. The president could raise and deploy troops, as well as borrow money without legislative approval, in order to "repel invasions or contain rebellions."
3. For the first time a Honduran constitution defined the role of the military: to defend the state against external enemies, maintain order, and insure the execution of the laws.
4. Military *fueros* were reaffirmed (Arts. 63–66).
5. The president was confirmed as commander in chief of the armed forces.

All of the provisions regarding the usurpation and the nullity of laws enacted under military pressure or conditions of popular tumult were retained. So, too, was the long list of *garantías* and the prohibition on their restriction, alteration, or violation (Arts. 98, 99, 102).

In 1869, President Medina persuaded Congress to summon a constituent assembly, which duly reformed Article 33 of the constitution, changing the presidential term to four years and installing him as president for the next term. Medina's political machinations could not prevent military defeat by liberal armies supported by forces from Guatemala and El Salvador. After 1871, with the victory of Honduran liberals allied with the new regime in Guatemala, more extensive emergency powers would appear in the constitution adopted in 1873. In 1880, for the first time, a state of siege clause allowed complete "suspension of the *imperio*" of the constitution

(1880 Constitution, Arts. 21, 47) along with the delegation of extensive legislative authority to the president, first adopted in 1865. Honduras thus followed the pattern of El Salvador, expanding the scope of regimes of exception in the latter part of the nineteenth century.

In some ways, the evolution of extraordinary powers delegated to the executive and the creation of state of siege provisions in Honduras exemplified developments in the Central American region.

- *1848 Constitution, Article 29, Section 14:* "In no case and with no pretext may the legislature concede extraordinary powers to the executive, nor expand those detailed in this constitution."
- *1865 Constitution, Article 25:* "The legislative may not, except in the cases determined in this constitution, concede extraordinary powers to the executive, nor expand those detailed in this constitution."
- *1865 Constitution, Article 26:* "The legislature may delegate the following powers to the executive: (1) legislate concerning police, finance, army and navy; (2) approve or decree statutes and regulations for corporate entities; . . . (3) manage the system of weights and measures, promote communication links; and (4) decree civil, penal, commercial and mining codes."
- *1873 Constitution, Article 25:* "The congress, in cases of internal or external war, may confer upon the Executive whatever extraordinary powers prudently deemed indispensable to achieve pacification" (followed in addition by the same list of powers to delegate as in 1865).
- *1880 Constitution, Articles 47, Section 5; 48:* "Congress may delegate to the Executive power to legislate in the areas of police, finance, army, navy, education, and development [*fomento*]."

The Honduran state of siege law entailed suspension of the rule of the constitution, which in Articles 6–11 detailed the liberal commitments to individual security, including habeas corpus, liberty, equality, and property. Honduras had achieved the "perfect" solution: all rights and no rights; limited government and unlimited government; separation of powers and delegation of legislative authority to the president. As the anarchy, foreign intervention, and internal wars of Honduras epitomized the tragedy of Central America from 1824 to the 1880s, the Honduran Constitution of 1880 exemplified the contradictions of liberal dictatorship. As in its Central American neighbors and Mexico, by the 1870s Honduran constitutional law incorporated the juridical foundations of tyranny. The contradictory amalgamation of liberal *garantías* and restrictions on legislative and executive authority, with regimes of exception and the military dominance of politics, consolidated a tradition of constitutional dictatorship.

This tradition persisted in the last decades of the nineteenth century and into the twentieth. From the 1880s until 1904, generals fought each other for the presidency, seeking to legitimate their rule with congressional sanction of their victories in chaotic elections. Typical was General Manuel Bonilla's use of a constituent assembly, under a state of siege and a suspension of the *imperio* of the constitution, to enact a reformed charter and confirm his election as president. This assembly delegated extraordinary powers to General Bonilla in 1906. With this authority Bonilla enacted new civil, criminal, and military codes, reorganized the court system, and modified the election laws. Despite Bonilla's ouster in a 1907 coup, the legislation he promulgated endured into the 1920s.

Honduras again faced national elections under a state of siege in 1919, though the "German threat" that had justified this proclamation had obviously ended. The current president insisted on maintaining the state of siege to meet the "continuing danger" to the country, at least until he had imposed his chosen successor. From the 1920s to the early 1980s, military officers generally headed Honduran governments; when not in the presidency, they constrained presidential and congressional initiative. These officers and their occasional civilian surrogates routinely used their authority to suspend constitutional *garantías*, declare states of siege, and rule by decree. As in El Salvador, constitutional dictatorship and military control of government had become the rule in Honduras in the nineteenth century and remained so throughout the twentieth. Elected civilian governments in the 1980s and early 1990s hesitated to make any effort to dismantle the foundations of Honduras's constitution of tyranny. The transition to civilian government and adoption of a new constitution in 1982 failed to eliminate the key role of regimes of exception (Arts. 187–88; Art. 247, Sec. 7) and the armed forces (Arts. 272–74) in Honduran politics.

Nicaragua

With the dissolution of the federal union, Nicaragua became the first Central American state to declare itself independent (1838). Regional animosities between the two major towns, León and Granada, continued from the colonial era into the nineteenth century. A conservative center, Granada, first allied itself with Guatemala, whereas León declared itself independent (1821). Both territories eventually united with Iturbide's Mexican Empire, but upon its dissolution, regional conflict within Nicaragua recurred.

Independence and a national constitution in 1838 failed to resolve internal conflicts or to prevent the immersion of Nicaragua in the intrigues and warfare that afflicted Central America until the 1870s. Like its isthmian neighbors, Nicaragua was pressured to repay its share of loans contracted by the federation from the British. In 1842, the British blockaded both coasts seeking to force payment. In addition, during the 1840s Nicaragua faced British guardianship of the "Miskito Kingdom" (Nicaragua's eastern coast), meddling by U.S. and British diplomats, scheming by investors competing for control of steamship and wagon lines, and a battle between the United States and England over control of potential canal routes across the isthmus.

Personalist and factional struggles defied efforts to consolidate a viable political order. As in Honduras and El Salvador, the commanders in chief of the armed forces came to play a more central role than even the presidents, who rarely completed their constitutional terms.[26]

The Constitution of 1838   The 1838 Constitution was the first of the constitutions of independent states in Central America. It stated that Nicaragua continued to "pertain by pact to the Federation of Central America" (Art. 1); not until 1858 would the country formally become a sovereign republic. The "conservation of liberty, equality, security, and property" were declared the first and most essential objectives of the sovereign government (Art. 6). Even before discussing the legislative, executive, and judicial branches, the first constitution of independent Nicaragua declared that the armed forces "were essentially obedient, instituted for public security, and prohibited from 'deliberation' " (Art. 9). The document assigned the security police to civilian authorities and guaranteed citizens the right to own and bear arms, "except in the case of tumult, rebellion, or attacks upon the constituted authorities" (Art. 13). This clause was later borrowed by constitution drafters in other parts of Central America.

The list of "rights and duties" incorporated in Articles 25–48 was a typical menu of the liberal principles shared by most of the constitutions of the era, except that it forbade the president to exact taxes even in times of emergency, a more restrictive role for the executive than that prescribed in Honduras or El Salvador. More tolerant in religious matters than many of the Spanish American republics (and a source of considerable friction within the country), the 1838 Constitution stipulated that the public exercise of religions other than Catholicism would not be prohibited (Art. 53).

Rather than president, the constitution named the chief executive officer the supreme director, borrowing from the constitutions in the Rio de la Plata region and Chile from 1810 to the mid-1820s. He would be elected for a nonrenewable two-year term and would appoint the commander of the armed forces, military and administrative officers, and ministers. He could also order the arrest and interrogation of persons suspected of conspiracy or treason. However, the supreme director was not extended any explicit emergency powers (beyond Article 176 of the federal constitution) nor was the legislature authorized to delegate legislative or other extraordinary power to the chief executive. Thus, while the supreme director could choose the military officers and also staff the central administration, he had relatively less constitutional authority than his Central American counterparts in the 1840s. Constitutional reconfirmation of the military *fueros* further enhanced the role of the military in the new Nicaraguan nation. Finally, all previous legislation not in conflict with the constitution would remain effective, including Spanish law and the military *ordenanzas*.

From 1838 to 1858, this constitution nominally prevailed in Nicaragua, though three draft constitutions (1842, joining Nicaragua with El Salvador and Honduras, 1848, and 1854) were debated and "approved" but never formally proclaimed.[27] These never-promulgated charters enhanced executive authority, allowed the suspension of particular civil rights and liberties, and introduced a variety of extraordinary powers in the case of internal disorders or threats to public tranquility.

Meanwhile, a number of external influences internationalized Nicaraguan politics: British control of eastern Nicaragua (the Mosquitia coast) and occupation of San Juan del Norte, which became Greytown (1847); U.S. penetration by steamship and transport entrepreneurs taking advantage of the California gold rush; and British-American rivalry over the construction of a canal across the isthmus. This rivalry, as well as that among competing capitalists from the United States, joined Nicaraguan politicians and business interests with foreign investors and invaders.

Nicaraguan liberals even resorted to a pact with filibusters, the most famous of whom, William Walker, became president of Nicaragua in 1856 at the head of a rabble army. An alliance of Nicaraguans, Costa Ricans, and Hondurans, supported by Cornelius Vanderbilt, whose business interests Walker threatened, eventually ousted the interloper. Refusing to drop his schemes for personal control over a Central American territory to be annexed by the United States, Walker was captured by British marines and handed over to Honduran forces. He died before a firing squad in Honduras in 1860.[28]

Conservatives, who in any case favored stronger executive authority and less ample individual *garantías,* noted that perturbation, agitation, and tumult had become "the normal state of our society." They blamed this on the lack of power of the executive branch to fulfill its mission: maintenance of order and public tranquility.[29] The defeat and discrediting of the liberal forces allied with Walker allowed conservative criticism to take constitutional form. Supported also by the sway of Carrera's antifederal conservative regime in Guatemala, Nicaraguan conservatives drafted and imposed a constitution that would endure until the 1890s—more than two decades after the liberals had regained power in most of Central America.

The Constitution of 1858   The new constitution had a president elected for a four-year term instead of a supreme director for two. The president was vested with a number of far-reaching powers in addition to heading the armed forces. These included (1) raising military forces and taking the measures necessary to control internal disturbances, even to the extent of forced loans from private citizens, (2) personally commanding the armed forces at his own discretion, temporarily leaving the presidency with an appropriate replacement, and (3) ordering the arrest and interrogation of suspects, when "public tranquility [was] threatened," and either releasing them within fifteen days or ordering their imprisonment or exile (Arts. 55, 56).

This last provision was unique in Central America. Executive authority to detain and arrest suspected conspirators or rebels was typically limited to forty-eight to seventy-two hours without judicial orders. Nowhere else during this period could the executive order longer periods of imprisonment, much less exile, except in the charter adopted in 1821 for Iturbide's Mexican Empire. Although the customary list of *garantías* followed, as well as the usual clause declaring void the acts of government officials who had usurped authority (Art. 95), presidential authority "when public tranquility was threatened" was extensive. If "order was subverted," the president could send "traitors and conspirators" into internal or foreign exile, making banishment a legal method of suppressing political opposition (Art. 56). Nicaragua shared this method of punishing political opponents with Venezuela and Colombia, both of which had adopted laws against "conspiracy" in the early 1830s (see chapter 5). In addition, when in recess the legislature could delegate a number of powers to the executive (Art. 42, Secs. 25–26); this list provided the model for a similar clause adopted by conservatives in the Honduran Constitution of 1865 (discussed above).

Seeking to limit the political role of the military, the 1858 Constitution prohibited officers from "deliberating," in language common to many of the Central American and South American documents of this period ("esencialmente obediente, instituída para seguridad común, en actual servicio le es prohibido deliberar"— Art. 98). Further, as in Honduras, military officers were forbidden to stand for election but were extended the traditional *fueros* (Art. 101) and the customary military *ordenanzas* applied to states of war. However, the charter stated that the military (*fuerza pública*) was instituted to provide "collective security" (Art. 98), which was interpreted as an internal political mission as well as protection against external threats. Though more ambiguous than those of Honduras and El Salvador, the constitution recognized a legitimate military role in national politics.

Presidential dominance, suspension of selected *garantías* in times of internal tumult, presidential authority to arrest, incarcerate, or exile suspects when internal order was subverted, and the de facto dominance of military authorities would reign in Nicaragua for the remainder of the nineteenth century. Although the Nicaraguan liberals had discredited themselves by collaborating with foreign invaders and filibusters, the victorious conservatives consolidated constitutional provisions for regimes of exception in Nicaragua quite similar to, if more "flexible" than, those enacted by liberal charters in Guatemala, El Salvador, and Honduras. When the Nicaraguan liberals lost power after the William Walker episode, conservatives stepped in to consecrate the institutions of constitutional dictatorship. The contending factions and parties might disagree on the role of the church in society, on the relationship between their country and the United States or Great Britain, and on the policies toward education, public works, and Indian communities, but they agreed on the need for extraordinary powers for the executive in times of turbulence, on the unavoidable role of the military in politics, and on regimes of exception that permitted suspension of the fundamental *garantías*.

When liberals returned to power in the early 1890s and adopted a new constitution (1893), they added the right of habeas corpus (Art. 28), overturned provisions linking the state to the Catholic church (Art. 47), expanded the list of individual *garantías,* and provided that all *garantías* (except the prohibition on the death penalty and confiscation of property) could be suspended by declaration of a state of siege. Article 82 (Sec. 34) allowed the legislature to declare the country in a state of siege; Article 93 (Sec. 18) conferred this authority on the president when the legislature was not in session.

For good measure, the 1893 Constitution added a separate constitutional definition of the role of the military: "to assure the rights of the nation, compliance with the law, and maintenance of public order" (Art. 134). Reforms in the 1890s, and from 1905 to 1913, confirmed these fundamental principles of Nicaraguan politics. Not until 1939 did important changes occur in constitutional language, when Anastasio Somoza Garcia supported reforms that further expanded executive authority in regimes of exception and broadened congressional power to delegate legislative authority to the president (Arts. 165, 220, 221). Changes in the numbering of these constitutional articles in 1948 and 1950 added no new extraordinary powers or exceptional regimes—not that any were needed to assure the periodic exercise of constitutional dictatorship by the Somozas and their surrogates.

Thus, by the mid-nineteenth century, constitutional dictatorship and military guardianship had become basic features of the Nicaraguan polity. These features endured into the twentieth century and buttressed the Somoza regime with legitimate instruments of tyranny from 1936 until 1979. They would also survive the revolution of 1979 to reappear in modified form in the Sandinista Constitution of 1986 (Arts. 95, 184–86). Like their predecessors in Mexico and Guatemala, Nicaraguan revolutionaries after 1979 preserved constitutional authority to suspend civil liberties and rights, exercise extraordinary powers, and in certain instances, rule by decree. They also reaffirmed the role of the military in politics, albeit the Popular Sandinista Army. Article 185 of the 1986 Constitution stipulated:

The President of the Republic may suspend, in all or part of the national territory, the rights and *garantías* consecrated in this constitution in the case of war or when national security, economic conditions or a national catastrophe demand it.

The decree [that suspends civil liberties and rights] may put into effect a State of Emergency, for a determined period, subject to extension. A Law of Emergency will specify the particulars. During the State of Emergency the President of the Republic will have the authority to approve the national budget and to send it to the Assembly for its information.

Article 186 listed certain rights and *garantías* that could not be suspended under the state of emergency. These included the right to life, religious freedom, and the right of a prisoner to be informed in a language that is understood of the reason for his or her detention.

Nineteenth-century liberals and conservatives, the Somoza dynasty, and the Sandinistas had agreed on the necessity, in times of crisis, to govern Nicaragua under constitutional dictatorship. They likewise agreed on the role of the armed forces as an essential branch of government and on the need to repress "criminal and anti-social activities" to defend "the revolution." The Sandinista constitution declared: "The Popular Sandinista Army is national and must . . . protect and respect the present constitution. . . . The State prepares, directs, and organizes popular participation in the armed defense of the fatherland through the Popular Sandinista Army (Title V, Arts. 95, 97). Sandinismo inherited older traditions than the struggle against the Somozas; their version of the constitution of tyranny continued to operate in Nicaragua after they lost the national elections in 1990. The so-called democratic government that succeeded them made no effort to eliminate the foundations of constitutional dictatorship bequeathed by nineteenth-century constituents to twentieth-century Nicaraguans.

Costa Rica

Geographically and politically isolated from the centers of colonial administration, the colonists of the central *meseta* of Costa Rica played no role in the independence movements of the first two decades of the nineteenth century. When it was learned, in 1821, that independence had been declared in Guatemala and Nicaragua (León), Costa Ricans were cautious. Consideration of options by the *ayuntamientos* in San José, Heredia, and Cartago resulted in responses typified by a declaration issued by the council in Cartago: "while time decides the outcome, we shall be peaceful spectators of the results."[30] Costa Ricans generally maintained their aloofness from Central American events and sought to manage their own affairs. They did, however, incorporate themselves formally into the federal union in 1824, adopt a state constitution in 1825, and remain, to their distress, a theater of operations for key battles fought by forces seeking to sustain or dissolve the federation during the next twenty years.

By 1829, however, Costa Ricans had edged closer to autonomy than most other territories of the federation. Energetic leadership by the state's first *jefe de estado*, Juan Mora Fernández (1824–1833), the early introduction of coffee production and export to Chile and England, and the homogeneous population were among the factors that set Costa Rica apart from its Central American neighbors. Nevertheless, internal rivalries among the four major towns of the *meseta* (Heredia, Cartago, San José, and Alajuela), personal feuds among local caudillos and their supporters, and unavoidable entanglements with federal or antifederal alliances brought intermittent warfare to Costa Rica as experienced in the rest of Central America.

Efforts to resolve the conflicts among the state's four major towns resulted in the unique *ley de ambulancia* in the mid-1830s. This law stipulated a rotation of government functions every four years among the four towns. When Costa Rica's second major caudillo, Braulio Carrillo (1835–1837, 1838–1842) suspended this law in favor of San José and adopted measures restricting the church and eliminating tithes, the other three towns joined in a *liga* and Costa Ricans fought the War of the *Liga*. In response, Carrillo declared the populations of Cartago, Heredia, and Alajuela "in rebellion against the constitution" and imposed martial law until January 1836, supposedly in accord with legislation of the Central American Federation. Carrillo was victorious but reestablished tithes as part of a settlement. Defeated in the 1837 elections, he took power through a military coup and remained in power, illegally, until 1842.

During this de facto government, Carrillo decreed the first post-1825 constitutional measures in Costa Rica: Ley de Bases y Garantías (March 8, 1841). This decree contained a list of civil liberties and *garantías*, on the familiar liberal model, and a provision for a lifetime president with extensive powers to "conserve the internal peace of the State," "raise and command the military forces necessary in times of war," preside over the "legislative" branch (*cámara consultiva*), and "legislate, suspend legislation, direct the administration of the State, provide for income and direct expenditures" (Arts. 4, 5).

In April 1842, Francisco Morazán, recently defeated by Guatemalan strongman Carrera, returned from exile in Peru. Seeking a base for military operations to restore the federation, Morazán allied himself with Carrillo's opponents, defeated Carrillo's military forces, and declared the Federal Constitution of 1824 in effect in Costa Rica. A June 1842 decree proclaimed Carrillo's *Bases y Garantías* and reinstituted the state Constitution of 1825; a subsequent decree in August declared null and void the acts of the usurper, Carrillo, since 1838.[31] Morazán's overriding concern with restoring the federation rather than with domestic affairs alienated the Costa Ricans. An alliance of political groups in San José and Alajuela sent military forces against Morazán, defeated him, and condemned him to death. The most important advocate of Central American union was executed on September 15, 1842, in San José.

The Constitution of 1844. Bickering over a successor led to a temporary agreement on José María Alfaro, who took office and called for a constituent assembly. This assembly created the first postindependence constitution of an independent Costa Rican state; after reform and further constitution writing (1847, 1848), Costa Rica was declared a republic in 1848.

From the outset, the 1844 Constitution distinguished Costa Rica from its Central American neighbors in a number of significant and unusual ways. Overall, the incipient Costa Rican coffee oligarchy and merchant class sought to control executive authority, establish civilian control over the military, and prohibit military jurisdiction over civilians. In addition, beginning in 1844, Costa Rican constitutions, made education a right of all citizens, noted dogmatically the "moral right of resistance to oppression," and incorporated some unique circumstances under which the rights of citizens were lost: for abandoning "his woman" (Art. 61, 1844); for "ingratitude to parents or abandoning his woman or children and notoriously failing to meet family obligations" (Art. 33, 1847; Art. 10, 1848); and for "scandalous and notorious abandonment of the duties of head of family" (Art. 52, 1859).

Despite the unique aspects of Costa Rican constitutions after 1844, the turmoil, civil war, and caudillismo of the period also were reflected in the evolution of regimes of exception and extraordinary powers in the six national charters adopted from 1844 to 1871. Unlike all the other Central American nations, however, no Costa Rican constitution during this era defined a constitutional role for the military, permitted civilians to be tried in military courts, or allowed the formal suspension of constitutional *garantías* without legislative approval. This did not prevent military intervention in politics and the expansion of presidential power. In May 1846, a law revising the judicial system restricted military *fueros*. On June 7, military commanders in the four main towns, Cartago, Heredia, Alajuela, and San José, overturned the 1844 Constitution. A new constitution, adopted by the constitutional convention that followed, restricted the "right of rebellion," substituting for the old language (Arts. 32, 46) "the right to protest directly to the legislature if the government violated the laws" (Art. 3, 1847).

The administration of President José María Castro Madriz (1847–1849) survived only briefly the incessant civil wars. It did, however, innovate in the area of presidential authority and the suspension of the constitutional order. In October 1847, faced with an uprising in Alajuela, the president convoked an extraordinary session of the Congress to "take measures which the Supreme Executive Power is not authorized to [implement on its own authority]." In accord with the permanent commission of the Congress but without clear constitutional authority for action, the president promulgated a decree "suspending the constitutional order and establishing martial law [*un régimen militar*], with the president at the head of the army as guardian of the law." This apparent breach of the constitution, under cover of approval by the permanent commission of the Congress, lasted until October 15, 1847, when the president decreed a return to the "full enjoyment of *garantías* stipulated in the Constitution."[32]

Castro Madriz based his actions on Article 110 (Sec. 3) of the constitution, authorizing the president to "conserve order, tranquility, security, and the integrity of the political regime" and requiring congressional approval of "efficacious measures to conserve public order." Congress subsequently determined in December 1847 that Article 110 (Sec. 3) should be understood to authorize unilateral action by the president "because everything cedes, and should cede, to conservation of the social order."[33] With this interpretation of the constitution, the Costa Rican legislature had resorted to the Machiavellian doctrine of reason of state; no constitutional limits mattered if security and survival of the state erased all legal constraint on government action.

Confronted by another rebellion in Alajuela in March 1848, Vice President Juan Rafael Mora Porras decreed "the constitutional order suspended and the country in a state of war, under military law. Therefore the Executive Power assumes supreme authority over all branches of the State." This included control of the judiciary and municipal councils. On May 15, 1848, the president restored the rule of the constitution.[34]

In the name of constitutional reform, the Congress adopted a virtually new constitution in November 1848, though the 1847 charter remained formally in effect. The 1848 reforms confirmed the ambiguous executive authority exercised by Castro Madriz. Article 77 provided "The president may take, on his own accord, the measures deemed necessary to defend the country against threats of external aggression, or internal commotion, informing the congress of the use made of this authority."

Threatened with a military coup in November 1849, Castro Madriz resigned; the elections following selected Mora Porras to complete the resigned president's term. Mora Porras went further than Castro Madriz in expanding presidential powers, suspending the Congress in January 1852 "in accord with the ample authority conferred by the Constitution." No constitutional clause authorized presidential dissolution of Congress, but the president relied on Article 77 (Sec. 2) until May 1852, when a new Congress convened. Again in 1856, faced with war against the filibuster William Walker, Mora Porras postponed legislative sessions indefinitely, commenting that "in the present circumstances the constitutional order is suspended 'to a certain degree.' " This ambiguous (but accepted) regime of exception prevailed until 1859.[35]

The domination of the executive branch by a president, Juan Rafael Mora Porras (1849–1853, 1853–1859)—who dissolved the Congress, directly commanded the armed forces (including the defeat of the filibuster William Walker in 1857), and enriched his friends and family with government favors—gave a different meaning to Costa Rican constitutionalism. Eventually, Mora Porras was ousted by a military coup arranged by civilian groups opposed to his reelection for a third term (1859). Thereafter, the evolution of constitutional regimes of exception in Costa Rica was generally marked by a return to legislative rather than executive determination of emergency conditions until the 1870s—and even then required legislative review of executive action if the constitution were suspended while the assembly was not in session.

Constitutional Development, 1844–1882   The evolution of regimes of exception in Costa Rican constitutional law is easily seen by comparing the terminology in the six constitutions during this period. In 1844 the legislature was charged with (1) "raising forces necessary to contain insurrections and repel invasions," (2) legislating the ordinances to govern the military, (3) conceding pardons or amnesties, by a two-thirds vote, in cases involving strictly political matters, when public welfare, tranquility, or security made such action advisable, and (4) overseeing strict and full compliance with the laws and constitution of the state and the republic and holding public officials accountable (Art. 106). Many of these functions were typically assigned to the executive branch in the rest of Central America. In addition, the particular duties and authority of the Senate and lower chamber focused attention on compliance with the constitution by public officials (Art. 126).

Even so, the executive (*jefe supremo del estado*) could "suspend, in agreement with the Senate, the execution of any law that causes grave danger to the State" and was charged with conserving internal order, tranquility, and security—in language reminiscent of almost all the early constitutions of the region. In cases of insurrection or invasion, the *jefe supremo* could also raise troops to deal with the crisis but must immediately advise the lower chamber or, if not in session, the Senate. The *jefe* was prohibited, without legislative approval, from directly commanding the armed forces. Finally, he could order the arrest of persons suspected of threatening public tranquility but must deliver such persons to a judge within forty-eight hours—slightly less than the customary three days and far from the fifteen days allowed in Nicaragua. No other emergency powers were enumerated; no authority to suspend part or all of the constitution existed.

Three years later the 1847 Constitution, which would endure only a year, introduced significant modifications. These included eliminating the Senate and creating a permanent commission of the legislature with legislative authority when the assembly was not in session, increasing the term of office of the executive from four to six years, and expanding executive authority. The executive could now (1) "command in person the armed forces when he deemed it convenient," (2) unilaterally decree loans and taxes, in the case of public disorder, or pledge public resources as collateral in order to meet the crisis, (3) decree and implement regulation governing the armed forces, and (4) assume responsibility for overseeing faithful adherence to the law and constitution by government officials (Art. 110). The last responsibility had previously pertained to the legislature. Still, no general authority to suspend part or all of the constitution or *garantías* appeared.

Following Guatemala's 1847 declaration of its status as a republic (rather than a state within the illusory federation), groups in Costa Rica favoring total independence and an end to even symbolic adherence to the federal union pressed for constitutional reform.

As indicated above, almost all of the 1847 document was modified or discarded rather than reformed. Despite the apparent illegality of such extensive changes on the pretext of "reform," the 1848 document survived until 1859, coinciding almost precisely with the political dominance of Juan Rafael Mora Porras.

The new constitution (1859) maintained a six-year presidential term and allowed for reelection at the will "of the people" (Art. 66). The president, with the agreement of the permanent commission, could suspend any law judged to cause "grave prejudice" to the republic (Art. 77). He could also raise troops, to repel invasions or repress any perturbation of public order, and command the armed forces directly and in person (though only by temporarily allowing the vice president or other official to assume executive authority). Most strikingly, the president could "take on his own account any measures deemed necessary to defend the country against aggression or internal commotion that threatens [the republic], while advising the congress of the use to which this authority has been put" (Art. 77, Sec. 21). This clause extended unlimited authority to the president to deal with "internal commotion" and was a clear constitutional foundation for presidential dictatorship.

Eleven years later a new constitution was adopted after the military intervention that prevented Mora Porras from serving a third term. Mora's heroic image with the population, due largely to his role in defeating the filibuster William Walker, made him a dangerous opponent. He returned to Costa Rica from exile, landing in Punta Arenas in September 1860. Defeated by government forces, Mora, like a number of prominent Central American caudillos during this era, fell to the executioner. Mora's death signaled a victory for Costa Ricans seeking to limit presidential dominance. The implementation of the new constitution, thus, was partly a reaction to Mora but also a renewed effort to constrain executive authority. The 1859 Constitution reduced the presidential term to three years, recreated the bicameral legislature of the 1844 Constitution, declared the subordination of the military to civilian authority, and added a long section of *garantías* (Arts. 7–20).

The 1859 Constitution also introduced a regime of exception that permitted the suspension of the constitution in its entirety by a three-fourths vote of the Congress "when the Republic was found in manifest and imminent danger" and suspension of the constitution was necessary to save it. The "suspension" would end when the danger disappeared (Art. 69, Sec. 7). It was also left to Congress, meeting in extraordinary session, to determine the number of forces needed to meet insurrections or invasions and to confer ranks in the military from lieutenant colonel and above.

Ten years later, in 1869, another military coup served as the transition to still another constituent assembly and adoption of a new constitution. This constitution changed little in regard to government structure or fundamental principles but went even further in seeking to constrain government authority. All acts of the legislative or executive branch that violated the constitution were declared a priori null and void (Art. 12). Another important innovation in the 1869 Constitution was the authority of the Supreme Court of Justice to suspend by a majority vote, at the request of any citizen or its own legal adviser, the implementation of legislative dispositions contrary to the constitution until Congress, in its next session, "definitively resolved the matter" (Art. 135). While still short of judicial review as it developed in the United States, this unprecedented judicial constraint on legislative authority was an important landmark in Central American constitutional institutions.

The general tendency toward institutionalizing constraints on government authority in Costa Rica did not entirely eliminate provisions for constitutional regimes of exception. A more limited but essentially similarly worded regime of exception clause appeared in the 1869 document. It authorized Congress to suspend the constitutional order with a three-fourths vote of the membership—but only for sixty days, unless a new declaration of "manifest and imminent danger" justified another sixty-day suspension—until a three-fourths vote could no longer be obtained to extend the suspension of the constitution. The president retained his authority to deploy troops to meet such conditions, without suspension of the constitution, but not to violate the *garantías* or to command the armed forces directly and personally.

It seemed that, as would occur later in Chile (see chapter 8), a struggle between a legislative political class, army officers, and president-politicians was being gradually won by the new *clase política* based in the coffee economy, finance, and commerce. But this new political class was divided by family and regional factions, occasioning ongoing political conflict. Elite dissension allowed a military arbiter to temporarily resolve the recurrent strife.

After almost half a century of independence, the inability of the factions within the political class to settle their differences paved the way for a military caudillo, and Costa Rica was governed for the first time by a genuine military ruler, Colonel Tomás Guardia.[36] Guardia was president from 1872 to 1876, commander in chief of the armed forces, and occasional acting president until his death in 1882. He played a critical transitional role in Costa Rican politics by seizing control of the government from a small group of prominent families and, at the same time, by inspiring a dread of dictatorship, arbitrary executive power, and military intervention in politics by the nation's political oligarchy. After Guardia, compromise was usually preferred to confrontation.

The constitution adopted by a constituent assembly under Guardia's administration would endure, with reforms and lapses (1917–1919), well into the twentieth century. In many respects the 1871 Constitution continued the trend of expanded *garantías* and the liberalization of Costa Rican politics. Habeas corpus was enshrined in the list of rights of citizens, along with the outlawing of the death penalty (except in cases of high treason, premeditated murder, and piracy) and prohibitions on trial of civilians by military courts or special tribunals. (In 1882 a further amendment made the death penalty unconstitutional.)[37]

In regard to the juridical foundations of the regimes of exception, however, the legislative authority to suspend the constitution found in the 1859 and 1869 documents was now extended to the permanent commission of the unicameral Congress in concert with the president (Art. 93, Sec. 3) and, when Congress was in recess, to the executive in concert with the permanent commission (Art. 102, Sec. 3). Even under Costa Rica's first genuinely military president, no constitutional clause assigned a constitutional mission to the armed forces. Only the clause declaring that "the military forces are subordinate to the civil authority, essentially passive, and never may deliberate" (Art. 22) sketched limits on, but not a constitutional mission for, the armed forces. This same language had appeared in each constitution since 1859 (Art. 18) and survived through the 1946 Constitution (Art. 22), making Costa Rica a rare case in which constitutionalization of a role for the military failed to occur in the nineteenth century despite recurrent military participation in coups and civil wars into the 1880s.

Costa Rica did not avoid militarism altogether; but even when political conflict resulted in the suspension of the constitution and regimes of exception, as occurred in 1891, 1892 (dissolution of Congress), 1900, and 1902, no constitutional rationale legitimated military coups. (As elsewhere, the Ordenanza Militar [1871], the Military Code of Justice [1898], and the Military Code [1900] assigned to the armed forces the mission of upholding the laws, the defense of the constitution, and the maintenance of internal order.) Beyond congressional authority to fix the size of the army" in times of peace, internal commotion, and external war" (1871, Art. 102), the armed forces did not achieve status as a fourth branch of government, as often occurred in other Spanish American constitutions.

Essentially the same language for regimes of exception found in the 1859 and 1869 Constitutions also survived in the 1946 and 1949 Constitutions. Marginal changes required a two-thirds rather than a three-fourths vote of Congress to suspend enumerated *garantías* rather than the entire constitution (Art. 82, Sec. 7). The same held true for the language imparting authority to the executive to suspend specified *garantías* when the Congress was not in session.

Thus by 1859, as modified in 1869 and 1871, the form and language of Costa Rica's basic constitutional regime of exception had been elaborated. Like its Central American neighbors, Costa Rica had developed a juridical foundation for constitutional dictatorship by the mid-nineteenth century that endured for more than a century. However, more stringent legislative controls over the executive, a clearer separation of legislative and executive authority, a requirement for three-fourths (or two-thirds) votes in the legislature to impose regimes of exception, and Costa Rican refusal to constitutionalize a political mission for the armed forces distinguished the country's political system from those of the rest of the region. These aspects of constitutional design, combined with social and economic developments that encouraged the democratization of Costa Rican politics, reduced the use of regimes of exception and softened Costa Rica's constitution of tyranny.

Into the 1990s, however, the foundations for its exercise remained part of the country's juridical baggage; a severe political and economic crisis of the sort that affected Chile from 1968 to 1973 or Brazil in the early 1960s could reactivate the operation of Costa Rican constitutional dictatorship. The limits on the military (*guardia*) and the strengthening of the country's party system and other civilian institutions make this unlikely, but not unthinkable, as long as the remaining elements of the constitution of tyranny are not dismantled.

5

Regimes of Exception in Venezuela, Colombia, and Ecuador

IN DRAMATIC CONTRAST TO CENTRAL AMERICA, INDEPENDENCE IN most of South America came after years of bitter warfare. Temporary victories and brutal setbacks involved troop movements over vast territories and destruction of much of the infrastructure from centuries of colonial rule. By the time the final strongholds of Spain surrendered in Peru and Bolivia (1824–1826), an exhausted, bloodied continent with only the most fragile of government institutions stood exposed to the whims of European economic and political initiatives and the vicissitudes of the international economy.[1]

As in Central America, dreams of union, experiments in federation and confederation, and the vision of "the Liberator," Simón Bolívar, of a great confederated Spanish American nation gave way to the nightmare of personal and ideological conflicts, civil war, regionalism, and political fragmentation. The leaders of the independence movements and their trusted lieutenants became "nationalists"; lesser caudillos justified their local and regional military bossism with the rhetoric of federalism or with calls for the defense of liberties purportedly violated by the government in national or provincial capitals. Albeit with significant regional and national variations, the first half century of political independence in Spanish South America brought incessant struggles for dominance among hundreds of caudillos and their personal armies.

These conflicts were evidenced in the spate of constitutions devised, reformed, cast off, and reinstated. Sharing the optimism of

North American and French revolutionaries that adopting so-called correct constitutional principles would ensure life, liberty, and the pursuit of happiness, South American elites spent much of the nineteenth century making and unmaking constitutions. As in Central America, constituent assemblies in Venezuela, Colombia, and Ecuador served to legitimate otherwise irregular presidential successions, to extend presidential terms, and to debate constitutional principles. Constitution making became a ritual that smoothed over departures from prescribed procedures for government alternation and anointed victors of internal wars.

Under permanent conditions of civil strife, severe racial and class cleavages within society, and the threat as well as the reality of foreign invasion, Spanish South Americans incorporated provisions for regimes of exception into even the earliest of constitutions. However, differences in national and regional circumstances generated distinctive constitutional and political developments in Venezuela, Colombia, and Ecuador after the dissolution of Bolívar's Gran Colombia.

VENEZUELA

On the pretext of creating a "conservatorship of the rights of Ferdinand VII," an elite cadre in Caracas established a "suprema junta conservadora" in April 1810. The initial act of independence in Venezuela consisted of rejecting the regency established in Spain and assuming local control in the name of the imprisoned king. Unlike other parts of Spanish America, however, the mask of Ferdinand only fleetingly disguised the motivations of Francisco de Miranda, Simón Bolívar, and other precursors of independence. By August, the Patriotic Society of Agriculture and Economy, ostensibly founded to stimulate agriculture and economic development, turned its meetings into political conspiracies aimed at independence.

Less than a year later, the supreme junta converted itself into a national Congress, derogated much Spanish legislation, and began drafting civil, criminal, and penal codes, new press laws, and a constitution. In July, the Congress declared that all Venezuelans had the rights of liberty, security, property, and equality—the essential rhetorical building blocks of liberalism in Spanish America for the rest of the nineteenth century. Four days later the Congress issued a declaration of independence and on December 21, 1811, adopted the first constitution in Spanish America.

The Constitutions of 1811 and 1819

The first Spanish American constitution, and the first of more than twenty in Venezuela during the next 150 years, preceded the Spanish Constitution of Cádiz. It borrowed ideological and organizational principles from the North American and French experiments. The Venezuelan charter created a federal regime that reserved to the "provinces" all powers not expressly delegated to the "general Authority of the Confederation."[2] The 1811 Constitution concentrated authority in the legislative branch, including the power to adopt "all laws and regulations necessary and proper" for carrying out the functions assigned by the constitution to "the Government of the United States" of Venezuela (Art. 72). A didactic description of the "rights of man in society" enumerated the limits on government authority and the civil liberties guaranteed to Venezuelan citizens. A section on "the duties of man in society" included the "golden rule" as Article 193 of the constitution.

Paraphrasing eighteenth-century liberal philosophy, the 1811 Constitution was more a declaration of principles than a formula for governance. It did, however, contain two articles that, while not fully developed regimes of exception, seemed to anticipate the internecine warfare to follow. Articles 133 and 134 guaranteed the provinces the republican form of government and provided for the use of the force necessary to protect them against domestic violence or invasion. This would justify the use of federal troops against local caudillos who failed to conform to national policies. Article 216 stated that any armed group congregated under any pretext other than government orders constituted "an attack against public security" and could be destroyed by force of arms. In the case of unauthorized unarmed groups, orders to disperse would be given first, but if resistance or strong opposition (*tenáz obstinación*) persisted, "then [they] may be destroyed by force of arms." This Venezuelan version of the British Riot Act (see chapter 1) disappeared with the 1811 Constitution; much more severe and comprehensive constitutional regimes of exception would follow.

The 1811 Constitution endured briefly and only in a small territory of Venezuela. Spanish reconquest in 1812 gave little opportunity to test the federal experiment. Bolívar and other key leaders of the movement against Spain, though self-declared liberals, were convinced that federalism, limited government, and legislative predominance all were inappropriate for Spanish American circumstances. After 1812, Bolívar frequently repeated his preference for centralist, executive-dominant regimes capable of meeting emergencies with energy and forcefulness. During and after the wars across northern and north central South America in the mid-1820s, a number of constitutional experiments imposed by Bolívar or his supporters captured the spirit of the Liberator's "Manifesto of Cartagena":

> I am of the opinion that unless we centralize our American governments, the enemy will obtain the most complete advantages; we shall be inevitably enmeshed in civil dissensions. . . .
> It is essential that Government correspond to the needs of the circumstances, of the times and men around it; if these be prosperous and serene, it ought to be mild and protective; but if [times] are calamitous and tumultuous, it must be ferocious [*terrible*] and arm itself in a fashion equal to the dangers [it faces], without concern with laws or constitutions while peace and felicity are not reestablished.[3]

Bolívar remained convinced of these sentiments until his death in 1830; as he roamed and warred from Venezuela to Colombia, Ecuador, Peru, and Bolivia, he carried this inspiration for authoritarian government.

More so than the idealistic charter of 1811, the second Venezuelan constitution, the so-called Constitution of Angostura (1819), represented a wartime proclamation with evident strategic motivation in addition to ideological and juridical underpinnings. Five years earlier, Bolívar had been invested by a "popular assembly" with "full powers" to prosecute the war and govern Venezuela. By the terms of this decree he exercised all legislative, executive, and military powers.[4] From 1815 to 1818, efforts to reinstate the 1811 charter and the federal regime by federalists and military caudillos opposed to Bolívar's dominance failed. Bolívar had established a center of operations in Guayana, with a provisional capital at Angostura (modern-day Ciudad Bolívar). A rump Congress meeting in this provisional capital proclaimed the Angostura Constitution on August 15, 1819.

Although maintaining most of the liberal didacticism of the 1811 document, the new constitution drastically altered the authority of the three branches of government.[5] First, the constitution established a unitary government: "The Republic of Venezuela is one and indivisible" (Title II, Art. 1). Congress would be convoked by the executive every January 15 and remain in session for two months. In "extraordinary" circumstances, this might be extended for twenty-five days. In the event of a "grave occurrence," the president could summon the Congress especially to deal with the urgent matter.

In contrast to the weak presidency of 1811, the 1819 Constitution granted the president broad authority in civil and military matters. He could serve two successive four-year terms and, most importantly, had almost unlimited powers in the case of "internal commotion that threatens the security of the state or in the event of sudden foreign invasion." In either of these circumstances, the constitution authorized the president "to suspend the *imperio* of the constitution in those places affected by the disturbance or insurrection" by decree. The same decree must convoke Congress to confirm or revoke the suspension of the constitutional regime (Sec. 3, Art. 20).

The 1819 Constitution fell short of Bolívar's preference for a lifetime president with virtually dictatorial powers, but it did permit the government comprehensive emergency powers. After 1819, no Venezuelan president would ever lack some sort of constitutional extraordinary powers to deal with internal commotion or insurrection, although the broad authority to suspend the *imperio* of the constitution disappeared in later charters.

Gran Colombia and the Cúcuta Constitution of 1821

Military successes and the incompetence of the Spanish liberals in prosecuting the war effort in South America allowed Bolívar to unify the colonial subdivisions of the former viceroyalty of New Granada. The Congress of Angostura proclaimed the existence of the República de Colombia in December 1819. Bolívar decreed a provisional government based upon the authority of the Congress of Angostura. On this flimsy foundation, the Congress became the "depository of the national sovereignty of Venezuelans and Granadines."[6] A law uniting the two territories was adopted in December 1819, with provisions for the future incorporation of Ecuador. Not until August 1821 did the Congress, now meeting in Cúcuta, approve a constitution for the new republic.

From 1821 to 1830, Bolívar served periodically as president, military leader, and symbol of the centralist regime adopted for the República de Colombia. To his dismay, local and regional caudillos, former compatriots of the independence struggles, liberals, federalists, and personal enemies opposed his vision of union, his obstinate insistence on centralized and personalist government, and his sometimes capricious exercise of power.[7] The 1821 Constitution for Gran Colombia incorporated the basic elements for executive domination of a centralized political system. It divided the country into departments and these into provinces, cantons, and parishes, the executive officers of which were appointed by, and responsible to, the president of the republic (Art. 8).

This centralist organization irked "Colombians" and "Venezuelans" who were divided into competing regional and personalist factions, the Venezuelans now forced to accept political control from Cúcuta or Santa Fé de Bogotá. Bolívar, alternating among president, military commander in continuing independence wars in Ecuador, Bolivia, and Peru, and dictator, never permanently unified these geographically, culturally, and economically disparate territories. Regional and national caudillos, such as General Francisco de Paula Santander in Colombia, Juan José Flores in Ecuador, and José Antonio Páez in Venezuela, resisted central authority—that is, Bolívar's dictatorship—and gradually came to symbolize a new nationalism that destroyed Bolívar's dream of union even before his death in 1830.

Despite the eventual failure of the Gran Colombia experiment, the 1821 Constitution captured the spirit of Bolívar's political vision for Spanish America, an amalgamation of Napoleonic executives within constitutional republics. This meant executives with life or long terms of office combined with centralized and comprehensive government authority, circumscribed, of course, by enumerated liberal *garantías*. These *garantías* could be suspended in times of crisis. When internal strife or other circumstances required, the executive, either on his own account or by legislative decree, could exercise extraordinary powers.[8]

A central feature of this Bolivarian model was broad and relatively unrestricted executive authority in constitutional regimes of exception. The 1821 Constitution provided two bases for constitutional dictatorship. Article 55 (Sec. 25) assigned Congress the authority "to grant to the Executive, during the present War of Independence, those extraordinary powers deemed indispensable in those places within the area of military operations, as well as in those places recently liberated from the enemy, but defining them as clearly as possible and delimiting the time of their validity to such as shall be absolutely necessary." Article 128 empowered the president "in times of internal commotion and armed conflict endangering the security of the Republic, and in cases of sudden invasion" to take (*dictar*) with prior consent of the Congress or, if

Congress were not in session, on his own authority, "whatever extraordinary measures, not within the normal sphere of his authority, that the case may require." In the latter case, the constitution required him to convoke Congress to confirm his extraordinary measures. In principle, this extraordinary power was limited in time and place to where it "may be indispensably necessary." Despite these provisions, Bolívar believed that the 1821 charter had given too much authority to the legislature; he favored still less restraint on executive discretion to deal with "internal commotion"—that is, with political adversaries.

These regimes of exception were less drastic than the complete "suspension of the *imperio* of the constitution" as allowed in the Angostura Constitution (1819). Given the permanent warfare, the temporary absences of Bolívar when acting as commander in chief of various armies, and the interim presidencies of the vice president from 1821 to 1830, Gran Colombia was governed continuously under regimes of exception. Constitutional dictatorship became the rule in Venezuela as well as in Colombia and Ecuador (see below). And the stylized language, *in the event of internal commotion or foreign invasion,* became the most common preface to provisions enumerating the times, places, and extent of extraordinary presidential powers in regimes of exception throughout northern and central South America.

In 1825, the Gran Colombian Congress established provincial assemblies (juntas) with limited autonomy for local and regional administration. The reforms acknowledged the limits of central government competence and regional demands for local control on certain economic and administrative issues. They also provided a legitimate operational base for forces favoring federalism or more regional autonomy. In this sense, the Gran Colombia experiment faced pressures comparable to those of the federation in Central America (1824–1838) but with more dramatic geographical barriers and socioeconomic differences separating the parts of the union. In the meantime, Bolívar had liberated Peru and Bolivia from Spanish control. In Bolivia (1826) the most radical version of the Bolivarian political model was adopted, including a president with life tenure (see chapter 6). Amid complex intrigues and personalist battles, Bolívar then attempted to create a confederation of Bolivia, Peru, and Gran Colombia.[9] This unrealistic yet visionary scheme provoked opposition practically everywhere on the continent; only Bolívar's closest followers failed to distance themselves from the Liberator's dream.

In 1827, the Gran Colombian Congress revoked Bolívar's extraordinary powers, accentuating the growing animosity between the president and a hostile legislature. Bolívar's personal enemies, federalists led by General and Vice President Francisco de Paula Santander, and Venezuelan autonomists all played a role in preventing the preservation of the union through constitutional reform. Santander's supporters proposed reforming the 1821 Constitution by deleting any mention of extraordinary powers for the executive.[10] This proposal was anathema to Bolívar, who called upon the assembly to reduce legislative authority and enhance executive power. It presaged a battle over the delegation of extraordinary powers and other regimes of exception in Venezuela, Colombia, and Ecuador for the next half century.

Exasperated with politics, Bolívar assumed emergency powers in an unconstitutional decree (*decreto orgánico*, August 27, 1828). He eliminated the vice presidency, named Santander as minister to the United States, reorganized internal administrative subdivisions, reserved to the president the right to appoint and dismiss public officials, and established a temporary dictatorship. When an assassination attempt followed on September 25, 1828, Bolívar outlawed secret societies (Masons and other groups of conspirators), eliminated freedom of the press, prohibited the teaching of the works of Jeremy Bentham, and suspended university instruction in jurisprudence, constitutional law, and universal law. He replaced these subjects with Roman civil law and canon law. Municipal government was also suspended. Bolívar even entered an alliance of convenience with clericals and included the archbishop in the council of state. More than a dozen anti-Bolívar leaders convicted of involvement in the assassination attempt were executed. Santander, who denied participation in the plot, received a death sentence. The sentence was subsequently commuted and Santander sent into exile.

Importantly, Bolívar also decreed an increase in the size of the standing army. He divided the country into four military regions, with commander-generals assigned political authority in each department and lower-ranking officers in provinces, cantons, and parishes. This militarization of territorial administration would be emulated in Central America, Peru, and Bolivia for long periods in the nineteenth century. For the moment, the Bolivarian vision of continental union had degenerated into a temporary military dictatorship.[11] Resistance to Bolívar resulted in insurrections headed by military officers supporting the restoration of the 1821 Constitution. Regional conflicts and demands for autonomy in Bolivia, Peru, Ecuador, and Venezuela made effective government impossible.

The constituent assembly promised by Bolívar for 1830 convened in Bogotá on January 20, 1830. A parallel constituent assembly convened by General Páez in Venezuela prevented the attendance of most Venezuelan delegates at the Bogotá sessions. The Venezuelan assembly adopted a new constitution that instituted a centro-federal scheme. This meant a unitary government with significant provincial autonomy. Páez became provisional president of the new nation.

Despite their differences with Bolívar and the desire for political autonomy, the Venezuelan constituents retained many features from the Constitution of Gran Colombia of 1821. This included provisions for extensive executive authority and regimes of exception. In contrast, the Colombian Constitution of 1830 (see below), and those for many years thereafter, deleted all reference to extraordinary powers and circumscribed or eliminated other regimes of exception. In both Venezuela and Colombia, however, provisions in later constitutions for congressional delegation of extraordinary powers to the executive and for other regimes of exception reflected the reaction to debates on the Bolivarian model and to Bolívar's brief dictatorship.

Simón Bolívar ostensibly retired to private life in March 1830. Even after his resignation, however, he continued to dream of reuniting Gran Colombia. His continuing intrigues could not prevent the eventual dissolution of the nation he founded and its fragmentation by the mid-1830s into three countries: Ecuador, Colombia, and Venezuela.

While Venezuela was never without provision for regimes of exception, from 1830 to 1864 its constitutions contained less draconian measures for such regimes than those in most of Spanish America. After 1864, however, executives routinely used expanded extraordinary powers against political opponents. These presidential powers were further enhanced in 1901 (Art. 89, Sec. 20) and 1904 (Art. 80, Sec. 8 [D]) to allow the president to suspend all constitutional *garantías* (except the right to life) "the exercise of which is incompatible with defense of the Republic." These foundations for constitutional dictatorship would survive the so-called redemocratization of the country from 1958 to 1990 and be used by elected civilian presidents to counter insurrection, riots, labor protests, and unruly political opponents. Venezuelan "democracy" never shed the protective umbrella of regimes of exception and press censorship into the 1990s.

The Constitution of 1830

The Venezuelan Constitution of 1830 was the country's first truly national constitution. It would endure for more than a quarter century and resulted largely from José Antonio Páez's charisma and his quest for autonomy from Gran Colombia. Páez's ability to manage internal politics from 1830 to 1848 with his *llanero* army, both as president (1831–1835 and 1839–1843) and as arbiter among political factions, contributed to a period of relative stability. His influence also permitted eliminating the military *fueros* and reducing the size and budget of the armed forces. Allying with landowners and foreign merchants, Páez allowed Venezuela to take advantage of the opportunity to develop coffee, cotton, and cattle exports, as also occurred in Costa Rica (see chapter 4).

Despite intermittent rebellions, caudillo uprisings, and widespread banditry, Páez's leadership made possible more than a decade of economic recovery and political consolidation. These gains would be challenged by the economic crisis of the late 1830s and early 1840s, when commodity prices declined and debt overwhelmed Venezuelan planters and merchants. Not until 1857, however, did liberals overturn the 1830 Constitution.

It is in some ways paradoxical that the 1830 Constitution and Páez's political influence from 1830 to 1848 is associated with conservatism in Venezuelan historiography. Although Páez allied with oligarchical families and foreign merchants to govern the country and was unwilling to confront the challenges of abolishing slavery and expanding the suffrage, the 1830 Constitution dutifully proclaimed the liberal guarantees of liberty, security, property, and equality. It also enumerated civil liberties and rights (Arts. 185–203), abolished torture, held officials responsible for the violation of citizens' rights (Arts. 201–04), and prohibited trial of civilians by military law (Art. 219). Neither at the national nor provincial levels could military and civil authority be exercised by the same government official, except the president (Art. 177).

Though unitary rather than federalist, the constitution was a compromise between the Bolivarian model and a federal regime such as that of the United States. It recognized the need for considerable local autonomy, creating indirectly elected provincial assemblies with important duties (Arts. 156–69). These included providing a list of candidates from which the president appointed the governor of each province. The constitution granted the president far-reaching authority but restricted his intervention in judicial proceedings and prohibited his personal command of the armed forces without congressional consent or his use of the armed forces to quell internal disturbances without prior sanction from the council of state. This council included among its members the vice president, a Supreme Court judge, and others named by the Congress. Article 118 provided for a constitutional regime of exception that was more circumscribed than similar clauses in the constitutions of Mexico, Central America, and most other South American countries during this period. Article 118 read:

> In the case of internal commotion and armed conflict that threatens the security of the Republic, or of sudden invasion, the President of the State will request that Congress, if it is in session, or if it is not in session the Council of State, . . . extend to him the following powers: (1) to call into service that part of the national militia judged necessary by Congress or the Council of State; (2) to require advance payment of taxes judged necessary or to negotiate loans for sums sufficient [to deal with the crisis], if ordinary revenues do not suffice; (3) to issue written orders for the appearance for interrogation or arrest of indicated persons, when informed that conspiracies against internal or international security exist, [but with the requirement] of placing such persons at the disposition of the judge of jurisdiction within three days; and (4) conceding amnesties or general and individual pardons.

Whereas the introductory language regarding "internal commotions or sudden invasion" mirrors the terms of the early Venezuelan and Bolivarian constitutions, the scope of the executive's extraordinary powers was limited in comparison with those discussed earlier. No other extraordinary executive powers were mentioned, no delegation of legislative authority was permitted, and no constitutional provision allowed for suspending civil liberties and rights (Arts. 185–209). Public officials were prohibited from issuing, obeying, or executing any order contrary to the constitution or the laws or any issued by illegitimate (*incompetente*) authorities.

However, in 1831 the government adopted the Law of Conspiracy. This law stipulated the death penalty in cases of treason and acts that threatened (*atentados*) public order. It remained effective until 1849, when reforms reduced the penalty for treason from death to perpetual banishment and, for conspiracy against the public order, from death to a maximum of ten years. The Law of Conspiracy was used frequently against political opponents from 1831 into the 1860s; banishment and exile became common for Venezuelan political leaders in the nineteenth century. At the same time, such legal repression did not require recourse to any regime of exception. However, legislative approval of presidential amnesty decrees was required. Leniency would be the exception necessitating congressional sanction. Congress frequently denied executive requests to pardon political enemies convicted of treason or conspiracy.

The 1830 Constitution also dealt with civilian control of the military. The militia rather than the standing army was to maintain internal order in the provinces, while the widely used constitutional prohibition on the armed forces from deliberation was included in the brief constitutional definition of the military role (Arts. 180–84). The abolition of the military *fueros* and legislation permitting freedom of worship (1834) brought bitter protests from military and church interests, even provoking an uprising in 1836, the so-called Revolution of the Reforms. Páez, called from his rural estate to support the constitution, defeated the rebels through negotiations, chicanery, and charismatic leadership. In practice, a professional national military developed later in Venezuela than anywhere in South America; caudillismo, self-promoted generals, bandits, and brigands dominated the country into the early twentieth century.

Public policies adopted by Páez and the presidents who governed with him behind the scene until the 1840s also seem more liberal than conservative, particularly regarding the economy. The government passed legislation that opened the economy to European capital, abolished colonial regulations limiting interest on borrowed money (Law of April 10, 1834), encouraged exports, and sought to incorporate Venezuela into the growing North Atlantic economy. All these policies conformed more closely to economic liberalism than to the neomercantilist, proclerical policies adopted by conservatives in Mexico, certain provinces of Argentina, and even in Colombia and Ecuador. Groups that elsewhere were closely identified with conservatism became the liberal opposition to Páez along with families and military caudillos identified with Bolívar.[12] For most elites, personalist, familial, and regional struggles for control of the state determined the composition of temporary alliances and ideological identity more than fundamental principles.[13]

Whatever label best characterizes this regime or its policies, the constitutional foundations of dictatorship in Venezuela were weaker in this period than those elsewhere in Spanish America. This did not prevent usurpation of authority, rebellions, rampant caudillismo, and political violence, but it did create the basis for a distinctive approach to constitutional rule in Venezuela in the early nineteenth century.

By the 1840s, opposition movements openly criticized policy and printed vicious satirical attacks on presidents and government officials in *El Venezolano* and other liberal propaganda sheets *(periodiquitos)*. In the 1846 elections, press polemics soared. The president resorted to the emergency powers of Article 118, asking the council of state for permission to call out the militia and increase the size of the army to suppress rebels.

At the president's request, Páez returned to head the national army and defeated the insurgents. His choice for president, José Tadeo Monagas, won the election in Congress. The liberal leader Antonio Leocadio Guzmán was tried under the conspiracy law as "conspirator, first class" for preaching social and political revolution. After a lengthy trial the presiding judge condemned Guzmán to death; he appealed to the Supreme Court, which upheld the sentence but asked the president to commute it. Monagas, already loosening his ties to Páez, reduced the sentence to "perpetual exile."

Several months later, Guzmán returned as minister of the interior in Monagas's cabinet and then served as vice president. Conservatives reacted immediately to Monagas's shifting loyalties and government appointments. They accused the president of increasing the size of the army and militia without the permission required by Article 118 and of deploying troops in violation of Article 121. On January 23, 1848, a liberal-inspired mob attacked the Congress to protest its challenge of the president. The Congress then created its own military guard. Another confrontation on January 24 left militia members, congressmen, and army officers dead and wounded. The next day, President Monagas requested emergency powers to conserve peace and public order.

In response, Páez rebelled "to defend congress and the constitution." Monagas's forces defeated the old caudillo. The coalition of oligarchs, centro-federalists, and military officers that had dominated Venezuela since 1827 had lost its hegemony. Like their counterparts in Chile from 1830 to 1860, they had attempted to institutionalize authoritarian but limited government, develop effective legislative institutions, limit the suffrage, and encourage integration of their export economy into the North Atlantic economic system. They hoped to consolidate oligarchic politics, establish order, and develop a system for government succession.

Venezuelan regionalism, caudillismo, and lack of cohesion among elites made this impossible. Economic fluctuations precipitated periodic political crises. But the fact that future events and political crises gradually moved the country toward a stronger executive and more comprehensive provisions for regimes of exception was not the legacy of Páez and the Constitution of 1830. It was the gift, rather, of the self-proclaimed liberal politicos who followed.

Civil War and the Constitutions of 1857, 1858

From the 1840s, divisions within the Páez coalition and the rise of the Liberal party, generated in part by economic crises and in part by increasing polarization over religious, economic, and political issues, submerged Venezuela in recurrent strife. In 1850, Congress sent the defeated Páez into exile. The Monagas family gained control of the executive branch of government and exercised power for a decade. Forced loans, confiscation of property, and repression of enemies became the rule. The 1830 Constitution remained in place but was ignored more than it was respected.

One Venezuelan author describing this period commented: "During the long rule of the Monagas [1848–1858] not a day passed in which someone was not persecuted as a rebel or conspirator. On the roads of the country it was not possible to travel except in convoys and with weapons in hand."[14] Corruption, personalism, and clientelism predominated in government circles as the resources of the state were used to reward followers of those in power. Much public land went to favored buyers. Conversely, legislation in the late 1840s permitted dismissal of public employees who participated in conspiracies or were not loyal to the government. Periodic purges of bureaucrats and university professors reinforced the personal and familial hold on the government by the Monagas and their supporters.

But a certain populism and spirit of democratization also prevailed. The first Monagas administration reformed the laws on credit and interest passed by the governments of the 1830s. It also expanded pension benefits for military families and retirees. In 1854 the government abolished slavery, with compensation for slaveholders, and a trend developed toward expanding the suffrage and enhancing political opportunities across social and racial lines.[15]

In 1856, the Congress illegally gave itself the right to reform the constitution through ordinary legislation rather than the process described in the 1830 Constitution. The 1830 charter prohibited the immediate reelection of the president. José Tadeo Monagas arranged for the Congress to change this prohibition as part of the reforms incorporated into the 1857 Constitution. This constitution confirmed the abolition of slavery, outlawed the death penalty for political crimes, and further democratized suffrage. It also allowed the Congress to appoint the next president—to no one's surprise, José Tadeo Monagas. In this sense, the 1857 transition in Venezuela was a clear example of the *succession constitutions* used by Spanish American caudillos to legalize *continuismo* and usurpation.

Although the 1857 Constitution remained in effect only briefly, it extended the presidential term and expanded considerably executive authority. The year before, Monagas had pushed through Congress the Law of Territorial Division, which allowed him to appoint directly the provincial governors. This reform upset the provincial caudillos accustomed to controlling their own fiefdoms under the 1830 Constitution. It also stirred up and divided liberal leaders who opposed efforts at centralizing political control in the national government, particularly in the presidency. Regarding constitutional regimes of exception, however, Article 54 of the 1857 charter only slightly changed the terms of Article 118 of the 1830 Constitution. Article 54 allowed Congress or, when not in session, the council of government to concede extraordinary powers to the president "in cases where there is *fear* of internal commotion, or external threat to public peace" (emphasis added).

Monagas rightfully feared internal commotion. Liberal dissidents and conservative leaders opposed another six years of his personalist rule. A military uprising led by the governor of the state of Carabobo spread to other regions. Rather than submerge the country in another civil war, and recognizing that he had lost too much support to survive in office, Monagas resigned in March 1858. He took refuge in the French legation. Efforts by opponents to remove him for trial brought protests from resident diplomats; ensuing diplomatic intervention led to a British and French naval blockade of Caracas's port, La Guaira.

The rebels named the governor of Carabobo, General Julián Castro, interim president but initially denied his requests for extraordinary powers. This (and other) legislative rejection of executive requests for extraordinary powers in Venezuela (as in Colombia) distinguished nineteenth-century politics in northern South America from congressional weakness in Mexico and most of Central America. However, the coup that brought Castro to power also undermined the evolving legitimacy of the political system, derived in part from formal adherence to provisions in the 1830 charter for periodic elections and the lack of patently illegal presidential succession since 1830.

The Castro government began an investigation into government irregularities since 1851, imprisoned and exiled Monagas's supporters and family members, and issued a list of persons temporarily banished from the country. For the first time since 1830, a rebellion had ousted a constitutional government; in the next decades this would occur frequently. Monagas's violation of the 1830 Constitution deprived him and his successors of the fragile basis of political legitimacy that had evolved in Venezuela.

The victorious insurgents briefly reinstituted the 1830 Constitution and then convened a constituent assembly both to legitimate the next government and to devise a new Constitution, which the assembly approved in 1858. For the first time, universal suffrage would be introduced and property requirements deleted for candidates to the lower chamber of the Congress. Divisions within the assembly between proponents of federalism and those who favored the maintenance of the centro-federal regime of 1830 did not prevent further political democratization.

The 1858 Constitution augmented considerably the responsibilities of a fourth or municipal branch of government added to the legislative, executive, and judicial powers in the 1857 Constitution. Moving even further toward regional and local autonomy than had the centro-federal regime of 1830, the 1858 Constitution provided for provincial legislatures elected by direct and secret vote. These legislatures had extensive control of the militia and of the appointment of national senators and judges and had broad authority to tax and even to modify internal administrative boundaries of the cantons and parishes. They were to exercise all powers not specifically delegated to the national government (Art. 128).

The 1858 Constitution also reinstated the prohibition on presidential reelection, discarded the council of government, and further limited the extraordinary powers of the executive. It restricted the period for which Congress could concede such powers to ninety days and required the actual existence of "internal commotion and armed insurrection that threatened the security of the Republic or sudden invasion" for such powers to be conferred upon the president. This amounted to a return to the 1830 Constitution, except that it eliminated the president's authority to order the arrest and interrogation of suspects and specified one additional extraordinary power: it established the requirement of a "passport" for internal and foreign travel (Arts. 95–98). This new restriction in times of emergency paralleled the added constitutional right to travel within the country and leave the country without a passport (Art. 17).

Inasmuch as the council of government had been eliminated, when Congress was not in session the president could convoke an "extraordinary council" composed of the Supreme Court justices, the vice president, and a minister who requested the concession of extraordinary powers. This council could confer extraordinary powers on the president by a two-thirds vote.

Although action by an extraordinary council was more cumbersome than that of the council of government of the past, the general thrust of the constitution regarding regimes of exception was to circumscribe government power, with the exception of the additional authority to regulate travel during periods of conflict or warfare. In particular, the stipulation that extraordinary powers could not be granted for more than ninety days was an important departure from the months or years of government by exception since 1819. Even so, certain legislators in the assembly voiced their concern about the propensity of Venezuela and the rest of Spanish America to be governed routinely by extraordinary powers. Dr. Miguel Palacio remarked:

> And the Extraordinary Powers? This is the shipwreck, the obstacle against which all the constitutions run aground. They have run aground and shall run aground. It seems that the Constitutions have been made for fair weather. When the emergencies occur and when the cataclysm arrives, then come difficult straits. The Romans called it dictatorship; we [call it] extraordinary powers [*facultades extraordinarias*].[16]

Unfortunately for Venezuela, even with its concessions to local autonomy and further restrictions on executive authority, the 1858 Constitution did not satisfy militant federalists, provincial caudillos, and ambitious liberal politicians.

Before the provisional government could call for elections and implement the new constitution, prominent liberal politicians and military officers plotted a new rebellion. In exile and then in Venezuela, the founder of the Liberal party (1840), Antonio Leocadio Guzmán, and his allies proclaimed their intentions to carry out a federalist revolution. Only one year after implementation of the constitution in December 1858, vicious civil war between federalists and centralists enveloped Venezuela and neighboring Colombia. For almost the next five years the country drowned in the blood of the federal wars, actually more a power struggle among political factions and personalities than a commitment to any consistent ideology. Unlike the contemporaneous Civil War in the United States, the federal war in Venezuela occurred after the abolition of slavery and, after more than 300,000 casualties, resolved little except which caudillos would control Caracas and dispense patronage in the provinces. Rather than confirming national unity, as in the United States, the federal war in Venezuela gave way to another half century of civil war and caudillistic control of semiautonomous states.

Federalist commanders issued decree laws to govern areas under their control; General Páez, called by government supporters from exile in New York, became an interim dictator (1861–1863) in Caracas. In a letter to the provisional president, Manual Felipe de Tovar, Páez had written: "A benevolent dictator is the only way to save the society."[17] He now declared his authority to be unlimited, thereby illegally suspending the 1858 Constitution for the duration of the war. He rescinded the liberal press laws and authorized provincial governors and their subordinates to arrest, imprison, and fine authors or presses that published antigovernment material. To finance the war, the Páez administration obtained foreign loans on disadvantageous terms, using as collateral the customs revenue and the nation's natural resources.

Gradually the war turned against the constitutionalists in favor of the federalists. During the struggle, Leocadio Guzmán's son, Antonio Guzmán Blanco, emerged as a prominent military and political leader of the federalist-liberal forces, along with the commander in chief, General Juan Falcón. Falcón and Páez negotiated an end to the war: amnesties and guarantees against retribution for all acts committed since 1830, a constituent assembly to meet to draft a new constitution, Falcón to serve as provisional president, and Guzmán Blanco as vice president. After years of vicious fighting and more than 300,000 deaths, Páez went back to exile in

Philadelphia. He died at the age of eighty-three in New York, after receiving honors and living in Argentina for a number of years.

The Federal Constitution of 1864 and Constitutional Reforms to 1904

The federalist victory produced a new constitution, which borrowed heavily from the federal charter adopted in Colombia in 1863 (see below). Venezuela became a federal regime. This nominal designation never made federalism a political reality, though it did accentuate the regional caudillismo, periodic uprisings, and personalist-familial struggles for power endemic to the country. First, victorious General Falcón assumed the presidency (1864–1868). Then, a revolt returned José Tadeo Monagas to power at the head of an ad hoc coalition of liberals and conservatives. The Monagas government retained the 1864 Constitution but attempted to reassert control by the federal government over the states and regional caudillos.

Monagas's return to power precipitated new plotting and military revolt by forces headed by Liberal party patriarch Leocadio Guzmán and his son, General Antonio Guzmán Blanco. After 1870 Guzmán Blanco dominated Venezuelan politics, governing as a dictator from 1870 to 1872, then occupying the presidency several times and more or less controlling handpicked successors in alternating terms. Guzmán Blanco initiated anticlerical, educational, and economic reforms typical of liberal governments throughout Spanish America in the last quarter of the nineteenth century. Foreign investment and the modernization of agriculture, transportation, and communication provided expanded economic opportunity, increased government revenues, and contributed to relative stability in comparison with the pre-1870 period. The lack of a truly national army and the persistence of regional caudillismo justified by federalism prevented consolidation of a national political system until the first decades of the twentieth century.

During the remainder of the nineteenth century, the 1864 Constitution was modified in several new constitutions adopted in 1874, 1881, 1891, and 1893. These changes reduced the number of states (then restored them, then reduced their number again), altered the relationship between state and federal authorities, modified the term of office of the executive and legislative officials, changed procedures for constitutional reform (1891), and even (in the 1881 Constitution) introduced a federal council on the model of the 1874

Swiss Constitution. This council appointed the president from its members but also exercised some of the functions previously assigned to the council of government in the Venezuelan charters of 1819, 1830, and 1857.[18]

In every case, the main incentive for calling constituent assemblies was to regularize presidential succession for interim presidents or dictators, increase or decrease the length of the presidential term, or allow the incumbent to remain in office despite prohibitions on reelection. In Venezuela, as clearly as anywhere in Spanish America, constitutional reform after 1864 became the key to resolving crises of presidential succession.

Whatever constitutional revisions occurred after 1864, however, the basic regime of exception clause of the Venezuelan Constitution remained unchanged until 1901. Then, the extraordinary powers of the executive in times of war, internal commotion, armed insurrection, or armed conflict among two or more states were expanded to include the suspension of those civil liberties or rights "whose exercise might be incompatible with defense of the republic or restoration of the constitutional order" (Constitution of 1901, Art. 89, Secs. 20, 21, 22). Until this modification, the language of the 1864 document prevailed:

> In the case of foreign war the Executive may: (1) request from the states the necessary assistance for national defense; (2) collect taxes in advance; (3) arrest or expel from the country citizens of the enemy country opposed to national defense; ... (7) suspend those rights whose exercise is incompatible with defense of the Republic, except that of life, with a prior declaration of those rights suspended and the delimitation of the locale or localities in which [suspension] is necessary. . . .
>
> In the case of armed insurrection against the political institutions of the nation, deploy the armed forces and exercise the powers enumerated in [Sections] 1, 2, and 5 in the preceding clause, with the object of restoring the constitutional order. (Arts. 15, 16)

No time limits were placed on the exercise of these powers nor was congressional approval necessary, though the constitution required the president to notify the Congress within the first eight days of its next session.

Acting as commander in chief of the armed forces and authorized to personally direct their operations, the president could unilaterally determine the existence of a rebellion or war or armed conflict among the states (almost any uprising involving caudillos from neighboring states) and then deploy the military to defend the republic or restore the constitutional order. Nevertheless, these powers were still more limited than those given the executive in the earliest Venezuelan constitutions. They did not allow the president to arrest dissidents or impose death penalties for political crimes nor to suspend the constitution or civil liberties and rights. The constitution did not authorize Congress to confer extraordinary powers on the president, but not until the Constitution of 1893 (Art. 122) were Congress and the state legislatures prohibited from conferring such powers on the executive.

In contrast, executive authority in times of external war included the suspension of most constitutional *garantías*. In the case of internal uprisings, with the approval of the council of government the president could use the armed forces to restore constitutional order (Arts. 77, 78). In this sense, though constitutional regimes of exception in Venezuela in the late nineteenth century were less comprehensive than they had been after independence or than they would be in the early twentieth century, the executive retained broad authority to unilaterally identify and then suppress so-called threats to the constitutional order.

The 1864 Constitution and its successors until the turn of the century also proclaimed that the armed forces were obedient and passive and prohibited them from "deliberation" while forbidding the exercise of military and civilian authority by the same officials (Arts. 97, 116). The constitution further proclaimed all government acts null and void when usurpation of authority had occurred and provided the same for any action taken due to direct or indirect military pressure or taken under pressure of subversive public demonstrations (Art. 104). These provisions, in the precise language of the 1864 document, were retained until 1901.

None of these safeguards spared Venezuela from the caudillismo of the nineteenth century or from the dictatorships that would follow from 1908 to 1935 and from 1948 to 1958. In 1904, the new constitution used by General Cipriano Castro (1899–1908) to legitimate his *continuismo* deleted the prohibition on the delegation of extraordinary powers to the president and provided for sweeping executive powers to meet the exigencies of external war, "internal commotion," and armed rebellion. It also introduced a formal nomenclature for declaring a regime of exception: "subversion of the public order" (*trastorno del orden público*). When there existed *trastorno del orden público,* the president could, among other actions, unilaterally arrest, confine, or deport "persons whose [presence] is contrary to reestablishment of peace; suspend all rights, except the right to life, whose exercise is incompatible with reestablishing order; and order trials for treason of Venezuelans who were, in whatever way [*de alguna manera sean hóstiles*], inimical to national defense" (Art. 80, Sec. 8).

Article 17 of the 1904 Constitution listed almost two pages of civil rights and liberties guaranteed to Venezuelans, subject to suspension "in the cases and under the terms detailed in Article 80 (8, 9)." This section of Article 80 read:

> The Attributes of the Federal Executive are:
> (8) To make use of the following powers, previous declaration of *trastornado el orden público,* in the cases of external war, internal commotion or rebellion, until peace is restored:
>> (A) ask the states their assistance for defense of national institutions and defense;
>> (B) accelerate tax collections;
>> (C) arrest, confine, or expel from the national territory individuals . . . contrary to reestablishment of peace;
>> (D) suspend the rights whose exercise are incompatible with defense of the country or reestablishment of order, with the exception of the right to life;
>> (E) designate to where the national government may be temporarily moved, if there is serious reason to do so;
>> (F) order the trial for treason to the Fatherland of Venezuelans who are inimical to national defense. . .
> (9) Deploy the armed forces . . . in the case of armed rebellion in any of the states of the union, after exhausting efforts at conciliation, in order to reestablish peace and order.

Expanding on the regime of exception provisions contained in the constitutions after 1864, Cipriano Castro's 1904 Constitution marked the end of the era of the regional caudillos. Castro created a military academy, began a program of military professionalization, and adopted the basis for constitutional dictatorship that would be used by his successor, Juan Vicente Gómez, to govern the country from 1908 to 1935. Gómez subverted the army to overthrow the absent President Castro and gradually instituted a personalist despotism. He suspended the *garantías* in 1913 to meet the threat of ex-president Castro's expedition to regain power. Thereafter he used extraordinary powers and periodic reforms of the constitution from 1914 to 1931 to retain the fiction of constitutional legitimacy for his tyranny. Even as capricious a dictator as Gómez wished to govern, whether as president or commander of the armed forces, under the apparent cover of law. In the 1950s, Venezuela's most recent dictator, Marcos Pérez Jiménez (1948–1958), also relied on constitutional reforms and concession by the constituent assembly of extraordinary powers to disguise his usurpation of power.

Almost identical language for constitutional dictatorship was retained in the constitutions of 1909 (Art. 82); 1914 (Arts. 19, 79); 1922 (Art. 19; Art. 79, Sec. 23); 1925 (Art. 36; Art. 100, Secs. 24–26); 1928 (Art. 36; Art. 100, Secs. 23–28), with the addition of outlawing communist propaganda; 1929 (Art. 36; Art. 100, Secs. 23–27); 1931 (Art. 36; Art. 100, Secs. 25–29); 1936 (Art. 36; Art. 100, Secs. 22–27); and 1947 (Art. 76; Art. 198, Sec. 18).

In 1958 Venezuela "returned" to democracy and in 1961 a new constitution marked this transition from authoritarian government. Article 190 (Sec. 6) gave the president authority "to declare a state of emergency and decree restriction or suspension of the *garantías* in the cases indicated in this Constitution." Title IX of the constitution, "On Emergency," stipulated that the president could exercise the authority of Article 190 "in case of emergency, commotion that perturbs the peace of the Republic, or grave circumstances that affect economic or social life." The president could also adopt "the indispensable measures [short of a declaration of emergency] to prevent subversion of the public order, if sound evidence existed that such subversion [*trastorno*] might occur" (Art. 244). While approval by the council of ministers and review by the Congress was required, the 1961 Constitution had provided even more bases for implementing regimes of exception than had its nineteenth-century predecessors. Perhaps more ominously, the 1961 Constitution recognized a much broader constitutional mission for the armed forces than had been customary in Venezuela in the nineteenth century. It provided that they were "organized by the state to assure the national defense, the stability of democratic institutions, and respect for the Constitution and the laws, compliance with which will always take precedence over all other obligations" (Art. 132). Two attempted coups in 1992 reminded Venezuelans that despite three decades of civilian rule, their constitution made the armed forces the ultimate authority in the case of threats to stability and to the existing political order.

Just as consolidation of national government took longer in Venezuela than in Mexico and parts of Central America, so it also took longer to solidify the constitutional foundations of dictatorship. But just as the language defining regimes of exception in the Mexican Constitution of 1857 found its way into the revolutionary charter of 1917, the language of constitutional dictatorship that was settled on in Venezuela in 1864 and modified in 1904 survived until the 1990s. One hundred and sixty years after Bolívar's death, Venezuelan governments had emergency powers and military resources that the Liberator would have envied (though he may still have objected to legislative constraints on presidential authority).

COLOMBIA

Colombian political history and constitutional development in the nineteenth century shared, superficially, many features of the rest of Spanish America: caudillismo, regionalism, political violence, civil wars, and struggles between federalists and centralists, clericals and anticlericals, and liberals and conservatives. Like neighboring Venezuela and Ecuador, modern-day Colombia formed part of Gran Colombia, splintered off after the death of Simón Bolívar, and faced years of uncertainty regarding the definitive boundaries of its national territory. In particular, doubt existed concerning the adhesion of the southwestern provinces to Ecuador and the pretensions of Panamanian autonomy. As in Venezuela, civil war in Colombia in the early 1860s resulted in a new constitution (1863) that eviscerated the role of the national government, signaling increased relative autonomy for the states.

In other respects, however, Colombia experienced political and constitutional developments unique in the region, some of them persisting to the present. First, as the capital of Gran Colombia, it suffered most intensely from the struggle between Bolívar and his supporters, who favored highly centralized, executive-dominated governments, and General Francisco de Paula Santander and the advocates (if only for tactical reasons) of provincial autonomy. This personal and ideological battle in the 1820s clearly defined several enduring themes in Colombian political life: executive versus legislative dominance; the relative power of central and provincial governments; the role of the national military versus provincial militias; and the extent of emergency powers or other extraordinary powers that would be allowed in Colombian constitutions.

By 1827 Santander was convinced that Bolívar had become, rather than the Liberator, "the Great Perturber of the Republic," and argued that it was necessary "to bind the colossal power which Bolívar exercises, to secure the rights . . . of citizens, and to divide executive authority in order to contain it. . . . I am for federalism as the only recourse left to us to save the national liberties."[19]

Second, the battles between economic liberals and neomercantilists took on explicit organizational and ideological form early in Colombian political evolution. Colombia is perhaps the only Spanish American nation where opposition by organized artisans to free trade policies played an important role in presidential politics prior to the 1850s.

Third, and similarly uniquely, the intense and bitter conflicts between antichurch liberals and conservative defenders of the role of the church led to the consolidation of identifiable liberal and conservative political organizations that became the basis for Colombia's two-party political system by the 1860s. Overlapping and crosscutting cleavages continued to exist, but the bellicosity of liberal attacks on the role of the church, the insistence on relatively short presidential terms (two to four years), and the effort to eliminate or drastically curtail presidential emergency powers and to impede central government intrusion into provincial politics gave Colombian liberalism a more clearly defined program than in Venezuela, Ecuador, or Central America. Indeed, the 1853 and 1863 Colombian constitutions were the only two charters in Spanish America without provision for regimes of exception in the entire nineteenth century.

A well-defined, even ferocious, conservative reaction to these liberal tendencies also developed. This reaction included identification with Bolívar rather than Santander, support for strong central government, and support for the traditional rights and privileges of the church. Conservatives were also slightly more likely to favor protectionism and local industry against the threats of foreign competition.[20] In contrast to Mexico, most of Central America, Venezuela, and most of South America, Colombian conservatism as a movement and as a political party reemerged triumphant in the 1880s at the height of liberal ascendance elsewhere. The Constitution of 1886, which survived until 1936, reaffirmed the centralist, authoritarian, executive-dominated regime that the liberals had seemingly destroyed after the 1840s. In the conservative charter was the restoration of the sort of provision for regimes of exception encouraged by Bolívar in 1821 and 1826. These provisions would serve as the foundations of constitutional dictatorship in Colombia until the beginning of the 1990s.

However, the legacy of the liberal victories from the 1840s and, in particular, the almost confederal Constitution of 1863 juxta-

posed the political reality of provincial autonomy, regional caudillismo, and violence as the arbiter of political differences to the
pretensions of centralized rule from Bogotá. In many respects,
modern-day Colombia, as it was from the 1850s into the 1880s, is a
conglomeration of regional fiefdoms plagued by private armies, political militia, bandits, and guerrilla bands over which the national
government and military is unable to attain control, despite the almost permanent state of siege under which the country has been
governed during much of the twentieth century.

Early Constitutional Development

The succession of previously recounted events in Spain and northern South America after 1808 brought the proclamation in 1811 of
Colombia's first constitution. This was an idealistic, provisional federalist charter called the Constitution of Cundinamarca. The constituent Congress that adopted this charter seemingly recognized its
idealistic pretensions, declaring (Art. 6) that the provinces "bind
themselves by a pact as permanent as the wretched human state
permits" and that a more well-thought-out constitution would follow on "a better occasion and a more tranquil time" (preamble).[21]

The 1811 Constitution vested government authority in a Congress composed of deputies representing the provinces but with all
powers not assigned to the Congress reserved to the states. A list of
the inalienable rights of the provinces delimited the authority of the
federal government (Art. 7). Congress had responsibility for foreign
relations, for relations with the Apostolic See, and for the *patronato*
(the appointment of church officials and the administration of
church affairs and revenues), responsibilities formerly exercised by
the king (Arts. 40, 41). No article of the constitution could be revoked without the approval of the provinces. Not until 1814 did an
amendment provide for an executive triumvirate elected by Congress; in 1815 this was modified to provide for a single "President of
the United Provinces of New Granada." In the meantime, resistance
in some provinces prevented unanimous ratification of the 1811
document until Bolívar prevailed militarily in Cundinamarca in
1814. By 1815 the Spanish reconquest headed by General Pablo
Morillo imposed itself in New Granada as well as Venezuela. The
federation dissolved.

In 1819, after a series of military victories in Venezuela and
Colombia, Bolívar's decree of September 11 established a provisional government in which the Congress of Angostura became the
depository of the national sovereignty.[22] The highly centralized,

executive-dominated regime imagined in the 1821 Constitution, including broad authority for the president with the possibility of the concession of extraordinary powers, departed radically from the legislative dominance and federalism of 1811. (The details of these provisions have been discussed above.) Thus commenced the fundamental constitutional tensions in Colombian politics, tensions that would not be resolved even late into the twentieth century.

By 1827–1828 the dissolution of Gran Colombia and its dismemberment into three or four nations seemed likely. Bolívar resisted, but the 1830 Constitution could not convince Páez in Venezuela or separatists in New Granada and Ecuador to forgo independence. This meant that the 1830 Constitution, which incorporated all of the former viceroyalty of New Granada, was stillborn.

Of historical interest is Title VII, a separate section of the constitution (Arts. 104–08) which defined the role of the armed forces to include the "maintenance of public order and to secure the observance of the laws." This provision was only maintained in the Constitutions of 1832 and 1843; thereafter, the constitutions of Colombia omitted separate constitutional titles regarding the armed forces until 1886. Even in 1886 the constitution assigned no specific role to the armed forces regarding the maintenance of internal order or law enforcement, though they were required "to bear arms when public necessity requires that they should do so in defense of the national independence and institutions of the country" (Art. 165).

Both liberals and conservatives seemingly preferred civilian control, though they fought bitterly over the extent of federalist versus centralist dominance, over limitations on the executive authority, and over religious issues. In the twentieth century, the codifications of the constitution in 1936 and 1945 retained the exact language of the 1886 charter regarding the military. The limited constitutional mandate of the Colombian armed forces and the late professionalization and modernization of the national army contrast markedly with most of the Central and South American cases.[23]

In addition to the limitations on military political participation, the legacy of the Santander-Bolívar conflict and the underlying ideological, religious, and political cleavages made the organization and scope of national government the permanent object of contention. The first constitution adopted for Colombia as a separate nation in 1832 was a compromise between hard-line centralism and federalism. It restored the centralist regime, with important concessions to the provinces in the form of provincial legislatures with extensive electoral and policy-making authority. It also reduced the term of office for most national officials but invested the president with limited emergency powers:

- *Article 108:* "In the case of grave danger arising from internal disorder or foreign attack which menaces the security of the Republic, the Executive shall meet with Congress, or, if it is not in session, with the Council of State, to consider the urgency of the situation as reported by the Executive and to grant him in whole or in part the following powers with such limitations as are deemed necessary: (1) To call into active service such part of the National Guard as may be necessary; (2) To collect in advance at a fair discount as much of the national taxes and revenues as may be deemed necessary, or to raise a sufficient sum by a loan if the ordinary revenues are inadequate to cover expenses, designating at the same time the funds from which and the time within which repayment shall be made; (3) Upon receipt of information that plots are being made against the peace and security of the Republic, to issue orders for the appearance or arrest of suspected persons in order to interrogate them or have them interrogated and to turn them over within seventy-two hours to the competent judge . . . ; (4) To grant amnesties and individual or general pardons."
- *Article 109:* "The Powers that may be granted to the Executive according to the foregoing article shall be limited solely to the time and objects indispensably necessary for the reestablishment of the peace and security of the Republic, and the Executive shall render to Congress at its next session an account of the manner in which they were exercised."
- *Article 110:* "The President of the Republic shall be responsible for all infractions of the Constitution and laws and for the abuse of powers entrusted to him by Article 108 of this Constitution, as well as any other misconduct in the exercise of his functions."

This limited regime of exception, providing as it did for extraordinary powers for the president but not for any suspension of constitutional *garantías*, nor for martial law or for immunity from liability for abuse or excesses, reflected a general concern in Colombia over the legacy of Bolívar. However, the compromise on the federalist-centralist debate left no one satisfied and the provinces became the domains of petty sovereigns. In response, the national

Congress in 1833 passed a law against conspiracy, similar to the 1831 Venezuelan legislation, imposing capital punishment for political crimes.

Amid intrigue and dissension, General Santander finished his term and was succeeded by José Ignacio de Márquez, who had served as vice president and interim president in the early 1830s. On the pretext of anger at the government's closure of nearly abandoned convents in the southern province of Pasto, some Bolivarians and avid clericals joined a revolt headed by General José María Obando. Obando called himself "Supreme Director of the War in Pasto, General-in-Chief of the Army, and Protector of the Religion of the Crucified." Although many church officials agreed with the government action, carried out by virtue of previous legislation regarding the minimum membership of religious convents, supporters of increased provincial autonomy and opportunistic caudillos joined the revolt.

Bloody civil war followed. It ended with a government victory. The most important general on the victorious side, Pedro Alcántara Herrán, was inaugurated president in May 1841. Intent on eliminating the constitutional foundations of provincial autonomy and the political base this represented for provincial governors, the government imposed a new constitution. The 1843 Constitution allowed the president to appoint and remove provincial governors (Art. 131) and generally subordinated provincial government and administration to the central government. Article 62 of the 1843 document even stipulated that "Senators and Representatives represent the Nation and not the Provinces in which they are chosen."

To deal with the threat of provincial caudillos, Article 101 assigned the president authority "to preserve the internal order and peace of the Republic, repel all foreign attacks or aggression, and repress any disturbances of the internal public order." The president could unilaterally "dispose of the land and sea forces for the defense and security of the Republic, for the maintenance or reestablishment of order and peace therein, and for other objects required by the public service."

However, the president was not authorized, while in office, to command the armed forces personally (Art. 101, Secs. 1, 4), and the regime of exception clause (Art. 108) of the 1832 Constitution was eliminated. The constitution prohibited the Congress from delegating any of its constitutional powers including, thereby, the power to levy taxes, authorize loans, or to take other measures to encumber the national credit—all matters authorized for the executive under the previous regime of exception provisions.

In the manner of most liberal constitutions of the era, an enumeration of rights and liberties, judicial protections, and official responsibility for violations of law were also included in the 1843 Constitution (Arts. 157–65). Reaction to the civil war of 1839–1840 pushed the country toward a more centralist, executive-dominated regime but did not create anything like the provisions for suspension of constitutional guarantees or unlimited regimes of exception adopted in parts of Central America, in Mexico, or in Ecuador, Peru, and Bolivia.

Despite internal wars, until the mid-1850s Colombia's presidents came to power via elections and completed their terms of office. Congress began to establish itself as a viable counterweight to the presidency; presidents were typically unable to impose their chosen successors even within the same party, and *continuismo*, the bane of much of Spanish America, did not take root in Colombia. A loose alliance of moderate liberals, former Bolívar supporters, and clericals sought to impose order and virtue, but not dictatorship, upon Colombian society. Nevertheless, attacks on liberal texts (such as Bentham's), the Jesuits' return to the country, the restoration of religious *fueros* and religious control of education, and the invocation to "God the Father, Son, and Holy Ghost" in the preamble to the 1843 Constitution all portended intensified political conflict.

President Pedro Alcántara Herrán was succeeded by his father-in-law, Tomás Cipriano de Mosquera (1845–1849), whose brother was archbishop of Bogotá. Mosquera had served under Bolívar when he was fifteen years old, risen to brigadier general by thirty, and came from a staunchly conservative family. As president, however, he proved flexible, pragmatic, and opportunistic. Making allies of selected liberal politicians and business interests, Mosquera reduced the government subsidy to the church.[24] Adopting some of the attitudes and economic policies of mid-nineteenth-century liberalism, Mosquera promoted exports, encouraged foreign investment in public works and transportation, promoted coffee production, carried out fiscal and monetary reforms, and renegotiated the foreign debt. In retrospect, the Mosquera administration could be viewed as a transition to Liberal party rule, but during its tenure, despite his eclectic policies, Colombian politics seemed on a moderately progressive yet still conservative course.

Colombian liberal intellectuals drew inspirations from French socialists during the 1840s, and the fall of Louis Phillipe in 1848 coincided with the presidential campaign at the end of Mosquera's term. The foundation of an artisan association in Bogotá, partly in response to the government's 1847 reduction of tariffs, allied a working-class organization favoring protectionism with liberal opponents to Mosquera's programs. In the elections that followed, the two groups that would form the modern parties of Colombian politics emerged: Conservatives and Liberals, but with the government (Conservative) forces split, thereby allowing a Liberal victory. This meant a peaceful transition via elections in 1849. The Liberal candidate, General José Hilario López, took office in April after being selected in the fourth ballot in Congress. Ominously, the Congress had been surrounded by protesting artisans and urban workers insisting on López's selection. The artisans, later known as the Sociedad Democrática, became the first significant urban, working-class pressure group in Colombian national politics and the first labor auxiliary of the Liberal party. While López was selected by Congress rather than on the battlefield, intimidation had clearly played a role. The president of the chamber wrote on his ballot: "I vote for General José Hilario López so that the deputies may not be assassinated."[25]

General López, now president (1849–1853), unleashed a torrent of liberal reforms that traumatized conservative Colombians and split his own party. Abolition of slavery headed the list, followed by numerous anticlerical measures, such as again expelling the Jesuits, allowing municipal councils to select parish priests, abolishing the *fueros* and tithes, establishing religious toleration, and proposing the formal separation of church and state. The government also promoted subdividing Indian communal lands and expanding freedom of the press. The failure to provide tariff protection for industry and artisans alienated an important support group of the administration, while the Conservatives attempted revolt in 1851 but were suppressed. Significantly, the rebels in Pasto and elsewhere questioned the legitimacy of López's election due to the pressure exerted outside the Congress by the artisan society and the workers. Meanwhile, the government sent Archbishop Mosquera and others into exile; the fundamental cleavage between anticlerical liberals and church supporters intensified.

Expecting defeat in the 1853 presidential elections, the Conservatives offered no candidate. Competition between the two main Liberal factions, labeled *gólgotas* (secular reformists who controlled Congress) and *draconianos* (more moderate Liberals, opposed to the abolition of capital punishment) gave victory to the *draconiano* candidate, General José María Obando. Obando, who cherished the sword of Santander as the symbol of Colombian nationality and liberalism, took office in April 1853, a little less than a month before the implementation of the 1853 Constitution. Bitter debates ensued over universal suffrage, separation of church and state, popular election of provincial governors (instead of presidential appointment as in the 1843 document), and drastic reduction in the size of the armed forces. Street violence in Bogotá between artisans and free-trade liberals exacerbated political tensions. The *gólgotas* managed to anger both the army, with their proposals to cut military forces, and the working class and manufacturers, with proposals for further tariff reductions. These were two key groups in the Obando coalition.

Despite the conflict, the 1853 Constitution entered into force in May. It expressed the liberal victory by enhancing the relative power of the legislature and by incorporating the major reforms of the early 1850s. This included abolition of slavery, separation of church and state, elimination of property and literacy qualifications for voters (though the provinces could and did undermine this democratic provision), introduction of direct and secret ballots, and an increase in the number of officials elected rather than appointed. For the first time, the preamble to Colombia's constitution read: "In the Name of God, Legislator of the Universe, and by the Authority of the People."

The 1853 Constitution reverted to more federal principles, with "full powers of local government reserved to the Provinces" (Art. 10). Executive powers were greatly diminished and those of Congress enhanced (Art. 23). In particular, no disbursement could be made for any sum not appropriated by Congress nor for an amount greater than that authorized (Art. 56). The constitution made no provision for delegation or assumption of extraordinary powers by the executive and failed even to mention the possibility of internal commotion, tumult, or insurrection. The closest it came to restricting individual liberties was in Article 5 (Sec. 8), wherein the right of peaceful assembly was conditioned by the warning that

> any meeting of citizens which makes its petitions or expresses
> its opinions upon any matters by arrogating unto itself the
> name or the voice of the People, or pretends to impose upon
> the authorities its will as the will of the People is seditious; in-
> dividuals composing such a group shall be tried on the charge

of sedition. The will of the People can only be expressed through the representatives of the People by mandate obtained in conformity with this Constitution.

In addition to lacking provisions for any regime of exception— the first constitution in Spanish America to do so—the 1853 Constitution authorized the Supreme Court to declare null those municipal ordinances repugnant to the constitution and laws of the republic. (As it turned out, this would include overturning ordinances that gave women the vote.) Likewise, the president could suspend from office officials who violated the constitution, subject to review by the Supreme Court (Art. 42, Sec. 6; Art. 54). Whereas a quasi-autonomy was created for the provinces, both citizens and the federal executive had recourse to national law to control local and regional officials.

The liberalized constitution had been in place briefly when a coup d'état followed in April 1854, headed by the commander of the Bogotá garrison, General José María Melo. Many believed that President Obando knew of and acquiesced in the *autogolpe*. Melo suspended the new constitution, closed Congress, made himself dictator, and then offered the government to Obando, who refused it.

The *gólgota* faction allied with Conservatives, and the legitimist claim of Tomás Herrera (the official presidential alternate or *designado*) managed to force the restoration of constitutional government by the end of the year. Vice president José Obaldía took power from Herrera and assembled Congress—which impeached President Obando. No dictatorship would survive more than eighteen months in nineteenth-century Colombia; but all Colombians were reminded by the 1854 coup that proposals to abolish the military or drastically curtail its resources and numbers could be risky.

In the confused succession that followed, a congressional coalition of Conservatives and Liberals enacted reforms that pushed Colombia closer to a thoroughly federal regime. Some Conservatives now supported federalism as a way to escape, in certain provinces, from the provisions of the liberal 1853 Constitution. In 1857, the Conservatives regained the presidency with Dr. Mariano Ospina Rodríguez. Once again, after the aberrant *golpe* by Melo, the opposition had returned to power via elections, this time the Conservatives taking over from the Liberals. The Conservatives now also controlled both houses of Congress. Under these circumstances, the Conservatives reformed the constitution regarding amendments, modifying the four-fifths requirement to that of a simple majority, as in the case of ordinary legislation.

Instead of restoring the centralized political regime of the past, however, the Conservative Congress recognized the reality of strong provincial/state autonomy and the potential for civil war if it insisted on the historical Conservative program. It therefore adopted a new constitution in 1858, the Granadine Confederation, more federalist than any since 1811. While the president retained the authority to use the armed forces to maintain order and to suppress conflicts among the states (Art. 43, Secs. 11, 20), again no provision was made for suspending all or part of the constitution nor for assuming or delegating extraordinary powers in times of crisis.

The Confederation was characterized by semiautonomous states governed by caudillo "presidents" and state assemblies. Quarrels within and among the states, as well as intrigue linking the federal government with partisan politics within the states, rapidly degenerated into civil war.[26] In 1860 the national Congress passed legislation making state officials criminally liable for turmoil in their states and subject to banishment if they disregarded the orders of national authorities.[27] Former president Tomás Mosquera, now president of Cauca state, announced that Cauca was severing relations with the national government and reassuming its sovereignty.[28] Several other state administrations followed with similar declarations, allied with Cauca, and named Mosquera "Supreme Director of War." The 1858 Constitution fell prey to the civil war; Mosquera's victorious forces took control of Bogotá in July 1861.

At the instance of Mosquera, a Provisional Pact of Union was adopted in September 1861. Acting as a radical Liberal, Mosquera attacked the church viciously, subordinating its officials to the government, expelling the Jesuits, and ordering the sale of church properties. Implementing the anticlerical measures was Rafael Núñez, a cabinet member who, twenty-five years later as a moderate Liberal allied with the Conservatives, would restore Conservative hegemony and even sign a concordat with the Vatican.[29]

The Liberal victory produced the first Colombian constitution since independence that provided for suspension of the constitutional rights and liberties of citizens when "peace was disturbed." Santander's "descendants," rather than Bolívar's, reintroduced regimes of exception into Colombian constitutional law. They could be implemented by the decree of a council consisting of the attorney general, justices of the Supreme Court, and the secretaries of state (Art. 6). The suspension would continue until the council judged that peace had been restored. Whereas the council could suspend the constitutional rights of citizens, the constitution prohibited the national government from putting down rebellions in the states without congressional authorization (Art. 30).

Military conflict continued between Conservatives and Liberals into late 1862; the last major Liberal victory at Antioquia in October confirmed Mosquera's success. He then convened a constitutional convention with no Conservative representation. The next constitution, that of 1863, would be no compromise; it was the product of Liberal military victory.

The Constitution of 1863

The new constitution established a federal regime in which the sovereign states united to form a "United States of Colombia." The national government had strictly enumerated powers; all other powers were within the exclusive jurisdiction of the states (Arts. 1, 16). Following the precedent set by the provisional pact of 1861, the Supreme Court could now declare national legislation unconstitutional and annul "any act of the National Congress or of the Executive of the United States [of Colombia] which ... attacks the sovereignty of the States ... by the vote of the States expressed by the majority of their respective legislatures" (Art. 25). Further, "with the exception of the National Congress, the Federal Supreme Court, and the Executive Power of the Nation, there shall be no federal officers having ordinary jurisdiction or authority in any of the States in time of peace" (Art. 20).

In addition to creating a state-dominant federal regime, the 1863 Constitution consecrated the liberal principles of freedom of expression, of the press, and of association and also eliminated the death penalty. For the first time, the right to possess arms and ammunition and to engage in their commerce in peacetime was also constitutionally guaranteed (Art. 15, Sec. 15). As in the 1861 pact, no mention was made in the preamble of God or divine inspiration; this constitution was written "in the name and by the authority of the People of the United Colombian States." It would be the last Colombian constitution that failed to acknowledge God's assistance. It also provided that "the law of nations is part of national law," especially in cases of civil war, allowing internal conflicts to be settled by "treaty" and rebels to be treated as "prisoners of war" (Art. 91). Article 91 did not provide for a regime of exception in the common sense; it did serve later, for example in 1867, as the basis for declaring "internal war" against state governments that resisted federal authority. It was intended to prevent the summary execution of rebels by insisting on their treatment as prisoners of war rather than criminals. (Rebellion was a serious crime; enemy soldiers were entitled to better treatment and lesser punishment.)[30]

The 1863 Constitution barely mentioned the national armed forces; each state could have its own army. Congress was prohibited from delegating any of its functions, and the executive had recourse to no extraordinary powers. Elected by state vote, the president would serve a two-year term and be ineligible for immediate reelection (Art. 75). The states were to rule, the federal government to administer the common enterprise. There existed no foundation for constitutional dictatorship, except within each of the semisovereign states, and virtually no effective national government at all. Under this constitution, Liberals would dominate the national government and those of most states until the 1880s.

Conservatives considered the anticlerical provisions of the 1863 Constitution intolerable; many dreamed of its abrogation and restoration of a strong central government capable of guaranteeing internal order and respect for religion. Within Liberal circles there also were Catholics who favored limited government and federalism while opposing the extreme anticlericalism and exaggerated autonomy of the states in the 1863 Constitution.

After the two-year term of Manuel Moro Murillo, General Mosquera began his third elected term in 1866. Again battling the church, the president now confronted Congress, dissolved it, declared the nation in a state of internal war, and assumed dictatorial powers under the cover of constitutional Article 91 in April 1866.[31] He repeatedly violated the constitution, exiled bishops, killed and incarcerated opponents, intruded into the affairs of the states, made Bogotá a federal district, and even waged war against Ecuador. Resistance to Mosquera by the presidents of several key states took as its banner restoration of the constitution. Calls to make war against the tyrant emanated from regional leaders in Santander and Antioquia.

Before the threats of renewed civil war were realized, a coalition of moderate Liberals and Conservatives won over the president's palace guard and ousted Mosquera in a coup. After his incarceration, suspension from presidential duties according to constitutional process by the Senate, and trial for treason ("attacking the Constitution of the Republic") under the provisions of the criminal code, he was granted a pardon, subject to accepting exile for three years. Leaders of the army proclaimed that it had "carried out the glorious movement of 23 May, overthrowing the dictatorship and, without disorders or bloodshed, reestablished the constitutional regime."[32] General Santiago Acosta succeeded Mosquera in the presidency, prudently requesting that Congress reward officers of the palace guard and other key units with promotions and military honors.

A bit more than a month after Mosquera's ouster, the government of Bolívar state refused to recognize the authority of the new president. On July 23, 1867, President Acosta, making use of his constitutional powers and under the authority of the Law of Public Order, declared the "Republic in a state of war against the government of the state of Bolívar, its agents and allies." This activated Article 91, putting into force the "laws of war" in the entire country.[33] Acosta imposed national authority in Bolívar, through negotiations with rebellious officers, and also suppressed uprisings in Tolima, where Mosquera had significnat support.

During the next thirteen years, Liberal presidents came and went on schedule; coups and uprisings within the states were just as routine, as were debates on, and modifications of, state constitutions. Each state held its presidential elections at different times; the federal president served only a two-year term. Virtually unceasing politics marred by ballot fraud and violence permeated Colombian life.[34] In some states, such as Antioquia and Tolima, the federal charter provided opportunities for Conservatives to gain political bases; by the mid-1870s, fissures within the Liberal ranks found independents and moderate Liberals advocating reforms to strengthen the national government. As in Argentina before 1861, regimes of exception within the Colombian states were as important or more so than federal provisions for suspension of *garantías* and internal war. Colombian presidents barely had the national power exercised by Argentine caudillo Juan Manuel de Rosas in the Rio de la Plata region from 1835 to 1852 (see chapter 7). This lack of strong national authority, however, did not protect Colombians against state and local emergency powers and the risks of civil war.

In 1875 the Liberal dissidents, or independents, supported Rafael Núñez for the presidency against the radicals' Aquileo Parra and Bartolomé Calvo for the Conservatives. The radicals' manipulation of the vote in Congress led to insurrection in Antioquia, Tolima, and then Cundinamarca, Boyacá, and Santander. For the moment, however, Núñez was unwilling to ally with the Conserva-

174 The Constitution of Tyranny

tives and the rebellion was defeated. Four years later, further Liberal fragmentation pushed Núñez into a coalition with the Conservatives and won him the presidency (1880–1882).

After a two-year interim Núñez was reelected, now with the clear support of Conservatives, and immediately faced insurrections in Santander, Boyacá, Cundinamarca, Magdalena, and parts of Bolívar state. Conservatives and independents joined temporarily in a new National party and defeated the insurgents by August 1885. Military victory by the coalition, which included Conservatives, meant the end for the 1863 Constitution. The National party declared it void and requested that the state governors send representatives to a constituent assembly. On August 4, 1886, a new constitution restored the unitary regime, created a strong executive, and made provision for the regimes of exception that would prevail in Colombia into the second half of the twentieth century.

Under the new constitution, whose preamble declared it written "in the name of God, Supreme Source of all Authority," military officers were authorized to "inflict immediate punishment in order to subdue a military insubordination or mutiny or to maintain discipline in the face of the enemy" (Art. 27). The government could "order the arrest or detention of persons seriously suspected of having committed a crime against the public peace" (Art. 28). Public education was to be organized and directed in accordance with the Catholic religion, and acts contrary to Christian morals or subversive of public order and committed in connection with or under the pretext of religious worship were "subject to the ordinary law" (Art. 40). The press "is free in times of peace, but . . . responsible for injuries to personal honor and for disturbance of the social order and public peace" (Art. 42).

In addition to these returns to the past (reminiscent of García Moreno's "remoralization" of Ecuadorean society in the 1870s, discussed below) and the expansion of government authority, provisions for regimes of exception appeared in the 1886 Constitution. First, the charter authorized Congress to "invest the President of the Republic temporarily with such extraordinary powers as necessity may require or the public convenience demand" (Art. 76, Sec. 10). This clause practically restored the powers given Simón Bolívar in the 1820s. Second, the president's term was lengthened to six years and he was charged with "maintaining public order throughout the national territory and reestablishing same when it has been disturbed" (Art. 120, Sec. 8). Most significantly, Article 121 declared:

In case of foreign war or civil commotion the President may, after consultation with the Council of State and with the written consent of all the Counselors, declare the public order disturbed and that a state of siege prevails throughout the Republic or a part thereof.

After such a declaration has been made, the President shall be vested with all the powers conferred by law to defend the rights of the Nation or repress the disturbance, and in case such shall not be sufficient he shall use the powers conferred by the law of nations. The extraordinary measures or decrees of a provisional nature within the said limits which the President may take shall be binding, provided they carry the signatures of all the Counselors.

The Government shall declare the restoration of public peace whenever the civil commotion or foreign war has ceased, and shall send to Congress a report of the actions taken. All officials shall be responsible for the abuse of extraordinary powers vested in them.

This basic regime of exception clause remained in effect until 1936, when it was slightly reformed (Art. 117, 1936). It remained in the codification of 1945 and survived, with only small changes, into the 1960s. By its terms, the "law of war" applied to "internal commotion" and "disturbance of public order"; the national government thereby could treat opponents or rebels as enemy soldiers.[35] Only in 1968 would constitutional reforms further modify government powers under the state of siege and expand them to include "economic emergency."[36]

After more than half a century of struggle to democratize Colombian politics, to limit presidential power, to constrain government authority, and to guarantee civil liberties and rights, the 1886 Constitution nominally restored the Bolivarian vision of a strong centralized government with recourse to extraordinary powers in times of crisis. The efforts of Bolívar's adversaries to eliminate extraordinary powers and other regimes of exception had allowed over forty years of experimentation with weak executives, deconcentration of government power, and recurrent civil strife.

Liberalism had failed to create unity or stability in Colombia just as it had in Venezuela. Misunderstood federalism generated quasi-feudal caudillismo, cynically justified by provincial sovereignty and individual liberty. Decades of constitutional dictatorship would follow, but no national government, even into the 1990s, would govern Colombia with the control over its national territory that developed in Mexico, Central America, or southern South America. Governance under state of siege and executive decree powers would become more common than routine government, but constitutional centralization of government authority would not overcome the political and military legacy in Colombia of these federal experiments of the nineteenth century.

In the short term, the Conservatives adopted several repressive legal measures to supplement the constitutional regimes of exception. First, a new press law promulgated on February 17, 1888, defined as subversive those publications that were harmful to society, encouraged disobedience to the law, attacked the church or the armed forces, offended the honor of government or religious officials, or incited class conflict. This law was used against the opposition press frequently; offending journalists could be arrested, jailed, and fined; offending publications could be suspended or permanently banned. Second, a law promulgated May 15, 1888, (called the Law of the Horses because it was passed after the governor of Cauca reported that decapitated horses had been found near Palmira) authorized the president, using extraordinary powers, to detain, arrest, imprison, exile, and divest persons of political rights in order to prevent or repress crimes against public order and property. The law also authorized the president to purge the military of disloyal personnel and to suspend any establishment that became the "source of revolutionary or subversive propaganda."[37] Liberal efforts to have this law repealed failed overwhelmingly in 1892; in 1893, Liberal leader Santiago Pérez denounced the use of extraordinary powers, which he claimed "undermined republican institutions by their very existence."[38]

Riots by angry workers and artisans in Bogotá provoked a state of siege decree on January 16, 1893. Police stations, jails, and homes of prominent government officials were attacked, and an estimated fifty persons died in the confrontations. The state of siege remained in effect until late February. It had now been used to contain a small popular insurrection; it would be used many more times against working-class movements in the future. Rafael Núñez declared that the "socialist scourge" had penetrated Colombia.[39] As in other parts of Spanish America, the regimes of exception invented to repress elite political opposition would be the legal basis for repressing social movements and political parties intent on democratizing the region's political systems.

Conservatives effectively excluded the Liberals from Congress after 1886 through rigged elections and persecution. They also made the public administration a party enclave. Legislation permitting the president to transfer judges to any post in the republic (the law of *transhumancia*) served as an instrument to intimidate and purge magistrates unwilling to defer to "the political interests of the regime."[40] Unable to regain the presidency through elections, the Liberals tried war. An uprising in 1895 was rapidly suppressed.

In 1896 the lone Liberal congressman, General Rafael Uribe Uribe, scathingly denounced the 1886 Constitution, the Conservative Congress, and the government's economic policies, its corruption, and its despotism:

> You [the Congress] do not consent to abrogate the unlimited powers [*omnímodas*], in order to replace constitutional normality for dictatorship, to substitute security for the state of anguish [*zozobra*] suffered by society, the result of the constant threat to its rights.
>
> The press law you expedited is nothing but legislative sanction for the state of arbitrariness to which this precious immanent right has been subjected. . . . You have done nothing to reform the defects in the electoral law and the recent abuses [*atropellos*] of the suffrage, . . . while sanctioning political proscription of the opposition parties. You have not derogated the Law of *transhumancia* that enslaves magistrates and judges to presidential volition. . . .
>
> Blood gushes from the sides, and tears from the eyes, of this poor nation, and there are some hundred predators [*hombres de presa*] that have fallen about her, terrifying alchemists! who have rushed to collect the blood and tears and turn them into gold for their exclusive benefit; and when Colombia, now pale and dying, appears to lay down in this coffin of the *Regeneración*,[41] the greedy vampires have perched on her and, slowly connecting their thousand fangs, have sucked, and continue sucking, the warm blood from her open veins.[42]

The Liberals were unable to convince the government to reform the political system to allow their reincorporation. Opposition meant subversion; the Liberals were not citizens but enemies. As in the Uruguayan struggle of the Blancos against the Colorados, only armed conflict remained as an alternative (see chapter 7).

From 1899 to 1902, Colombia suffered the War of a Thousand Days, the bloodiest of its internal wars since independence. Government decrees provided that rebels be treated as common criminals and that they be tried in military courts. Between 75,000 and 100,000 dead (perhaps 2 percent of the population—a bit more, proportionately, than the losses in the U.S. Civil War) and widespread destruction of property and infrastructure were the consequences. A bitter legacy of partisan hatred and guerrilla warfare also resulted; these would be resurrected in the 1940s and 1950s to produce hundreds of thousands more victims in *La Violencia*.[43] The Liberals lost the war, and Colombia lost Panama in 1903 as the United States supported the autonomist movement against the national government. In the same year, congressional elections were again held under state of siege.

The Liberals did not regain the presidency in Colombia until 1930, but General Rafael Reyes (who had put down the Liberal uprising of 1895) was elected to the presidency in 1904 and began efforts at reconciliation by naming Liberals to his cabinet. Reyes's political slogan, "Less Politics and More Administration," echoed the familiar antipolitical, antidemocratic themes of Bolívar, Portales in Chile (see chapter 8), Ramón Castilla in Peru (see chapter 6), and Linares in Bolivia (see chapter 6). Reyes illegally dissolved the Congress and replaced it with a "national assembly"; three deputies were chosen from each department by departmental councils, with obvious government intervention. Reyes's national assembly introduced a system of proportional representation in congressional elections and other elective entities as part of the president's effort to provide minimal guarantees to the Liberals.

An assassination attempt against the president strengthened his resolve to govern virtually as a dictator, to repress opponents, both Conservatives and Liberals, and at the same time to design reforms that permitted reconciliation. When his efforts to have the council extend his presidential term failed, and facing protests by university students, Reyes resigned rather than massacre the sons of the elite. The laws of the rump assembly were declared void; a Congress elected in 1910 adopted constitutional reforms that reduced the presidential term to four years, prohibited immediate reelection, and guaranteed the minority party at least one-third of the seats in the legislature, a method of coopting the opposition adopted under similar circumstances in Uruguay (see chapter 7).[44]

The 1910 reforms returned Colombia to constitutional government. After another twenty years of limited Liberal participation in

Congress and, sometimes, in the cabinet, Conservative rule finally ended with the election of a Liberal president in 1930—but not before President Miguel Abadía Méndez sent the army, in late 1928, to suppress a strike in the banana zone of Santa Marta. This action left several thousand dead and wounded. The transition to a Liberal president was also marred by violence and a brief civil war in the departments of Santander and Boyacá.

Until 1946, legally elected Liberal presidents governed the country. Episodic provincial violence, repression of labor and new political movements by police and the military, and use of extraordinary powers were reminders of the foundations of Colombian government. After 1946, despite a stronger legislature and political party system than elsewhere in South America, with the possible exceptions of Chile and Uruguay, Colombians lived under state of siege and were subject to presidential decree powers more often than not. In 1949, President Mariano Ospina Pérez dissolved the Congress, declared a state of siege, gave extraordinary powers to the provincial governors, and assigned the police the mission of enforcing the press and radio censorship. The Liberal party was again banned from public assembly and association.[45]

Colombians would spend most of the next two decades under states of siege. In some respects, this results from the uniquely vicious and prolonged political violence suffered by the country in the decades after World War II, followed by a proliferation of guerrilla movements. (Later, the terrorism by drug cartels would be added to the list.) In part, however, this development resulted from Colombia's history of nineteenth-century political violence and its accommodation to the Spanish American formula for constitutional dictatorship.

A new constitution promulgated in 1991 maintained this tradition. In its chapter 6, *estados de excepción*, Colombia was provided "new" language for the constitution of tyranny:

Article 213: "The President of the Republic, with the approval of all his ministers, may declare a State of Internal Commotion in all or part of the Republic for no more than ninety days, with two extensions of equal time, the last requiring approval of the Senate of the Republic, in the case of grave perturbation of the public order that imminently threatens institutional stability and security of the State, or civil peace [*convivencia ciudadana*], and which cannot be confronted with the use of ordinary police powers. . . .

The legislative decrees issued by the government [during the state of emergency] may suspend laws incompatible with the State of Commotion and will cease in their effect as soon as [the government] declares restored the public order. The government may extend the application [of such laws] for ninety days. . . . In no case may civilians be investigated or tried by military justice."

Article 214: "[During states of emergency] human rights and fundamental liberties may not be suspended. In all cases international law on human rights will be respected. A future law will regulate the attributes of the government during states of exception and establish judicial controls and *garantías* to protect these rights. . . .

The President and ministers . . . and other functionaries . . . shall be responsible for any abuses committed in the use of the authority [conceded to them by the state of emergency]."

Article 215 added a more limited state of emergency to meet threats to the economic, social, and ecological order of the Republic, allowing presidential decree laws for thirty days, with two thirty-day extensions, but no more than ninety days in a calendar year.

Updated to include an environmental and social rationale for regimes of exception, modernized to provide formal legislative and judicial oversight, and moralized by reference to international standards for human rights, the 1991 Colombian Constitution expressed the traditional Spanish American sentiment: the country could not be governed without provisions for regimes of exception, even temporary constitutional dictatorship. Bolívar would have objected to the nuisance of judicial and congressional review, but he would have appreciated the broad authority granted to the president for three months (renewable twice) to save the fatherland from internal commotion and from threats to the security of the state and to the *convivencia ciudadana.*

ECUADOR

Ecuador, the "estado del sur de Colombia," exhibited significant differences from both Venezuela and Colombia in its first half-century of independence. From the outset, military elites and opposing caudillos determined the outcome of political development. Presidential succession rarely gave even the appearance of a legal transfer of power through elections, in contrast to Colombia and Venezuela to the 1850s, and efforts to limit the term and powers of the president failed. Prominent national leaders considered seriously the idea of monarchy, even inviting Spanish and French protectorates on several occasions. Ultimately, however, Ecuadoreans failed both to establish a monarchy and to solve the dilemmas of legitimacy and peaceful regime succession posed by independence from Spain.

With few exceptions, military battles rather than elections decided the timing of regime changes. Personal struggles for power couched in vituperative journalistic assaults accompanied everything from the poisoning of archbishops to assassinations of presidents and would-be presidents, public whippings of political opponents, torture of prisoners, and the operation of secret police and espionage networks. More so than in Venezuela or Colombia, the historical description of the years from 1830 to the 1880s in Ecuador may be designated with the names of the dominant caudillos: General Juan José Flores, 1830–1845; General José María Urbina, 1845–1860; Dr. Gabriel García Moreno, 1860–1875.

Unlike Colombia, and less so even than in Venezuela, in Ecuador no modern political party system developed until the early twentieth century. And when elections or plebiscites did occur, a much smaller percentage of the population could vote than even in Venezuela and Colombia. The most participatory of Ecuadorean national elections involved approximately 5 percent of the population in 1875; previously, property, income, literacy, and other restrictions meant much lower rates of suffrage.[46] This resulted in part from the fears Ecuadoreans on the coast and in Quito had of Indian rebellion and racial strife, since the Indian and *casta* (mulatto and *zambo*) population comprised perhaps 80–85 percent of the 600,000 inhabitants in 1830. It also resulted from the aggressive and often brutal repression of opposition by temporarily incumbent governments, whether liberal or conservative. Regionalism also contributed to the lack of a national party or political system; not even a decent wagon road connected the main port of Guayaquil to the highland capital of Quito until the 1870s.

Ecuador also is unique in having been dedicated, by its president and Congress, to "the Sacred Heart of Jesus" (1873) and having made Catholicism a requirement for citizenship (1869). The Ecuadorean church gained more privileges during this period than had the Holy See in the times of the Hapsburgs. Indeed, the political role of both the church and the military, important institutions in most of Spanish America, was more pronounced in Ecuador than elsewhere in northern South America.[47]

Two other key features also shaped nineteenth-century Ecuadorean history. The nation's first president, General Juan José Flores, had been Bolívar's key lieutenant in this region, and he dominated Ecuador (1830–1845) with an army predominantly composed of Venezuelans and Colombians. This foreign element in Ecuadorean politics made place-of-birth requirements for the president a central issue in constitutional debates during most of the century—an issue shared with Peru during the early years of that country's independence. It also engendered resentment over Flores's Bolivarian political models, the role of the military in controlling the country, and Flores's schemes for a monarchy in Ecuador, perhaps with assistance from other caudillos in Bolivia or Peru.[48]

Finally, Ecuador faced a variety of external threats during the first half-century of independence that greatly influenced internal politics and constitutional development. Some of these threats resulted from the machinations of Flores, after his exile in 1845, and of other leaders who sought Peruvian, Colombian, Bolivian, Chilean, and even Spanish and French support for their political ambitions. Wars with Colombia and Peru (1859, 1861, 1863) involved domestic political forces in collusion with foreign caudillos. Though Ecuador never won a war in the nineteenth century, it lost little territory.

Given all this, it should not be surprising that no Ecuadorean political leader desired to govern without recourse to extraordinary powers or other regimes of exception. Nor should it be surprising that debates of the extent, duration, legality of exercise, and abuses of such powers permeated political life throughout the nineteenth century.

Early Constitutional Development and Regimes of Exception, 1830–1843

As in other parts of northern South America, the independence movements in what was to become Ecuador originated in juntas proclaiming their loyalty to the king of Spain in response to the Napoleonic invasion of the Iberian peninsula. In August 1809, a junta in Quito sought to establish autonomy from the peninsular regime in the name of "the preservation of true religion" and "the defense of the legitimate monarchy." This junta survived briefly and then collapsed due to internal conflicts and the effective countermoves of Spanish officials in Peru and New Granada.[49] Repression by the royal officials followed swiftly, with hundreds of rebels imprisoned and some executed in their cells. Riots in Quito led to hundreds more casualties. A new junta restored order, but the turmoil and resentment eventually led to a declaration of independence and a controversial constitution in 1812.

This constitution, called Artículos del Pacto Solemne de Sociedad y Unión Entre las Provincias que Forman el Estado de Quito, bore little resemblance to the documents drafted in Colombia and Venezuela in 1811. Indeed, the Quito Constitution of 1812 adopted a centralist organization with authority vested in a "general congress" that would tolerate no religion but that of the Holy Church and proscribe from political rights (*vecindad*) anyone who did not profess Roman Catholicism. Moreover, the new state of Quito declared that it "recognizes and will recognize as its Monarch, Ferdinand VII, as soon as he is free of French domination" (Art. 5). The constitution combined this reaffirmation of monarchy and loyalty to Ferdinand VII with an eclectic mixture of liberal principles, separation of powers, and confused lines of government authority.[50] It was effective only briefly, if ever; Spanish royalists reestablished authority and subjected Quito to the control of the viceroy at Lima.

Only with the Bolivarian victories in northern South America and those of General San Martín in the south (see chapter 6) did independence movements again seem plausible in Ecuador. In 1820, a movement headed by the Venezuelan León de Febrés Cordero proclaimed independence in Guayaquil. Military victories in 1821–1822 by General Antonio José de Sucre, Bolívar's closest ally, took control of Ecuador from Spain and brought it into Gran Colombia. This meant government under the umbrella of the 1821 Bolivarian Constitution for Colombia, with its powerful executive and its provision for comprehensive regimes of exception.

From 1822 to 1830, Ecuador became a subordinate state within the new Colombian nation, dominated by Venezuelan and Colombian officials and military forces. It also served as a base for Bolívar's campaigns into Peru and Bolivia, thereby involving Ecuador immediately in international wars and accumulating for the new state a significant debt. In practice, Ecuador supplied double or triple the resources that Venezuela and Colombia did in the Peruvian and Bolivian campaigns.

Ecuador declared independence in May 1830, with the dissolution of Gran Colombia, but would be dominated for the next fifteen years by the Venezuelan general who had been Bolívar's ally: General Juan José Flores. Treachery marked Ecuador's beginnings. General Sucre, seeking to restore the state into the confederation, was assassinated; suspicion that General Flores was implicated never abated. Whatever the merits of this suspicion, Flores played the role of Páez in Venezuela and Santander in Colombia after Bolívar's death. Even after his ouster and exile in 1845, Flores continually plotted his return to power, managed a brief comeback as commander in chief of the armed forces in the early1860s (like Páez in Venezuela), and died on active duty in 1864.

Independence meant the need for a constitution, which General Flores duly had prepared in 1830. Tactical concerns required keeping open the opportunity for Ecuador's reincorporation into the Republic of Colombia, and given Flores's situation, the constitution recognized as Ecuadoreans natives of the other states of Colombia and military personnel in the service of Ecuador at the time of the declaration of independence (Arts. 2–9). Ritual enumerations of liberal principles, rights, and liberties were combined with extensive executive authority in a nominally federal charter. The constitution gave the name of Ecuador to the three departments of Guayaquil, Quito, and Azuay, with lesser jurisdictions called provinces, cantons, and parishes—a familiar pattern by this time in other parts of Spanish America. Most official posts were to be filled by the executive, including those of cabinet officers, bishops, high-ranking military officers, and judges. Most important, the Constitution of 1830 included comprehensive emergency powers for the president in times of "internal commotion" or foreign invasion, along with routine responsibility for conserving internal order and external security of the state (Art. 35, Sec. 1):

> The Powers of the President are:
> 1. To conserve internal order and external security of the State;
> 2. To convene the Congress for its ordinary sessions; and extraordinarily when required for the welfare of the fatherland; . . .
> 4. Deploy the national militia for internal security, and the army for defense of the nation, and command it in person with express consent of Congress;
> 5. Take, on his own initiative, when Congress is not in session, whatever measures are necessary to defend and free from danger, in the case of foreign invasion or threat of internal commotion; subject to prior acknowledgment of danger by the Council of State.

In addition to these broad executive powers, the 1830 Constitution conserved the military *fueros* of the colonial era and explicitly provided a constitutional mission for the Ecuadorean armed forces: "The duty of the armed forces is to defend the independence of the Fatherland, uphold its laws, and maintain public order" (Arts. 51, 52, 58). Thus from Ecuador's first constitution, no president was without recourse to emergency powers, and the military forces had a constitutional mission in internal politics. Constitutional dictatorship and the prominent role of the armed forces in Ecuador was a legacy of the first days of independence. This legacy would be expanded upon, modified, and debated—but never overturned—for the next century and a half.

Adoption of the 1830 Constitution was followed by years of political and military unrest. Supporters of Bolívar immediately revolted, seeking reincorporation of Ecuador into the Colombian federation. Flores successfully overcame this threat and several others, but the fiscal condition of the new republic was fragile. The salaries and maintenance of the military forces required over 75 percent of the budget. Another uprising in 1833, this time by liberals influenced by an English officer, Colonel Francis Hall, stimulated the first serious public debate concerning extraordinary powers in independent Ecuador.

Flores requested extraordinary powers from Congress to confront the uprising. El Quiteño Libre, a political club that opposed the role of the church, upheld Benthamite principles, and demanded an end to the domination of Ecuador by foreign military elements, circulated a pamphlet titled *Las Facultades Extraordinarias.* It argued forcefully against these extraordinary powers, as did leading liberal congressmen such as Vicente Rocafuerte. Rocafuerte was a former opponent of Bolívar and had also battled grants of extraordinary powers to executives during his residency in Mexico. Beyond their opposition to extraordinary powers, the Quiteño Libre group also attacked the military, criticized Flores's use of troops to intimidate voters, and advocated replacing the foreign army with a national militia.

Although Rocafuerte would later negotiate an alternation of power with Flores, for the moment the Congress granted Flores the powers he requested to deal with the so-called uprising, although with Congress in session it was not clear that this was constitutionally permissible. Flores sent members of the Quiteño Libre society into exile, stifled its publications (which merely accused the government of tyranny, despotism, corruption, and oppression), and persecuted its members. Previous personal animosity between Hall and Flores clearly influenced the tone of the conflict; Hall's racial epithets (calling Flores a "little mulatto") and other indiscretions certainly had little calming effect.

Soon thereafter, Congress granted extraordinary powers to Flores and he headed toward Guayaquil to deal with the rebellion. Soldiers assassinated Colonel Hall and several other society members in Quito who headed an uprising in the capital. A full-scale insurrection followed, based in Guayaquil, which had become the center of liberal opposition to the conservative regime in Quito. With the intellectual leadership of Vicente Rocafuerte, a distinguished internationalist who advocated liberal principles for Ecuadorean government, the so-called War of the Chihuahuas engulfed the country.[51]

Betrayal by one of his military allies delivered Rocafuerte to Flores; the loss of Quito to rebels led Flores to negotiate with Rocafuerte. Concessions by both leaders resulted in Flores's promise not to seek another term and to support Rocafuerte for president. Resistance by the forces at Quito forced Rocafuerte and Flores to battle as allies against José Félix Valdivieso, who had made himself head of a provisional government. Flores's victory over Valdivieso near Ambato in January 1835 was followed by Rocafuerte's ascension to the presidency. Flores, military hero and "defender of the constitution," became commander in chief of the armed forces. The man Rocafuerte had called a "ferocious tyrant" now was "my esteemed friend" and invested with emergency powers "to govern the Department of Guayas in case of invasion or insurrection."[52] As the transition from Flores to Rocafuerte was irregular, the new president called for a constituent assembly to legitimate the new government. This pattern characterized the rest of the nineteenth century in Ecuador, as in Central America, Venezuela, Peru, and Bolivia. Constitutions followed coups as victors in political conflicts or war sought the symbolic legitimacy of constitutional rule.

Rocafuerte's efforts to exclude the clergy and active-duty military personnel from the assembly provoked controversy, but the constitution neither eliminated the ecclesiastical *fueros* nor diminished the constitutionally defined role of the military. To the contrary, Article 85 of the 1835 Constitution declared "there shall be permanent military naval and land forces for the external defense of the State and to conserve internal order." Despite Rocafuerte's liberal background and previous opposition to extraordinary powers, the 1835 charter authorized Congress to concede to the executive "whatever extraordinary powers it considers necessary" in the event of "internal commotion or foreign invasion" (Art. 64). If Congress were not in session, the council of government could concede emergency powers to the executive, including collecting taxes in advance, increasing the size of the military, and ordering the arrest, interrogation, banishment, internal and foreign exile, or temporary dismissal from public employment of those suspected of "conspiracy" against the government (Art 65).

Faced with ongoing political intrigues, financial crises, and international conflicts, President Rocafuerte made ample use of extraordinary powers, confirming his newly developed opinion, later conveyed to General Flores during the latter's second presidential term (1839–1843) that "the only way to maintain a government in America . . . and to save the people from the bloody claws of the ferocious restorers of liberty and the fatherland is with clubs, clubs, and more clubs."[53]

After a four-year term filled with efforts at political reforms, initiation of public works, and even establishment of military academies, Rocafuerte left office in 1839 and returned to Guayaquil as the provincial governor. Maintaining his personal and ideological differences with Flores, he nevertheless avoided violent confrontations and secured Flores's military support throughout most of his administration. In keeping with the private pact between the two leaders for alternation in office, Rocafuerte engaged in political intrigues and criticism of Flores's second administration but also continued to provide counsel and correspond with his sometime ally.

Flores faced a number of difficulties in his second term. He had little control over some, including chronic fiscal crises, widespread currency counterfeiting, a serious yellow fever epidemic in Guayaquil in the early 1840s, minor military mutinies, and persistent regionalism. Other difficulties stemmed from his own eclectic, arbitrary, and authoritarian policies and political style. His avarice, rampant corruption in public administration, and manipulation of congressional elections provoked recurrent unrest. His halfhearted attacks on the privileges of the church, use of an official press to slander opponents, and schemes to establish a monarchy in the central Andean nations in collusion with Spain and in collaboration with Bolivian caudillo-in-exile Andrés Santa Cruz (see chapter 6) all contributed to increasing opposition.

Finally, a head tax on white and mestizo citizens, similar to the tax that provoked anger against liberals in Central America in the

1830s, enraged many of the affected population. Intended to increase revenue, the tax offended highlanders greatly by degrading their status to that of Indians, who had paid such tribute for centuries. Such a leveling device made popular resistance far more intense than it would have been as simply a tax protest. If that were not enough, tariff increases intended both to protect highland industry and to increase customs receipts clashed with the interests of Guayaquil merchants.

Flores's manipulation of congressional elections also led to a unique institutional crisis. Opposition congressmen, and even some disenchanted supporters, refused to convene, making congressional action impossible for lack of a quorum. This further convinced Flores, who preferred legal and constitutional means (or at least the appearance thereof) to naked force, that the republican institutions adopted for Ecuador in 1830 and 1835 were inappropriate for the country's social and cultural conditions.

In October 1842, the president convoked a constitutional convention for January 1843. Flores attempted to pack the convention with his supporters, including government and military officials, but opponents such as Rocafuerte and president-to-be Colonel José María Urbina also gained access. General Flores preferred a constitution more like the Bolivarian model: a strong executive in a centralized system, long terms of office, and extensive extraordinary powers when needed. He also sought "to prepare the spirit of the nation for the establishment of a system of government which, although preserving the republican name, would approach a constitutional monarchy as far as possible."[54]

Labeled "the Charter of Slavery" by opponents, the Constitution of 1843 gave Flores less than he wanted but went far in establishing a constitutional dictatorship. Executive power was greatly enhanced and the legislature was to meet only once every four years, for ninety days, unless called by the executive into "extraordinary session." A "Permanent Commission" of five senators had extensive legislative functions when Congress was not in session. This included "declaring when the Fatherland was in danger" and conceding extraordinary powers to the president as stipulated in Article 62 of the constitution (Art. 52). Article 62 declared:

> In the case of foreign invasion or armed internal commotion,
> the Executive Power, with the consent of Congress, or of the
> Permanent Commission, if the former is in recess, may collect

taxes in advance; contract debts by pledging the public credit; increase the size of the military as believed necessary; unite in the hands of a single person civil and military power; issue pardons and general amnesties in the territory affected by the insurrection; arrest, interrogate, or cause to be interrogated those suspected of the crime of conspiracy, placing them at the disposition of a judge of jurisdiction within three days; moving them to another part of the Republic, for a time period [considered] absolutely necessary; transferring the government's residency, when the capital is threatened, until the danger ceases.

Article 63 further provided that these extraordinary powers would be limited in time and to the purposes strictly necessary to "reestablish the tranquility and security of the Republic." In an indirect and slippery fashion, the constitution also authorized the president to take a number of drastic actions, with the consent of the Senate or the permanent commission of the legislature. In practice this meant that five senators could authorize the president to arrest, banish, and incarcerate citizens; suspend judicial proceedings, the Congress, and its sessions; and unilaterally redirect budgeted funds to purposes other than those indicated by Congress (Art. 62). The constituent assembly, composed mostly of Flores's supporters, was to name the first president and vice president to serve under the new constitution, as well as senators and members of the permanent commission (Transitory Art. 1).

In addition, the 1843 Constitution added a unique clause declaring that while the military was essentially obedient and could not deliberate, it was "independent of the political authority in its specialized functions, but still obligated to provide the assistance requested [by civil authorities] in conformity with the law." Military *fueros* were also retained (Arts. 83–86). Perhaps it was not a charter of slavery, but it was most definitely the constitutional foundations of dictatorship.

Resistance to implementing this constitution and a plethora of other political and economic conflicts submerged the country in civil war. Seeking to assuage opponents in Guayaquil and to reduce tensions in the highlands, Flores reversed his policies both on the new head tax and the higher tariffs. Concessions were futile, and after a number of minor confrontations a revolt broke out in Guayaquil. Peruvian military support for the rebels (due in part to

Flores's earlier assistance to General Santa Cruz against the Peruvian regime) and their control of the country's main port eventually brought Flores's defeat.

Even in defeat, however, Flores exacted a so-called treaty from the victors, the Tratado de La Virginia (named after the hacienda in which it was signed). This agreement theoretically guaranteed him a full salary as commander in chief of the armed forces, protection for his supporters against persecution, and respect for his honors and rank of military officers, in exchange for his "voluntary" departure from the country for two years—after which time he could return. Both the victors and Flores failed to respect this agreement. Flores spent most of the next ten years plotting against the Ecuadorean government, planning invasions, and moving from Europe to the United States and to Central America almost as a filibuster or pirate. Always, he justified his plans with patriotic rhetoric and bitter complaints about his adversaries' failure to honor the treaty of 1845.

Politics and Constitutional Development, 1845–1860

The March 6 Revolution that defeated General Flores was followed by three civilian presidents (1845–1851) and two military presidents (1851–1859). The initial chore of the revolution was to constitutionalize its victory. Beginning in October 1845, a constituent assembly met for four months in the highland town of Cuenca. Reacting to Flores, the new constitution expanded the suffrage, disallowed any but native-born Ecuadoreans from serving as president, took the power of the *patronato* from the president, and, more generally, sought to liberalize political life.

Shifting somewhat the balance of power from the executive to the legislature, the Congress was to convene every year for sixty days without convocation by the executive. The 1845 Constitution mandated Congress to fix the maximum size of the military in peacetime and prohibited delegation of legislative authority to any person, authority, or "corporation" (Art. 43). As in the past, the president would be elected by the Congress.

Although the assembly consciously attempted to limit executive powers, the 1845 Constitution retained, or only slightly modified, most of the extraordinary powers accorded the president in the 1835 Constitution, and even most of the regime of exception provisions found in the "charter of slavery" of 1843 (Arts. 71, 74, 75). Determination by Congress of "grave danger," as a result of internal commotion or foreign invasion, justified exercising presidential emergency powers. Even without such a determination, a number of drastic measures might be permitted by Congress (Art. 71). As expected, the president was to "conserve internal order and the external security of the State" (Art. 70).

The president lost the authority to command the armed forces in person without congressional permission, and it was left to Congress to resolve any doubts regarding interpretation of the constitution. Still, not even the liberal reaction of 1845 eliminated extensive provisions for regimes of exception. Further, the liberals expanded the constitutional mission of the military to include "maintaining public order, sustaining observance of the constitution and the laws," subject to the constitutional authorities and "the subordination and direction of the Executive Power and its agents" (Art. 105). As in the 1843 Constitution, the constituents in 1845 gave themselves power to name the first president and vice president to serve under the new charter and also to enact "laws and decrees necessary for the establishment of this Constitution" (Arts. 143–45).

By 1852, further internal strife generated two more constitutions, each adopted essentially to constitutionalize governments coming to power as a result of irregular regime succession. These charters made provision for "extraordinary powers" for the president and delegation of special powers in the event of "internal commotion" or foreign invasion. They also gave the executive even broader and vaguer authority. In addition to the now customary clauses evolved since 1830, the constitution of 1851 extended presidential authority to deal with the crimes of sedition and rebellion, not just conspiracy, whenever the "welfare or security of the Republic require" (Art. 59).

The political role of the military now included "defending the independence and dignity of the Republic against all offenses or external aggression, maintaining internal order and assuring execution of the laws." In 1852, the list of extraordinary powers that Congress or the council of government might concede to the president in times of "grave danger due to internal commotion or foreign attack that threatens the security of the State" increased still further (Art. 73), though the duty of the armed forces to "defend the dignity of the Republic" was deleted from the otherwise similarly defined constitutional mission.

Whether liberals or conservatives, clericals or anticlericals, all of Ecuador's military and civilian governments availed themselves of extraordinary powers and ruled through regimes of exception. The country's sixth constitution, that of 1852, legitimized the removal of a civilian president and the formal assumption of power by General José María Urbina. It was, in many respects, a modification of the charter of 1845, but it provided for indirect popular election of the president by provincial assemblies instead of selection by Congress (Art. 59). The president would serve a four-year term without the possibility of immediate reelection.

Urbina adopted policies that ejected the Jesuits from the country, intervened in selecting church personnel, outlawed capital punishment, encouraged free primary education, and abolished slavery. In matters of political dominance, like his liberal compatriots elsewhere, Urbina relied upon military force, in particular a battalion of black soldiers from the coast whom he called "my canons" (*canónigos*).[55] Ineligible for reelection, Urbina engineered the victory of his military colleague, General Francisco Robles, in 1856.

Robles faced increased opposition from clerical forces led by soon-to-be dictator Dr. Gabriel García Moreno. Civil war, conflict with Peru over land in the east ceded by Ecuador to British creditors but claimed by Peru, and the resurgence of regional caudillismo brought the nation to the brink of chaos. Congress granted the president extraordinary powers to deal with the war with Peru. The government moved the capital from Quito to Riobamba and then again, without congressional authorization, to Guayaquil. The rebels created a provisional government, but military encounters continued into late 1859. Eventually a triumvirate that included García Moreno recalled General Juan José Flores from exile in Peru. Urbina, Robles, and other liberals now began fifteen years of exile and intrigue against Ecuadorean governments.

Autocracy and Theocracy, 1860–1875

In Ecuador a new era began, a unique period of conservative reaction and practically theocratic government. To impose and "legalize" this new order required even more comprehensive regimes of exception and extraordinary powers than previously. To consecrate their victory, the García Moreno forces first required a new constitution, as had all their predecessors. Presided over by the returned first president of the republic, General Juan José Flores, a constituent assembly met in Quito in January 1861. It elected García Moreno interim president, adopted a new constitution, and then named García Moreno president for the first term under the new charter.

The 1861 Constitution introduced to Ecuador direct popular suffrage, lifted property restrictions on citizenship, and substituted proportional representation for regional representation. These apparently democratizing changes favored the highland conservative base of the new regime. In accord with García Moreno's views, the new constitution further centralized power and further empowered the executive branch while weakening the legislature. Reversing the reforms of the liberal regimes, the legislature would now meet only every two years, for sixty days, unless convoked into extraordinary session by the president.

The 1861 Constitution accorded to the president the gamut of authority now common in Ecuador, including special prerogatives to deal with emergencies or subversion with congressional or council of government consent (Arts. 66–70). The president could also delegate these extraordinary powers to subordinates (Art. 72). Significantly, the constitutionally defined mission of the armed forces was now reduced to "defense of the Republic and conservation of internal order," perhaps as an effort by García Moreno and the conservatives to establish civilian control of the military (Art. 99).

García Moreno adopted an aggressive foreign policy, leading to conflict with Peru and war with Colombia. In 1864 General Flores died in military service, thus ending his dream of another presidency. García Moreno proposed a French protectorate, flirted with monarchy, and entered into a concordat with Rome (1863) that greatly favored the church. Internally, the president initiated important public works (including a road between Quito and Guayaquil), attempted to assert civilian control over the military, and returned education to the church.

Liberal reaction was immediate. The government met assassination attempts, threats of invasion by exiles from Peru, and ongoing political plotting with repression. García Moreno expanded the secret police network, summarily executed captured prisoners involved in rebellion or sedition, had prisoners tortured, and murdered opponents. In a letter to General Flores, he wrote that his enemies obliged him "to execute the worst of them. I am alert, maintain regular espionage, and have inspired a good deal of fear in them" (*les he inducido bastante miedo*).[56] Although the constitution prohibited banishment and exile, García Moreno did not hesitate to use these measures against opponents, confident that he did God's work as he sought to moralize the nation.

His theory of government was clear: "Terrible, quick and energetic repression is the only way to cure the wicked" (*malvados*).[57] His moralizing mission made the secret police and armed forces integral instruments of public policy, attacking political enemies as well as adulterers, drunks, gamblers, and corrupt priests (those priests who did not support his policies). At the end of his first term, García Moreno selected a successor whom he believed would carry on his program and allow him to rule covertly. He was wrong. As his successor exhibited independence in his cabinet appointments and policies, García Moreno began a campaign to oust him. Under pressure from opponents and stripped of extraordinary powers by the Congress in 1867, President Jerónimo Carrión resigned. Succeeded by an aged vice president, who also resigned shortly thereafter, and then by the president of the Senate, President Carrión's departure left the country in political limbo. Elections followed to fill his unexpired term; opposing factions temporarily agreed on Dr. Javier Espinosa, who took office in January 1868.

Espinosa's moderation and his appointment of liberal opponents of García Moreno angered the latter. A devastating earthquake in Imbabura Province that destroyed the towns of Otaválo and Ibarra gave García Moreno a chance to again demonstrate his energy and charisma in the supervision of the rescue and reconstruction effort. In 1869, however, unwilling to accept the likelihood of electoral defeat, García Moreno gained the support of key military garrisons and returned to power by coup d'etat. Requiring legitimacy for this new regime, García Moreno followed the now well developed Spanish American pattern; he convened a constituent assembly and packed it with supporters. Meeting in Quito in May 1869, the assembly adopted a theocratic charter, called by García Moreno's adversaries the "Black Charter of Slavery to the Vatican."[58]

In addition to the central political role given to the church and the outlawing of non-Catholic religious practice, the 1869 Constitution made citizenship dependent upon "being Catholic" (Art. 10, Sec. 1). Citizenship could be suspended for "membership in organizations prohibited by the Church" (Art. 13, Sec. 1). More generally, Ecuadoreans were afforded "the right of unarmed assembly, so long as they respect religion, morality and public order. Such associations are under the vigilance of the Government. No Catholic organizations established in the Republic may be closed or dissolved without the agreement of the Holy See" (Art. 109).

Beyond its theocratic and intolerant character, the 1869 Constitution increased still further the routine and extraordinary powers of the executive branch, extended the term of the presidency to six years, and allowed immediate reelection for one subsequent term (Art. 56). The country was divided into provinces, cantons, and parishes, with a governor, *jefe político,* and lieutenant serving as the appointed direct agent of the president in each of these jurisdictions. The president had authority over "whatever has as its purpose the conservation of internal order and external security, in conformity with, and assuring conformity with, the Constitution and the laws" (Art. 59). On his own initiative, and for the first time in Ecuadorean constitutional development, the president could declare a state of siege, in accord with the Congress or (if not in session) the council of state (composed of a church official, the president's ministerial appointees, one property owner eligible to serve in the Senate, and two judges). Such a declaration could occur when there was actual or threatened internal commotion or foreign attack. Thus, Ecuadorean conservatives established constitutional state of siege provisions seventeen years earlier than their Colombian counterparts (1886).

Under the state of siege provisions (Art. 61), the government could practically suspend all the *garantías* ritually extended to Ecuadoreans in the constitution (Arts. 87–110) and specifically could

> order the search of the residences of suspicious persons; take them prisoner, move them to other parts of the Republic, or exile them for a determined period of time; order the confiscation of ammunition and weapons and proceed with their discovery and seizure; prohibit publications or meetings that, in the government's judgment, favor or incite disorder; increase the size of the armed forces and call the national guard into service; impose a war tax on those who promote or support the foreign war or internal strife; subject authors, accomplices or supporters of the crimes or external attack or internal commotion to military law and impose the punishments specified under military regulations, even after the state of siege has ended.

The state of siege clause introduced most of the elements of martial law, with the exception of the right of military authorities to legislate and initiate policy on their own accord. It provided comprehensive foundations for constitutional dictatorship. García Moreno intended to assert civilian control: the constitution limited its definition of the military mission to "defense of the Republic and conservation of internal order." It also reiterated the familiar terminology stipulating that "the armed forces are essentially obedient, not deliberating" (Arts. 84, 85).

To avoid the risk of elections, the assembly allowed itself to name the next president and Supreme Court judges and to adopt, even after promulgation of the constitution, "the laws, decrees or resolutions it deems necessary" (Transitory Art. 117). Nominated president, García Moreno took office August 10, 1869; the nation's new national motto, which survived late into the twentieth century, became *Religión y Patria.*

In 1873, García Moreno had the Ecuadorean Congress dedicate the country to the Sacred Heart of Jesus.[59] Church officials and religious orders took charge of educational and health institutions. Great emphasis was placed on evangelical work among the Indian population. However, García Moreno also encouraged an important public works program, including a road network, both to move troops and to more effectively integrate the distinctive regions into a nation.

Unceasing opposition to García Moreno took the form of assassination plots, local uprisings, and even student revolts. In 1871, an Indian rebellion around Riobamba, incited by government intrusions into Indian life, brought the death of a number of tax collectors enforcing the new school tax. Government troops forcefully quelled the revolt after a number of towns suffered damage and looting by Indian forces.

Ecuadorean exiles in Peru and Panama also continually plotted against what liberal intellectual Juan Montalvo had called, in an inflammatory pamphlet, *La dictadura perpetua.*[60] He wrote: "García Moreno divided the people of Ecuador into three equal parts: one, he assigned to death, a second to exile [*destierro*], the last to servitude."[61] Montalvo proclaimed that "it is the duty of every [Latin] American to point out the traitors of the common fatherland, of every republican to fight despotism and its perpetuation, of every worthy man to rise up against iniquity.[62] The archbishop of Quito threatened to excommunicate persons reading the Montalvo pamphlet, but when García Moreno had himself reelected in 1875, a group of discontented liberals and young military officers plotted his assassination. He was murdered, after attending church, on August 6, 1875.

Ecuadorean Regimes of Exception after 1875

A struggle for power followed, both within the ranks of García Moreno's supporters and between them and liberal opponents. Antonio Borrero y Cortázar, a moderate liberal serving as interim president (1875–1876), attempted to reconcile conservative and liberal factions, promising to "protect the religion of our fathers" even as he rejected the 1869 Constitution and the use of extraordinary powers. Borrero proclaimed that "a government of popular and legitimate origins does not need, like tyrannical and oppressive governments, states of siege and *consejos de guerra,* . . . as the means to protect themselves from the conflicts that from time to time threaten them."[63]

Despite these noble sentiments, Borrero requested that the council of state, meeting in extraordinary session, invest him with extraordinary powers and allow declaration of a state of siege on May 9, 1876, to confront an insurrection. On September 11, 1876, the president again declared a state of siege in all the republic for four months.[64] Borrero resisted calls for a constituent assembly, fearing both the conservative and militant liberal factions. A prominent cabinet minister, Manuel Gómez de la Torre, declared, "We are in possession of the power, and we are not so innocent as to disarm ourselves of the ample faculties which the Constitution of García Moreno concedes to us."[65] Though the president boasted that civil liberties and rights were respected, the nation continued under state of siege.

Leading liberal caudillos and military officers returned from exile by 1876 and joined to overturn the interim regime. General Ignacio de Veintemilla, a graduate of the Colegio Militar created by Vicente Rocafuerte and commander of the Guayaquil garrison, headed the revolt initiated September 8, 1876. Borrero controlled Quito and declared the country under a state of siege; Veintemilla dominated the coast and the customs revenue over which so many Spanish American coups were fought in the nineteenth century. Military action was delayed while the rebels in Guayaquil awaited an arms shipment.

In Guayaquil the municipal council disavowed President Borrero's authority and that of the constitution. It accused Borrero of betraying liberal principles and refusing to abrogate the Black Charter of Slavery. On its own authority, it declared the 1861 Constitution in effect, named General Veintemilla *jefe supremo* of the nation and captain-general of its armies, and invested him with "full powers necessary for this effect" ("la suma de poderes que le fuese necesario para tal objeto").[66]

Veintemilla fit the mold of Spanish American military caudillos. He had served both conservative and liberal presidents, commanded garrisons in the capital and provinces, participated in mutinies and rebellions, lived in exile, and served in the presidential palace. President Borrero wrote of Veintemilla that [He] was "neither conservative nor liberal . . . he distinguishes perfectly between cognac and brandy, rum and gin; in Paris as in Quito he has lived gambling and drinking by night, sleeping by day." Unfortunately for Borrero, he also knew how to inspire loyalty from his troops, enthusiasm in the crowd, and adulation from "his women and camp followers."[67]

Veintemilla knew the importance of the customshouse and rebelled when Borrero sought to replace him as commander of the Guayaquil garrison. After deposing Borrero, he announced that the 1861 Constitution would replace that of 1869. Decrees in 1877 secularizing education, limiting political participation by the clergy, suspending the concordat with Rome, and reinstating the law of Gran Colombia (asserting government exercise of the *patronato*) provoked protests and rioting in Quito. The death of the archbishop by poisoning further inflamed the clericals and led to revolt.

Until the 1869 Constitution was officially replaced, Veintemilla used its martial law provisions to prosecute conservative opponents and prisoners. Conspiracies by conservatives to bring Borrero back from exile and supposed dangers of war with Colombia further justified repression. *Consejos de guerra* and extraordinary powers became the main instruments of government; imprisonment, exile, and occasional execution of opponents made clear the general's intent to hold on to power. Like his predecessors and Spanish American compatriots, he desired to formally legitimize his government. This required the orchestration of still another constituent assembly, convened in Ambato in July 1877. In 1878 it named Veintemilla interim president and in May adopted a new constitution. Before the constitutional convention adjourned, it had granted General Veintemilla extraordinary powers to deal with the supposed emergency situation facing the country.

The 1878 Constitution incorporated many of the principles of Spanish American liberalism in the nineteenth century, including abolition of the death penalty for political crimes, prohibition of immediate reelection, and expansion of the *garantías* of citizens. It also retained provisions for extensive extraordinary powers "in cases of internal commotion or foreign invasion" for limited times, places, and purposes but without the 1869 Constitution's state of siege clause (Arts. 80, 81). In certain respects these provisions were even more draconian than those of García Moreno, extending the period during which "suspects" could be detained without court appearance to ten days, allowing creation of military government "where the president finds it convenient," and permitting the president to use public funds at his discretion, except those designated for education or health (Art. 80).

An important innovation in the 1878 charter provided that "military officers shall not obey orders that have as their object attacks upon the national authorities or that are manifestly unconstitutional or illegal" (Art. 109). Not only would the usual regimes of exception be retained, but the military would, apparently, determine the legality and constitionality of civilian and military orders. Ecuador had formally introduced "judicial" review with bayonets. As had become customary, the constituent assembly designated the next president: General Veintemilla. Governing with extraordinary powers, Veintemilla resorted to progressively harsher and more arbitrary measures to maintain power, provoking anger from his past liberal allies as well as from conservatives and ex-allies of García Moreno. Prominent opponents not banished or sent into exile were sentenced to prison for sedition, conspiracy, or violations of the press laws. Some spent years in fetters (*grillos*).

The congressional elections in 1880 occurred under a regime of exception; Veintemilla delegated extraordinary powers to his provincial governors who, in turn, manipulated the elections and vote count. The elected Congress became a servile rubber stamp for the president.[68] Taking advantage of the increased customs receipts at Guayaquil as a result of the war between Chile and Peru (1879–1883), Veintemilla augmented the army and raised military salaries.

As the presidential elections approached, Veintemilla cynically renounced the extraordinary powers, only to have his sycophantic Congress reconcede them to him, ostensibly to meet the threat of war with Colombia. This took place without the formal executive request required by the constitution.[69] Unwilling to relinquish office at the end of his term, he staged an *autogolpe* in March 1882, with five months remaining. Pretenses of legitimacy were dropped as he established an outright dictatorship. An unlikely opposition coalition that included military officers seeking their turn in the presidency held itself together long enough to defeat Veintemilla. Overcome at Guayaquil in July 1883, the general went into exile on a British vessel and did not return to Ecuador until the first decade of the twentieth century.

A new government meant another succession constitution. It was delivered by a constituent assembly, which met in Quito from late October 1883 to early 1884. With more or less balanced representation between conservatives and liberals in the convention, the

1884 Constitution provided for a somewhat more significant legislative role, including annual sessions for sixty days. Extraordinary sessions still required convocation by the president. The constitution attempted to limit executive authority, with prohibitions on violations of the *garantías,* intervention in judicial proceedings, and dissolution of the Congress or suspension of its sessions (Art. 91).

Nevertheless, the Congress or, if not in session, the council of state could still concede vast extraordinary powers to the president in cases of "internal commotion or foreign invasion." Inclusion of two senators and one deputy from Congress in the council of state implied more control over the concession of such powers to the executive. The president was also prohibited from naming more generals and colonels to the army than authorized by Congress. Officers were again directed not to obey illegal or unconstitutional orders—a double-edged sword at best (Arts. 123, 127).

The 1884 Constitution was as close as Ecuador would come in the nineteenth century to controlling the executive and reducing the scope of constitutional regimes of exception. Three conservative civilian governments followed, including a presidential term for Antonio Flores, son of the country's first president (1888–1892). President José María Plácido Caamaño rededicated the country to the Sacred Heart of Jesus and resurrected other policies of García Moreno. From 1883 to 1887, he faced regional revolts and coup attempts headed by liberal leader General José Eloy Alfaro Delgado, who would later serve two terms as president (1895–1901, 1906–1911). The conservative oligarchy that ruled the country, virtually an extended family group of Caamaño and Flores kin called *la argolla* (the ring) by its critics, jailed, tortured, exiled, and executed liberal opponents.

In 1884, the council of state conceded President Caamaño extraordinary powers to suppress an uprising led by Alfaro. Ignoring the constitutional prohibition on capital punishment for political crimes, liberal opponents and guerrilla fighters (*montoneros*) were executed under military law. In 1886, Congress extended the death penalty to treason, arson, pillage, and piracy, thereby legalizing execution of political adversaries without recourse to military tribunals.[70]

The liberal uprisings and invasions from Peru continued into the next presidential term and were met again with concession of extraordinary powers to the president. Although political strife persisted and liberal guerrillas harassed the incumbent administrations into the 1890s, the Constitution of 1884 survived until 1897—longer than any constitution since the country's independence in

1830. The conservative restoration, like the governments of Flores and García Moreno and also the liberal governments prior to 1895, little tolerated opposition, made extensive use of extraordinary powers, and relied on the military and police to sustain their rule.

On June 5, 1895, before the presidential elections could be completed, mob violence and a liberal uprising in Guayaquil ended the domination of conservative governments. In a revolution financed by ascendant cacao interests on the coast, Alfaro returned from Central American exile, unilaterally abrogated the 1884 Constitution, and decreed the restoration of the 1878 charter. Opposition by the church hierarchy to the enemy knocking at the gates of the Republic of the Sacred Heart of Jesus presaged civil war—a religious, political, and military conflict. Withal, Alfaro's chaplain blessed the cannons of Alfaro's artillery and celebrated mass for the soon-to-be president.

Alfaro's liberalism produced attacks on church privilege but did not eschew repression. He formed a corps of *garroteros*, much like Rosas's *mazorca* in Buenos Aires or Díaz's *bravi* in Mexico—thugs operating as secret police to terrorize his opponents. In March 1896 he called for a convention to produce still another constitution that would, of course, legitimize the liberal revolution. Like his conservative enemies, Alfaro sought to pack the convention with supporters, forbid participation of the opposition (in this case particularly priests and religious), and control the elections to follow. Like the conservative military officers who preceded him in the presidency, the liberal General Alfaro needed a constitution to certify the legitimacy of the new regime and a constituent assembly to name him president. One day after the convention approved the 1897 Constitution, it named Eloy Alfaro president.

The 1897 Constitution changed church-state relations, but little else of significance. Constitutional dictatorship remained the heart of the body politic. Liberal authoritarianism, analogous to that of Mexico, had replaced the Republic of the Sacred Heart of Jesus. Opposition media was attacked and government-supported media subsidized. The government manipulated elections, ramrodded the Congress, and stacked the judiciary with loyalists after purging conservative judges. *Ley fuga* reigned. Revolts against the government occurred in 1897 and 1898, partly in response to new legislation adversely affecting the church. After a conservative revolt, the liberal government restored laws permitting confiscation of property belonging to insurgents.[71] In 1900, legislation creating civil registries for recording births, marriages, and deaths further angered the conservatives.

Despite the conservative opposition, Alfaro successfully orchestrated the election of General Leonidas Plaza Gutiérrez as his successor. The government candidate received 65,000 of the 75,000 votes cast. Plaza had served in the armies of El Salvador, Nicaragua, and Costa Rica and participated in the liberal forces that defeated Veintemilla at Guayaquil in 1883. He served in Alfaro's national assembly (1896–1897) and had also been governor of Azuay Province. He would again be president from 1912 to 1916.[72] Plaza attempted reconciliation and disbanded the secret police—but he broke with Alfaro, who carried out a coup in 1906 when Plaza's chosen candidate was selected president. From 1901 to 1916, insurrections reflecting factionalism within the liberal governments afflicted the country, even as the conservatives gradually accommodated themselves to electoral politics.

After the 1906 insurrection, Alfaro again ruled as *jefe supremo,* interim president, and constitutional president, after first calling for still another constitutional convention. The convention adopted a new charter in 1906. When Alfaro's chosen successor, coastal businessman Emilio Estrada, died in 1911 only months after taking office, it took five years of civil war to determine the next president. Liberals confronted each other, Alfaro against Leonidas Plaza and Julio Andrade. Fighting in 1912 left 3,000 dead; taken prisoner, Alfaro and other rebel leaders were dragged from a jail cell and murdered by a mob.[73] An assassin also killed Andrade, and Plaza became president for the second time (1912–1916).

Military garrisons and caudillos still decided who was president; from 1895 to 1920, military expenditures accounted for almost 30 percent of national budgets, exceeded only by debt service as the government became seriously indebted to private banks. Political violence was the rule; extraordinary powers and regimes of exception still legitimated tyranny. Every Ecuadorean constitution in the nineteenth century had provided for ample extraordinary powers, several for suspending enumerated civil liberties and rights, and one (1869) for a practically unlimited state of siege and martial law. Parallel to the regimes of exception, the constitutional mission of the armed forces compelled military officers to evaluate the constitutionality and legality of orders from civilians or superior officers. The armed forces' prominent role in politics had been constitutionally guaranteed.

Ecuador's last nineteenth-century constitution, in 1897, ratified a liberal revolution that secularized the state and reiterated the legal foundations for dictatorship (Arts. 94, 95, 98, 99, 125–31). The

1906 Constitution did the same (Arts. 80, 81, 83, 84, 97, 117–23). Succession constitutions in 1925, 1938, 1945 (after the restoration of the 1906 charter), and 1946 reconfirmed the tradition, as did Ecuador's 1978 Constitution (Art. 78, Sec. n). In the nineteenth century, the juridical foundations of dictatorship were firmly embedded in Ecuadorean constitutional law—as they would also be in neighboring Peru and Bolivia. They endured into the 1990s, despite further reforms during the twentieth century.

As Ecuador entered the last decade of the twentieth century, the president could declare a state of "national emergency" to meet external threats and grave internal commotion or catastrophe. He could suspend all constitutional *garantías* except the right to life and prohibitions on involuntary exile (Art. 78). He also had decree powers for economic emergencies that approximated the expansive Venezuelan and Mexican presidential prerogatives. The armed forces remained the guardians of the constitution and the arbiters of national politics (Art. 128). As elsewhere in Spanish America, Ecuador's nineteenth-century foundations of constitutional dictatorship legitimated twentieth-century political repression.

6

Regimes of Exception in Peru and Bolivia

ALMOST A DECADE AFTER VENEZUELANS PROCLAIMED INDEPENDENCE from Spain and adopted South America's first republican constitution, an Argentine general heading a predominantly Chilean army and supported by naval forces commanded by a British officer proclaimed independence for Peru. Even then, the center of royal authority and military power remained ambiguously independent until the Argentine, José de San Martín, stepped aside (1822) and permitted the Colombian armies of Simón Bolívar and José Antonio de Sucre to invade from the north, defeating Spanish forces in the Andean highlands. At Ayacucho in December 1824, General Sucre's combined force of Colombians, Peruvians, freed slaves, and mulattos defeated the army of Peru's last viceroy, José de la Serna. A hopeless last stand by royalists besieged in Callao, Lima's port, ended with Spanish capitulation in January 1826. But support for Spain, the king, and the traditional order persisted; fear of republicanism, liberalism, and disorder permeated the upper strata of Peruvian society.[1]

From the first signs of rebellion in Upper Peru (later Bolivia) in 1809, Peruvian Viceroy José Fernando de Abascal began reorganizing administrative jurisdictions and expanding royalist military capabilities. On his own initiative, and at times blatantly resisting the *cortes* at Cádiz, he reestablished order over the Upper Peruvian provinces in 1810, though they were formally assigned to officials in Buenos Aires. He then reinforced the army in Guayaquil (1812) and sent an army against rebels in Chile (1813).

Abascal also eventually defeated the *criollo* and Indian armies that had sacked cities and slaughtered the garrison at La Paz in 1814. The "rebellion of Pumacahua," named for the aged Indian cacique who had fought on the Spanish side against Túpac Amaru in the 1780s and now joined *criollo* dissidents opposing royalists policies, left many Peruvian *criollos* convinced again that Spanish imperialism was preferable to Indian rebellions.[2] The restoration of absolute monarchy in Spain and the abrogation of the 1812 Constitution (1814–1820) coincided with vigorous viceregal repression of rebels in Peru. Abascal retired in 1816, proud of his contributions to the monarchical cause and still disdainful of liberal principles and demands for reform of the colonial regime.

Most Peruvian *criollos* had no desire for independence. The extension of warfare, banditry, and sedition from the independence struggles of the Rio de la Plata region into Upper Peru caused anxiety among elites who depended primarily upon patronage in the royal bureaucracy, colonial commercial monopolies, stringent export-import controls, and hegemony over Chile and other subordinate jurisdictions. Free trade meant loss of captive markets, increases in prices of food imports required to sustain Lima, and "unfair" competition from northern ports, such as Guayaquil, or southern ports, such as Valparaíso. Added to the decades-long decline of mining and commerce, the short-term economic dilemmas in Lima intensified Peru's dependence upon the imperial system rather than generating support for the liberal reforms demanded in Buenos Aires, Chile, or Venezuela.[3]

In short, most Peruvian elites had much to lose and much to fear from independence. Even those *criollos* significantly influenced by the liberal principles of the Enlightenment seemed to prefer concessions and reforms on the part of Spain—more jobs, more influence in peninsular affairs, more opportunity for social mobility, and more protection against the so-called dangerous classes (Indians, blacks, and *castas*)—to independence.

The Lima *criollo* elite shared a desperate fear of social revolution and race war with their Mexican counterparts. Memory of the thousands dead and the widespread devastation and ferocity of the Túpac Amaru revolt of the 1780s made the "Indian danger" a central concern. In Peru, "conserving internal order" meant much more than controlling bandits or rebels; it was an easily decoded message to "whites" that Indian insurrection always threatened.[4] The conscription and arming of black slaves from the countryside near Lima by San Martín in his campaign against the royalists from 1821 to 1822 further frightened Peruvian landowners and urban elites. Devastation of rural estates by roving bandits and rebel troops heightened their anxiety.

In contrast to Mexico, however, foreign troops would liberate Peru and impose republican regimes instead of allowing the creation of a conservative empire such as that forged by Iturbide from 1821 to 1823 (see chapter 3). In the words of Timothy Anna, "The event was accomplished, the deed was done, the Peruvians still had not decided."[5]

In contrast, although the creation and independence of Bolivia was closely connected to that of Peru, rebellions in Upper Peru preceded the movements in Venezuela and Buenos Aires that ultimately separated the southern provinces and northern South American colonies from Spanish rule. The first declaration of independence by an American colony of Spain, albeit in the name of the deposed King Ferdinand VII, was by a junta in La Paz in July 1809. Suppressed shortly after by troops from Cuzco, this first autonomist movement resulted in the execution of its principal leaders and the exile of more than a hundred "rebels."[6]

Officially part of the viceroyalty of Buenos Aires since the administrative reforms of the late eighteenth century, Upper Peru also suffered repression by an army from Rio de la Plata. Into the mid-1820s, royal armies struggled to control the urban centers of Upper Peru while guerrilla forces and bandits controlled much of the countryside. As the independence movement in Buenos Aires gained strength and rebels invaded Upper Peru, the highlands served frequently as a battlefield.[7] Distributing arms to Indian allies by both royalists and rebels eventually resulted in increased levels of violence and Indian uprisings. After 1816, however, royalists regained control of most of the region.

Both royalists and supporters of independence in Peru and Buenos Aires viewed Upper Peru as potentially part of their administrative jurisdiction or national territory. After 1776, Upper Peru pertained to the viceroyalty of the Rio de la Plata; due to war, troops from Peru, the viceroyalty to which the mines of Potosí and the towns of the highlands had belonged through most of the colonial period, had reoccupied the territory.

Ironically, the royal commander in Upper Peru, the *criollo* Pedro Olañeta, precipitated the separation of what became Bolivia from the last bastion of royal authority in Peru. Olañeta despised the liberal military officers sent from Spain to Peru from 1821 to

1823 and opposed the restored Constitution of Cádiz even more than had Viceroy Abascal. In February 1824, Olañeta proclaimed an absolute monarchy in Chuquisaca in the name of Fernando VII, overthrew the Spanish constitution, and named himself "Commander of the Provinces of the Rio de la Plata." At Ayacucho in December 1824, the royalist forces defeated by Sucre vainly waited for reinforcements from Olañeta. Olañeta even engaged in minor battles against his royalist compatriots while reserving his forces to fight against the rebels. General Sucre, the victorious commander at Ayacucho, went after Olañeta in Upper Peru. After convincing many of Olañeta's troops to mutiny, Sucre defeated the remaining royalist forces. Olañeta, indirectly the founder of Bolivia, died in battle against mutinous troops in early 1825.[8]

This left Upper Peru in the hands of Sucre, at the orders of Bolívar, and submerged in the chaotic regionalism and personalism that had resulted from more than fifteen years of war and intrigue. Local and regional elites, preferring autonomy to subordination to either Peru or Buenos Aires, prevailed upon Sucre to create an independent nation; in 1825, delegates meeting in Chuquisaca declared Upper Peru independent. Dr. Casimiro Olañeta, nephew of the general defeated by Sucre, renounced his royalist ties and became a key Sucre adviser and intermediary between local elites and the Colombian expeditionary force. To assure Bolívar's support, the constituent assembly named the new republic Bolívar, later changed to Bolivia. What had once been the colonial *audiencia* of Charcas was now the Republic of Bolivia. This region, first to proclaim independence, would be the most chaotic polity in South America during the remainder of the nineteenth century.

Immediately after independence, both Bolivia and Peru experienced short-lived dictatorships by Bolívar followed by more than half a century of political violence, instability, and constitutional experimentation. Attempts by caudillos in Peru and Bolivia to unite these territories, or to append part of Bolivia to Peru, made it difficult to disentangle domestic from international politics into the 1840s. The short-lived Peru-Bolivia Confederation (1836–1839) of General Andrés Santa Cruz, the self-styled Napoleon of South America, provoked war with Argentina and Chile, leaving both Peru and Bolivia the worse for Santa Cruz's South American version of manifest destiny.

Always, however, *criollo* elites and urban dwellers in these two republics lived in fear of Indian rebellion, racial conflicts, and uprisings of the poorer classes. Thus, the debates over federalism versus centralism, legislative versus executive dominance, the role of the church, and other institutional issues were often subordinate to concerns over civil-military relations and struggles to ensure law and order. In these struggles the protagonists were often military officers from the generation of Ayacucho, those who had fought in the independence wars and would dominate Peruvian and Bolivian politics into the 1860s. The geographical isolation of Andean towns, the difficulty of communication and transportation, and the survival of localism made the dispersed garrisons the key political actors and resources in the first sixty years of independence.

As in Central America, constitutional debates and reforms were confounded by the immediate politics of presidential succession. Principled debates over legislative versus presidential authority, especially over limits on executive power and control of appointment of military officers and other public officials, could not be separated from the personal antagonisms and passions of the moment. Usually military victories rather than political philosophy or elections determined the outcome.

Neither Peru nor Bolivia established effective civilian governments until late in the nineteenth century; government by, and constitutional provision for, regimes of exception characterized politics in these two republics from the moment of independence. Peru would have the dubious distinction of initiating its independent existence under a regime of exception and suspending its first constitution on adoption. During the first sixteen years of independence, Peru adopted five constitutions: 1823, 1826, 1828, 1834, and 1839. Peruvian executives would never be without extraordinary powers to confront emergencies, and the military became the most important political institution in the country.

In Bolivia, independence meant a temporary dictatorship under the Bolivarian Constitution of 1826, followed by recurrent changes of government and constitutions from 1826 to 1880: 1831, 1834, 1839, 1843, 1851, 1861, 1871, 1878, and 1880. Bolivia's first national constitution, promulgated by Santa Cruz in 1831, allowed for "the suspension of any of the formalities of the constitution or the law" when "the security of the Republic requires" (Art. 132). Extraordinary powers could be conceded to the president to confront invasion or "internal commotion" (Arts. 74, 75). No Bolivian government after 1831 would lack this flexibility. Regimes of exception and de facto dictatorships became the rule.

INDEPENDENCE AND REGIMES OF EXCEPTION
IN PERU

Constitutional development in Peru began during the wars of independence, with the 1821 proclamations of General San Martín that established temporary military dictatorships. This was followed by the short "Bases de la Constitución Política de la República Peruana" issued by the Supreme Government Junta in 1822. San Martín's Provisional Statute of October 1821 concentrated all power in "the Protector" (that is, San Martín) whose authority derived "from the rule of necessity, force, and reason and the requirements of public welfare" (Art. 1). As generalissimo of land and sea forces, "the Protector" had as his primary duty the liberation of all parts of the Peruvian territory and could "increase or decrease the size of the armed forces as deemed necessary" (Art. 2). This all-powerful executive could also impose taxes, request "voluntary" contributions, and exact forced loans to pay for public expenses. "The Protector" also could appoint and remove all public officials.

The Provisional Statute defined as "treason" and "sedition" almost any resistance to government policy (Art. 3). Formation of any "secret association opposed to the legitimate authority" was outlawed. Freedom of the press was authorized, subject to future regulations (Arts. 3, 4). Obviously a wartime effort to legitimate martial law, the Provisional Statute nevertheless provided insight into the authoritarian premises of certain independence leaders and *criollo* elites. Over time, less severe versions of such constitutional regimes of exception would compete with idealistic liberal principles amid the political violence and rapid-fire constitution making and unmaking that characterized Peru into the 1880s.

San Martín lacked both the predisposition and the will to govern Peru. In failing health, and with Spanish troops still a threat, he traveled to Guayaquil to plan with Bolívar the forthcoming military campaign against the Spanish armies in Peru and Upper Peru. Dissatisfied with his conversations with Bolívar, San Martín arrived in Peru and returned political power to the constituent Congress. He left shortly after for Chile and then, via Argentina, went into self-imposed exile in Europe, which left Peru up for grabs.

There would be no lack of potential takers for the next fifty years. The 1822 Bases de la Constitución Política de la República Peruana declared that Peru's to-be-adopted constitution should protect liberty, freedom of the press, personal security and inviolability of the home, property rights, equality before the law, and privacy of correspondence (Art. 9).[9] The document also didactically asserted the main tenets of French and North American liberalism—separation of powers, need for an independent judiciary, taxation to be imposed only by the legislature, and a prohibition on life-tenure executives.

Recognizing the pivotal role of the military, it also declared "there will be armed forces as determined by Congress each year. Their purpose will be to maintain the external and internal security of the State, at the orders of the Executive Power." Before the constituent assembly had even elaborated a constitution for Peru, it decreed a central political role for the new nation's armed forces. Even so, few of the members of the assembly could have suspected that no civilian president would govern Peru until the 1870s.

War continued to ravage the highlands; Lima suffered alternating occupations and raids by rebels and royalists. Pressured by military setbacks and the rebel army, the constituent Congress dissolved the governing junta that had replaced San Martín. On February 27, 1823, it appointed José de la Riva Agüero as Peru's first president. With misgivings, Riva Agüero requested assistance from Bolívar who sent 4,000 troops commanded by Sucre. Thus began the intervention that culminated the independence struggle at Ayacucho in 1824 and in Upper Peru in 1825.

Constitutional Development, 1823–1839

Before the decisive battle at Ayacucho, the Congress pondered a constitution for Peru. Royalist troops briefly retook Lima, and the Peruvian Congress, under pressure from mutinous and unpaid troops of the Lima garrison, dispensed with the president, naming Sucre supreme commander of the combined Colombian and Peruvian forces and assigning him broad executive powers (*amplias facultades*). Arguably, the first of Peru's civil-military *golpes* had ousted the nation's first president and imposed the first of many regimes of exception.

In August a group of congressmen named the Marquis de Torre Tagle president. Riva Agüero and his supporters in the Congress refused to accept this decision. Peru had two presidents, a supreme military commander, a Spanish viceroy, and a royal army— all waiting for Bolívar, the Liberator, to play the leading role in the final act of the drama.[10] With the military situation deteriorating for the rebels in Peru and Upper Peru during most of the next year, the Peruvian Congress conferred upon Bolívar "the highest military and political authority with the power required by the difficult circumstances." In November 1823 the constituent Congress, dominated by liberal sentiment, approved Peru's first constitution. Unique among the Spanish American nations, the first constitution of Peru itself was promulgated subject to a regime of exception. Congress declared that "implementation of the constitutional articles incompatible with the authority and power conferred upon Bolívar as Liberator would be postponed [*quedaba en suspenso el cumplimiento*]."[11]

Barely implemented, and then only briefly in 1827, this constitution nevertheless merits the same attention as the Apatzingán Constitution (1814) in Mexico (see chapter 3). Both charters reveal the idealism and contradictions of nineteenth-century Spanish American liberalism. Similar also in many ways to the first constitutions in northern South America (1811–1814), Peru's 1823 Constitution proclaimed that sovereignty resided essentially in the nation and its exercise in the officials to whom power had been delegated. It established a tripartite separation of powers in the tradition of Montesquieu rather than that of the North American experiment, with a dominant legislature—but in a presidential rather than parliamentary regime.

The constitution afforded to Peruvians (including the majority of Indians, free blacks, and *castas* who would never see or comprehend the document) all the common liberal rights and liberties, even adding the right to resist oppression.[12] It also reflected the tentativeness of Peruvian liberalism: all members of the Congress were required to take an oath "to defend the Catholic Religion . . . and prevent the exercise of all others in the Republic" (Art. 52).[13] Ominously, it also stated: "If the Nation does not conserve or protect the legitimate rights of the individuals who form it, the social contract is assailed; anyone who violates any of its fundamental laws loses the protection of this pact" (Art. 4).

Unlike the largely symbolic influence of the Mexican 1814 charter, this first expression of Peruvian liberalism contributed a highly significant, ironic, and lasting element to Peruvian politics. Article 60 (Sec. 27) charged the Congress with "protecting freedom of the press in a fashion that its exercise may not be suspended or abolished." This required an "organic law," which the constituent Congress promulgated with the constitution in November 1823. The first section of the press law declared that all Peruvians "have the right to manifest their ideas in the press . . . with the exception of publications referring to the Holy Writings, religious dogma, religious morality, and discipline of the Church" (Art. 2).

Of even greater long-term political significance, Article 6 listed as "abuses of press freedom" the following: "publication of maxims or doctrines that directly conspire to overturn or destroy the religion of the republic or its political constitution; publication of doctrines or maxims that tend to incite rebellion or perturbation of public tranquility; direct incitement to disobey any law or legitimate authority; promoting such disobedience through invective or satire." These "abuses of press freedom" were subject to criminal sanctions of varying severity (Arts. 9–24). For example, an article considered "subversive in the first degree" could lead to a jail sentence of six years, "subversive in the second degree" to four years, and "subversive in the third degree" to two years (Art. 16).

This "organic law," with later amendments in procedures for a posteriori censorship and penalties for so-called abuses of press freedom, survived subsequent constitutional reforms and adoption of new constitutions. It provided permanent government authority for repressing political adversaries and opposition media into the twentieth century.[14] Combined with the provisions for suspension of constitutional *garantías* and the executive authority required to conserve internal order and repress subversion included in later constitutions, the press law was an important contribution of the independence era liberals to constitutional dictatorship in Peru.

The 1823 Constitution provided for a president to be elected for four years (and forbade immediate reelection) by Congress from among candidates selected by a body called the Senado Conservador. Composed of representatives of the provinces elected to twelve-year terms, this Senado was also responsible for supervising compliance with the constitution and the laws and, at the request of the president, determining the "responsibility" of the executive power or Supreme Court for "abuses of power" (Art. 90). The Congress retained budgetary and tax power and authority to create militias and determine the size of the armed forces. Executive authority extended to "all matters related to conservation of internal order and external security, subject to the Constitution and the law" (Art. 79). As supreme commander of the armed forces, the president could appoint all officers from the rank of colonel and above and command the armed forces in person, but in both cases only with the consent of Congress. The only emergency power afforded the president was the authority "if demonstrably required by public security" to arrest or detain persons and put them at the disposition of a judge within twenty-four hours. This clearly represented much more limited extraordinary powers than typically encountered by the mid-1820s in Spanish America.

In contrast to the early constitutions of northern South America and Mexico, the first Peruvian constitution included a lengthy description and definition of the role of the armed forces. The constitution eliminated the military *fueros* in spirited language proclaiming that "every soldier is nothing more than an armed citizen in defense of the Republic" (Art. 179). However, the constitution established three distinct types of armed forces—army, civic militia, and police guards—each with its own constitutional mission. These missions were, respectively, internal security, public security, and "private" security (ridding the roads of bandits and pursuing delinquents). In the case of "declared revolution" or "invasion," any of these three forces could be deployed as needed, with the consent of the Congress or, if in recess, of the Senado Conservador. Even if the liberal constituents failed to recognize the utopian nature of certain aspects of their charter, they accurately anticipated the central challenges of Peruvian politics: ridding the roads from Lima of bandits, conserving internal order, and establishing political stability.

In February 1824 the Congress reaffirmed that, due to the exigencies of the war of liberation, supreme power would remain with Bolívar and all constitutional articles, decrees, and legislation incompatible with Bolívar's military, executive, and legislative authority remained "suspended." Congress then declared itself in recess. The following February, meeting as scheduled, Congress again extended Bolívar's temporary dictatorship and authorized him to legislate concerning the organization of the republic.[15]

The Bolivarian Constitution

In 1826 Bolívar proposed a new constitution for Peru, the *constitución vitalicia*, or constitution with a lifetime presidency. Bolívar still dreamed of uniting Peru, Bolivia, and Gran Colombia into a vast republic under his direction. By the time the Peruvian Congress reviewed the *constitución vitalicia*, it had already received approval in Bolivia (see below). Over the objections of Ramón Castilla, later president, the Congress approved Bolívar's constitution and the council of state decreed it the law of the land on November 30, 1826. But on January 27, 1827, an uprising in Lima overturned this constitution, reinstituted the 1823 Constitution, and called for a constituent assembly. Bolívar had already left Peru. His adversaries in Peru and Colombia made impossible his exercise of executive authority in Peru and, soon, in Colombia as well.

The 1826 Bolivarian Constitution incorporated some elements of the Venezuelan Angostura Constitution of 1819 (see chapter 5) and added a much more centralist and authoritarian administrative regime. In Bolívar's view, this constitution combined the best attributes of monarchy and democracy, guaranteeing civil liberties and rights and also ensuring maintenance of law and order.[16] To ensure this order, the 1826 Constitution included a variety of regimes of exception and gave the lifetime executive overwhelming authority. The legislative branch, divided into three chambers—tribunes, senators, and censors—was created through indirect elections by strictly qualified electors. It was to meet for two months each year and could not convoke itself or legislate without the presence of 50 percent plus one of its members (Art. 39). Among its general powers, the legislature could "invest the President, in times of war or extraordinary danger, with those powers deemed indispensable for the salvation of the State" (Art. 30, Sec. 5).

The constitution also gave the president ample authority without congressional delegation of extraordinary powers. This included dismissal of the vice president and all ministers; adoption of regulations and ordinances for better enforcement of the constitution and the laws; personal command, in war and peace, of the armed forces; and deployment of the national militia. The president could also appoint all army and navy officers, establish military schools, grant pensions to the families of retired officers, and suspend any public official for three months (Art. 83). The constitution did prohibit the president from arresting persons, confiscating property, and interfering with elections (Art. 84). Bolívar sought order, not tyranny; constitutional dictatorship, if necessary, not blatant despotism. Thus, the "suspension of the constitution or of the rights corresponding to Peruvians, can only occur in the circumstances stipulated in this Constitution, and only with specification of the time during which such a suspension is to last" (Art. 50).

On the role of the military in Peru or Bolivia, the 1826 Constitution had little to say except that "there will be in the Republic permanent armed forces composed of an army, navy, and, in each province, a corps of national militia" (Arts. 134–36). The constitution also established a military reserve (*resguardo*) to combat clandestine commerce (Art. 137). Bolívar's constitution endured only briefly, but its assertion that there would be a permanent armed force in the republic proved correct. The armed forces would consistently play a central role in Peruvian politics well into the twentieth century.

Bolívar recognized the futility of his continued leadership in Peru or Bolivia when he left for Colombia in late 1826. The personal ambitions of Peruvian and Bolivian caudillos, emergent nationalism like that in Ecuador, and the complexity of regional and local conflicts prevented consolidation of centralized authority over northern South America and the central Andes. Bolívar even counseled certain supporters, such as Andrés Santa Cruz, in Peru and Bolivia, to "forget plans for America" and to ride the rising tide of nationalism.[17] In early 1827, mutinies among the Colombian troops stationed in Lima and widespread political unrest presaged an end to Bolívar's influence in Peru.

An interim government under General Santa Cruz convened a constituent Congress in extraordinary session, operating theoretically under the provisions of the 1823 Constitution. Santa Cruz (1826–1827) lost the presidency to General José de La Mar (1827–1829), appointed by the constituent Congress for a term of four years. General La Mar had been born in Cuenca, Ecuador, and General Santa Cruz in Bolivia. Both had served as officers in the Spanish army. The struggle for power among Santa Cruz, La Mar, and other caudillos continued for the next decade.[18]

Constitutional Change, 1828–1839

Despite the passionate arguments for federalism, the constituent Congress of 1827, faced with internal instability, the threats of war with Colombia, Ecuador, and Bolivia, and the shadow of Bolívar, adopted a centralist constitution in 1828. It included provisions mandating a convention in five years to consider constitutional reform, thereby forcing a constitutional debate in 1833. It also introduced provincial juntas in the tradition of the 1812 Spanish Constitution, a concession to proponents of federalism and increased local autonomy.

Mindful of the dangers of presidential excesses and the recent experience with Bolívar, the constituent assembly provided that "the exercise of the presidency may not be for a life-term nor inherited." Instead, the president was given a four-year term, with immediate reelection permitted for one additional term (Art. 84). The charter also required Peruvian birth of the president, so as to exclude caudillos such as Juan José Flores, Andrés Santa Cruz, and José de La Mar of Ecuador and Bolivia from the contest for political power in Peru (Art. 85). In this it failed miserably; these foreign-born military leaders, and others, plotted, warred, and governed from 1828 until the 1860s.

Peruvian constitutional scholars frequently note the influence of the U.S. Constitution on the constituent assembly that adopted the 1828 Peruvian document. Bolívar and other more conservative *criollos* were appalled by the supposed consequences of federal experiments in Mexico, Central America, and Argentina. Writing to his colleague, General O'Leary, Bolívar called federalism "the obligation to fragmentation and the ruin of the State." He added: "I believe it would be better for our America to adopt the Koran rather than the government of the United States, even if it were the best in the world."[19]

Though concerned with the limits of presidential power, Peruvian elites preferred order to exaggerated liberalism. The 1828 Constitution gave the president authority to command the armed forces and militia in times of international threat or internal subversion. He was also to ensure internal security, to name military officers from the rank of colonel and above, subject to legislative confirmation, and to review the decisions of military tribunals (Art. 90). The legislature could confer extraordinary powers upon the president for specified periods, when required by public security—with a two-thirds vote in both houses of the Congress (Art. 48, Sec. 23).

This last requirement, along with prohibitions against presidential postponement of elections or suspension of legislative sessions, indicated a particular concern with control over executive authority and emergency powers (Art. 91). In this respect, the 1828 Constitution reflected an effort by the liberals to strengthen the relative position of the legislature in Peruvian politics. However, the constitution created both the crimes of "sedition" and "attack upon public security" and assigned directly to the armed forces the constitutional mission of assuring internal order and enforcement of the laws of the land (Arts. 48, Sec. 23; Arts. 145, 169). Even in its most liberal moment, the Peruvian elite anticipated that the need would arise to invoke emergency powers, to declare regimes of exception, and to use the armed forces to put down seditious movements, guarantee public security, and defend law and order.

The assembly that adopted the 1828 Constitution also recognized the fragility of its creation. Article 177 stipulated that in July 1833 a national convention would convene to review and reform the 1828 charter, in part or entirely. In 1833 the caudillo-president of the moment, Agustín Gamarra, who had prevailed against numerous mutinies, rebellions, and conspiracies,[20] summoned an extraordinary session of the Congress parallel to the constitutional convention. This meant that the upcoming presidential elections and the recurrent civil strife overshadowed debates over constitutional principles.

Few changes were made to the 1828 Constitution, but the overall thrust was to further restrict presidential authority and to prohibit immediate reelection. Of particular importance, the constitution eliminated the president's unilateral control over appointments of prefects, subprefects, police commanders, and other public officials, as well as his authority to promote military officers and expand the officer corps. This reform undercut the key props of the political system: patronage, clientelism, and praetorianism.

Constitutional reform was complicated by the battle over presidential succession and marred by a *pronunciamiento* by General Pedro Pablo Bermúdez, the government's candidate to succeed Gamarra. In part, the Bermúdez *autogolpe,* supported by Gamarra, responded to a plot by liberal leader Francisco Javier de Luna Pizarro to arrange a confederation with Bolivia and impose General Santa Cruz as president.[21] The inability of the Congress to comply in a timely fashion with the indirect elections of the next president called for by the 1828 Constitution also precipitated the uprising. When Gamarra's term ended, the national convention designated General Luis José de Orbegoso president, rather than Gamarra's candidate, General Pedro Pablo Bermúdez.

Questioning the legality of this action, Gamarra reminded the Congress that "public security is the supreme law of states" and that Peru's public security would vanish the moment that the "legitimate authority left office and was replaced by a usurper installed by the spirit of faction and intrigue [the Congress]."[22] After unsuccessful efforts to resolve personal and political differences with Orbegoso, Bermúdez and Gamarra resorted to force. The attempted military coup led to violent confrontations between troops and civilians in Lima.[23] The convention delegated extraordinary powers to Orbegoso to deal with the crisis. Once again routine politics could not produce government succession; the legislators turned to a regime of exception.

Temporarily victorious over Orbegoso, Bermúdez decreed deportation of prominent liberal leaders and suspended legislative sessions "until the legal order [could] be restored."[24] The coup attempt degenerated into civil war as civilian resistance in Lima and

support for the government by military opponents to Gamarra and
Bermúdez restored Orbegoso.

Another constitution followed. From the time of its adoption in
June 1834 until Peru joined Bolivia in an ill-fated confederation
under General Santa Cruz (1836–1839), no government was able to
control the country. Military coup followed military coup as the
personalist ambitions of the caudillos led to frequent uprisings, interim presidents, and political chaos. Regimes of exception became
the rule, as did the expectation that military officers rather than
civilians determined the destiny of the nation. Despite the chaotic
political situation, the 1834 Constitution provided a certain continuity of basic principles. This included a moderate liberalism, a
slightly expanded list of *garantías*, continued concern with legislative controls over the budget and executive authority, and reliance
upon regimes of exception to meet political crises.

Article 51 (Sec. 27) iterated, in clearer language, the legislative
delegation of *facultades extraordinarias* to the executive to combat sedition or invasion enunciated in Article 48 (Sec. 23) of the 1828
Constitution. The language regarding the role of the armed forces
in maintaining internal order and upholding the laws was identical.
So, too, was the ritualistic prescription: "the armed forces are essentially obedient; they may not deliberate" (Arts. 139, 140). One
important addition, however, stipulated that "any act of Congress . . . or the Executive Power, taken under the influence of military intervention or popular tumult, is null" (Art. 174). The
constitution did not specify who would determine that such an
event had occurred, leaving the decision, in practice, to the military
caudillo able to secure temporary control of the government. In effect, victorious military commanders could engage in the functional
equivalent of judicial review of presidential and congressional acts.

In a comparative sense, Peruvian provision for regimes of exception in both the 1828 and 1834 constitutions was more restrictive than in many parts of Spanish America. Executives had no
constitutional authority to suspend the constitution, to declare a regime of exception unilaterally, or to suspend operation of the legislature. Whatever the reality of Peruvian politics during this
period, a reality hopelessly mired in caudillismo and incessant civil-
military coup making, the juridical foundations of constitutional
dictatorship remained relatively narrow and emphasized legislative control.

In contrast, the political role of the armed forces was clearer
and more overt in Peru than in most of South America. The mili-

tary caudillos of the "generation of Ayacucho" dominated national politics, while policy and constitutional debates concerning the role and the relative autonomy of the armed forces received more attention than debates on the extent of extraordinary powers of the executive or provisions relating to suspension of constitutional *garantías*. This would remain true into the 1880's.[25] Not until 1872 would Peru have its first civilian president.

Significantly, the country's first major political party called itself *civilista*. Civil-military relations, intramilitary feuds and personal antagonisms, assassinations of presidents, former presidents, and ministers, and recurrent local uprisings made even the provisions for constitutional exception less important in Peru than was the control of the barracks and armories.

Meanwhile, from 1836 to 1839 Peruvian politics became enmeshed again with those of Bolivia. Santa Cruz, now the dictator of Bolivia, constructed the Peru-Bolivia Confederation in collaboration with Orbegoso and other allies of convenience in Peru. This confederation, composed of the State of South Peru, the State of North Peru, and Bolivia, conferred in quasi-constitutions "the exercise of the sum total of all State Power in the hands of His Excellency, Captain General, Supreme Chief of the United Army, Andrés Santa Cruz, with the title of 'Supreme Protector.' "[26]

This temporary confederation, destroyed in part by war with Chile and Argentina and in part by opponents within Peru and Bolivia who joined the invading Chilean armies, was an aberration in Peruvian development. The so-called constitutions of this confederation lacked even the formal appearance of Spanish American constitutions since the example of Cádiz in 1812. They added nothing to Peruvian constitutional evolution, though the comprehensive powers of the Protector were reminiscent of Bolívar's *constitución vitalicia*.

The Constitution of 1839

With the dissolution of the Peru-Bolivia Confederation, the military victors, headed by former president Agustín Gamarra, attempted to purge Santa Cruz's supporters from the army and government. They also sought to overcome the perceived weaknesses of the 1823, 1828, and 1834 constitutions by imposing a more centralized, authoritarian, and executive-dominated political regime. Having "seen the liberal charters shredded and the nightmare of international and civil wars, the desire for peace and order predominated."[27]

A constituent Congress meeting in Huancayo in August 1839 named Gamarra, who with Ramón Castilla had allied himself with the Chileans against Santa Cruz, the provisional president. The Congress also adopted repressive measures against future revolutionaries and those guilty of "sedition" or "conspiracy." Sanctions for these crimes included confiscation of property, exile, and loss of citizenship. One of the decrees even stipulated that "those who maintain correspondence with the exiles and those who carry the correspondence and do not deliver it to the prefect of the department, will be considered seditious."[28]

Unlike the yearlong debates preceding adoption of the earlier constitutions, it took the postwar constituent Congress only three months to devise a new charter for Peru. The spirit of the new constitution and its focus on order and pacification were made clear in the provisions for loss of citizenship for "armed rebellion or popular sedition against the government and constituted authorities" (Art. 10). The constitution also eliminated the right of habeas corpus and the requirement that a judicial order precede deportation. In 1839, the romantic liberalism of the independence period gave way to the conservative appeal to order, while legislative dominance succumbed to that of the president.

In comparison with earlier constitutions, executive authority was significantly expanded and the presidential term extended to six years (Art. 78). The Congress could determine that "the Republic was in danger" and concede to the executive the powers necessary to "save it" (Art. 55, Sec. 26). In addition to any extraordinary powers conferred when the "Fatherland is in danger," the president was to maintain internal order and external security, using the armed forces and militia as required in cases of sedition (Art. 87, Secs. 1, 12, 14). A new council of state, which might include as many as three military officers and three ecclesiastics among its fifteen congressionally appointed members, could also declare when the fatherland was in danger and grant the president "whatever specific powers [were] necessary to save it" (Art. 103, Sec. 4). In times of "political tumult" this council could function with only eight members and "take whatever measures suitable to save the Fatherland" (Art. 109). The president could also suspend or transfer any public official for up to three months when this "serves the public interest" (Art. 87, Sec. 10). This clause made the entire public administration a personalist satrapy; every military officer and bureaucrat chose among fealty, renunciation, and rebellion.

Each of these new instruments provided broad, vague, and almost unlimited authority to suspend constitutional guarantees or otherwise govern under a comprehensive regime of exception. The 1839 Constitution also dropped any pretense of local government by dividing the country into departments, provinces, and districts whose administrators were named by the president. In each province and district the chief administrative officer acted as police commander (*intendente de policía*) "to maintain order and public safety" and "to enforce the constitution, the laws of congress, and the decrees and orders of the Executive Power" (Art. 139, Secs. 1, 2; Art. 143).

Moreover, the president could delegate extraordinary powers to his administrative subordinates (for example, in 1843 the prefect of Moquegua, Domingo Nieto, was given these powers in all of southern Peru to deal with rebels).[29] This meant that constitutional *garantías* could be suspended by the provincial police commander, who then dealt with "rebels" with "whatever measures were necessary to save the Fatherland." Even when the fatherland was not in need of salvation, the military prefects exercised the powers of Spanish colonial captains-general, allowing military law and *ley fuga* to be applied against so-called bandits.

Regarding the military, however, the 1839 Constitution moved in a different direction, deleting any constitutionally prescribed mission to conserve internal order or even to uphold the constitution. Article 145 merely indicated that "the armed forces consist of the army, navy and national guard," and Article 146 added the customary language borrowed from the French revolutionaries of the 1790s prohibiting military political intervention: "the armed forces are essentially obedient; they may not deliberate." An important formal, if ineffective, discouragement to military coups was added in Article 152: "There are no other means to obtain the Supreme Executive Power than those designated in this Constitution." This was followed by the declaration that all acts of those who usurp the supreme power, even if in conformity with the constitution, are null (Art. 153) and that any effort to legitimize demands by claiming to represent the "sovereign people" was a criminal attack on "public security" (Art. 172). As in the past, lack of clear assignment of authority to enforce these provisions left the interpretation of *usurpation* in the hands of the temporarily victorious garrison commanders.

Peru, following to some extent the example of Chile after 1833, became a more authoritarian and more centralized political regime. Coups, mutinies, rebellions, and insurrections continued from 1840 to 1845, but there now existed clearer constitutional foundations for the dictatorships and regimes of exception that followed. Taking power in 1839, President Gamarra also had ambitions to unite Peru and Bolivia—but this time under his own tutelage and Peruvian dominance. Defeat of Gamarra's troops and his death at Ingavi, Bolivia, in November 1841 plunged Peru back into political upheaval while confirming the political independence and territorial integrity of Bolivia. The Chilean government mediated the peace settlement signed in Acora, near Puno, in June 1842.

At Gamarra's funeral in Lima, the officiating priest and Peru's leading conservative ideologue, Bartolomé Herrera, preached that Gamarra's death, like earthquakes and floods, was God's punishment for replacing God's laws with liberalism and for allowing religion, mankind's consolation and the necessary condition for tranquility and conservation of nations to be ridiculed":

> Why have we fallen into the abyss? Why has this country so rich in resources and talent and valor suffered this humiliation of having its territory profaned? . . . The reason is that the principle of obedience perished with emancipation. We find ourselves since 1820 in a state of habitual rebellion. . . . Coming down the mountain, we broke the tablets of the law, because the passions we blindly worshiped were not compatible with this gift of heaven.[30]

The battle over presidential succession among several military officers, including the apparent constitutional successor, General Francisco de Vidal, resulted in victory for Manuel Ignacio Vivanco, another of the officers who fought at Ayacucho. Vivanco declared himself supreme director of Peru and required that all public officials and military officers swear an oath of personal allegiance. A firm believer in authoritarian government and the need to reestablish the principle of obedience, he suspended the 1839 Constitution. Vivanco was opposed by liberals and by dissident military officers such as Domingo Nieto and Ramón Castilla. The latter formed a "supreme government junta" until the 1839 Constitution could be reinstated.[31] In 1844 Castilla finally defeated Vivanco, who fled into exile. He restored the 1839 charter as a practical instrument for his first term of office (1845–1851)—a term that was a milestone in Peruvian development.

Ramón Castilla provided leadership previously unknown in Peru. Made possible in part by an export boom based on bird dung fertilizer (guano) and in part by Castilla's skillful coalition building, incipient modernization included construction of South America's first railroad from Lima to Callao, a surge of foreign investment, administrative reorganization, and programs of military professionalization. Castilla's career included service in the royal army and in the independence movements. He had participated in several insurrections and experienced exile and a legendary trek through the Amazon. Castilla combined charisma with professional talents. As a mestizo he symbolized an emergent Peruvian nationalism; as Gamarra's minister he had signed the first guano contracts that would bring wealth to a new merchant and financial class, symbolize their dependence on foreign investment and governments, and encourage the modernization of infrastructure into the 1870s. The guano revenues gradually reduced the foreign debt and accounted for some of the changes in public administration, but Castilla's leadership also permitted a new tone in national politics.[32] As a revolutionary leader in 1854–1855, he decreed an end to slavery and abolition of Indian tribute. Like the Chilean military hero and president, Manuel Bulnes, 1841–1851 (see chapter 8), Castilla at least encouraged the legislature to function. In 1848, Peru approved a national budget adopted according to constitutional norms for the first time.

Castilla's presidency did not end the recurrent plotting and rebellions, but it did mark a turning point in Peruvian socioeconomic and political history. Succeeded in office by General José Rufino Echenique and then responsible for Echenique's 1854 ouster, Castilla returned to power from 1855 to 1862. During this second period two new constitutions were adopted. The first, in 1856, sought to legitimate the movement that Castilla led against Echenique. A national convention convoked by the victors named Castilla provisional president, derogated the Constitution of 1839, and issued a provisional statute in 1855[33] and a constitution in 1856.

Constitutional Development, 1856–1879

Castilla had allied himself, for the moment, with radical forces in Peru influenced by the romantic liberalism of revolutionary Europe in 1848. He purged the army of Echenique supporters and sent key opponents into exile. The government decreed abolition of the Indian tribute, which had provided approximately 20 percent of its revenue, while recognizing that "providence had, with the extraordinary gift of guano, eliminated the fiscal deficit, which was the only justification for [the tribute's] maintenance."[34]

The 1856 Constitution, to Castilla's displeasure, was a drastic reversal from that of 1839. It returned dominant power to the legislature and sought to limit the influence of the church and to reduce the size and resources of the armed forces. The liberals maintained constitutional provisions against sedition and attacks on public security and added in Article 5 the crime of high treason (*lesa patria*). However, they also eliminated the death penalty, added freedom of association and peaceful assembly to the list of *garantías*, and deleted the loss of citizenship for attacking the constituted authorities.

The Congress was now to meet once a year (Art. 48), not twice, and retained the authority to "declare when the Republic is in danger and adopt, within constitutional limits, measures appropriate to save it" (Art. 55, Sec. 20). This was the only regime of exception clause in the 1856 Constitution. No provision was made for concession of extraordinary powers to the emasculated executive, who now was to serve four years, not six as stipulated in 1839. Of course, Congress might find it necessary to assign the president extraordinary powers "to save the nation."

The Constitution of 1856 also reaffirmed the internal security mission of the armed forces and insisted that "military obedience be subordinate to the Constitution and the laws"—a double-edged sword inviting military interpretation of the constitutionality and legality of directives or policies. Combined with the constituent Congress's efforts to limit the number of general officers and the size of the armed forces (Arts. 121–22), eliminate military *fueros*, and control promotions, the constitution challenged the aspirations and corporate interests of the armed forces.

The 1856 Constitution was an anomaly in Peruvian institutional development. It was an institutional framework compatible neither with president Castilla's own powerful personality and charismatic leadership nor with the political power of the new social groups rising from the economic expansion of the 1850s. In some ways a reaffirmation of the liberal principles of 1828 and 1834, the 1856 Constitution challenged conservative and clerical interests by attacking public collection of tithes and the military *fueros*.

Castilla objected to a number of the constitution's provisions, especially those that made Congress rather than the president responsible for military promotions, and to a clause that implied that military officers should judge the legality or constitutionality of policies and directives prior to compliance (Art. 118). The constituent convention had also decreed that public criticism of the constitution that incited disobedience to its strictures constituted a criminal act.[35]

A conservative reaction against the 1856 Constitution combined with a personalist struggle against Castilla led by his erstwhile enemy, the former supreme director Manuel Ignacio Vivanco, led to a revolt based in Arequipa. The rebels temporarily occupied the Chincha islands, source of the guano that financed Peru's public sector and secured the national debt. They also gained a foothold at Callao, which remained under siege from mid-1857 into 1858.

President Castilla first had to defend the constitution to which he objected, suffer the criticisms of the constituent convention (still in session), and defeat militarily the conservative opposition. Writing to the minister of war and navy in October 1857, Castilla made clear his views on the need for extraordinary powers to deal with civil war and rebellion.

> The state of war is, by its nature, extraordinary and abnormal. It requires, therefore, correspondingly extraordinary measures, beyond routine procedures. The slow working of civilian law can never be appropriate for suppressing rebellions, since the crime is committed in battle, and the perpetrators identify themselves with the clamorous sound of cannon. All later inquiry [investigation into the matter] is useless.[36]

When the Callao garrison surrendered in 1858 and Vivanco fled to Chile, Castilla turned his attention to the radical liberals.[37] Meanwhile, as the constituent assembly debated guano contracts, national finance, and church-state relations, a military unit commanded by a colonel invaded the assembly and forced its closure. Military anger at congressional interference in promotions, support for Castilla, support for the church against abolition of tithes, and the generalized political strife all contributed to this dramatic termination of the constitutional convention that had adopted the 1856 Constitution. The colonel later alleged that the convention had perpetuated itself illegally since the constitution had already been promulgated—and that, in any case, his military *fuero* made him immune from prosecution. The government decreed that the case would be heard by the next Congress.[38]

In March 1858, Castilla's army occupied Arequipa after a lengthy and bloody siege; he decreed soon after that elections would be held under the terms of the 1856 Constitution, offering himself as a candidate for the presidency. (He had served as provisional president from 1855 to 1858.) Castilla's election for a second term and the installation of a new Congress failed to eliminate con-

flict between the government and legislature. The new Congress
sought to condemn the colonel responsible for invading the convention in 1857. This and other incidents provoked a crisis; Congress
declared the fatherland in danger but then suspended its sessions
until July of 1859, leaving Castilla in charge.

Writing in the liberal *El Constitucional* in defense of the 1856
Constitution, prominent intellectual, jurist, and journalist Benito
Laso sarcastically attacked what he perceived as the bulwarks of Peruvian politics: authoritarian presidents, militarism, bureaucratic
servilism, and the church.

> Unfortunately it is so common for those who find themselves
> in power to act independently and to command others with
> despotic pride, that they rarely act as mere administrators, ser-
> vants of the law. Being in power means for them to be masters
> of all and arbiters of the destiny of the fatherland.
>
> Taking away from the president the vast power to which he
> is accustomed to appoint at his whim the *jefes políticos* . . . in or-
> der to have subjects blindly obedient to his will, to decentralize
> the administration of the state and to create departmental
> juntas with quasi-legislative power, . . . to take away the au-
> thority of the president to make generals and officers of any-
> one he pleases, . . . all this is unthinkable for a Peruvian
> government. . . .
>
> How can the presidents tolerate loss of the most important
> resource for dominating the people, taking from them the
> constitutional authority to name *jefes* and generals at their
> pleasure, when this attribute makes them absolute masters
> and provides the inducements to obtain the loyalty of [the
> military]?
>
> [Like the French] shall we also suffer the "principle of au-
> thority," the sacred words of the despots and their support-
> ers . . . ? Our mandarins have in their favor the ignorance of
> the masses, and above all the perverse education bequeathed
> us by our fathers, the Spanish, born under the yoke of the in-
> quisition, and educated in superstition and fanaticism.[39]

The liberals' defense of the 1856 Constitution could neither
persuade its detractors nor overcome the political crisis. The very
militarism that Laso asserted made presidents masters of Peru likewise made them prisoners of the military garrisons in Arequipa,
Ayacucho, Callao, Lima, and other lesser towns. Every barracks,

every general, every squad of soldiers was a potential threat to any government. Conservatives and liberals alike used the soldiers to suppress opponents, used the press law to stifle critical journalists and political adversaries, and applied extraordinary powers when the "Fatherland [was] in danger" to banish, exile, or execute "rebels," "bandits," and "traitors."

To complicate matters, Peru found itself at war with Ecuador, which sought to settle its debts with British creditors by ceding land in territory claimed by Peru (see chapter 5). After defeating the Ecuadorean forces, Castilla called the Congress into extraordinary session, which the legislators converted, without legal foundation, into a constituent assembly. A failed assassination attempt against Castilla attributed to liberal opponents sparked a purge of political adversaries, followed by debates on a new constitution.

President Castilla could influence but not control the Congress. In any case, he was not a liberal ideologue nor a conservative troglodyte. He preferred a flexible, centralist, authoritarian constitution in the spirit of the Chilean charter of 1833 (see chapter 8). He was willing to sacrifice military and ecclesiastical *fueros* and government collection of church tithes to liberal supporters in order to obtain a strengthened presidential role in directing modernization and development. He was also willing to mollify conservatives with a subsidy for the church amounting to more revenues than those lost by failure to collect tithes. For the military, Castilla could offer a program of military rearmament, professionalization, elimination of congressional meddling in promotions, and enhanced status.

With these basic compromises, the Congress adopted a new constitution in 1860. This constitution would endure, with brief interruptions and amendments (1867–1868, 1879–1881), until 1920. It consolidated the centralist, presidentialist regime but allowed for significant legislative participation in policy making, constitutional reform, and control over executive action. Above all else, however, it provided enough solace to the church and military and sufficient constitutional latitude for the government to implement regimes of exception "when the Fatherland was in danger" and thereby ensure law and order.

The 1860 Constitution prohibited the public exercise of any religion but the Roman Catholic Apostolic (Art. 4) and assigned the president the exercise of the *patronato,* with approval of clerical appointments by the Congress. This was followed, in the section titled *garantías nacionales,* with a definition of the crime of *lesa patria,* claiming to arrogate sovereignty (Art. 5). A regime of exception clause, similar to that in the 1839 charter, conferred on the Congress the authority to "declare when the Fatherland is in danger" and to suspend basic civil liberties and rights, such as freedom of assembly and association, as well as restrictions on arrest without a warrant and on internal relegation, banishment, or exile (Art. 59, Sec. 20). The president regained the authority to control the armed forces and police, though he could only command the armed forces personally with the permission of Congress or, when in recess, of the permanent commission of the legislature (Art. 96). Article 117 stipulated that all officials concerned with security policy and public order "depend immediately upon the Executive, who will appoint and remove them in conformity with the law."

The 1860 Constitution also reaffirmed the constitutional mission of the armed forces to secure internal order and compliance with the law (Art. 199). However, the issue of military obedience and subordination to civilian authority was not resolved. Article 119 read: "The [question of] military obedience will be governed by the law and military regulations." Thus the central political dilemma of the relative autonomy and political responsibility of the Peruvian military had been left to "future legislation" rather than being resolved in the constitutional debates. This outcome distinguished Peru from all its South American neighbors. In Peru it proved easier to agree upon constitutional constraints upon executive authority, to define the relative power of the executive and legislative branches, and to circumscribe regimes of exception than to adopt definitively the common nondeliberation clause that defined the constitutional limits of military action elsewhere in Spanish America.

In 1867, a short-lived constitution adopted to legitimate an insurgent liberal regime solved this problem by readopting earlier language: "military subordination is subject to the constitution and the law." This clause again made the military formally responsible for assessing the constitutionality of policy directives and orders (Art. 116). With the restoration of the 1860 Constitution in 1868, the issue of judicial review with bayonets once again depended upon legislative rather than constitutional regulation.

During the ten years after Castilla left office in 1862, Peru suffered a series of brief military dictatorships and interim presidencies, with the fatherland frequently "in danger." Spanish claims on the Chincha islands led to a short but disruptive war that brought Colonel Manuel Prado to power. Former president Castilla led the opposition forces and, when he died in 1867, his second in command temporarily gained the presidency. Violence prevailed. It reached its zenith in 1872 with the assassination of imprisoned President-General José Balta, the hanging of the deposed military putschists' bodies from the towers of the Lima cathedral, and their public burning. Politics in Peru remained a dangerous adventure into the 1880s.[40]

Parallel to this period of political violence, technological and economic modernization brought new social and economic groups into Peruvian politics. Railroad construction, financial speculation, and the rise of a more cosmopolitan urban commercial elite gave rise to a *civilista* movement that ultimately produced the country's first civilian president, Manuel Pardo (1872–1876). However, even Pardo, who sought to counterbalance the army with a national guard, relied heavily on close ties to key military officers and garrisons to fend off rebel movements. His successor, ex-dictator General Manuel Prado, faced numerous conspiracies and an intensifying financial crisis resulting from a chronic budget deficit, inability to pay foreign creditors, and a bloated public payroll. Several presidents and former presidents were assassinated in the 1860s and 1870s, including Manuel Pardo in 1878. The following year Peru found itself at war with Chile (1879–1883). The country lost significant amounts of territory, as well as nitrate deposits in the southern desert that might have replaced guano as a major source of public revenue.

In 1879, President Prado sailed for Europe to obtain financial assistance for the war; an uprising in Lima led by Nicolás Piérola resulted in a new wartime government, which issued the Provisional Statute of 1879.[41] By January 1881, Chilean troops occupied Lima, then sacked and looted the Peruvian capital. Guerrilla resistance continued in the highlands, but the Treaty of Ancón in October 1883 formalized the Peruvian loss of territory.

Military officers and patriots blamed defeat on the failure of the government and civilians to support the heroic efforts of Peruvian naval and land forces against difficult odds. The apparent consensus was that Peru required stronger government, better prepared military forces, and an end to the corruption and inefficiency of prewar administrations. Until almost the end of the century the military would reassume control of Peruvian politics. Not until 1920 would the 1860 Constitution be replaced. In the intervening years, the central issue in Peru remained the militarization of politics.

The basic provisions in the 1860 Constitution for regimes of exception allowing suspension of *garantías* when "the Fatherland is in danger" remained in place (Art. 59, Sec. 20). The constitution charged the armed forces with assuring internal order and compliance with the laws (Art. 119). In 1897, when the Peruvian Congress adopted habeas corpus legislation over the objection of the president, the law provided that habeas corpus would not be available to those arrested as a result of suspension of the *garantías* in accord with the constitution (Art. 59, Sec. 20).[42] Civil liberties and rights disappeared in times of "danger"; constitutional dictatorship prevailed.

Until the end of the nineteenth century, the struggle for power and control of the state prevented peaceful regime succession and consolidation of civilian government. Nevertheless, *civilistas* and military elites, liberals and conservatives alike, had reached at least one fundamental agreement: Peru could not be governed without control over freedom of assembly, freedom of association, freedom of the press, and government authority to suspend the *garantías* "when the *patria* is in danger." The maintenance of internal order required recurrent recourse to regimes of exception or, alternately, to civil-military coups justified "to save the fatherland."[43] This principle was not only the dominant constitutional doctrine, it depicted the essence of Peruvian politics to the end of the twentieth century. Peru alternated between constitutional regimes of exception and coups justified by the supposed need to save the fatherland.

Between 1895 and 1919, a tenuous succession of civilian governments seemed to portend a gradual consolidation of the institutions of the 1860 Constitution. A great increase in foreign investment, expansion of mining, and increased coastal export agriculture brought prosperity but also the beginnings of labor strife and Peru's introduction to the politics of class conflict. Soon regimes of exception would be needed to control opposition political movements and demands for social justice.

In 1919, former president Augusto Leguía carried out a coup d'état, claiming that he came to office "to liquidate the old order" and to "detain the advance of communism."[44] Periodic strikes and Indian uprisings to reclaim land appropriated by the haciendas had frightened rural elites, foreign investors, and industrialists. To legitimate the new order, Leguía derogated the 1860 charter and imposed a more liberal constitution in 1920. For the first time, a Peruvian constitution dealt with workers' rights and industrial relations, much like the Mexican 1917 Constitution. Article 58 promised government protection and new educational opportunities for

Indians. Moreover, the 1920 Constitution limited executive power and guaranteed civil rights and liberties; their suspension was, for the first and last time in Peruvian history, prohibited.

In practice, however, Leguía nullified the constitution and ruled as a dictator. Using the army against workers and Indian rebellions in the early 1920s, he then moved against the press, newly organized university students, and political dissidents. During his eleven-year reign (1919–1930), he imprisoned and exiled opponents while ignoring the prohibitions against suspending *garantías*. With the constitution amended to permit presidential reelection, Leguía survived until the 1929 stock market crash ended the orgy of public works and construction projects that prosperity had allowed to soften the dictatorship.

The shock of economic collapse and the burden of eleven years of resentment allowed a military coup to depose Leguía in 1930. After his ouster, a new constitution adopted in 1933 reaffirmed the armed forces constitutional mission to "guarantee the Constitution and laws of the Republic and to maintain public order" (Art. 213) and restored presidential authority to suspend individual rights and liberties during emergencies or when state security required (Art. 70).[45] This authority was supplemented by several laws designed to repress political dissidents and "antisocial" ideas (*doctrinas disociadoras*). The most important of these were the 1932 Emergency Law passed by the constituent assembly that adopted the 1933 Constitution, the 1937 Social Defense Law, and the 1937 Law of Social Defense and Internal Security of the Republic. The 1932 law defined crimes against institutional stability and social welfare: incitement of military coups, incitement to disobey the law, the diffusion of alarmist news, among other such crimes. The government was also authorized to suspend meetings that might disrupt public tranquility and to close down locales or organizations that incited actions that threatened public order. The 1937 law added a ban against communist propaganda and organizations seeking to diffuse communist or other antisocial doctrines. Even more draconian, the 1938 law listed a number of crimes against public and social tranquility and assigned to military courts-martial civilians who committed crimes against internal peace. Capital punishment applied "depending on the gravity and circumstances of the crime."[46]

Alternating military and civilian governments would retain the authority conferred by the 1933 Constitution and by supplemental national security legislation until 1968, when a new type of military regime promised to more radically transform the country

(1968–1980). Military coups in 1948, 1962, and 1968 were justified by the constitutional mission assigned to the armed forces in the 1933 Constitution.[47]

When the military governments after 1968 exhausted their energy and left Peru in shambles, the country adopted still another constitution in 1979. It purportedly restored democracy and civilian government after twelve years of military rule. However, it enhanced the political role of the armed forces and provided for two basic regimes of exception that justified constitutional dictatorship: state of emergency (in the case of perturbation of peace or internal order, catastrophe, or grave circumstances that affect the life of the nation) and state of siege (to confront war, civil war, or imminent danger thereof). During a state of emergency, the 1979 Constitution authorized the armed forces to assume control of internal order at the request of the president. No congressional approval was required.

The state of emergency provisions in the 1979 charter resembled the authority of the president in Article 70 of the 1933 Constitution, though it required that the decree specify which *garantías* were suspended. In the case of state of siege, the 1979 Constitution suspended all *garantías* except those specifically exempted by the state of siege decree. Commenting on these provisions, Enrique Chirinos Soto, a delegate to the constitutional assembly and a member of one of Peru's most important reformist parties in the twentieth century, the Alianza Popular Revolucionaria Americana (APRA), declared: "The first duty of government is to govern. To govern, within the law, it needs regimes of exception like those we have approved."[48] In the 1980s, these provisions of the new constitution were used to put much of Peru under state of siege in the fight against the *Sendero Luminoso* insurgency.[49]

From Bolívar in the nineteenth century to the military rulers, their civilian successors under civilian President Fernando Belaúnde Terry (1980–1985), and then the *Apristas* (1985–1990), Peruvians agreed: without provision for constitutional dictatorship Peru could not be governed. Born under a regime of exception with the suspension of the 1823 Constitution, Peru continued to rely routinely upon regimes of exception and military force to govern its people into the last decade of the twentieth.

Confronted by economic crisis and the intensified revolutionary insurgency of *Sendero Luminoso*'s guerrillas, Peru's president, Alberto Fujimori, illegally suspended the 1979 Constitution in April 1992 and instituted rule by decree. He promised an early plebiscite, elections, and a new constitution to legitimate his *autogolpe*. The draconian powers provided in the 1979 Constitution's regimes of exception did not satisfy President Fujimori; he faced congressional opposition that impeded implementation of his neoliberal economic reforms, including a massive privatization of public enterprises and assets. Like Peruvian caudillos of the past, Fujimori preferred dictatorship to the annoyance of politics. He dissolved Congress and promised, with his military allies, to carry out the historic mission of Peruvian caudillos and the armed forces: to "save the Fatherland"—this time from itself.[50]

BOLIVIA

In February 1825, Antonio José de Sucre, commander of the army that defeated Spanish forces at Ayacucho, declared the provinces of upper Peru liberated from Spanish oppression. Sucre convoked an "Assembly of the Representatives of Upper Peru" to determine their future. Localism prevailed; the assembly resisted reunification with Peru or Buenos Aires and declared Bolivia independent in August 1825. Named for Simón Bolívar, Bolivia consisted of the poor amalgamated provinces of colonial Upper Peru. Site of the most important colonial silver mines, Bolivia's independence wars further decapitalized the already depressed mining sector. Abandoned and flooded mines littered the territory. The Bolivian rural economy was also devastated.[51]

Bolivia, with a population of a little over a million, was a collection of Indian communities, large rural estates, dispersed villages, and small towns, each with its local caudillos and armies. Most of its people lived in the highlands, several days' travel from the Pacific Ocean. Transportation by mule trains or carts to the coast was difficult and costly, making most Bolivian products uncompetitive and raising significantly the price of imported goods. The only port available to the new state was that of Cobija, which by the 1830s had a population of seven hundred. Bolivia never established control over its Pacific desert territory. Eventually, Chilean settlement, foreign investment, ineffective diplomacy, and war would mean the loss of Bolivia's Pacific region, leaving the nation landlocked.[52]

Geographical isolation, difficult topography, a predominantly rural population, the majority non-Spanish-speaking Indians, and a primitive economy condemned Bolivia to an extreme version of the difficulties of the new nations of Spanish America. The most Indian of the South American republics, perhaps 70–80 percent,

Bolivian society remained highly segregated, stratified, and rigid during the nineteenth century.

Taxes on Indians and exploitation of their labor contributed disproportionately to public revenues and private wealth until mining recovered late in the nineteenth century. The Indians participated little in "national" life, lacking awareness of, or commitment to, a Bolivian nation. Nineteenth-century governments alternately sought to impose liberal principles on the Indian communities, thereby destroying the communal system and making Indian land a marketable commodity, or to defend the communal lands and the Indian tribute that accompanied it. Thus, although excluded from conventional political participation, the indigenous people felt the impact of changing government policies, sometimes resisting violently, sometimes passively, and sometimes succumbing to the inevitable.[53] Contestants in national politics were the minority European, Creole, and upwardly mobile *cholo* (mestizo) population who dominated the urban districts. Literacy and property requirements limited the active electorate drastically; in the 1870s, less than twenty thousand voted in national elections.

Elections typically brought violence. Votes were cast in public and voters wishing to oppose official candidates were forced to run the gauntlet of government thugs. Electoral violence and government manipulation of the suffrage exacerbated the regionalism and parochialism characteristic of nineteenth-century Bolivia. The pattern of dispersed urban centers with their local interests and military garrisons combined with the adverse economic and international factors to impede the development of a strong national oligarchy and an effective political system until the 1880s.

Yet, like their counterparts elsewhere, Bolivian conservatives and liberals debated constitutional principles and experimented with numerous constitutions from 1826 to 1880. Integral to these debates were conflicts over the relative authority of executive and legislative branches, control of the military, and the scope of extraordinary powers for the executive in times of "internal commotion" or "threats to the security of the Republic." Eleven constitutions, assorted constitutional reforms, and abortive constituent assemblies framed a canvas of violence, disdain for the law, and recurrent coups and civil wars.[54]

Almost continual plotting, uprisings, conspiracies, and barracks revolts confounded the consolidation of a national political system. Legal, peaceful government succession rarely occurred. The list of nineteenth-century presidents includes numerous interim, provisional, de facto, and transitory executives, some of whom served only days. Between 1829 and 1850, one caudillo, General José Miguel Velasco, was president five times for terms ranging from several months to slightly more than two years.[55] From 1825 to 1899, every Bolivian president faced uprisings and coup attempts; several were assassinated in office, others after leaving office, and almost all failed to complete their terms. Nowhere else in Spanish America did so many presidents and former presidents participate personally in assassinations, executions, direct command of barracks revolts, and large-scale insurrections. Into the 1870s, personalism in Bolivian politics extended to dagger thrusts, gunshots at close range, summary executions, and even trampling opponents under the hooves of caudillo steeds.

In Bolivia, more than elsewhere in Spanish America, the national treasury, though always impoverished, and the posts of the public administration were war booty for victorious caudillos and their supporters. Bolivian historian Augusto Guzmán remarked that the Bolivian president "was not a simple ruler or representative of the people, but rather, most of the time, made himself lord, master, and owner of the nation."[56] As elsewhere, however, even the most cynical caudillos sought a veneer of respectability and legitimacy for their governments in constitutional conventions, splendid declarations of their love of civil liberties and rights, and rigged elections. This was true despite the comparatively insignificant role in Bolivian politics, at least to the 1870s, of ideological differences concerning basic political principles and the organization of the state.

Unlike Colombia, Venezuela, Argentina, Central America, Mexico, and even Peru, no serious federalist proposals emerged until the 1870s. Debates over commercial, agricultural, or sectoral policies, conflicts among organized class or occupational interests, and disputes over religious toleration were also less important in Bolivia than elsewhere in Spanish America before 1880.[57] Elite agreement to exclude and control Indians restricted their political participation except in instances of local uprisings over national land policies or encroachments on their communities. Liberal economic doctrine did not seriously challenge neomercantilist protective policies until the 1860s.

Until at least the 1870s, Bolivian politics centered unambiguously on personal power and control of limited state resources. Typically this required a military victory followed by convocation of Congress or a constitutional convention that selected a provisional, interim, transitory, or constitutional president. Not until 1855 did a Bolivian president, Manuel Isidoro Belzú, retire from office peacefully rather than suffer assassination or deposition by armed revolt. Even then, he imposed his son-in-law, General Jorge Córdova (1855–1857), as his successor.

Bolivian constitutions reflected this political reality. From 1825, Bolivia would never be without provisions for constitutional regimes of exception, ample presidential powers, and a central political role for the military. Bolivian presidents would have the authority to send adversaries into "internal exile" if they chose not to voluntarily leave the country, to suspend the rights of "subversives," and to exercise extraordinary powers that were either self-conferred, conceded by Congress, or constitutionally authorized under the state of siege provisions introduced in 1861 (Art. 11). However, the scope of constitutional dictatorship and the balance of power between the president and Congress became central issues in national politics. When the last nineteenth-century constitution was promulgated in 1880, Congress had achieved some constitutional and political control over the previously unchecked presidential tyranny that prevailed earlier in the century.

Exercise of extraordinary powers depended on the support of the army or, more accurately, of the most important regional garrisons and on maintaining the neutrality of retired, exiled, and pensioned officers. In turn, this required a military budget that usually amounted to 40–50 percent of government revenues. Payments to retirees and pensioners often exceeded by 50 percent the costs of maintaining the standing army.[58] While armies were small, perhaps 1,500–5,000, officers might account for 40–50 percent of all personnel. Even so, these armies were little more than paid retainers of the caudillos officered by "generals" and "colonels" without training in military academies. To meet the costs of these garrisons, governments that theoretically monopolized the silver market though the *bancos de rescate* resorted to debased currency, forced loans, requisition of supplies, sequestration of property, forced labor, and pillage.[59]

So extreme was the Bolivian experience that by 1878 the constitution included a separate section on "the conservation of public order," the basic stipulations of which were retained in constitutional reforms in 1880 (Arts. 26, 27), the last nineteenth-century charter, and in the 1938 Constitution (Arts. 34–38). This concern with internal order as a distinctive constitutional issue prevailed into the late 1960s. Section IV of the 1967 Constitution, Conservation of Public Order (Arts. 111–15), essentially replicated the language of the charters of 1878, 1880, 1938 (Arts. 34–38), 1945 (Arts. 34–38), and 1947 (Arts. 34–38).

Independence and the Constitution of 1826

From its first constitution, Bolivia would never lack the foundations of constitutional dictatorship. The nation began under the authority of Sucre's predominantly Colombian Army of Liberation. In a decree on February 9, 1825, Sucre asserted his authority over Upper Peru as commander of the revolutionary army, "while an assembly of deputies deliberates the destiny of the provinces denominated Upper Peru." This decree anticipated Bolivia's subsequent history of militarism, caudillismo, and civil wars. It prophetically stipulated that "the liberation army shall respect the decision of the assembly, so long as it conserves order, unity and concentration of power to avoid anarchy." It added that "intervention by the military in the deliberations of the assembly will void those acts in which the military interferes."[60] Composed of representatives selected by each *cabildo*, this assembly proclaimed Bolivia an independent nation, separate from Peru and Rio de la Plata, on August 6, 1825.

Meanwhile, Simón Bolívar had sent the assembly a draft constitution, preceded by a self-effacing disclaimer concerning his own legislative abilities and a reminder of the terrible experiences suffered by other new nations.

> I have brought all my resources to the fore to give you my opinions on how to organize free men, with the principles adopted by advanced nations [*pueblos cultos*]; though the lessons of experience only demonstrate long periods of disaster, interrupted by lightning flashes of fortune. What guides can we follow in the shadow of such fearful [*tenebrosos*] examples?
>
> Legislator! Your duty is to overcome the conflict between two monstrous enemies . . . both of which will attack simultaneously: tyranny and anarchy from an immense ocean of oppression, that surrounds a small island of liberty, besieged permanently by the violence of the waves and hurricanes.[61]

Central to Bolívar's solution to this dilemma was a lifetime president "who in our constitution will be like the sun in the universe, central, firm and life-giving."[62] The assembly adopted a modified version of his proposal, accepting the lifetime president but rejecting his advice to avoid establishing an official church. It gutted his proposal to abolish slavery by adding the provisions that the freed slaves "shall not leave the property of their masters, except as shall be determined in a special law" (Art. 11).

In Bolivia, as in Peru, the Bolivarian Constitution was never fully implemented. It did, however, establish constitutional precedents that survived into the twentieth century: centralism, presidential dominance, and a constitutional definition of a political role for the armed forces in maintaining internal security. The constitution also provided authority to protect state security by suspending "constitutional formalities" under "extraordinary circumstances." Article 128 was the first, if not the most comprehensive, of Bolivia's constitutional regimes of exception:

> If in extraordinary circumstances, the security of the Republic requires the suspension of some of the formalities of this section [section V, detailing the administration of justice and certain civil liberties and rights], the legislative chambers may so decree; if these are not in session, the Executive may do so, informing the legislature of his actions in the next session, and assuming responsibility for any abuses committed.

Article 157 added that, in suspending the rights conferred in the constitution, the government "must specify the period during which the suspension will prevail."

From 1825 to 1828, Sucre and the Army of Liberation dominated Bolivia. Despite personal reservations about the lifetime presidency and the wisdom of assuming executive power in Bolivia, Sucre accepted the presidency from the constituent assembly. Efforts to effect tax and administrative reforms, including abolition of the Indian tribute, to attract foreign investment in the depressed mining sector, to reactivate the royal mint, and otherwise to stimulate the economy, failed. Sucre did successfully confiscate church lands, close small monasteries, and take control of collecting tithes.

As Bolívar's closest lieutenant, Sucre was the target of anti-Bolivarian sentiment in both Peru and Bolivia. His reforms offended landowners and urban taxpayers, while abolition of the Indian tribute eliminated the most important source of government revenue. This, combined with resentment against the Army of Liberation and the costs of its maintenance, encouraged attacks on Sucre by local caudillos. Bolívar's departure from Peru in 1827, threats of war between Gran Colombia and Peru that potentially involved Bolivia, and an eventual assassination attempt led in 1828 to Sucre's resignation. This was accompanied by an agreement, the Treaty of Piquiza, to remove foreign troops from the country and adopt a new constitution.[63]

With his departure, a series of temporary presidents and caudillos jockeyed for power. The assembly named Marshall Andrés Santa Cruz as president. He had served briefly as Peruvian president and would, during his entire lifetime, intrigue to unite Peru and Bolivia. He shared this objective with Peruvian leaders, including President Agustín Gamarra, who had stated clearly an intent to consolidate Peruvian control over Bolivia: "Bolivia and Peru will come to terms and we shall form of them the Peruvian nation, not the Bolivian. Peru has never been Bolivian. Bolivia has always belonged to Peru."[64] Santa Cruz's government (1829–1839) would be dominated by the issue of Peruvian-Bolivian federation or unification.

Constitutional Development Under Santa Cruz

Taking office in May 1829, Santa Cruz derogated the 1826 Constitution and decreed an anticonspiracy law (Ley de Conato). The law afforded him ample authority to exile, imprison, and otherwise repress political opponents. Fancying himself the Napoleon of South America, he adopted imperfect versions of Napoleonic civil and penal codes for Bolivia. He also established new colleges and medical and military schools. He devoted himself to equipping and controlling the army and to preparing a new constitution that legalized his dictatorship.

Treated as a reform of the 1826 charter, the 1831 Constitution provided that Bolívar's powerful president would now be elected indirectly by parish juntas for a four-year term, instead of a lifetime, but could be reelected indefinitely. Presidential authority was virtually omnipotent, ranging from control over the entire public administration, the armed forces, and the national guard and police to the ability to dissolve the Congress and rule by decree, with assent by the council of state. The constitution established the armed forces as a permanent government institution, and this would never change in Bolivian constitutional history (Arts. 141–42). Typical of nineteenth-century Spanish American constitutions, it added the language of the French revolutionary proscription of military participation (*deliberación*) in politics that would be contradicted thereafter by Bolivian reality: "the armed forces are essentially obedient, in no case may they deliberate" (Art. 143).

The fundamental regime of exception clause also departed little from the 1826 Bolivarian scheme. Article 132 stated:

> If in extraordinary circumstances, the security of the Republic requires suspension of any of the formalities prescribed by this Constitution and the law, the legislature may so decree. If the legislature is not in session, the Executive, with the assent of the Council of State, may do so as a provisional measure, with the responsibility of informing the legislature, and responding for any abuses committed.

In the case of "sudden invasion" or "internal commotion" the president could be invested with extraordinary powers by the council of state, thereby suspending enumerated civil rights and liberties (Arts. 74–75). When in session, the legislature could also give the president "whatever authority is deemed necessary for the salvation of the State" in times of war or "extraordinary danger" (Art. 19). In short, the constitution made the president a virtual dictator; in times of war, internal commotion, "extraordinary danger," or threats to the security of the state he had unlimited power. This made the presidency invaluable but also meant that it would be bitterly and permanently contested.

From 1831 until the end of the century, with the exception of the 1839, 1878, and 1880 constitutions (see below), caudillos used constitutional reforms to legitimate new governments and sought to enhance further the routine and extraordinary power of the presidency in times of "danger," external threats, or "internal commotion." Intermittent efforts to strengthen the legislature, limit presidential authority, shorten presidential terms, and forbid immediate reelection were finally institutionalized in the 1880s. Delayed economic development, lack of an integrated agrarian elite, and regional isolation militated against the evolution of effective national legislative and judicial counterweights to the president. In the 1831 Constitution, congressional sessions were limited to three months a year and could be suspended by the president. In 1834, under Santa Cruz's direction, a reformed constitution limited congressional sessions to once every two years.

The 1831 Constitution served as the basic foundation for executive dictatorship. Its 1834 successor further weakened the legislature and limited presidential accountability to acts of treason, illegally "staying" in office, and usurpation of the constitutional authority of other branches of government (Art. 73). Otherwise, the president could not be held legally accountable for official acts, an important departure from the 1831 charter that had made him "responsible for all administrative acts according to the Constitution"

(Art. 71). The 1834 reforms also retained the unique clause of 1831 that prohibited Congress from confirming a new president if a military uprising ousted the previous president—that is, Santa Cruz—unless the outgoing president had violated the constitution and was legally deposed.

Santa Cruz ruled Bolivia from 1831 to 1839, perennially involved in plots with caudillos and presidents in neighboring Peru. Sharing with some Peruvians the dream of a united Peru-Bolivia (under his own direction, of course), he was often granted extraordinary powers to protect Bolivia against invasions or to quell internal uprisings. In 1833, for example, the Congress invested him with authority to "take measures to protect the integrity of the [country's] institutions and public order."[65] To this end, Santa Cruz allied himself with Peruvian president Orbegoso against the rebellious forces of outgoing President Gamarra. Authorized by the Peruvian Congress in 1834 to ask for Santa Cruz's military assistance to end the civil war in Peru, Orbegoso eventually agreed to Peruvian financing of a Bolivian army commanded by a designee of the Bolivian president.

Santa Cruz sent a Bolivian army into Peru, and Orbegoso transferred the extraordinary powers delegated to him by the Peruvian Congress to the Bolivian president, an unusual occurrence even for the magical realism of Spanish American politics in the nineteenth century. In Peru, former adversaries Gamarra and Felipe Salaverry (another of Sucre's lieutenants at Ayacucho) united to fight "the second war of Peruvian independence" against Santa Cruz and his Peruvian supporters. Salaverry declared "war to the death" against Santa Cruz, promising tax exemptions for those who killed Bolivians. After several ragged engagements, Salaverry's forces were defeated and he was executed following a trial by a *consejo de guerra.*[66]

These events left Santa Cruz dominant in Peru and Bolivia, whereupon he created the Peru-Bolivia Confederation. Unable to consolidate control of the confederation's internal adversaries, he was ultimately defeated in 1839 by a Chilean army, assisted by Peruvian, Bolivian, and Argentine opponents of the confederation. So ended Santa Cruz's dream; he spent the rest of his life in exile conspiring to return to power in Bolivia.

Reform, Reaction, and "Restoration," 1839–1851

The defeat of Santa Cruz and the dissolution of the confederation in 1839 necessitated reorganization of the political system and, naturally, a new constitution. General José Miguel Velasco, turncoat commander of Santa Cruz's southern army, assumed the presidency provisionally, supported by the victorious Chilean General (soon to be President) Manuel Bulnes. Meanwhile, a constituent assembly worked on a new constitution and a rebellious caudillo, General José Ballivián, proclaimed himself "Provisional Supreme Chief of the Republic," adding that "any Bolivian who did not submit to his authority within thirty days will be considered an enemy of Bolivia and treated as such." The assembly proclaimed Ballivián a "traitor and outlaw" to be captured "dead or alive." Promotions were promised to any soldier or officer who "brought him in."[67]

Santa Cruz's defeat and the influence of the Chilean occupation resulted in the first Bolivian constitution to reduce executive authority and enhance that of the legislature. In its preamble, which denounced the "pretended confederation of Peru and Bolivia" and invalidated the 1834 charter, the assembly delegates made clear that the 1839 Constitution was a reaction to Santa Cruz's ten-year (1829–1839) reign and to the plans of Peruvian and Bolivian caudillos to unify the two territories.

The new constitution made the president legally accountable for administrative acts, reduced his appointment power, prohibited executive dissolution of the Congress and dismissal of judges, forbade immediate presidential reelection, and eliminated the vice presidency. Congress was prohibited from investing the executive with extraordinary powers beyond those enumerated in the constitution. This was an important effort to end the delegation of "whatever power is deemed essential" to meet threats of external invasion or internal commotion. It restricted presidential authority to expel, exile, deprive of property or liberty, or punish citizens, to interfere in court proceedings, and to impede elections called for by the constitution (Art. 78). It also forbade the president to prevent those elected from taking office or to dissolve Congress or suspend its sessions. If the constitution had been implemented, the constitutional dictatorship created by Bolívar and perfected by Santa Cruz would have ended.

The framers of the 1839 charter also sought to redefine the military mission—"to defend the freedom and independence of the Nation" (Art. 139), to create militia (*guardia nacional*) in each department subject to civilian authority, to prohibit military courts or "special commissions" from trying civilians (Art. 163), and to secure military subordination to civilian authority. Article 142 stated: "All military officers of the Republic are subject to the orders of the person who, according to this Constitution, should succeed as President, the day on which, according to [the Constitution] the constitutional term ends. Whoever violates this article commits the crime of treason against the fatherland."

Despite these efforts to curtail militarism and depart from the presidentialism of Bolívar and Santa Cruz, the 1839 Constitution remained strongly centralist, with the prefect of each department and district the "immediate constitutional agent of the Executive power" (Art. 120). Within their jurisdictions, prefects exercised supreme military and civil authority over order, security, politics, and the economy. This included applying decrees issued by the president under still ample, though delimited, emergency powers. The constitution sought explicitly to reduce the scope of presidential extraordinary powers. The new regime of exception provisions (Arts. 79–81) were more restrictive than in most of Spanish America. Bolivia would never have more constitutional constraint on its presidents than in 1839:

- *Article 79:* "In the case of grave danger which threatens the security of the Republic, caused by internal commotion or external invasion, the Executive shall apply to the Congress . . . [requesting] concession of the following powers: (1) increase in the size of the permanent army and call to active service of the national guard; (2) [financing of the military effort]; (3) . . . arrest of those who conspire against the tranquility of the Republic, putting them at the disposition of a judge within 72 hours; . . . (4) naming of generals on the battlefield; (5) to concede amnesties and pardons for political crimes."
- *Article 80:* "If [the threat] occurs while Congress is not in session the Council of Ministers may invest the president with the authority specified in the previous article."
- *Article 81:* "[The authority in articles 79 and 80] shall be limited to the time indispensable to reestablish the tranquility and security of the Republic, and the executive shall report to congress on the use made of such authority in the next legislative session."

President Velasco (1839–1841) was unable to implement the 1839 Constitution or to consolidate his government. Continued intrigue by Gamarra and other Peruvians and by Santa Cruz in exile, Ballivián, and assorted Bolivian caudillos, ignited new uprisings. Supporters of Santa Cruz ousted Velasco in 1841. Gamarra invaded Bolivia in another effort to unite the two territories, or at least to annex a part of Bolivia, and to prevent the return of Santa Cruz from his Ecuadorean exile. Velasco, ever the survivor, turned over loyal southern troops to Ballivián before departing for Argentine exile. At Ingavi in November 1841, President Gamarra died leading his defeated army. Despite his earlier intrigues, support for Gamarra, and frequent failed coup attempts, Ballivián's victory made him a hero of Bolivian nationalists instead of the "outlaw and traitor" he had been labeled by Congress in 1839. He led his army into Peru: Puno, Tacna, Moquegua, Arica, Tarapacá. Further military encounters and guerrilla resistance in Peru against his forces resulted in a peace treaty in June 1842.

Ballivián returned to Bolivia, repressed conspiracies by remaining Santa Cruz supporters, symbolically delivered power to the Congress he convoked in Sucre, and dutifully accepted appointment as provisional president. A new constitution was now necessary to replace the 1839 charter and to legitimate Ballivián's forthcoming election as constitutional president (1843–1847). He had come to power as a military hero. His constitution restored the all-powerful presidency, lengthened the presidential term to eight years, augmented presidential patronage in the bureaucracy, courts, and military (to the rank of colonel), and allowed the executive to dissolve the Congress "if it exceeded its constitutional authority" (Art. 43) and again limited its sessions to alternate years. Legislative authority shrank significantly, while that of the executive expanded to include even issuing the *ordenanzas* for the army and national guard.

Ballivián's critics called his constitution the *ordenanza militar*, reflecting their perception that it was essentially a charter for military dictatorship. In contrast to the 1839 Constitution, the president was now authorized "in cases of external danger or internal commotion" to "take whatever security measures he deems convenient, reporting the measures taken to the congress, or if it is not in session to the National Council" (an advisory body made up of legislators, judges, a military officer, a religious official, and a minister of finance) (Arts. 45–46).

The president could take "whatever security measures he deems convenient" without limitation, without congressional review, and without reference to the civil rights and liberties of Bolivian citizens. He could do this whenever there existed "internal commotion" or "external danger": in the Bolivia of the 1840s that meant always. Ballivián had thus surpassed Bolívar and Santa Cruz; unilateral presidential determination of the existence of external danger or internal commotion suspended all civil liberties and rights, including the long list of *garantías* commencing with liberty, security, property, and equality before the law (Arts. 86–98).

Ballivián fully used these provisions, creating a primitive network of secret police and paid informers to control political opponents. Though no more repressive than his predecessors and successors, his constitution derailed the 1839 movement toward more protection for civil rights and liberties and a more significant role for Congress. While Bolivia would never again have such unlimited provisions for constitutional dictatorship as those adopted in the 1843 Constitution, it would also never again so limit presidential emergency powers and the scope of regimes of exception as it had in 1839.

Ballivián survived numerous barracks revolts and conspiracies, including support for his enemies by Peruvian President Ramón Castilla, whom he had taken prisoner and offended at Ingavi. He could not, however, survive the mercurial rise of rival caudillo Manuel Isidoro Belzú, who gained control of the La Paz garrison in 1847. Defeated, Ballivián delegated power to General Eusebio Guilarte, president of the council of ministers. Guilarte clung to office for ten days before Belzú's forces prevailed. A year later he was assassinated in Cobija as Belzú persecuted his adversaries.

Belzú feigned support for General and expresident Velasco. Abandoning Ballivián's 1843 charter, a new Congress was convened to confirm Velasco and to reform the 1839 Constitution. The proposed reforms included limitations on the scope of extraordinary powers and reductions in the personnel and budget of the armed forces.[68] This provoked an uprising at the Oruro garrison that sparked antigovernment movements in several northern towns. Belzú decided to end the charade of support for Velasco. He took charge of the rebellious garrisons and in appeals to urban *cholos* and Indians encouraged the pillage of cities where Velasco's supporters resisted, including La Paz and Cochabamba.

Belzú was Bolivia's first populist president. He imposed himself on most of Bolivia with direct appeals to the underclasses and attacks on the urban elite. Revisionist historians have seen his support from artisans and the urban poor as the first overt clash between neomercantilists and a rising group of miners, foreign investors, merchants, and "liberals" favoring "free trade" and relaxation of state controls on the economy.[69]

Whatever the real commitment of Belzú to defend the plebes and colonial monopolists against a supposed liberal threat, a new Congress convened in Sucre and obsequiously designated the victorious caudillo provisional president. After a botched assassination attempt against Belzú by Colonel (later the president, 1871–1872) Agustín Morales, whose home had been looted, Congress suspended the constitution and invested Belzú with extraordinary powers. All of Belzú's administrative subordinates were likewise given such powers to conserve public order and confront the threat to internal security.

In September 1851 a new constitution was promulgated, providing for the direct election of the president for a shortened (five-year) term.[70] Contrary to the abortive reforms of 1848, it also buttressed the tradition of constitutional regimes of exception. Indeed, in some respects the 1851 Constitution more clearly restricted the exercise of civil liberties and rights than previous constitutions. First, Article 23 stated: *the enjoyment of* garantías *and rights that this constitution concedes to all men . . . is subordinated to compliance with this obligation: respect [for] and obedience to the law and the constituted authorities* (italics in the constitution). Second, the Congress could declare the fatherland in danger as a result of internal commotion or external war and invest the executive with extraordinary powers to reestablish order and peace. This declaration suspended the constitutional regime until the Congress declared the "end of extraordinary powers" (Art. 50, Secs. 12, 13). Third, the president might invest himself with these same powers, with the assent of the council of ministers (appointed by the president), under the same conditions. The president was to report to Congress on the use made of this authority, but no provision was made for congressional oversight or removal of such powers (Art. 76, Secs. 26–28).

Although the president and ministers were legally responsible for violations of the law, unlike in earlier charters, Article 76 provided a blank check for the chief executive. His authority was unlimited if he and his ministers decided that the "fatherland [was] in danger." The president retained the traditional authority to conserve internal security, name military officers to the rank of colonel, organize and direct the militia (*guardia nacional*), exercise the *patronato* (naming religious officials), staff the public administration, and convoke the Congress and electoral colleges. The 1851 charter thus further reinforced the institutions of constitutional dictatorship established by Bolívar and Santa Cruz.

Constitutional Development, 1851–1880

Belzú was the first Bolivian president to complete his constitutional term, overcoming assassination attempts, mutinies, uprisings, and internal wars. In 1855 he surprised Congress, meeting in Oruro, with a farewell speech that included the following lament: "Revolution in the south, revolution in the north, revolution fomented by my enemies, by my friends, . . . My God! They have condemned me to a state of permanent warfare. . . . Bolivia has made itself ungovernable."[71] Despite his apparent exasperation, Belzú used the electoral process and the government-controlled press to secure congressional selection of his son-in-law, General Jorge Córdova, as his successor. He was appointed minister plenipotentiary in Europe, given a fitting salary, and then left the country. Like Santa Cruz, he spent much of the rest of his life unsuccessfully plotting a return to power. In 1865 he was killed in a coup attempt against Mariano Melgarejo.[72]

Santa Cruz and José María Linares, inveterate *golpista*, former congressman, minister, prefect of Potosí, and former interim president, had opposed Córdova in the presidential elections and, since his investiture, both sought to oust him. Shortly after taking office, Córdova faced his first serious revolt from northern garrisons who ostensibly supported Linares's claims against irregularities in the recent elections. Declaring "the fatherland in danger," Congress conferred extraordinary powers on the president and suspended its sessions.[73] Córdova annulled the amnesty decrees with which he had attempted to mollify the opposition, suppressed the rebellions ruthlessly, and imprisoned opponents. New revolts followed.[74]

In the August 1856 congressional sessions a cabinet minister, seeking to impress the Congress with the government's achievements and to flatter the president, revealed the pathetic political situation: "Five conspiracies suppressed in less than fifteen months, not a single victim on the gallows, a few temporary incarcerations, five amnesty decrees . . . prove the moderation of the government in using the extraordinary powers [conferred by Congress].[75] In September 1857, an artillery unit at Oruro proclaimed Linares provisional president. The aristocratic, moralistic Linares had dedicated decades to achieving the presidency; once again he challenged an incumbent caudillo.

The Congress responded predictably, investing Córdova with extraordinary powers and suspending its sessions until the revolt had been suppressed. Bolivian historian Alcides Argüedas relates the following speech by Córdova to his troops:

> My sons, it is time to save the fatherland. I need your help, and I promise you after victory all the booty of the city. I declare you owners of lives and property [*vidas y haciendas*]. . . . Kill without mercy the burghers [*hombres de levita*]. . . . If you die in

the fray your families will receive pensions. If the poor [*cholos*]
leave their trenches, disarm and denude them, the same for
old women: the young girls are yours.[76]

It is not clear whether these instructions properly fell within the
extraordinary powers with which Congress had invested the president. In any case, unable to obtain victory after three days of skir-
mishing, Córdova fled to Oruro. Learning that garrisons in La Paz
and Sucre had pledged support for Linares, Córdova took refuge in
Peru, and Linares, Bolivia's first civilian chief executive (1857–
1861), became de facto president, proclaiming "my only mission is
to moralize the country."[77] Personally austere, disdainful of Belzú's
and Córdova's populism, and committed to putting the government's affairs in order, Linares made severe budget cuts. This included eliminating sinecures in the public administration and the
army. The number of paid soldiers was reduced from 6,000 to
1,200, and the customary government subsidies to what passed for
newspapers were abolished.

Opposition to Linares surfaced quickly from those disappointed
not to share in the booty of the ascendant dictator and also from the
garrisons. Linares openly adopted a dictatorial regime in 1858, declaring martial law on March 31, 1858:

> [Considering that] the battle between revolution and reaction
> demands intrepidity so that weakness does not compromise the
> great interests of the fatherland; toleration of the press' licen-
> tiousness has opened a bottomless abyss; that the material or-
> der is threatened. . . . [The government therefore decrees] that
> all crimes against the security of the State will be removed from
> the jurisdiction of the ordinary courts and that the govern-
> ment, confirming summarily the veracity of the charges, [in
> each case] will submit the accused to the discretional measures
> it decides to take.[78]

Linares chose not to wrap his dictatorship in the cloak of the
constitution, nor to adopt a new one—a rare patrician, even colonial, resort to the moralistic repression of evil. He despised the liberal pretenses of the Congress, the press, and the postcolonial
constitutional order. Like Diego Portales in Chile (see chapter 8),
Linares viewed militarism as the key obstacle to political stability in
Bolivia. He sought:

to destroy the domination of the saber, so lamentable for the Hispanic American Republics, to make the military understand they are the friends and protectors of civilians, not their executioners; that to require respect for the institutions, the privileges [*fueros*], and independence of the fatherland is their first duty; . . . that the sword of honor is converted into the dagger of the assassin when it determines the fortune of a country.[79]

Linares's most prominent supporters would be known in the 1870s as constitutionalists and antimilitarists, seeking to end the recurrent coups, enhance the role of Congress, and constrain executive authority. However, Linares's own disdain for constitutional solutions, his preference for dictatorship, his personal crusade against corruption, and his severe repression of political opponents could not withstand the reaction of resentful officers and office seekers.

After an unsuccessful assassination attempt that killed look-alike General Juan José Prudencio, Linares created a *consejo de guerra* to investigate and punish the perpetrators. Draconian sentences followed, including the execution of a priest involved in the conspiracy. Supported by Peruvian President Castilla, supporters of Belzú and Córdova made new efforts to depose Linares. In response, Linares decreed that the press "should not discuss administrative acts, political questions, and [must] refrain from all publications that compromise the public order."[80] Besieged by enemies, broken by poor health, and betrayed by his closest civilian and military advisers—Ruperto Fernández, Manuel Antonio Sánchez (prefect), and General José María Achá—Linares was removed from office.[81] His three former collaborators established a triumvirate and called for congressional elections and the meeting of a constituent Asamblea Nacional. They sent Linares into exile in Chile and arrested his loyal ministers. He died a few months later.

The elections for the Asamblea Nacional were more open than customary, giving rise to a the government composed of competing proto-parties: the Rojos—Tomás Frías, Mariano Baptista, and Adolfo Ballivián among the most notable (all future presidents)—and the Azules in opposition. After some debate, the Asamblea Nacional selected General Achá as provisional president, adopted a new constitution (1861), and approved a reformed press law. The 1861 Constitution endured only briefly; then anarchy engulfed the country. However, the possibility of more genuine legislative debate in the 1861 Asamblea did reflect the diffusion into Bolivia of mid-century Spanish American liberalism. This included efforts to limit presidential prerogatives, to shorten the presidential term (to three years in 1861), and to make the president and his ministers legally accountable for all official acts (Arts. 44, 52). A directly elected unicameral legislature, with greatly expanded budgetary power and control over military promotions, would meet annually. The constitution forbade legislative concession of extraordinary powers or "supreme power" to the executive (Art. 10).

This apparent limitation on the most frequently used regime of exception was accompanied by a caveat in the case of war and also the first state of siege clause in Bolivia's constitutional history. In the case of war, the legislature could "invest the president with the power necessary to save the State" (Art. 26, Sec. 13). Article 11, the new state of siege clause, read as follows:

> In the case of internal commotion that puts in danger the Constitution or the authorities created by it, a state of siege will be declared in the department or province where order is perturbed, all constitutional rights and liberties [*garantías*] thereby being suspended. During this suspension the Executive Power will limit itself to arresting or removing persons from the territory affected to other places in the Nation, if they do not prefer [voluntarily] to leave the country. Under no circumstance is torture permitted. . . . Likewise, persons are not to be transferred to unhealthy places nor a distance of more than fifty leagues. As soon as order is reestablished, they will be permitted to return to their homes and tried [according to the procedures and *garantías* of the constitution].

Thus, all the *garantías* (Arts. 3–9) could be suspended if internal commotion put the constitution or the government "in danger."

Faced with continued uprisings, the government invoked the state of siege provisions for the city of La Paz, leaving Colonel Plácido Yáñez, prefect of the city, in command of the garrison. Yáñez imprisoned leading Belzú supporters, including expresident Córdova. On October 23, 1861, on the pretext of a *belcista* plot to overthrow the government, Yáñez ordered the murder of Córdova and sixty-nine others in their jail cells. Two days after his death, Córdova was "sentenced" to death by a *consejo de guerra*. Achá then proposed calling elections for a special Congress in 1862 to approve constitutional reforms that would allow the executive to take preventive and repressive measures against sedition. The opposition (Rojos) protested. Attempting to quell them, Achá revoked the decree convoking the convention but could not assuage his enemies.[82]

The tension between order and liberty, identified by Bolívar in his 1825 letter to the first constitutional convention, was clear in the 1861 Constitution. The solution was the prohibition on the concession of extraordinary powers, the adoption of a state of siege provision, limitations on the presidential term and appointment power, and new pressures for a still stronger executive.

As Achá's three-year term neared its end, he vacillated in choosing a successor before settling on General Sebastián Agreda, one of several contenders, including former president Belzú, Adolfo Ballivián (son of the former president and leader of the Rojos), and General Mariano Melgarejo. Achá attempted to isolate Melgarejo, who was serving as prefect of Cochabamba, reassigning him to the same post in Santa Cruz. Melgarejo feigned compliance but delayed his departure from Cochabamba. Finally, Belzú's intrigues, the Rojos's maneuvers, and Melgarejo's ambition produced a coup in the last days of 1864, prior to the scheduled presidential elections.[83]

Mariano Melgarejo ruled Bolivia from 1864 to 1871. His surname became a synonym for brutal, unrestrained, depraved caudillismo.[84] He courted foreign investors, signed boundary agreements with Brazil and Chile alienating Bolivian territory and natural resources, and ruled with capricious violence. Despoliation of the Indian communities through the sale and theft of communal lands rewarded the caudillo's civilian and military adherents. Melgarejo lacked the popular support of Belzú or the aristocratic support of Linares. He relied on his army (the Colorado regiment), which was left to pillage, confiscate property, exact "loans" from the towns, and terrorize opponents. He dissolved the municipal councils and centralized all revenues in the national treasury "which became synonymous with his person." He "canceled" the 1861 Constitution and proclaimed "I will rule Bolivia as long as I please; whoever challenges me I shall hang in the center of the plaza."[85]

Challenged initially by former president Belzú, Melgarejo killed him at the presidential palace in La Paz in 1865 after Belzú's forces had apparently achieved military victory.[86] He then suppressed revolts in Potosí, Cochabamba, and Santa Cruz. Melgarejo had participated in army revolts since the 1840s, first as a sergeant, now as a general. His rise coincided with new guano and mineral finds (silver and nitrate) in the southwest and with an increase in commercial relations with Britain, Chile, Brazil, and Argentina. Accommodating the incipient mining oligarchy, Melgarejo bypassed the government monopoly on silver purchases for favored entrepreneurs, relied on tax revenues from guano and nitrate exports, and dismantled the neomercantilist policies that had dominated Bolivia into the 1860s.[87] He bestowed valuable business concessions on foreign capitalists for a pittance, though it must be noted that encouraging investment in Bolivia required a plentitude of generosity. Melgarejo also loved to entertain foreign dignitaries and to receive the plaudits—and in the case of Chile, even a military commission—from European and South American governments.

Constitutions inspired no respect in Melgarejo, but even he ordered his advisers to devise a new one and his Congress to approve it. An oft-repeated anecdote reports the following from a drunken Melgarejo at a state banquet celebrating the promulgation of the 1868 charter: "I want the *doctor* who just spoke to know, and all the honorable congressmen also, that the 1861 Constitution, which was a good one, I stuck in this [left] pocket and that of 1868, which is even better according to these *doctores,* I stuck in this other pocket, and that no one but me rules Bolivia."[88] Such candor raises a question concerning the significance of nineteenth-century constitutions, not only in Bolivia but elsewhere in Spanish America. Why be concerned with constitutional clauses when government by rifle, sword, lance, and dagger was the rule?

Indeed, Melgarejo promulgated the 1868 Constitution, on a whim, on October 1, 1868—a month earlier than stipulated in the constitution's Transitory Article 1. Melgarejo desired congressional approval of boundary and commercial treaties with Chile and Brazil, at the insistence of these two nations. The treaty with Brazil recognized Brazilian sovereignty over more than one hundred thousand square kilometers, including valuable rubber lands. In exchange, Melgarejo obtained access to several Brazilian rivers but abrogated Bolivian claims to much of the Amazon Basin. Brazil decorated him with the Gran Cruz del Imperio.[89] The Chilean treaty (1866) provided for the common ownership of nitrate resources between latitudes twenty-three and twenty-five and promised Chilean companies tax relief. In recognition for his peaceful resolution of Chilean-Bolivian disputes, the Chilean minister in Bolivia made Melgarejo a general in the Chilean army.[90]

These agreements angered Bolivian nationalists. It required almost two years of terror, intimidation, and persuasion to obtain approval of the treaties even by a legislature that Melgarejo had convened. From this "constituent legislature" Melgarejo also extruded the 1868 Constitution, "a suit made to order, a dress coat tailored for a tyrant,"[91] for not even Melgarejo wished to rule naked: the vestments of the constitution civilized barbarity and legalized dictatorship. They also satisfied the Chileans and Brazilians, who refused to rely on agreements with other than constitutionally legitimate authorities. Only constitutional governments could redraw boundaries, extend long-term mineral concessions, and promise not to increase export taxes. A treaty with a de facto president was feeble; a treaty with a legitimate government could more reasonably require compliance.

Melgarejo's 1866 agreement with Chile, abrogated by a Bolivian government in the mid-1870s, would lead to war. Nevertheless, it is revealing that even Melgarejo required a constitution for international legitimacy as well as internal convenience, and that the 1868 Constitution, precipitated by Chilean and Brazilian insistence on congressional ratification of their treaties with the Melgarejo government, followed precedent.

In many ways Melgarejo's constitution simply reflected the traditional debates in Bolivia over the relative authority of the legislature and the president, the length of presidential terms, the possibility of immediate reelection, and the extent of presidential control in staffing the public administration, the judiciary, and in military promotions. The aberrant unicameral legislature of 1861 was replaced by the conventional bicameral Congress. Deputies and senators would be chosen by direct election, but Congress would meet only every two years. As with Santa Cruz's 1831 and 1834 Constitutions, the president could be reelected indefinitely for four-year terms. Congressmen enjoyed immunity from arrest for opinions expressed and for any other cause during their tenure. If the president failed to convoke the Congress as stipulated in the constitution, the legislators "shall meet [without such convocation] on the date and in the place [Sucre] specified" (Art. 32).

Catholicism remained the state religion, and public exercise of other religions was prohibited (Art. 4). Centralism, presidential dominance, and a clear constitutional mission for the armed forces also prevailed. The armed forces were charged with "conservation of order, respect for social *garantías,* and defense of the independence and integrity of the nation" (Art. 87). The 1868 Constitution also promised Bolivians the gamut of civil rights and liberties now expected: property, liberty, freedom of movement and of the press, and immunity from trial by "special commissions" or military tribunals. It even "guaranteed" respect for "intellectual property" and inventions.

Even if Melgarejo never read his constitution, as some claim, it epitomized Spanish American liberalism.[92] That meant that provisions were also made for emergencies, internal commotions, danger to the state, and for constitutional dictatorship. This had become part of Bolivian constitutional practice. Melgarejo and his advisers, like their predecessors, wished to rule as constitutional authorities, to dignify the abominable with constitutional principles and a presidential sash.

Any armed force, or group of persons that claimed to exercise the sovereign rights of the people, committed sedition (Art. 27). Such sedition might require the president "to take the measures necessary" to suppress it. However, civil liberties and rights could be suspended in the case of "internal commotion" only by decree of the council of ministers (appointed by the president). This allowed the president to "act as circumstances demand, with the sole and exclusive object of taking the necessary measures to put down the insurrection" (Art. 20). The president could transfer persons within the national territory or arrest them if they refused voluntary exile. They could not be sent to "unhealthy places" or more than fifty leagues from their residence (Art. 21). When the "internal commotion" had been put down, "the *imperio* of the Constitution again prevails" (Art. 22). In these respects, Melgarejo's constitution afforded more latitude for constitutional dictatorship than the constitutions of 1839 and 1861 but less than earlier and later documents. It failed to address the issue of extraordinary powers, neither authorizing nor prohibiting legislative concession of such authority to the president. Likewise, the state of siege provision of the 1861 Constitution was dropped. Perhaps the president's duty to "conserve and defend internal and external security of the State, according to the Constitution" was deemed sufficient.

Melgarejo's pathetic international initiatives, the minting of debased coinage (popularly labeled *Melgarejos*), his brutality, drunken orgies, and eccentric love life along with the routine uprisings faced by all Bolivian presidents finally brought an end to his government. On November 25, 1870, General Agustín Morales marched his troops into La Paz and was proclaimed "Supreme Chief of the Revolution." Discarding Melgarejo's constitution, the new authorities relied on the 1861 Constitution to declare all opposition towns to be in a state of siege. Morales called upon the Indian population to support the new government, promising restoration of the lands appropriated by foreign investors, friends, family, and supporters of Melgarejo. Only after a bloody all-day battle in La Paz in January 1871 did Melgarejo flee. Exiled in Lima without financial resources except a small military pension from Chile, Melgarejo was killed by a relative of his lover, Juanita Sánchez, in November 1871.

His successor, Agustín Morales (1870–1872), had been an active anti-*belcista* since his house was sacked in the 1849 uprising in Cochabamba. After his failed assassination attempt against Belzú, he fled the country, returning to serve in the Linares government (1857–1861), then leading uprisings against Linares and Achá. Melgarejo made him a general in reward for suppressing a revolt, then condemned him to death for conspiracy, then commuted the sentence to internal exile. Morales escaped to Peru—from whence he returned to oust Melgarejo. Morales nicely fit the mold of Bolivia's nineteenth-century caudillo presidents. Congress proclaimed him president with 10,473 votes of the 14,186 cast.[93]

Morales sought to reverse Melgarejo's land policies, returning some land to Indian communities and ceasing the minting of the debased coins. He mistakenly proclaimed that "no more tyrants would rule Bolivia."[94] However, his brief administration witnessed the opening of new silver mines at Caracoles in the southern (later Chilean) desert, the expansion of nitrate production in the Atacama desert, and the first contracts for railroads (1872) needed to carry nitrate from the Mejillones fields and the silver mines to Antofagasta. Elimination of the government silver monopoly and an end to protective tariffs continued the liberal economic policies of the Melgarejo administration.[95]

Before his assassination in 1872, President Morales also promulgated a new constitution. Approved on October 9, 1871, by the National Constituent Assembly meeting in Sucre, it was treated as a reform of the 1861 Constitution. The assembly had declared null the decrees of the Melgarejo government, including the agreements with the Anglo-Chilean Nitrate and Railway Company in Antofagasta. This eventually provoked the Chilean-Bolivian conflict that would lead to the War of the Pacific (1879–1883).[96] In addition, the assembly witnessed the first serious debates on federalism in a Bolivian constitutional convention. As a result, the 1871 Constitution defined the country as a "representative, democratic republic" instead of a "republic, one and indivisible" (Art. 1). Overall, after debating several draft constitutions, few significant changes were made in the 1861 document.

Presidential dominance and the broad responsibility for "conserving and defending the internal and external security of the State" and the "rank of Captain General of the armed forces inherent in the Presidency" reaffirmed the patterns of Bolivian politics since 1825. The centralist administrative system was retained, with the prefect of each department the immediate agent of the president, exercising direct authority in regard to order and security, administration, and the economy (Art. 91).

The most vocal advocate of federalism, Lucas Mendoza de la Tapia, pointed to this presidentialist-centralist tradition as the source of Bolivia's political woes: "Despotism and insurrections have infected [*desmoralizado*] politics. . . . Political morality is impossible under the centralist system, in which men are everything and principles nothing. Sinecure-mania is the natural product of this system."[97] Some delegates attacked federalism as the abandonment of Bolívar's dream; others noted that arguments for federalism were overreactions to Melgarejo's tyranny.[98]

The delegates eventually rejected federalism but, in a departure from the past, the constitution allowed public exercise of religions other than Catholicism in immigrant *colonias*. This was an effort to join other Spanish American nations in attracting European settlers and investment, rather than evidence of increased religious toleration for Bolivians. Success in this regard proved disastrous in the next decade as Chilean and British firms gobbled up the Pacific coast mineral wealth that had enriched the Bolivian government with tax revenues in the 1870s and then was lost in the War of the Pacific (1879–1883).

Melgarejo's arbitrary dictatorship also made the state of siege provisions in the 1861 charter and the broader issue of extraordinary powers important subjects at the 1871 convention. The delegates debated the causes of Bolivian political instability and caudillismo, seeking institutional and policy responses for the future. Intent on limiting executive authority and reducing legislative obsequiousness, the delegates decided to return more closely to the circumscribed regime of exception provisions in the 1839 Constitution. Article 19 stipulated:

> Neither Congress, nor any association, nor any popular assembly can concede extraordinary powers to the Executive, nor the sum of public power [*la suma del poder público*] nor extend him supremacies [*supremacías*] by which the lives, honor, or property of Bolivians are put at the mercy of the Government. . . . Deputies who promote, stimulate, or effect such acts are unworthy of public trust [*confianza nacional*].

In the case of "threats to the security of the Republic" in which "internal commotion or external war causes grave danger," the president could request from Congress the following authority: expansion of the armed forces and activation of the militia, special measures to finance the actions taken to meet the threat, and internal exile or arrest of those conspiring against "the tranquility and security of the Republic" if those involved refuse voluntary exile (Art. 21). If Congress were not in session, these powers could be conferred by the council of state or, if this were not possible, by the council of ministers. The president and his ministers were legally liable for any abuses committed in the exercise of this authority. Moreover, all acts that exceeded the constitutional authority of officials were, ipso facto, null (Art. 33). These provisions resembled earlier efforts to control executive authority and enhance legislative control. Restricting the presidential term to four years without possibility of immediate reelection (Art. 69) further indicated the intent of the 1871 delegates to deter presidential caudillismo and *continuismo* and to narrow the legal foundations for constitutional dictatorship.

Congress attempted to assert itself from 1871 to 1872, reducing the administration's discretionary budget (*gastos extraordinarios*) and threatening military expenditures. Vociferous debates over tax concessions to foreign investors and Morales's public and private excesses exacerbated legislative-executive tensions.[99] Morales reacted violently, marching troops to the Congress and personally closing an empty congressional session with vehement slurs on the legislators' honor and patriotism:

> My People. As the chief magistrate of Bolivia I come here today to close this assembly, whose seats, today deserted, have been occupied by a pack of traitors, despicable, corrupt [*vendidos*] men, who far from fulfilling their mission, have abused their power and authority to perturb and block the work of the government, accusing me of having violated the laws.
> ...What could be expected of men without work, who can only live off the sweat of the poor. . . .
> Do you know they accused me of being a thief. Me! Accused by these worthless ones who have tried to usurp your rights.
> . . . Gentlemen, I close this Assembly and I declare to the country that the congressmen of '72 have been corrupt traitors.[100]

Seeing conspirators everywhere, Morales offended a number of supporters with accusations of disloyalty. After an exchange of insults with a colonel whom he accused of plotting against him, the colonel shot and killed the president.

Morales's death (1872) allowed the civilian Rojos to temporarily assume control of the government. First, Tomás Frías, president of the council of state, assumed the interim presidency according to the 1871 Constitution. Elections followed, making Adolfo Ballivián the chief executive. Upon his death, Tomás Frías (1874–1876) again assumed the presidency, facing new garrison uprisings.[101]

Frías signed a treaty with Chile in 1874 confirming the basics of Melgarejo's agreements of 1866. His efforts to govern in accord with the constitution and complete Ballivián's presidential term failed. When he requested that his minister of defense, Hilarión Daza, defend the government against new uprisings, Daza decided that Frías's neutrality in the upcoming elections would prevent him from becoming president. Daza's public rationale for the coup he effected had a very modern sound to it: "The government had betrayed republican principles by favoring one of the candidates in the presidential elections; public order was threatened, the economic situation was difficult and the treasury empty; the government coalition was excessively exclusivistic, preventing the 'best elements' from assuming public positions."[102]

Like military officers in Chile, Uruguay, Brazil, Bolivia, El Salvador, and Guatemala in the 1960s and 1970s, Daza effected a coup to "defend the constitution and republican institutions." He promised to "create a strictly constitutional government."[103] Instead, he relied on the Colorado regiment, angered the legislature, and even saw his ministers resign in protest over his crude methods of government. A small landowning and mining elite had finally formed a permanent oligarchy to challenge absolute presidential dominance.

Making the Chilean-Bolivian territorial disputes and the contracts with the Antofagasta Nitrate and Railroad Company a nationalist crusade, Daza rejected the Melgarejo and Frías agreements. This pushed Bolivia (and due to a secret treaty signed in 1873, also Peru) toward war with Chile. Relations were broken in early 1878 after Daza imposed a new tax on the nitrate and railroad interests, contrary to the 1866 and 1874 agreements.[104]

Meanwhile, following routine practice, Daza called a constituent convention in 1877, which dutifully named him provisional president. A new constitution followed in 1878; it would be, with minor reforms in 1880, the constitutional framework for Bolivia until 1938. The 1878 Constitution was the culmination of Bolivian constitutional development after 1826. It represented a limited victory for the forces seeking to prevent *continuismo* for the president and to delimit, if not eliminate, the extent of extraordinary powers under states of siege. The president was to serve four years without the possibility of immediate reelection. He would be elected directly by voters or, if no candidate received an absolute majority, by Congress, from among the three candidates with the highest vote totals (Art. 85). This made control of legislative elections and the Congress a target for those seeking power. Congress would meet each year for sixty to ninety days, with the possibility of special sessions by agreement of both chambers or convocation by the executive (Arts. 39–42).

Despite the growing importance of the legislative branch, presidential dominance prevailed, as did centralism. Presidential patronage, command of the military, and the *patronato* were reaffirmed (Art. 89). The office of president included the "inherent rank" of captain-general of the army (Art. 90), and the president was responsible for "conserving and defending internal order and external security, in accord with the Constitution" (Art. 89, Sec. 23). This had become standard language in Bolivia's constitutions.

A special section of the constitution was dedicated to "the Conservation of Public Order" (Arts. 26–30). The language of this section was barely altered from 1878 until the 1960s:

- *Article 26:* "In the case of grave danger resulting from internal commotion or external war, that threatens the security of the Republic, the chief executive, with the approval of the Council of Ministers, may declare a state of siege, in that part of the country when it is necessary, and for the time thought indispensable."
- *Article 27:* "The declaration of the state of siege has the following effects: [the executive may increase the size of the army, make financial arrangements to pay for the measures taken, from internal or external sources, reduce the public payroll, municipal budgets, etc.]

   Garantías may be suspended for individuals who plot against public tranquility of the Republic [lists all the measures that may be taken against such persons, including internal exile, arrest, or voluntary external exile, censor mail, restrict travel, etc.]."

These basic provisions served Bolivian governments from 1878 into the 1990s. Despite prohibitions on applying these restrictions to congressmen, in the 1880s and 1890s civilian governments even violated this provision in order to remove opponents from Congress during the presidential selection process.

With the 1878 Constitution promulgated, Bolivia went to war with Chile. President Daza's ineptitude, cowardice, and unwillingness to risk the Colorado regiment in battle effectively took Bolivia out of the war by 1880.[105] Daza's military failure, corruption, and inability to maintain the loyalty of the army meant deposition. Ousted by a coup in late 1879, he fled—accused of having sold out to the Chileans. When he returned to face these charges under military escort in 1894, he was assassinated on his way to the capital.

Daza was succeeded by General Nicolás Campero, one of Bolivia's few European-trained military officers. Campero called a constitutional convention, which named him president and ratified the 1878 Constitution with minor changes. This constitution (1880) would be Bolivia's last in the nineteenth century. Campero, playing a role similar to that of General Manuel Bulnes in Chile in the 1840s, committed himself to a more effective role for the legislature, to constitutional government, and to consolidating a national political system. He also sought peace with Chile.

Serving his full four-year term, he abided by a promise to refrain from interfering in the 1884 presidential elections, despite his preference for fellow officer and founder of the Liberal party, General Eliodoro Camacho. These elections were a turning point in Bolivian politics, bringing the first of Bolivia's civilian Conservative party presidents to power. Mining magnates replaced garrison commanders as Bolivian presidents. This group would dominate the country until the end of the century, monopolizing the presidency and dominating the legislature through orchestrated elections, periodic repression of opponents, and liberal use of the state of siege provisions in the 1880 Constitution.

Vote buying, railroad construction (making possible more effective movement of troops), and incipient professionalization of the army reduced the power of local caudillos. A more prosperous national treasury ensured the salaries of public officials and the military, as rubber and tin gradually replaced silver exports as the major source of private and public revenue. Presidents now completed their four-year terms, influenced the choice of their successors, and were forced to negotiate with opponents in the legislature. A fragile political party system was developing.[106]

Always, however, temporary constitutional dictatorship was necessary to deal with adversaries. Presidents Gregorio Pacheco (1884–1888), Aniceto Arce (1888–1892), Mariano Baptista (1892–1896), and Severo Fernández Alonso (1896–1899) all used the state of siege provisions during their tenure. Acre used the state of siege to suppress a major Liberal uprising led by Colonel José Manuel Pando in 1890 and to ensure Baptista's election. Baptista left it in place as "a preventive measure." Fernández Alonso used the state of siege in efforts to control the "federal revolution" in which Pando's "Liberal" army ousted him, ending Conservative rule."[107]

When Liberals replaced Conservatives in the first decades of the twentieth century, they followed the practices of their predecessors. The Liberals dropped their support for federalism and buttressed the centralist-presidentialist system. The state of siege provisions remained an often-used instrument to control the opposition. In 1914, for example, Ismael Montes's Liberal government declared a state of siege to repress the Republican party opposition through arrests, internal exile and deportation, and closure of opposition newspapers.[108]

The Republican party platform included proposals to further restrict executive powers under the state of siege clause, to strengthen constitutional *garantías,* and to increase legislative and judicial autonomy. When they finally gained power in a July 1920 coup, they enacted none of these reforms. Rather, Republican presidents relied on the state of siege provisions to sustain their governments. In 1923, President Bautista Saavedra declared a state of siege to confront a miners' strike at Uncía. Union leaders were arrested and several dozen miners and family members killed when troops fired into a crowd.[109] The government also closed opposition newspapers to prevent dissemination of information on the strike. Later in 1923, Saavedra exiled opposition leaders. His successor, Hernando Siles (1924–1928), also used the state of siege to control political opponents, strikes by public employees and teachers, and student demonstrations. The Siles government also accused the Soviet Union of inciting rebels and Indian uprisings, which were ruthlessly suppressed.[110]

After more than half a century of coups, militarism, and constitutional instability (1826–1884), Bolivia experienced a quarter-century of oligarchic rule by mine owners, financiers, exporters, and *hacendados.* These civilian governments, Conservative, Liberal, and Republican, relied on the juridical foundations for constitutional dictatorship consolidated in 1880 to govern the country. Even after more than another century of socioeconomic change and a social revolution initiated in 1952, Bolivia would be subject to virtually the same constitutional bases for state of siege and with the same constitutional mission of the armed forces: to maintain internal order and act as saviors of the fatherland. Constitutional dictatorship and the militarization of politics "to save the nation" was the legacy of Bolivia's nineteenth-century development.

This legacy of the nineteenth century would survive new constitutions and reforms in 1938, 1945, 1947, 1961, and 1967. It would not be eliminated with the 1952 Revolution and would be reinforced by the challenges of the decades after the 1959 Cuban Revolution. Twelve years after the social revolution of 1952 began, the commander of the armed forces, General Alfredo Ovando Candía, reportedly told President Víctor Paz Estenssoro that he would "take him either to the airport or the cemetery"—as the military once again sought to rescue the *patria* from chaos.[111] The constitution adopted in 1967 conserved the language of Bolivian state of siege clauses, including presidential authority to suspend the *garantías* of selected persons, impose taxes, make expenditures necessary to meet the crisis, and increase the size of the armed forces.

When elections once again were permitted, in 1978, they occurred under a state of emergency, with police and the military on full alert. The use of state of siege and executive decree powers persisted after the restoration of civilian presidents in the 1980s. For example, Paz Estenssoro's return to power and his implementation of a neoliberal economic program brought a hunger strike by miners in 1985. Labeling this strike a *conmoción interna,* the president declared a state of siege. He claimed this was necessary to confront a movement that "seeks to supplant the authority of the State, exercising for these ends arbitrary pressures and public incitement to disobedience to the constituted authorities."[112]

Into the 1990s, Bolivians sustained the institutions of constitutional dictatorship bequeathed by Bolívar, Belzú, Achá, Melgarejo, Daza, and Campero. The country's penal code identified crimes against internal security, against public tranquility, and against government officials in the exercise of their legitimate authority. Sedition (Art. 121) and conspiracy (Art. 123) were also defined in a manner reminiscent of the nineteenth century. And of course the armed forces remained the guardians of internal security, public tranquility, and the institutions of the fatherland.

7

Regimes of Exception in Argentina, Uruguay, and Paraguay

CREATED AS AN ADMINISTRATIVE UNIT IN 1776, THE TERRITORY OF the viceroyalty of the Río de la Plata stretched from Tierra del Fuego to Upper Peru and from the Andes to the Atlantic. During the independence wars, Upper Peru gained autonomy as Bolivia. The province of Paraguay separated from the viceroyalty in 1811 and the region across the Río de la Plata north of Buenos Aires became the new nation of Uruguay in 1828. After almost half a century of internal and international wars, the remaining provinces of the Río de la Plata formed the Argentine Republic.

Constitutional development in the Río de la Plata region was in some ways unique. Political experimentation in Uruguay and Argentina involved fewer constitutions and ended earlier than in most of Spanish America. Uruguay adopted its first and only nineteenth-century constitution in 1830. Though numerous provisional statutes, interprovincial treaties, and two abortive constitutions (1819, 1826) expressed a commitment to nationhood among the provinces of the Río de la Plata, no accepted federal constitution existed in Argentina until 1860, no national president until 1862, and no national capital until 1880.[1] After 1860, however, only minor reforms modified the national charter.[2] Paraguay failed to enact a true constitution until 1870.

Despite the limited number of constitutional experiments, firm foundations for constitutional dictatorships similar to those developed elsewhere in Spanish America were constructed in Uruguay and Argentina by midcentury. In Paraguay, after sixty years of personalist rule, constitutional dictatorship took form in the 1870 charter and remained integral to Paraguayan constitutions into the 1990s.

ARGENTINA

From the 1780s, expansion of the cattle economy and establishment of meat processing enterprises (*saladeros*) had shaped the structure of economic and political confrontation for the Río de la Plata region. Commercial and livestock interests in Buenos Aires favored dismantling the Spanish mercantile system and opening the economy to international trade. They were opposed by artisans of the interior provinces who had relied on Spanish protectionism and links to the Upper Peruvian mining centers for their limited prosperity. Leaders of the interior resisted Buenos Aires's control of the rivers connecting them to the coast and of the customs revenues, and they resisted its presumed political hegemony over the rest of the viceroyalty. In Buenos Aires, merchants and bureaucrats associated with colonial monopolies also opposed relaxation of trade restrictions and the growing influence of European liberalism but shared *porteño* feelings of superiority over the provinces.

Perhaps nowhere else in Spanish America did Spanish colonial commercial policy make as little sense and engender as much hostility as in Buenos Aires. The arrival of an expanded Spanish administrative contingent after 1776 intensified this hostility by curtailing the power of the *cabildo* and downgrading the status of the *criollo* socioeconomic elite.[3] Intermittent periods of direct trade with Europe and Brazil, associated with wartime exigencies from the 1790s, further whetted the appetite of advocates of freer trade and produced corps of political activists in the port city.

In late 1804 Spain again found itself at war with Britain. When the British destroyed the Spanish fleet at Trafalgar in 1805, naval interdiction by the British fleet made normal communications with Buenos Aires virtually impossible. A British invasion in 1806 reinforced the *criollos'* disdain for the Spanish elite and encouraged pride in local political and military initiative. The Spanish viceroy fled to the interior; multiracial *porteño* and provincial militia (*patricios, aribeños*) led by Santiago Liniers, a French army officer in the royal service, defeated the British. A subsequent British attack in 1807 also failed, after which the *audiencia* deposed and arrested the viceroy and replaced him with Liniers, the interim military governor. Liniers decreed freer trade, thereby buttressing the localist forces and angering the monopoly merchants and colonial bureaucrats. With Spanish authority undermined and the *criollo* militia the prime power in the port, news of Ferdinand VII's abdication and the assumption of Joseph Bonaparte in Spain encouraged radical separationists. Some *porteños* initially accepted the authority of the *junta central* in Spain; others urged immediate independence.

Across the river in Montevideo, Governor Francisco Javier Elío was distrusted by Liniers and his *criollo* supporters. Liniers attempted to replace Elío with a less adamantly royalist officer. He resisted and the local *cabildo* established a governing junta composed entirely of *peninsulares*. Until 1814–1815, Montevideo would be a key royalist base in the Río de la Plata. Like-thinking Spaniards sought to emulate this decision in Buenos Aires in 1809, which in effect was an attempted coup, but *criollo* troops led by Cornelio Saavedra prevented the *golpe*.[4]

Appointed by the Seville junta that resisted the French occupation of Spain, a new viceroy, Viscount Balthazar de Cisneros, arrived in Buenos Aires in 1809. Cisneros symbolized the weak but important thread connecting the deposed king, the Spanish resistance, and the colonies. Caught in the conflict between free traders and the mercantilist faction, and unsuccessful in efforts to restore the power of the Spanish garrison vis-à-vis the colonial militia, Cisneros was deposed by a *cabildo abierto* he convoked on May 25, 1810. Though Argentine independence came formally in 1816, this coup marked the effective end of Spanish rule.

From 1810 to 1819, when the first short-lived constitution was adopted for the provinces of the Río de la Plata, extensive debates occurred over the legitimate source and exercise of sovereignty after the collapse of Spanish authority. These debates, and the political conflicts of which they were part, generated a number of transitory governments in some ways reminiscent of France in the 1790s. These governments faced the dual challenge of pursuing the independence war against Spain as far away as Upper Peru and Chile while attempting to establish and sustain political authority for the Río de la Plata region.[5]

Politics and Constitutional Experiments, 1811–1820

For the first half century of independence, the political and economic differences between the coast and interior provinces and between localist and nationalist sentiment in Buenos Aires were translated into battles of centralists (*unitarios*) and federalists, between those in Buenos Aires who insisted on monopolizing the benefits of international trade and customs revenues and those who proposed making the port a national capital of an Argentine republic. In the words of James Scobie, this was truly the history of "a city and a nation."[6] It was also the history of regionalist caudillo militarism and constitutional dictatorship.

Constituent assemblies, congresses, triumvirates, supreme directors, governors, and provisional governments in Buenos Aires and the interior provinces promulgated a series of proto-constitutions and constitutional decrees from 1811 to 1820. Each of these decrees included a bill of rights (*decreto de seguridad individual*) and a separate guarantee of press freedom. Each also made provision for suspension of these rights by invocation of a regime of exception, often through investing the executive with full authority ("lleno de facultades"), with extraordinary powers, or with the power to suspend the bill of rights. From 1811 to 1860, as army officers, militia commanders, caudillos, and their civilian allies toppled juntas, governors, and presidents, Argentine national and provincial charters included provisions for constitutional dictatorship.

Following the coup of May 25, 1810, Cornelio Saavedra ordered Cisneros's arrest and assumed the presidency of a new junta that initially pledged its loyalty to Spain. Despite the eventual conflict between Saavedra and the most liberal intellectuals, such as Mariano Moreno, the junta represented the proindependence merchants and political radicals.[7] Thus, more clearly than elsewhere in Spanish America, the origins of independence in Buenos Aires were found in a military coup. Armies of the caudillos of Buenos Aires and the interior would dominate the region for most of the nineteenth century, establishing a central role for violence and military power in the politics of the Río de la Plata.[8]

The Saavedra junta and the confusing succession of juntas, congresses, triumvirates, and directorates that followed from 1810 to 1829 wanted to establish control over the old viceroyalty. They failed dismally, as royalists and separatists in Montevideo, Asunción, and Upper Peru rejected *porteño* leadership and defeated military units sent to secure compliance with the *porteño* junta's decrees.[9]

In Córdoba, initial resistance was led by the *intendente* and former viceroy Liniers, who remained loyal to Spain. When the Buenos Aires militia defeated Liniers's forces, Mariano Moreno, secretary of the junta, ordered the execution of Liniers and his officers. His justification of this order anticipated the spirit of Argentina's future constitutional provisions for regimes of exception, extraordinary powers for executives, and merciless repression of political opponents. His Rousseauistic liberalism melded state terrorism with insincere appeals to popular sovereignty and to constitutionalism, while his adherence to intolerant Hispanic Catholicism led him to recommend a secret police force to denounce all enemies of the government. Enemies were those not fully committed to Moreno's version of the patriot cause.

This view would become an important element of Argentine political culture, making adversaries into heretics, critics into criminals, and political opponents into enemies of the state and threats to the security of the fatherland. It was shared by Argentine liberals and conservatives. It would justify murder, savagery, and mayhem for much of the nineteenth century and would culminate in a "dirty war" in which thousands of "subversives" would perish or "disappear" from 1976 to 1983.[10] To defend the rights of the people and the legitimate provisional government against treason, as Moreno put it, "we have decreed the sacrifice of these victims, to protect the lives of thousands of innocents. Only the terror of this punishment can serve as warning to their accomplices."[11] Insisting on an immediate declaration of independence and centralized control by the Buenos Aires junta over the viceregal territory, Moreno's inquisitorial Jacobinism proved unsustainable. An effort by Moreno and his supporters to wrest control of the militia from Saavedra failed. He resigned from the junta and died at sea on his way into European exile. With Moreno's departure, the junta was reconstituted into a *junta grande* that included representatives of the interior provinces. The junta conceded extraordinary powers to Saavedra, who created a new "court of public security" and gave ample police functions to the local garrisons. He also authorized the creation of *juntas provinciales*.[12]

Successive military defeats in Paraguay, Upper Peru, and Montevideo undermined the junta. Saavedra lost control to a triumvirate, which dissolved the *junta grande* and the *juntas provinciales*. This triumvirate represented the extreme centralists and economic liberals of Buenos Aires, dominated by the secretary of the junta, Bernardino Rivadavia. Rivadavia's design to unify the provinces under *porteño* direction would be the focus of the most important political conflicts in the Río de la Plata region for the next half century.

The triumvirate toyed with a plan for constitutional monarchy, flirted with the British for support by promising direct access to the Buenos Aires market, and adopted Argentina's first bill of rights, accompanied by its first formal provisions for a regime of exception. A press law issued in April 1811,[13] and amended by the triumvirate government, ended a priori censorship and allowed for "freedom of the press"—so long as publications did not "compromise public tranquility, the conservation of the Catholic religion, or the constitution of the State, [with] such criminal abuses to be punished as provided by law."[14] The triumvirate also issued a decree on "personal security," the nine articles of which captured Spanish American liberalism's essential conception of human rights and their limitations. Most of this decree would eventually find its way into the Constitution of 1853:

> Every citizen has the sacred right of protection of life, honor, liberty and property. The possession of this right, the basis for civil liberty, and foundation of social institutions, is what is called "personal security" [*seguridad individual*]. [To this end the following decree guarantees the following: due process, inviolability of domicile without proper warrant, no period of *incomunicado* beyond ten days, abolition of torture and humiliation in the jails, freedom of travel, no involuntary exile, freedom of press, etc.]
>
> Art. 9. Only in the remote and extraordinary case of threats to public tranquility or security of the fatherland may the government suspend this decree, while the threat endures, reporting to the Assembly, justifying its decision, and assuming responsibility [for any abuses committed].[15]

Thus Argentina's first bill of rights and guarantees of press freedom were accompanied by provisions for a regime of exception. It permitted suspension of these rights to conserve public tranquility or security of the fatherland. From this time (1811), Argentina would never be without constitutional foundations for dictatorship.

For the moment, the exigencies of civil war directly threatened "public tranquility and security of the fatherland." Royalists supported by Ferdinand VII's sister, Princess Carlota of Brazil, attempted a new restoration in Buenos Aires in July 1812. Martín Alzaga, hero of the defense of Buenos Aires against the British invasions (1806–1807), and other leaders of the unsuccessful coup were executed and their bodies hung in the main plaza of Buenos Aires. Numerous unsuccessful rebels and deposed governors would follow in their path over the next fifty years.

The recently founded Patriotic Society (Sociedad Patriótica), led by José de San Martín, Carlos Alvear, and Bernardo de Monteagudo under the slogan "Independence, Constitution, and Democracy," took advantage of the 1812 uprising to oust the first triumvirate and establish a more aggressive independence initiative. Under the authority of an October 8, 1812, decree that created a "provisional government" for an entity called United Provinces of the Río de la Plata, San Martín reorganized the militia that was created in 1806 and imposed new revenue measures discriminating against Spaniards to finance the war against Spain. Article 5 of the decree recognized the "bill of rights" and regime of exception provisions issued by the first triumvirate.[16]

The new government, a second triumvirate, acting as the Supremo Poder Ejecutivo under the terms of a decree published March 6, 1813, survived until 1814. The assembly assigned to the plural executive most of the powers associated with presidents in Spanish America, including authority "to suspend the decree of personal security [1811] in the case of invasion or threat of invasion, rebellion or other grave threat to the security of the state, advising the constituent Assembly of the action taken within 24 hours."[17] In early 1814, the assembly replaced the plural executive with a "supreme director," who inherited all the powers of the second triumvirate.[18] The first supreme director, Gervasio Antonio de Posadas, resigned in January 1815. He was followed by Carlos Alvear for three months, and then by several forgettable successors. Posadas sought to oust the Spanish from Montevideo but had also declared José Artigas, the Uruguayan caudillo and proponent of federalism, to be an "outlaw . . . enemy of the fatherland" and offered six thousand pesos' reward for the federalist leader "dead or alive."[19]

In his tenure as supreme director, Alvear captured Montevideo and decreed (March 28, 1815) capital punishment for those who "attacked the government, invented or spread false information, encouraged desertion by the soldiers, those who conspired, or who knowing of conspiracies failed to inform the authorities." A special commission would try these cases in Buenos Aires, no matter where the crime occurred. Those judged guilty of attacking the established government, directly or indirectly, would be executed within twenty-four hours.[20] The army sent against Artigas mutinied at Fontezuelas in April 1815. Alvear resigned the supreme directorship and was prevented from assuming military command.

This crisis resulted in the dissolution of the assembly and the reassumption of sovereignty by the *cabildo*. A military commission named by the mutinous officers brought several assembly delegates to trial, imposing exile or prison sentences in some cases. Artigas gained further support among the littoral provinces, advancing the federalist cause against the pretensions of Buenos Aires. In response to the creation of "provinces duly dependent upon the authority [*suprema*] of the State," local caudillos in Entre Ríos and Corrientes aligned themselves more closely with Artigas and the Provincia Oriental del Río de la Plata, created in 1814. Meanwhile, Ferdinand VII had returned to Spain, and royalist victories in Upper Peru and Chile threatened the independence movement.

Reassuming popular sovereignty in April 1815, the *cabildo* directed the election of a provisional government to exercise the "supreme executive authority" until a Congress representing all the provinces could meet and devise a constitution for the United Provinces. The *cabildo* named a Junta de Observación composed of "virtuous citizens" to enact a provisional charter for governing the territory.[21] The resulting elections made General José Rondeau director of state; in his absence, Colonel Ignacio Alvarez Thomas, leader of the Fontezuela mutiny, took military command and the *cabildo* political control. On May 5, 1815, the Junta de Observación issued the "Provisional Statute for the Direction and Administration of the State."[22] Alvarez Thomas remained in office as director of state until a garrison uprising forced his resignation on April 16, 1816, and Brigadier General Antonio González Balcarce replaced him.[23]

Departing little from the liberal underpinnings of earlier proto-constitutions, the 1815 Provisional Statute commenced with a declaration of the rights of man in society—the liberal menu of life, liberty, equality, and security, spiced with the Spanish "right" of honor (Art. 1).[24] A separate section reaffirmed the decrees of personal security and the press law of 1811, followed by slightly more restrictive language than that in force from 1811 to 1815 providing for a regime of exception. The "bill of rights" (the 1811 decree on personal security) could not be formally suspended, but

> when, in a very remote and extraordinary case, that compromises public tranquility or the security of the Fatherland, it is not possible to respect them [*no pueda observarse quanto en él se previene*], the authorities who find themselves in this difficult [*fatal*] situation shall report the reason for their conduct to the

Junta de Observación and the Cabildo, who shall examine the
motives for the measures taken and the time for which they
shall persist. (Sec. 7, Chap. I, Art. XXI)

The Provisional Statute also reenacted the press law of October
26, 1811, with a number of innovative additions, including provision for a *cabildo*-sponsored newspaper dedicated to examining the
injustices and abuses of power committed by government officials
(Chap. II, Art. VI). It remained criminal, however, to "compromise
the public tranquility, conservation of the Catholic Religion, or the
Constitution of the State" in the press. Another innovation of the
Provisional Statute was to include lengthy sections on the army,
navy, provincial militia, and civic militia. While their constitutional
mission was neglected, the statute provided for important areas of
military autonomy from civilian meddling and respect for the military *ordenanzas*. It also included a puzzling provision commanding
the civic militia—but not the army, navy, or provincial militia—to
resist unconstitutional orders of the director of state and defend the
Junta de Observación and the *cabildo* against executive usurpation
of authority (Chap. III, Art. X).

Efforts to enact a constitution by the assembly of the United
Provinces had failed, despite preparation of several draft proposals
by federalists, unitarists, and the Patriotic Society.[25] The Provisional
Statute, which allowed the provinces to name their own governors
and exercise legislative authority within their jurisdictions, was explicitly an interim measure until a constitution could be adopted.
However, continued internal strife and war against royalist troops
prevented a constitutional convention convoked in 1815 from
achieving its goals. Instead, it adopted two additional provisional
statutes (1816, 1817), both of which maintained the regime of exception clauses of 1811 to 1815, and on July 9, 1816, it proclaimed
the independence of the United Provinces of the Río de la Plata.
Formally independent, the provinces would not be united in fact for
many years to come.

Congress preceded its declaration of independence by appointing as director Juan Martín de Pueyrredón, who had been a triumvir in 1811–1812. In June 1816, a Portuguese invasion of the
provincia oriental (Uruguay) ousted Artigas. He fought for three
more years before meeting defeat at Tacuarembó in January 1820.
Artigas, with several hundred fighters, escaped the battlefield littered with corpses; he continued guerrilla resistance for several
more months before retiring for life to Paraguay in September

1820.[26] San Martín's heroic crossing of the Andes into Chile soon resulted in a Chilean independence proclamation. At Buenos Aires, however, the director's efforts to control the provinces by interdicting the river trade precipitated armed resistance by the caudillos of Santa Fé and Entre Ríos.

From 1816 to 1819, relations between Buenos Aires and the provinces remained tense. In 1819 Congress adopted a national constitution. Some of the constituents clearly preferred a monarchy to end the chaos endemic since 1810. Opposition to the constitution stemmed both from its provision for a centralist state (referred to as unitarism in Argentina) and the presumption that its framers favored imposing a constitutional monarch. Cautiously, however, the constitution provided only for the traditional three branches of government, neglecting any definition of the form of state. This left open the possibility of constitutional monarchy on the Spanish or British model.

The chief executive was again denominated director, elected now for a five-year term instead of the shorter terms (six months, one year, two years) of the proto-constitutions from 1811 to 1817. Elected indirectly by the two houses of Congress, the director was commander in chief of the armed forces and was given broad authority to "oppose the invasions of foreign enemies, prevent conspiracies, and quell popular uprisings" (Sec. II, *Poder Executivo* LXXX). He could name unilaterally all generals of the armed forces, ambassadors, government ministers and, with the consent of the Senate, bishops and archbishops.

The 1819 Constitution reflected the urban elite's fear of the power of rural-based caudillos and the irregular gaucho forces that sustained them. It created a corporate Senate, with military, ecclesiastical, and even university representatives to counterbalance provincial senators. Senators and deputies in the lower house were required to meet property or education requirements. The Congress would elect the chief executive or director in open written elections, each ballot signed by the respective congressman.

The constitution reaffirmed the 1811 press law and the provisions of the 1811 decree on personal security, including exact replication of the regime of exception clause from the 1815 Provisional Statute with the sole modification of substituting the Congress as legislative authority for the *cabildo* and the Junta de Observación (Sec. V, Chap. I, Arts. CIX–CXXII). The Catholic religion remained the state religion. Failure to respect it was a crime, but no prohibition existed on public exercise of other faiths. Here the dominant influence of the British merchants and diplomats was visible, as it had been since 1810.[27] The constitution outlawed Indian tribute, slavery, and titles of nobility. Unlike the 1815 statute, no constitutional provision was made for the armed forces or the militia.

As a creation of the Buenos Aires centralists, the 1819 Constitution was dead on delivery. The provinces immediately declared their opposition and Pueyrredón sent an army into Santa Fé. His army defeated, the director resigned. Central authority evaporated as caudillos proclaimed self-rule throughout the interior.[28] Pueyrredón's replacement, José Rondeau, was defeated at Cepeda outside Buenos Aires in 1820. The victorious provincial caudillos demanded abrogation of the 1819 Constitution, acceptance by Buenos Aires of federalism (really localism), free navigation of the rivers, and respect for the autonomy of provincial commerce and administration.

The fruit of independence was bitter for the *porteños*. Ten years of war and constitutional experimentation had resulted in the balkanization of the Río de la Plata. In Buenos Aires the Congress resorted to a new regime of exception, authorizing the interim director to "take extraordinary measures of defense" to defend the fatherland, but without suspending the decree of personal security.[29] Shortly thereafter Congress dissolved itself and the supreme director delivered "the Supreme Direction of the State" into the hands of the *cabildo*. Now, however, the Buenos Aires *cabildo* spoke only for the province and the port—not for the United Provinces of the Río de la Plata.

A Junta de Representantes then assumed the legislative (sovereign) power in Buenos Aires Province, naming the governor and conferring upon the new provincial executive full authority (*el lleno de facultades*) for the next eight months to meet the immediate crisis.[30] In so doing, even in the chaos of 1820, the legislators limited the executive emergency powers, prohibiting exercise of judicial functions, imposition of new taxes, creation of new public posts or appointment of military officers above the rank of colonel, declaration of war, and ratification of treaties, among other restrictions. He could, however, "order the arrest and detention of persons who threatened public order and tranquility."[31]

Executive emergency powers and regime of exception provisions were already so entrenched in Argentine constitutional principles by 1820 that even the hapless Junta de Representantes automatically conferred them on the governor. When the Junta

named Martín Rodríguez governor (1821–1824), he received *lleno de facultades* without any limitation for three months—virtually a constitutional dictatorship on the Roman model. The Junta conferred this power to achieve "the only and supreme law of States, public welfare [*salud pública*]."[32] The provincial victory over Buenos Aires was ratified by the Treaty of Pilar on February 23, 1820.[33] In June 1820, Portuguese and *porteño*-supported troops defeated Artigas, provoking the incorporation of the *banda oriental* (Uruguay) into the Brazilian empire as the Cisplatine Province. The provinces of the Río de la Plata reverted to dismembered *republiquetas* just as Bolívar created Gran Colombia after the 1819 Congress of Angostura, the liberals in Spain reimposed the Constitution of 1812, and San Martín liberated Lima in 1821.[34]

Balkanization meant internecine strife. Several provinces declared themselves independent republics. From 1820 to 1825, all the provinces except Buenos Aires adopted their own constitutions, tax systems, and provisions for regimes of exception to protect the security of the state.[35] The first of these was Santa Fé in 1819 under Estanislao López who, invested with extraordinary powers, dominated the province for almost twenty years. Article 19 of the province's Provisional Statute declared that "selection of his *caudillo* constitutes one of the most essential acts of human freedom." López insisted on universal suffrage, a gaucho plebiscite, to approve his constitutional dictatorship. Article 34 of the statute afforded the governor "full authority" (*un lleno de facultades*), accompanied by a list of imaginary rights and *garantías* extended to citizens (Arts. 35–37, 46–47, 49, 50–53).

Into the early 1850s, modifications of these provincial constitutions included regimes of exception and provision for the exercise of extraordinary powers by the reigning caudillo-governor. The most famous of the Argentine caudillos, Juan Manuel de Rosas, who ruled Buenos Aires province and, indirectly, much of the interior from 1829 to 1852, emulated López's plebiscitary legitimation for his "full authority" but obtained also "the sum of sovereign power" (*la suma del poder público*) in 1835 (see below).

Illustrative are the articles from provincial provisional statutes and constitutions in Córdoba (1821), Entre Ríos (1822), San Juan (1825), Jujuy (1839), and Tucumán (1852):

• *Córdoba Provisional Reglamento, 1821, Articles 108 and 109*, replicated section III, chapter 2, articles 6 and 7 of the 1817 Reglamento Provisorio.

- *Entre Ríos Provisional Constitutional Statute, 1822, Article 78*, conferred on the executive the power "to prevent conspiracies, quell uprisings, and resist all foreign invasions" while "using at his discretion appropriate methods."
- *San Juan, Carta de Mayo, 1825, Article 22*, prohibited the suspension of articles of the constitution "unless required by the general welfare [*salud pública*]"; suspension requires a two-thirds plus two vote of the legislature.
- *Jujuy Provincial Statute, 1839, Article 59*, provided that personal security (bill of rights) may not be suspended without approval by the Junta General, or when in recess, by the permanent commission in the extraordinary cases of treason or conspiracy against the fatherland, and then only for the apprehension of the delinquents.
- *Tucumán Provincial Statute, 1852, Article 42*, provided that the House of Representatives may not invest the executive with extraordinary powers except in the case of internal commotion or external invasion, and for the time absolutely necessary to restore public order ("salvar al orden público"). *Article 43* provided that these powers may only extend to the arrest of persons deemed to threaten public order or to confine them within the province or to require that they leave the province.

The urge to legitimize even the power of cattle baron warlords with proto-constitutions or constitutions applied in the Río de la Plata as it did in Bolivia, Peru, and northern South America. If force determined who ruled, those who ruled sought some shred of evidence that popular sovereignty and juridical right cloaked their actions.[36] Adopting such charters did not prevent the caudillos, who had temporarily defeated Buenos Aires in 1820, from warring on each other. When the caudillo of Entre Ríos, Francisco "Pancho" Ramírez, sought in 1821 to impose his will in Córdoba and Corrientes, Estanislao López's forces defeated, captured, and murdered him. His head was displayed in an iron cage in the plaza of Santa Fé.[37] Decapitated heads of the vanquished displayed in public dramatized the risks of alleged treason, subversion, and threatening the security of the fatherland during the first half of the nineteenth century.

Intra- and interprovincial conflicts did not end the quest for federation or some other institutional expression of a nascent nationalism. The Treaty of Pilar (1820) provided for eventual federation and the meeting of a Congress to adopt an acceptable constitution. Efforts in this direction persisted, with treaties, pacts, and abortive constituent congresses occurring from 1821 to 1831. A Confederal pact adopted in 1831 by Buenos Aires, Entre Ríos, and Santa Fé served for twenty years as the reservoir of national sentiment and the pretext for preventing the formation of a national government.[38] It provided for a "Representative Commission of the Governments of the Littoral Provinces" (a legislature) and the future meeting of a "General Federal Congress" to constitute a federal republic, when the remaining provinces were "fully free and tranquil." After 1820, dissension among the provincial warlords allowed Buenos Aires to reassert itself gradually and to dominate the waterways, customs revenues, and international commerce. Still, the *porteño* liberals, unitarists, and commercial elite were a minority attempting to impose alien philosophical and political reins on the gaucho horsemen and caudillos of the provinces.

In Buenos Aires, after a year of virtual anarchy (the best estimate for 1820 is that twenty-four governments rose and fell, with three on June 20 alone), the administration of Martin Rodríguez (1821–1824) initiated sweeping reforms. Inspired by Minister Bernardino Rivadavia's European and Benthamite liberalism, the government introduced a land policy (emphyteusis) based on leasing extensive tracts of public lands at low rates to privileged cattle interests that in turn secured the foreign debt. This further opened the economy to the British and other merchants. Rivadavia also created a university in Buenos Aires, abolished the colonial *cabildo* (thereby separating police functions from administration of justice), and sought to professionalize the province's military forces. An effort was also made to reduce the privileges and functions of the church and to institutionalize a provincial system of government in which a legislative branch selected the governor, granting him broad administrative authority.[39] Both Rodríguez and his successor, General Juan Gregorio de la Heras, a hero of San Martín's Chilean and Peruvian campaigns, exercised extraordinary powers conferred by the legislature.

Campaigns against the southern Indians permitted an expansion of the large private cattle estates. Combined with an influx of British merchant capital and growth in trade, this brought limited prosperity to Buenos Aires. Commerce produced increasing import duties that now accounted for over 80 percent of the province's revenues. The political elite rewarded itself with *estancias* from the newly conquered lands and further developed the *saladero* enterprises.

In 1824, with the Spanish defeat at Ayacucho (see chapter 6), the British extended formal recognition to the United Provinces of the Río de la Plata. A loan from the Baring Brothers merchant banking house, ostensibly for consolidation of the public debt and for public works, created great controversy both because the government received only 50 percent of the negotiated million pounds sterling after discounts and commissions and because most of the funds were expended for the war (1825–1828) against Brazil for control of Uruguay (*la banda oriental*).

In the same year, another effort began to enact a national constitution, with a constituent Congress called to Buenos Aires. From 1824 to 1826, extensive debates and political machinations produced interim "fundamental laws" and agreements on procedures for ratification of the new constitution. A modified unitarist constitution followed in 1826.[40] Like its predecessor of 1819 and the earlier proto-constitutions, the 1826 charter incorporated most of the bill of rights and press freedom provisions customary since 1811 (Arts. 159–73), followed by provision for their suspension, now by Congress, when the security of the fatherland was threatened. Article 174 provided that "all the above dispositions relative to personal security may not be suspended except in the case of imminent danger compromising public tranquility or the security of the fatherland, in the judgment and by special disposition of the congress." As in 1811, threats to public tranquility or security of the fatherland justified suspension of civil rights and liberties.

An executive elected for five years with authority to appoint all the provincial governors [Arts. 130–36) and to control the armed forces, combined with the division of Buenos Aires province into two and the nationalization of Buenos Aires as the federal capital, among other provisions, spelled disaster. Both provincial caudillos and federalists in Buenos Aires rejected the constitution. Rivadavia's policies had created numerous enemies—clerical interests, those disadvantaged by land and banking reforms, and disaffected military officers among the most visible—and few allies. Ideological and political opposition to the constitution was thus reinforced by enemies of the new president's policies in Buenos Aires. Rivadavia, who had been selected president by the constituent Congress, served briefly, then resigned amid renewed civil war.

The Rosas Dictatorship, 1829–1852

Again there existed no national government. Futile decrees of a powerless national Congress and a provisional president maintained the fictive presence of national sovereignty until 1829, but civil war, caudillo militia, and provincial assemblies exercised authority in the interior. Buenos Aires reverted to provincial government under Colonel Manuel Dorrego, who acknowledged the autonomy of the provinces, negotiated a British-imposed solution for the *banda oriental*—Uruguayan independence in 1828—and accepted the name Confederation of the Río de la Plata instead of United Provinces. Dorrego attempted to negotiate treaties with the interior provinces, looking toward eventual consolidation of a confederal polity.

Discontented army units returning from the Uruguayan front rebelled; in the name of the unitarists, they deposed and executed Dorrego. Juan Manuel de Rosas, leading *estanciero,* militia commander, declared federalist, and defender of the Catholic religion, ousted Dorrego's assassin and was given extraordinary powers as "provisional governor" of Buenos Aires in a peace treaty (Convención de Barracas, August 24, 1829).[41] Both the federalists of the interior provinces and the unitarists wished to create some constitutional foundations for a national political system. They hoped to reduce Buenos Aires's hegemony and end its control over international trade, the customs revenues, and tariff policy. Generally, the provinces favored protectionism and resented both Buenos Aires's taxes on their products and the privileges granted to British and European merchants.[42]

From the time of his investiture with extraordinary powers by provincial authorities, Rosas opposed creation of a national government or adoption of a national constitution, supposedly until the provinces had established internal stability.[43] He maintained this position, as a pretext for his own unrestrained rule, until he was ousted in 1852. His position benefited cattle and commercial interests in Buenos Aires, the church ("Before we were federalists, we were Catholics, and we must remember our obligations to God"), some foreign merchants, and caudillos in other provinces. With his allies in the provinces he shared resources in exchange for the delegation of authority to make foreign policy or otherwise exercise power on their behalf.

The first grant of extraordinary powers to Rosas was made that he might

> regulate, in conformity with the exigencies of present circumstances, the interior administration of the provinces in all their branches . . . to thwart the attacks that the anarchists design

against them; and to ensure order and public tranquility. . . .
In order to promote these objects *he is invested with the extraordinary powers which he may judge necessary* until the meeting of
the next legislature, to which he shall give an account of the
use which he has made of this special authorization.[44]

On August 2, 1830, a law expanded these powers so that Rosas
could "make use of these powers, according to his judgment and
conscience, to adopt those measures deemed useful [*conducentes*] to
rescue the province from the dangers that . . . menace its political
existence and civil liberty." Emulation followed. In September 1831,
the province of Corrientes authorized its governor "to take all measures necessary and convenient [in order to] "end all these problems" (*cortar todos los males*).[45] Having completed his first three-year
term of office, Rosas refused reappointment and led a military campaign against hostile Indians to the south of Buenos Aires. Victorious in this campaign, he returned to the governorship, after first
refusing the legislature's offer of reappointment.

Rosas assumed office after the interim governor had declared it
impossible to administer the province due to civil and interprovincial wars as well as economic difficulties. The legislature conferred
upon Rosas "the sum total of public authority" (*la suma del poder
público*), despite the debates that had occurred from 1831 to 1834 in
the legislature over "extraordinary powers" and despite a draft constitution for the province in 1833 that had explicitly prohibited investing the executive with such authority except in cases of
rebellion or invasion, and then only for three months.[46] Rosas accepted appointment only upon the condition that a plebiscite affirm his dictatorial powers. A plebiscite in Buenos Aires on March
26–28, 1835, in which citizens verbally said yes or no to local officials, made Rosas constitutional dictator by a vote of 9,716 to 4.[47]

Monopolizing revenues from international trade, controlling
the rivers, and delaying all efforts to draft a national constitution,
Rosas used terror, a private, politicized police force (*mazorca*), his
private militia (Colorados), and alliances with provincial caudillos to
maintain himself in the saddle.[48] He completely dominated the
provincial legislature, the bureaucracy, the army, and the militia.
He supported and received support from the church, which allowed his likeness to be placed upon altars. Political exiles in Chile,
Montevideo, and Europe bemoaned the tyranny of the dictatorship;
its origins, however, were in delegations of "full authority" to Rosas
by duly constituted legislatures. This was periodically reinforced by

investiture with further authority and honors by provincial legislatures from 1835 to 1851.[49] Rosas installed a terrorist regime with the veil of legitimacy. He

> used terror as an instrument of government, to eliminate enemies, to discipline dissidents, to warn waverers and, ultimately, to control his own supporters. Terror was not simply a series of exceptional episodes, though it was regulated according to circumstances. It was an intrinsic part of the Rosas system, the distinctive style of the regime, its ultimate sanction. Rosas himself was the author of terror, ordering executions without trial by virtue of the extraordinary powers vested in him. . . . The incidence of terrorism varied according to pressures on the regime, rising to a peak in 1839–1842, when French intervention, internal rebellion, and unitarian invasion threatened to destroy Rosas' state.[50]

Rosas always faced challenges from external or internal enemies; he never lacked some rationale for exercising extraordinary powers. The threats of "the savage unitarists," and the need to defend federalism and protect the sacred Catholic religion against liberals and Masons, provided suitable pervasive enemies. The war against Santa Cruz in Bolivia and Peru (1837–1838), pretensions to reincorporate Paraguay into the confederation, resistance to the Anglo-French blockades (1838–1840, 1845), and the siege against Montevideo (1843–1851) further justified repression of internal adversaries. Slit throats, decapitated heads of enemies displayed in public squares, bodies of the executed hung from lampposts, gunshots by Rosas's *mazorca* thugs through residential windows to "encourage" the flight of opponents, summary executions, and military impressment became routine methods of saving the fatherland from its enemies.[51] After his military victories, Rosas routinely executed captured enemies and confiscated their property for distribution among his allies.

Rosas's rule was a lengthy regime of exception, exceeding the tenure of more modern terrorist governments built on similar juridical foundations in Argentina, Chile, Uruguay, and Brazil from the 1960s through the 1980s. Like his twentieth-century terrorist compatriots, Rosas had supporters, represented important religious, ideological, economic, and social interests, and had some foreign allies. Otherwise, he could not have stayed so long in power. He bullied but also rewarded provincial supporters, gave land taken from the Indians to soldiers and officers, and inspired rural, conservative opponents of citified imported liberalism. He also had on his side the legal tradition of regimes of exception in the Río de la Plata commencing in 1811, and the legislative delegation of full authority, as constitutional legitimation.

Finally, in 1852, an army headed by Justo José de Urquiza, leading caudillo of Entre Ríos province, backed by British, Brazilian, Uruguayan, and provincial adversaries, defeated Rosas at Monte Caseros. Rosas responded with a letter to the provincial legislature:

> Honorable representatives: the time has arrived to return to you the investiture of governor of the province and the sum total of power with which you deigned to honor me. I believe that I have fulfilled my duty as have all the representatives, our fellow citizens, and my compatriots and companions in arms. . . . In the countryside, and wounded in the right hand, excuse me for writing this note with a pencil and in scrawling letters.[52]

The constitutional dictator returned to the legislature the sovereign powers it had delegated to him and sailed for exile in England. He died in Southhampton in 1877.

The 1853 Constitution

Rosas's defeat again raised the question of a constitution for the Argentine federation. The victorious caudillo, Urquiza, assembled the provincial governors at San Nicolás and proposed a constituent assembly in Santa Fé. Meanwhile, the governors, many of whom had supported Rosas and were invested with "full authority" by their provinces, would confer such authority on Urquiza as "provisional director" of the confederation under the terms of the Accord of San Nicolás.[53] Most political leaders in Buenos Aires objected to the Urquiza plan, referring especially to the "omnipotent" powers conferred upon the "provisional director," despite their previous submission to even broader authority (*la suma del poder público, lleno de facultades*) for earlier provincial executives and for Rosas. Illustrative was the proclamation of Bartolomé Mitre, who later served as provincial governor and national president and exercised state of siege authority under the 1853 Constitution.

> [I shall be told that General Urquiza will not abuse this authority that is without precedent in our history] I believe this. . . .

But even if [Urquiza] does not abuse this power, he will still be a despot, because a despot, as I have said and demonstrated previously, is whoever acts without legal constraint, checks and balances [*entidad que le sirva de contrapeso*], or lack of legal liability for his actions.

This authority [created by the Accord of San Nicolás] may dispose of the national income, without a budget, and without rendering accounts to anyone.

It may regulate commerce on the rivers as if it were a sovereign legislative body.

It may exercise internal and external sovereignty without previous or later sanction.

It may declare war.

It may quell revolutions.

It may deploy the military forces of the Confederation, as if we were at war [with external enemies] and therefore command them directly.

In the sphere of human possibilities, I do not know what other power may be conferred on an authority. . . . In one hand is placed the resources [*la plata*] and in the other bayonets, at its feet is placed the nation, its peoples, and the law.[54]

Mitre exaggerated, but only slightly. These same powers had been vested in numerous Argentine executives in Buenos Aires and the provinces. The temporary investiture of Urquiza with such powers, particularly since he sought to negotiate with provincial governors, with the elite in Buenos Aires, and to avoid the draconian measure of Rosas, was natural considering the constitutional precedents from 1811. The Accord of San Nicolás and the previous agreement among four governors at Palermo (April 16, 1852) had expanded somewhat the scope of executive authority provided for by the 1831 Federal Pact that had founded Rosas's rule. However, Urquiza did not receive *la suma del poder público*. On the other hand, Mitre was correct. Argentine constitutional evolution had incorporated the legal foundations of dictatorship and tyranny.

Most political and military leaders in Buenos Aires opposed the Accord of San Nicolás and Urquiza's policies toward the province. Exasperated by provincial obstinance, Urquiza dissolved the legislature and imposed a provincial governor, Vicente López. When López resigned, unable to consolidate his authority, Urquiza made himself governor of Buenos Aires. He apparently intended to convert the port into the federal capital, nationalize customs revenues, and divide the province in two, much as had been proposed in the 1826 Constitution.

A military uprising in Buenos Aires prevented Urquiza from carrying out his plans, its leaders calling for the reestablishment of autonomous provincial government. The military leaders of the revolt proclaimed their intentions to support the legitimate provincial authorities and summoned the legislature into session, thereby confirming their "patriotic mission" and their recognition of civilian authority. This was consistent with Argentine development to this time; with one exception, no constitution had established a mission for the armed forces, and sovereignty had been vested in legislative institutions, despite their delegation of extraordinary powers or "full authority" to executives. Urquiza was forced to recognize the impossibility of imposing his authority militarily on Buenos Aires; the province would maintain its autonomy until 1862.[55]

In the meantime, a constituent assembly meeting at Santa Fé adopted a constitution for the Argentine federal republic. The delegates to the convention included leading Argentine intellectuals who, from exile and within the country, had opposed Rosas and had experienced constitutional and political conflicts in Europe, North America, and neighboring Spanish American republics. At the convention, the framers of the 1853 Constitution considered the *Federalist Papers*, took inspiration from the authoritarian Chilean 1833 Constitution (see chapter 8), borrowed from French, Swiss, and British legal traditions, and incorporated (virtually unchanged) provisions from the U.S. Constitution. They even studied the 1849 California state constitution.

The most important influences in the 1853 Constitution, however, were the accumulated Río de la Plata experiments, particularly the failed 1819 and 1826 constitutions and the draft constitution submitted by Juan Bautista Alberdi. Alberdi had written a polemic entitled *Bases and Points of Departure for the Political Organization of the Argentine Republic,* in which he recognized the colonial, confederal, federal, and unitary elements in Argentine constitutional development.[56] He argued that a constitution must reflect the "true and faithful history of a people," requiring a melding, in the Argentine case, of advanced constitutional principles with the particular history of political conflict in the region. Alberdi, like Sarmiento, Mitre, and the other liberals of the 1850s, focused on the need to impose order on the masses, protect the civil liberties and rights of the elite, gradually educate the population, promote economic development, and create conditions that would make democratic, republican institutions more viable in the future. Such a vision required a strong executive and provision for emergency powers.[57] Alberdi argued:

> [To stimulate] industrial and commercial development give the executive all possible power . . . to defend and conserve order and peace. . . . [This is] the magic wand that will give us [immigrant] population, roads, industry, education and liberty.
>
> I do not see why in some cases total power [*facultades omnímodas*] should not be given to overcome backwardness and poverty, when it is given to conquer disorder, which is nothir.g more than the offspring of the former. [To achieve this] it is necessary . . . to suppress the rights of the multitude, [giving the vote only to] the propertied and educated.
>
> Between the absence of government and dictatorship a normal government is possible; this is a constitutional president who may assume the powers of king in the instant that anarchy disobeys him as a republican president. If order, that is to say, the life of the constitution, requires this flexibility of power entrusted with enforcing the Constitution, with even more reason, it is required for those enterprises contributing to material progress and the grandeur of the nation.[58]

Alberdi fondly remembered Bolívar's call for the creation in Spanish America of "kings under the name of presidents" and urged that Argentina "give to the executive all the power possible . . . but give it to him by means of a constitution."[59]

Sarmiento, the great advocate of education, future president (1868–1874), vitriolic opponent of Rosas's tyranny, and firm supporter of the Chilean authoritarian presidents during his exile in that country, was even more emphatic: "A Constitution is not the rule of conduct for all persons. The Constitution of the popular masses is the ordinary law, the judges, and the security police. It is the educated classes who need a Constitution that assures their liberty of action and thought; the press, the forum, property, etc."[60] Sarmiento would use the emergency powers of the 1853 Constitution to suppress provincial revolts in the 1870s.

The 1853 Constitution, as amended in 1860 and thereafter, remains the basis of Argentine politics in the 1990s. It devised a mixed federal system. On the model of the U.S. Constitution, the provinces select their own governors and legislatures, reserving all powers not explicitly delegated to the federal government. However, a strong federal executive could "intervene" in the provinces "to guarantee the republican form of government, to repel foreign invasions, and, at the request of the constituted authorities, sustain or reestablish them if they are deposed by sedition or invasion from another province" (Art. 6, as amended). This power of intervention virtually allowed the receivership of provincial government, with the president naming interim governors and controlling or closing the provincial legislature.

The 1853 constituents prohibited congressional delegation of *facultades extraordinarias* or *la suma del poder público* to the president, provincial governors, and legislatures (Art. 29). This was obviously a response to over forty years of abuse of this practice and, in particular, to the power exercised by Rosas from 1835 until 1852. However, they provided for broad state of siege authority, adopting the French lexicon and the example of the Chilean 1833 Constitution (see chapter 8). The president could "declare in state of siege one or various points of the nation, in the case of external attack, for a period of time limited by the Senate. In the case of internal commotion, the president has this authority only when Congress is in recess, since this authority corresponds to [the Senate]. This authority is limited by Article 23" (Art. 86, Sec. 19).

Article 23 authorized the Congress,

> in the case of internal commotion or external attack that endangers the exercise of this constitution and the authorities created by it, to declare in state of siege the province or territory in which order is disturbed, thereby suspending constitutional guarantees [in that territory]. During this suspension the president may not, on his own accord, convict persons nor impose sentences. He may only arrest persons and transfer them to places within the nation, if they do not prefer to leave the country [voluntary exile].

With the 1853 Constitution, Argentina adopted definitive language on regimes of exception. More than a century of jurisprudence would define and redefine the authority of Congress and the president under Articles 23 and 86, but the fundamental resolution of the conflict between liberty and order had been determined: suspension of constitutional *garantías* to preserve order and the intervention of the provincial governments to contain internal uprisings and maintain "republican" government would be permitted. The state of siege declaration required no limit on the duration of the regime of exception and no limit on presidential authority except the prohibition on executive determination of criminal culpability and the imposition of penalties (fines, prison, capital punishment). Persons could be detained, interrogated, and lose all other constitutional protections for an indeterminate period.

Though this constitutional solution would prevail, Buenos Aires initially refused to join the federation, opposing nationalization of its revenues, federalization of the city as national capital, and dominance of a provincially imposed president (Urquiza). The province therefore reconstituted itself, adopting its own charter in 1854 and naming Mitre as governor. The 1854 Buenos Aires Constitution prohibited delegation of extraordinary powers to the executive but also provided for declaration of a state of siege in the case of internal commotion or external invasion (Art. 110). The provincial governor, named by the legislature for a three-year term, could, under the state of siege, arrest persons and transfer them within the province, with the requirement that the legislature be informed of this action within twenty-four hours. While the extent of government authority under the provincial state of siege provision was less precisely stipulated than in the 1853 Constitution of the confederation, one essential agreement had been reached, if implicitly, between Buenos Aires and the provinces. Argentines would be subject to a state of siege as the basic regime of exception—even if the city and the provinces could not yet agree on the formation of a nation.

For the next six years, negotiations and military skirmishes failed to resolve the differences between the provinces and Buenos Aires. In 1859, another confrontation between the forces of President Urquiza's confederation and Mitre's Buenos Aires province afforded Urquiza a military victory. Buenos Aires agreed to join the confederation on the condition that its proposed amendments to the 1853 Constitution be adopted by the provinces. The major concerns—delaying federalization of Buenos Aires and guarantees of the provincial revenues for five years after nationalizing customs revenue—were among other amendments accepted in October 1859. Argentina finally implemented the national constitution in 1860, as General Urquiza completed his constitutional presidency in March 1860.

An uprising in the province of San Juan and rejection by the Congress of Buenos Aires's deputies (elected under provincial rather than federal law) made it impossible for Urquiza's successor to consolidate the apparent victory of the nationalists. A final military engagement on the plains of Pavón in Santa Fé province (September 17, 1861) was indecisive. Urquiza decided to withdraw from the conflict, leaving Mitre in control of Buenos Aires and as "provisional president" of the republic. The confederation invested Mitre with extraordinary powers, notwithstanding the prohibition on such investiture in the 1853 Constitution.[61] Subsequent negotiations between Mitre and Urquiza, calling for elections of a new Congress, and a compromise making Buenos Aires the national capital for five years permitted Mitre to become national president in 1862.

Mitre and his successors into the mid-1870s gradually overcame the vestiges of provincial caudillismo, using the state of siege and intervention provisions of the amended 1853 Constitution. In 1880 Buenos Aires was made the federal capital. Nevertheless, both *porteño* localist sentiment and resistance by regional caudillos to the political solution of 1860 continued to plague Argentina from 1862 into the 1880s. In 1862 the dominant caudillo in La Rioja led an unsuccessful uprising against Mitre's government; again in 1866 Mitre faced rebellion in the same province. Tactical alliances and federal subsidies for provincial supporters allowed Mitre, using the powers of federal intervention, to overcome these rebellions and several others. Temporary federal intervention was converted into lengthy periods of "transitional" rule over dissident provinces by presidential appointees. The application of the state of siege provisions and federal intervention in the provinces became routine, although the Supreme Court asserted in 1865 its right to declare presidential decrees unconstitutional.[62] (Not until 1885 did the court assert this power regarding congressional legislation.) Only once, on the occasion of the Paraguayan War (see below), did a president declare a state of siege to confront an external threat. On the numerous occasions that presidents imposed a state of siege to meet internal disorders or rebellions, Congress never exercised its constitutional authority to reject the state of siege decree.[63]

Unable to impose his own successor in 1868, Mitre himself became a source of instability in 1874 when he failed to win the presidential elections. President Domingo Faustino Sarmiento (1868–1874), his successor, had already imposed state of siege provisions and intervened against Ricardo López Jordán, the last great caudillo of Entre Ríos whose adherents had assassinated Urquiza in 1870. Confronted by numerous provincial disturbances, Sarmiento frequently resorted to the federal "intervention" authority (Art. 6), relying on military officers to restore order, impose appointed governors, and overcome resistance by provincial legislatures.[64] In response to Mitre's 1874 uprising, Sarmiento imposed censorship on the press and declared a state of siege in Buenos Aires.[65]

Interestingly, the military units supporting Mitre claimed that the president had violated the constitution and that:

> when the authorities scandalously exceed constitutional limits and when the rights and liberties of citizens are trampled by those sworn to uphold them. . . . the army cannot be expected to continue to serve as a hateful instrument against free institutions, for whose defense and maintenance they are sustained by the people. . . . In such cases the path of resistance is the way of the Constitution and patriotism.[66]

Though unsupported by constitutional text, the "duty" of the army embedded in the oaths of fealty required of military officers to uphold the constitution, as its leaders interpreted it, had also taken hold in Argentina. This duty perdured for the next century; the military junta that took power in 1976, like its predecessors from the 1930s to 1966, echoed Mitre's military collaborators a century earlier:

> Profoundly respectful of constitutional powers, the natural underpinnings of democratic institutions . . . the armed forces assumed control of the government. [It] is precisely to ensure the just protection of the natural rights of man that we assume the full exercise of authority; not to infringe upon liberty but to reaffirm it; not to twist justice but to impose it. After reestablishing an effective authority, which will be revitalized at all levels, we will turn to the organization of the state, whose performance will be based on the permanence and stability of judicial norms which will guarantee the primacy of law and the observance of it by the governors and the governed alike.[67]

Political violence again marred the presidential succession in 1880. The victorious candidate, General Julio Roca, was one of the officers who had overcome Mitre's forces in 1874. He had served as President Nicolás Avellaneda's minister of war, commanded the army that carried a campaign of extermination against the Indians south of Buenos Aires (the so-called conquest of the desert), and defeated the *porteño* militia of Governor Carlos Tejedor. The military engagements between Tejedor's provincial army and the federal troops left some three thousand casualties; the immediate consequences included the definitive resolution of the longstanding question of a national capital. With Tejedor's assent, Congress federalized Buenos Aires, standing armies in the provinces were outlawed, and the province of Buenos Aires soon constructed a new capital at La Plata, thirty miles from Buenos Aires.

Accompanied by a massive wave of foreign immigration and investment, railroad construction, commercial growth, and expansion of the agrarian economy, Argentine political development from 1880 to World War I concentrated power and the ability to manipulate elections in the presidency.[68] The rise of a reformist political party, the Unión Cívica Radical, its alliance with modernizing sectors of the armed forces, and demands for electoral reforms during a brief but deep economic depression brought new rationales for political violence from 1891 to 1893. It was met by the now customary state of siege and federal intervention in the affected provinces. Indeed, the 1892 presidential elections were held under a state of siege, with opposition politicians in jail, hiding, or exile.[69]

After manipulating the election of two surrogate presidents in the mid-1890s, General Roca returned to the presidency in 1898. He represented the Argentine positivists' commitment to order and progress: that is, progress made possible by order. In this sense he mirrored contemporary events in Mexico under Porfirio Díaz. Seeking to consolidate national power and to professionalize the Argentine military, Roca established the Superior War College and contracted a German military mission to "provide Argentina with military leadership capable of countering Chile's recent gains."[70]

The emergent Radical party protested electoral fraud and vote buying with abstention, demanding honest elections and universal suffrage. The rise of an anarchist labor movement in the 1880s and the creation of the Argentine Socialist party in 1894 introduced new "threats to the Constitution and the authorities created by it" (Art. 23). National governments repeatedly imposed states of siege to combat political protests and general strikes from 1896 to 1910.[71] The new professional army would be deployed against striking workers and political protesters frequently, but never against foreign enemies. From the country's first general strike in 1902 to the Radical party's use of the military in 1919 and 1921–1922 against workers in Buenos Aires and southern Patagonia, constitutional dictatorship and military repression became routine in twentieth-century Argentina.

Until 1902, the state of siege decree usually applied only to designated provinces or the federal district. After 1905 it became more common to suspend simultaneously constitutional rights and liberties (Arts. 14–19) in the entire country.[72] Article 23 of the constitution stated that declaration of a state of siege entailed "suspension of constitutional guarantees." The constitution prohibited the president from convicting or applying criminal penalties during the state of siege but not from detaining and confining those who threatened or perturbed public order. Argentina was governed under state of siege decrees for approximately 45 percent of the period from 1930 to 1970. Under the several military regimes from 1930 to 1976, and the harsher dictatorship from 1976 to 1983, the state of siege provisions became the legal foundation for vicious repression of dissidents legitimized by numerous decrees of the military junta, including the "Act to Consider the Conduct of Those Persons Who Prejudice the Higher Interests of the Nation."[73]

The "dirty war" of the 1970s that left thousands "disappeared" had its precedent in the mass graves of Río Gallegos in the early 1920s and its juridical underpinnings in Argentina's institutions and practice of regimes of exception since 1811.[74] The military dictatorship from 1976 to 1983 could rightfully claim its inspiration in Argentina's past, legitimation for its actions in the 1853 Constitution, and precedent for its "salvation" of the fatherland in the words of the country's nineteenth-century liberal and conservative heroes: Moreno, Rosas, Sarmiento, Mitre, and Roca.

URUGUAY

La banda oriental (the eastern bank) between the Uruguay River and the Atlantic Ocean had some 50,000 residents in 1810. It had been contested by Spanish and Portuguese monarchs since the sixteenth century, penetrated by British merchants in the seventeenth and eighteenth, and served as an alternative to Buenos Aires as the entry depot for European trade. The region's major economic activity was hunting wild cattle and the *saladeros*. Strategically important as the entrance to the Río de la Plata, the *banda oriental* also served as a buffer between Brazil and the Río de la Plata provinces. The Portuguese Colonia do Sacramento, established in 1680 on the north bank of the river, had harbored smugglers, outlaws, and bandits; the Spanish created a fort at Montevideo in 1726 to counter the Portuguese threat. Recognizing its potential as an alternative port, the government at Buenos Aires immediately prohibited international commerce at Montevideo.

After 1776, with the creation of the Río de la Plata viceroyalty, the Spanish expelled the Portuguese from Colonia do Sacramento,

but Spanish-Portuguese competition for control of the region persisted. Likewise, as Montevideo grew and prospered it engendered
commercial and political rivalry with Buenos Aires. This rivalry
would influence significantly Argentine and Uruguayan political
development. Temporary liberation from Buenos Aires's dominance
during the British invasions (1806–1807) intensified pressures for
greater autonomy in the *banda oriental.* When Montevideo's governor, Francisco Elío, supported the authority of the captive king,
Ferdinand VII, and the Liniers government in Buenos Aires hesitated, the opening shots were fired in a battle that would make
Uruguay independent two decades later.[75]

Independence came only after years of destructive civil wars,
the temporary incorporation into the Portuguese (1817–1824) and
Brazilian (1824–1825) empires, and a war between Brazil and the
United Provinces for control of the territory (1825–1828). British
mediation ended the war but allowed the United Provinces of the
Río de la Plata and Brazil to veto provisions of the to-be-adopted
Uruguayan constitution to which they objected. Article 10 of the
Preliminary Peace Treaty (1828) also stipulated that for five years
from the adoption of a constitution for Uruguay, Brazil and the
United Provinces would protect the legal government of the new
republic against armed uprisings. This article left Argentina and
Brazil to determine which government that might be. Only after
1835 would the new republic "be considered perfectly and absolutely independent."[76] The failure of Argentina's 1826 Constitution, the rampant caudillismo in the Río de la Plata region, and the
rivalry among Uruguayan caudillos from 1828 into the 1850s made
Uruguayan sovereignty illusory for years to come.[77]

From 1810 to 1853, Uruguayan constitutional and political development was integrally connected to that of the provinces of the
Río de la Plata. In principle, the press laws and personal security (bill of rights) decrees and the correlative regime of exception
provisions adopted in Buenos Aires from 1811 applied to the *banda
oriental.* Reality was otherwise, with Spanish, Portuguese, and Brazilian occupation before 1814 and after 1817. From 1815, factions
and armies in both Montevideo and the interior shared resources,
leadership, alliances, and enemies with counterparts in the Argentine provinces. Uruguayans led "Argentine" armies; "Argentine"
commanders faced off in Uruguayan civil wars.

In the 1830s, the major political parties in Uruguay, Colorados
and Blancos, were linked with Rosista and anti-Rosista movements
across the river. Between 1832 and 1852, Rosas's liberal enemies

used Montevideo as a base for anti-Rosas intrigues. Rosas refused to recognize Uruguayan independence, his Uruguayan supporters sometimes feigning preference for reunification with the United Provinces under a confederal formula. Only after Rosas's defeat by Urquiza at Monte Caseros in 1852 did Uruguay's independence gain Argentine recognition.[78]

La Banda Oriental, 1810–1830

Until 1814, Montevideo remained an outpost of royalist military presence and, until 1820, the most likely port of disembarkation for a Spanish army of reoccupation. Like many independence leaders, José Artigas, Uruguay's George Washington, had served as an officer in Spanish military units, including fighting the British in the 1806–1807 invasions. He led local resistance against the Spanish and also against *porteño* armies seeking, between 1811 and 1819, to establish control over Uruguay. From 1811, he was designated Jefe de los Orientales and exercised virtually unlimited political and military authority, although he implicitly recognized the sovereign power of the congresses and "popular representative assemblies" that convened in the province. In many respects, Artigas's social and political ideas, including the abolition of slavery, agrarian reform, extreme federalism, and local political initiative, were more radical than those of the cosmopolitan liberals of Buenos Aires.[79]

Artigas became the most important champion of confederation in the Río de la Plata, sending instructions with his delegates to the 1813 convention at Buenos Aires that provoked refusal by the *porteño* elite to seat the Uruguayans at the assembly.[80] He insisted on equal, virtually sovereign status for the provinces of the confederation, rejecting a strong central government and Buenos Aires's hegemony.[81]

Allied with caudillos of the littoral provinces, he controlled much of the countryside even after losing Montevideo to the Spanish and then to the Portuguese (1817). His Liga Federal (1814–1815) established an alternative to centralized rule from Buenos Aires; he headed a fierce guerrilla resistance to Spanish, Brazilian, and *porteño* armies until 1819. Defeated by Portuguese-Brazilian forces, to the pleasure and with the collaboration of the unitarists at Buenos Aires, Artigas retreated to Paraguay, never to return to the country that reveres him as its first citizen. He played no role in the establishment of Uruguayan independence in 1828 nor in the elaboration of the nation's 1830 Constitution.

Montevideo and the interior remained under Portuguese control until 1822, then passed to newly independent Brazil. It was theoretically governed under the Portuguese 1822 Constitution, which was a copy of Spain's Cádiz Constitution (1812), and then under Brazil's 1824 Imperial Constitution. This constitution contained a typical regime of exception provision, allowing suspension of constitutional guarantees. Article XXXV stipulated:

> In the case of rebellion or enemy invasion that threatens the security of the State, a special act of the legislature may suspend for a specified time some of the formalities that guarantee civil rights and liberties [*liberdade individual*]. If the Assembly is not in session, and if the Fatherland faces imminent danger, the Government may exercise this same authority as a provisional measure, but only until the urgent necessity that motivated its use has passed.

Under this provision the authorities were "responsible for any abuses committed" in the implementation of the regime of exception.

Thus Uruguay's first constitutional regimes of exception, setting aside the decrees from Buenos Aires beginning in 1811, were contained in the 1822 Portuguese and 1824 Brazilian imperial constitutions. In practice, it was governed until 1821 by both a governor–captain general who combined civil and military authority and the governor of Montevideo. In 1821, the *cabildo* of Montevideo requested formal incorporation into the Portuguese empire; in 1822, the *banda oriental* became the Portuguese *provincia cisplatina*.[82] This status, never entirely formalized, changed in 1824 when Brazil took control of the territory and the 1824 imperial constitution was imposed. Like the Portuguese 1822 Constitution, it was never fully implemented in the *banda oriental*.

In 1825 a small band of Uruguayan and *porteño* rebels, known in Uruguayan history as the heroic Thirty-three, invaded the Brazilian province from Buenos Aires. War ensued between Brazil and the United Provinces. After creating a provisional government in August 1825 headed by a governor–captain general and enacting several constitutive decrees, insurgents in Montevideo swore fealty to the 1826 Buenos Aires–inspired unitarist constitution in March 1827. The next month the assembly adopted a press law similar to that of Buenos Aires's 1811 regulations.[83] This made Uruguay subject to the regime of exception provisions contained in the 1826 Argentine charter (see above) and to the authority of the provisional government created in July 1827—before Rivadavia's resignation.[84]

With neither the Brazilians nor the Argentines able to prevail in the war and Uruguayan territory again a battleground, Britain imposed Uruguayan independence on the adversaries. Created as a buffer state between the two largest South American nations, Uruguay implemented its first national constitution in 1830. It was elaborated by the General Constituent and Legislative Assembly, which convened in November 1828, and approved on September 10, 1829.[85] After scrutiny by Brazil and the government of the United Provinces of the Río de la Plata, according to the terms of the 1828 peace settlement, it entered into force in July 1830.

The 1830 Constitution

Unlike its Spanish American neighbors, Uruguay passed the nineteenth century without significant constitutional reform. Three important factors inhibited constitutional innovation in Uruguay after the 1830 charter's promulgation: (1) the Brazilian and Argentine tutelage recognized in this charter (an often forgotten antecedent to the infamous Platt Amendment imposed by the United States on Cuba in 1902); (2) the extraordinarily difficult amendment procedures contained in Article 159 (a special constituent assembly with double the number of senators and representatives, explicitly charged with constitutional reform, adopting them by three-quarters vote); and (3) the almost perpetual international and internecine wars from 1832 to the 1870s, with concomitant Brazilian and Argentine interventions.

Instead of constitutional reform, the constitution was stretched, violated, used to justify tyranny, remembered as a battle cry by opposing armies promising to restore its sanctity or, in the case of several de facto and military governments, temporarily ignored. Though abused and maligned, the 1830 Constitution also became an important symbol of nationalism and legitimacy, with Blancos, Colorados, military dictators, and provisional presidents seeking legitimacy through bare bones compliance with the rules for presidential succession.

The 1830 Constitution borrowed liberally from Argentina's 1826 charter but also reflected the constitutional debates and conflicts in Spanish America and Europe from 1811 to the late 1820s. Advocates of an executive with extensive authority prevailed, despite the rejection of the proposal by the influential José Ellauri for a ten-year presidency and *amplias facultades* for the executive in order to reestablish authority and overcome the "reigning state of anarchy."[86] In some respects, the 1830 Constitution reflected the most progressive liberal doctrines, including prohibition on military officers serving in the legislature, authority for the legislature to bring government ministers to the Congress for questioning (*llamado a sala*), and failure to prohibit public exercise of religions other than Roman Catholic. (In 1831 the Chamber of Representatives eliminated military *fueros;* final approval and promulgation of this reform occurred in 1838.)[87]

In other respects, the 1830 Constitution adopted the conservative spirit of the anti-Artigas aristocrats. It provided for a centralized administrative system with *jefes políticos* for each department named by the president. These *jefes* were responsible for "all governmental matters," thereby extinguishing the ember of local representative institutions (Art. 121). This proved true despite provision for *juntas económicas-administrativas* as advisory bodies manned by prominent local citizens (Art. 122). Voting and citizenship requirements excluded illiterates (after 1840), servants, peons, day workers, soldiers, the "notoriously vagrant," and "drunks" (Art. 11). Presidential control over the electoral machinery developed quickly, making the legislature much less independent than was suggested by reading the constitutional text.

The president was to be elected by the general assembly for a four-year term, without the possibility of immediate reelection. Legislators voted with signed ballots read publicly by the secretary of the legislature (Art. 73). This effort to discourage presidentialism on the Bolivarian model prevented *continuismo* but not presidential dominance of the government and electoral system.

The constitution obliged the president to attend with priority to the "conservation of order and tranquility within the country, and external security" (Art. 79). He was also commander in chief of the armed forces but could only directly take command with approval by two-thirds of both chambers of the Congress (Art. 80). The president also had extensive appointment power in the civil bureaucracy and military, sole authority to appoint and remove ministers, exercise of the *patronato* (appointment of religious officials), and authority to "take whatever security measures deemed expedient [*medidas prontas de seguridad*] in grave cases of internal commotion or external invasion, reporting immediately to the Assembly, or if in recess, to the Permanent Commission [of the legislature] of the measures taken and motivation for so doing" (Art. 81).

This clause was adopted from similar language in the 1828 Chilean constitution (Art. 81, Sec. 12). Presidential authority to "take whatever security measures deemed expedient" was neither restricted nor qualified elsewhere in the constitution. While the bill of rights (*seguridad personal*) and other *garantías* could only be suspended by the legislature or the permanent commission in the case of treason or conspiracy against the fatherland, and then only for apprehension of the perpetrators (Art. 143), the broad presidential authority in Article 81 made delegation of extraordinary powers redundant. Uruguayan presidents had virtually unlimited authority when quelling "internal commotion." Moreover, "anyone who attacks or provides means to attack the present Constitution, after it is approved, published and implemented, shall be tried and punished for the crime of high treason [*lesa-nación*]" (Art. 151). These provisions, only slightly modified, survived in all the Uruguayan constitutions to 1967.

Uruguay's constituent assembly of 1828–1829 had provided, "in the cases of treason or conspiracy against the Fatherland," for both legislative suspension of civil liberties and rights (Art. 143) and constitutional dictatorship by the president (Art. 81). These provisions had been only briefly debated in the constitutional convention, with the delegates sharing the view expressed by Santiago Vásquez that: "in urgent cases, such as conspiracy, the authorities should not be impeded from taking expedient measures in order to save the Fatherland."[88] Although Vásquez preferred legislative to executive exercise of emergency powers, he argued that to confront conspiracy it was not possible to reconvene the assembly if it were not in session, and it was thus necessary to allow the permanent commission of the legislature (two senators and five deputies) to suspend civil liberties and rights.[89] Vásquez expressed some doubts about the lack of precision in Article 81 (*medidas prontas de seguridad*) but in this case, also, debate was limited.

From the first presidential administration, the precise meaning and scope of *medidas prontas de seguridad* were debated in the legislature. Almost inexorably, presidential authority to confront "internal commotion" and "conserve public tranquility" was upheld. In June 1832 the president informed the general assembly that due to an Indian uprising in Bella Unión he had "taken extraordinary measures to protect lives and property in the countryside." Invoking Article 81 of the constitution, the president ordered that *medidas prontas* be taken, "whose exact nature can only be determined by circumstances of the moment," including "whatever measures deemed convenient to protect lives and property."[90] As required by Article 80, the message further requested from the legislature permission for the president to take direct command of the troops, if this should become necessary. After extensive debate, the legislature agreed to this request, despite some legislators' objections to leaving to presidential determination whether, and if, circumstances required his direct command of the army. Some legislators objected to this blank check on the direct command of the army. None suggested that presidential authority to take *medidas prontas de seguridad* had been exceeded.

In 1832–1833, the legislature debated further the president's authority under Article 81, as the president invoked this authority to fight banditry, cattle rustling, violent crime, and rebellion in the rural districts It rejected only the presidential power to impose taxes without legislative approval as part of the *medidas prontas de seguridad*. Indeed, in February 1833 the assembly condoned as proper *medidas prontas de seguridad* the suspension from legislative duty and the arrest of legislators whom the government accused of conspiracy and support for a rebel movement. This repression of opposition legislators was approved despite clear constitutional language making the chamber of deputies exclusively responsible for impeaching senators and deputies (Art. 26, Sec. 2).[91]

In 1844 an opposition legislator, Manuel Herrera y Obes, denounced the gradual accretion of "dictatorial powers" by the president, including "attacks on liberty and civil rights [*seguridad de los ciudadanos*] and the investiture of a military officer with unlimited power [*facultades omnímodas*] in violation of constitutional articles 134 and 144, on the pretext of the requirements of conserving public tranquility."[92] Legislators sought unsuccessfully to restrict presidential authority under Article 81 in 1853 and 1873, in the latter case through an "interpretive law" that the president vetoed. This law would have held the president and all administrative officials criminally liable for violations of Articles 83 and 136 [privation of personal liberty and punishment or imprisonment without due process] in applying the *medidas prontas de seguridad*.[93]

The sweeping authority accorded the president to take "medidas prontas de seguridad," combined with legislative authority to suspend civil liberties and rights, became the legal foundation for constitutional dictatorship in Uruguay. These provisions also served as the constitutional justification for the counterinsurgency campaign and state terrorism of the 1970s, over 150 years after the constitutional debates of 1828–1829.[94]

From the 1830s to the turn of the century, presidential authority was so extensive and executive control of elections so pervasive
that opposition candidates had virtually no possibility of winning
the presidency. One Uruguayan historian attributes the incessant
rebellions, coups, and de facto governments characteristic of the
country in the nineteenth century directly to the 1830 Constitution:

> One of the principal causes of the revolutions that bled and ru-
> ined the country for long decades, was this electoral system [*go-
> bierno elector*]. And this resulted not so much from the ill
> intentions of the rulers, but from the ill conceived mechanisms
> of the Constitution. Revolutions are explained and justified as
> the only instrument available to the parties to conquer
> power.[95]

Political Development, 1830–1918

Even after the promulgation of the 1830 Constitution, the desire of
some Argentines to reincorporate Uruguay into Argentina, and
that of some elites in Montevideo for annexation, produced instability in the *banda oriental*. Argentine caudillo Juan Manuel de Rosas supported several major rebellions against Fructuoso Rivera,
Uruguay's first president, and continued to meddle in Uruguayan
politics after Rivera left office. Rivera had returned the favor by giving exile and support to the unitarists from Buenos Aires, Rosas's
sworn enemies. Keeping command of the army after leaving the
presidency (a device emulated from Chile to Central America late
into the twentieth century by revolutionaries and reactionaries
alike), he continued to oppose Rosas and his Uruguayan allies. Rivera, thus linked to the Argentine unitarists, became the personal
embodiment of Uruguay's Colorado party. His companion in arms,
then his adversary and the country's second president, General
Manuel Oribe, joined forces with Rosas. Oribe's supporters became
the nuclei of the Blanco party. These labels, first adopted in the
mid-1830s as a result of the colored banners displayed by the opposing factions, stuck; Blancos and Colorados remained the two
major parties in Uruguay into the 1980s, albeit with numerous personalist and ideological divisions.

Argentine unitarists and federalists again made Uruguay a battleground from 1836 to 1851, this time adding a struggle for control of the Uruguayan presidency. Oribe and Rosas dominated the

countryside and the Colorados prevailed in Montevideo. Rosas besieged the port with Argentine and Uruguayan forces from 1842 to 1851; France and England maintained sea lanes open for the Colorados and the predominantly foreign-born population of the city. (Among the foreign fighters in Montevideo was Giuseppe Garibaldi, later the hero of Italian independence.) Britain and France countered with a not always effective blockade of Buenos Aires from 1838 into the late 1840s.[96] Meanwhile, only the defeat of Rosas by Urquiza and his Brazilian and Uruguayan allies consolidated Uruguayan independence.

These events, knows as the Guerra Grande, damaged Montevideo little but left the countryside in ruins, exalted the role of military leaders, and left a Brazilian army to "maintain order" into the mid-1850s.[97] Blancos and Colorados alike confiscated cattle, property, and money from their adversaries in the name of saving the fatherland. Armies helped themselves to beef, sold stolen hides to finance the military campaigns, and pressed peons into military service. These practices continued into the 1870s, inhibiting development of a modernized agrarian economy. Presidential and legislative authority to adopt *medidas prontas de seguridad* and suspend civil liberties and rights would not be translated into effective control of the country until the advent of military governments after 1876.

Continued Brazilian and Argentine meddling and support for Blanco and Colorado caudillos generated a series of rebellions, military coups, and de facto governments from 1855 to 1865.[98] Efforts by Paraguayan dictator Francisco Solano López to aid the Blancos against Brazilian intervention in 1865, combined with Argentina's refusal to allow Paraguayan troops to cross its territory, provoked the Paraguayan War (1865–1870). This war compromised Uruguay's political sovereignty as its government joined a triple alliance against Paraguay.[99]

These international dimensions of Uruguay's internal affairs made the defense of sovereignty and the 1830 Constitution a matter of national pride, even when caudillos and politicos did not adhere literally to its prescriptions. Colorado and Blanco leaders assassinated their opponents, attacked incumbent governments, and sought aid from foreign armies but rarely suggested the need for a new constitution. This remained the case despite the failure of the Blancos to regain the presidency from the mid-1860s until 1958. Despite frequent uprisings and political violence, they at most called for electoral reforms, some restraint on presidential authority, and power sharing via appointing opposition leaders to administrative, police, and military posts.

When President Venancio Flores was assassinated in 1868, he was succeeded by the minister of war, General Lorenzo Batlle. Civil war again broke out in 1870, the so-called revolution of the lances, lasting until 1872 when Argentine mediation allowed the Blanco rebels control of four *jefaturas políticas* and thereby of police and elections in four departments, along with 500,000 pesos in cash.[100] From this time, the tenuous pacts affording the Blancos control of many rural districts, along with political bribes, reduced but did not eliminate political violence and insurrections. Still, the 1830 Constitution had not been effectively implemented. Neither political order nor peaceful presidential succession had been achieved. Civil war and government ineptness left a public debt that required over 45 percent of revenues to service, and customs revenues accounted for over 85 percent of income—sure signs of a fragile government and weak fiscal system.

Unlike their counterparts in Costa Rica and Chile, the heterogeneous rural elite in Uruguay failed to strengthen legislative institutions sufficiently to curtail executive hegemony. Instead, civil wars produced extraconstitutional power sharing pacts that allocated the country's departments and legislative seats among the Blanco and Colorado factions. Eventually the landowners relied on the army to impose social peace, to protect private property, to reform the rural police, to "discipline" vagrants and the rural labor force, and to dictate the legal foundations for rural development: the 1875 Código Rural.[101] Exasperated with endemic disorder and the seeming irrelevance of liberal discourse in Montevideo to the needs of the countryside, leading *estancieros* of the newly formed Asociación Rural (1871) called for an end to traditional politics, namely party and caudillo politics, and for a new "politics of work, of order, of stability and of progress."[102] In the 1870s, supported by merchants and financiers linked to foreign capital and the Asociación Rural, professional military officers replaced the caudillos.

Reorganized and modernized in the recent Paraguayan War (1865–1870), the army became a centralizing and nationalizing force previously lacking in Uruguay. Symbolized by a decree forbidding private ownership of the Remington rifle, adopted for the army in 1876, the centralized state imagined in the 1830 Constitution began to control effectively the national territory.[103] Krupp cannons, Mauser rifles, and the extension of telegraph, road, and

rail networks across the country marked the end of regional caudillismo, widespread banditry, and rural disorder.

Following the resignation of President Francisco Antonio Vidal,
colonels Lorenzo Latorre (1876–1880) and Máximo Santos (1882–
1886), along with General Máximo Tajes (1886–1890) sought legitimation in elections that approximated constitutional norms,
though Latorre exercised power as dictator from 1876 to 1879. He
deposed President José Ellauri amid an economic crisis and the im-
mediacy of electoral violence. Ellauri fled to Buenos Aires and the
legislature named Pedro Varela to finish Ellauri's term. Varela and
Latorre agreed with Blanco caudillos to honor the power-sharing
pacts of the early 1870s, thereby preventing civil war.

Unable to consolidate his administration, Varela resigned in
1876 and Latorre received *la suma del poder público* from a crowd of
several thousand supporters in the plaza.[104] First overseeing a provisional government, then named as constitutional president in
1879, he ruled fiercely, "imposing on the country the discipline
of the barracks."[105] In the spirit of 1870s positivism he made law
and order the basis for programs of administrative and economic
reform.

Shortly after assuming power, Latorre authorized the *jefes politicos* to send police across department boundaries, eliminating the
de facto sanctuary offered to criminals who crossed administrative
lines. A new Código de Policía sought to professionalize law enforcement, requiring literacy, frequent rotation of police personnel
among the departments, better salaries and equipment, and at least
a sergeant in command of each rural post. This code was adopted in
October 1876, after full review and modification by members of the
Asociación Rural.[106] Bandits, cattle rustlers, and impudent workers
went to jail or did forced labor. Political enemies "disappeared" or
were assassinated, jailed, or sent into exile.

Landowners and merchants praised Latorre's authoritarian
government. Though fierce by Uruguayan standards, he never exercised the "full authority" of Rosas in Argentina or the patrimonial, personalist rule of José Gaspar Rodríguez Francia and the
elder López in Paraguay (see below). Latorre negotiated with
Blanco regional caudillos and relied on professionals, *estancieros*,
merchants, and foreign legations for advice on major policies. Indeed, frustrated with the legislature's delay in adopting a number
of proposed reforms and wishing to secure the assembly's blessing
for continued rule, Latorre resigned in 1880. Echoing the words of
Sucre in the 1820s, he lamented that he had become disillusioned

"to the point of thinking that ours is an ungovernable country."[107] When the assembly accepted his resignation, Latorre went to Argentina. The threat of his return to power haunted Uruguayan politics to the end of the century.

His successors elevated further the role of the military in politics and society, though both Santos and Tajes also relied to a great extent on civilian ministers and party leaders. A military code adopted in 1884, still in effect in the 1970s, gave military courts jurisdiction over civilians "in times or states of war . . . with or without declaration of war, in international or internal conflicts" (Art. 63).[108] This code, combined with the executive authority to take *medidas prontas de seguridad* and the legislature's power to suspend civil liberties and rights, expanded the role of the armed forces in regimes of exception. Article 525 of the code referred also to the military's role in "maintaining or reestablishing public order."[109] Written by civilian lawyers and legal scholars, the Código Militar and the Code of Military Justice would serve the authoritarian governments of the 1970s as a legal basis for widespread political repression. Similar outcomes would occur in Chile as a result of a military code adopted in the 1830s (see chapter 8).

Not until 1890 did the officers give way to civilian presidents.[110] This did not mean an end to presidential assassination, illegal succession, or informal pacts of pacification. After President Juan Idiarte Borda's assassination during the 1897 revolt, the provisional president dissolved the legislature and declared himself dictator. In 1899, however, the dictator was "elected" constitutional president by the reconvened assembly. In the meantime, the peace settlement gave the Blancos control of six departments—an increase of two from the agreements of the 1870s—and 200,000 pesos in cash for the "expenses of pacification."[111] Thus the hegemony of the presidential party, still contemplated by the constitution, was diluted by political strife and the conquests of civil war. Electoral reform followed, making the ballot box somewhat more viable for the opposition and reducing the necessity to resort to arms to gain political representation.[112]

From Batlle Ordóñez to Tupamarosí

Strong leadership by Colorado politico and twice-president José Batlle y Ordóñez (1903–1907, 1911–1915) eventually produced a new constitution in 1918 along with numerous social and economic reforms. Batlle y Ordóñez faced an insurrection in 1903–1904 but committed himself to institutionalizing constitutional rule. He refused to allow the general assembly to reelect him in 1907, an unconstitutional succession, despite considerable popular support for this alternative.[113] In 1912, a constitutional reform supported by Batlle y Ordóñez changed the procedures for future modifications of the constitution. This reform allowed convocation of a constituent assembly with a two-thirds vote by the legislature. Reforms approved would be submitted to the electorate for ratification.[114]

A principal focus of the constituent convention, and the primary motive for Batlle y Ordóñez's quest for constitutional reform, was to reduce presidential power. Inspired by the Swiss collegiate presidency, Batlle y Ordóñez successfully orchestrated the adoption of a mixed system with a president and a Consejo Nacional de Administración, despite the opposition by Blancos and a group within the Colorados calling themselves Riveristas (after the party's founder and the country's first president). In an effort to consolidate the power sharing won by the Blancos in recurrent civil wars, the new constitution guaranteed a one-third minority party representation on the executive council.

Nevertheless, the 1918 Constitution preserved the president's duty to conserve internal order and tranquility, his role as commander in chief of the armed forces, and most of the civil and military patronage powers. It changed the key article concerning presidential authority to confront external invasion and internal commotions to read: "to take whatever security measures deemed expedient . . . informing the Council and the General Assembly, or if not in session, the Permanent Commission [of the Assembly] within twenty-four hours of the measures taken. This authority is limited by the dispositions of Articles 80, 152 and 168" (Art. 79, Sec. 19).

The limitations were important, but not major, innovations. Article 80 limited presidential action to the arrest of those threatening national security, with the requirement that detainees be presented to a judge within twenty-four hours; Article 152 prohibited punishment or incarceration without due process; Article 168 reiterated the provision of the 1830 Constitution allowing only the legislature or, if in recess, the permanent Commission to suspend the bill of rights (*seguridad individual*) to confront treason or conspiracy against the fatherland—and then only to apprehend suspects (*delincuentes*).

The 1918 Constitution also retained the provision from 1830 that defined as "high treason" (*lesa nación*) "any attack, or providing the means to attack, the present Constitution" (Art. 175). Those provisions regarding presidential powers in times of "internal commotion" and the legislature's authority to suspend the bill of rights were essentially retained, with minor revisions, in the 1934 Constitution (Art. 30; Art. 158, Sec. 18); that of 1942 (Art. 30; Art. 157, Sec. 18); and that of 1952 (Art. 31; Art. 168, Sec. 17)—conceded to a collegiate executive; and in the charter of 1967 (Art. 31; Art. 85, Sec. 7; Arts. 253, 330).

Thus Uruguay's unusual constitutional development and its inability to consolidate a stable political system in the nineteenth century did not prevent it from sharing a key characteristic with its Spanish American neighbors: provisions for constitutional dictatorship that survived into the twentieth century. The basic authority of the executive to take "whatever measures deemed expedient" to confront rebellions and internal disorder was established in 1830 and altered little into the mid-twentieth century. Likewise, the country's basic regime of exception provisions, allowing the legislature to suspend the bill of rights to deal with treason and conspiracy against the fatherland, hardly changed from 1830 to 1967. Military responsibility for maintaining or restoring internal order was added later, in the 1884 Código Militar and, as in Chile, entailed military jurisdiction over civilians in times of "internal war."[115]

Although known for its democracy after World War II, Uruguay had established the constitutional foundations of tyranny from 1830. Faced with intense social conflict and the threat of the Tupamaro guerrillas in the late 1960s and early 1970s, Uruguay's president sent a message to the general assembly in April 1972:

> The country faces a grave situation provoked by seditious organizations.
>   This [situation] constitutes treason and conspiracy against the Fatherland. The members of the subversive organizations [by their actions] have committed the crime contemplated in Article 330 of the Constitution, high treason [*lesa nación*], since they have brought the nation to a state of internal war.
>   Therefore, and in accord with articles 31, 85 (7) 253, and 330 of the Constitution, I request that the General Assembly (1) agrees to suspend civil liberties and rights [*seguridad individual*]; (2) declares that a state of internal war exists, with application of the pertinent constitutional and legal dispositions.[116]

The 1830 Constitution and the 1884 Código Militar would be the legal foundations for the repression of the Tupamaros and of the political opposition to the civil-military dictatorship, though the authoritarian regime eventually suspended the constitution and political party activity while using antiterrorism legislation adopted in 1972 to combat its enemies.[117]

However, when the civil-military dictatorship established after 1976 failed to gain support for its proposed new constitution in 1980, in contrast to its Chilean counterpart, Uruguay returned to its nineteenth-century foundations for constitutional dictatorship. The country's unique version of presidentialism and constitutional dictatorship had survived the nineteenth century to "conserve internal order," suppress conspiracy and "high treason," and defend the security of the state in the twentieth. Uruguay's constitution of tyranny remained in place as the nation approached the twenty-first century.

PARAGUAY

First a part of the Viceroyalty of Peru and then an *intendencia* within the viceroyalty of Buenos Aires, Paraguayan territory in 1800 contained some 100,000 residents dispersed in a vast countryside. From 1607 until 1767 Jesuits had administered the Guaraní Missions virtually as a separate kingdom; after 1767, the confiscation of the mission estates resulted in a decline of the rural economy. Harassed by the Portuguese, threatened permanently by hostile Indians, governed by decree from Buenos Aires, and located twelve hundred miles by river from the Atlantic, Paraguay developed as a backward agricultural economy exporting *yerba mate* (Paraguayan tea), tobacco, sugar, honey, and hides.

Natural river barriers and difficult terrain added to Paraguay's physical and cultural isolation. A cadre of Spanish officials, militia commanders, merchants, and landowners formed a tiny social and political elite. Many of the population were native Guaraní Indians and Guaraní-speaking mestizos who worked the fields, engaged in artisanry, and lived at subsistence levels. Few Paraguayans had any formal education.[118]

By 1800, Paraguayans resented obligatory militia service and decrees and taxes from Buenos Aires as much as they did Spain's neglect. Buenos Aires had been refounded by an expedition from Asunción in 1580; since that time the twelve hundred miles from the port to Asunción had been Paraguay's tenuous link to international trade. When the *porteños* sought to replace Spanish domination with their own after 1810, Paraguayans resisted successfully.

They avoided the civil strife of unitarist-federalist conflict as in Argentina and Uruguay for the next fifty years, experiencing instead a unique sequence of personalist dictatorships: José Gaspar Rodríguez de Francia (1811–1840), Carlos Antonio López (1841–1862), and Francisco Solano López (1862–1870). The last of these embroiled Paraguay in a war against Brazil, Argentina, and Uruguay that left the nation in ruins. Only at the end of the war did Paraguay adopt its first real constitution, imposed in 1870 by the Brazilian and Argentine armies of occupation.

Independence and Dr. Francia

Events in Buenos Aires and Montevideo in 1810 upset the lethargic tranquility of Asunción. Spanish officials and royalists sought support from a Portuguese army to defend themselves against the revolutionary juntas downriver. *Criollos* in Asunción initially proclaimed their allegiance to the Spanish Council of Regency (July 1810) but soon thereafter rejected both Spanish rule and the demands by the junta at Buenos Aires to recognize its authority. In May 1811 the *cabildo* of Asunción, influenced by Doctor of Theology José Gaspar Rodríguez de Francia, declared its independence from Spain and its autonomy from Buenos Aires—after first defeating a *porteño* army commanded by Manuel Belgrano.

A Paraguayan Congress created a two-consul executive to govern the country in 1813; by 1814, Francia called another Congress, which conferred upon him the title Supreme Dictator of the Republic for five years. In 1816 the Congress made Francia Perpetual Dictator and decreed that "the Republic will have a General Congress whenever the Dictator deems it necessary" and that the churches should praise from the pulpit "love and respect for the orders of our Supreme Government."[119] Francia remained *el supremo* until his death in 1840.

Francia has been both vilified and celebrated by Paraguayan historians. His policies—isolation of Paraguay from external influence, restrictions on foreign visitors, decrees forbidding Spaniards and *criollos* from intermarrying in order to encourage *mestizaje*, attacks on the *criollo* and Spanish social elite, nationalizing of much of the nation's lands to create public enterprises that financed the government, and establishing an army to buttress his rule and defend the country against invasion—were intended to keep the country free "from contamination by that foul and restless spirit of anarchy and revolution." Francia wished "to preserve order, subordination, and tranquility."[120] Retrospectively, his policies are regarded favorably by Paraguayan nationalists and antiliberals.[121] Other Paraguayans see in Francia's administration only a primitive personalist dictatorship.

Francia took possession of the Crown lands and those of the religious orders. Leases, direct state production, and sharecropping financed public expenditures and built a subsistence economy. By 1840 almost fifty thousand persons earned their livelihood as tenants on public land; they were assisted with credit, tools, and clothing.[122] Francia governed the country as a large rural estate. Government officials were his personal administrators, the army and police his foremen and enforcers. Personally austere, Francia ruled without constitutional constraints until his death. No constitutional or legislative restriction on his power required provision for regimes of exception. His word was law, his orders disobeyed at great risk, his treatment of criminals and conspirators harsh. He spared no effort in building the Paraguayan army, directly appointed members to the Asunción *cabildo* until he dispensed with it in 1825, ordered the torture of those charged with plotting against his government, and confiscated their property to add to the public enterprises.[123]

Francia ruled directly and personally, doing the government account books, setting prices for commodities, training his cavalry, granting or refusing couples permission to marry (for example, an Indian woman and a white man), and ordering the widening of city streets. He rotated provincial officials frequently and retired many to government farms and ranches. Always concerned with order and economy, Francia instructed his officials to "enforce the peace, arrest troublemakers, clear the land of vagabonds and suspicious characters."[124] Judicial decisions were based, subject to his review, on the *Recopilación de las Leyes de las Indias,* the accretion of Spanish colonial legislation.

Francia replaced the king and royal officials in Paraguay. His legacy was a relatively egalitarian, backward fortress, free from the foreign debts and international complications that afflicted the rest of Spanish America. His personal life-style precluded ostentation, his probity and fierce repression of official corruption set examples unsurpassed in nineteenth-century Spanish America. However, he bequeathed to a nation without a printing press a retrograde political system that was unequal to the task of economic modernization. According to expatriate Juan Andrés Gelley, writing from Buenos Aires, "Paraguay is in complete darkness from that which occurs in the world: it had been dead for twenty-five years."[125]

Carlos Antonio López

Within hours of Francia's death, three army officers formed a junta "to safeguard public order and avoid anarchy."[126] A coup in January 1841 deposed this inept junta. A triumvirate followed, announcing it would call a Congress. Carlos Antonio López, who had passed the Francia regime at his ranch in the interior, returned to Asunción and began plotting with military commanders. Another coup in February, led by Mariano Roque Alonso and his civilian secretary, Carlos Antonio López, took control of Asunción and called a Congress for March. The Congress orchestrated by López and Roque Alonso named them co-consuls for a term of three years; no written constitution emerged and only vague instructions were given to the co-executives to defend the republic, regulate commerce, and manage foreign affairs.

López was a landowner and lawyer, one of the few educated men in Asunción. Roque Alonso proved more suited for the barracks than for directing the destiny of the nation. Gradually he allowed López, "the corpulent despot," to take charge. Unlike Francia, López had carnal and material appetites to match his oversized body. Soon, he and family members acquired large haciendas, enjoyed public revenues as private sinecures, and awarded supporters with public revenues and government posts. Like Francia, however, he repressed opposition fiercely; a large Paraguayan exile community grew in Buenos Aires.

A Congress met in 1844 and adopted a proto-constitution called "The Law that Establishes the Political Administration of the Republic of Paraguay." It created a centralized regime dominated by the executive López, who was given a ten-year term. The executive had full authority "whenever necessary to conserve order and public tranquility" ["cuantas veces fuese precisa para conservar el orden i la tranquilidad pública"].[127] Congress was to meet every five years. Five years later the Congress approved all of López's actions and adjourned. In 1854 it reelected him for another ten years. With his son, Francisco Solano López, as commander of the army and clearly the designated successor, no serious constitutional reforms nor any effective political opposition occurred. On his deathbed in 1862, López named his son vice president.

When his father died, Francisco Solano convened a Congress to confirm his succession, after first ordering the arrest of several notables he thought might object. Even so, several delegates dared to question the propriety of filial inheritance of the presidency, suggesting that it might be time for Paraguay to have a constitution like its neighbors. Under the watchful eyes of the military, the Congress named Solano López president for ten years. Arrests and confiscation of opponents' properties followed. New groups of exiles found their way to Buenos Aires.

Unlike his father, Solano López sought a role for Paraguay in southern cone politics. Taking sides in 1863 with the Blancos in Uruguay, he engaged his country in war with Brazil, Argentina, and their Uruguayan allies. Despite a strong army and heroic resistance, Paraguay suffered monumental losses of life and property in a losing effort. Solano López died in battle March 1, 1870, after a Brazilian army already controlled Asunción.[128] At the war's end, males constituted less than 20 percent of Paraguay's estimated population of 220,000. Asunción's major dilemma was finding enough wagons to take bodies for burial. A Brazilian occupation army remained in the country and pulled the strings of puppet presidents until 1876. It imposed a provisional government and Paraguay's first constitution in November 1870.

Finally, under Brazilian imperial tutelage and the intellectual inspiration of the most liberal groups in Buenos Aires, Paraguay adopted a recognizable constitution. It provided for universal adult suffrage (for those over eighteen years), the most complete list of civil liberties and rights in South America, freedom of the press, a clear prohibition on Congress's interference in freedom of religion, abolition of slavery, and elimination of special privileges and *fueros* (Arts. 18–26). It also established criminal liability of government officials for "intervening in elections or coercing voters" (Art. 27).

In response to the dictatorial threesome from 1813 to 1870, the constitution prohibited the congressional delegation of extraordinary powers, or the *suma del poder público*. It declared "dictatorship null and inadmissible in the Paraguayan Republic," making anyone who formulated, consented to, or approved such a measure "guilty of the crime of 'traitor to the Fatherland'" (Art. 14). However, Paraguay's imported liberalism also included the mechanisms required for repression of "internal commotion" and "defense of the constitution and the government." Article 9 stipulated that

> in the case of internal commotion or external attack that threatens the operation of this constitution and the authorities created by it, a state of siege shall be declared in all or part of Paraguayan territory, for a specified period. During this time

the authority of the president shall limit itself to the arrest of suspects and their transfer to points within the Republic, if they do not prefer voluntary exile.

Congress was to declare a state of siege in the case of internal commotion or approve and terminate such a declaration made by the president when Congress was not in session (Art. 22). Article 102 (Sec. 17) conferred on the president the unilateral authority to declare a state of siege in the case of external attack. It also stipulated that the state of siege should terminate when "the conditions [that precipitated the declaration] have ceased to exist." However, the constitution did not detail the legal consequences of declaring a state of siege, which *garantías* were suspended, or the extent of government authority during the state of siege. The president was not to assume *la suprema del poder público*, to supersede judicial authority, nor to ignore due process, but unlike other such provisions in Spanish America no elaborated regime of exception clause was inserted nor was reference made to a "to-be-adopted" organic law regulating the state of siege.

The 1870 Constitution remained in effect, if not in force, until 1940. In the next eighty-five years Paraguay had forty-four presidents, most of whom experienced considerable internal commotion and adapted the ambiguity of the state of siege clause to suit their immediate needs. For thirty-five years after the adoption of the 1870 charter, with brief interludes, military officers dominated the presidency. These war heroes formed the nucleus of the Colorado party, a loose coalition of personalist factions that shared the martyrdom of López's defeat. Brazilian and Argentine meddling confounded the plotting and the assassinations of presidents, former presidents, and would-be presidents, punctuated by periodic revolts, that gave governments good pretexts for using dictatorial powers.

In 1877 President D. Cándido Barreiro confronted a revolt with a declaration of state of siege, fulfilling his promise to "maintain peace and public order with a firm hand."[129] Barreiro's death in 1880 brought a coup led by war hero Bernardino Caballero, who would dominate Paraguayan politics as kingmaker, party leader, and senator in the decades after leaving the presidency. Caballero's cynical Manifesto to the People, issued after the arrest and forced resignation of the vice president, sounded all too familiar in nineteenth-century Spanish America.

The illustrious President of the Republic, D. Cándido Barreiro, has just died and in the duty of maintaining imminently threatened peace and order, I have taken command of the national forces until the Honorable Congress of the Nation can meet and adopt those measures warranted by the circumstances.

For this purpose all measures to guarantee order have been taken. I assume this responsibility willingly in the name of the salvation of the country and its institutions. The people may be assured that it will be my first duty to guarantee the lives and interests of all inhabitants of the Republic.

You may rest assured that my greatest desire is to fulfill the Constitution and the laws of the Nation.[130]

Caballero's words, or words like them, would be often repeated as presidents came and went from 1880 until 1904, some through election, others through coup, but always exercising the broad powers conferred by the 1870 charter. Occasionally, states of siege were imposed to meet electoral violence or the threat of revolt. Constitutional dictatorship became a ready tool of incumbent administrations. Between 1880 and 1904, Colorado presidents controlled elections and violently repressed antigovernment candidates. Electoral fraud, intimidation, and disdain for legality made political opposition both risky and thankless. With the rise of a loose opposition coalition, identified as liberal to distinguish it from the government's Colorado party, insurrection seemed the only plausible method for overcoming government electoral manipulation. Such methods naturally provoked repression, as occurred with most elections in the 1880s and 1890s.

In the early 1890s, minor military mutinies and full-scale coup attempts failed. President Juan Gualberto González invoked the state of siege provisions to suppress a liberal revolt in 1891; many leading liberals were imprisoned and others fled to exile. In 1894, however, he could not resist a Brazilian-orchestrated coup that allied former presidents generals Caballero and Escobar with General Juan Bautista Egusquiza. President Egusquiza adopted a modified Uruguayan model for incorporating the opposition without ceding hegemony: liberals were allowed to elect two senators and four deputies in 1895. Not until the revolt of 1904 did the military president on duty, despite the use of the state of siege provisions, lose to liberal rebels supported by Argentina. The Colorados lost to the liberals, but with minor changes the basic pattern of politics prevailed into the 1930s. Presidents now held office for a year or two instead of three to four. Between 1904 and 1924, only one president completed his term of office.

After the Chaco War against Bolivia (1932–1935), Paraguay adopted a new constitution; its regime of exception provisions confirmed the presidential authority to declare a state of siege (Art. 52) and added a constitutional mission for the armed forces unspecified in the nineteenth century: "the custody and defense of the order and of the sovereignty, territorial integrity, and honor of the Republic, as well as the defense of this [1940] Constitution" (Art. 18). As commander of the armed forces, the president thus had both state of siege authority and everyday responsibility for conserving internal order and defending the constitution and the honor of the Republic. Moreover, in 1940 all civil liberties and rights could "be limited by law as exigencies of the public order may require" (Art. 35).

Late to adopt its first constitution, Paraguay departed from many (but not all) of its Spanish American neighbors also in expanding executive authority and providing more draconian regimes of exception in the twentieth century than it had in the nineteenth. It likewise had the distinction of constitutionally outlawing "the preaching of hatred or class conflict" in its 1940 Constitution (Art. 35) before most other Latin American nations (Peru being a notable exception) adopted anti-Marxist constitutional and legislative measures later in the 1940s.

Despite these differences, Paraguay, like Argentina and Uruguay, had typical provisions for executive and legislative implementation of regimes of exception to counter internal commotion, subversion, treason, and rebellion. The Paraguayan constitutional provisions resembled those of Argentina more than those of Uruguay but were imprecise enough so that the president could take action more like the *medidas prontas de seguridad* of Uruguay than the more delineated measures authorized for the Argentine executive. Whatever differences existed, however, Paraguay had provided more than adequate constitutional foundations of dictatorship in the nineteenth century that endured to the end of the twentieth.

8

Regimes of Exception in Chile

SINCE THE MID-SIXTEENTH CENTURY, CHILE HAD BEEN A GARRISON colony at war with the southern Indian tribes. It was a poor frontier colony of three discernible economic regions: the sparsely settled mining districts of the *norte chico* from Copiapó to Quillota; Santiago and the agricultural estates of the central valley; and the territory from Concepción south of the Bio-Bio River—the Indian frontier. Subsidized militarily and economically by Spain and Peru, Chilean agrarian and mineral exports failed to pay even the costs of imported sugar and yerba mate (Paraguayan tea) into the nineteenth century.

Commercial and political domination by Lima had been resented and resisted by settlers, landowners, merchants, and bureaucrats since the sixteenth century. Administrative reorganization in the last decades of the eighteenth century left Chile an autonomous captaincy-general, no longer directly subject to the viceroy of Peru. Economic reforms and expanded public works had improved the colony's situation, but it remained a backwater of the empire and a drain on Spanish and Peruvian treasuries.

At the time Chileans learned of Napoleon's invasion of Spain in mid-1808, approximately one million people resided in the colony, including perhaps two hundred thousand Indians in the south. A few *criollos* viewed the turmoil in Spain as an opportunity to achieve independence; most Chileans saw the events in Europe as an interruption of legitimate Spanish rule. Confrontations occurred between those professing to favor the temporary exercise of authority by a local junta, as in Spain and elsewhere in Spanish America, and those favoring submission to the French authorities in Spain. The former were concentrated in the *cabildo*, while the latter adhered to Governor Francisco Antonio García Carrasco and the *audiencia*.

313

Unlike the capable administrators who had governed Chile in the last decades of the eighteenth century, Carrasco lacked experience and political skills. His inept response to the news of the May 1810 events in Buenos Aires, including the arrest and deportation to Lima of leading *criollos* on charges of subversion, provoked anger in Santiago. The *audiencia* attempted to calm the situation by announcing Carrasco's resignation and his replacement by the octogenarian Conde de la Conquista, Mateo de Toro Zambrano, whose rank as brigadier of the royal armies gave him a rightful claim to the governorship. This failed to pacify the local elite. On September 18, 1810, a *cabildo abierto* convened in the *tribunal de consulado* in Santiago, accepted the governor's resignation, and proclaimed the creation of a national junta.[1]

Although September 18 is celebrated as Independence Day in Chile, this junta (as its counterparts elsewhere) swore to "govern and protect the rights of the king during his captivity." This mask of loyalty to the king donned by the Chilean junta earned it recognition from the Council of Regency in Spain, the only junta so recognized in Spanish America. Not until 1818 would Chileans formally declare their independence. During the two decades following the 1810 *cabildo abierto,* a confusing succession of juntas, assemblies, congresses, dictatorships, directorates, and presidents sought to establish their authority in Chile. These governments adopted several proto-constitutions and four formal charters (1818, 1822, 1823, and 1828) before the final consolidation of the constitutional order in 1833. Civil war between 1810 and 1814 was followed by the restoration of Spanish rule from 1814 to 1817. San Martín's successful expedition across the Andes brought to power Chile's founding father, Bernardo O'Higgins, from 1818 until his abdication in 1823. After O'Higgins's departure to Peru, renewed civil war among contending personalist, family, and ideological factions produced several constitutional experiments, resulting finally in the establishment of the 1833 centralist, executive-dominated political system that would survive with reforms in the 1870s until 1925.

The 1833 Constitution and the Chilean autocratic republic became the envy of the other Spanish American nations, as from the early 1830s Chile largely avoided the caudillismo, fragmentation, and disorder characteristic of the region. This constitution stood unamended until 1870, when the immediate reelection of the president was prohibited after four chief executives had served two five-year terms each from 1831 to 1871. Many writers call the system established by the 1833 Constitution the "Portalian state," in honor of Diego Portales, the conservative merchant and politician who directed policy making in the 1830s. Others regard post-1833 Chile as "the last and most beautiful chapter of Spanish colonial history."[2]

The 1833 Constitution, and the political system it sanctioned, perfected and frequently implemented the regimes of exception that became familiar to other Spanish Americans in the nineteenth century and that included the delegation of extraordinary powers to the executive to meet political emergencies, suspension of civil liberties and rights, limitations on press freedom, government control of elections, repression of political opposition, and imposition of states of siege. More favorable political and economic conditions, the geographical compactness of the 700-mile territory from Copiapó to the Bio-Bio River, the homogeneity of the landowning oligarchy, and the country's less severe regionalism compared with the Río de la Plata, northern South America, or Central America allowed Chileans to consolidate these foundations of constitutional dictatorship earlier than other Spanish Americans. While Chile was the first Spanish American nation to adopt constitutional provisions for state of siege, its other regimes of exception differed little in form and content from those adopted elsewhere. After 1833, however, Chile would become the model for achieving political stability through constitutional dictatorship.

POLITICAL EXPERIMENTS AND INDEPENDENCE, 1810–1818

From 1810 to 1814, a period labeled *patria vieja,* or old fatherland, by Chilean historians, the personalities and ambitions of competing founding fathers, such as Juan Martínez de Rozas, José Miguel Carrera and his two brothers, the Larraín family (which dominated the early legislatures and judiciary), and Bernardo O'Higgins, dominated politics and the course of rebellion. The national junta of September 18, 1810, was followed by experiments with a Congress and then the brief dictatorship of José Miguel Carrera. Feuds between Carrera, the omnipresent Larraín family, and the eventual military hero of independence, Bernardo O'Higgins, prevented the formation of a national consensus. Rivalry between officials in Santiago and a junta at Concepción further confused political authority. Adding to the disarray, the U.S. consul, Joel Poinsett, allied himself with the Carrera faction, provoking Spanish, *criollo,* and British hostility. In this period of political confusion, the first printing press arrived in Chile and the first national paper, *La Aurora de*

Chile, initiated a tradition of inflammatory journalism that would characterize Chilean politics in the nineteenth century.

Several decrees sought to establish the basis for provisional authority in the Chilean colony: the Reglamento Provisional de la Junta Gubernativa (1810), the Reglamento Para el Arreglo de la Autoridad Ejecutiva Provisorio de Chile (1811), and the Reglamento Constitucional Provisorio (1812). Only the last of these, imposed virtually at bayonet point by the Carrera dictatorship, had the basic elements of the Spanish American proto-constitutions— consideration of the origins of sovereignty, the manner of its delegation by the people to a newly constituted authority, its division among three branches of government, and provisions for civil rights and liberties along with provisions for their suspension when required by "threats to public welfare."

The 1812 *reglamento* proclaimed that "no decree, statute [*providencia*] or other order, that emanates from any authority or tribunal outside Chilean territory will have any effect, those who attempt to enforce them will be punished as criminals against the State [*reos de Estado*]" (Art. 5). In some respects this was a revolutionary document, reserving to the sovereign people ample authority and declaring that if the authorities acted against the general will as expressed in the constitution "in that moment power returns to the people who will punish that act as high treason." However, the 1812 charter still deferred to Ferdinand VII, albeit with the caveat that "he will accept our Constitution in the same fashion as that of the Peninsula [the Cádiz Constitution, 1812]" (Art. 3). Thus the Chileans did not follow the Venezuelan lead, though the Venezuelan declaration of independence was printed in the seventh issue of *La Aurora de Chile* on March 26, 1812.³

Anticipating the more precise regimes of exception of later Chilean charters, the 1812 Reglamento Constitucional Provisorio established basic citizens' rights to the security of their persons, homes, possessions, and documents; due process in legal proceedings; press freedom (as long as it did not offend the church, honor of persons, or good customs); equality before the law; and freedom of movement (Arts. 16, 18, 24). It then stipulated that "the government may arrest [persons] for crimes against the State" subject to appeal to the Senate. Civil liberties and rights could be suspended "only in the case of threats to the welfare of the Fatherland" ("en el caso de importar a la salud de la Patria amenazada") (Art. 26). In the midst of civil war from 1812 to 1814, the government used these provisions to justify repressing royalists and other opponents of the incumbent administration. Despite the increasingly revolutionary journalism of independence supporters, however, never did the governments from 1810 to 1814 overtly call for independence from Spain.

Fearful that despite protestations of loyalty the Chileans would follow the Venezuelan and New Granadian path toward independence, the Peruvian viceroy sent a military expedition to restore order in Chile. It first disembarked at the southern island of Chiloé, which still depended directly on the viceregal authority, gathered recruits, and went to Valdivia where the royalists had established control. The expedition then went by sea to Talcahuano and captured Concepción, where part of the garrison switched allegiance. These victories temporarily secured control of southern Chile for Spain.

A second royalist expedition commanded by General Gabino Gaínza entered Chile in early 1814. Defeating armies led by Carrera, O'Higgins, and Juan Mackenna, the royalists took Chillán and Talca in the southern part of the central valley. Thereafter, a stalemate developed. British commodore James Hillyar mediated a treaty (the Treaty of Lircay) whereby Chile swore fealty to Ferdinand VII and would send deputies to the *cortes* in Spain and suppress display of the Chilean flag, introduced in 1812.

Before Lircay the 1812 charter was supplanted by the 1814 Reglamento Para el Gobierno Provisorio. The junta had dismissed Carrera and replaced him in March with Francisco de la Lastra as supreme director. Lastra assumed the "absolute powers" previously exercised by the 1810 Junta. The supreme director was given "full and unrestricted" authority (*facultades amplísimas y ilimitadas*) for eighteen months, except for making peace treaties, declaring war, and establishing new businesses and taxes. In these cases he was required to consult the Senate (Arts. 1, 2, 5). The 1814 document, unlike its 1812 predecessor, made no mention of civil rights and liberties, nor did it require provision for regimes of exception, given the "full and unrestricted" authority of the executive. Imprisoned by the royalists, Carrera rejected the Treaty of Lircay, as did the viceroy, who desired a return to the old order rather than an acceptance of the extent of autonomy agreed to by his commander in the field. Carrera escaped, overthrew the Lastra government on July 23, 1814, and reimposed a personal dictatorship.

The Peruvian viceroy now sent General Mariano Osorio to resolve the Chilean matter. Ironically, Osorio sought to obtain Chilean adherence to the Cádiz Constitution, already abrogated by

Ferdinand VII in Spain. Carrera mockingly informed Osorio that the king had declared traitors all who upheld the 1812 charter. Thus, after 1814 both royalists and *criollo juntistas* purportedly fought for Ferdinand VII. In practice, O'Higgins and Carrera sought independence, but when Carrera failed to support O'Higgins's army at Rancagua in October 1814, General Osorio's victory ended the *patria vieja*. The remnants of the rebel forces fled to Mendoza, along with prominent *criollos*. José de San Martín welcomed O'Higgins and planning began for the campaign that would ultimately liberate Chile and Peru (1817–1825).

For the next three years the Spanish administration purged separatists, cleansed the army and bureaucracy of suspected sympathizers, and discriminated blatantly against *criollo* leaders. When Chileans protested, Governor Francisco Casimiro Marcó del Pont was reputed to have told his entourage: "I shall not leave the Chileans even tears with which to weep."[4] Repression alienated even the moderate *criollos;* guerrilla resistance against the Spanish persisted while San Martín prepared his expedition in Cuyo. Until 1817 Chile remained in Spanish control. The proto-constitutions from 1810 to 1814 had eclectically provided for regimes of exception and, alternately, for full and unrestricted power for the executives. They had not, however, created a recognizable constitutional benchmark for later Chilean regimes. They are historical curiosities rather than significant juridical antecedents of Chilean constitutionalism.

INDEPENDENCE UNTIL 1828

Crossing the Andes in early 1817, San Martín's army defeated a royalist force at Chacabuco, north of Santiago. Mobs in Santiago ransacked the homes and property of royal officials and supporters. San Martín and O'Higgins entered the capital on February 14, 1817. After San Martín declined the *cabildo's* offer to rule Chile and supported the candidacy of O'Higgins, the cabildo conferred upon O'Higgins the supreme directorship of the colony. His first months in office were spent in the field against royalist armies in a war that continued into the 1820s, but by mid-1818 the territory from Copiapó to Concepción was liberated from Spanish rule. His proclamation of independence in Talca in February 1818 symbolically ended Chile's ties to Spain.

O'Higgins fancied himself a liberal in the tradition of the Bourbon reforms of the late colonial period, influenced also by Francisco de Miranda and the secret, Masonic-inspired revolutionary group called *logia lautarina*.[5] This lodge, dedicated to the independence of Spain's American colonies, swore its members to secrecy and required that adherents who gained key positions in any of the liberated colonies submit for approval the names of those they would appoint to high military or government positions. O'Higgins's critics viewed him as an agent of an extranational, anticlerical, Masonic conspiracy. They blamed him for the executions of the three Carrera brothers and the assassination of the guerrilla hero Manuel Rodríguez.

O'Higgins's liberalism did not mean serious attachment to civil liberties and rights, to legislative control of policy, to elections, or to faith in common people. He believed that "it was necessary, with people like the Chileans, to confer good upon them by force" when other means failed.[6] Liberalism demanded constitutional legitimation for government benevolence, imposed by force or otherwise. To this end, O'Higgins promulgated a constitution in 1818 and another in 1822. The 1818 Constitution was written by a handpicked commission and ratified in a limited plebiscite. Eligible voters cast their yes or no votes in registries supervised by parish priests. Adopted in the name of "Omnipotent God, Creator and Supreme Legislator," it gave O'Higgins a six-year term as supreme director, with the possibility of an additional four-year term. A five-person Senate, named by O'Higgins before the plebiscite, had little real legislative authority but could amend the constitution "as circumstances require" (Arts. 5–6).

O'Higgins's conception of government and his personal disposition differed radically from those of Artigas in the *banda oriental* or, later, of Argentine dictator Juan Manuel de Rosas and the other, less enlightened supreme directors in the Río de la Plata region. He intended to institute strong, centralized government but not a tyrannical dictatorship. He looked to "the inalienable right of the people to give themselves the form of government most suited to their needs" for the legitimation of his directorship.[7] In the Roman Senate he found justification for benevolent dictatorship: "From the beginning I was charged with the Supreme Directorship, without limitation of powers. In the same way, the free state of Rome, in moments of greatest crisis, used to hide the tables of the law beneath a veil and entrust absolute power to a Dictator."[8]

O'Higgins also recognized that the manner of installing the 1818 Constitution did not conform properly to the liberal ideal: a constituent convention followed by an elected legislature exercising the sovereign authority. He felt justified by circumstances to substitute the appointed commission, the plebiscite, and an advisory Senate for the ideal until it was possible for a more representative constituent assembly to modify the 1818 charter (Title III, Chap. 1). Nevertheless, this first constitutional expression of O'Higgins's rule little inhibited a draconian personalist and centralist regime.

Despite his reformist bent, the constitution established the Roman Catholic religion as the "only and exclusive religion of the State of Chile . . . its protection, conservation, purity and inviolability will be one of the foremost duties of the directors of society, who shall never permit public exercise of another religion contrary to that of Jesus Christ" (Title II, Art. Unico). After displaying the menu of the liberal "rights of man in society"—*seguridad individual,* honor, property (*hacienda*), liberty, and civil equality—the charter was spiced with provisions allowing suspension of these and other rights. The prohibition on search and seizure in the "sacred" home of each person could be suspended "in urgent cases determined by the Senate" (Title I, Chap I, Art. 5). Freedom of the press was guaranteed so long as "it did not offend public tranquility and the Constitution of the State, and conservation of the Christian religion" (Art. 11). Privacy of correspondence could be violated when "the general welfare of the State required" ("cuando por la salud general y bien del Estado, fuese preciso") (Chap. II, Art. 8). Arrests of citizens were prohibited without evidence of wrongdoing and making known the charges within eight days, except when "some danger threatens the Fatherland" (Title V, Chap. III, Art. 21).

This smorgasbord of vague recipes for suspending civil rights and liberties was accompanied by a section on the "obligations of social man." These obligations included:

> complete submission to the Constitution of the State, its statutes and laws . . . ; obey, honor and respect all magistrates and public officials . . . ; assist with some share of wealth to [pay for] the ordinary expenses of the State; and in extraordinary circumstances or times of danger, sacrifice as much as possible [*lo mas estimable*] to conserve its existence and liberty. (Title I, Chap. II, Arts. 1–3)

The charter also afforded virtually unlimited power to the supreme director. Conjoining the authority and ceremonial distinctions of viceroy and captain-general (Title IV, Art. 4), the executive commanded the armed forces and militia and was responsible for staffing the public administration and "seeing to the development of agriculture, industry, commerce, mining, the mail service, and roads." He was to give special attention to "extinguishing the internal divisions that ruin States" (Title IV, Chap. I, Art. 16) and would have "general supervision of all branches and resources [caudales] of the State" (Title IV, Chap. I, Art. 19).

In one important respect the 1818 Constitution restricted executive authority: the supreme director "may not intervene in any criminal or civil matter before the courts, nor alter the administration of justice, nor the appeal process in the exclusive jurisdiction of the Courts of Appeal" (Title IV, Chap. II, Art. 1). Unlike the *suma de poder público* or *lleno de facultades* exercised by directors and directorates in the Río de la Plata, executive authority in the 1818 Chilean scheme was powerful but not unlimited. Constitutional dictatorship under O'Higgins did not include the capricious intromission in the everyday administration of justice found in Paraguay, Buenos Aires, the provinces of the Río de la Plata, and Bolivia.

Despite his executive powers, O'Higgins's government lacked institutional support. He was a military hero tied to the army of San Martín and the *logia lautarina*. This made him, in the view of some Chilean *criollos,* an appendage of the government at Buenos Aires. A clause in the 1818 Constitution charging the supreme director with "maintaining the closest alliance with the Supreme Government of the United Provinces of the Río de la Plata" reinforced this perception (Title IV, Chap. I, Art. 9). A number of difficulties undermined O'Higgins's position. They included conflicts with the church, opposition to his introduction of Protestant teachers to develop a Lancasterian system, opposition to his efforts to abolish entailed estates (*mayorazgos*), poor relations with "his" Senate, unsuccessful tax and economic reforms, and personalist intrigues. The supreme director gradually lost the support of the landowning and merchant elite and the small group of key families—that is, the political class—that would govern the country from the 1830s to the end of the century.

Speculation in tobacco and other commodities by the supreme director's finance minister and charges of ministerial corruption further eroded the moral base of the administration. O'Higgins's generosity to former royalists who swore loyalty to Chile and the return of their confiscated property, accompanied by political intrigues regarding a new constitution proposed in 1822, alienated his supporters. A debate concerning a loan secured in London, failure to pay the fleet in Valparaíso, and a threat to replace the popular general, Ramón Freire, as commander of the army at Concepción all contributed to O'Higgins's eventual downfall.[9]

In 1822 two of the country's five senators left on diplomatic missions. A third decided to leave public office. O'Higgins proposed that the Senate temporarily suspend its sessions and confer upon the supreme director full legislative authority. The Senate resisted O'Higgins's plan; he decided to reform the 1818 Constitution. Controlling elections to a preparatory convention that met from July to October, he imposed on the delegates his preferences for a strong executive and a powerless legislative branch. The convention promulgated the 1822 Constitution on October 30.

Provincial uprisings ensued and quickly affected Santiago. The Concepción intendant, General Ramón Freire, led troops against Talca and threatened to strike toward Santiago. The northern city of La Serena followed Freire's lead, and O'Higgins's opponents in Santiago called for his ouster. After an emotional farewell speech, O'Higgins abdicated in late January 1823, transferring power to a national junta. Six months later he left for Peruvian exile, from which he would never return. Chileans would later view this as a heroic gesture to spare the country bloodshed; in 1823 his opponents wished him, at best, good riddance.[10]

O'Higgins observed the last stages of Bolívar's Peruvian campaign in 1824 at the Liberator's side. He supported an uprising in Chile at Chiloé in 1826 and hoped that the conservative governments after 1830 would invite him to return to the nation he had helped to forge. His return involved too many political risks. No invitation materialized. Still in exile, O'Higgins died in 1842.

The 1822 Constitution had precipitated the provincial revolts that ended O'Higgins's rule. It was, however, Chile's first fully elaborated charter and its preamble trumpeted the victory of republicanism and enlightenment: "the fundamental and invariable principles proclaimed from the birth of the revolution, such as division and independence of the branches of government, the representative system, the election of the chief executive, responsibility of government officials for their actions, individual *garantías.*" Despite these appeals to "the revolution," the constitution failed to define Chile as a republic—this would not occur until 1823. It also retained the language of 1818 on religious intolerance. In part, this resulted from O'Higgins's indecisiveness regarding the most appropriate form of government for the country, preferring, as he did, to await the examples of Mexico, Colombia, Peru, and Argentina, or even the possibility of joining the Río de la Plata confederation.[11]

Opponents of the new constitution could not argue that it further expanded O'Higgins's powers. The classical division of authority into executive, legislative, and judicial branches was translated into a supreme director, elected for six years with the possibility of a second four-year term; a corporativist Senate, including religious, military, judicial, congressional, and university representatives; a chamber of deputies, composed of representatives selected in complex departmental elections supervised by the *cabildos* (Title IV, Chap. I, Arts. 17–36); a *cortes* of representatives (to carry out legislative tasks and oversight when the Congress was not in session); and an independent judicial branch headed by a Tribunal Supremo de Justicia (Title VII, Chap. I).

The supreme director retained control over the armed forces, authority to appoint all general officers subject to legislative approval, and most patronage powers in the civil and ecclesiastic bureaucracy. However, new posts requiring public expenditures could not be created without legislative acquiescence. The supreme director was charged with "all matters conducive to conservation of public order and security of the State" and could be conceded extraordinary powers (*facultades extraordinarias*) by the legislature in the "case of imminent danger to the State" for the period necessary to meet such a threat (Title V, Chap. II, Art. 121). This introduced one of the most important bases for exceptional regimes in Chile during the nineteenth century: legislative concession of extraordinary powers to the executive. It went no further in this respect than earlier such provisions in the Río de la Plata, while providing more legislative control than in the 1818 charter. It also precluded the maintenance or renewal of the extraordinary powers beyond the time necessary to take immediate measures (*providencias muy prontas*) to meet the "danger to the state." Further, the charter prohibited the supreme director's interference in the deliberations of the legislature or its suspension during scheduled sessions, subject to prosecution for "treason against the Fatherland" (Art. 118). Even the supreme director's appointment of *delegados directoriales,* departmental administrators who combined civilian and military authority, was subject to legislative approval (Title VI, Chap. I, Arts. 143–144).

Thus, the 1822 Constitution provided ample executive authority and included important bases for constitutional dictatorship, but in many respects it restricted the supreme director more than had the 1818 charter. It was not the constitution itself, but O'Higgins's personality, style, and policies, that provoked his ouster.

Political uncertainty followed O'Higgins's abdication. A barrage of political slogans, ideologies, and political experiments flooded the country for the next six years. Internal warfare, rebellions, and further constitutional experiments prevented consolidation of political authority. Regional factions, though not as strong as in neighboring republics, nevertheless supported superficial federalist projects in their desire to gain autonomy from Santiago or to increase their influence in national politics.

The national junta that replaced O'Higgins immediately adopted a provisional statute, the Reglamento Orgánico Provisional (January 29, 1823), giving itself "all the powers necessary to conserve internal order and external security" (Art. 6). It decreed that when "imminent danger threatened public security" persons could be arrested and turned over to the judicial authorities, and it also readopted the press law of 1813. In February the junta accepted General Freire as head of state. A month later a new provisional regime was created by the publication of the Reglamento Orgánico y Acta de Unión del Pueblo de Chile, approved by delegates from the provinces. This document created a chief executive, now called "jefe supremo del estado," with the same powers as those exercised by the supreme director under the 1818 charter, and an appointed Senate (Arts. 2–4). The *jefe supremo* was directed to afford all possible aid to Peru in completing its liberation from Spain, and the future Congress was advised to adopt measures "to assure unity, public tranquility, civil rights and liberties" (Art. 39). Chile temporarily returned to executive dictatorship, essentially conforming to the 1818 charter, as modified by the 1823 Reglamento Orgánico y Acta de Unión.

Freire assumed the provisional supreme directorship the day after this decree's promulgation. The newly elected Congress confirmed him as supreme director for a three-year term and set about drafting a new constitution. The temporary intellectual ascendance of conservative Juan Egaña resulted in the adoption of a most unusual, lengthy, and complex constitution in the last days of December 1823.

The 1823 Constitution combined incompatible ingredients, kneaded by an ardent but inexpert baker. It concocted a republic without elected representatives, assigned contradictory authority to legislators and the executive, and contained a strange section on "National Morality" (Title XXII). This section charged the legislature with passing laws that "form a moral code detailing the obligations of citizens in all stages of life . . . transforming laws into customs, and customs into civic and moral virtues." In one respect, however, Egaña shared the concerns of his contemporaries. In the case of "external attack or internal commotion," the supreme director imagined in the 1823 Constitution could "dictate offensive or defensive urgency measures," and then consult with the Senate (Title II, Art. 18, Sec. 9). A number of unique, moralistic, and impractical provisions distinguished Egaña's creation, though he finally designated Chile a republic, provided constitutional foundations for the armed forces (Title XX), and called for Congress to adopt military *ordenanzas*. This latter afterthought would eventually produce legitimation for *consejos de guerra* and the trial of civilians for subversion by military tribunals in the late 1830s, but Egaña could not be blamed for the particulars at that late date.

Neither liberals nor conservatives could abide the 1823 Constitution. It was an aberration, devoid of consistent principles and impossible to implement. The regime of exception clause allowing executive action to meet internal commotion or external threats neither expanded nor delimited earlier such authority but, as in much of the 1823 document, it confused the manner of its exercise or control. Moreover, the Senate's authority to "suspend temporarily the actions of the Directorate if grave and dangerous results or violation of the law might occur" (Art. 38, Sec. 3) virtually guaranteed irresolvable conflicts between the supreme director and the legislature.

The 1823 Constitution was never operational. The day after its promulgation, General Freire left the capital at the head of an expedition to liberate the island of Chiloé, the last Spanish outpost. Initially unsuccessful, he returned to Santiago in June 1824. On July 14 he resigned, telling the Senate he could not implement the 1823 charter. The Senate conferred broad powers on Freire and agreed to suspend the implementation of the constitution and to consider reforms. Instead, in November, it declared the constitution null and void. In the interim, the Freire government confiscated the possessions of the regular clergy, thereby rupturing church-state relations. Regional uprisings and Freire's inability to organize effectively the public administration undermined the government. Soon, only Santiago recognized the provisional government and Freire. Coquimbo, under the leadership of General Francisco Antonio Pinto, and also Concepción, resorted to home rule by provincial assemblies. Freire ordered the convocation of another Congress in July 1825, but only Santiago sent representatives.

Congress then suspended Freire from the supreme directorship. He returned the favor, dissolving Congress by force and organizing a "directorial council." (This was the last time a Chilean chief executive dissolved Congress until a military coup in 1924.) Heading the council was José Miguel Infante, the most avid proponent of federalism in Chile. In January 1826, the council divided the country into eight new provinces and contemplated installing a federalist constitution. Finally victorious against the Spanish at Chiloé, Freire returned to Santiago in March 1826 and called a new Congress into session, then resigned the supreme directorship.

In July, Manuel Blanco Encalada was elected president, the first time that title was given to Chile's chief executive. Freire received appointment as captain-general, a rank attained only by San Martín and O'Higgins. Congress then approved a federal system for Chile and produced a draft federalist constitution. Meanwhile, the army went unpaid, the treasury was depleted, banditry plagued the countryside, and provisional presidents rapidly succeeded one another. The newspaper *El Cometa* reported: "The country is travelling to its ruin."[12]

Civil strife so increased that Congress requested Freire to reassume the presidency, after an abortive coup by Colonel Enrique Campino, who entered the Congress on horseback with his escort. Freire accepted, defeated several opposition armies, then resigned again. On May 5, Vice President Francisco Antonio Pinto succeeded him, and in August 1827 the country reverted to a unitary form of government. All this had occurred without a new constitution and without an operating constitution since 1823. Pinto's moderate liberal administration would fill this vacuum in 1828.

THE 1828 CONSTITUTION AND THE FAILURE OF LIBERALISM

The 1828 Constitution symbolized the temporary victory of the liberal factions over the patrician, merchant, and colonial oligarchy. However, Chilean liberals were divided among federalists and centralists, anticlericals and moderate Catholics, populists and those favoring restricted suffrage. Personal and family allegiances often determined the composition of coalitions and governments. From 1823 to 1828, the liberals had been unable to consolidate the institutions of a liberal political system. Leading liberals believed this would finally be achieved with the 1828 charter.

Vice President Francisco Antonio Pinto, who became the first president after the promulgation of the 1828 Constitution, advised his compatriots in the overleaf of the constitution that "the solemn day of consolidation of our liberty has arrived."

These laws are not the product of force but of reason. The times in which fate condemned us to blind obedience to unlimited authority have ended. . . . These laws define limits, they require an inviolable respect for the National will and individual rights.

. . . the Constitution assures our Holy religion. [It] establishes the most formidable guarantees against the abuse of all authority against excesses of power. Liberty, equality, property, the right to publish your opinions, and to present your complaints and petitions to the organs of national sovereignty are sheltered against all attack.

The representative system . . . is established in our fundamental charter, with the precautions necessary to preserve it in all its purity. . . .

The executive power has been given all the vigor required to work well, and deprived of means that could be used in a contrary sense. . . .

The government has enough energy to stop crime and to reward virtue; enough stability to confront on its own rebel manipulations and the disorders occasioned by disobedience.

Pinto restated the dilemma for liberals since Bolívar's first proclamations: smash "anarchy," disorder, and rebellion while curbing dictatorship and despotism, and protect civil liberties and rights without allowing "excessive" freedom of the press and political opposition. He claimed that the 1828 Constitution had cut the Gordian knot—and he was proved wrong.

The 1828 charter retained the privileged position of the church (Art. 3) but outlawed the vestiges of aristocratic entail (*mayorazgos*), thereby offending the most patrician of landowners. And while guaranteeing freedom of the press, it provided for the future adoption of a special press law that, when adopted and later reformed, significantly curtailed political expression (Art. 18). Borrowing language from Spanish liberals, perhaps as a result of the influence of Spanish intellectual José Joaquín de Mora in the constitution's formulation, Article 16 allowed "search and seizure" in private homes (*allanamiento*) "in cases of resistance to the legitimate government." Given the broad legal interpretation of *resistance* in liberal Spain, this left ample authority for political repression.

While limiting executive authority to a much greater extent than previous Chilean constitutions, the 1828 charter permitted the president "to deprive persons of their liberty . . . when the general interest required, putting the arrested person at the disposition of a judge within twenty-four hours." Potentially more ominous, the president could "in the cases of grave and unexpected external attack or internal commotion *take whatever security measures deemed expedient,* immediately advising the congress, or if in recess, the Permanent Commission, of the measures taken and his motives" (Art. 12, emphasis added). The final words of this clause, *estando a su resolución,* left unclear whether Congress might overturn, undo, or merely express dissatisfaction over the president's actions. Since the 1828 Constitution endured only briefly, this issue was mute. In 1830, however, Uruguay adopted an identical clause, eliminating only these last four words. The Uruguayan provision lasted into the twentieth century and became that country's principal foundation of constitutional dictatorship (see chapter 7). Similar provisions, worded slightly differently, appeared in the Costa Rican constitutions of the 1840s and 1850s (see chapter 4).

Though not without provisions for suspending civil liberties and rights, and potentially, for constitutional dictatorship, the 1828 charter went a long way toward enhancing legislative control of the executive and the military. Congressional control over budgets and taxes, the size of the armed forces, the creation of government positions, the authority of administrators, and appointments to the Supreme Court began a tradition of legislative checks on the executive. After 1860 consolidation of these checks gradually distinguished Chilean politics from the rest of Spanish America. For the moment, however, the 1828 Constitution died with the liberal defeat of 1830. Conservative factions, the landowners, the merchants associated with Diego Portales (called *estanqueros* after Portales's tobacco monopoly or *estanco*), supporters of ex–Supreme Director O'Higgins, and staunch clericals attacked the 1828 charter as an expression of imported utopian ideology. A dispute over the vice presidential election in 1829 served as a pretext for a conservative rebellion.[13] Conservatives cynically rebelled against the government in the name of restoring the rule of law under the 1828 charter that they abhorred.

Estanquero Manuel José Gandarillas urged the creation of a national junta to replace Congress. Provisional President Francisco Ramón Vicuña refused to cooperate but was forced out of Santiago on November 12, 1829. Civil war followed. In January 1830, Freire broke relations with General Joaquín Prieto and left Santiago to head a liberal reaction. In mid-April 1830 a decisive military victory at Lircay, north of Talca, by General Prieto, *intendente* of Concepción, gave the conservatives victory.

During the 1829–1830 civil war, several interim governments had failed to restore order. These included a temporary grant of full authority (*poderes omnímodos*) to Freire, a forty-two day provisional presidency of Francisco Ruiz Tagle, his resignation, and the assumption of the presidency by Vice President José Tomás Ovalle. Just before the battle at Lircay, Ovalle named Diego Portales minister of foreign relations, war, and the interior—effectively creating a ministerial dictator. With Ovalle ill, Portales ruled Chile in league with Prieto, Prieto's nephew, Colonel Manuel Bulnes, and Manuel Rengifo, who became minister of finance. Portales cashiered the liberal army officers, many of them heroes of the independence wars, including De Lastra, Freire, and Pinto. He also implemented a campaign to reestablish law and order, persecuted the opposition press, and ordered severe punishment for those guilty of common crimes. Troops were dispatched to the countryside to eliminate highwaymen and cattle rustlers. Taken together, Portales's policies created an atmosphere in Chile after 1830 of "fear and trembling."[14]

President Ovalle died in March 1831. Portales orchestrated General Prieto's election in April but refused to take the oath as vice president, wishing to avoid succession if some misfortune affected Prieto. He then temporarily withdrew from the government, removing himself to Valparaíso.[15] He continued to advise Prieto and exercise influence in government until his formal return to the cabinet in 1835. Some believed that Portales participated in politics to revenge himself against those who had deprived him of the *estanco* contract. Others emphasized his distaste for liberalism and the disorder following independence. Whatever the motivation, his solution for Chile involved the restoration of law and order, a strong centralized government, fiscal integrity, and an end to conspiracy and intrigue. Portales began through repression and administrative skill to create a new political order for Chile. In this he would be assisted by Finance Minister Manuel Rengifo, British investment, and the discovery of silver at Chañarcillo near Copiapó. The victory of a Chilean army against the Peru-Bolivia Confederation in 1839 would buttress this political system after Portales's assassination in 1837.

In the short term, both conservatives and liberals had feigned defense of the 1828 Constitution as the rationale for the 1829–1830 civil war. Both sides claimed to serve the cause of legitimacy and constitutionalism. Elections for Congress and then the inauguration of General Prieto as president in 1831 purportedly conformed to constitutional norms. In February 1831, the *cabildo* of Santiago called for the reform of the 1828 charter, ostensibly still in operation. The same fiction was reiterated in June by Senator Manuel Gandarillas.[16] In September the Congress adopted a law providing for reform of the 1828 Constitution. The constitutional convention began its deliberations in October; after extensive debates and modifications of the initial draft elaborated by Mariano Egaña, the new constitution was promulgated on May 25, 1833. Congressional elections under the new constitution occurred in December.

The 1828 charter had prohibited reform until 1836. No matter. After two years of sessions the convention had approved the following: the constitution that would enshrine the strong executive, various provisions for regimes of exception, and foundations of constitutional dictatorship that would govern Chile (with modifications in 1874) until 1925. Prieto and Portales began to transform the country, using the state of siege and the delegation of extraordinary powers to govern with dictatorial authority. For more than a third of the period from 1833 to 1861, the country lived under regimes of exception.[17]

THE 1833 CONSTITUTION

Portales's style left little room for constitutional principles. He declaimed against unbridled democracy, favoring decisive and pragmatic action unconstrained by legal principles or constitutional limits. While Portales focused on action, other conservative leaders and intellectuals wanted to constitutionalize the new regime, formalize its institutions, and legitimize its practices. The most important author of the new constitution, Mariano Egaña, called for establishment of a centralized, authoritative regime that precluded "anarchy in the shadow or name of popular rule, liberal principles, republican government." Portales urged creation of a "strong, centralizing government, in order to set the citizens on the straight path of order and virtue."[18]

The 1833 Constitution accomplished these objectives. It also made constitutional reform quite difficult. First, a motion to discuss constitutional reform had to specify which article or articles would be debated and had to be supported by at least 25 percent of the members of the chamber in which it was introduced. If the debate occurred, the Congress could approve, in principle, only the "necessity" to reform the designated articles. This action required two-thirds support in the Senate and chamber of deputies. Substantive debate on the constitutional reform could not occur until the next

Congress convened. It then would be treated as ordinary legislation, except that the constitutional reform law had to originate in the Senate (Art. 40). Thus were erected the hurdles of the presidentially dominated Senate and the presidential veto (Arts. 165–68).

The constitution created a centralist system with a strong executive, given authority over "all matters affecting the conservation of internal public order and external security" (Art. 81). The president was also authorized to issue those regulations and instructions "deemed convenient" to insure implementation of the law, supervise judicial behavior, extend ordinary sessions of Congress for up to fifty days, name and replace ministers, diplomats, intendants, governors, and councillors of state at his pleasure, name judges of the higher courts from lists proposed by the council of state, and name high church officials, military officers, and certain other public officials with approval by the Senate (Art. 80). The president could veto congressional legislation, without the possibility of congressional override and without the possibility of reconsideration by Congress in the current session (Art. 45). As commander of the armed forces, the president could deploy them on his own initiative and personally command operations in the field with the approval of the Senate. In the latter case, he could reside anywhere in the country occupied by Chilean forces, in effect exercising the presidency from battle headquarters.

In the provinces and lesser jurisdictions, the president appointed intendants, governors, subdelegates, and inspectors as his direct agents. All pretense of provincial initiative, let alone federalism, disappeared. (Not until 1844 was the virtually viceregal authority of these administrators fully elaborated in regulations for internal administration of the state.) The power of Congress to approve annually the budget, taxes, and the force levels of the armed forces, and its powers to censure ministers, provided potential checks on the executive. Until later in the century, however, as in much of Spanish America, the executive and his agents controlled elections, thereby blunting legislative checks on presidential action. As elsewhere, the Chileans adopted the language of France's 1791 constitution asserting the subordination of the armed forces to civilian authority—"La fuerza pública es esencialmente obediente. Ningún cuerpo armado puede deliberar" (Art. 157).

The constitution permitted the reelection of the president for a second term of five years; to 1871, all presidents remained in office for ten years. The intendants and governors controlled the election of senators and deputies within their jurisdictions. The president, his ministers, and advisers made lists of official candidates; only rarely did more than a handful of opposition candidates overcome the government electoral machine in the various departments.

Writing in 1874, when electoral reforms modified this system, future president Domingo Santa María (1881–1886) commented that "during the long life of this political code there is no case of a person occupying a seat in the senate that had not been selected by the President."[19] Describing the Prieto government, but with comments applicable to all Chilean administrations into the 1870s, Chile's great liberal historian of the nineteenth century, Diego Barros Arana, observed: "The national congress, constituted in a form of elections in which the government's adversaries took no part, habitually demonstrated the most absolute deference" to the president.[20]

Suffrage limitations restricted the vote through property or income requirements. Literacy requirements also applied, but lax enforcement and deliberate delays in implementing them allowed landowners to enroll their tenants as voters and militia commanders to do likewise with their troops. After 1840, Congress allowed those already registered to continue to vote, applying literacy requirements selectively to new voters. In this fashion the rural work force and militia became voting cattle for the incumbent government and their landowner supporters. General Prieto called this system, and the 1833 Constitution, "a means of putting an end to the revolutions and disturbances which arose from the confusion in which the triumph of independence left us. For this reason the system of government to which the republic was subjected . . . may be called autocratic in view of the great authority or power . . . concentrated in the hands of the citizen elected president."[21]

To put an end to revolutions and disturbances, the constitution provided an array of regimes of exception. In April 1839, the Ordenanza General del Ejército, which was adopted "under the authority of Article 161 of the constitution and the law of 31 January 1837" (which had conceded virtually unlimited extraordinary powers to the executive), added provisions for martial law. These provisions, with some alterations, survived a new constitution in 1925 and served as the legal rationale for actions of the military junta that ousted President Salvador Allende in 1973.

The most important regimes of exception in the 1833 Constitution provided for: (1) delegation of extraordinary powers to the president, (2) congressional or presidential proclamation of a state of siege (the first such provisions in a Spanish American constitution), and (3) suspension of civil liberties and rights, due process, and press freedom, and dilution of protection against search and seizure in domiciles. Military jurisdiction over civilians in cases of sedition, conspiracy, insurrection, treason, and rebellion were added with the military Ordenanza of 1839.

Article 36 (Sec. 6) allowed Congress "to authorize the president of the republic to use extraordinary powers, always with the requirement that the powers conceded be expressly detailed and limited to a stipulated time period." This provision was made use of liberally until its revision in 1874, when an amendment more tightly circumscribed the proper objectives of congressional "exceptional laws" (see below). Articles 82 (Sec. 20) and Article 161 permitted the Congress to declare "one or more points of the republic in state of siege, in the case of internal commotion," thereby "suspending the *imperio* of the constitution in the territory affected by the declaration." Under the authority of these articles, the Congress could suspend civil liberties and rights, enact any laws needed to meet the emergency, or delegate power to the president to do the same.

On his own authority the president could declare a state of siege in the event of external attack, and if the Congress were not in session and with the approval of the council of state, he could do so in the case of internal commotion. Since Congress was in ordinary session from June 1 until September 1 each year (Art. 52), the president had state of siege authority during nine months of the year. If Congress reconvened prior to the termination of the declared state of siege period, then the state of siege proclamation would be considered by Congress as a proposed law, remaining in effect until Congress acted (Art. 82, Sec. 20). In practice, presidents after the early 1840s limited the duration of the state of siege decrees to the time remaining before Congress was to reconvene, thereby complying a priori with Article 82.[22]

During a state of siege, and in cases when Congress conceded the president extraordinary powers, he was prohibited from sentencing and punishing those accused of violating the law or emergency decrees. He could, however, arrest, detain, and transfer such persons to any place in the country, a practice that was institutionalized as "relegation," internal exile, and house arrest. Unlike other such provisions in neighboring countries, voluntary exile was not constitutionally afforded the accused as an alternative.

Even these limitations were indirectly circumvented after the issuance of the Military Ordenanza in 1839, which President Prieto

ordered "distributed to . . . civil, military and ecclesiastical authorities" under the authority of Article 161 of the constitution and "the
law of 31 January 1837."²³ This decree, which conserved and defined the military *fueros* for active-duty and retired personnel, made
the intendant of each province the *comandante jeneral de armas*,
thereby conjoining military and civilian authority (Title LII, Art. 1).
The Ordenanza gave the intendant broad powers for military and
civil administration but prohibited troop movements across provincial boundaries without the express permission of the appropriate
government minister (Art. 4).

The Ordenanza prohibited any fiesta or public act in which
numerous persons would assemble without the governor's, intendant's, or other acting commander's approval and without the
"adoption of measures convenient to avoid disorder" (Title LIII,
Art. 4). It also imprecisely introduced the concept of *provincia de
asamblea,* referring to any territory within the republic "in which
war exists," and conferred upon the commanding officer in the *provincia de asamblea* the authority to "issue the decrees [*bandos*] that he
finds conducive [to best carrying out his functions]" (Title LIX, Art.
13). (Of interest, the first decrees of the military junta that ousted
President Salvador Allende in 1973 were also characterized as *bandos,* issued in the circumstance of internal war.)²⁴

In addition, the Ordenanza provided that all conspiracies in
which civilians (*paisanos*) and military personnel participated together would be subject to the jurisdiction of military tribunals (*consejos de guerra*). Conspiracy included distributing pamphlets that
"tend to alter public tranquility" ["el delito de fijar pasquines que
conspiren a alterar la tranquilidad pública"] (Title LXXVII, Art. 2).
This provision was reminiscent of the Spanish 1774 *Pragmática* (See
chapter 2). Military personnel having knowledge of conspiracies
and not revealing it to superior officers or inducing others to participate in any seditious act affecting the security of military instal-
lations could be sentenced to death. Punishments would also apply
for "inducing, or illegally assembling persons for whatever other
reason." Any person who "contributes to the desertion of army personnel, suggests or supports this crime, by hiding the deserter, buys
him clothes or arms, or other sort of disguise, shall be tried by military courts" (Title LXXIII, Art. 1).

The jurisdiction of the *consejos de guerra* applied within and
without the national territory, once the government ordered the
army to "act defensively or offensively . . . against its enemies" (Title
LIX, Art. 1). In short, the combination of the regimes of exception

in the 1833 Constitution and the Ordenanza General del Ejército gave Chile the legal foundations for martial law.

To counterbalance military power and to bring it under civilian control, Portales also reorganized the national guard, made it an electoral as well as a military asset of the government, and participated personally as a lieutenant colonel. Two days after the victory at Lircay, a decree created the "civic artillery" of Santiago, headquartered in La Moneda palace. According to historian Francisco Encina, by June 1831 the civic guard had over 25,000 troops, uniformed, drilled, and newly equipped. This national guard greatly outnumbered the army during the next decades.

All this did not entirely overcome Portales's initial disappointment with what he viewed as the constitution's overemphasis on civil liberties and rights and the insufficient power it gave the government to confront "the threats of those who would overturn authority."[25]

> One cannot come to terms with men of law; for what devil of a purpose serve Constitutions and bits of paper if they are not capable of remedying a known problem, or one that is going to occur . . . by taking the measures needed to end them. . . .
>
> In Chile the law serves no purpose but to produce anarchy, the absence of punishment, libertinism, eternal lawsuits. . . . If I take prisoner a person I know is conspiring I violate the law. Be damned the law that keeps government from freely taking action at the opportune moment.
>
> . . . This respect for delinquents, or suspected delinquents will finish the country rapidly. . . . I know how to say, with the law or without it, this lady called Constitution must be violated when the circumstances are extreme.[26]

Portales need not have worried. Virtually from its promulgation, the government made use of the extraordinary powers and state of siege authority of the 1833 Constitution. This allowed successful suppression of several conspiracies and abortive coups from 1834 to 1836.[27] Prieto's reelection in 1836 brought new conspiracies; on November 9, 1836, the Congress gave Prieto extraordinary powers to detain and transfer anywhere in the republic any person in order to confront the danger. In response to threats of new incursions by General Freire, who was exiled and deprived of his military rank, Portales had Congress approve a law on January 27, 1837, that ordered all government officials "to execute, within twenty-four hours, and without any delay beyond assuring the identity of the person, . . . any person who returns from exile without government authorization or who leaves the place where he has been confined." On January 31, 1837, Congress declared the entire country in a state of siege, due to the war against Peru and Bolivia (see chapter 6), authorizing the president to "make use of all power he finds prudent." The only limitation prohibited sentencing and punishing suspects without a court trial or a trial by tribunals "that the president may establish."[28] Prieto and Portales governed by decree, reorganized the government, and administered justice and injustice. In 1838 Congress met once, on February 4, and did not function again until 1839.

On February 2, the government created *consejos de guerra* in the capital of each province. These *consejos* had jurisdiction over the crimes of sedition, rebellion, insurrection, and conspiracy (*sedición, tumulto, motín, conspiración*). They could apply capital or other punishment without the possibility of appeal. In some cases lieutenants and captains with no legal or political experience headed these military tribunals. In these conditions, the government presided over congressional elections in March 1837.

On April 7, 1837, three respected citizens convicted of conspiracy by the *consejo de guerra* in Curicó swung from the gallows for "conversations that in better times would hardly have been noticed."[29] The mood in much of the country was reminiscent of the gloom and fear brought by the Spanish *reconquista* (1814–1817). Two months later, a garrison commanded by Colonel José Antonio Vidaurre rebelled in Quillota, took Portales prisoner, and assassinated him. The uprising was quickly suppressed, but Portales had been eliminated. A special *consejo de guerra* in Valparaíso condemned twenty-three participants in the plot, though eventual commutations to exile saved all but ten from execution. The government also arrested Senator Diego José Benavente, who had been in communication with Vidaurre. This appeared to violate Article 15 of the constitution regarding the *fueros* of senators, but a three-senator commission determined that the extraordinary powers legislation had suspended the constitution. Senator Gandarillas objected and proposed instead the derogation of the January 31 law that had conferred extraordinary powers on the executive.[30] The Senate rejected this proposal, but Benavente was freed after the tribunal determined he had not participated in the uprising. More significantly, precedent had been set for ignoring congressional immunities during the exercise of extraordinary powers and state of siege provisions. This precedent would hold in the next decades.

With Portales's death, the Prieto administration softened its repressive policies. The *consejos de guerra* were instructed not to execute their sentences without review by higher military authorities, except in the cases of sedition or persons captured in flaganti during rebellions. Nevertheless, the government retained the draconian authority conferred upon it in January 1837 while focusing its attention primarily on the war against the Peru-Bolivia Confederation.

Victory at the battle of Yungay and the end of the war terminated the period stipulated for the exercise of the extraordinary powers. On May 31, 1839, General Prieto announced: "With the present decree I declare ended the use of the extraordinary powers conferred on the government by the law of 31 January 1837."[31] In an effort at reconciliation, Prieto also decreed the reincorporation of most of the surviving liberal officers cashiered in 1830, and he reinstituted their pensions and benefits for widows and orphans. Three months later he also abolished the permanent *consejos de guerra*.

When Congress convened in June 1839, Prieto reported decorously on the last two years and sought approval for the actions taken under the extraordinary powers. This he obtained, but only after a discussion precipitated by Rafael Valentín Valdivieso, deputy for Santiago, over the constitutionality of the original decree, since it did not properly delimit the powers conferred on the president and specify their duration.[32] Valdivieso supported Prieto but questioned the permanent validity of the laws that reorganized the public administration and the courts without subsequent congressional approval.

With presidential elections approaching, political activity increased. A liberal Sociedad Patriótica formed to challenge the government and opposition newspapers attacked the government. Prieto invoked the press law to repress the opposition. Under this law, juries decided whether violations had occurred. In 1840 Prieto was angered by a decision that liberated the editor of *El Diablo Político,* Juan Nicolás Alvarez, whose paper had accused the government of "many crimes," including the illegal abrogation of the 1828 Constitution, and had called upon patriots to "overthrow the tyranny." Accused of sedition and defamation, Alvarez's trial became a circus, a sardonic theater of opposition to the government—and he was acquitted. Disturbances followed, with the police intervening to restore order. The government declared Santiago Province in a state of siege on February 10, 1840, arresting dissidents and seeking to create the "proper" climate for the upcoming congressional elections. Nevertheless, the government allowed a small number of opposition candidates to be elected to the Congress, making the 1840 legislature an important arena for supporters of reform.

Almost as soon as Congress began debates, Melchor de Santiago Concha, a liberal deputy from Ovalle, proposed a constitutional reform limiting the scope of extraordinary powers conceded to presidents. He urged that such delegation also specify the duration of the concession, prohibit legislation by the executive and the creation of special courts, and make all decree laws under the extraordinary powers provisional, subject to future legislative approval. The proposal was not seriously discussed, but its spirit came to prevail as Congress and the president gradually accepted the notion that decree laws under the extraordinary powers or state of siege required congressional approval when the Congress reconvened.[33] Thus, a state of siege for Santiago Province in 1846 for eighty-five days, for Santiago and Aconcagua in 1850 for sixty days (cut short by a special session of Congress), for Santiago and Valparaíso in 1851 for forty-two days, and the already mentioned decree for Santiago on February 10, 1840, all conformed to this pattern.[34]

President Prieto had chosen at his successor General Manuel Bulnes, his nephew and the commander of the army that had defeated Santa Cruz's Peru-Bolivia Confederation. Bulnes had earlier been successful in Indian wars and in eradicating bandits in the south. A career military officer with moderate views, he fortuitously found himself engaged to marry the eldest daughter of his rival, independence hero and ex-president Francisco Antonio Pinto. This left only the most staunchly clerical and conservative factions as serious adversaries. Bulnes's desire for conciliation with the liberals provided an ideal opportunity for a nonviolent election and presidential succession. For the first time in Chilean history a peaceful government transition occurred with Bulnes's inauguration in 1841. During the next decade his great popularity, his support for development of legislative and judicial institutions, and his refusal to become a caudillo like other contemporary Spanish American leaders served to solidify the Portalian state. Chile's victory against the Peru-Bolivia Confederation had thus provided a basis for solidarity and popular leadership that spared the country much of the disorder experienced elsewhere.

What would most distinguish Chile from other Spanish American republics in the nineteenth century, a remarkable constitutional continuity, would owe much to Bulnes's acceptance of congressional exercise of budgetary authority, including that over the military, and the development of a tradition of ministerial responsibility to Congress. Influenced by Belgian practice, Congress adopted the system of interpellation, a questioning of ministers called to Congress to explain or defend government policy. Combined with budgetary controls and delays in passing government-sponsored legislation, interpellation moved the country toward a quasi-parliamentary system from 1841 to 1891, gradually enhancing the role of the legislature relative to the president. In November 1841, Congress suspended its consideration of the budget bill and authorization for tax collection until the executive submitted a legislative package that included expanded congressional oversight of public expenditures. Agreement by Bulnes meant the de facto abrogation of a constitutional prerogative of the president: the designation of matters to be considered in extraordinary sessions of Congress.

Bulnes's implicit recognition of the legitimacy of legislative checks on government policy did not mean he was willing to forego presidential intervention in elections, especially to control the Senate, or to abdicate presidential dominance. (Indeed, no opposition candidate won a Senate seat before 1874.) It did mean, however, that he understood the rising influence of Chile's political oligarchy: a small group of intermarried extended kinship groups that controlled the large rural estates, the militia, and the Congress. Oligarchy buttressed by endogamy and *compadrazgo* forged a political class across ideological and party lines.[35] Bulnes successfully presided over the inauguration of this oligarchic republic.

Economic growth with investment in mining, agriculture, and public works contributed to the consolidation of the political system. Manuel Rengifo returned to the finance ministry and supervised government economic policy with great success until his death in 1845. Bulnes confronted serious opposition only during congressional elections and the fight over presidential succession at the end of the decade. In each of these cases the extraordinary powers and the state of siege were invoked to maintain control.[36]

Bulnes began his presidency with a general amnesty for political exiles and with the restoration of honors to San Martín, O'Higgins, and other heroes of independence ostracized by Prieto and Portales.[37] In 1842 legislation reincorporated the military officers purged by Portales after 1830, including General Freire, who was eventually compensated for the property he had lost as a result of his political and military resistance to Portales. Bulnes also named liberal civilians and military officers to high government posts. Bulnes faced virtually no internal opposition during the first three years of his presidency, though the administration was divided between factions less tolerant of liberal ideas and practices and those favoring further liberalization. The former were lead by Manuel Montt, who would be president from 1851 to 1861, and the latter by Ramón Luis Irarrázaval.

On January 10, 1844, the government promulgated the law regulating the internal administration of the state. This law defined the authority of the intendants, governors, subdelegates, and inspectors, emphasizing their role in conserving internal order and suppressing popular tumults, unauthorized public demonstrations, conspiracy, and rebellion.[38] Their authority would suffice to harass and repress political opponents, labor leaders, union organization, and after 1880, the nascent socialist movements, even without recourse to regimes of exception.[39]

Anticipating the 1846 presidential elections, Bulnes moved Montt to the interior ministry and brought Antonio Varas to the justice ministry. This left the liberal view unrepresented in the higher echelons of the administration. From the time of this cabinet change, preparations for congressional and presidential elections evoked an increasingly militant and offensive press. Angered, the government sponsored a more repressive press law to replace that of 1828 and used its provisions to stifle opposition.[40] Liberal intellectuals and opposition politicians, influenced by European socialism and fearful of Montt's succession to the presidency, agitated against the government, calling for an end to electoral manipulation and administrative abuses by the intendants. The government met minor conspiracies from 1847 to 1850, and a serious uprising in 1850, by arresting opponents and imposing jail terms or exile.[41]

In 1849 the Bulnes government spared no resource to fill the Congress with adepts. Only four opposition candidates won seats, one of these due to the literal enforcement of the electoral law by the intendant in Valparaíso, who was promptly labeled a traitor by government ministers. José Victorino Lastarria, a prominent liberal intellectual and congressman, proposed reforms to limit the scope of extraordinary powers delegated by the legislature to the president. The proposal also required that the congressional *comisión conservadora* determine the existence of an internal commotion by a five-sixths vote before the president could declare a stage of siege.

Government ministers objected that the proposed reforms were unconstitutional. After ten days of debates, the chamber of deputies surprisingly approved the reform, only to have it tabled by the Senate—until 1866.[42]

In 1850 the recently created Society of Equality, inspired by the 1848 revolutionary events in Europe and the writing of the physiocrats, held numerous public demonstrations against the government. It also attacked the Catholic church in its newspaper *El Amigo del Pueblo*. Claiming that Manuel Montt, Bulnes's chosen successor, "represents states of siege, deportations, exile, military tribunals, judicial corruption, assassination of the people, torture in criminal justice, the [repressive] press law, usury, and repression in all respects," the Society of Equality provoked reaction.[43]

In early November 1850 news arrived in Santiago of an uprising in Aconcagua. The Santiago intendant outlawed the Society of Equality and "all similar organizations," closed opposition newspapers, arrested "conspirators" and "seditionists," and forced others into exile. The president declared a state of siege for Santiago and Aconcagua provinces for sixty days, commencing November 7.[44]

The coming presidential elections complicated Bulnes's last year in office. The votes of militia, tenant farmers, and government employees guaranteed victory for Manuel Montt, his chosen successor. However, the ambitions of Bulnes's cousin and intendant in Concepción, General José María de la Cruz, encouraged resistance by regional interests in the south and north, especially in Concepción and La Serena, by liberals (though Cruz was a conservative) and by the president's personal enemies. Cruz had been among the conservative generals that brought his uncle, Joaquín Prieto, to power in 1830, was a respected military officer and a favorite of Concepción merchants jealous of Santiago's domination. His candidacy, which divided the army, was serious and also paradoxical. Born an aristocrat, he was supported by "the people" against Manuel Montt, who was born poor, had risen to power, and was supported by the Santiago oligarchy.

An armed uprising in Santiago led by a colonel was put down easily by the government in April 1851 but cost over one hundred lives. This provoked still another state of siege decree for Santiago and Valparaíso provinces. By the time of the presidential elections in June 1851, peace had been restored. Montt won an easy victory and took office as scheduled on September 18, 1851.

The opposition declared the election invalid due to the obvious government intervention, fraud, and intimidation. Expecting violence, Congress had passed a law at Montt's request extending the president's extraordinary powers for a year, beginning September 14, 1851—a thoughtful bequest to the incoming president.[45] Cruz's deposition as intendant was the last straw. Armed revolt in La Serena (actually initiated before Montt assumed the presidency), followed by a revolutionary movement in Concepción, initiated a brief civil war.[46] Bulnes, now commander of the southern army, defeated Cruz's forces by the end of 1851, but not without unusually high casualties on both sides (2,000 dead and 1,500 wounded at the battle of Loncomilla in December 1851). The northern rebellion also collapsed.[47] To confront this challenge, Congress had given Montt extraordinary powers to arrest and move persons within the country, increase the size of the army, exceed the budget, and remove all government officials on his own authority.[48] After one year, this was limited to suspending civil liberties and rights and then canceled in June 1853. Chilean legislators had become sensitive to the scope and duration of extraordinary powers, though few challenged the need for them.

Having defeated the rebels, Montt moved quickly to reunite the army, issue selective amnesties, and reward his supporters. Bulnes received 50,000 pesos for his "services during the events of 1851."[49] Once the extraordinary powers had been dropped, Montt renewed efforts to form liberal-conservative coalitions and took direct actions to satisfy some of the regional demands that had originated the 1851 war. He was reelected without opposition in 1856.

Confrontations with the church and with liberals followed in the next three years, but no serious rebel movements challenged government authority. The formation of a clerical Conservative party in 1857 and a party of secular conservatives and moderate liberals, the National party (or Montt-Varista party), on the part of the government, framed the upcoming presidential elections. Montt apparently intended to impose his minister of the interior, Antonio Varas, who was viewed as a hardliner (as had been Montt in 1851). Liberals demanding electoral reform and stronger guarantees of civil liberties and rights detested Varas; so too did the clerical Conservative party for his support of the government in its conflicts with the church.[50]

Facing challenges both from liberals and conservatives, the government emphasized its "moderation" and chose a slate of congressional candidates campaigning under the slogan Liberty with Order (*libertad en el orden*). The unusual alliance of ultramontane conservatives, liberal *exaltados*, and personal enemies of Montt and Varas eventually gave the polyhedral opposition fourteen seats in the

Congress. They demanded complete amnesty for political prisoners and exiles. Montt accepted only a more limited measure that excluded political exiles, except those individually approved by the president.[51] The most radical opposition leaders, such as Benjamín Vicuña Mackenna, Manuel Antonio Matta, Guillermo Matta, and Justo and Domingo Arteaga Alemparte (who would later found the Radical party), urged a constitutional convention and drastic modifications of the Portalian state.[52]

Meanwhile, in response to newspaper attacks on the government and alleged conspiracies in 1857 and 1858, the government arrested opposition leaders. In December the intendant of Santiago, who had prohibited political meetings, arrested 180 so-called conspirators at the Club de la Unión. A new state of siege was declared for Santiago, Valparaíso, and Aconcagua in anticipation of armed confrontation. Rebellion broke out in Copiapó in January 1859, followed by lesser incidents in San Felipe, Talca, and Talcahuano. Reacting to the uprising in Copiapó led by mining magnate and flamboyant liberal Pedro León Gallo, on January 20 the Congress granted Montt the now customary extraordinary powers for one year to arrest and detain conspirators and seditionists, to prevent or quell internal commotions, to increase the size of the army, to expend funds without budgetary limitations, and to remove public officials at his own discretion.[53] In contrast to the late 1830s, the Congress now restricted the scope and duration of extraordinary powers given to the executive. This practice would not be institutionalized through constitutional reform until 1874, but the legislative proposals of Lastarria and other liberals of 1849 were gradually gaining de facto acceptance.[54]

Gallo organized and financed an army of miners that marched toward Coquimbo in March 1859 and won initial encounters with government forces but was defeated near La Serena by General Juan Vidaurre Leal, who had also quelled the 1851 rebellion. Minor outbreaks of violence followed in Santiago and Valparaíso. On September 18, 1859, General Vidaurre Leal was assassinated in Valparaíso during a Te Deum celebrated in the cathedral. In the south, revolutionaries had allied with Indian leaders to challenge the government. This provoked a guerrilla war of skirmishes and ambushes that lasted more than a year before the government restored peace. After its victory, the government tried the conspirators and sought to apply sanctions under the "law of civil responsibility for internal commotions" passed on November 5, 1860. This law made revolutionaries financially responsible for damage caused in their uprisings, a return to the confiscating of property of political opponents typical of the early nineteenth century. It also meant that the families of rebels lost their property and income.[55]

The political crisis faced by the Montt government had been exacerbated by an economic recession, partly the result of lower prices for Chilean exports, partly the result of internal violence. Antonio Varas, in a patriotic gesture, announced that he would not be Montt's successor but requested an extension of the extraordinary powers for the president for another eleven months, until November 1860. As minister of the interior, Varas would preside over the elections and therefore would not be the government's candidate. This personal decision calmed the political atmosphere briefly, while the diverse factions began the search for the next president. The ultraconservatives preferred the return of General Bulnes, the liberals had several potential candidates, and the moderate conservatives and liberals united in the National party insisted on Varas's candidacy. Varas again rejected the offer, this time in writing, in January 1861.[56]

In March, congressional elections reaffirmed National party control over the legislature, returning Bulnes and other notables to the Senate and Varas to the chamber of deputies. After one more offer of the presidential candidacy to Varas in April, Montt surprised the country by designating Senator José Joaquín Pérez as the official candidate. Pérez was a candidate of conciliation; he inspired neither great enthusiasm nor opposition. The indirectly selected electors made him their unanimous choice, and he assumed the presidency on September 18, 1861.

Calling for national unity, Pérez formed government coalitions during the next ten years in which all political factions participated. His slogan, "A Government of All and for All," reassured the adversaries of the Montt decade and contributed to healing the wounds of the body politic. The legislature assumed an ever more important role in the political system, controlling budgets and cabinet appointments and sometimes taking the initiative in policy making. A recognizable political party system was taking shape, with three main ideological components: conservative, liberal, and radical. In August 1865 the Law of Responsibility was repealed; not even a brief war with Spain in 1866 induced the government to ask for extraordinary powers or to declare a state of siege in Valparaíso when it was bombarded by a Spanish fleet.[57] In 1866, Pérez was reelected without opposition.

Pérez governed for ten years without invoking the state of siege provisions, without asking for extraordinary powers, and without facing serious violent opposition. During his administration the issue of constitutional reform again took center stage, with proposals from the liberals for electoral reforms, greater protection for civil liberties and rights, and the reduction of executive and legislative authority under states of siege. As a first step in the lengthy process of constitutional reform spelled out in the 1833 Constitution, the Congress declared its intent to modify the constitution in 1865.[58]

After Pérez's election for a second term and the end of the war with Spain, the debate on constitutional reform resumed. José Victorino Lastarria remained a vocal proponent of the reforms he had suggested in 1849 concerning the extraordinary powers and state of siege provisions in the 1833 charter. He had proposed reforms in the 1864 Congress regarding sedition and search and seizure in homes, including eliminating military jurisdiction over civilians as provided in the 1839 and 1852 Ordenanza.[59] He had also joined Melchor de Santiago Concha in proposing constitutional reforms concerning the state of siege authority of the executive, lamenting that for "about half of the last 31 years the Republic has been under the weight of extraordinary powers and states of siege, under the authority the Constitution provides to obviate itself and enthrone the rule of force."[60]

Lastarria failed to persuade his colleagues; no constitutional reform passed until 1870, and then only a bar on the immediate reelection of the president, ending forty years of ten-year presidencies. However, in 1867 Congress formally passed legislation initiating the reform of Article 36 (Sec. 6) and others, and in 1869 an electoral reform barred voting by army and navy enlisted personnel and police. This removed thousands of votes from presidential control.[61] It did not end electoral manipulation or corruption but did presage a trend toward a more competitive political system.

During the following administration, of President Federico Errázuriz Zañartu (1871–1876), constitutional reforms further modified electoral procedures and voter eligibility, added the rights of peaceful assembly, association, petition, and "freedom of education" to the bill of rights, and amended provisions regarding state of siege and extraordinary powers.[62] As a deputy in the Congress, Errázuriz had proposed constitutional reforms in the late 1840s and suffered persecution during the Montt presidency. He intended to encourage moderation in Chilean politics and had authored the

1870 reform that introduced the six-year presidency without possibility of immediate reelection. Judicial reforms in 1875 virtually ended military and ecclesiastical *fueros*[63] Article 36 (Sec. 6) of the constitution now read:

> Congress has exclusive authority to adopt laws of exception of temporary character, not to exceed one year, restricting personal liberty and freedom of the press, and to suspend or restrict the exercise of freedom of assembly, when required by urgent necessity to defend the state, the constitutional regime, or internal peace. If such laws establish penalties, application thereof shall be effected by the existing tribunals.

Amendments to Article 102 and 161 redefined executive authority concerning states of assembly and siege.

> There will be a Council of State . . . with three members selected by the Senate and three by the Chamber of Deputies, [and five presidential appointees to include a judge resident in Santiago, an ecclesiastic, a general admiral, an official from the finance office, and a person who has been a government minister or diplomat, or an intendant, governor, or mayor].
>
> The Council of State may agree to declare one or more provinces affected or threatened by foreign invasion in a state of assembly (Art. 102).
>
> When one or various points of the Republic are declared in state of siege, in accord with Article 82 (20), the President of the Republic may exercise only the following authority: (1) to arrest persons in their own homes or in other places that are not used for detention or imprisonment of common criminals; (2) to move persons from one department to another within the Republic on the continent in the territory between the port of Caldera to the north and the province of Llanquihue to the south.
>
> Measures taken by the President of the Republic by virtue of the [state of] siege may not last beyond the state of siege itself, and may not violate the constitutional immunities guaranteed to Senators and Deputies. (Art. 161)

These reforms ended the "suspension of the *imperio* of the constitution" under states of siege effective since 1833, prohibited unlimited concessions of extraordinary powers to the executive, and gave the council of state authority to decree the "state of assembly," though this lacked clear legal definition outside the military Ordenanza. In addition, the Comisión Conservadora of the Congress was expanded to include deputies as well as senators, and its seven members were charged with "overseeing observance of the Constitution and the laws, and protecting individual *garantías*" (Art. 58, Sec. 1). This included informing the president of abuses by administrative officials and, when the president failed to end them and punish his subordinates, holding the president personally responsible "as if the abuses were executed by his orders and with his consent" (Art. 58, Sec. 2).

While important, these reforms were accompanied by provisions in the 1875 criminal code modeled on Spanish and Belgian legislation that defined crimes against the internal security of state. These would survive almost verbatim until late in the twentieth century. Political dissidence in various forms became a common crime (*delitos contra la seguridad interior*) that allowed severe government repression. The *código penal* provided government officials and police with the authority to combat unruly crowds, political protests, and, later, union organization and strikes without recourse to regimes of exception. The identification of political crimes in the code legitimated routine repression. Still, Congress had clearly emerged as a counterbalance to the president. Each year it adopted laws authorizing maximum force levels for the army, navy, and national guard, the stationing of troops in Santiago, and government tax collection (this, every eighteen months). Presidentialism had not ended, but the legislature had established control over government operations and the military.

Likewise, the emergence of Congress's central role in the political system did not mean the elimination of constitutional foundations for regimes of exception nor that consensus existed for this. To the contrary, only a few legislators favored any further erosion of provisions for emergency authority. In practice, however, neither Congress nor the president used this authority again until the direct challenge of congressional authority by President José Manuel Balmaceda (1886–1891) resulted in the civil war of 1891.[64] During the War of Pacific (1879–1884) in which the Chilean victory brought the annexation of the mineral wealth of the Atacama desert, no regime of exception was imposed. Not even the incipient labor conflicts of the 1880s and continued electoral conflicts precipitated use of extraordinary powers or states of siege.

From 1886 to 1891, however, the enhanced congressional role was directly challenged. President José Manuel Balmaceda had come to office as bountiful nitrate duties dramatically increased public revenues. Nitrate and commercial expansion accompanied by government investment in transport, docks, education, and construction produced a transitory prosperity. Gradually, disputes over government nitrate policy, bickering over ministerial appointments, and an economic crisis in 1889–1890 eroded the government's coalition. Strikes in the northern nitrate districts put down by troops in 1890 added to the discontent.[65] Balmaceda's intention to support his friend, wealthy landowner Enrique Salvador Sanfuentes, as the government's presidential candidate in 1891 intensified opposition in the Congress.

In his battles with the congressional opposition, Balmaceda came to view interpellation and the censure of ministers as unpatriotic, though he had vigorously supported these established practices as a congressman. He refused to reconvene Congress at the request of the *comisión conservadora* in 1890. When Congress met in June, he offended the legislature with reference to a "bastard parliamentary system" that had led to a "dictatorship of congress."[66] The Senate and chamber of deputies censured the cabinet, headed by Sanfuentes, and decided to postpone the approval of legislation on the army, the budget, and authorization for tax collection until an acceptable cabinet was constituted. Temporary resolution of the cabinet crisis failed to end the conflict. In January 1891, Balmaceda declared he would operate with last year's budget.

This was clearly unconstitutional; Congress called it dictatorship. A congressional majority (89 of 126) resolved to depose Balmaceda, form a revolutionary junta headed by naval captain Jorge Montt, and nullify the congressional elections scheduled for February 1891. This action was taken "to restore the *imperio* of the constitution and the individual *garantías* that have been violated." The navy supported the congressional majority "in order to make the president understand that the navy obeys the constitution."[67] Both factions in the dispute violated the constitution in the name of its defense; personal rancor, family feuds, congressional and presidential obstinacy, and conflicting economic interests drove the institutional crisis toward civil war.

On January 7, 1891, Balmaceda decreed that since an important part of the navy, in the name of the Congress, had "mangled the constitution, destroying internal order and public peace," he had "assumed the exercise of all powers necessary to administer the state and to maintain internal order, thereby suspending all laws that impede the use of whatever authority is required to assure order, internal tranquility, and external security of the state."[68] While there existed no constitutional basis for such a decree, Balmaceda, like his opponents, claimed to be defending the constitutional order. In the course of the civil war, on May 11, 1891, Balmaceda's rump Congress conceded to him extraordinary powers. These exceeded those permitted by the 1874 constitutional reforms, including the authority to declare a state of siege or assembly and to make expenditures without budget law constraints.[69] The civil war that lasted seven months and left more than 10,000 casualties divided Congress, the army, and Chilean society. Balmaceda filled the prisons with opponents. Requisitioning property to finance the war authorized by the Ley de Requisiciones (July 22, 1891) and executions of captured "constitutionalists" further angered his adversaries.[70]

The revolutionary junta subsequently declared from its headquarters in Iquique that all acts of the president, the Congress elected in March 1891, and the courts established in Valparaíso were void. Congressional forces, commanded by the German military adviser whom Balmaceda had contracted to professionalize the Chilean army, General Emil Körner Henze, defeated Balmaceda's supporters near Valparaíso in late August 1891 with an army largely composed of northern miners.

For the first time in sixty years a Chilean government was toppled by force. The victors, however, viewed their success as a restoration of legitimate government and a return to constitutional rule. They called themselves "constitutionalists." Balmaceda took refuge in the Argentine legation, waited until his presidential term ended on September 18, and committed suicide. Some of his supporters were summarily executed; hundreds went to jail cells as political prisoners, some tried for alleged crimes committed in their service during the deposed president's government.

The war confirmed congressional dominance; until a military coup in 1924, the 1833 Constitution remained in effect—now interpreted as the foundation for a "parliamentary republic." Jorge Montt, president of the junta of 1891, continued as chief executive until his election as constitutional president (1891–1896). He took office in late December 1891, purged the army and the public administration of Balmacedistas, but also declared a partial amnesty benefiting most of the late president's supporters. In August 1894 he decreed a general amnesty as a gesture of conciliation.

Soon after taking office, Montt agreed with Congress on a law that put elections into the control of autonomous municipalities, destroying much of the presidential influence over the Senate and chamber of deputies that had prevailed since 1833. The reorganization of the military, the adoption of a compulsory military service law (1895), and large expenditures for the armed forces eventually reconciled the losers in 1891 to the new regime. By 1900 this led to the dissolution of the national guard created by Portales, growth of the army, and its further professionalization under German direction.

In 1893 and in 1894 Jorge Montt would be the last Chilean president to declare a state of siege in the nineteenth century. In both instances Balmacedistas and officers of the Balmaceda army provoked the decrees with attacks on military barracks in Santiago. Unlike his predecessors, Montt suspended the state of siege, except in Santiago province, for the March 1894 congressional elections, seeking to enhance the legitimacy of the electoral process. The Balmacedista uprisings had not prospered and a small number of congressmen futilely objected to Montt's insistence on the maintenance of the state of siege. Montt's ministers argued that it served a "preventive" purpose and would be revoked in good time.[71] Thereafter, concern turned from oligarchic conspirators toward the growing labor movement. The president proposed legislation outlawing strikes and disruption of economic activity; he also enlarged the army and intensified the modernization program directed by General Körner.

Jorge Montt presided over congressional elections in 1894 in which the Balmacedistas' newly organized Liberal Democrat party obtained significant representation in the Senate and Chamber of Deputies. The Demócrata party, Chile's first workers' party, also elected one deputy. Anarchist and syndicalist influence began to be felt in the mines, on the docks, and among urban workers and artisans. Despite these challenges, the president completed his term peacefully. He was followed by five successive administrations that governed until 1919 without resort to states of siege or extraordinary powers, even with the rising influence of anarchists and socialists and the increase in demands for political and economic reforms.

From 1894 to 1919 no Chilean government used regimes of exception. The military and police routinely harassed and arrested union leaders and protesters, attacked the workers' press, and spied on anarchist and socialist leaders. Dramatic brutality occasionally left hundreds or even thousands dead: Valparaíso, 1903; Santiago Red Week, 1905; Santa María de Iquique, 1907; Valparaíso, 1913. Not until the massive protests by the short-lived Workers Assembly on National Nutrition (AOAN, 1918–1920) and a wave of strikes from 1918 to 1919 did Congress once again confer extraordinary powers on a Chilean president. In February 1919, Congress gave President Juan Luis Sanfuentes (1915–1920) extraordinary powers for sixty days under state of siege provisions for Santiago, Valparaíso, and Aconcagua provinces. This law repeated the concession of authority to declare a state of siege or assembly (*estado de asamblea*) made by Congress to President Balmaceda in 1891, though no external threat existed. This was a dangerous precedent, given the military jurisdiction over civilians implied by a state of assembly. Only one senator, Demócrata party representative Malaquías Concha, voted against this action.[72]

In 1924 a military coup ended the reign of the 1833 Constitution. The parliamentary republic had been unable to respond successfully to the challenge of industrialization, labor conflict, the rise of socialist and communist political movements, and the demands of a new era. The military junta imposed a state of siege in Santiago, Valparaíso, and Aconcagua for fourteen days, totaling sixty-four days under regimes of exception from 1895 to 1924.[73] On September 11, 1924, the military junta dissolved Congress, justifying this by questioning the validity of the March 2 congressional elections. It also proclaimed that it would respect the constitution and the independence of the judiciary and would soon call for a constitutional assembly. Not since the Carrera coup of 1811 and Freire's action in the mid-1820s had the military closed Congress. It would not occur again until 1973.[74] After 1925, however, Chilean governments would more frequently resort to regimes of exception.[75]

THE 1925 CONSTITUTION

Political theatrics allowed President Arturo Alessandri to take a six-month leave, return to the country, preside over a constitutional convention, and then resign—thereby almost achieving a legitimate constitutional transition. The new constitution shifted the balance of power back to the president and introduced direct popular election of the executive and senators. Congress retained budgetary authority and could override presidential vetos, but it lost control over the cabinet and the authority to prevent tax collection. The constitution formally recognized the role of political parties and gave Congress responsibility for choosing the president from the two highest vote-getters if no candidate received an absolute majority. Thus the Congress was not emasculated, merely prevented from replicating the 1891 debacle.

Regarding regimes of exception, the 1925 Constitution made few important changes from that of 1833 as amended in 1874. This was no longer a matter of debate but of consensus. The president had the authority to declare a state of siege in part or all of the country in the case of internal commotion, when the Congress was not in session, and, exclusively, to declare a state of assembly in the case or threat of external war (Art. 72, Sec. 17). In a state of assembly, military tribunals had jurisdiction over civilians, making this regime of exception particularly serious. Article 44 (Secs. 12, 13) of the 1925 Constitution essentially replicated the amended 1833 charter's provisions regarding the concession of extraordinary powers "in the urgent necessity of defending the state" and "to conserve the constitutional regime or internal peace." While the state of siege was limited to restrictions on personal freedom, the extraordinary powers allowed restrictions on press freedom and freedom of assembly—but only for six months instead of a year as previously.

The first use of this authority occurred in 1933 (Law 5163, April 28) when Congress gave the president extraordinary powers to subject persons to house arrest or detention in places other than jails for common criminals, to censure the press, to impede the circulation of printed matter that tended to alter the public order or subvert the constitutional regime, and to search homes without warrants.[76] Such concessions of extraordinary power became routine; from 1933 to 1958, sixteen separate laws imposed almost four years of these regimes of exception on the country. This did not include at least a dozen state of siege decrees during the same years.[77]

Despite minor modifications, the basic regimes of exception used in Chile until 1973 were those promulgated in 1833 as amended in 1874. The 1925 Constitution offered only small alterations, supplemented by several national security laws from the 1930s to 1973. At the time of the 1973 military coup that ousted President Salvador Allende, this tradition of regimes of exception and extraordinary powers provided General Augusto Pinochet Ugarte with an institutional and historical tradition to justify his *golpe,* including the *consejos de guerra* of Portales and the military Ordenanza of 1839, the states of siege and assembly of 1833, 1874, and 1925, the draconian extraordinary powers of 1837–1839 and the many concessions of such powers that followed, the deposition of Balmaceda by the Congress "to restore the constitutional order," and the panoply of laws for the internal security of the state passed after 1931.[78]

General Pinochet and the military junta issued *bandos* at the outset of their rule, "constitutional acts" restricting civil liberties and rights up to 1980, and a new constitution in 1980. The 1980 Constitution greatly expanded the types of regimes of exception and the constitutional role of the armed forces.[79] In seventeen years of military rule, however, Pinochet and his advisers added little to, and borrowed much from, Chile's juridical foundations for constitutional dictatorship.[80] Chile had created the legal basis for tyranny in 1833. Reinforced by the national security legislation enacted from the 1930s to the 1970s and made harsher by the 1980 Constitution, the military codes, and the organic laws for the armed forces adopted by the Pinochet government, these foundations of constitutional dictatorship and military jurisdiction over civilians impeded the country's effective democratization into the 1990s.

9

Regimes of Exception in the Dominican Republic

SHARING THE ISLAND OF HISPANIOLA WITH HAITI, THE DOMINICAN Republic was conceived in bloody racial warfare and international intrigue. After independence in 1844, it suffered periodic Haitian invasions. British, French, and U.S. meddling added to the country's grief. In 1861, Spain restored a colonial regime (1861–1864) at the request of the country's president, who had been conceded extraordinary powers by the legislature.[1] Fearful of Haiti, disdained by the racist slavocracy in the United States that threatened annexation, and plagued by internal wars, the Dominican Republic suffered into the twentieth century from a legacy of personalist dictatorships, chronic insurrections, and foreign intervention.[2]

Settled by Spain shortly after Columbus's first voyage to the Western Hemisphere in 1492, Hispaniola had been the target of pirates, corsairs, and Spain's European rivals since the sixteenth century. By the late eighteenth century, the western third of the island, Saint-Domingue, belonging to France, was the most affluent colony in the Antilles. A slave economy, Saint-Domingue exported sugar and other products to the newly expanding market of the recently independent United States.

Slave revolts periodically disrupted the economy and terrorized white and mulatto planters. In 1791 a new revolt occurred in the northern part of Saint-Domingue. The uprising spread and became more politically complex as British, French, and Spanish colonists in the eastern portion of the island, the present-day Dominican Republic, sought to use the disorder for their own ends. Divisions between blacks and mulattos and among various European and

354

Spanish colonial interests, and also the impact of the French Revolution, resulted in a bloody insurrection, culminating with Haitian independence in 1804.[3]

Opposition to French rule and fear of the spread of the slave revolt from Saint-Domingue provoked large-scale emigration from the Spanish-dominant eastern territories of the island in the last decade of the eighteenth century. From 1789 until 1810, the population decreased by perhaps two-thirds.[4] The remaining Spanish colonists preferred Napoleonic troops and French administration to the rule of radical black or mulatto revolutionaries. Although traditional agriculture and ranching predominated rather than the plantations as in Saint-Domingue, the Spanish resisted Haitian military decrees abolishing slavery. Thus, the French were able to establish a temporary military government supported by the Spanish Dominicanos fearful of subjugation or extermination by the Haitians.

In 1808, however, Dominican forces responded to the French invasion of Spain with a military attack against French forces. The alliance of Spanish guerrillas and British forces in Spain and Portugal facilitated the surrender of Santo Domingo to a British fleet in 1809. When the British left a year later, the impoverished colony of some seventy-five thousand was returned to Spain virtually at the moment that colonials in Venezuela were initiating their independence from Spanish rule (April 1810). In the next decade, abortive revolts and conspiracies based in Haiti, Caracas, and among local French, Italian, or Spanish residents portended a break from Spain. However, the fears of whites and mulattos of the spread of violence and racial persecution, should Haiti dominate the Spanish colony, inhibited serious independence movements.

The Haitians, in turn, feared French or other European efforts at reconquest and the reimposition of slavery. Many Europeans abhorred the "black republic" and pointed to the brutal internal strife and the plight of white planters and merchants in Haiti as justification for a military expedition to destroy the new nation. The anticipation of such an expedition, which would invade the eastern part of the island, Santo Domingo, and then push into Haiti, greatly concerned Haiti's president, Jean-Pierre Boyer. Boyer recruited local allies and urged them to proclaim independence from Spain and declare their support for incorporating Santo Domingo into the Haitian Republic. Such a declaration resulted on the Haitian frontier in November 1821.

Other Dominicans took a different tack, favoring the union of Santo Domingo with the new state of Gran Colombia propitiated by

Simón Bolívar (see chapter 5). In December 1821, a coup d'état occurred in the town of Santo Domingo; the rebels proclaimed the Independent State of Spanish Haiti. When authorities in Caracas failed to respond expeditiously to this movement, Boyer marched into Santo Domingo in February 1822 at the head of an occupation army. Thus began the so-called independence of the Dominican Republic. For the next twenty-two years the island of Hispaniola was politically unified. By the terms of the Haitian Constitution of 1816, a president for life governed the island. In reality, military force was the cornerstone of political rule. Haitian policies in Santo Domingo attacked the foundations of Spanish property law, imposed mandatory military service, prohibited the use of Spanish in official documents, and required that primary education be in French. Resentment and resistance that had incubated over the years gave birth to a secret society dedicated to Dominican autonomy and independence. Leaders of La Trinitaria—for its slogan, "God, Fatherland, and Liberty"—sought allies among opponents to President Boyer within Haiti.

An uprising in Haiti in January 1843 finally ousted Boyer from office after twenty-five years of political and military dominance. Only months after he and his family sailed into exile, a "popular revolutionary junta" overturned Boyer's appointees and took power in Santo Domingo. Despite efforts by the new Haitian government to ferret out the Trinitarian leadership, pressures for independence grew. In February 1844 matters came to a head; a coup led by the Trinitarian group presaged independence. Faced with internal opposition from former Boyer supporters, the new Haitian president, Charles Herard, nevertheless mounted an invasion of the eastern territory. Defeated on the battlefield, he was then overthrown in Port-au-Prince. Subsequent Haitian efforts to restore unity by military force failed. As elsewhere in Spanish America, from the armies of the independence movement emerged the dominant military caudillos in the first decades of independence: Pedro Santana (president, 1844–1848, 1853–1856, 1858–1860, and captain-general, 1861–1865, under the Spanish restoration) and Buenaventura Báez (president, 1848–1853, 1856–1857, December 1865 to May 1866, 1868–1874, and December 1876 to March 1878).[5]

Intermittent Haitian military incursions and diplomatic maneuvers left Dominican independence insecure into the late 1850s. The new nation sought protection from Europe, particularly from France and Britain after 1848, and also from the United States. Ultimately, though no serious Haitian intervention occurred after the defeat of Haitian dictator Soulouque ("Faustin I") in 1855, President Santana made the unique decision of requesting the reannexation of the Dominican Republic to Spain (1861) as protection against the Haitians and perhaps in fear of U.S. intervention like that in Nicaragua in the mid-1850s (see chapter 4). Santana was named captain-general of the restored Spanish province.

Spanish administration (1861–1865) proved disastrous. A new movement, the so-called War of Restoration (1863–1864), reestablished independence. The Haitian government, preferring a weak, slave-free, independent neighbor to a Spanish colony with a growing slave population, assisted the Dominicans with money, supplies, and sanctuary in the fight against Spain. The war again left the country in shambles, indebted and politically fragmented.

Military caudillos competed for regional and national power for the next fifteen years. Between 1865 and 1879 the country had twenty-one governments and over fifty rebellions.[6] During this period, Buenaventura Báez, the second president (1848–1853) and Santana's principal adversary, returned to the presidency several times. He served his fourth term from 1868 to 1874, his fifth and last from 1876 to 1878. Failed negotiations on annexation to the United States, the circulation of practically worthless paper currency, and corruption were central political issues in an era characterized by instability and violence.

Thus, from the time of independence from Haiti in 1844 until the early 1880s, the Dominican Republic endured unending warfare, turmoil, and political conflict. Superimposed on this political nightmare were a spate of liberal constitutions proclaiming the sanctity of civil liberties and rights, the division of powers among executive, legislative, and judicial branches of government, and the regimes of exception necessary to cloak, if only shabbily, barbaric dictatorships.

CONSTITUTIONAL DEVELOPMENT, 1844–1879

From the outset, the threat of foreign invasion and internal war and the lack of political legitimacy were reflected in the nation's constitutions. Indeed, an integral element of the chaos of Dominican politics from 1844 until 1882 was frequent constitutional reform. Reforms, revisions, and modifications, or "new" constitutions were enacted in 1854 (February and December), 1858, 1865, 1866, 1868, 1872, 1874, 1875, 1876, 1877, 1878, 1879, 1880, 1881, 1887, and 1896.

By the end of the nineteenth century, though beginning later than other Spanish American republics, the Dominicans had done more constitution making than any of their Spanish American brethren. Some of these were succession constitutions, necessary to legitimate governments that came to power through force. Others were little more than constitutional amendments that modified election procedures, redefined executive or legislative authority, and changed the length of presidential terms to allow incumbents to maintain themselves in power.[7] Very little of this constitution making and reform reflected fundamental disagreement on the form of government or on nineteenth-century liberal principles. No serious federalist experiments took place; no proposals for constitutional monarchy prospered. Some conflict did occur over the role and privileges of the Catholic church and over proposals to abolish the military *fueros,* echoing liberal-conservative debates elsewhere in Spanish America.

Always, however, the country was defined as a centralized republic with the conventional division of power among three branches of government. Always, citizens were given *garantías* encompassing the civil liberties and rights expected of civilized nations in the nineteenth century. And, always, the constitutions provided that these rights and liberties could be suspended, that Dominicans could be governed under comprehensive regimes of exception. In practice, Dominicans were governed by comprehensive constitutional regimes of exception from the moment of independence. They would continue to be so governed into the 1990s.

The 1844 Constitution

Prior to the Haitian invasion in 1822, Santo Domingo had shared with other Spanish American colonies the Cádiz Constitution (1812), its recision (1814–1820), and its restoration (1820). The substance of liberal civil rights and liberties, the notion of the separation of powers, and the basic framework of nineteenth-century constitutions in Spanish America were all familiar to political elites in Spanish Haiti.

Even before the victory against the Haitians had been consolidated, the governing central junta issued a decree (July 1844) convoking elections for deputies to a constituent Congress. Convened in September 1844, the Congress approved the country's first constitution by the first week in November. In many ways it resembled the Central American documents of this era, and their Cádiz predecessor, with enumerated rights and liberties of citizens, the abolition of slavery, prohibitions on confiscation of property, and even the right of free primary education (Arts. 14–38). In other respects, however, the 1844 Constitution contained the most exaggerated, comprehensive, and contradictory provisions for regimes of exception found anywhere in Spanish America during this period. Likewise, the constitutionalization of the internal political role of the military was more evident and even more inclusive than customary in most of Spanish America.

Conflicts between the constituent assembly and the governing junta marred the constitutional convention. More importantly, saber rattling by the soon-to-be first president of the republic, General Pedro Santana, engendered truly far-reaching provisions for regimes of constitutional exception. Santana preferred an executive with complete military authority over the entire population. He settled for a temporary regime of exception clause (Art. 210), wrested from the assembly by a squadron of calvary.[8] Article 210 of the first Dominican constitution read:

> During the present war, and while a peace treaty is not signed, the President of the Republic, may freely organize the army and navy, mobilize the national guard, and take all measures he believes opportune for the defense and security of the Nation; being authorized, therefore, to issue all orders, regulations and decrees that are convenient, without any liability for his actions [*sin estar sujeto a responsabilidad alguna*].

Born of warfare and racial strife in the shadow of imminent and recurrent invasions by Haiti, the constitutional foundations of the Dominican Republic rested upon the broadest regime of exception imaginable: unlimited authority of the executive to "issue all orders, regulations and decrees that are convenient."

Pedro Santana, the first Dominican president-caudillo, assumed powers beyond those exercised by Bolívar, San Martín, and O'Higgins in the independence wars. He used this authority in his several presidencies during the next two decades, as did his adversaries in their presidencies, to murder, imprison, and exile opponents, deliver booty to his troops and supporters, and to govern as a modern-day viceroy or captain-general. In the sardonic words of Selden Rodman: "Santana's first term in power (1844–48) was fairly uneventful. The paternalistic ruler established courts under the Napoleonic code, imposed curfews, ordained strict work codes, granted high salaries to himself and his staff, printed paper money to pay off the standing army, and executed several batches of conspirators suspected of hatching plots to unseat him."⁹

The 1844 Constitution included the following:

1. A clause (Art. 200) that allowed the declaration of a state of siege, and the corresponding suspension of *garantías* and martial law, in all or part of the republic, in time of war or "internal commotion." In the case of war, the state of siege declaration would be made by the president. In the case of "internal commotion," the president could declare a state of siege when Congress was not in session, being obligated thereafter to convoke the Congress and seek its "pronouncement" on the situation. (This clause made the Dominican Republic the second Spanish American republic to incorporate a state of siege clause into its constitution. The language of the clause was similar to that of Chile's 1833 Constitution. In 1853 Argentina would follow, then Bolivia in 1861 and El Salvador in 1864.)

2. Congressional authority to delegate to the executive, in time of war, "whatever extraordinary powers [were] deemed indispensable for public security," detailing them as far as possible, and limiting the time during which they may be exercised (Art. 94, Sec. 15). Although it limited the duration and suggested the specification of the extraordinary powers conceded, this clause resembled its similitude in the 1833 Chilean charter.

3. Presidential authority "in cases of armed internal commotion that threatens the security of the Republic, and in the case of sudden armed invasion" to use the powers delegated by the Congress pursuant to Article 94 (Sec. 15), or if Congress is not in session, "to take whatever other measures, not contrary to the Constitution, that preservation of the public interest (*cosa pública*) requires, giving account of these measures to Congress as soon as it convenes" (Art. 102, Sec. 13).

4. Authority for military officers to serve as provincial administrators (*jefes superiores políticos*) and, "while the present war lasts," to exercise military and civil authority (Art. 144).

5. Constitutional definition of the role of the armed forces to include "defense of the State, against internal aggression and internal commotions, and guardian of public liberties" (Art. 183), but with the familiar language declaring that "the armed forces are essentially obedient and passive; no armed corps may deliberate" (Art. 184).

Constitutional Reform, February 1854

Despite numerous reforms, these foundations of constitutional dictatorship and provisions for a central military role in politics in the Dominican Republic would never be significantly modified in the remainder of the nineteenth century. In the short term, the opposition to Article 210 and Santana's dictatorship persisted, leading to a congressional resolution calling for a special session to enact constitutional reforms. The resolution referred to seventy articles, including Article 210; reforms were promulgated February 27, 1854, the tenth anniversary of independence.

The reforms retained congressional authority to delegate extraordinary powers to the executive when deemed necessary to maintain the security of the state (Art. 68, Sec. 15). The executive conserved the authority to exercise the powers conferred under Article 68 (Sec. 15) to suppress internal commotions threatening state security and to resist external invasion (Art. 77, Sec. 18). The amended constitution also included provisions for the declaration of a state of siege by the Congress, or by the executive when the Congress was not in session (Art. 147). No change occurred from the 1844 charter in defining the constitutional mission of the armed forces, but "deliberation" by any group of the armed forces was made a criminal offense: rebellion (Art. 129). While Santana's controversial Article 210 was deleted, a new Article 161 further expanded presidential authority "until a peace treaty is signed." The chief executive could promote officers in the military forces and appoint and dismiss governors of the provinces. These officials would exercise overlapping civil and military authority.

The Constitution of December 23, 1854

In September 1854, Santana, again president of the republic after another insurrection, convoked Congress into extraordinary session. He presented it with a new draft constitution that he claimed was more suitable for confronting the crisis facing the nation than the amended February charter. This constitution, adopted in December 1854, considerably enhanced executive authority. The now entrenched state of siege provisions were to be implemented by the executive "in the case of *imminent* or actual invasion or internal commotion" (Art. 62, emphasis added). Moreover, the president could "take whatever measures he believes indispensable for the conservation of the Republic" in the cases of internal commotion, rebellion, invasion, and "when he has been informed that there exists some plot against the security of the state" (Art. 35, Sec. 22). This gave the Dominican president unlimited authority to deal with subversion, its threat, rebellion, or internal commotion.

Constitutional dictatorship had been consolidated. For good measure, a transitional article of the constitution provided for two consecutive six-year terms in office for the incumbent president, though neither Santana nor any other president successfully completed such a long tenure. Again, the resemblance to Chile's 1833 charter is marked, though the Chileans provided for the possibility of two consecutive five-year terms.

Constitutional Reforms and Revision, 1854–1879

With lapses (1858, 1861–1865, 1866, 1872) and reforms, the Constitution of December 1854 reigned until 1879. It was reinstituted several times after being replaced temporarily with alternative charters and, from 1861 to 1864, with the reimposed Spanish colonial regime. In none of the alternative charters, however, did provisions for state of siege disappear, though the short-lived 1858 Constitution, and its revisions in 1865 and 1866, restricted executive authority and prohibited delegating extraordinary powers by Congress to the president. The 1858 charter also expanded the constitutional mission of the armed forces, adding the charge "to maintain public order and sustain observance of the Constitution and the laws" (Art. 132).[10]

In 1872, the reestablishment of the 1854 Constitution reconfirmed the president's emergency powers in "cases of armed internal commotion, rebellion or enemy invasion" (Art. 35, Sec. 22) and restored exclusive authority to the executive to declare a state of siege in all or part of the country in the event of "foreign invasion or internal commotion" (Art. 62). Further reforms in 1874 slightly limited executive and military authority during periods of state of siege and, in particular, prohibited subjecting civilians to military law. They also added a novel clause restricting freedom of the press. It read: "The authorities may suspend, for immediate submittal to the censor, any publication that manifests ideas that subvert order or public tranquility" (Art. 23).

Additional tinkering from 1875 to 1880 established and then amplified congressional authority to declare a state of siege and suspend for limited periods enumerated *garantías* (for example, Art. 38, Sec. 20, reforms of 1875), as well as executive authority to suspend certain *garantías* in order "to reestablish constitutional order when threatened by armed uprising" (for example, Art. 66, reforms of 1879). The 1875 reforms (Art. 62) reconfirmed similar presidential emergency powers to those enumerated in 1854 and also detailed the scope of government authority during periods of state of siege (Arts. 97–99).

Thus, while the 1854 Constitution was periodically derogated, reinstated, and then derogated, revised, reformed, and then again discarded, only to be once again revived, it remained the benchmark for regimes of exception in Dominican constitutional law. All constitutions that followed contained a number of provisions for regimes of exeception. Most contained the clauses introduced in 1854 (or even 1844), with the addition from 1872 to 1880 of executive authority to suspend enumerated *garantías* in times of internal commotion or in order to restore public order. These very same clauses, with slightly modified language, appeared in Dominican constitutions into the 1960s.[11]

POLITICS AND CONSTITUTIONAL CHANGE AFTER 1879

The last two decades of the nineteenth century brought increased foreign investment and some prosperity to the Dominican Republic. Government encouragement of immigration, public works programs, increased sugar production, and foreign investment stimulated commercial speculation and the rise of a small middle class. As in Mexico, Guatemala, and parts of South America, this physical and economic modernization also permitted consolidation of political control by a personalist dictator through expansion and reequipping of the armed forces and elimination of competing caudillos.

In the Dominican Republic this strongman was Ulises Heureaux, nicknamed "Lilis." Of Haitian and West Indian descent, General Heureaux ruled as constitutional president (1882–1884), puppet master (1884–1886), and president-dictator (1887–1899). During these last twelve years, he had the 1881 Constitution amended to allow for the indirect election of the president and extension of the presidential term to four years. The constitution's ample provisions for regimes of exception and presidential authority to "restore constitutional order, altered by armed revolution" (Art. 53) made Heureaux a constitutional dictator.

In the aftermath of the 1879–1880 rebellion, General Gregorio Luperón delegated authority in Santo Domingo to Heureaux.

Though Luperón headed the rebel forces, he refused to assume the presidency; elections made Archbishop Fernando Arturo de Meriño constitutional president in 1880. Heureaux, as minister of the interior, commanded troops that put down two minor rebellions against a government that abolished the right to political asylum in foreign embassies.

In May 1881, Meriño decreed the suspension of the constitution, while Congress considered reforms he proposed to the 1879 charter. He instructed Congress to give priority to exacting more severe punishment, including capital punishment, for conspiracy; conferring military, as well as civil, powers on the governors of provinces and districts, powers they, de facto, had; and giving greater authority to the executive "so that he can govern with fewer restraints [*trabas*]." In the interim, the president "assumes all power."[12]

The constituent assembly approved the 1881 Constitution in late November; it remained in effect until November 1887. It reaffirmed the Dominican tradition of regimes of exception and constitutional dictatorship. Its regime of exception provisions, with the deletion after 1908 of Article 54 (see below), remained in effect until 1942.[13] (In 1942, an additional regime of exception—the "state of emergency"—was added "when national sovereignty is exposed to a grave and imminent threat," [Art. 33, Sec. 8; Art. 48, Sec. 8].

What, then, were the foundations for constitutional dictatorship promulgated in the Dominican Republic in 1881?

- Congress could "decree a state of siege and suspend for a limited time" freedom of speech, press, assembly and organization, in private and public, the rights of privacy of correspondence and private papers, the prohibition on arrest without warrant, the right to be advised of the reason for arrest within forty-eight hours, the prohibition on lengthy periods of being *incomunicado* or in jail longer than prescribed by law (Art. 25, Sec. 20).
- To restore constitutional order, altered by armed revolution, "the president may declare a state of siege, when congress is not in session and for as long as the perturbation [of constitutional order] endures" with the same effects as listed above in Article 25, section 20 (Art. 53).
- In the cases of armed rebellion, the president could also "decree any other measures of a temporary nature necessary to reestablish public order" (Art. 54).
- Each province and canton was presided over by a "Civil and Military Governor," named by the president, who would carry out

the constitutionally defined mission of the armed forces to "defend independence, liberty of the Republic, maintain public order, the Constitution and the laws" (Arts. 77, 85).

With the 1881 Constitution, the president had no need of congressional delegation of extraordinary powers. Article 54 added broad authority reminiscent of that conferred on the Chilean (1828) and Uruguayan (1830) presidents early in the nineteenth century and on the Costa Rican chief executive in 1859. Indeed, the only relief from virtually complete military administration of the country was the abolition of military *fueros* and the prohibition on trying civilians in military tribunals (Arts. 85, 88).

General Heureaux was elected to succeed Archbishop Meriño in accord with the 1881 Constitution. After his two-year term, he stepped down but retained control over the military. In 1887 he returned to the presidency and did not relinquish power until his assassination in 1899. Heureaux ruled through terror and co-optation. He used foreign loans to finance his bureaucracy and repression, creating a praetorian army to enforce his will. The army absorbed 70 percent of the national budget.[14] The loans that made payment of the secret police, the army, and the bloated bureaucracy possible were secured by the customs revenues. Failure to meet the repayment obligations eventually provoked threats of European intervention and prompted U.S. efforts to mediate.

After his death, this dilemma would lead to recurrent threats of European intervention and, ultimately, to the long-term U.S. occupation of the country (1916–1924). In the short term, however, Heureaux manipulated the imperial ambitions of the United States and European powers as he pragmatically repressed opponents. The perennial threat of Haitian invasion or internal dissidence legitimated tyranny as the president sought to "save the fatherland" or to "restore constitutional order."[15]

President Heureaux's personalist dictatorship made fear and corruption the foundations of government. He ordered the "surplus population" of Santo Domingo's fortress prison "thrown to the sharks at the base of the cliff, along with the garbage."[16] Combining repression with greed, he lavishly appropriated public funds and resources for himself and supporters. Still, Heureaux insisted on periodic elections and constitutional reforms to sanctify his dictatorship. He had the 1881 Constitution amended in 1887, further restricting civil rights and liberties and adding to presidential prerogatives. The freedom of press clauses now ended with the words "subject to the laws," that is, to any restriction decreed by the government (Art. 11). The presidential term was extended to four years, and the president was to be elected indirectly instead of directly (Arts. 42–44). In times of foreign war (for example, any small incursion by rebels from Haiti), the president could "place on trial for treason to the Fatherland those Dominicans who are hostile to national dignity and defense" (Art. 28, Sec. 3).

Again in 1896 Heureaux convoked Congress to amend the constitution, unreformed since 1887. No important changes from the 1881 and 1887 charters occurred regarding regimes of exception, except for a clause providing that international human rights law (*derechos de gentes*) would become part of national constitutional law. Therefore, "treaties among the belligerents may be used to put an end to civil wars, who [the belligerents] should respect the humanitarian practices of Christian, civilized peoples" (Art. 106). Heureaux's enemies did not wait for the next constitutional reform to legitimate his perpetuation in power. Assassination ended his rule in 1899—without "respect for the humanitarian practices of christian and civilized people."

Political instability followed Heureaux's assassination. A wicked game of presidential musical chairs accompanied by the orchestral meddling of U.S. imperialism exhausted the country's energy and finances. Provisional presidents suspended the 1896 (really the 1881, amended in 1887 and 1896) Constitution, then repromulgated it in 1902. It remained theoretically in operation until further revisions in 1907.

After 1905, Dominican politics was dominated by the United States. Commercial, strategic, and geopolitical concerns fostered military protection for "American lives and property," then occupation and economic subjugation. The military occupation from 1916 to 1924 and the U.S. control over customs revenues until 1941 made the country virtually a U.S. colony. Between 1916 and 1924, the Dominican constitution was replaced with martial law.[17] This did not prevent more constitution making. New constitutions adopted in 1907 and 1908 differed little from the late nineteenth-century charters. Much the same could be said regarding the charters of 1924, 1927, 1929, and 1934. In 1942 a new regime of exception, the "state of emergency," was added by General Rafael Leonidas Trujillo, but except for renumbering, the other provisions of the 1881 charter remained essentially unchanged.[18]

The temporary restoration of elected government and constitutional reform (1924, 1927) was followed in 1930 by the beginning of three more decades of tyranny. General Trujillo, the commander of the national guard created by the U.S. occupation government, effected a coup, had himself elected constitutional president, and shortly thereafter suspended constitutional *garantías*. This he did, ostensibly, to meet the emergency conditions wrought by a hurricane that devastated Santo Domingo. The civil liberties and rights of Dominicans would be suspended and violated from that moment until Rafael Leonidas Trujillo's assassination in 1961. Trujillo was among the most despotic of Latin American dictators in the twentieth century, but the legal foundations for his tyranny were in place, ready for his exercise, long before 1930.[19]

Like Peru, the Dominican Republic had initiated independence under a sweeping regime of exception. Following Chile, its first constitution (1844) contained provision for the delegation of extraordinary powers to the president and for the declaration of a state of siege to suppress internal commotion or external threats. Like most of Spanish America, it experienced over half a century of rampant caudillismo. Besting, or worsting, the other Spanish Americans, it adopted more constitutions in the nineteenth century than any other Spanish American country.

From the outset, provisions for delegating extraordinary powers to the executive and a classic state of siege clause formed the legal basis of constitutional dictatorship. The armed forces were also assigned a clear internal political role. In the nineteenth century, government by regime of exception became commonplace in Dominican political life. In the 1990s the country has not yet overcome these constitutional foundations for tyranny.

10

Regimes of Exception, Civil-Military Relations, and Spanish American Politics

> There is no freedom at all if the power to judge is not separate
> from legislative and executive power. If it were joined to execu-
> tive power, the judge would have the force of oppressor. . . . All
> would be lost if the same man or body of principals or nobles,
> or men from among the people exercised these three powers.
>
> —*Montesquieu*

SPANISH AMERICANS EXPERIMENTED WITH MORE THAN ONE HUNDRED
constitutions in the nineteenth century. After the breakdown of the
Spanish Empire they attempted to create political regimes able to
reconcile the socioeconomic and political legacy of colonialism with
liberal constitutionalism. Neither the political institutions nor the
socioeconomic structure of the former colonies permitted easy
transition to stable constitutional government.

Following fifteen years of destructive warfare (1810–1825), the
new nations came to independence with shattered economies, ineffective administrative and fiscal systems, and no national identity.
Civil and other wars, racial and religious conflicts, brigandage,
boundary disputes, foreign intervention, and factional struggles for
political domination bled the nascent states during most of the
nineteenth century. This was the era of the caudillos—the charismatic warlords, landowners, and would-be regional or national
bosses. It was also the era of constitutional experimentation, na-

tional consolidation, and the entry of independent Spanish America into the world economy.

Spanish American political leaders recognized their dilemmas, even as they contested for power and plundered the meager resources of the public treasuries. Caudillos, congresses, presidents, and rebels raised armies to defend their privileges or wrest them from others, but they also passionately debated institutional alternatives that might moderate or end the bloodshed and establish governments both sufficiently energetic to maintain order and sufficiently restrained to promote liberty.

In some respects, Spanish American political leaders faced the same challenge as any elite seeking to create new political institutions. Nineteenth-century Spanish and French politics were at least as contentious, involving restored monarchies, emperors, fragile republics, populist dictators, military involvement in governance, and recurrent civil conflicts as formerly absolutist societies struggled to create a consensual political order. In both countries, as well as in Prussia, the recreation of legitimacy after the demise of traditional absolutism proved difficult.[1] Dictators, monarchs, and military rulers criminalized political opponents and resorted to states of siege in successive constitutions as they sought to replace the imperium of divine right with the new catechism of popular sovereignty.[2]

The Spanish Inquisition, Machiavelli, Calvin, Hobbes, and Rousseau provided obvious answers to the question of how to treat political and religious dissenters: with persecution and repression. However, in a new era that celebrated constitutionalism and citizenship rather than monarchy and vassalage, the question of what to do with enemies became more complex. This was as true in nineteenth-century France, Spain, Italy, and Germany as it was in Spanish America. Theoretically, such persons were entitled to basic civil liberties and rights. In fact, after 1824, every Spanish American constitution, with the exception of Guatemala's 1851 charter, had a bill of rights (a list of *garantías*). By the end of the nineteenth century, provision for at least the right of habeas corpus existed in all of South America and the similar writ of *amparo* in parts of Central America.

There were 103 national constitutions adopted in Spanish America in the nineteenth century. They are listed in table 1.

Habeas corpus, *amparo*, and other *garantías* restricted government authority. (See table 2.) The obvious solution no longer applied when absolute monarchy gave way to constitutionalism, at least not without constitutional legitimation and special repressive

TABLE 1

Spanish American National Constitutions in the Nineteenth Century

	Number	*Date*
Argentina	3	1819, 1826, 1853
Bolivia	11	1826, 1831, 1834, 1839, 1843, 1851, 1861, 1868, 1871, 1878, 1880, (does not include 1836 Confederation)
Chile	5	1818, 1822, 1823, 1828, 1833
Colombia	8	1811, 1832, 1843, 1853, 1858, 1861, 1863, 1886
Costa Rica	6	1844, 1847, 1848, 1859, 1869, 1871
Dominican Republic	15	1844, 1854,[1] 1854,[2] 1858, 1866, 1872, 1874, 1875, 1877, 1878, 1879, 1880, 1881, 1887, 1896
Ecuador	11	1830, 1835, 1843, 1845, 1851,[3] 1852, 1861, 1869, 1878, 1884,[4] 1897
El Salvador	7	1841, 1864, 1871, 1872, 1880, 1883, 1886
Guatemala	2	1851, 1879
Honduras	6	1839, 1848, 1865, 1873, 1880, 1894
Mexico	6	1814, 1822, 1824, 1836,[5] 1843, 1857 (does not include Maximilian's 1865 imperial charter)
Nicaragua	3	1838, 1858, 1893
Paraguay	1	1870
Peru	8	1823, 1826, 1828, 1834, 1839, 1856, 1860, 1867 (does not include 1836 Confederation)
Uruguay	1	1830
Venezuela	10	1811, 1819, 1830, 1857, 1858, 1864, 1874, 1881, 1891, 1893
Total	103	

Note: Total does not include the numerous proto-constitutions, provisional statutes, *reglamentos,* and organizational decrees discussed in the text. Confederal and state constitutions also are not included.
   1. Constitution promulgated February 25, 1854.
   2. Constitution promulgated December 16, 1854.
   3. Often referred to as the 1850 Constitution.
   4. Often referred to as the 1883 Constitution.
   5. Constitution effective January 1, 1837.

legislation. Often, penal codes (beginning with that of Spanish liberals in 1822) outlawed certain types of political opposition and permitted censorship of public expression and publications that offended, defamed, or merely criticized the government or public officials.[3] Illustrative was Peru's 1823 press law that forbade the publication of uncensored works "treating the Holy Scripture, articles or dogmas of the Republic's religion, religious morality . . .

TABLE 2
Civil Liberties and Rights (*Garantías*) in Spanish
American Constitutions

	Constitutions Including Clause	
Type of Clause	*Number*	*Percentage*
Enumerated civil liberties (*garantías*, derechos*, etc.)	99	96
Official state religion	83	81
Prohibition of public freedom of worship	55	54
Property, liberty, equality and security (the liberal menu clause)	58	59[a]
Prohibition of torture	49	48
Suspension or limitation of some *garantías* within the the same clause	99	100[a]
Sedition or subversion	14	14

[a] Excludes cases missing enumerated rights.

[and] maxims or doctrines that conspire to overturn the Republic's religion, or its political constitution, [or which] are intended to incite rebellion or perturbation of public tranquility, or inciting directly to disobey the law or legitimate authority; provoking [to this end] with satire or invective."[4]

Religious intolerance was usually explicitly provided for in early Spanish American constitutions, by establishing an official state church, prohibiting freedom of worship (or, at least, public freedom of worship), and linking government legitimacy and power to the Catholic church. For example, the Peruvian 1860 Constitution declared: "The Nation professes the Roman Apostolic Catholic Religion, the State protects it, and does not permit the public exercise of any other [religion]" (Art. 4).

Only six Spanish American republics ended the nineteenth century without an official state religion clause; Colombia had been in this category but a conservative victory reestablished Catholicism as the official faith in the 1886 Constitution. The following constitutions had no official state religion clause:

- Colombia: 1853, 1858, 1861, 1863
- El Salvador: 1880, 1883, 1886
- Guatemala: 1879
- Honduras: 1880, 1894
- Mexico: 1857

- Nicaragua: 1893
- Venezuela: 1819, 1830, 1858, 1864, 1874, 1881, 1891, 1893
- Central American Federation (Nicaragua, Honduras, and El Salvador):   1898
- Gran Colombia: 1821

Gradually, public exercise of non-Catholic religions was permitted in the nineteenth century, especially, but not only, where liberals gained ascendance. This trend secularized political repression, although in some instances reversals also occurred. Most dramatic was the case of Ecuador under García Moreno (1861–1865, 1869–1875), where non-Catholics lost citizenship and civil rights in order "to raise a wall of division between lovers of the true God and those who serve the devil."[5] Even where presidents failed to emulate Philip II's Catholic intolerance, government protection of the church and its officials from ridicule, insult, and slander persisted. Press laws and penal codes prohibited behavior to which the church objected, linking political and religious circumscription of public and private behavior.

The following constitutions had no prohibitions on public freedom of worship:

- Argentina: 1819, 1326, 1853
- Colombia: 1811 (New Granada), 1843, 1853, 1858, 1861, 1863, 1886
- Costa Rica: 1844, 1848, 1859, 1869, 1871
- Dominican Republic: 1844, 1854 (1, 2), 1858, 1872
- El Salvador: 1841, 1864, 1871, 1872, 1880, 1883, 1886
- Guatemala: 1851, 1879
- Honduras: 1839, 1873, 1880, 1894
- Mexico: 1857
- Nicaragua: 1838, 1858, 1893
- Paraguay: 1870
- Uruguay: 1830
- Venezuela: 1819, 1830, 1857, 1858, 1881, 1893
- Central American Federation (Nicaragua, Honduras, and El Salvador):   1835, 1898
- Gran Colombia: 1821
- Peru-Bolivia Confederation: 1836

For example, the Guatemalan Constitution of 1879 guaranteed the exercise of all religions in public places of worship *(templos)*, but this did not extend to "acts of subversion or practices incompatible with peace and public order, nor [did] it give the right to refuse compliance with civil and political obligations" (Art. 24).

The church-state question reflected the more fundamental problem of legitimating government power when stripped of divine providence. In the United States and Spanish America, confused appeals to natural law, meaning sometimes God's law and sometimes a vague claim of moral status for reason or the imperatives of nature, sanctified the new order. This meant only that the sovereign, but not the political order itself, had lost divine appointment. When the latter occurred, the polity stood naked against those who would challenge its legitimacy, the authority of particular governments and public policies.

Despite the initial optimism of the philosophers of the Enlightenment about applying reason to human affairs, constitutions did not (and cannot) of themselves solve the overwhelming problems of creating effective, legitimate political systems. Securing acceptance for any constitutional order is a dilemma for all polities. However, when properly designed and based on principles that the polity comes to accept or already accepts, a constitution may be a cornerstone for the legitimation of a new political system or government. In addition to this symbolic legitimating function, it may also provide a formula for governance. Such an outcome requires fortuitous circumstances and effective political leaders. Conversely, constitutions may provide a juridical foundation for dictatorship and tyranny. This they frequently did in nineteenth-century Spanish America.

Constitutional debates in the former Spanish colonies were informed by an awareness of political developments in Europe and the United States. For example, the French 1814 Constitution that gave the executive authority "to issue the ordinances necessary for enforcement of the law and for the security of the State" (Art. 14) was emulated in Spanish America but also resisted by opponents of executive dominance. An insurrection in Paris in 1830 overturned the king's ordinance that dissolved the legislature and his declaration of a state of siege. A new constitution was adopted that prohibited him from suspending the constitution or civil rights and liberties. This was also noted in Spanish American debates over the desirability of regimes of exception and the proper scope of legislative and executive authority. Spanish Americans similarly considered the 1831 Belgian charter, adopted in response to events in Paris in 1830, that expressly forbade suspension of the constitution, in part or in its entirety (Art. 130) and the Spanish 1837, 1845, and

1848 enactments that authorized suspension of constitutional *garantías* and use of states of siege.[6]

Spanish American constitution makers were also influenced by their own failed or marred experiments. Constituent assemblies drew on the accumulated experiences of their contemporaries, copying, modifying, and adapting distinct versions of federalism and centralism, separation of powers, church-state relations, and regimes of exception. They also experimented with different judicial and administrative systems, suffrage requirements, and electoral procedures. At the end of the nineteenth century, however, only Mexico, Venezuela, and Argentina had retained even formal aspects of federalism. The centralist tradition prevailed.

Occasionally, Spanish America also resorted to Bonapartism, installing dictatorships with coerced approval in staged plebiscites, as had the first Napoleon in 1799 and again in 1802. Constitutional provisions for lifetime presidents and delegation of full sovereign powers to caudillos, such as Juan Manuel de Rosas in Argentina and Rafael Carrera in Guatemala, offered a republican alternative to monarchy and a buffer against the dangers of liberalism.

As in Europe and North America, the initial stages of constitutionalism in Spanish America created oligarchic republics but not democracies. Not even minimal conditions for democratic politics—that is, a broad (if not universal) suffrage, fair and free elections, liberty for political opposition, and equality before the law—existed in the nineteenth century. Rather, where personalistic dictatorship or exaggerated presidentialism did not prevail, Spanish Americans established oligarchic, exclusionary political systems. Property, income, literacy, race, gender, and religious restrictions limited political participation, as in the United States and Europe.

Beyond the typical concerns of nineteenth-century constitution makers in Europe and North America, three interrelated issues particularly plagued Spanish American politics: the extent of political and religious tolerance to be afforded to adversaries (religious dissenters, opposition politicians, the press, critics of government policy), the role of the military and militia in the new political systems, and the scope of constitutional regimes of exception. These issues still afflict Spanish America in the twentieth century. Details of the political resolution of these issues for particular Spanish American nations have been presented in the preceding chapters. Generally, Spanish Americans permitted less political and religious tolerance than Britain or the United States and even somewhat less than

France after 1830, though in Spain, Portugal, and other parts of Europe political and religious intolerance was at least as fierce as in Spanish America.

Political tolerance and civil liberties are as dangerous and as essential to societies in the 1990s as they were in the 1820s, and the supposed champions of liberty sometimes remain its worst enemies. F. A. Hayek, author of the *Constitution of Liberty* and idol of the temporarily ascendant neoliberals dominating (not just) Latin American politics and economic policy in the twentieth century's last decade, proclaimed:

> When an external enemy threatens, when rebellion or lawless violence has broken out, or a natural catastrophe requires quick action by whatever means can be secured, powers of compulsory organization, which nobody normally possesses, must be granted to somebody. Like an animal in flight from mortal danger society may in such situations have to suspend temporarily even vital functions on which in the long run its existence depends if it is to escape destruction.[7]

Nineteenth-century liberalism, intent on preventing a resurgence of absolutism and protecting the new political order, had recourse to such "powers of compulsory organization" and to repressive legislation and penal codes that proscribed a variety of forms of political opposition under the rubric of sedition. Half of the Spanish American nations studied—Argentina, Bolivia, Chile, Colombia, Costa Rica, the Dominican Republic, Honduras, and Venezuela—included antisedition clauses in one or more constitutions in the nineteenth century. Antisedition legislation and repressive press laws were even more common than constitutional provisions.

The most favored constitutional instruments for confronting political opposition were regimes of exception. These included delegation of extraordinary powers to executives and other officials, suspension of civil liberties and rights, and constitutional dictatorship. Conservatives eventually accepted the basic principles of constitutionalism, it not the liberal enthusiasm for a secular order and expanded suffrage. They also came to share the liberals' methods for defending the constituted order. Catholic doctrine on just war[8] and the legacy of the Spanish Inquisition, along with reasons of state, melded with the liberals' "defense of the constitution": "whatever is required to insure the survival of the state must be done by the individuals responsible for it, no matter how repugnant such an act may be to them in their private capacity as decent and moral men."[9]

Protection of national security and the constitutional order justified repression of opponents: traitors, subversives, conspirators, religious dissenters, monarchists, and assorted "enemies." Later the list included anarchists, socialists, communists, fascists, and other ideological deviants. These enemies threatened public tranquility, endangered the institutional order, occasioned internal commotions, conspired against the legitimate authorities, worshipped the wrong god, offended the honor of presidents, military officers, or senators, demanded changes in government policy or presidents, and called an ogre an ogre.

Any of these offenses might require repression. Liberals and conservatives alike resorted to fines, imprisonment, torture, deportation, exile, or execution to punish political delinquency in the United States, Europe, and Spanish America. Such threats to the polity in Europe and Spanish America frequently precipitated implementation of regimes of exception. This became routine long before the rise of the post-1950s national security doctrines that justified the antipolitical military dictatorships in Spanish America and Brazil after 1964, extending in some cases into the 1990s.[10]

Despite such precautions, nowhere did liberty flourish, nowhere did regimes of exception protect the constitutional order, uphold civil liberties and rights in the long term, or promote consolidation of republican institutions. Indeed, temporary lack of use (but not necessarily formal elimination) of regimes of exception occurred in the two countries that exhibited the clearest movement away from caudillismo and that saw an enhanced role for the legislature and political parties: Chile (1861–1891) and Colombia (1863–1886).

In the twentieth century, the fear of adversaries, from anarchists and communists to religious fundamentalists, still justifies the existence and implementation of regimes of exception. Hayek, like his nineteenth-century counterparts in Europe and Spanish America (but without adding to their insight or sophistication), followed his call for "emergency powers" with a discussion of how constitutional design should limit them: the same agency should not both declare the existence of an emergency and assume emergency powers; the declaring agency (for example, the council of state, the permanent commission of the legislature, or the Congress) should then renounce its other powers and retain only the authority to revoke the emergency decree; authority should exist after the emergency passes to confirm or rescind the measures adopted by the government during the crisis.[11]

Although Hayek clearly recognized that "emergencies have always been the pretext on which the safeguards of individuals have been eroded" and was concerned to limit these dangers with institutional checks, he readily accepted the necessity for constitutional dictatorship, apparently much more fearful of popular sovereignty than of any regime of exception. In this respect he shared the preferences of Spanish conservative Juan Donoso Cortés, who proclaimed that between the tyranny of the many and the tyranny of the monarch, he preferred the latter.[12]

Hayek's notion that "all power rests on pre-existing opinions, and will last only so long as those opinions prevail" surprisingly neglects the convincing power of state terrorism, coercion, and the disposition to use these to sustain personalist, party, and military-dominated authoritarian regimes of all ideological persuasions. This neglect led Hayek to attack democracy as "the name for the very process of vote-buying, for placating and remunerating those special interests which in more naive times were described as 'sinister interests.' "[13] As did European and Spanish American elites in the nineteenth century, Hayek feared the implications of universal suffrage, of demands for social justice (in his words, "legalized corruption") that required progressive taxation or "unequal treatment" for certain groups in society.[14] While Hayek would never have approved the arbitrary, predatory politics of nineteenth-century Spanish American caudillos and governments, the solution he advocated for political emergencies in his "model constitution" was no different: regimes of exception and outlawing those who threaten society—with some attention to the design of exceptional regimes so as to limit the potential for abuse.

This was the Spanish American solution in the nineteenth century; it remains so in the twentieth. In this sense, Hayek was correct about the power of preexisting opinions. As long as he and others presume the need for regimes of exception, fit them into constitutions, and prefer tyranny of the sovereign to the tyranny of the many, such devices continue to figure as constitutional legitimation for outrages.

In the sixteen Spanish American nations considered in this study, only two of 103 national constitutions in the nineteenth century were without provision for regimes of exception. Both of these were adopted by Colombian liberals (1853, 1863).[15]

TABLE 3
Regimes of Exception in Spanish America

Type of Regime of Exception	Number	Percentage of Total
Number of constitutions with regime of exception clause	101	98
Constitutions with multiple constitutional rationale for regimes of exception	95	92
Clause(s) for suspension of some civil liberties and rights	97	94
Clause(s) making possible suspension of all civil liberties and rights	34	33
Clause permitting legislative delegation of "extraordinary powers" (*facultades extraordinarias*) to the executive	44	42
Clause permitting unilateral presidential suspension of constitution	19	18
State of siege clause	32	31

Note: In cases where there is not explicit constitutional authority to suspend all civil liberties, the code *suspension of some* is used, even when in practice all civil liberties may have been suspended during states of siege (for example, Chile 1833–1874). Thus the table underestimates the extent to which regimes of exception curtailed civil liberties and rights.

The most common types of regimes of exception were (1) vague and unilateral executive authority "to take the necessary measures" or "to take the actions deemed convenient" to meet external or internal threats; (2) delegation to the executive by the legislature or other entity of all encompassing or enumerated extraordinary powers; (3) declaration of a state of siege (or emergency, internal commotion, or threat to public tranquility) concomitantly granting exceptional authority to presidents, other officials, military officers, or even judges; and (4) suspension of some or all civil liberties and rights. (See table 3.)

In constitutions that gave presidents vague and unilateral authority to meet threats to national security and respond to emergencies, it was difficult to distinguish between regimes of exception and a permanent, if latent, constitutional dictatorship. For example, the constitutions of Chile in 1828, Uruguay in 1830, and Costa Rica in 1848 allowed the president, without consultation or institutional restraint, "to take the security measure necessary" (*medidas prontas de seguridad*) to meet disturbances to public tranquility or threats of danger to the polity. This type of unbridled constitutional dictatorship by presidents was the least common regime of exception, but it survived formally into the twentieth century in Uruguay and the Dominican Republic. Illustrative language is that from Bolivia's 1843 charter (Arts. 45, 46): "In the case of external threat or internal commotion, the President of the Republic will take whatever security measures he deems expedient [*conveniente*], reporting his actions and the reasons for them to the legislature, or if in recess to the National Council." The list below shows the countries where presidential rule by decree and suspension of the constitution occurred, with the constitutional rationale for such action indicated in its Spanish phrasing.

- Argentina: 1819 (I)
- Bolivia: 1834 (CL), 1843 (M), 1851 (CL)
- Chile: 1823 (D), 1828 (M)
- Costa Rica: 1848 (T), 1859 (T)
- Dominican Republic: (1852 (2) (T), 1872 (T), 1881 (TM), 1887 (TM), 1896 (TM)
- Ecuador: 1830 (TC)
- Gran Colombia: 1821 (ME, TL)
- Guatemala: 1851 (D)
- Mexico: 1814 (TE), 1822 (T)
- Uruguay: 1830 (M)
- Venezuela: 1811 (M, T) 1819 (IL)

Key: CL = both TL and TC: "tomar las medidas necesarias"; D = "decretar providencias hostiles o defensivas de urgencia"; I = "suspender el imperio de la constitución"; IL = "suspender el imperio cuando el congreso está en receso"; M = "medidas prontas de seguridad"; ME = "todas aquellas medidas extraordinarias que sean indispensables"; T = "tomar las medidas necesarias"; TC = "tomar las medidas con previa calificación del peligro del Consejo"; TE = "tomar medidas que estime conducentes"; TL = "tomar las medidas cuando el congreso está en receso"; TM = "podrá decretar otras medidas de carácter transitorio, que sean necesarias al reestablecimiento del orden público."

This list excludes all state constitutions, for example, within the Central American Confederation, the Colombian states when federal systems made provisions for state regimes of exception more important than the national charter, and the provincial statutes in the Río de la Plata.

Delegation of extraordinary powers to the executive by Congress or another entity might entail virtual rule by decree or a much more precise enumeration of particular powers. For example, the president might be given the authority to detain, arrest, and send "conspirators" or "rebels" into internal or external exile, to deploy troops, to spend funds without prior legislative approval, to impose special taxes, or even to confiscate property. Such extraordinary powers might be delegated, in turn, to ministers, provincial administrators, regional police chiefs, and local mayors. Delegation of "full authority" (*lleno de facultades, la suma del poder público*) created a constitutional dictatorship, sometimes for a specified duration and sometimes without any definite temporal restriction beyond the vague "while the emergency persists." Ecuador's 1835 charter, for example, allowed Congress, in the event of an internal commotion or external war, to concede to the executive "whatever extraordinary powers it considers necessary." Peru's 1839 Constitution allowed the council of state to "declare the fatherland in danger and grant [the president] whatever specific powers deemed necessary to save it," (Art. 103, Sec. 4), and Venezuela's 1857 Constitution permitted Congress or, if not in session, the council of government to concede extraordinary powers to the president "in cases where there is fear of internal commotion or external threat to public peace" (Art. 54).

The following list identifies those constitutions permitting congressional delegation of decree powers to the president:

- Bolivia: 1826, 1831, 1834, 1851, 1861
- Chile: 1822, 1833
- Colombia: 1886
- Dominican Republic: 1854 (1)
- Ecuador: 1835
- Guatemala: 1879
- Honduras: 1839
- Mexico: 1843, 1857
- Nicaragua: 1858
- Peru: 1826, 1828, 1834, 1839
- Venezuela: 1857
- Central American Federation (Nicaragua, Honduras and El Salvador):   1824, 1835
- Gran Colombia: 1821

When noncongressional entities had authority to impose regimes of exception, the composition of these government agencies became an important political concern. (See table 4.) A council of government or council of state could consist of legislative and presidential appointees, strictly presidential appointees, or a collection of representatives from the judicial, legislative, and executive

TABLE 4

Noncongressional Delegation of Extraordinary Powers, Ten Countries

Country and Year	Entity That Concedes Extraordinary Powers
Bolivia	
1831	Consejo de Estado
1834	Consejo de Estado
1839	Consejo de Ministros
1851	Consejo de Ministros
1868	Consejo de Ministros
1871	Consejo de Estado
1878	Consejo de Ministros
1880	Consejo de Ministros
Chile	
1833	Consejo de Estado
Colombia	
1832	Consejo de Estado
1861	Consejo de Estado
1886	Consejo de Estado
Costa Rica	
1847	Comisión Permanente (legislature)
1848	Comisión Permanente (legislature)
1871	Comisión Permanente (legislature)
Ecuador	
1830	Consejo de Estado
1835	Consejo de Gobierno
1843	Comisión Permanente
1845	Consejo de Gobierno
1851	Consejo de Estado
1852	Consejo de Estado
1861	Consejo de Estado
1869	Consejo de Estado
1878	Consejo de Estado
1884	Consejo de Estado
1897	Consejo de Estado
El Salvador	
1886	Consejo de Ministros
Guatemala	
1879	Consejo de Ministros
Mexico	
1836	Supremo Poder Conservador
1857	Consejo de Ministros; Comisión Permanente (legislature)
Peru	
1839	Consejo de Estado
1860	Comisión Permanente (legislature)
Venezuela	
1857	Consejo de Gobierno
1858	Consejo Extraordinario (includes Supreme Court)
1893	Consejo de Gobierno

Note: Noncongressional delegation includes the permanent commission of the legislature but not approval by the full Congress or by the Senate or lower chamber.

branches plus the church and the armed forces. For example, the 1833 Chilean charter provided for an eleven-person Consejo de Estado, six named by Congress (three by each chamber) for three-year terms and five named by the president. These appointees were specified as follows: a justice of the higher courts resident in Santiago, a religious functionary, a general rank officer from the army or navy, a department chief from the finance ministry, and a citizen who had previously been a cabinet minister, diplomat, intendant, provincial governor, or municipal official.[16]

In some cases, prohibitions on the congressional delegation of legislative authority coexisted with ample presidential decree powers or authority under a state of siege. In these cases, the principle of separation of powers was respected; this merely defined the method of imposing regimes of exception without curtailing their scope or effects. This was true, for example, in Ecuador (1845), Bolivia (1851), Argentina (1853), and El Salvador (1871). The list below shows those constitutions prohibiting the delegation of emergency powers:

- Argentina: 1853
- Bolivia: 1839, 1851, 1878, 1880
- Colombia: 1832, 1843, 1858, 1863
- Dominican Republic: 1854 (1, 2), 1858, 1866, 1872, 1874, 1875, 1877, 1878, 1879
- Ecuador: 1845, 1851, 1852, 1861, 1878, 1884, 1897
- El Salvador: 1871, 1872, 1880, 1883, 1886
- Honduras: 1894
- Mexico: 1824, 1836
- Nicaragua: 1893
- Venezuela: 1857, 1858, 1881, 1891, 1893
- Central American Federation (Nicaragua, Honduras, and El Salvador):   1898

Declarations of a state of siege, a state of internal war, internal commotion, or the existence of threats to public tranquility or national security entailed varying political and legal consequences from country to country and from time to time within countries. At first, a state of siege implied limitless government authority and military jurisdiction over civilians. In Chile (before 1874), the Dominican Republic, and Spain, declarations of states of siege virtually implemented martial law, suspending civil liberties and rights and subjecting civilians to military tribunals. In these cases, military officers and *consejos de guerra* became masters of lives and property without recourse to judicial or administrative remedy.

In other cases, state of siege decrees imposed constitutional dictatorship but without subjecting, or fully subjecting, civilians to military courts-martial. Argentina's 1853 state of siege clause authorized Congress or, if not in session, the president (with approval of the council of state) to declare one or various parts of the republic in a state of siege, thereby "suspending constitutional rights and liberties" but limiting the president to "the arrest of persons and their transfer from one point to another within the republic, if they do not choose voluntary exile" (Art. 23; Art. 64, Sec. 27; Art. 83, Sec. 19).

In still other instances, the state of siege or the declaration that there existed any of a number of eventualities (such as internal commotion, urgent circumstances, threats to public tranquility, tumult, rebellion, threats to the constitutional order, conspiracy, or external attacks) invoked regimes of exception that suspended only enumerated civil liberties and rights, conferred temporary powers on the executive (for example, to detain and arrest, incarcerate, and relegate to internal exile) and did not subject civilians to military law.

No presumption concerning the precise constitutional and legal implications of the state of siege or any other constitutionally designated state of exception could be made without examining the constitutional provisions, statutory elaboration, and practice in each case. Similarly, it was necessary to determine where authority was vested (the president, council of state, cabinet, Congress, the permanent commission of the Congress, or another entity) to implement these regimes of exception.

Despite this variation, several facts stand out. Ten of the sixteen nations studied adopted state of siege clauses in the nineteenth century; only Ecuador subsequently eliminated state of siege in favor of other regimes of exception. In some cases, states of siege resulted in constitutional dictatorship, almost equivalent to the delegation to the executive of "full sovereign authority" (*la suma del poder público*). For some countries this became routine during long stretches of the nineteenth century; for example, Chile for over half the period from 1837 to 1861, in most of Argentina prior to 1861, in Guatemala until 1865, in the Dominican Republic from independence in 1844, and in Paraguay after 1870. In much of Spanish America, constitutional dictatorship became the rule rather than the exception. The following list shows when Spanish American countries adopted the state of siege:

- Chile: 1833
- Dominican Republic: 1844
- Argentina: 1853
- Bolivia: 1861
- El Salvador: 1864
- Ecuador: 1869 (later deleted)
- Paraguay: 1870
- Honduras: 1880
- Colombia: 1886
- Nicaragua: 1893

Costa Rica, Guatemala, Mexico, Peru, Uruguay, and Venezuela had no constitutional state of siege clause, although all had other provisions for regimes of exception, except Colombia's 1853 and 1863 constitutions. The "constitution" (Estatuto Provisional del Imperio Mexicano) adopted by the French Emperor Maximilian on April 10, 1865, did contain provision for a state of siege (Art. 40). However, no true Mexican constitution contained state of siege provisions.

Even when full constitutional dictatorship was avoided, the extraordinary powers of the executive under regimes of exception could destroy the fortunes and families of political opponents in the name of saving the fatherland. One clear example was delegation of authority to impose special taxes, to advance tax collections, or to make expenditures without congressional approval. For example, Nicaraguan constitutional reforms in 1893 permitted the president, in cases of invasion or rebellion, "to decree a general loan, voluntary or forced, reporting on expenditures made [with these funds] to the Assembly in its next session" (December 1893). The constitutions listed below gave budget or tax authority to the president during regimes of exception:

- Argentina: 1819
- Bolivia: 1826, 1831, 1834, 1839, 1843, 1851, 1868, 1878, 1880
- Chile: 1823, 1828
- Colombia: 1886
- Costa Rica: 1847, 1848, 1871
- Dominican Republic: 1844, 1854 (1, 2), 1872, 1877, 1881, 1887, 1896
- Ecuador: 1830
- El Salvador: 1864, 1871, 1872, 1880, 1883, 1886
- Guatemala: 1851

- Honduras: 1848, 1865, 1873, 1880, 1894
- Mexico: 1814, 1822
- Nicaragua: 1858, 1893
- Peru: 1826
- Uruguay: 1830
- Venezuela: 1811, 1819, 1864, 1874, 1881, 1891, 1893
- Gran Colombia: 1821

This list includes cases where budget and tax authority are included in the constitutional definition of the regime of exception; it does not include cases where *facultades extraordinarias* delegated by Congress could include budget and tax authority: for example, Mexico's constitutions of 1857 or 1917.

Despite this feature of Spanish American constitutionalism, a gradual, if uneven, tendency emerged toward circumscribing government emergency authority, particularly that of the executive, and strengthening legislative institutions. In some countries this tendency moderated the more draconian aspects of regimes of exception. In particular, constitutional protection against confiscation of property, summary execution, and executive supression of legislative and, to a lesser extent, judicial authority indicated a growing concern among political elites that regimes of exception should not simply legitimate presidential dictatorship. This concern is evident in state of siege provisions that require prior congressional approval and that transform constitutional dictatorship into more limited regimes of exception. (See table 5.) The list below shows examples of limitations on state of siege powers:

- **Chile** (1833, amended 1874): President may impose house arrest or detain in places that are not jails for common criminals; transfer to other parts of the country between Caldera and Llanquihue; but not violate the constitutional *garantías* of deputies and senators; duration not to exceed the emergency for which the state of siege is put into effect (Art. 152, Sec. 161). Habeas corpus is automatically suspended but not other *garantías*.
- **Argentina** (1853): All *garantías* may be suspended. President may not punish on his own authority; must allow detainees to leave the country if they desire (voluntary exile). President may not assume judicial functions or reopen already decided cases.
- **Bolivia** (1880): *Garantías* are not automatically suspended with state of siege but "may be suspended for selected persons, identified as plotting against the tranquility of the Republic"; inter-

TABLE 5
Legislative State of Siege Powers

Type of Provision	Number of Constitutions	Percentage
Legislature given primary responsibility for declaration of state of siege	22	67
President given primary responsibility for declaration of state of siege	7	22
President can declare a state of siege only when the legislature is out of session	17	53
President must receive approval for a declaration from another government body if the legislature is out of session	8	25
Legislature is automatically called into session with a presidential declaration	3	9
Legislature must confirm the executive action if it is automatically called into session	2	6
Legislature must confirm the executive action in its next session	5	16
Legislature must review executive action in its next session	16	50
State of siege powers are delineated in the constitution	17	53

Note: Thirty-two of the 103 national constitutions in the nineteenth century contained state of siege clauses. (*N* = 32)

nal exile is permitted but no more than fifty leagues from one's place of residence and not to unhealthy places (*lugares no malsanos*); *garantías* of congressmen cannot be suspended in state of siege. Detainee may choose "voluntary" exile outside the republic.
• **Nicaragua** (1893): Civilians may not be tried in special commissions or courts-martial. State of siege decree defines scope of emergency powers and limits.

Finally, while regimes of exception permitted complete suspension of civil liberties and rights in some cases, in others they permitted suspension of certain *garantías,* often for limited periods. These temporary suspensions of civil liberties and rights fell short of constitutional dictatorship while still permitting extensive political repression and persecution of political opponents. After 1865, no Spanish American constitution lacked provisions for suspension of some civil liberties and rights; many allowed suspension of all constitutional protection of individual rights to meet designated emergencies. The list below identifies regimes of exception formally permitting the suspension of all *garantías:*

- Argentina: 1819, 1853
- Bolivia: 1834, 1843, 1851, 1868, 1878, 1880
- Chile: 1822, 1828
- Colombia: 1861, 1886
- Costa Rica: 1848, 1859
- Dominican Republic: 1844, 1854 (1, 2), 1872, 1881, 1887, 1896
- Ecuador: 1830, 1835
- El Salvador: 1883
- Guatemala: 1879
- Honduras: 1880
- Mexico: 1814, 1836
- Paraguay: 1870
- Peru: 1839
- Uruguay: 1830
- Venezuela: 1811, 1819
- Central American Federation (Nicaragua, Honduras, and El Salvador): 1898
- Gran Colombia: 1821

Below are listed the constitutional regimes of exception permitting the partial suspension of *garantías:*

- Argentina: 1819, 1826, 1853
- Bolivia: 1826, 1831, 1834, 1839, 1843, 1851, 1861, 1868, 1871, 1878, 1880
- Chile: 1818, 1822, 1823, 1828, 1833
- Colombia: 1832, 1843, 1858, 1861, 1886
- Costa Rica: 1838, 1859, 1869, 1871
- Dominican Republic: 1844, 1854 (1, 2), 1858, 1866, 1872, 1874, 1875, 1877, 1878, 1879, 1880, 1881, 1887, 1896
- Ecuador: 1830, 1835, 1843, 1845, 1851, 1852, 1861, 1869, 1878, 1884, 1897
- El Salvador: 1864, 1871, 1872, 1880, 1886
- Guatemala: 1851, 1879
- Honduras: 1839, 1873, 1880, 1894
- Mexico: 1814, 1822, 1824, 1836, 1843, 1857
- Nicaragua: 1838, 1858, 1893
- Paraguay: 1870
- Peru: 1823, 1826, 1828, 1834, 1839, 1856, 1860, 1867

- Uruguay: 1830
- Venezuela: 1811, 1819, 1830, 1857, 1858, 1864, 1874, 1881, 1891, 1893
- Central American Federation (Nicaragua, El Salvador, and Honduras): 1824, 1835, 1898
- Gran Colombia: 1821

Illustrative language in constitutions suspending enumerated civil liberties and rights appears below:

- **United States** (1787): "The privilege of the writ of habeas corpus shall not be suspended unless when in cases of rebellion or invasion the public safety may require it" (Art. 1, Sec. 8).
- **Spain** (1812): "The king may not deprive any person of liberty nor impose any punishment. . . . Only in the case when the security and welfare of the State require may the king issue orders to this effect, but only on the condition that the detainee be put at the disposition of the court or judge of the jurisdiction" (Art. 172, Sec. 11).
- **Central American Federation** (1824): "Only in the cases of tumult, rebellion, or armed attack on the constituted authorities may [the council, assemblies, or other authorities] (1) disarm the population or confiscate any type of weapon a person legally carries or has in his home; (2) impede popular meetings that have as their object honest pastimes [*placer honesto*], political conversation, or the assessment of the conduct of public officials; (3) set aside the sacred legal formalities regarding search and seizure in private homes, privacy of correspondence, and arrest and detention; (4) create special courts or commissions to try certain crimes, or for a certain class of citizens or inhabitants" (Art 176).
- **Imperial Brazil** (1824): "In the case of rebellion or enemy invasion that threatens the security of the State, a special act of the legislature may suspend for a specified time some of the formalities that guarantee civil rights and liberty [*liberdade individual*]. If the Assembly is not in session, and if the Fatherland faces imminent danger, the Government may exercise this same authority as a provisional measure, but only until the urgent necessity that motivated its use has passed" (Art. 179, Sec. 35).
- **Chile** (1833): "The congress may enact exceptional laws of a temporary nature, for no more than one year, to restrict personal liberty, of the press, and to restrict freedom of assembly, when

required by the overriding necessity of the defense of the State, or the conservation of the constitutional regime, or internal peace" (Art. 36, Sec. 6).

Efforts to tinker with provisions for regimes of exception focused on several constitutional design issues: (1) assignment of authority to determine the existence of an emergency; (2) allocation of authority to impose the regime of exception, for example, to the president, the president with council of state approval, the cabinet, the Congress, or another entity; (3) limitation on the duration of the regime of exception, and provisions for extending it; (4) definition of the territory in which the regime of exception would apply, for example, "in all the territory of the nation or any part thereof"; (5) assignment of authority to revoke, revise, or end the regime of exception; and (6) definition of the scope of extraordinary authority conferred on officials to deal with the emergency, ranging from "to take all the measures necessary," to authority only to arrest and detain certain individuals while retaining the protection of other civil liberties and rights. Also of concern were which civil liberties and rights might be suspended, the availability of administrative or judicial restraints on government authority during the regime of exception, and remedies afforded, if any, after the fact, for any abuses committed while the regime of exception prevailed.

Whittling away at the virtually unlimited extraordinary powers typical in the early nineteenth century, later constitutions often required approval by ministers, permanent commissions of the legislature, or by one or both houses of the Congress, if in session, for the imposition of exceptional regimes. By design, legislatures in most of Spanish America met infrequently. They rarely convened for more than ninety days once a year, sometimes every two years. (The exaggerated case of General Juan Flores's 1843 Ecuadorean Constitution that had the legislature convene every four years was not emulated, but at one time or another Bolivia, Chile, Colombia, Honduras, Mexico, Nicaragua, and Peru had constitutions that specified ordinary congressional sessions every two years, or less frequently.) Under these constitutional provisions, presidential exercise of exceptional authority could hardly be prevented by requiring prior legislative approval. The subsequent revocation or rectification of presidential initiative was both politically and practically more difficult. Constitutions stipulating that congress meets every two years or less frequently are listed below:

- Bolivia: 1834, 1843, 1851, 1868
- Chile: 1822
- Colombia: 1886
- Ecuador: 1835, 1843, 1861, 1869, 1878
- Honduras: 1865, 1873, 1880
- Nicaragua: 1858
- Peru: 1839

In some cases, permanent congressional commissions remained in session, with assorted duties ranging from the exercise of limited legislative authority to the oversight of the public administration and convening of extraordinary sessions of the Congress. (See table 6.) The existence of these permanent commissions provided some leverage for Congress in controlling presidential action and facilitated the convocation of extraordinary congressional sessions. Five nations—Argentina, Colombia, Mexico, Paraguay, and Uruguay— came into the twentieth century with expanded legislative sessions. At least in principle, this increased the chance that the use of regimes of exception might be, or was required to be, considered a priori by the Congress. In addition, the scope of government authority during regimes of exception might be curtailed and limits placed on their duration, subject to extension by legislative or executive action. However, no clear trend developed from more to less draconian regimes of exception or from more to less extensive executive authority.

Spanish American politics varied irregularly in the design and use of regimes of exception into the twentieth century. In Chile, the state of siege of the 1833 Constitution (which was emulated by the Dominican Republic, Argentina, and Bolivia) permitted constitutional dictatorship. It was used rarely after 1861, redefined in 1874, and subjected to expanded legislative controls until the 1891 civil war. Chile's 1925 Constitution and subsequent national security legislation again enhanced government and executive authority during regimes of exception. From 1930 to 1957, seventeen different laws and decree laws conferred extraordinary powers on the president, apart from multiple presidential state of siege decrees.[17] This pattern continued from 1958 to 1973. The 1980 Constitution imposed by the military junta headed by General Augusto Pinochet further expanded the scope of exceptional regimes.

In Colombia, the only country studied where regimes of exception were temporarily eliminated in national charters (1853, 1863), the 1886 Constitution instituted a state of siege provision that al-

TABLE 6

Constitutions with Permanent Legislative
Commissions and Their Powers

Country and Constitution	Commission Powers
Chile	
1822	O, LA, C
1828	O, LA, C
1833	O
Costa Rica	
1844	O, C
1847	LA
1848	
1871	LA
Ecuador	
1843	LA, O
Guatemala	
1879	O, C
Mexico	
1836	O, C
1843	C
1857	O, C
Paraguay	
1870	O
Peru	
1823	O, C (Senado Conservador)
1860	O
Uruguay	
1830	O, C

Note: O: Oversight only
LA: Some legislative authority
C: Power to convene extraordinary sessions

lowed virtual constitutional dictatorship. Constitutional reforms thereafter both expanded and curtailed regimes of exception but never eliminated provisions for the state of siege, which became a routine practice in Colombian politics. This remained true into the twentieth century; from 1958 to 1988, Colombian presidents exercised decree powers more than 75 percent of the time.

A new Colombian constitution adopted in 1991 reaffirmed the basic principles of regimes of exception, dedicating a lengthy section to *estados de excepción,* including the declaration of a "state of internal commotion." This declaration, requiring the approval of all cabinet ministers, allowed "the suspension of all laws incompatible with the State of Internal Commotion," albeit with some effort to limit the duration and scope of presidential authority and to protect "human rights and fundamental liberties" (Arts. 213, 214).

What did not change, regardless of debates, amendments, successive constitutions, the rise of new social movements and political parties, and the diverse ideological underpinnings for twentieth-century revolutions, was the acceptance of regimes of exception as an essential ingredient of Spanish American constitutionalism. This held for the Mexican 1917 Constitution, the 1944–1954 abortive revolution in Guatemala, the 1952 Bolivian revolution, the forging of Costa Rican liberal democracy and abolition of the armed forces after 1948, and the 1979 Nicaraguan revolution. It was taken for granted to such an extent that it transcended the clashes among conservatives, liberals, socialists, fascists, and communists. It had become a hegemonic first principle of constitution making and everyday politics.[18] In practice, no matter what constitutional limitations were put on government authority during regimes of exception, legislatures and courts found it extremely difficult to overturn decisions made for reasons of state while regimes of exception prevailed and even more difficult to constrain executive and military actions while the "emergency" persisted or was declared to exist. This meant that the acceptance of regimes of exception as a basic principle was a political threshold that, once crossed, made the subsequent protection of civil liberties and rights extraordinarily difficult.

The juridical fiction that justified regimes of exception was that the survival of society itself was threatened. When the very existence of the polity or the constitutional order was presumed at stake, it seemed implausible to restrict government initiative to save the fatherland from foreign or domestic enemies. No matter the wording of constitutional clauses, it became almost impossible to impose effective constraints on executive, legislative, and military actions during regimes of exception. In short, government action to confront emergencies justified all sorts of abuse, persecution, and repression.

Although in a few cases, such as Colombia at midcentury, presidents were "tried" for corruption and the abuse of power, no prosecutions occurred for inappropriate use of extraordinary powers during regimes of exception. Judicial protection of citizens against government action was virtually unknown in nineteenth-century Spanish America, even in cases where citizens were supposedly protected by the right of habeas corpus or the writ of *amparo*. These rights could be suspended when most needed, namely, during government exercise of emergency powers that stripped citizens of other rights and liberties. Judges depended on the executive for appointments and faced intimidation when they were not creatures of the president. This remained a weakness in systems with supposed separation of powers into the twentieth century. It was the result, in part, of a weak, executive-dominated judiciary, in part, of the lack of a legal tradition that permitted judicial review of legislative and executive decisions, despite an effort to emulate the U.S. model in a few cases (seven constitutions of the 103 studied).

The Argentine case is illustrative. Argentine judges theoretically served during "good behavior," immune from executive manipulation. In 1865 the Supreme Court had decided that a de facto government "exercised provisionally all national powers . . . with the right of the triumphant revolution, assented to by the people."[19] The courts gradually accepted broader powers for de facto governments and never overturned a state of siege declaration nor successfully resisted the authority of *golpistas.* Nevertheless, the Supreme Court was purged in 1946, 1955, 1966, 1973, and 1976, when it appeared that the full authority of new governments might be challenged.

Likewise, the impeachment of presidents occurred nowhere (though some were tried for "treason" after deposition by military coup), and rarely did effective control by Congress or the judiciary develop over ministerial action. The denunciation of abuses might serve ex post facto to legitimate ousting presidents in coups or to incite insurrection, but few politicians proposed eliminating regimes of exception once in power. Nowhere were effective restraints on government authority during regimes of exception institutionalized, though in Chile the custom of ending regimes of exception when Congress reconvened limited their duration. Unlike routine legislative controls over the executive, rejection of executive-proposed legislation, or even withholding of approval of cabinet appointments, legislative control over executive power in the case of internal commotion, threats to national security, or subversion proved largely illusory, no matter what the constitutional design for such exigencies.

This use of regimes of exception prevailed despite the supplementary powers in criminal codes to repress subversion, mayhem, and murder. Spanish criminal ordinances dating from the colonial era, and updated by nineteenth-century governments, gave broad discretion to provincial administrators, the military, and the police to deal with "bandits," "rebels," and dissidents. "Bandits," in particular, could be tried in military courts or summarily executed if they "offered resistance."[20] This authority, transferred from Spanish captains-general to provincial administrators in Ecuador, Peru, Chile, and elsewhere after independence, gave broad latitude in suppressing dissidents. (Into the twentieth century, political opponents, guerrilla fighters, most of the leaders of the Mexican revolution, and Nicaragua's nationalist hero Augusto César Sandino, for example, were labeled "bandits" by the governments they fought). The device of labeling opponents as bandits could not be used, of course, where no "crime" existed and the regime of exception served to buttress incumbent governments and to legitimate the repression of political opposition whose only offense was to be in opposition.[21] It also was not possible when regimes of exception disguised irregular succession and dictatorship in the costume of constitutionalism.

Once extraordinary powers were conferred, Vincent Ostrom's apocalyptic vision became reality:

> Those who exercise the ultimate authority to govern and simultaneously command the legitimate use of force in a society may, in their passion to do good, seek to eliminate all obstacles that stand in their way. These are the circumstances that yield the most extreme forms of oppression in human societies. Great dangers arise whenever human beings with strong convictions about the rightness of their cause are authorized to use instruments of evil to do good. The results can reach genocidal proportions.[22]

The results may be equally terrible when those who exercise unlimited sovereign authority do so in their own interest or in the interest of party, faction, religious conviction, or greed.

Spanish American caudillos and constitutional theorists understood this dilemma long before Ostrom rightly compared the Copeland formula for supporting "free world" anticommunists with the Lenin formula. The Copeland formula prohibited "all 'organized political activity not favored by the government,' and [created] an unlimited center of power [with] extensive instrumentalities for repressive action." The Lenin formula entailed "a unified leadership exercis[ing] command over a revolutionary movement in much the same manner that an autocratic imperial government exercises unity of power in its command over society."[23]

However, neither Leninism nor authoritarian capitalism nor the post-World War II cold war confrontation of superpowers was responsible for Spanish American regimes of exception and political intolerance. The national security doctrines of the Spanish American civilian and military intellectuals who created fierce dictatorships after 1964 were little more than new versions of the "just war" and "reasons of state" doctrines. Provisions for protecting the security of the state and militarizing public administration and law enforcement had been implemented in Bourbon Spain. They were updated and "constitutionalized" in nineteenth-century Spanish American provisions for regimes of exception. The immediate rationale for repression was new; the basic principles, language, methods, and consequences were familiar.

What is not clear is whether constitutional design can effectively restrain these tendencies once regimes of exception are accepted as part of the constitutional framework. This refers especially to expansive executive authority to take the measures necessary to meet emergencies, to broad delegation of legislative authority, to suspension of civil liberties and rights, to elimination of official responsibility for actions taken during exceptional regimes, and to the application of military law and courts-martial to civilians.

There is no good evidence from Spanish America that such an outcome is possible. Even the limited regime of exception provision in the U.S. Constitution regarding the suspension of habeas corpus has been abused "to save the nation," with courts unwilling to restrain executive authority during the emergency.[24] When, as in Spanish America, the authority and autonomy of courts is much weaker and the constitutional tradition of regimes of exception stronger, the effective enforcement of limitations on government authority, once the regime of exception is in place, is less likely. This has been the experience in Spanish America, Brazil, Spain, France, and Germany as well as in most of postcolonial Africa and Asia.[25]

This conclusion does not imply that all effort to define tightly and to control the application and scope of regimes of exception is futile. It does suggest that once regimes of exception, whether by decree, delegation of extraordinary powers, suspension of civil liberties and rights, or state of siege (or the equivalent with other nomenclature) are incorporated into constitutions, severe political constraints exist in enforcing limits in their implementation. Once provisions for constitutional regimes of exception exist, the difficulties in limiting government action under such provisions makes allocating authority to determine that an "emergency" exists and the

TABLE 7
Legislative Extraordinary Majorities and Regimes of Exception

Country and Year	Requirement
Peru	
1828	Two-thirds vote of both houses of Congress for concession of extraordinary powers
1834	Same as 1828
Mexico	
1843	Two-thirds vote of both houses of Congress for concession of extraordinary powers
Costa Rica	
1859	Three-fourths vote of Congress to suspend the *imperio de la constitución*
1869	Same as 1859, but limited to sixty days
1871	Same as 1869
Bolivia	
1851	Two-thirds vote of Congress to concede extraordinary powers

authority to implement, revoke, and terminate a regime of exception a critical constitutional design problem. Appeals to reasons of state, national security, and the defense of "our way of life" lead easily to the passionate exercise of government power and to tyranny.

With this in mind, a few Spanish American nineteenth-century reformers sought to require extraordinary legislative majorities to implement exceptional regimes, to limit them to sixty days, to require congressional approval for their extension, and to tightly limit executive authority during their rule. (See table 7.) Costa Rica's 1859 Constitution, for example, required a three-fourths vote in the Congress to approve the imposition of exceptional regimes and Chile, after 1874, limited the effects of state of siege to arrest and detention but without suspending other civil liberties and rights or imposing martial law.

Even these controls proved largely inadequate, mainly because executives manipulated elections, packed legislatures, and staffed the judiciary with sycophants. Unless the electoral process is fair, free, and includes effective guarantees for opposition candidates as well as a free press and independent judiciary, constitutional checks and balances cannot preclude the implementation of regimes of exception nor abuses while they endure. Contrary to Hayek's assertions, democracy is a necessary, if not sufficient, condition for the protection of civil rights and liberty. However, even when democracy is supplemented by constitutional limits and civil and criminal remedies against officials for abuses during states of emergency, regimes of exception are invitations to dictatorship and tyranny. This was the Spanish American experience throughout the nineteenth century. It remained so in the twentieth.

With legislatures packed with supporters of incumbent presidents or incoming caudillos, judges appointed (and removable) by the executive, and military officers and public officials from provincial administrators to local bosses dependent on government favors, presidentialism prevailed. When even these advantages failed to secure law and order, military intervention either buttressed the government or toppled it, almost invariably in the name of defending the constitution, meeting threats to national security, ending corruption, or ousting a government that had violated the constitution. In the latter case, the victors sought typically to justify their actions to consolidate the new government by using a regime of exception, followed by plebiscites, constitutional reform, or the adoption of a succession constitution. This pattern is illustrated, though not completely revealed, in the number of constitutions that included transitory clauses whose purpose was to legitimate the continuation in office of the incumbent or de facto president. Of the 103 national constitutions studied, eighteen had this feature, though seven of these were adopted in the Dominican Republic. This did not always indicate a military coup but frequently resulted from military influence over the constituent assembly. Sometimes this meant literally surrounding the Congress or entering with troops; at other times, intimidation sufficed. Listed below are constitutions with transitory clauses retaining the president in power:

- Bolivia: 1851, 1868, 1871, 1880
- Colombia: 1853, 1858
- Dominican Republic: 1844, 1854 (1, 2), 1875, 1877, 1881, 1887
- Ecuador: 1861
- El Salvador: 1872
- Guatemala: 1879
- Honduras: 1880
- Mexico: 1857
- Peru-Bolivia Confederation: 1836

In either case, the centrality of military force to Spanish American politics reinforced the constitution of tyranny, making violence the arbiter of government succession and political conflict more often than elections. Again, however, it was necessary to look at least in part to constitutional design and legal tradition for an explanation of the role of the military in the Spanish American nations. In most of Spanish America the military had been made a fourth branch of government.

THE MILITARY AS THE FOURTH BRANCH
OF GOVERNMENT

Military officers and military caudillos were singularly prominent in nineteenth-century Spanish American politics. This was particularly evident before the rise of modern political parties in some countries after the 1870s, but continues to be true in the last decade of the twentieth century. Violence by armed bands and the "national military" in the early nineteenth century often determined government succession and policy; development of more professional national armies after the 1880s overcame caudillismo and regional resistance to permit consolidation of national authority.[26]

The role of the military in Spanish American politics stemmed from a long Iberian tradition that frequently fused civil and military authority. This was reinforced by the Bourbon reforms in eighteenth-century Spain and Spanish America. Provincial intendants exercised centralized civil and military authority; military *fueros*, extended to colonial militias in Spanish America, made the military a privileged corporate group.

The wars of independence destroyed Spanish political authority and left the new nations without effective administrative infrastructure. The military leaders stepped naturally into this vacuum, reaffirming the privileges and jurisdiction of the armed forces conferred by the royal ordinances. This included authority over "bandits," application of *ley fuga*, and general responsibility for upholding the laws and guaranteeing "public tranquility."

Added to the Iberian tradition came constitutional definition of the role of the armed forces. The Spanish American constitution makers recognized the salience of the military; in their efforts to design new political systems they seemingly felt compelled to define a role for the armed forces. Borrowing from the French prohibitions on military participation in politics (see chapter 2), they also contradictorily supplied ample rationale for the permanent military involvement in policy making, implementation, and government succession.

Of the 103 constitutions reviewed in this study, over 80 percent directly defined the role of the armed forces, much as the powers

TABLE 8
Constitutional Role of the Armed Forces

Type of Constitutional Mission	Number of Constitutions	Percentage
Mission Stipulated in the Constitution	83	81
Includes maintaining internal order	47	46
Includes upholding laws	32	31
Includes both maintaining internal order and upholding laws	32	31
Military *fueros* recognized	84	82
Excludes military jurisdiction over civilians	23	22
Prohibits fusion of military and civil authority	22	21

Note: Constitutions may include several or all types of missions. (*N* = 103)

and duties of the president, Congress, and judiciary were constitutionally stipulated. The armed forces were not merely an instrument for national defense; they had their own constitutional status. (See table 8.)

Congress and the president might have budgetary control, influence in appointing, promoting, and retiring officers, and power to establish ordinances that governed military life, but the constitutions created the military and assigned them their duties. Despite prohibitions on deliberation and the constitutional subordination to civilian authority, broad constitutional justification also existed for military action to protect the fatherland, defend the constituted order, maintain law and order, and uphold the laws. In every constitution that assigned the armed forces the responsibility to uphold the laws, they were also given the mission of maintaining internal order. Listed below are those countries and constitutions whose armed forces had the mission of maintaining internal order and upholding the laws:

- Colombia: 1832, 1843
- Dominican Republic: 1858, 1866, 1874, 1875, 1878, 1879, 1880, 1881, 1887, 1896
- Ecuador: 1830, 1835, 1845, 1851, 1852
- El Salvador: 1864, 1871, 1872, 1880, 1883, 1886
- Honduras: 1865, 1873, 1894
- Nicaragua: 1893
- Peru: 1828, 1834, 1856, 1860, 1867

In a few cases the military even had a mandate to supervise elections, to ensure proper presidential succession and, indirectly, to guard against legislation "adopted during popular tumult." Constitutional clauses specifying that laws adopted without proper authority were "null and void," without defining who determined that this had occurred, also provided pretexts for the military "defense of the constitution" against presidential or congressional "usurpation." Constitutions that voided laws adopted under the pressure of popular tumult are listed below:

- Bolivia: 1839, 1851
- Dominican Republic: 1877, 1878, 1879, 1880, 1881, 1887, 1896
- Ecuador: 1845, 1851, 1852, 1861, 1878, 1884, 1897
- El Salvador: 1841, 1864, 1871
- Honduras: 1848, 1865, 1873, 1880
- Peru: 1834
- Venezuela: 1864, 1874, 1881, 1891, 1893
- Central American Federation (Nicaragua, Honduras, El Salvador):   1835

The following constitutions had usurpation clauses:

- Bolivia: 1871, 1878
- El Salvador: 1841, 1864, 1871, 1872
- Honduras: 1848, 1865, 1873, 1880
- Nicaragua: 1858
- Paraguay: 1870
- Peru: 1834, 1839, 1856, 1860, 1867
- Venezuela: 1811, 1864, 1874, 1881, 1891, 1893
- Central American Federation (Nicaragua, Honduras, El Salvador):   1835

Whereas the usurpation clauses may be viewed as an effort to maintain government action within constitutional limits, the ill-defined authority to enforce such clauses invited military intervention. The clauses making null and void those laws adopted under popular pressure or during "tumult" even more clearly encouraged the military to perform its constitutional mission to uphold the laws, maintain public tranquility, and defend the existing political order. Inasmuch as the military played a key political role almost everywhere in nineteenth-century Spanish America, with the notable exceptions of Colombia and Chile, it is not possible to attribute militarism to the usurpation clauses or any other particular constitutional provisions. It is suggestive, however, that the countries on the list of those in which constitutions provided that laws adopted under "popular pressure" were null and void are among those with the weakest civilian institutions: Bolivia, the Dominican Republic, Ecuador, El Salvador, Honduras, Peru, and Venezuela. In these countries caudillismo lasted longer, modern political parties developed later, and legislatures constrained executive action less than in Argentina, Chile, Uruguay, Colombia, and Costa Rica.[27]

Whether the clauses were a response or encouragement to military intervention, or both, they provided the constitutional rationale and reinforced the use of regimes of exception as routine political expedients. Testimony to this is provided by the numerous military proclamations cited that referred to constitutional duties and the defense of the fatherland when acting to oust governments, repress opponents of governments, and create new governments. Claims that governments had taken illegal actions continued to justify military coups in the twentieth century, as the examples of Brazil (1964), Chile (1973), and Argentina (1976), among many others, clearly illustrate. Again, this does not mean that without such rationale there would be no military coups in Spanish America. It only means that without such clauses no constitutional justification would exist for the military to assume the mission of "judicial review with bayonets."

Even where no usurpation clause exists, the constitutional mission of defending the constitution, upholding the laws, and assuring public tranquility provides an easy legal basis for military action. In this sense, the military does not intervene in politics, as often presumed. It carries out its constitutional task, as it understands it or claims to understand it, as an essential component of the political system—like the president, Congress, judiciary, and other constitutionally created institutions. In the words of the Supreme Command of the Armed Forces in El Salvador in 1961 (and in similar words by hundreds of military officers since the early nineteenth century): "Disassociative forces mobilized throughout the republic in a program of agitation designed to undermine and destroy the institutions of the fatherland. . . . The armed forces could do nothing less than confront the emergency and fulfill their constitutional mandate to guarantee public order and respect for law."[28]

As a fourth branch of the constitutional regime, the armed forces carried out their mission. They did not intervene in politics for they were a central, if not the central, arbiter in the political system, not merely by caprice but by constitutional design. This tradition has reasserted itself forcefully after 1964, and nowhere is it more noticeable than in Chile's 1980 constitution (see chapter 8). This constitutional mission of the armed forces has not been entirely eliminated anywhere except Costa Rica. It is an essential part of the constitution of tyranny.

Spanish Americans recognized this danger from the time of independence. They sought to limit military involvement in politics by emulating the French prohibition on "military deliberation" and restricting the fusion of military and civil authority. This last provision, incorporated in the 1830 Gran Colombian Constitution, survived the nineteenth century in Ecuador, Colombia, and Venezuela but was interpreted to mean *in normal circumstances;* that is, not during regimes of exception. In any case, military officers often served as provincial administrators, blurring the line between civil and military duties.

Efforts were also made in a number of countries to prevent subjecting civilians to military law. At the beginning of the twentieth century, however, only Costa Rica and Ecuador formally protected civilians against military law, trial by courts-martial, and summary execution when the fatherland was in danger, when internal commotion disturbed public tranquility, or when usurpation of authority by incumbent governments threatened the constitutional order. This was among the most telling debilities of Spanish American constitutions in protecting civil rights and liberties.

In further efforts to limit military participation in politics, Spanish American constitutions sometimes prohibited military officers from standing as candidates for elective office or, at least, forbade their candidacies in the territorial jurisdiction where they were stationed. While this caused some resentment, few military officers cared to serve in Congress, preferring administrative appointments, especially as provincial governors. These provisions usually failed, however, to keep officers out of the presidency; in the cases of Peru, Bolivia, El Salvador, Honduras, and Uruguay, all with prohibitions on military officers running for public office, presidents were more frequently military officers than civilians. Constitutions prohibiting active military from running for office (interpreted as any office) are listed below:

- Bolivia: 1861, 1871, 1878, 1880
- Chile: 1822
- El Salvador: 1841, 1871

- Honduras: 1848, 1865, 1873, 1880, 1894
- Mexico: 1824, 1836, 1843
- Nicaragua: 1838, 1858
- Peru: 1867
- Uruguay: 1830
- Venezuela: 1858
- Central American Federation (Nicaragua, Honduras, and El Salvador):   1898

Presidents depended on the armed forces as the bulwark of public administration, for law enforcement, management of public works, and control of political opposition. Army and national guard units also "supervised" elections and sometimes directly intimidated legislators who resisted presidential policies. The imposition of presidential successors, or a president's inability to do so, also often depended on control of key garrisons and the support of leading officers. Troops determined electoral outcomes and government longevity; they enforced, or failed to enforce, regimes of exception when imposed. Their constitutional mission of upholding the laws, defending the constitution, and maintaining internal order legitimated their roles as arbiters of national politics and as enforcers of the constitution of tyranny.

ENEMIES, SUBVERSIVES, HERETICS, AND TYRANNY

Underlying the formal constitution of tyranny is an intolerance for religious, social, and political pluralism shared by the Spanish Inquisition, Rousseau's revolutionary general will, witch burning, holy wars (whether jihad or crusade), fascism, and Stalinism. When opponents are heretics, witches, or subversives, when they are put outside the normal protection of the law that applies to persons rather than dangerous beasts, repression becomes virtue, torture a means of salvation (for the victim as well as the torturer), and murder a way of extirpating cancerous cells from threatened social organisms. When the body politic is allegedly in mortal danger from savage enemies, no countermeasures are too drastic, no defense unimaginable. As Chile's General Augusto Pinochet declared in 1975, "When confronted by communist penetration, [that] represents the destruction of the basic moral foundations from which the Western and Christian civilizations derive . . . society is under the obligation of drastic self-defense." Argentina's General Leopoldo Fortunato Galtieri agreed, proclaiming in 1980: "[given the circumstances] it was necessary for the Argentine Army and the other armed security and police forces to come together to eradicate that scourge . . . that jeopardized the very existence of the Fatherland. . . . In this country there was not, and could not have been, any violations of human rights. There was a war, an absurd war, unleashed by a treacherous and criminal barbarism." In Guatemala in 1982, General José Efraín Ríos Montt warned "the men of subversion" that they would "not be found murdered along the roadside; anyone who breaks the law will be shot, but not murdered." And in El Salvador, General Carlos Humberto Romero called on his compatriots to join him in 1979 in a "patriotic crusade" to eradicate "dissociative, subversive, and terrorist groups"[29]

Regimes of exception often serve as legal devices for legitimating this political repression. Adding a constitutional role for the military to such regimes weakens the fragile constitutional barriers devised to limit the use and abuse of constitutional dictatorship, suspension of civil liberties, and violation of fundamental human rights.[30] To overcome this legacy in Spanish America (and elsewhere) requires profound changes in fundamental political attitudes, in the premises of constitutional design, and in the role of the military in politics. It also requires a conscious celebration of tolerance that makes unthinkable, or at least unacceptable, the legal conversion of persons into enemies outside the law and without human rights. Regimes of exception, whether based on the doctrine of just war or reasons of state, tend to make the unthinkable not only thinkable but doable and to result in tyranny. This was the Spanish American experience in the nineteenth century; it has not ended as the twenty-first century nears.

Spanish American constitution makers in the nineteenth century did not resolve the dilemmas of political intolerance, the role of the military in the polity, and regimes of exception. Spanish America remains a region where the legitimacy of political pluralism is fragile, where the armed forces exercise direct and indirect control over government policy and succession, and where regimes of exception routinely justify the loss of civil rights and liberties while legalizing dictatorship. As in the nineteenth century, the resolution of these three key problems depends on changes in political attitudes; on strengthening civilian institutions, particularly political parties, legislatures, public administration, and the judicial system; and on abolishing or severely limiting regimes of exception. Without such radical changes, transitions to elected civilian governments guarantee neither democracy nor constitutional rule.

Ideological restrictions on political competition, press censorship, laws that criminalize supposed insults to government and military officials, and maintenance of the constitutional prerogatives of the armed forces are incompatible with real democratization. This cannot be overcome with managed elections and orchestrated plebiscites. The quasi-autonomy of the armed forces regarding their budgets, military laws and courts, and the appointment of branch commanders further impedes democratization. Finally, subjecting civilians to the authority of military courts or courts-martial for political offenses, including supposed threats to national security, terrorism, or the violation of arms control laws is inherently contradictory to constitutional democracy and inimical to the protection of basic civil rights and liberties. Crimes may be tried in ordinary civilian courts; the militarization of justice promotes injustice.

The foundations of constitutional dictatorship survived the nineteenth century to be the pillars of Spanish American politics as the twentieth century ends. The constitution of tyranny is intact; the consequences between 1959 and 1992 include thousands more incarcerated, tortured, "disappeared," and murdered, from the islands of the Caribbean to the highlands of Guatemala and the steppes and archipelagos of the Argentine and Chilean Patagonia.

The display of severed heads and dangling corpses in plazas and forests favored by Peruvian, Uruguayan, Argentine, Salvadoran, and Honduran caudillos in the nineteenth century has given way to corpses floating in rivers, left on the sides of roads, or dumped in mass graves in clandestine cemeteries. The rack and thumbscrews gave way to the parrot's perch and the *parrilla*.[31] What has not given way is the constitution of tyranny.

Notes

Bibliography

Index

Notes

INTRODUCTION TO PART 1

1. France's Louis XVI was executed after conviction in January 1793 by the National Convention for "conspiring against liberty and threatening the security of the State." The end of absolutism was the beginning of prosecutions for threats to national security and "defense of the [new] constitution." Louis XVI had purportedly conspired to restore absolute monarchy, thereby violating the 1791 charter of the constitutional monarchy that he had accepted and that also stipulated that the royal personage of the king was "inviolable and sacred" (Art. 2, Constitution of 3 September 1791). See Javier Valle-Riestra, *La Responsabilidad Constitucional del Jefe de Estado* (Lima: Benítez-Rivas and Montejo, 1987).

2. Alexis de Tocqueville, *Democracy in America,* ed. Philip Bradley (New York: Knopf), 1:9. Cited in Vincent Ostrom, *The Intellectual Crisis in American Public Administration,* 2d ed. (Tuscaloosa: University of Alabama Press, 1989), 69–70.

3. The precise origin of the term *caudillo* is uncertain, though it is explained as a derivation of an Arabic word meaning leader. It generally refers to strong, charismatic leaders in Spanish America and Spain. An eighteenth-century antecedent may have been the urban militia formed in Galicia in 1701. Called *caudillatos,* the militia was formed from peasant troops with the purpose of coastal defense against pirates and "enemies of the crown." Reforms gradually upgraded the status and arms of the *caudillatos,* who by 1762 were grouped in one-hundred member units (*trozos*) under the command of a sergeant major called the *caudillo principal.* See Félix Colón de Larriátegui, *Juzgados Militares de España y Sus Indias,* (Paris: Emprenta de C. Farcy, 1828), 2:462–63.

4. Cited in Arturo E. Sampay, *Las Constituciones de la Argentina (1810/1972),* 2 vols. (Buenos Aires: Editorial Universitaria, 1975), 59.

CHAPTER 1. CONSTITUTIONAL GOVERNMENT AND
REGIMES OF EXCEPTION

1. The philosophical and juridical evolution of the concept of *salus publica* as the supreme law is detailed in Pedro Cruz Villalón, *El Estado de Sitio y la Con-*

stitución: La Constitucionalización de la Protección Extraordinaria del Estado (1789–1878) (Madrid: Centro de Estudios Constitucionales, 1980). Cruz Villalón, (p. 193) provides the following text from Cicero (*De Legibus*, 3:8) as the classical Roman formulation: "Militiae summum ius habento, nemini parento: ollis salus publica suprema lex esto." In England, the most unambiguous statement of the law of necessity is by Thomas Hobbes: "It belongeth of right, to whatsoever man, or assembly that hath the sovereignty, to be judge both of the means of peace and defense, and also of the hindrances, and disturbances of the same; and to do whatsoever he shall think necessary to be done, both beforehand, and for the preserving of peace and security. . . ." *The English Works of Thomas Hobbes of Malmesbury,* comp. and ed. Sir William Molesworth (Aalen, Ger.: Scienta 1966) reprint of 1839 edition, 3:163–64. See also Giovanni Botero, *Reason of State,* trans. P. J. Waley and D. P. Waley (New Haven: Yale University Press, 1956); Friederich Meinecke, *Machiavellism: The Doctrine of Raison d'Etat and Its Place in Modern History,* trans. D. Scott (New York: Praeger, 1965). A modern treatise on "reasons of state" is Carl Friedrich, *Constitutional Reason of State: The Survival of the Constitutional Order* (Englewood Cliffs, N.J.: Prentice-Hall, 1957).

2. On the British common-law prohibition against seditious libel and the Federalist antirepublican sedition law in the United States, see Frank Maloy Anderson, "The Enforcement of the Alien and Sedition Laws," *American Historical Association Annual Report, 1912:* 115–126; John C. Miller, *Crisis in Freedom: The Alien and Sedition Laws* (Boston: Harvard University Press, 1951); Zechariah Chafee, *Free Speech in the United States* (Cambridge: Harvard University Press, 1948); James Morton Smith, *Freedom's Fetters: The Alien and Sedition Laws and American Civil Liberties* (Ithaca: Cornell University Press, 1956).

3. Cited in Clinton L. Rossiter, *Constitutional Dictatorship, Crisis Government in the Modern Democracies* (Princeton: Princeton University Press, 1948), 31.

4. Cited in Brian Loveman and Thomas M. Davies, Jr., eds., *The Politics of Antipolitics: The Military in Latin America,* 2d ed. (Lincoln: University of Nebraska Press, 1989), 281.

5. Cited in ibid., 238.

6. See Cruz Villalón, *El Estado de Sitio y la Constitución,* 127; and see A. V. Dicey, *Introduction to the Study of the Law of the Constitution* (London: Macmillan, 1924). Dicey provides a long note, "Duty of Soldiers Called Upon to Disperse an Unlawful Assembly" (512–16), in which he reviews the text of a report concerning the actions of soldiers commanded by a Captain Barker in a "riot" in 1893. The report notes, among other things, that "the question whether, on any occasion, the moment has come for firing upon a mob, depends . . . on the necessities of the case."

7. Dicey's chapter, "Nature of Parliamentary Sovereignty," cites Blackstone's *Commentaries:* "The power and jurisdiction of Parliament, says Sir Edward Coke, is so transcendent and absolute, that it cannot be confined, either for causes or persons, within any bounds. . . . It hath sovereign and uncontrollable authority in the making, confirming, enlarging, restraining, abrogating, repealing, reviving and expounding of laws, concerning matters of all possible denominations, ecclesiastical or temporal, civil, military, maritime, or criminal:

this being the place where that absolute despotic power, which must in all governments reside somewhere, is entrusted by the constitution of these kingdoms." Dicey, *Law of the Constitution,* p. 39.

8. For a detailed discussion of the concept and law of habeas corpus, see R. J. Sharpe, *The Law of Habeas Corpus* (Oxford: Oxford University Press, 1976).

9. See Juan Rebora, *El Estado de Sitio y la Ley Histórica del Desborde Institucional* (La Plata: Facultad de Ciencias Jurídicas y Sociales, 1935); Clodomiro Bravo Michell and Nissim Sharim Paz, *Restricciones a las Libertades Públicas* (Santiago: Editorial Jurídica de Chile, 1958).

10. For example, the constitution of El Salvador in 1886 provided that the cases in which a state of siege could be declared, and government authority during the "state of siege," would be determined by law. The Law of State of Siege, passed by the constituent assembly in 1886, specified that a state of siege could be declared in cases of "external war, rebellion or sedition," indicated that under the state of siege "treason, rebellion and sedition" were subject to military authority and military courts, and detailed the powers of the president, military, and other government officials during the state of siege. The Law of State of Siege thereby operationalized the constitutional articles on the state of siege.

11. Rossiter, *Constitutional Dictatorship,* chap. 2.

12. On the development of political theory regarding executive authority, sovereignty, and royal prerogative, see C. Mansfield, Jr., *Taming the Prince: The Ambivalence of Modern Executive Power* (New York: Free Press, 1989).

13. Dicey, *Law of the Constitution,* deals with this issue in terms of "flexible" versus "rigid" constitutions and compares French with British institutions (469–76). In more general terms, the issues involve distinctions between constituent versus legislative authority, the special (if any) procedure for constitutional amendment versus ordinary legislation, and the authority of ordinary legislatures to suspend, modify, or delete constitutional rules. Given Dicey's views on British parliamentarism, he is critical of the "rigidity" of French institutions, particularly since they failed "to provide any adequate means, such as those adopted by the founders of the United States, for rendering unconstitutional legislation inoperative" (475).

14. See B. O. Nwabueze, *Constitutionalism in the Emergent States* (Rutherford: Fairleigh Dickinson University Press, 1973). The author provides a number of case studies of the operation of regimes of exception in Africa and Asia in the twentieth century.

15. Bravo Michell and Sharim Paz, *Restricciones,* 122–30; Rebora, *Desborde Institucional,* 140–45.

16. On the varieties of regimes of exception, see Gregorini Clusellas, *Estado de Sitio y la Armonía en la Relación Individuo-Estado* (Buenos Aires: Ediciones DePalma, 1987); Cruz Villalón, *El Estado de Sitio y la Constitución;* Carl Friedrich, *Constitutional Government and Democracy,* rev. ed., (Boston: Ginn and Co., 1950), chap. 26, "Constitutional Dictatorship and Military Government"; Rossiter, *Constitutional Dictatorship;* Frederick M. Watkins, "The Problem of Constitutional Dictatorship," *Public Policy* 1 (1940): 324–79; Rebora, *Desborde*

Institucional. Rodrigo Borja Cevallos, *Derecho Político y Constitucional*, vol. 1 (Quito: Casa de la Cultura Ecuatoriana, 1971), divides "regimes of juridical exception" into two types: states of siege (temporary suspension of constitutional guarantees, expansion of executive authority in all or part of a nation to confront internal or external emergency) and regimes of martial law (subordination of civil authority to military authority with accompanying suspension of normal constitutional procedures, including civil rights and liberties) and provides normative discussions of each type.

17. However, even Dicey, *Law of the Constitution,* who acknowledges the "power, right, or duty of the Crown and its servants, or, in other words, the Government, to maintain public order, or in technical language, the King's peace, at whatever cost of blood or property may be in strictness necessary for that purpose" (defined as martial law) and the legitimacy of indemnity acts (the post hoc "legalization of illegality" for government officials), argues that the indemnity acts do not cover "acts of spite or extortion" or "reckless cruelty to a political prisoner, or still more certainly, the arbitrary punishment or the execution of a political prisoner" (228–33). In comparing British practice with French *droit administratif* (324–401), Dicey comments that the French system rests on two leading ideas: "that the government, and every servant of the government, possesses, as representative of the nation, a whole body of special rights, privileges, or prerogatives as against private citizens, and that the extent of these rights, privileges, or prerogatives is to be determined on principles different from the considerations which fix the legal rights and duties of one citizen towards another" and "the necessity of maintaining the so-called 'separation of powers' " which means that "the government and its officials ought (whilst acting officially) to be independent of and to a great extent free from the jurisdiction of the ordinary Courts. . . . No part of revolutionary policy or sentiment was more heartily accepted by Napoleon than the conviction that the judges must never be allowed to hamper the action of the government" (333–35).

18. See Charles Tilly, Louise Tilly, and Richard Tilly, *The Rebellious Century 1830–1930* (Cambridge: Harvard University Press, 1975). On the history of food riots and other popular demonstrations, see George Rudé, *The Crowd in History* (New York: John Wiley and Sons, 1964); M. Beloff, *Public Order and Popular Disturbances, 1660–1714* (London: Cass, 1938); F. O. Darvall, *Popular Disturbances and Public Disorder in Regency England* (New York: A. M. Kelley, 1934); E. J. Hobsbawm, *Primitive Rebels: Studies in Archaic Forms of Social Movements in the Nineteenth and Twentieth Centuries* (New York: Praeger, 1959). For a discussion of the intellectual and political challenge of organized labor to liberal regimes in Europe and Latin America and an excellent bibliography on the topic, see James O. Morris, *Elites, Intellectuals and Consensus: A Study of the Social Question and the Industrial Relations System in Chile* (Ithaca: New York State School of Industrial and Labor Relations, 1966).

19. Rossiter, *Constitutional Dictatorship,* 36–37.

20. J. J. Rousseau, *The Social Contract* (New York: Dutton, 1935), chap. 8, "Of Civil Religion." Rousseau went even further, arguing that though the government cannot compel *belief* in whatever "civil religion" is adopted, "it can

banish from the State all who fail to do so, not on grounds of impiety, but as lacking in social sense, and being incapable of sincerely loving the laws and justice, or of sacrificing, should the need arise, their lives to their duty. Any man who, after acknowledging these articles of faith, proceeds to act as though he did not believe them, is deserving of the death penalty."

21. For example, the Venezuelan 1961 Constitution authorizes the president of the republic "to dictate extraordinary economic or financial measures when required by the public interest and when such measures have been authorized by special legislation" (Art. 190, Sec. 8). Inasmuch as the Venezuelan state is responsible, according to the constitution, for a broad range of social and economic "rights" of the citizenry, economic "emergencies" may include price increases ("la indebida elevación de los precios") or, more broadly, "abusive manipulations which tend to obstruct or restrain economic freedom" (Art. 95). Other Latin American cases are discussed in later chapters.

22. See Friedrich, *Constitutional Government*, 577–88; Rossiter, *Constitutional Dictatorship*, 8–13. Rossiter notes that "the fact remains that there have been instances in the history of every free state when its rulers were forced by the intolerable exigencies of some grave national crisis to proceed to emergency actions for which there was no sanction in law, constitution or custom, and which indeed were directly contrary to all three of these foundations of constitutional democracy." Rossiter cites Abraham Lincoln on this score as follows: "Every man thinks he has a right to live and every government thinks it has a right to live. Every man when driven to the wall by a murderous assailant will override all laws to protect himself, and this is called the great right of self defense. So every government, when driven to the wall by a rebellion, will trample down a constitution before it will allow itself to be destroyed. This may not be constitutional law, but it is fact." Notwithstanding Rossiter and Abraham Lincoln, in addition to fact it is also government lawlessness and, potentially, governmental tyranny.

23. Rousseau, *Social Contract*, chap. 10.

24. Rossiter, *Constitutional Dictatorship;* Friederich, *Constitutional Government;* Clusellas, *Estado de Sitio y la Armonía;* and Cruz Villalón, *El Estado de Sitio y la Constitución*, are among the few systematic studies carried out in this area.

25. See John Lynch, *Spanish Colonial Administration, 1782–1819: The Intendant System in the Viceroyalty of the Río de la Plata* (London: Athlone, 1958), 63–68.

26. See ibid., especially chaps. 1 and 3; E. Christiansen, *The Origins of Military Power in Spain, 1800–1854* (London: Oxford University Press, 1967); Stanley Payne, *Politics and the Military in Modern Spain* (Stanford: Stanford University Press, 1967); David B. Ralston, *The Army of the Republic: The Place of the Military in the Political Evolution of France, 1871–1914* (Cambridge: MIT Press, 1967); John Whittam, *The Politics of the Italian Army, 1861–1918* (London: Croom Helm, 1977); Gordon Craig, *The Politics of the Prussian Army, 1640–1945* (New York: Oxford University Press, 1964).

27. See Christon L. Archer, *The Army in Bourbon Mexico, 1760–1810* (Albuquerque: University of New Mexico Press, 1977); Leon G. Campbell, *The Military and Society in Colonial Peru, 1750–1810* (Philadelphia: The American

Philosophical Society, 1978); Allan J. Kuethe, *Military Reform and Society in New Grenada, 1773–1808* (Gainesville: University Presses of Florida, 1978); Lyle N. McAlister, *The "Fuero Militar" in New Spain, 1764–1800* (Gainesville: University of Florida Press, 1957).

28. For the Latin American case, see Augusto Varas, ed., *La Autonomía Militar en America Latina* (Caracas: Nueva Sociedad, 1988).

29. Dicey, *Law of the Constitution*, 295–302.

30. This assumption is the outcome of at least four centuries of political struggle among monarchs, aristocrats, bourgeois elites, and the people in Europe. During hundreds of years of conflict and ideological and philosophical debate, absolute monarchy gave way to constitutional monarchy, followed by periods of very limited popular participation in politics and governance. Only after the mid- to late-nineteenth century did the principle of universal male suffrage begin to be accepted as the source of representative or plebiscitary authority. See Raymond Grew, ed., *Crises of Political Development in Europe and the United States* (Princeton: Princeton University Press, 1978), for a general framework and case studies (United Kingdom, Belgium, Scandinavia, United States, Spain and Portugal, France, Italy, Germany, Russia, and Poland). Each of the case studies discusses the problems of establishing national identity, political legitimacy, political participation, "penetration" (growth of scope and functions of state activity), and distribution (economic and social justice). While this framework is not all-inclusive, the case studies provide succinct overviews of the ideological and philosophical debates and political conflicts experienced in each of the countries treated from the feudal era into the twentieth century. The book also provides useful short bibliographies for each case.

31. See, for example, Christopher Clapham and George Philip, eds., *The Political Dilemmas of Military Regimes* (London: Croom Helm, 1985); and Nwabueze, *Constitutionalism*, especially chap. 8.

32. For overviews on this topic, see Edwin Lieuwen, *Arms and Politics in Latin America* (New York: Praeger, 1960, 1961); John J. Johnson, *The Military and Society in Latin America* (Stanford: Stanford University Press, 1964); Salvador Maria Lozada, *Las Fuerzas Armadas en la Política Hispanoaméricana* (Buenos Aires: Colección Esquemas, Editorial Columba, 1967); Loveman and Davies, *Politics of Antipolitics;* Alan Roquie, *El Estado Militar en America Latina* (Mexico, D.F.: Siglo XXI, 1984).

33. An excellent overview of provisions for regimes of exception in Spanish American constitutions in the 1980s and of the diffusion of such practices into international law and treaties concerning human rights is Felipe González Morales, Jorge Mera Figueroa, and Juan Enrique Vargas Viancos, *Protección Democrática de la Seguridad del Estado* (Santiago: Programa de Derechos Humanos, Universidad Academia de Humanismo Cristiano, 1991). See, especially, chap. 2.

34. Thus, according to Linares Quintana, forty-four articles of the Argentine Constitution of 1853 are practically identical to articles in the U.S. Constitution ("Comparison of United States and Argentine Constitutional Systems" *University of Pennsylvania Latin American Review* 97 [1948–1949]: 641–64). See,

also, J. R. Vanossi, *La Influencia de la Constitución de los Estados Unidos de Norte-américa en la Constitución de la República Argentina* (1976); and Alejandro M. Garro, "The Role of the Argentine Judiciary in Controlling Governmental Action Under a State of Siege," *Human Rights Law Journal* 4, no. 3 (1983): 311–37.

CHAPTER 2. IBERIAN ORIGINS OF SPANISH AMERICAN REGIMES OF EXCEPTION AND CIVIL-MILITARY RELATIONS

1. For the influence of Roman law and institutions on Spain and Spanish America, see William Glade, *The Latin American Economies: A Study of Their Institutional Evolution* (New York: Van Nostrand, 1969), especially chap. 2. Carlos Fuentes, *The Buried Mirror: Reflections on Spain and the New World* (Boston: Houghton Mifflin, 1992), chaps. 1–3, provides a beautifully written introduction to Spain's triculturalism, from the Iberian guerrillas resisting Rome, to the Spanish caudillos (the word is adapted from an Arab word meaning leader), the Moorish occupation, the Christian *reconquista*, the Inquisition, and the expulsion of Jews. Fuentes also brilliantly describes the "dilemmas of the Spanish character" brought to the New World after 1492: "its image of sun and shadow dividing the soul as they divide the bullring. Tolerance or intolerance? Respect for the point of view of the other, the right to criticize and inquire, or the inquisition? Ethnic mixture or racial purity? Central or local authority? Power from above or power from below? And, perhaps the question that contains them all, tradition or change? These alternatives would divide the Hispanic world, in Europe and the Americas, for many centuries" (88).

2. Recurrent dynastic wars in the 1470s among contenders for the Castilian and Portuguese crowns, motivated partly by competing claims to African colonies and outposts, resulted in the Treaty of Alcáçovas-Toledo (1479–1480). This gave the Portugese the Azores, the Madeiras, and the Cape Verde islands, "and lands towards Guinea," and gave Spain the Canaries. The papal bull *Aeterni Patris* (1481) sanctified the treaty. This was part of the legal claim of Portugal to Africa, and Spain's claim, later, to the territories discovered to the west in North and South America. See Bailey W. Diffie and George D. Winius, *Foundations of the Portuguese Empire, 1415–1580*, vol. 1 (Minneapolis: University of Minnesota Press, 1977).

3. For overviews of Spanish administration and the colonial system, see C. H. Haring, *The Spanish Empire in America* (New York: Oxford University Press, 1947); J. H. Elliot, *Imperial Spain* (New York: New American Library, 1964); Charles Gibson, *Spain in America* (New York: Harper and Row, 1966); Stanley J. Stein and Barbara H. Stein, *The Colonial Heritage of Latin America* (New York: Oxford University Press, 1970); James Lockhart and Stuart Schwartz, *Early Latin America: A History of Colonial Spanish America and Brazil* (New York: Cambridge University Press, 1983); Lyle N. McAlister, *Spain and Portugal in the New World, 1492–1700* (Minneapolis: University of Minnesota Press, 1984); Mark Burkholder and Lyman L. Johnson, *Colonial Latin America* (New York, Oxford University Press, 1990).

4. See James Lockhart, *Spanish Peru, 1532–1560* (Madison: University of Wisconsin Press, 1968).

5. *Recopilación de Leyes de los Reynos de las Indias* (Madrid: Gráficas Ultra S.A., 1943), Libro I, Título XVIII.

6. *Recopilación,* Libro III, Título III, Law XXVI.

7. Haring, *Spanish Empire.* The Bourbons relied on the military to consolidate their victory in the War of the Spanish Succession, which ended in 1713. Gradually, military officers came to play more visible and diverse roles in regional and local government, and civilians were subjected to military jurisdiction in matters ranging from "insults to military patrols" to banditry.

8. Laura Rodríguez, "The Spanish Riots of 1766," *Past and Present* 59 (May 1973): 117–46.

9. Título XVII, Ley I, De los bandidos, salteadores de caminos y facinerosos. D. Felipe IV. en Madrid por pragm. de 15 Junio y 6 de Julio de 1663. Modo de proceder contra los bandidos y salteadores que anden en quadrillas por caminos ó despoblados; Ley X, D. Carlos III. por Real decreto de 2 Abril, inserto en céd del Cons. de 5 de Mayo de 1783, y Real instruccíon de 19 Junio de [1]784 cap. 8. Pena de los bandidos contrabandistas ó salteadores que hiciesen resistencia á la Tropa destinada á perseguirlos. (*Novísima Recopilación*). This last decree made "bandits" who "resisted" subject to military justice in *consejos de guerra.* If they resisted with firearms or blades (*armas blancas*) they could be executed; otherwise, they could be imprisoned for ten years.

10. Christiansen, *Origins of Military Power,* 9.

11. For varying interpretations of independence movements in Spanish America, see John Lynch, *The Spanish-American Revolutions, 1808–1826* (New York: W. W. Norton, 1973); Richard Graham, *Independence in Latin America* (New York: Knopf, 1972); Salvador de Madariaga, *The Fall of the Spanish American Empire,* rev. ed. (New York: Collier, 1963); William Spence Robertson, *The Rise of the Spanish-American Republics: As Told in the Lives of Their Liberators* (New York: Appleton, 1918).

12. The impact of eighteenth-century philosophical and political currents in Spanish America is treated in Arthur P. Whitaker, ed., *Latin America and the Enlightenment,* 2d ed. (Ithaca: Great Seal Books, 1961); John Tate Lanning, *The Eighteenth Century Enlightenment in the University of San Carlos de Guatamala* (Ithaca: Cornell University Press, 1956).

13. Stanley G. Payne, *Politics and the Military in Modern Spain* (Stanford: Stanford University Press, 1967), 1–4.

14. On the French occupation and the extent of Spanish collaborationism, see Richard Herr, *An Historical Essay on Modern Spain* (Berkeley: University of California Press, 1974), chap. 5; Raymond Carr, *Spain 1808–1975,* 2d ed. (Oxford: Clarendon, 1982), especially chap. 3; Gabriel Lovett, *Napoleon and the Birth of Modern Spain,* 2 vols. (New York: New York University Press, 1965), especially vol. 2, chap. 13, "The Collaborators." On the Bayonne Constitution, see Carlos Sanz Cid, *La Constitución de Bayona* (Madrid, 1922).

15. Decree of January 22, 1809, cited in Herr, *An Historical Essay,* 71.

16. In discussing the Constitution of 1812 or Cádiz Constitution, I have used the version reprinted in Emilio Alvarez Lejarza, *Las Constituciones de Nic-*

aragua (Madrid: Ediciones Cultura Hispánica, 1958). Also useful are R. Verduin, ed. and trans., *Manual of Spanish Constitutions, 1808–1931* (Ypsilanti, Mich.: University Lithoprinters, 1941); Luis Sánchez Agesta, *Historia del Constitucionalismo Español*, 2d ed. (Madrid: Centro de Estudios Constitucionales, 1964). Excerpts of key provisions of the Cádiz Constitution in English appear in W. N. Hargreaves-Mawdsely, *Spain Under the Bourbons, 1700–1833: A Collection of Documents* (London: Macmillan, 1973), 238–41.

17. Herr, *An Historical Essay*, 72.

18. Carr, *Spain 1808–1975*, 97. See, also, Vicente Palacio Atard, *La España del Siglo XIX, 1808–1898* (Madrid: ESPASA-CALPE, S.A., 1978), especially chap. 2, "La Reforma Política: De la Asamblea de Bayona a las Cortes de Cádiz. La Constitución de 1812."

19. Christiansen, *Origins of Military Power*, 9. Spanish law afforded the *fuero* to soldiers in criminal matters and extended it to officers in both civil and criminal actions. Book III, Title XI, of the *Recopilación* contained regulations dating from the first decade of the seventeenth century detailing the provisions of the military *fueros*, tribunals of first and appellate jurisdiction for cases involving military personnel in particular colonies, and authorization for officers to waive their *fueros* in commercial contracts a priori.

20. Cited in Carr, *Spain 1808–1975*, 108. Palacio Atard, *La España del Siglo XIX*, 443–50, also emphasizes the inability of Napoleon to take advantage of his numerical strength due to the necessity to disperse his forces in the peninsular war against British armies and Spanish guerrillas.

21. Carr, *Spain 1808–1975*, 110.

22. Christiansen, *Origins of Military Power*, 17.

23. Decree of Valencia, 4 May 1814. Reprinted in English in Hargreaves-Mawdsley, *Spain Under the Bourbons*, 243–46.

24. Christiansen, *Origins of Military Power*, 18–21.

25. See J. L. Comellas, *Los Primeros Pronunciamientos en España 1814–1820* (Madrid, Consejo Superior de Investigaciones Científicas, Escuela de Historia Moderna, 1958); Payne, *Politics and the Military*, chap. 2, "The Era of Pronunciamientos"; J. Fontana Lazaro, *La Quiebra de la Monarquía Absoluta, 1814–1820 (La Crisis del Antiguo Régimen en España)* (Barcelona: Ediciones Ariel, 1971); Miguel Artola, *La Burguesía Revolucionaria (1808–1869)* (Madrid: Alianza Editorial, 1973), 43–57.

26. Payne ends the first paragraph of his impressive study of the military in Spanish politics with the assertion that "nearly all nineteenth-century Spanish political history is a record of the search for a viable structure of government" (*Politics and the Military,*). Much the same could be said for Latin America. See, for example, Mario Rodríguez, *The Cádiz Experiment in Central America, 1808–1826* (Berkeley: University of California Press, 1978).

27. In part this resulted from the lack of resources with which to maintain the numerous armies and guerrilla commanders produced by the "war of independence" against the French and from the inability to distribute enough patronage to satisfy all elements of the military along with the needs of civil society. See Carr, *Spain 1808–1975*, 123–26; Palacio Atard, *La España del Siglo XIX*, chap. 4.

28. Thus Christiansen (*Origins of Military Power,* 22) affirms that the "liberal" *pronunciamiento* of Colonel (soon to be General) Riego in 1820, which forced Ferdinand VII to swear allegiance to the Cádiz Constitution, proclaimed the Constitution of 1812 to give their movement respectability but "held their men together by promises of reduced service, cash bounties, retirement grants, and no America" (that is, not being sent to Spanish America to fight against the independence movements). Riego eventually became governor of Zaragoza and a member of the *cortes;* officers received pay increases; but politicization of promotions, assignments, and even the military courts severely debilitated the Spanish military establishment. Divisions between royalists and "liberals" persisted. Riego was eventually executed and other liberal officers persecuted after the French invasion of 1823 to reaffirm the rule of Ferdinand VII.

29. Herr, *An Historical Essay,* chap. 5–6; Carr, *Spain 1808–1975,* 129–46. See, also, R. Marsh Smith, *Spain: A Modern History* (Ann Arbor: University of Michigan Press, 1965), for a description of the complexity and fragility of Spanish governments from 1820 through the mid-nineteenth century; and Alberto Gil Novales, *Las Sociedades Patrióticas (1820–1823). Las Libertades de Reunión y de Expresión en el Orígen de los Partidos Políticos,* 2 vols. (Madrid: Editorial Tecnos, 1975).

30. Christiansen, *Origins of Military Power,* 24–27.

31. Carr, *Spain 1808–1975,* 124.

32. Cruz Villalón, *El Estado de Sitio y la Constitución* (notes on pp. 320–22 reprint key articles of the Law of April 17, 1821). Some members of the *cortes* presented this law as a logical *application* of late eighteenth-century royal decrees (1783–1784) regulating the punishment of bandits, smugglers, robbers, highwaymen, and their accomplices, who resisted the troops sent to capture them.

33. Cruz Villalón, *El Estado de Sitio y la Constitución,* 332.

34. The Holy Alliance joined the major monarchies of Europe in an effort to roll back the revolutionary tide of liberalism and constitutionalism. In Spain, Ferdinand VII's advisers sought to purge the liberals from the military and imprison, banish, and otherwise repress the masons, the press, and other progressive forces. See Pedro Pegenaute, *Represión Política en el Reinado de Fernando VII: Las Comisiones Militares (1824–1825),* in *Cuadernos de Trabajos de Historia,* vol. 3 (Pamplona: Universidad de Navarra, 1974); Carr, *Spain 1808–1975,* 146–51; Palacio Atard, *La España del Siglo XIX,* 152–68; Herr, *An Historical Essay,* 81. Herr suggests that "only the opposition of the French commander prevented him [Ferdinand VII] from reviving the Inquisition." Excerpt from the Treaty of Verona reprinted from Hargraves-Mawdsley, *Spain Under the Bourbons,* 256–57.

35. Manuel Tuñón de Lara, *La España del Siglo XIX (1808–1914)* (Paris: Librería Española, 1971), 63.

36. Ibid., 59.

37. Payne, *Politics and the Military,* chap. 2, surveys the *pronunciamientos* of this period.

38. See Miguel Artóla, *La España de Fernando VII*, vol. 26, of *Historia de España*, ed. R. Menéndez Pidal (Madrid: Espasa-Calpe, 1978, c. 1968.); Salvador de Madariaga, *Spain* (New York: Scribner's, 1930); Carr, *Spain 1808–1975*, 143–46; Mark J. Van Aken, *Pan-Hispanism* (Berkeley: University of California Press, 1959); Carlos A. Villanueva, *Fernando VII y los Nuevos Estados* (Paris: C. Ollendorff, 1912).

39. Lovett, *Napoleon and the Birth of Modern Spain;* Karl Marx and Friedrich Engels, *Revolution in Spain* (New York: International Publishers, 1939); William Spence Robertson, *France and Latin American Independence* (New York: Octagon, 1967).

40. The prologue to Ramiro Borja y Borja, *Las Constituciones del Ecuador* (Madrid: Ediciones Cultura Hispánica, 1951), by Manuel Fraga Iribarne includes a list ("que no pretende ser exhaustiva") of Latin American constitutions from 1811, by country (VIII–X n. 3).

41. José Pareja Paz-Soldán, *Las Constituciones del Perú* (Madrid: Ediciones Cultura Hispánica, 1954), 47 n. 98.

42. Simón Bolívar, *Proyecto de Constitución para la República Boliviana* (Lima, 1826), *Con Adiciones Manuscritas de Antonio José de Sucre* (Caracas: Cromotip, 1978).

INTRODUCTION TO PART 2

1. See John Lynch, *Spanish American Revolutions*, and "The Origins of Spanish American Independence" in *The Cambridge History of Latin America*, ed. Leslie Bethell (Cambridge: Cambridge University Press, 1985), 3:3–50; Richard Graham, *Independence in Latin America* (New York: Knopf, 1972). On Mexico and Central America, particularly, see Timothy Anna, "The Independence of Mexico and Central America" in *The Cambridge History of Latin America*, ed. Leslie Bethell (Cambridge: Cambridge University Press, 1985), 3:51–94; Michael C. Meyer and William L. Sherman, *The Course of Mexican History*, 2d ed. (New York: Oxford University Press, 1983), pt. 4; Rodríguez, *Cádiz Experiment;* Ralph L. Woodward, Jr., *Central America, A Nation Divided*, 2d ed. (New York: Oxford University Press, 1985).

2. *Reglamento Provisional Político del Imperio Mexicano* (1822); *Constitución Política de Bolivia* (1826); *Constitución Política Para la República Peruana (Constitución Vitalícia de Bolívar)*, 1826.

3. According to Fuentes, "Rousseau perhaps had the greatest influence that any single writer has ever had on the history, sensibility, and the literature of Spanish America. He represented the writers of the Enlightenment, professing new principles of social and religious organization, against the monarchy and against the church, against the divine right of kings and in favor of popular sovereignty," *Buried Mirror*, 240–41.

4. See chapter 10 for a list of the Spanish American constitutions included in this study. Jorge Guier, *Historia del Derecho* (San José, C.R.: Editorial Costa Rica, 1968), 2:1093, suggests that the "real constitutional history" of Latin

America begins with the unitarian constitution adopted in the Río de la Plata in 1819, followed by Gran Colombia (1821), Chile (1822, 1823), Imperial Brazil (1824), Mexico and Central America (1824), Peru and Bolivia (1826), Chile (1826), Río de la Plata (1826), Chile (1828), Peru (1828), and Uruguay (1830). However, on the next page Guier cites a more extensive list, beginning with the 1814 Mexican Constitution, offered by Pedro Henríquez Ureña, *Historia de la Cultura en America Hispánica*, 7th ed. (Mexico, D.F.: Fondo de Cultura Económica, 1947).

5. Cited in Alcides Argüedas, *Historia General de Bolivia, 1809–1921* (La Paz: Ediciones Puerta del Sol, 1967), 65.

6. Lynch, *Spanish American Revolutions*, 394, citing correspondence of Bolívar to Flores, 9 November 1830, *Cartas*, ix, 376.

7. José Pareja Paz-Soldán, *Derecho Constitucional Peruano*, 4th ed. (Lima: Ediciones Librería Studium, 1966), 5.

8. Heraclio Bonilla, "Peru and Bolivia from Independence to the War of the Pacific," in *The Cambridge History of Latin America*, ed. Leslie Bethell (Cambridge: Cambridge University Press, 1985), 3:558.

CHAPTER 3. REGIMES OF EXCEPTION IN MEXICO

1. Lynch, *Spanish American Revolutions*, 300–04.

2. For a discussion of the extent to which social and economic stress and popular protests contributed to the independence movement in Mexico, see Eric Van Young, *Hacienda and Market in Eighteenth-Century Mexico* (Berkeley: University of California Press, 1981).

3. Michael C. Meyer and William L. Sherman, *The Course of Mexican History*, 2d ed. (New York: Oxford University Press, 1983); Timothy Anna, *The Fall of Royal Government in Mexico City* (Lincoln: University of Nebraska Press, 1978); Brian R. Hamnett, "Royalist Counterinsurgency and the Continuity of Rebellion: Guanajuato and Michoacán, 1813–1820," *Hispanic American Historical Review* 62 (Feb. 1982): 19–48; Margaret L. Woodward, "The Spanish Army and the Loss of America, 1810–1824," *Hispanic American Historical Review* 48, no. 4 (Nov. 1968): 586–606.

4. Meyer and Sherman, *Course of Mexican History*, 288–92; Lillian E. Fisher, *The Background of the Revolution for Mexican Independence* (Gainesville: University of Florida Press, 1966); Hugh Hamill, *The Hidalgo Revolt: Prelude to Mexican Independence* (Gainesville: University of Florida Press, 1966).

5. Anna, *The Fall of the Royal Government;* Hamnett, "Royalist Counterinsurgency," 5.

6. Rodríguez, *Cádiz Experiment;* Woodward, *Central America*.

7. Reprints of these documents can be found in Felipe Tena Ramírez, *Leyes Fundamentales de Mexico (1808–1983)*, 12th ed. (Mexico, D.F.: Editorial Porrúa, S.A., 1983), 21–22, 28–31.

8. Meyer and Sherman, *Course of Mexican History*, 294. Amnesty orders appeared in 1816, 1817, and 1818—at which time almost thirty thousand amnesties had been issued (Hamnett, "Royalist Counterinsurgency," 45).

9. Meyer and Sherman, *Course of Mexican History,* 292.

10. Tena Ramírez, *Leyes Fundamentales,* 32–58. The Cádiz Constitution of 1812 is also reprinted here, 59–104.

11. Copies of the Treaty of Córdoba and Plan de Iguala can be found in ibid., 113–19.

12. Interestingly, this preceded the liberal Law of April 17 (1821) in Spain, which subjected civilians who threatened the "security of the state" to military tribunals (see chapter 2).

13. This is eight years after the official creation of state of siege provisions in Spain. See Cruz Villalón, *El Estado de Sitio y la Constitución,* 329.

14. Paul J. Vanderwood, *Disorder and Progress: Bandits, Police and Mexican Development* (Lincoln: University of Nebraska Press, 1981), 32.

15. Meyer and Sherman, *Course of Mexican History,* 324, 328–30. For a colorful description of the internal wars and personal rivalries of this period, see Lesley Byrd Simpson, *Many Mexicos* (Berkeley: University of California Press, 1964).

16. Cited in *Antología del Pensamiento Social y Político de America Latina* (Washington, D.C.: Unión Panamericana, Secretaría General de la Organización de los Estados Americanos, 1964), 242–43.

17. Ignacio Burgoa, *Las Garantías Individuales* (Mexico, D.F.: Editorial Porrúa, S.A., 1965), 109.

18. Ibid., 110.

19. Ibid., 111.

20. See Tena Ramírez, *Leyes Fundamentales,* 304–402.

21. Gloria Fuentes, *El Ejército Mexicano* (Mexico, D.F.: Grijalbo, 1983), 41.

22. Tena Ramírez, *Leyes Fundamentales,* 478–81.

23. Important sources on Mexican liberalism in the nineteenth century include Charles A. Hale, *Mexican Liberalism in the Age of Mora, 1821–1853* (New Haven: Yale University Press, 1968); Daniel Cosío Villegas, *Historia Moderna de Mexico,* 9 vols. (Mexico, D.F.: Editorial Hermes, 1955–1974); L. B. Perry, "El Modelo Liberal y la Política Práctica en la República Restaurada, 1867–1876," *Historia Mexicana* 23 (1974): 646–94; Justo Sierra, *Juárez: Su Obra y Su Tiempo* (Mexico, D.F.: Universidad Autónoma de México, 1948); Jesús Silva Herzog, *El Pensamiento Económico, Social, y Político de Mexico, 1810–1964* (Mexico, D.F.: Fondo de Cultura Económica, 1967), especially chaps. 8–11.

24. Richard Sinkin, "The Mexican Constitutional Congress, 1856–1857. A Statistical Analysis," *Hispanic American Historical Review* 53, no. 1 (Feb. 1973): 1.

25. Ibid., 7.

26. Cited in Tena Ramírez, *Leyes Fundamentales,* 681.

27. See Paul Vanderwood, "Genesis of the Rurales: Mexico's Early Struggle for Public Security," *Hispanic American Historical Review* 50, no. 2 (May 1970): 323–44. Vanderwood's article references sources for congressional debates on the extraordinary powers and controversies over abuses by the *Rurales.* Also of interest is Cosío Villegas, *Historia Moderna,* 1:368–97, and Meyer and Sherman, *Course of Mexican History,* 24.

28. Jan Bazant, *Alienation of Church Wealth in Mexico: Social and Economic Aspects of the Liberal Revolution, 1856–1875* (Cambridge: Cambridge University Press, 1971); Walter W. Scholes, *Mexican Politics During the Juárez Regime, 1855–1872* (Columbia: University of Missouri Press, 1957); Richard Sinkin, *The Mexican Reform, 1855–1876: A Study in Liberal Nation Building* (Austin, Tex.: Institute of Latin American Studies, 1979).

29. Vanderwood, *Disorder and Progress,* chap. 12.

30. Ibid., 169.

31. Ibid., 120, 171.

32. William S. Stokes, *Latin American Politics* (New York: Crowell, 1959), 392–93.

33. Burgoa, *Las Garantías Individuales,* 189.

34. Tena Ramírez, *Leyes Fundamentales,* 895.

35. Salvador Hernández, "El PRI y El Movimiento Estudiantil de 1968" (Mexico, D.F.: El Caballito 1971), 104–05; Paul Sigmund ed. *Models of Political Change in Latin America,* New York: Praeger, 1970, 38–44.

36. In 1951 a reform expanded this authority to economic emergencies, though Article 49 had previously prohibited expansion of the scope of delegated emergency powers.

37. The exception to this pattern is Cuba, partly because Cuban independence came in the twentieth century and the country lacked nineteenth-century constitutional foundations, and partly because the Cuban Revolution rejected limited government, resorting to a modified Leninist model in the 1976 Constitution.

CHAPTER 4. REGIMES OF EXCEPTION IN CENTRAL AMERICA

1. The political reforms of the Cádiz Constitution allowed for representation in the Spanish *cortes* from the colonial regions and for a system of local government (*diputación provincial*) that combined appointees of the central government (the *jefe politico* and *intendente*) with seven elected representatives of districts (*partidos*) within a province. Tensions developed over an advisory role versus a policy-making role for the *diputación provincial.* What were essentially administrative subdivisions for the Spanish became potential political centers for the Central Americans both before independence and after, thereby sowing the seeds of localism and regionalism. See Rodríguez, *Cádiz Experiment,* for a detailed treatment of these issues.

2. See ibid.; Lynch, *Spanish American Revolutions;* Woodward, *Central America;* Héctor Pérez-Brignoli, *A Brief History of Central America,* trans. Ricardo B. Sawrey and Susana Stettri de Sawrey (Berkeley: University of California Press, 1989). Though there was an independence decree from Central America in 1821, arguments continue as to whether Central American independence dates from before or after separation from the Mexican Empire.

3. See Ricardo Gallardo, *Las Constituciones de la República Federal de Centro-America,* 2 vols. (Madrid: Instituto de Estudios Políticos, 1958), for the historical background on nineteenth- and twentieth-century efforts at Central American

union. This study also reproduces the various constitutional documents seeking to create a federal republic in Central America. See also Alejandro Marure, *Bosquejo Histórico de las Revoluciones de Centroamérica, Desde 1811 Hasta 1834,* 2 vols. (Guatemala City: Ministerio de Educación Pública, 1960); Miles Wortman, *Government and Society in Central America, 1680–1840* (New York: Columbia University Press, 1982).

4. The discussion that follows in this chapter relies upon the constitutional texts reproduced in Hernán G. Peralta, *Las Constituciones de Costa Rica* (Madrid: Instituto de Estudios Políticos, 1962); Universidad Nacional Autónoma de Honduras, *Recopilación de las Constituciones de Honduras (1825–1965)* (Tegucigalpa, 1977); Alvarez Lejarza, *Las Constituciones de Nicaragua;* Ricardo Gallardo, *Las Constituciones de El Salvador,* 2 vols. (Madrid: Ediciones de Cultura Hispánica, 1961); Luis Mariñas Otero, *Las Constituciones de Guatemala* (Madrid: Instituto de Estudios Políticos, 1958).

5. Mariñas Otero, *Las Constituciones de Guatemala,* 287–88.

6. Gallardo, *Las Constituciones de El Salvador,* vol. 1.

7. Universidad Nacional Autónoma de Honduras, *Recopilación de las Constituciones de Honduras,* 201–13.

8. Alvarez Lejarza, *Las Constituciones de Nicaragua,* 365–94; Peralta, *Las Constituciones de Costa Rica,* 205–26.

9. Alvarez Lejarza, *Las Constituciones de Nicaragua,* 377.

10. Primer estatuto político de la provincia de Costa Rica, 17 Marzo, 1823; Segundo estatuto político de la provincia de Costa Rica, 16 Mayo, 1823, in Peralta, *Las Constituciones de Costa Rica,* 147–66.

11. See David Bushnell and Neil Macaulay, *The Emergence of Latin America in the Nineteenth Century* (New York: Oxford University Press, 1988), chap. 12; Bruce B. Solnick, *The West Indies and Central America to 1898* (New York: Knopf, 1970), chaps. 8–9; Ralph L. Woodward, Jr., "Central America from Independence to c. 1870," in *The Cambridge History of Latin America,* III: ed. Leslie Bethell (Cambridge: Cambridge University Press, 1985), 471–506.

12. Reprinted in Gallardo, *Las Constituciones de la República Federal de Centro-America,* 739–72.

13. See Woodward, "Central America from Independence to c. 1870," for a detailed consideration of isthmian conditions during this period. Also of value are Ciro Cardosa and Hector Pérez, *Centroamerica y la Economia Occidental (1520–1930)* (San José: EDUCA, 1977); T. L. Karnes, *The Failure of Union: Central America, 1824–1975,* rev. ed. (Tempe: Arizona State University Press, 1976).

14. On the influence of U.S federalism and European ideology in Central America, see Gallardo, *La Constituciones de la República Federal de Centro-América* 1:285–347.

15. Mariñas Otero, *Las Constituciones de Guatemala,* 119.

16. Acta en que se reforman algunos artículos de la ley constitutiva de la república, 1855, reprinted in ibid., 419–21.

17. Mariñas Otero, *Las Constituciones de Guatemala,* 150.

18. Gallardo, *Las Constituciones de El Salvador,* 1:544–99. See also Gallardo, *Las Constituciones de la República Federal de Centro-America.*

19. Solnick, *West Indies and Central America,* 137; Carlos Monge Alfaro, *Historia de Costa Rica,* 17th ed. (San José, C.R.: Librería Trejos, 1982), 196–99; Jorge Sáenz Carbonell, *El Despertar Constitucional de Costa Rica* (San José, C.R.: Libro Libre, 1985).

20. Gallardo, *Las Constituciones de El Salvador,* 2:601–27, discusses politics and constitutional reform between 1841 and 1864. In the 1864 Constitution a state of siege clause appeared for the first time in Salvadoran constitutional law.

21. Ibid., 2:356–57.

22. Ibid., 1:609.

23. For brief overviews of Honduras from independence to the 1870s, see Rubén Barahona, *Breve Historia de Honduras,* 5th ed. (Mexico, D.F.: Editorial Azteca, 1955); Latin American Bureau, *Honduras, State for Sale* (London, 1985), 17–21; William S. Stokes, *Honduras* (Madison: University of Wisconsin Press, 1950), chaps. 2 and 3.

24. Latin American Bureau, *Honduras,* 19.

25. For a summary of the relationships among Central American caudillos during this period, see Woodward, "Central America from Independence to c. 1870," 480–92.

26. Alvarez Lejarza, *Las Constituciones de Nicaragua,* 82–97.

27. Ibid., 457–530.

28. Karl Bermann, *Under the Big Stick: Nicaragua and the United States Since 1848* (Boston: South End Press, 1986), 51–102; Alvarez Lejarza, *Las Constituciones de Nicaragua,* 105.

29. Alvarez Lejarza, *Las Constituciones de Nicaragua,* 106–07. On Walker's exploits, see Woodward, "Central America From Independence to c. 1870," 136–46; William Walker, *The War in Nicaragua* (New York: Goetzel, 1860).

30. Peralta, *Las Constituciones de Costa Rica,* 281–86.

31. Saenz Carbonell, *El Despertar Constitucional,* 377–78.

32. Cited in Sáenz Carbonell, *El Despertar Constitucional,* 430, and Decreto 64, 15 October 1947, in ibid., 431.

33. Ibid., 433.

34. Ibid.

35. On this, see Decreto 3, 27 February, 1856; Decreto 9, 11 April 1856.

36. This did not mean an absence of conspiracies, rebellions, and military uprisings previously. Mercedes Muñoz Guillén estimates that, between 1821 and 1849, Costa Rica suffered fifteen military conspiracies, six rebellions, and six successful coups. *El Estado y la Abolición del Ejército, 1914–1949* (San José, C.R.: Editorial Porvenir, 1990), 23. See, also, Rafael L. Obregón, *Hechos Militares y Políticos* (Alajuela, C.R.: Museo Histórico Juan Santamaría, 1981).

37. Reform of 1871 Constitution, Article 45, implemented 26 April 1882.

CHAPTER 5. REGIMES OF EXCEPTION IN VENEZUELA, COLOMBIA, AND ECUADOR

1. For overviews of independence movements in Spanish America that include valuable material on northern South America, see Lynch, *Spanish Amer-*

ican Revolutions; Malcolm Deas, "Venezuela, Colombia and Ecuador, The First Half Century of Independence," in *The Cambridge History of Latin America,* ed. Leslie Bethell (Cambridge: Cambridge University Press, 1985), 3:507–38; David Bushnell, "The Independence of Spanish South America," in *The Cambridge History of Latin America,* ed. Leslie Bethell (Cambridge: Cambridge University Press, 1985), 3:95–156; Miguel Izard, *El Miedo a la Revolución, Lucha por la Libertad en Venezuela 1777–1830* (Madrid: Editorial Tecnos, 1979); David Bushnell, *The Santander Regime in Gran Colombia* (Newark: University of Delaware Press, 1954); Frank MacDonald Spindler, *Nineteenth Century Ecuador: An Historical Introduction* (Fairfax: George Mason University Press, 1987); Mark J. Van Aken, *King of the Night: Juan José Flores and Ecuador, 1824–1864* (Berkeley: University of California Press, 1989).

2. References to Venezuelan constitutions are to the copies reprinted in Luis Mariñas Otero, *Las Constituciones de Venezuela* (Madrid: Ediciones Cultura Hispánica, 1965). The 1811 and 1819 charters are reprinted at pp. 127–97. I have also relied in some cases on material in José Gil Fortoul, *Historia Constitucional de Venezuela,* 5th ed., 3 vols. (Caracas: Ediciones Sales, 1964).

3. Translated from Mariñas Otero, *Las Constituciones de Venezuela,* 12. Of great value for Bolívar's political thought and communication with a wide range of caudillos and personages of importance in the independence struggles is Simón Bolívar, *Obras Completas,* 3 vols. (Caracas: Ministerio de Educación Nacional de los Estados Unidos de Venezuela, n.d.).

4. See Augusto Mijares, *La Evolución Política de Venezuela 1810–1960* (Buenos Aires: Editorial Universitaria de Buenos Aires, 1967).

5. Bolívar wanted to add a fourth branch of government called the Moral Authority. While this was not accepted in Colombia and Venezuela, Bolívar continued to press this idea in later constitutional debates in Bolivia and Peru. See Banco Hipotecario de Crédito Urbano, *El Libertador y la Constitución de Angostura de 1819* (Caracas, 1970); Pedro Grases, comp., *Los Proyectos Constitucionales del Libertador* (Caracas: Ediciones Conmemorativas del Bicentenario del Natalicio del Libertador Simón Bolívar, Congreso de la República, 1983). A volume published in Caracas in 1978 under the auspices of the National Academy of History and Lagoven, S.A., included a facsimile copy of the draft constitution for Bolivia in 1826 with the notes of Bolívar's trusted colleague, Antonio José de Sucre, and a bibliographical preface by Pedro Grases. See Bolívar, *Proyecto.*

6. William Marion Gibson, *The Constitutions of Colombia* (Durham: Duke University Press, 1948), 36.

7. See Lynch, *Spanish American Revolutions,* chaps. 6–8; J. M. Siso Martínez, *Historia de Venezuela,* 9th ed. (Venezuela: Editorial Yocoima, 1967), 275–405; J. L. Salcedo-Bastardo, *Historia Fundamental de Venezuela,* 9th ed., rev. (Caracas: Universidad Central de Venezuela, 1982), 217–321; John Lombardi, *Venezuela, The Search for Order, The Dream of Progress* (New York: Oxford University Press, 1982), 133–56.

8. For an excellent treatment of the Bolivarian-Napoleonic model and its diffusion into Peru, Bolivia (1826), and Ecuador (1843), see Frank Safford, "Politics, Ideology, and Society in Post-Independence Spanish America," in *The*

Cambridge History of Latin America, ed. Leslie Bethell (Cambridge: Cambridge University Press, 1985), 3:347–421 (especially 364–70).

9. For summaries of the period 1821–1830, see Gibson, *Constitutions of Colombia;* Lynch, *Spanish American Revolutions;* Mariñas Otero, *Las Constituciones de Venezuela;* Bushnell, *Santander Regime.*

10. Mariñas Otero, *Las Constituciones de Venezuela,* 30–31.

11. Siso Martínez, *Historia de Venezuela,* 446–47; Mariñas Otero, *Las Constituciones de Venezuela,* 30–31; Bushnell, *Santander Regime,* chap. 21.

12. See Bushnell and Macaulay, *Emergence of Latin America,* 102–07; Lombardi, *Venezuela,* 157–78.

13. Siso Martínez, *Historia de Venezuela,* 481–84; Bushnell and Macaulay, *Emergence of Latin America,* 102–07; Gil Fortoul, *Historia Constitucional de Venezuela,* chap. 1.

14. Cited in Siso Martínez *Historia de Venezuela,* 526. See, also, Salcedo-Bastardo, *Historia Fundamental,* 376–82 on commotions and violence.

15. During the period 1852–1858, negotiations were ongoing among certain political leaders in Venezuela, Colombia, and Ecuador for the reestablishment of some sort of confederal union. In each case, domestic opponents of confederation offered resistance. See Gil Fortoul, *Historia Constitucional de Venezuela,* 3:243–46.

16. Cited in ibid., 126.

17. Salcedo-Bastardo, *Historia Fundamental,* 379. Gil Fortoul, *Historia Constitucional de Venezuela,* 3:136–37, quotes "the cynical remarks of Antonio Leocadio Guzmán in the 1867 Congress" in this respect: "I don't know where they got the idea that the people of Venezuela have some sort of love for the Federation, when they don't even know what the word means: this idea came from me and others who said to ourselves: given that all revolutions need a slogan and that the Valencia Convention didn't want to baptize the Constitution with the title of Federation, we invoked this idea; because if our opponents had supported Federation, we would have supported Centralism."

18. Mariñas Otero, *Las Constituciones de Venezuela,* 44–52; Siso Martínez, *Historia de Venezuela,* 597–626.

19. Communication from Santander to Alejandro Vélez, May 17, 1827, cited in Bushnell, *Santander Regime,* 357.

20. For competing interpretations of this period, see Helen Delpar, *Red Against Blue: The Liberal Party in Colombian Politics 1863–1899* (University: University of Alabama Press, 1981); Robert H. Dix, *The Politics of Colombia* (New York: Praeger, 1987), 1–30; Jorge P. Osterling, *Democracy in Colombia: Clientelist Politics and Guerrilla Warfare* (New Brunswick: Transaction, 1989), 45–72; Charles W. Berquist, *Coffee and Conflict in Colombia, 1886–1910* (Durham: Duke University Press, 1978); Agustín Cueva, *The Process of Political Domination in Ecuador,* trans. Danielle Salti (New Brunswick: Transaction, 1982).

21. Cited in Gibson, *Constitutions of Colombia,* 9. I have made some small changes in Gibson's translation for consistency with translations of the other constitutions throughout this study.

22. Ibid., 36.

23. The distinctive evolution of the Colombian national military forces is mentioned by a number of authors as partial explanation for the dominance of civilians in nineteenth-century politics. See R. Maullin, *Soldiers, Guerrillas and Politics in Colombia* (Lexington, Mass.: Lexington Books, 1973); A. P. Maingot, "Colombia," in *The Military in Latin American Socio-Political Evolution: Four Case Studies,* ed. L. N. McAlister (Washington, D.C.: Center for Research in Social Systems, 1970); 127–95; J. Mark Ruhl, *Colombia, Armed Forces and Society* (Syracuse: Maxwell School of Citizenship and Public Affairs, Syracuse University, 1980).

24. Gibson, *Constitutions of Colombia,* 136–37.

25. Cited in Dana Gardner Munro, *The Latin American Republics: A History,* 2d ed. (New York: Appleton-Century-Crofts, 1950), 358.

26. Hubert Herring, *A History of Latin America* (New York: Knopf, 1961), 504–05.

27. Delpar, *Red Against Blue,* 6–8; Gibson, *Constitutions of Colombia,* 192–94; Bushnell and Macaulay, *Emergence of Latin America,* 210–19.

28. Cited in Delpar, *Red Against Blue,* 11.

29. Osterling, *Democracy in Colombia,* 68–69.

30. Gibson, *Constitutions of Colombia,* 268–70.

31. Pablo E. Cardenas Acosta, *La Restauración Constitucional de 1867, Historia de un Contragolpe de Estado* (Tunja, Colombia: Departamento de Extensión Cultural de Boyacá, 1966), 37–40.

32. Cited in ibid., 72.

33. Decree issued 23 July 1867, reprinted in ibid., 112–13.

34. Delpar, *Red Against Blue,* chap. 5.

35. See Gustavo Peñagos, *Interpretación y Desarrollo de la Reforma Constitucional* (Bogotá, 1972); Alvaro Gómez Hurtado, *La Reforma del Artículo 121 de la Constitución. El Estado de Sitio, Debate en el Senado de la República,* vol. 1, comp. Héctor C. Samper (Bogotá: Imprenta Nacional, 1962).

36. Secretaría Jurídica de la Presidencia, *Historia de la Reforma Constitucional de 1968* (Bogotá: Imprenta Nacional, 1968).

37. Delpar, *Red Against Blue,* 143–44.

38. Cited in ibid., 155.

39. Cited in ibid., 156. See David Sowell, "The 1893 *bogotazo:* Artisans and Public Violence in Late Nineteenth-Century Bogotá," *Journal of Latin American Studies* 21, pt. 2 (May 1989): 267–82.

40. Milton Puentes, *Historia del Partido Liberal Colombiano,* 2d ed. (Bogotá: Editorial PRAG, 1961), 446.

41. *Regeneración* was the name given by Núñez and his followers to the post-1886 regime.

42. Cited in Puentes, *Historia del Partido Liberal Colombiano,* 450, 459. The cited passages barely convey the force and vitriol of the attack on the government and its personages.

43. See Germán Guzmán, *La Violencia en Colombia* (Cali, Colombia: Ediciones Progreso, 1968).

44. Munro, *Latin American Republics,* 364–65.

45. Vernon Lee Fluharty, *Dance of the Millions: Military Rule and the Social Revolution in Colombia, 1930–1956* (Pittsburgh: University of Pittsburgh Press, 1966), 110–17.

46. Spindler, *Nineteenth Century Ecuador,* 8; George I. Blanksten, *Ecuador: Constitutions and Caudillos* (Berkeley: University of California Press, 1951), chaps. 1 and 3; Herring, *History of Latin America,* 525–32.

47. See Manuel Gálvez, *Vida de Don Gabriel García Moreno,* 2d ed. (Buenos Aires: Editorial Difusión, 1942); Juan Ignacio Larrea Holguín, *La Iglesia y el Estado en el Ecuador. La Personalidad de la Iglesia en el Modus Vivendi Entre la Santa Sede y el Ecuador* (Seville: Escuela de Estudios Hispanoamericanos, 1954); Pedro Moncayo, *El Ecuador de 1825 a 1875. Sus Hombres, Sus Instituciones y Sus Leyes* (Santiago: R. Jover, 1885); Oscar Efrén Reyes, *Breve Historia General del Ecuador,* 4th ed., 2 vols. (Quito: Editorial Fray Jodocko Ricky, 1950); Julio Tobar Donoso, *La Iglesia Ecuatoriana en el Siglo XIX* (Quito: Editorial Ecuatoriana, 1934).

48. See Van Aken, *King of the Night;* Safford, "Politics, Ideology, and Society"; Deas, "Venezuela, Colombia and Ecuador"; Ralph Haskins, "Juan José Flores and the Proposed Expedition Against Ecuador, 1845–1847," *Hispanic American Historical Review* 27 (Aug. 1947): 467–95.

49. Spindler, *Nineteenth Century Ecuador,* 16–18; Borja y Borja, *Las Constituciones del Ecuador,* LXII–LXIII. The references to constitutional texts in this chapter rely upon Borja y Borja as well as Homero Izquierdo Muñoz, *Derecho Constitucional Ecuatoriano* (Quito: Editorial Universitaria, 1980); Rodrigo Jacome Moscoso, *Derecho Constitucional Ecuatoriano* (Quito: Imprenta de la Universidad Central, 1931).

50. Borja y Borja, *Las Constituciones del Ecuador,* 9–23.

51. Spindler, *Nineteenth Century Ecuador,* 26–30; Van Aken, *King of the Night,* chaps. 3–4. A fascinating treatment of the international and Ecuadorean role of Rocafuerte is found in Jaime Rodríguez, *The Emergence of Spanish America: Vicente Rocafuerte and Spanish Americanism, 1808–1832* (Berkeley: University of California Press, 1975).

52. Cited in Van Aken, *King of the Night,* 97–99.

53. Ibid., 124.

54. Potestad to first secretary of state, no. 26, Quito, 16 January 1843, in AMAE (foreign ministry) Madrid, Correspondencia, Ecuador, Legajo 1458. Cited in ibid., 187.

55. Spindler, *Nineteenth Century Ecuador,* 47.

56. Benjamín Carrión, *García Moreno, El Santo del Patíbulo* (Buenos Aires: Fondo de Cultura Económica, 1959), 437.

57. Ibid., 440.

58. Ibid., 667.

59. On García Moreno, see F. García Calderón, *Latin America, Its Rise and Progress* (London: Unwin, 1913); Richard Pattee, *García Moreno y el Ecuador de Su Tiempo,* 3d ed. (Mexico, D.F.: Editorial Jus, 1962); Friederich Hassaurek, *Four Years Among Spanish Americans* (New York: Hurd and Houghton, 1867); J. Lloyd Mecham, *Church and State in Latin America: A History of Politico-Ecclesiastical Relations* (Chapel Hill: University of North Carolina Press, 1934);

Spindler, *Nineteenth Century Ecuador*, chaps. 5–6; Curtis A. Wilgus, ed., *South American Dictators During the First Century of Independence* (New York: Russell and Russell, 1963).

60. Spindler, *Nineteenth Century Ecuador*, 84. Spindler includes a good sampling of Montalvo's biting political satire and venom. His Ph.D. thesis (Frank Macdonald Spindler, "The Political Thought of Juan Montalvo," American University, 1966) provides a detailed study of Montalvo's political thought and the dilemmas of early independence politics in Ecuador.

61. Carrión, *El Santo del Patíbulo*, 698.

62. Spindler, *Nineteenth Century Ecuador*, 84.

63. Cited in Luis Robalino Dávila, *Orígenes del Ecuador de Hoy* (Quito: Editorial Casa de la Cultura Ecuatoriana, 1966) 1:72–73.

64. Ibid., 150.

65. Spindler, *Nineteenth Century Ecuador*, 95.

66. Robalino Dávila, *Orígenes del Ecuador de Hoy*, 1:139.

67. Ibid., 132, 133.

68. Ibid., 362.

69. Ibid., 2:89–90.

70. Enrique Ayala, *Lucha Política y Orígen de los Partidos en Ecuador*, 3d ed. (Quito: Corporación Editora Nacional, 1985), 189–92.

71. Spindler, *Nineteenth Century Ecuador*, 170.

72. Ibid., 184–85.

73. David W. Schodt, *Ecuador: An Andean Enigma* (Boulder: Westview, 1987), 44–47; Linda Rodríguez, *Ecuador 1830–1940;* Oscar Efrén Reyes, *Breve Historia General del Ecuador*, 12th ed. (Quito, n.d.), 245–46.

CHAPTER 6. REGIMES OF EXCEPTION IN PERU AND BOLIVIA

1. See R. A. Humphreys and John Lynch, eds., *The Origins of the Latin American Revolutions, 1808–1826* (New York: Knopf, 1965); Lynch, *Spanish American Revolutions;* Jorge Basadre, *La Iniciación de la República. Contribución al Estudio de la Evolución Política y social del Peru*, 2 vols. (Lima: Editorial E. Rosay, 1929–1930); Basadre, *Chile, Peru y Bolivia Independientes* (Buenos Aires: Salvat Editores, 1948); Mariano Felipe Paz-Soldán, *Historia del Peru Independiente*, 4 vols. (Lima: Imprenta El Havre, 1868–1870); Frederick Pike, *The Modern History of Peru* (New York: Praeger, 1967).

2. Leon G. Campbell, *The Military and Society in Colonial Peru, 1750–1810* (Philadelphia: American Philosophical Society, 1978); Timothy E. Anna, *The Fall of Royal Government in Peru* (Lincoln: University of Nebraska Press, 1979); Carlos Daniel Valcárcel, *Túpac Amaru. Precursor de la Independencia* (Lima: Universidad Nacional Mayor de San Marcos, 1977); Boleslao Lewin, *La Rebelión de Túpac Amaru y los Orígenes de la Emancipación Americana* (Buenos Aires: Hachette, 1957); Jorge Cornejo Bouroncle, *Túpac Amaru. La Revolución Precursora de la Emancipación Continental*, 2d ed. (Cuzco: Editorial H. G. Rozas, 1963); Thomas M. Davies, Jr., *Indian Integration in Peru* (Lincoln: University of Nebraska Press, 1970).

3. See Heraclio Bonilla, "Peru and Bolivia from Independence to the War of the Pacific," in *The Cambridge History of Latin America,* ed. Leslie Bethell (Cambridge: Cambridge University Press, 1985), 3:539–82; Basadre, *Chile, Peru y Bolivia;* Pike, *Modern History.*

4. See Davies, *Indian Integration,* 4; Valcárcel, *Túpac Amaru.*

5. Anna, *Fall of Royal Government in Peru,* 238. Anna provides an excellent basic bibliography on Peruvian independence.

6. See Herbert Klein, *Bolivia: The Evolution of a Multi-Ethnic Society* (New York: Oxford University Press, 1982), 90–92.

7. Klein, *Bolivia,* chap. 4 and the bibliographic references on pp. 283–84.

8. Ibid., 96–98; Anna, *Fall of Royal Government in Peru,* 226–36.

9. Reprinted in *Constituciones Políticas del Peru, 1821–1919* (Lima: Imprenta Torres Aguirre, 1922), 27–32.

10. Basadre, *Chile, Peru y Bolivia,* 60–65; Anna, *Fall of Royal Government in Peru,* chap. 9.

11. Basadre, *Chile, Peru y Bolivia,* 61, 60.

12. This provision, along with the loss of citizenship for men "who without cause abandon their spouses, or notoriously fail to meet family obligations" bears a striking resemblance to clauses in the Costa Rican 1825 State Constitution. I have not been able to determine the manner of diffusion, if any.

13. "Todo Diputado antes de instalarse al Congreso para ejercer su cargo prestará juramento ante el Presidente del Senado en la forma siguiente: Juraís a Dios defender la Religión Católica, Apostólica, Romana, sin admitir el ejercicio de otra alguna en la República? Si, juro."

14. Reprinted in Ricardo Aranda, *La Constitución del Peru de 1860 con Sus Reformas Hasta 1915, Leyes Orgánicas, Decretos, Reglamentos y Resoluciones Referentes a Ellas Coleccionadas y Anotadas,* 2d ed. (Lima: Librería e Imprenta Gil, 1916), 245–63. This is followed by documentation on reforms in the press law during the nineteenth century.

15. José Pareja Paz-Soldán, *Las Constituciones del Peru* (Madrid: Ediciones Cultura Hispánica, 1954), 154–56.

16. Ibid., 163–68.

17. Basadre, *Chile, Peru y Bolivia,* 72.

18. Ibid., 125–36.

19. Cited in Pareja Paz-Soldán, *Derecho Constitucional Peruano,* 66.

20. Ibid., 73–74.

21. Basasdre, *Chile, Peru y Bolivia,* 143–48; Basadre, *La Iniciación de la República,* 1:276–78.

22. Cited in Basadre, *La Iniciación de la República,* 1:284–85 n. 133.

23. Basadre, *Chile, Peru y Bolivia,* 144–45; Pareja Paz-Soldán, *Las Constituciones del Peru,* 190–91.

24. Basadre, *La Iniciación de la República,* 1:305–06.

25. Illustratively, in 1857 a military unit led by a colonel invaded the constituent congress and forced its dissolution, alleging that the congress had exceeded its authority by continuing to deliberate after promulgation of the 1856 Constitution. Even after Peru's defeat by Chile in the War of the Pacific, civil-

military relations remained a central issue in the constitutional debates of 1879, 1919, and 1933. See Felipe de la Barra, *Objetivo. Palacio del Gobierno, Reseña Histórico-Cronológica de los Pronunciamientos Políticos y Militares de la Conquista a la República y que Permitieron la Ocupación del Palacio de Gobierno* (Lima: Librería Editorial Juan Mejía Baca, 1967). De la Barra lists twelve governments from 1827 to 1963 that completed their legal term without deposition.

26. See the constitutions of each of the three federated states reprinted in *1821–1919 Constituciones Políticas del Peru*, 191–200.

27. Basadre, *Chile, Peru y Bolivia*, 183–84.

28. Ibid., 183.

29. Ibid., 240.

30. Bartolemé Herrera, *Escritos y Discursos* (Lima: Librería Francesa Científica, 1929), 1:17–21.

31. Basadre, *Chile, Peru y Bolivia*, 247.

32. Pike, *Modern History of Peru*, 91–94.

33. Ibid., 102–09; Basadre, *Chile, Peru y Bolivia*, 248–51.

34. Basadre, *Chile, Peru y Bolivia*, 271; Pike, *Modern History of Peru*, 66.

35. Pike, *Modern History of Peru*, 105–08; Basadre, *Chile, Peru y Bolivia*, 279.

36. Alberto Tauro, ed., *Ramón Castilla, Ideología* (Lima: Ediciones Hora del Hombre, 1948), 53–54.

37. Pike, *Modern History of Peru*, 103–04; Basadre, *Chile, Peru y Bolivia*, 283.

38. Basadre, *Chile, Peru y Bolivia*, 283.

39. Benito Laso, *El Poder de la Fuerza y el Poder de la Ley* (Lima: Ediciones Hora del Hombre, 1947), 66–83.

40. See Pike, *Modern History of Peru*, chaps. 4 and 5, for commentary on the colorful and at times bizarre methods of control and repression used by presidents and dictators.

41. Estatuto Provisorio expedido por el jefe supremo de la República, Doctor Nicolás Piérola, el 27 de diciembre, 1879. Reprinted in *Constituciones Políticas del Peru*, 343–46.

42. Article 21. This law is reprinted in Aranda, *La Constitución del Peru de 1860*, 240–44. The Congress first passed the law in 1893. Vetoed by the president, the Congress returned it to him in 1897 for promulgation as provided in the constitution.

43. For example, in the debates over the clause permitting suspension of *garantías* by the executive in the 1933 Constitution (Art. 70), members of the constituent assembly opposing the draft charter argued that the 1919 Constitution had not permitted suspension of *garantías* and that the government "sought to legalize dictatorship and tyranny." The government majority in the assembly prevailed, insisting that "the government should count on the necessary constitutional mechanisms . . . when required by the security of the State." Luis Alarcón Quintana, *Orígen y Proceso de la Constitución de 1933, Los Debates de la Constituyente* (Lima: Editorial Científica S.R.I., 1978), 226–31.

44. Cited in Frederick Pike, *The Politics of the Miraculous in Peru* (Lincoln: University of Nebraska Press, 1986), 33.

45. Alarcón Quintana, *Orígen y Proceso;* Daniel M. Masterson, *Militarism and Politics in Latin America: Peru from Sánchez Cerro to Sendero Luminoso* (New York: Greenwood, 1991).

46. José Pareja Paz-Soldán, "Comentarios a la Constitución Nacional" (Ph.D. diss., Universidad Católica del Peru, 1959).

47. Masterson, *Militarism and Politics,* 266.

48. See the discussion on Article 231 (*Del Régimen de Excepción*) of the Peruvian 1979 Constitution in Enrique Chirinos Soto, *La Nueva Constitución al Alcance de Todos* (Lima: Editorial Andina, 1979), 258–62.

49. Cynthia McClintock, "Sendero Luminoso: Peru's Maoist Guerrillas," *Problems of Communism* 32 (Sept.–Oct. 1983): 19–34; McClintock, "Peru's Sendero Luminoso Rebellion, Origins and Trajectory," in *Power and Popular Protests: Latin American Social Movements,* ed. Susan Eckstein (Berkeley: University of California Press, 1989), 61–101.

50. Fujimori also reverted to early nineteenth-century Peruvian presidential behavior in purging the judiciary, seeking to control the entire government apparatus without restraint through patronage and emasculation of the judicial branch of government.

51. According to historian Herbert Klein, in each year from 1825 until well into the 1850s, Bolivia had a net deficit in its legal trade account that could only be met by illegal exports of silver and an active contraband trade. Klein indicates that the Bolivian economy was, if anything, in worse condition at midcentury than it had been at independence. See Klein, *Bolivia,* 125; see, also, Herbert S. Klein, *Parties and Political Change in Bolivia, 1880–1952* (Cambridge: Cambridge University Press, 1969), especially chap. 1.

52. Klein, *Bolivia,* 4–5.

53. See Erwin P. Greishaber, "Survival of Indian Communities in Nineteenth-Century Bolivia: A Regional Comparison," *Journal of Latin American Studies* 8, no. 2 (1980): 233–69; Greishaber, "Survival of Indian Communities in Nineteenth Century Bolivia (Ph.D. diss., University of North Carolina, 1977); Bonilla, "Peru and Bolivia from Independence," 539–82.

54. Ciro Félix Trigo, *Las Constituciones de Bolivia* (Madrid: Instituto de Estudios Políticos, 1958), 38–63.

55. For a list of Bolivia's presidents in the nineteenth century, see ibid., 533–35.

56. Augusto Guzmán, *Historia de Bolivia,* 2d ed. (La Paz-Cochabamba: Ediciones los Amigos del Libro, 1973), 137.

57. A brief synopsis of the economic and class underpinnings of caudillo politics is provided in James Dunkerley, *Orígenes del Poder Militar en Bolivia. Historia del Ejército 1879–1935* (La Paz, Bolivia: Quipus, 1978), chap. 1. Dunkerley includes a very useful bibliography on nineteenth-century Bolivia.

58. Klein, *Bolivia,* 123–35; Bonilla, "Peru and Bolivia from Independence," 576–81; Dunkerley, *Orígenes del Poder Militar,* 18–20; A. Mitre, "The Economic and Social Structure of Silver Mining in Nineteenth Century Bolivia" (Ph.D. diss., Columbia University, 1977).

59. Trigo, *Las Constituciones de Bolivia,* xx.

60. *Decreto de 9 Febrero de 1825,* reprinted in ibid., 157–58.
61. *Mensaje,* in ibid., 168.
62. Ibid.
63. Basadre, *Chile, Peru, y Bolivia,* 86–87, 135.
64. Cited in ibid., 135.
65. Alcides Argüedas, *Historia General de Bolivia (El Proceso de Nacionalidad) 1809–1921* (La Paz: Ediciones Puerta del Sol, 1967), 95.
66. Basadre, *Chile, Peru y Bolivia,* 143–46, 164.
67. Ibid., 191.
68. Trigo, *Las Constituciones de Bolivia,* 90–93.
69. Dunkerley, *Orígenes del Poder Militar,* chap. 1. For related material on Peru, see Paul Gootenberg, "North-South: Trade Policy, Regionalism and *Caudillismo* in Post-Independence Peru," *Journal of Latin American Studies* 23, part 2 (May 1991): 273–308.
70. Reform efforts to further restrict presidential "extraordinary powers" failed in 1848. Trigo, *Las Constituciones de Bolivia,* 91–92.
71. Basadre, *Chile, Peru y Bolivia,* 315.
72. Ibid., 368–69.
73. Ibid., 317; Argüedas, *Historia General de Bolivia,* 179.
74. Argüedas, *Historia General de Bolivia,* 180–81.
75. Ibid., 178.
76. Ibid., 181.
77. Ibid., 187.
78. Ibid., 192.
79. Basadre, *Chile, Peru y Bolivia,* 323.
80. Argüedas, *Historia General de Bolivia,* 202.
81. Basadre, *Chile, Peru y Bolivia,* 326–31.
82. Ibid., 326–29.
83. Argüedas, *Historia General de Bolivia,* 244–47; Basadre, *Chile, Peru y Bolivia,* 365–74.
84. Basadre, *Chile, Peru y Bolivia,* 366–67. See Tomás O'Connor d'Arlach, *Dichos y Hechos del General Melgarejo* (La Paz: Ediciones Puerta del Sol, n.d.).
85. Cited in ibid., 29.
86. Guzmán, *Historia de Bolivia,* 143–45.
87. For a short synopsis of Melgarejo's economic policies, see Klein, *Bolivia,* 135–41.
88. Cited in Basadre, *Chile, Peru y Bolivia,* 372.
89. Ibid., 375–76.
90. Ibid., 375.
91. Trigo, *Las Constituciones de Bolivia,* 102.
92. Ibid., 103–04.
93. Argüedas, *Historia General de Bolivia,* 319.
94. Cited in Basadre, *Chile, Peru y Bolivia,* 380.
95. Klein, *Bolivia,* 141–45.
96. Brian Loveman, *Chile: The Legacy of Hispanic Capitalism,* 2d ed. (New York: Oxford University Press, 1988), 167–71.

97. Cited in Trigo, *Las Constituciones de Bolivia*, 107–08.

98. Federico Díez de Medina, *Breves Reflexiones Acerca del Principio Federativo y Sobre el Orígen de Nuestras Guerras Civiles* (La Paz: Imprenta de la Unión Americana, 1871). Cited in Trigo, *Las Constituciones de Bolivia*, 109.

99. Basadre, *Chile, Peru y Bolivia*, 380–83.

100. Cited in Argüedas, *Historia General de Bolivia*, 325–26.

101. See Basadre, *Chile, Peru y Bolivia*, 383–89; Argüedas, *Historia General de Bolivia*, 344–56.

102. Cited in Argüedas, *Historia General de Bolivia*, 368.

103. Ibid., 370.

104. Loveman, *Chile*, 167–73.

105. Basadre, *Chile, Peru y Bolivia*, 477–88.

106. Klein, *Bolivia*, chap. 6; Klein, *Parties and Political Change*, pass.

107. Basadre, *Chile, Peru y Bolivia*, 586–607; Klein, *Bolivia*, 159–83.

108. Basadre, *Chile, Peru y Bolivia*, 603–05.

109. Klein, *Bolivia*, 172–73. Munro, *Latin American Republics*, comments on the Saavedra government: "Constitutional guarantees were suspended under the so-called 'state of siege' during the greater part of his term, and there was little freedom of the press" (274).

110. Basadre, *Chile, Peru y Bolivia*, 658–60.

111. Cited in Cornelius H. Zondag, "Bolivia's 1952 Revolution, Initial Impact and U.S. Involvement," in *Modern Day Bolivia: Legacy of the Revolution and Prospects for the Future*, ed. Jerry R. Ladman (Tempe, Ariz.: Center for Latin American Studies, 1982), 37.

112. Cited in Gonzalo Molina, "El Estado de Sitio en Bolivia," in *Estados de Emergencia en la Región Andina*, ed. Diego García-Sayán (Lima: Comisión Andina de Juristas, 1987), 168.

CHAPTER 7. REGIMES OF EXCEPTION IN ARGENTINA, URUGUAY, AND PARAGUAY

1. For discussions of constitutional and political evolution during this period, with copies of key decrees, interprovincial pacts, and constitutional debates, see Arturo E. Sampay, *Las Constituciones de la Argentina (1810/1972)*, 2 vols. (Buenos Aires: Editorial Universitaria de Buenos Aires, 1975); Alfredo Galletti, *Historia Constitucional Argentina*, 2 vols. (La Plata: Editora Platense, 1972); Emilio Ravignani, *Historia Constitucional de la República Argentina*, 3 vols. (Buenos Aires: Casa Jacobo Peuser, 1926); *Documentos Relativos a la Organización Constitucional de la República Argentina*, 2 vols. (Buenos Aires: Facultad de Filosofía y Letras, 1911).

2. A brief constitutional history and official versions of the amendments are found in Ciro Félix Trigo, "Introduction," *Constitución de la Nación Argentina* (Buenos Aires: Ediciones DePalma, 1971).

3. For background to the independence movements in English, see James R. Scobie, *Argentina: A City and a Nation*, 2d ed. (New York: Oxford University Press, 1974); David Rock, *Argentina, 1516–1987* (Berkeley: University of Cali-

fornia Press, 1987); Ricardo Levene, *A History of Argentina*, trans. William Spence Robertson (Chapel Hill: University of North Carolina Press, 1937); John Lynch, "The River Plate Republics from Independence to the Paraguayan War," in *The Cambridge History of Latin America*, ed. Leslie Bethell (Cambridge: Cambridge University Press, 1985), 3:615–76.

4. Galletti, *Historia Constitucional Argentina*, 175–77; Lynch, *Spanish American Revolutions*, 40–44.

5. A summary of the governments during this period appears in Levene, *History of Argentina*, and Ravignani, *Historia Constitucional*.

6. Scobie, *Argentina*.

7. On Moreno's political ideas, see Galletti, *Historia Constitucional Argentina*, 216–24; José Luis Romero, *A History of Argentine Political Thought* (Stanford: Stanford University Press, 1963), chap. 3; Nicolas Shumway, *The Invention of Argentina* (Berkeley: University of California Press, 1991), chap. 2.

8. Luis Alberto Romero, *Los Golpes Militares, 1812–1955* (Buenos Aires: Carlos Pérez Editor S.A., 1969, 7.

9. For treatments of the independence movements, social implications of the conflicts, and political divisions among independence forces from 1810 to 1825, see Klein, *Bolivia*, chap. 4; Rock, *Argentina*, chap. 3; Tulio Halperín-Donghi, *Politics, Economics, and Society in Argentina in the Revolutionary Period*, trans. Richard Southern (Cambridge: Cambridge University Press, 1975).

10. Shumway, *Invention of Argentina*, chap. 2. On the "dirty war," see Donald C. Hodges, *Argentina's 'Dirty War'* (Austin: University of Texas Press, 1991).

11. Manifiesto de la Junta con motivo de la conspiración de Córdoba, cited in Galletti, *Historia Constitucional Argentina*, 1:223.

12. Ibid., 240; Rock, *Argentina*, 82–83.

13. Decreto de seguridad individual y de libertad de imprenta. Cited in Galletti, *Historia Constitucional Argentina*, 1:246–47, and reprinted 1:569–72.

14. Cited in ibid., 246–47.

15. Decreto de seguridad individual, 23 November 1811. Reprinted in ibid., 571–72; see also Sampay, *Las Constituciones de la Argentina*, 120–21.

16. Creación de un Gobierno Provisorio. Reprinted in Galletti, *Historia Constitucional Argentina*, 1:573–74.

17. Reprinted in Sampay, *Las Constituciones de la Argentina*, 144–45.

18. Ibid., 146.

19. Galletti, *Historia Constitucional Argentina*, 1:323.

20. Ibid., 326.

21. Acta por la cual el Cabildo resume provisoriamente la autoridad soberana (hoja suelta). Reproduced in *Registro Nacional* (1815), 305–06, and cited in Galleti, *Historia Constitucional Argentina*, 1:328.

22. Sampay, *Las Constituciones de la Argentina*, 211–32.

23. Levene, *History of Argentina*, 292; Lynch, *Spanish American Revolutions*, 66–68.

24. Estatuto provisional para la dirección y administración del estado dado por la junta de observación, 5 May 1815. Reprinted in Sampay, *Las Constituciones de la Argentina*, 211–32.

25. Creación del triunvirato y de la junta conservadora, 23 September, 1811; Proyecto de constitución de la sociedad patriótica para las Provincias Unidas del Río de la Plata en la América del Sur, 1813; Proyecto de constitución para las provincias de la plata, formado por una comisión especial designada por el segundo triunvirato, 1813. Reprinted in ibid., 107, 177, 191.

26. Russell H. Fitzgibbon, *Uruguay: Portrait of a Democracy* (New Brunswick: Rutgers University Press, 1954).

27. Rock, *Argentina*, 95–96; H. S. Ferns, *Britain and Argentina in the Nineteenth Century* (London: Clarendon, 1960).

28. Rock, *Argentina*, 92–94.

29. Galletti, *Historia Constitucional Argentina*, 1:387.

30. On the origins of the junta, see ibid., 432.

31. Ibid., 410–11.

32. Ibid., 434.

33. Reprinted in ibid., 401–03.

34. Bartolomé Mitre, *Historia de Belgrano* (Buenos Aires, 1902), 4:124–25.

35. Sampay, *Las Constituciones de la Argentina*, 29 n. 134.

36. Juan P. Ramos, *El Derecho Público de las Provincias Argentinas*, 3 vols. (Buenos Aires: Facultad de Derecho y Ciencias Sociales, Universidad de Buenos Aires, 1914–1916).

37. Rock, *Argentina*, 97.

38. See Galletti, *Historia Constitucional Argentina*, 1:398, 399–408; Sampay, *Las constituciones de la Argentina*, 27–34, 327–31, for provincial pacts and the Confederal Pact of 1831.

39. On these reforms, see Galletti, *Historia Constitucional Argentina*, 1:482–89; Rock, *Argentina*, 98.

40. Galletti, *Historia Constitutional Argentina*, 1:492–522.

41. Ibid., 2:46–47.

42. See Miron Burgin, *The Economic Aspects of Argentine Federalism, 1820–1852* (Cambridge: Harvard University Press, 1946).

43. Nota confidencial de S.E. el Sr. Gobernador de la Provincia de Buenos Ayres al Sr. General Quiroga, 3 February 1831. Reprinted in Sampay, *Las Constituciones de la Argentina*, 330–31.

44. Levene, *History of Argentina*, 404, emphasis added.

45. For discussion of the debates over the *facultades extraordinarias* for Rosas and in the provinces, see Enrique M. Barba, *Unitarismo, Federalismo, Rosismo* (Buenos Aires: Ediciones Pannedille, 1972), chap. 7; Víctor Tau Anzoátegui, "Las Facultades Extraordinarias y la Suma del Poder Público en el Derecho Provincial Argentino (1820–1853)," *Revista del Instituto de Historia de Derecho* 12 (1961): 66–105; Ricardo Zorraquin Becu, *El Federalismo Argentino*, 2d ed. (Buenos Aires: La Facultad, 1953), chaps. 1–2.

46. Galletti, *Historia Constitucional Argentina*, 2:249–50.

47. Ibid., 258.

48. Rock, *Argentina*, 106–13; John Lynch, *Argentine Dictator Juan Manuel de Rosas, 1829–1852* (Oxford: Clarendon, 1981), especially chaps. 5 and 6; Er-

nesto Palacio, *Historia de la Argentina,* 5th ed. (Buenos Aires: A. Peña Lillo, 1968), 1:48, 334–56.

49. Galletti, *Historia Constitucional Argentina,* 2:260.

50. Lynch, "River Plate Republics," 3:643–44.

51. A list of the major rebellions against Rosas is found in Levene, *History of Argentina,* 416–22; Lynch, *Argentine Dictator,* chap. 6.

52. Levene, *History of Argentina,* 440.

53. L. A. Romero, *Los Golpes Militares,* 70.

54. Cited in James R. Scobie, *La Lucha por la Consolidación de la Nacionalidad Argentina, 1852–1862* (Buenos Aires: Hachette, 1964), 44–45.

55. For proclamations and letters of the military leaders, see L. A. Romero, *Los Golpes Militares,* 69–84.

56. Juan Bautista Alberdi, *Bases y Puntos de Partida para la Organización Política de la República Argentina,* 5th ed. (Buenos Aires: Rosso, 1960).

57. On Alberdi's political ideas, see Shumway, *Invention of Argentina,* chap. 7; Galletti, *Historia Constitucional Argentina,* 2:337–59.

58. Cited in Galletti, *Historia Constitucional Argentina,* 2:355–56.

59. Cited in Shumway, *Invention of Argentina,* 153.

60. Cited in Sampay, *Las Constituciones de la Argentina,* 59.

61. Justo Arosemena, *Estudios Constitucionales Sobre los Gobiernos de la América Latina* (Paris: Librería Española i Americana de E. Denne, 1878), 1:183.

62. Alejandro M. Garro, "The Role of the Argentine Judiciary in Controlling Governmental Action Under a State of Siege," *Human Rights Law Journal* 4, no. 3 (1983): 324.

63. Ibid., 319.

64. Ambrosio Romero Carranza, Alberto Rodríguez Varela, and Eduardo Ventura Flores Pirán, *Historia Política de la Argentina,* 3 vols. (Buenos Aires: Ediciones Pannedille, 1975). Volume 3 discusses the numerous provincial disturbances and the use of the "intervention" and state of siege authority by Mitre and Sarmiento. See, for example, "El Ministro del Interior encarga al Governador de Entre Ríos que, usando de las facultades del estado de sitio, haga cesar la aparición de varios diarios enterrianos que hacen propaganda subversiva en contra del Gobierno National (1867)"; "Decreto del Presidente de la Cámara Legislativa de Entre Ríos, declarando en estado de sitio la provincia, por authorización del Presidente de la República," (1874) in *Documentos Relativos,* 2:153, 245.

65. L. A. Romero, *Los Golpes Militaros,* 90.

66. Cited in ibid., 94–96.

67. Cited in Loveman and Davies, *Politics of Antipolitics,* 199–200.

68. Romero Carranza et al., *Historia Política,* chaps. 5, 6; Rock, *Argentina,* chap. 5.

69. Romero Carranza et al., 3:383–85.

70. Cited in Frederick Nunn, *Yesterday's Soldiers: European Military Professionalism in South America, 1890–1940* (Lincoln: University of Nebraska Press, 1983), 123.

71. Rock, *Argentina,* 130–31. For overviews of socioeconomic development during these years, see Galletti, *Historia Constitucional Argentina,* 2:659–70; Rock, *Argentina,* 131–72.

72. Garro, "Role of the Argentine Judiciary," 319.

73. For a discussion of these decrees, see Frederick E. Snyder, "State of Siege and Rule of Law in Argentina: The Politics and Rhetoric of Vindication," *Lawyer of the Americas* 15, no. 3 (1984): 503–20.

74. For a fierce justification of the dirty war, see Osiris G. Villegas, *Testimonio de un Alegato* (Buenos Aires: n.p., 1990).

75. See Washington Reyes Abadie, *Crónica General del Uruguay,* 3 vols. (Montevideo: Ediciones de la Banda Oriental, n.d.); Lynch, *Spanish American Revolutions; Alberto Zum Felde, Proceso Histórico del Uruguay,* 5th ed. (Montevideo: Arca, 1967), chaps. 1–2.

76. Ravignani, *Historia Constitucional,* 3:377–83.

77. For sources on independence movements in Uruguay, see Héctor Gros Espiell, *Las Constituciones del Uruguay* (Madrid: Ediciones Cultura Hispánica, 1956), 9–48; Lynch, *Spanish American Revolutions,* 88–104.

78. See Zum Felde, *Proceso Histórico,* chaps. 4–5; Juan E. Pivel Devoto, *Historia de los Partidos Políticos,* 2 vols. (Montevideo: Garcia & Cia., 1942).

79. Héctor Gros Espiell, *La Formación del Ideario Artiguista* (Montevideo, Garcia & Cia., 1951), 18; Gros Espiell, *Las Constituciones del Uruguay,* 13; Emilio Ravignani, *La Participación de Artigas en la Génesis del Federalismo Rioplatense* (Buenos Aires, 1939).

80. For a discussion of these instructions and the rejection of the Uruguayan delegates, see Ravignani, *Historia Constitucional,* 1:216–39.

81. Gros Espiell, *Las Constituciones del Uruguay,* 21–23.

82. Alfredo Castellanos, *La Cisplatina, la Independencia, y la República Caudillesca 1820–1838,* 3 vols. (Montevideo: Ediciones de la Banda Oriental, 1974), 3, 56.

83. David Bushnell, *Reform and Reaction in the Platine Provinces, 1810–1852,* (Gainesville: University of Florida Monograph, No. 69, University Presses of Florida, 1983), 134–35.

84. Ravignani, *Historia Constitucional,* 3:360, reprints the decree creating the provisional government. "Sobre organización del gobierno provisorio—Sus deberes y facultades."

85. Gros Espiell, *Las Constituciones del Uruguay,* 37; *Actas de la Asamblea General Constituyente y Legislativa del Estado,* 3 vols. (Montevideo, 1896).

86. Gros Espiell, *Las Constituciones del Uruguay,* 39; Francisco Bauza, *Estudios Constitucionales* (Montevideo: La Librería Nacional, 1887).

87. Bushnell, *Reform and Reaction,* 69; *Actas de la H. Cámara de Representantes,* 6 vols. (Montevideo, 1905–1908), 3, 83.

88. Justino E. Jiménez de Arechaga, *El Poder Ejecutivo y Sus Ministros,* 2 vols. (Montevideo: A. Barreiro y Ramos, 1913), 2:114.

89. Ibid.

90. Ibid., 118.

91. Ibid., 131–38.

92. Ibid., 139.

93. The text of this proposed law is reprinted in ibid., 140–42.

94. See the debates in República Oriental del Uruguay, Ministerio del Interior, *Ley de Orden Público. Suspensión de la Seguridad Individual y Estado de Guerra Interna* (Montevideo, 1972). For discussion of the jurisprudencial history regarding *medidas prontas de seguridad,* suspension of civil liberties and rights, and military jurisdiction over civilians, see León Cortinas Peláez, *Poder Ejecutivo y Función Jurisdiccional* (Mexico, D.F.: Universidad Autónoma de Mexico, 1982), 60–68, 142–46.

95. Zum Felde, *Proceso Histórico,* 131.

96. Ibid., 156–61.

97. José Pedro Barrán and Benjamín Nahum, *Historia Rural del Uruguay Moderno,* 3 vols. (Montevideo: Ediciones de la Banda Oriental, 1967, 1971), vol. 7, pt. 7, 44–57.

98. Charles Kolinski, *Independence or Death: The Story of the Paraguayan War* (Gainesville: University of Florida Press, 1965), 13.

99. See John Hoyt Williams, *The Rise and Fall of the Paraguayan Republic, 1800–1870* (Austin, Tex.: Institute of Latin American Studies, 1979), chaps. 12–13.

100. Barrán and Nahum, *Historia Rural,* vol. 1, pt. 1, 499–516.

101. Cited in ibid., 410.

102. Ibid., 486–87.

103. Zum Felde, *Proceso Historico,* 201–03.

104. Ibid., 203.

105. Ibid., 208.

106. Barrán and Nahum, *Historia Rural,* vol. 1, pt. 1, 487–98.

107. Cited in Munro, *Latin American Republics,* 204.

108. Cited in *Ley de Orden Público,* 135.

109. Ibid.

110. For a detailed treatment of the socioeconomic changes, especially in the rural sector, that underlay political change, see Barrán and Nahum, *Historia Rural,* vol. 2.

111. Munro, *Latin American Republics,* 205.

112. Zum Felde, *Proceso Historico,* 209.

113. An interesting study of Batlle y Ordóñez's role in Uruguayan politics is Milton I. Vanger, *The Model Country: José Batlle y Ordóñez of Uruguay, 1907–1915* (Hanover, University Press of New England, 1980).

114. Gros Espiell, *Las Constituciones del Uruguay,* 60.

115. See the debates in *Ley de Orden Público.*

116. Ibid., 122–23.

117. See Germán W. Rama, *La Democracia en Uruguay* (Buenos Aires: Cuadernos de Rial, 1987), 163–78; Juan Rial, "Los Militares en Tanto 'Partido Político Sustituto' Frente a la Redemocratización en Uruguay," in *La Autonomía Militar en América Latina,* ed. Augusto Varas (Caracas: Nueva Sociedad, 1988), 197–229; Latin Amerian Bureau, *Uruguay: Generals Rule* (London, 1980); Charles Guy Gillespie, *Negotiating Democracy, Politicians and Generals in Uruguay*

(Cambridge: Cambridge University Press, 1991). In chapter 3, Gillespie details the sequence of the repressive measures—President Gestido's ban on the socialists (1967), Pacheco's rule by emergency decree, curbs on the press and anti-terrorism measures (1969), the suspension of habeas corpus (1971), and the declaration of internal war—that preceded the Law of State Security and Public Order, subjecting civilians to military tribunals.

118. For the administrative development of Paraguay in the eighteenth century and the Paraguayan independence movement, see Lynch, *Spanish Colonial Administration*, 104–17; Williams, *Rise and Fall*, chap 1.

119. Cited in Williams, *Rise and Fall*, 48.

120. Cited in Lynch, *Spanish Colonial Administration*, 112.

121. See, for example, the highly laudatory treatment of Francia in E. Bradford Burns, *The Poverty of Progress: Latin America in the Nineteenth Century* (Berkeley: University of California Press, 1980), 128–30.

122. Richard Alan White, *Paraguay's Autonomous Revolution, 1810–1840* (Albuquerque: University of New Mexico Press, 1978), 120–21.

123. Williams, *Rise and Fall*, chaps. 4 and 5.

124. Ibid., 89.

125. Cited in ibid., 101.

126. Ibid., 102.

127. Arosemena, *Estudios Constitucionales*, 1:290.

128. See Kolinski, *Independence or Death;* B. Capdevielle and C. Oxibar, *Historia del Paraguay* (Asunción: Colegio de San José, n.d.), chaps. 9, 10; Rodolfo Ortega Peña and Eduardo L. Duhalde, *Mariscal Francisco Solano López, Pensamiento Político* (Buenos Aires: Editorial Sudestada, 1969), 144–214.

129. For the first thirty years after the war, see Harris Gaylord Warren, *Rebirth of the Paraguayan Republic: The First Colorado Era, 1878–1904* (Pittsburgh: University of Pittsburgh Press, 1985).

130. Cited in ibid., 52.

CHAPTER 8. REGIMES OF EXCEPTION IN CHILE

1. See Simon Collier, *Ideas and Politics of Chilean Independence, 1801–1833* (Cambridge: Cambridge University Press, 1967); Lynch, *Spanish Colonial Administration*, 127–49; Brian Loveman, *Chile: The Legacy of Hispanic Capitalism*, 2d ed. (New York: Oxford University Press, 1988), chap. 4; Basadre, *Chile, Peru y Bolivia*, chap. 1.

2. Julio Heise González, *150 Años de Evolución Institucional* (Santiago: Editorial Andrés Bello, 1960), 45.

3. Collier, *Ideas and Politics*, 109.

4. Cited in Loveman, *Chile*, 114–15.

5. See Robertson, *Rise of the Spanish-American Republics*, chap. 2, "Francisco Miranda."

6. Loveman, *Chile*, 117.

7. Collier, *Ideas and Politics*, 242.

8. Cited in ibid., 241, n. 2.

9. Loveman, *Chile*, 118.

10. Alywin, Patricio, "Discurso del Presidente Patricio Aylwin en Ceremonia Conmemorativa del Natalício del General Bernardo O'Higgins." Reprinted in *Fuerzas Armadas y Sociedad* 5, no. 3 (July–Sept. 1990): 29–30.

11. Collier, *Ideas and Politics*, 252.

12. Cited in ibid., 290.

13. Ricardo Donoso, *Las Ideas Políticas en Chile* (Mexico, D.F.: Fondo de Cultura Económica, 1946), 97–107; Collier, *Ideas and Politics*, 326–35.

14. Collier, *Ideas and Politics*, 352.

15. Luis Galdames, *Historia de Chile*, 9th ed. (Santiago: Zig Zag, 1944), 341–48; Donoso, *Las Ideas Políticas*, 101–04.

16. Donoso, *Las Ideas Políticas*, 104.

17. Simon Collier, "Chile from Independence to the War of the Pacific," in *The Cambridge History of Latin America*, ed. Leslie Bethell (Cambridge: Cambridge University Press, 1985), 3:586.

18. Loveman, *Chile*, 124.

19. Cited in Donoso, *Las Ideas Políticas*, 108.

20. Diego Barros Arana, *Un Decenio de la Historia de Chile, 1841–1851*, 2 vols. (Santiago: Imprenta y Encuadernación Universitaria, 1905, 1906), 1:6.

21. Cited in Loveman, *Chile*, 124.

22. Jorge Huneeus, *La Constitución ante el Congreso*, 2d ed. (Santiago: Imprenta Cervantes, 1891), 150.

23. *Ordenanza Jeneral del Ejército* (Santiago: Imprenta de la Opinión, 1840), at the unnumbered pages prior to p. 3.

24. For a work supporting the necessity of the coup and the military junta's *bandos*, see Rafael Valdivieso Ariztia, *Crónica de un Rescate (Chile 1973–1988)* (Santiago: Editorial Andrés Bello, 1988).

25. Cited in Donoso, *Las Ideas Políticas*, 11.

26. Cited in ibid., 110–11.

27. Francisco Encina, *Historia de Chile*, 20 vols. (Santiago: Editorial Nascimento, 1949).

28. Cited in Barros Arana, *Un Decenio*, 1:12–13.

29. Ibid., 16.

30. Ibid., 21.

31. Cited in ibid., 57.

32. Ibid., 59–60, 60 n. 4.

33. Ibid., 106.

34. Huneeus, *La Constitución Ante el Congreso*, 2:151–52.

35. *Compadrazgo* is a common term of fictive kinship prevalent throughout Spain and Latin America; it means, literally, "godmother" and "godfather" for baptism, marriage, etc.

36. Loveman, *Chile*, chap. 5; Antonio Huneeus Gana, *La Consitiución de 1833* (Santiago: Editorial Splendid, 1933), 51–54.

37. Ricardo Anguita, *Leyes Promulgadas en Chile, Desde 1810 Hasta el 1 de Junio de 1912*, 6 vols. (Santiago: Imprenta Barcelona, 1912), 1:356. "Amnistia— Se concede a todos los chilenos desterrados politicos," 23 October 1841.

38. Réjimen interior—Lei general sobre la materia. Reprinted in ibid., 1:416–34.

39. Article 48 authorized intendants to "use the armed force at his disposition" in order to suppress any "riot, tumult or insurrection."

40. On the press laws, see Iván Jaksić, "Sarmiento's Role in the Chilean Press, 1841–1851," in *Sarmiento: Author of a Nation,* ed. Tulio Halperín, Iván Jaksić, and Francine Masiello (Berkeley: University of California Press, forthcoming).

41. Huneeus Gana, *La Constitución de 1833,* 150–51.

42. Huneeus, *La Constitución Ante el Congreso,* 148–49.

43. Basadre, *Chile, Peru y Bolivia,* 207–08; Jaime Eyzaguirre, *Historia de Chile* (Santiago: Zig Zag, 1973), 2:566–69.

44. Barros Arana, *Un Decenio,* 2:232.

45. Facultades estraordinarias—Se conceden al Presidente de la República por el término de un año. Reprinted in Anguita, *Leyes Promulgadas en Chile,* 1:590.

46. Barros Arana, *Un Decenio,* 2:535–41.

47. Luis Galdames, *Historia de Chile,* 9th ed. (Santiago: Zig Zag, 1944), 417–18; Domingo Amunátegui Solar, *Historia de Chile* (Santiago: Editorial Nascimento, 1933), 2:32–34.

48. "Facultades estraordinarias—Se conceden al Presidente de la República," 15 September 1852. Reprinted in Anguita, *Leyes Promulgadas en Chile,* 1:601.

49. Ibid., 620. This was a substantial sum of money; in the mid-1850s, a general's salary was six hundred pesos per year and that of a colonel, five hundred pesos.

50. Loveman, *Chile,* 163–65.

51. "Amnistia a los que tomaron parte en los sucesos de 1851," 30 July 1857. Reprinted in Anguita, *Leyes Promulgadas en Chile,* 2:44.

52. Galdames, *Historia de Chile,* 433–36; Benjamín Vicuña Mackenna, *Historia de los Diez Años de la Administración Montt* (Santiago, Imprenta Chilena, 1862).

53. Basadre, *Chile, Peru y Bolivia,* 227; "Facultades estraordinarias—Se conceden al Gobierno las que se indican," 20 January 1859. Reprinted in Anguita, *Leyes Promulgadas en Chile,* 2:80.

54. Huneeus Gana, *La Constitución de 1833,* 57.

55. Basadre, *Chile, Peru y Bolivia,* 229; Encina, *Historia de Chile,* 13:386–88.

56. Encina, *Historia de Chile,* 13:394–96.

57. Reprinted in Anguita, *Leyes Promulgadas en Chile,* 2:200.

58. Basadre, *Chile, Peru y Bolivia,* 393.

59. José Victorino Lastarria, *Proyectos de Lei i Discursos Parlamentarios* (Santiago: Imprenta de la Libertad, 1870), 1–13.

60. Ibid., 18.

61. Anguita, *Leyes Promulgadas en Chile,* 2:236, 251–56.

62. Ibid., 343–51; see Huneeus Gana, *La Constitución de 1833,* 63–75, for discussion of the 1874 reforms. See also Mario Bernaschina González, *Consti-*

tución Política y Leyes Complementarias, 2d ed. (Santiago: Editorial Jurídica de Chile, 1958); Fernando Campos Harriet, *Historia Constitucional de Chile*, 3d ed. (Santiago: Editorial Jurídica de Chile, 1963), 313–16; Alcibiades Roldán, *Elementos de Derecho Constitucional de Chile*, 2d ed. (Santiago-Valparaíso: Imprenta-Litografía Barcelona, 1917).

63. Anguita, *Leyes Promulgadas en Chile*, 2:384–89.

64. On the civil war, see Loveman, *Chile*, 180–88; Harold Blakemore, "The Chilean Revolution of 1891 and Its Historiography," *Hispanic American Historical Review* 45 (Aug. 1965): 393–421.

65. Basadre, *Chile, Peru y Bolivia*, 510–19; Loveman, *Chile*, 180–88.

66. Loveman, *Chile*, 184–85.

67. Deposición de Balmaceda, de sus Ministros i Consejeros de Estado, 1 January 1891. Reprinted in Anguita, *Leyes Promulgadas en Chile*, 2:173–75; Nulidad de la convocatoria a elecciones hecha por el Gobierno de Balmaceda. Reprinted ibid., 175–76. See also Estado Mayor General del Ejército, *Historia del Ejército de Chile* (Santiago: Talleres Morgan Marinetti, 1985), 7:96–98.

68. Nulidad de los actos del Tribunal establecido por la Dictadura con el nombre de Corte de Apelaciones de Valparaíso, 26 June 1891. Reprinted in Anguita, *Leyes Promulgadas en Chile*, 3:181.

69. Lei que da al Presidente de la República facultades estraordinarias, 11 May 1891. Reprinted in ibid., 2:153.

70. Julio Heise González, *Historia de Chile, El Período Parlamentario 1861–1925*, 2 vols. (Santiago: Editorial Andrés Bello, 1974), 1:100–04. Lei sobre requisiciones, 22 July 1891. Reprinted in Anguita, *Leyes Promulgadas en Chile*, 3:158.

71. See Gonzalo Vial, *Historia de Chile, 1891–1973*, 4 vols. (Santiago: Santillana, 1983), 2:101–16. By the time Jorge Montt used the state of siege provisions, constitutional amendments in the late 1880s and renumbering of the clauses changed the old Article 161 to 152, (stipulation of presidential authority under state of siege, as amended in 1874), old Article 36 (Sec. 6) to 27 (Sec. 6) (leyes excepcionales y de duración transitoria . . .) and old Article 82 (Sec. 2) to 73 (Sec. 20) (presidential and congressional authority to declare state of siege). Anguita, *Leyes Promulgadas en Chile*, 2:259, 279; Manuel Rivas Vicuña, *Historia Política y Parlamentaria de Chile*, 3 vols. (Santiago: Ediciones de la Biblioteca Nacional, 1964), 1:29.

72. Peter DeShazo, *Urban Workers and Labor Unions in Chile, 1902–1927* (Madison: University of Wisconsin Press, 1983), 160–65; Loveman, *Chile*, 202–07; Carlos Andrade Geywitz, *Elementos de Derecho Constitucional Chileno*, 2d ed. (Santiago: Editorial Jurídica de Chile, 1971), 284.

73. Elena Caffarena de Jiles, *El Recurso de Amparo Frente a los Regímenes de Emergencia* (Santiago, 1957), 22.

74. Carlos Andrade Geywitz, *Génesis de las Constituciones de 1925–1980* (Santiago: Editorial Jurídica de Chile, 1988), 25.

75. Caffarena de Jiles, *El Recurso*, 22 n. 1.

76. Ibid., 121.

77. Ibid., 22, 111–31.

78. See Hugo Frühling, Carlos Portales, and Augusto Varas, *Estado y Fuerzas Armadas* (Santiago: Flacso, 1982); Ana María Zuniga San Martin, *Legislación Sobre Seguridad del Estado, Control de Armas y Terrorismo* (Santiago: Editorial Jurídica de Chile, 1985).

79. See Roberto Garretón Merino, "Los Estados de Excepción al Servicio de la Doctrina de la Seguridad Nacional, la Experiencia Chilena," in *Estados de Emergencia en la Región Andina,* ed. Diego Garcia-Sayán (Lima: Comisión Andina de Juristas, 1987), 129–57.

80. The 1980 Constitution created a number of regimes of exception and added substantial authority and autonomy for the armed forces but, despite some concepts borrowed from Germany on the political proscription of subversive movements and parties, relied on Chilean antecedents from 1833 and 1925 combined with the previous laws on internal security of the state.

CHAPTER 9. REGIMES OF EXCEPTION IN THE DOMINICAN REPUBLIC

1. Selden Rodman, *Quisqueya: A History of the Dominican Republic* (Seattle: University of Washington Press, 1964), 71–74.

2. For a four-page list of civil wars, coup attempts, conspiracies, insurrections, and rebellions from 1844 to 1916, see Richard Pattee, *La República Dominicana* (Madrid: Ediciones Cultura Hispánica, 1967), 157–62.

3. Frank Moya Pons, "Haiti and Santo Domingo: 1790–c. 1870," in *The Cambridge History of Latin America,* ed. Leslie Bethell (Cambridge: Cambridge University Press, 1985), 3:237–75; T. O. Ott, *The Haitian Revolution, 1789–1804* (Knoxville: University of Tennessee Press, 1973).

4. Moya Pons, "Haiti and Santo Domingo," 245.

5. Valentina Peguero and Danilo de los Santos, *Visión General de la Historia Dominicana* (Santo Domingo: Universidad Católica Madre y Maestra, 1981), 234–37.

6. Ibid., 237; Moya Pons, "Haiti and Santo Domingo," 274.

7. Manuel Arturo Peña Batlle, *Constitución Política y Reformas Constitucionales, 1844–1942,* 2d ed. (Santo Domingo: Publicaciones ONAP, 1981), vol. 1. *passim.*

8. Ibid., 6.

9. Rodman, *Quisqueya,* 62.

10. The 1858 Constitution was briefly reinstated by President Báez after the country regained independence from Spain in 1865. Article 140, which prohibited issuing of paper money, was excepted from the reinstatement.

11. For example, see Constitution of 1966, Articles 37 (Secs. 7, 8). State of siege clauses, the suspension of constitutional *garantías* clauses, and explicit constitutional roles for the armed forces are elements of all the constitutions after the mid-nineteenth century. These are reprinted in Peña Batlle, *Constitución Política,* vols. 1 and 2.

12. This decree is reprinted in Peña Batlle, ibid., 2:4.

13. 1942 reforms (Art. 33, Sec. 8; Art. 48, Sec. 8).

14. Franklin Knight, *The Caribbean*, 2d ed. (New York: Oxford University Press, 1990), 222–23. See also Rodman, *Quisqueya;* Sumner Welles, *Naboth's Vineyard: The Dominican Republic, 1844–1924*, 2 vols. (New York: Payson and Clark, 1928).

15. Rodman indicates that racism also played a part in Heureaux's repressive methods. He quotes the president's remarks to an American correspondent: "The black man can only be ruled by fear . . . and the half-breed is even more treacherous" (*Quisqueya*, 93).

16. Ibid., 102.

17. See Bruce J. Calder, *The Impact of Intervention* (Austin: University of Texas Press, 1984); Howard Wiarda, *The Dominican Republic* (New York: Praeger, 1969), 30–31. Wiarda comments that "the Dominican pattern had been one of recurrent periods of utter chaos and absolute despotism. . . . During its independent history, between 1844 and 1930 the country had fifty presidents (one for every 1.7 years) and thirty revolutions (one for every 2.9 years). With the exception of Venezuela, the Dominican Republic had more constitutions than any other country in the world" (33).

18. See Peña Batlle, *Constitución Política*, 2:168–69, 177–78, 218, 258–59, 327, 333, 370, 375, 476, 481, for the relevant clauses in the constitutions from 1907 to 1934.

19. On the Trujillo regime, see Jesús de Galíndez, *The Era of Trujillo*, ed. Russell H. Fitzgibbon (Tucson: University of Arizona Press, 1973); G. Pope Atkins and Larman C. Wilson, *The United States and the Trujillo Regime* (New Brunswick: Rutgers University Press, 1972); German E. Ornes, *Trujillo: Little Caesar of the Caribbean* (New York: Nelson, 1958); Wiarda, *Dominican Republic.*

CHAPTER 10. REGIMES OF EXCEPTION, CIVIL-MILITARY RELATIONS, AND SPANISH AMERICAN POLITICS

1. France adopted new constitutions, protoconstitutions, or "constitutional laws" in 1791, 1793, 1795, 1799, 1802, 1804, 1814, 1815, 1830, 1848, 1852, 1870, and 1875. Spain, after the Bayonne (1808) and Cádiz (1812) charters, returned to the ancien régime in 1814, the Cádiz charter in 1820, absolute monarchy in 1823, the Monarchical Statute (1834), the Cádiz charter (1836), a new constitution in 1837 and 1845, a nonimplemented new charter (1855–1856), the Additional Act (1856), a new charter in 1869, and another new charter in 1876.

2. See Cruz Villalón, *El Estado de Sitio y La Constitución*, chaps. 2–5, for political and constitutional developments in France and Spain regarding states of siege and martial law. Also of use are Joseph Carret, *L'organisation de l'Etat de Siège. Politique d'après Loi du 3 Avril 1878* (Dijon, 1916); Rossiter, *Constitutional Dictatorship*, chaps. 3 and 7, on Germany and France.

3. Examples of the criminalization of political opposition and the operation of such press laws are discussed in the chapters above, on Venezuela, Colombia, Peru, and Chile. Typically, violations resulted in both fines and incarceration on conviction.

4. Peruvian Press Law, 12 November 1823, Titles I and II, in *La Constitución del Perú de 1860 con Sus Reformas Hasta 1915*, 2d ed. (Lima: Librería y Imprenta Gil, 1916).

5. Cited in Hubert Herring, *A History of Latin America* (New York: Knopf, 1961), 530.

6. Cruz Villalón, *El Estado de Sitio y la Constitución*, 244–48, 268–76.

7. F. A. Hayek, *Law, Legislation, and Liberty* (Chicago: University of Chicago Press, 1979), 124.

8. Spanish political theorist Francisco de Vitoria wrote: "First, in the just war one may do everything necessary for the defence of the public good. This is obvious, since the defence and preservation of the commonwealth is the purpose of war. . . . It is [also] lawful to avenge the injury done by the enemy, and to teach the enemy a lesson by punishing them for the damage done." See Anthony Pagden and Jeremy Lawrance, eds., *Francisco de Vitoria: Political Writings* (Cambridge: Cambridge University Press, 1991).

9. Carl J. Friedrich, *Limited Government, a Comparison* (Englewood Cliffs, N.J.: Prentice-Hall, 1974), 88–89. See also Friedrich, *Constitutional Reason of State;* Friedrich, *Constitutional Government and Democracy,* chap. 26.

10. See Loveman and Davies, *Politics of Antipolitics,* for translated speeches by military officers justifying the coups and military regimes' policies in this period.

11. Hayek, *Law, Legislation and Liberty,* 125.

12. See Juan Donoso Cortés, *Obras Completas* (Madrid, 1970), "Discurso de la Dictadura"; "Proyecto de ley sobre estados excepcionales presentado a las últimas Cortes por el Ministerio de Diciembre," discussed in Cruz Villalón, *El Estado de Sitio y la Constitución*, 341. Donoso Cortés's language is revealing: "Asi, señores, la cuestión, como he dicho antes, no está entre la libertad y la dictadura; si estuviera entre la libertad y la dictadura, yo votaría por la libertad, como todos los que nos sentamos aquí. Pero la cuestión es ésta, y concluyo: se trata de escoger entre la dictadura de la insurrección y la dictadura del gobierno; puesto en este caso, yo escojo la dictadura del gobierno, como menos pesada y menos afrentosa. Se trata de escoger entre la dictadura que viene de arriba y la dictadura que viene de abajo; yo escojo la que viene de arriba, porque viene de regiones más limpias y serenas; se trata de escoger, por último, entre la dictadura del puñal y la dictadura del sable: yo escojo la dictadura del sable, porque es más noble. Señores, al votar nos dividiremos en esta cuestión, y dividiéndonos, seremos consecuentes con nosotros mismos. Vosotros, señores, votaréis, como siempre, lo más popular; nosotros, señores, como siempre, votaremos lo más saludable." Cited in Lozada, *Las Fuerzas Armadas,* 54–55 n. 42.

13. Hayek, *Law, Legislation and Liberty,* 103–04. Chapters 16–18 are an attack on majoritarian democracy, politics, and socialism as the greatest threats to human freedom. Hayek argues that representative assemblies elected by majorities must be deprived "of the power to grant discriminatory benefits to groups or individuals. . . . Nobody with open eyes can any longer doubt that the danger to personal freedom comes chiefly from the left" (129).

14. Ibid., 103–04.

15. Even in these two cases, regimes of exception were incorporated into state constitutions within the federal republic. Nevertheless, only in these two Colombian charters did national constitutions in Spanish America in the nineteenth century lack provision for regimes of exception.

16. Roldán, *Elementos de Derecho Constitucional de Chile*, 478–86.

17. Patricio Aylwin Azócar, "Prologo," in Elena Caffarena de Jiles, *El Recurso de Amparo Frente a los Regímenes de Emergencia* (Santiago, 1957), 10–11.

18. The exception to this pattern was the Cuban Revolution after 1959. It was an exception, however, only in language and in ideological justification for the restriction of civil liberties and rights. The Cuban leadership did not implement a constitution until 1976, relying on "revolutionary authority" for sixteen years after Fidel Castro ousted Fulgencio Batista. Thereafter, the principle "within the revolution everything, outside of the revolution, nothing" joined Fidel with Hobbes and Lenin rather than with the French, Spanish, and Spanish American constitutional tradition. Articles 61 and 63 of the Cuban constitution made it illegal to exercise freedom in opposition "to the existence and purposes of the socialist state" and to "the Cuban people's decision to build socialism and communism." This socialist version of *reason of state* provided the legal foundations for Cuba's constitution of tyranny. The Fourth Party Congress added to this a new rule giving the party central committee "exceptional powers" to overrule all other government authorities in "unpredictable situations."

After the Cuban revolutionaries ousted Batista, they instituted emergency military tribunals to try counterrevolutionaries and Batista supporters. Precedent for the trial of civilians by military courts existed in 1896 military regulations and was reaffirmed in Act 425 amending the 1938 Social Defense Code. Revolutionary courts under the authority of the minister of the revolutionary armed forces had jurisdiction over "any activity deemed a threat to the state," much like the *consejos de guerra* in times of internal war used by Chilean governments in the 1830s and by the military junta after the 1973 coup. See *Area Handbook for Cuba*, 2d ed. (Washington, D.C.: U.S. Government Printing Office, 1976), 434–36.

19. Garro, "Role of the Argentine Judiciary," 313 n. 6.

20. See Ley I. D. Felipe IV en Madrid por pragmática de 15 de Junio y 6 de Julio de 1663, Modo de proceder contra los bandidos y salteadores que anden en quadrillas por caminos y despoblados; 5 September 1781, órdenes a los Capitanes Generales de las provincias de Andalucia y Extremadura; Ley II. D. Carlos III por Real órden de 14 y céd. del Consejo 27 May 1783. Persecución de malhechores; breve determinación de sus causas, y execución de las penas que merezcan; Ley X. D. Cárlos III. por Real decreto de 2 April, inserto en céd. del Cons. de 5 May 1783, y a Real instrucción de 19 June de [1]784 cap. 8, Pena de los bandidos, contrabandistas ó salteadores que hiciesen resistencia á la Tropa destinada á persequirlos. Ley VIII. D. Carlos IV. por órdenes 30 March 1801, y 10 April [1]802, insertas en circular del Consejo 28 April, Los salteadores de caminos y sus cómplices, aprehendidos por la Tropa en las pobla-

ciones, queden sujetos al Juicio militar. Reprinted in Colón de Larriátegui, *Jusgados Militares*, vols. 1 and 2.

21. Outlawing persons or groups for their political beliefs and objectives, rather than punishing criminal behavior, has a modern form in the German *verfassungsschutz* and the Spanish *defensa de la constitución,* emulated by the Chilean 1980 Constitution. The theory is that it is "necessary to guarantee the constitutional order against *enemies,* even when they have committed no crime and have not violated the constitutional order" (emphasis added). See Ignacio de Otto Pardo, *Defensa de la Constitución y Partidos Políticos* (Madrid: Centro de Estudios Constitucionales, 1985), 17.

22. Vincent Ostrom, "Cryptoimperialism, Predatory States, and Self-Governance," in *Rethinking Institutional Analysis and Development,* ed. Vincent Ostrom, David Feeny, and Hartmut Picht (San Francisco: International Center for Economic Growth, 1988), 61.

23. Ibid., 45–54.

24. See n. 22 in chapter 1 for a reference to President Abraham Lincoln's violation of U.S. citizens' rights during the Civil War.

25. See Nwabueze, *Constitutionalism.*

26. See Nunn, *Yesterday's Soldiers,* for details on this process in Brazil, Argentina, Chile, and Peru.

27. It must be noted, however, that Chile's 1925 Constitution incorporated a usurpation clause and sedition clause (Arts. 3 and 4) and the equivalent of an "undue pressure by the military" clause voiding any official act or law implemented as a result of pressure by the armed forces (Art. 23). This clause immediately preceded the only constitutional treatment of the armed forces, the standard nondeliberation clause familiar since the 1811 Venezuelan charter borrowed this language from the French constitutional monarchy.

28. Cited in Mariano Castro Morán, *Función Política del Ejército Salvadoreño en el Presente Siglo* (San Salvador: UCA/Editores, 1984), app. 11, 397–99.

29. See Loveman and Davies, *The Politics of Antipolitics,* pp. 193–303, for these declarations and many others by Latin American military officers.

30. Garro estimates that between 1930 and 1969 "a person might have been detained for 17 years, five months and 18 days [in Argentina] for during that period the state of siege was decreed no less than 11 times, and on three of those occasions it was extended for several years in succession (1941/1945; 1951/1955; and 1958/1963)." "Role of the Argentine Judiciary," 320.

31. The parrot's perch and the *parrilla* refer to two modes of torture frequently used in parts of South America during the military dictatorships from the 1960s to the 1990s.

Bibliography

Alarcón Quintana, Luis. *Orígen y Proceso de la Constitución de 1933. Los Debates de la Constituyente*. Lima: Editorial Científica S.R.I., 1978.

Alberdi, Juan Bautista. *Bases y Puntos de Partida para la Organización Política de la República Argentina*. 5th ed. Buenos Aires: Rosso, 1960.

Alvarez Lejarza, Emilio. *Las Constituciones de Nicaragua*. Madrid: Ediciones Cultura Hispánica, 1958.

Amadeo, Santos P. *Argentine Constitutional Law*. New York: Columbia University Press, 1943.

Ameringer, Charles D. *Democracy in Costa Rica*. New York: Praeger, 1982.

Amunátegui Solar, Domingo. *Historia de Chile*. 2 vols. Santiago: Editorial Nascimento, 1933.

Anderson, Frank Maloy. "The Enforcement of the Alien and Sedition Laws," *American Historical Association Annual Report, 1912*. 115–26.

Andrade Geywitz, Carlos. *Elementos de Derecho Constitucional Chileno*. 2d ed. Santiago: Editorial Jurídica de Chile, 1971.

———. *Génesis de las Constituciones de 1925–1980*. Santiago: Editorial Jurídica de Chile, 1988.

Anguita, Ricardo. *Leyes Promulgadas en Chile, Desde 1810 Hasta el 1 de Junio de 1912*. 6 vols. Santiago: Imprenta Barcelona, 1912.

Anna, Timothy. *The Fall of the Royal Government in Mexico City*. Lincoln: University of Nebraska Press, 1978.

———. *The Fall of the Royal Government in Peru*. Lincoln: University of Nebraska Press, 1979.

———. *Spain and the Loss of Empire*. Lincoln: University of Nebraska Press, 1983.

———. "The Independence of Mexico and Central America." In *The Cambridge History of Latin America*, ed. Leslie Bethell. Cambridge: Cambridge University Press, 1985, 3:51–94.

Antología del Pensamiento Social y Político de América Latina. Washington, D.C., Unión Panamericana, Secretaría General de la Organización de los Estados Americanos, 1964.

449

Aranda, Ricardo. *La Constitución del Perú de 1860 con Sus Reformas Hasta 1915, Leyes Orgánicas, Decretos, Reglamentos y Resoluciones Referentes a Ellas Coleccionadas y Anotadas*, 2d ed. Lima: Librería e Imprenta Gil, 1916.

Archer, Christon L. *The Army in Bourbon Mexico, 1760–1810*. Albuquerque: University of New Mexico Press, 1977.

Area Handbook for Cuba. 2d ed. Washington, D.C.: U.S. Government Printing Office, 1976.

Argüedas, Alcides. *Historia General de Bolivia (El Proceso de Nacionalidad), 1809–1921*. La Paz: Ediciones Puerta del Sol, 1967.

Arosemena, Justo. *Estudios Constitucionales Sobre los Gobiernos de la América Latina*, 2 vols. Paris: Librería Española i Américana de E. Denne, 1878.

Artola, Miguel. *La España de Fernando VII. Vol. 26 of Historia de España*, ed. R. Menéndez Pidal. Madrid, Espasa-Calpe, 1978, c. 1968.

———. *La Burguesía Revolucionaria (1808–1869)*. Madrid: Alianza Editorial, 1973.

Astrosa Herrera, Renato. *Código de Justicia Militar Comentado*. 3d ed. Santiago: Editorial Jurídica de Chile, 1985.

Astrosa Sotomayor, Renato. *Jursidicción Penal Militar*. Santiago: Editorial Jurídica de Chile, 1973.

Atkins, G. Pope, and Larman C. Wilson. *The United States and the Trujillo Regime*. New Brunswick: Rutgers University Press, 1972.

Ayala, Enrique, coordinador. *Política y Sociedad, Ecuador: 1830–1980*. Quito: Corporación Editora Nacional, 1980.

———. *Lucha Política y Orígen de los Partidos en Ecuador*. 3d ed. Quito: Corporación Editora Nacional, 1985.

Aylwin, Patricio, "Discurso del Presidente Patricio Aylwin en Ceremonia Conmemorativa del Natalício del General Bernardo O'Higgins." *Fuerzas Armadas y Sociedad* 5, no. 3 (July–Sept. 1990): 29–30.

Ballbé, Manuel. *Orden Público y Militarismo en la España Constitucional (1812–1983)*. Madrid: Alianza Editorial, 1983.

Banco Hipotecario de Crédito Urbano. *El Libertador y la Constitución de Angostura de 1819*. Caracas, 1970.

Bañon Martínez, Rafael, and Thomas M. Barker, eds. *Armed Forces and Society in Spain, Past and Present*. New York: Columbia University Press, 1988.

Barahona, Rubén. *Breve Historia de Honduras*. 5th ed. Mexico, D.F.: Editorial Azteca, 1955.

Barba, Enrique M. *Unitarismo, Federalismo, Rosismo*. Buenos Aires: Ediciones Pannedille, 1972.

de la Barra, Felipe. *Objetivo, Palacio del Gobierno, Reseña Histórico-Cronológica de los Pronunciamientos Políticos y Militares de la Conquista a la República y que Permitieron la Ocupación del Palacio del Gobierno*. Lima: Librería Editorial Juan Mejía Baca, 1967.

Barrán, José Pedro, and Benjamín Nahum. *Historia Rural del Uruguay Moderno*. 3 vols. Montevideo: Ediciones de la Banda Oriental, 1967, 1971.

Barros Arana, Diego. *Un Decenio de la Historia de Chile, 1841–1851*. 2 vols. Santiago: Imprenta y Encuadernación Universitaria, 1905, 1906.

Basadre, Jorge. *La Iniciación de la República. Contribución al Estudio de la Evolución Política y Social del Perú.* 2 vols. Lima: Editorial E. Rosay, 1929–1930.

———. *Chile, Peru y Bolivia Independientes.* Buenos Aires: Salvat Editores, 1948.

———. *Los Fundamentos de la Historia del Derecho,* 2d ed. Lima: Editorial Universitaria, 1967.

———. *Historia de la República del Peru, 1822–1933.* 17 vols. Lima: Editorial Universitaria, 1968–1970.

Bauza, Francisco. *Estudios Constitucionales.* Montevideo: La Librería Nacional, 1887.

Bazant, Jan. *Alienation of Church Wealth in Mexico: Social and Economic Aspects of the Liberal Revolution, 1856–1875.* Cambridge: Cambridge University Press, 1971.

Beezley, William H. "Caudillismo: An Interpretive Note." *Journal of InterAmerican Studies* 11 (1969): 345–52.

Beloff, M. *Public Order and Popular Disturbances, 1660–1714.* London: Cass, 1963.

Bermann, Karl. *Under the Big Stick: Nicaragua and the United States Since 1848.* Boston: South End Press, 1986.

Bernaschina González, Mario. *Constitución Política y Leyes Complementarias.* 2d ed. Santiago: Editorial Jurídica de Chile, 1958.

Berquist, Charles W. *Coffee and Conflict in Colombia, 1886–1910.* Durham: Duke University Press, 1978.

Bielsa, Rafael. *El Estado de Necesidad en El Derecho Constitucional y Administrativo* 2d ed. Buenos Aires: Reque de la Palma Editores, 1957.

Blakemore, Harold. "The Chilean Revolution of 1891 and Its Historiography." *Hispanic American Historical Review* 45 (Aug. 1965): 393–421.

Blanksten, George I. *Ecuador: Constitutions and Caudillos.* Berkeley: University of California Press, 1951.

Bolívar, Simón. *Obras Completas.* 3 vols. Caracas: Ministerio de Educación Nacional de los Estados Unidos de Venezuela, n.d.

———. *Proyecto de constitución Para la República Boliviana Lima, 1826.* Caracas: [s.n.] 1978.

Bonilla, F. *Legislación Peruana. Ley Orgánica y Código de Justicia Militar.* Lima: Editorial Mercurio S.A., 1966.

Bonilla, Heraclio. "Peru and Bolivia from Independence to the War of the Pacific." In *The Cambridge History of Latin America,* ed. Leslie Bethell. Cambridge: Cambridge University Press, 1985, 3:539–82.

Borja Cevallos, Rodrigo. *Derecho Político y Constitucional,* vol. 1. Quito: Casa de la Cultura Ecuatoriana, 1971.

Borja y Borja, Ramiro. *Las Constituciones del Ecuador.* Madrid: Ediciones Cultura Hispánica, 1951.

Botero, Giovanni. *Reason of State.* Trans. P. J. Waley and D. P. Waley. New Haven: Yale University Press, 1956.

Box, Pelham H. *Origins of the Paraguayan War.* Urbana: University of Illinois Press, 1927.

Brading, David. *The First America: The Spanish Monarchy, Creole Patriots and the Liberal State, 1492–1867.* Cambridge: Cambridge University Press, 1990.

Bravo Michell, Clodomiro, and Nissim Sharim Paz. *Restricciones a las Libertades Públicas.* Santiago: Editorial Jurídica de Chile, 1958.

Brazil. *Constituçoës Do Brasil.* 6th ed. 2 vols. ed. Carlos Eduardo Barreto, São Paulo: Ediçao Saravio, 1971.

Buergenthal, Thomas, Jorge Mario García Laguardia, and Rodolfo Piza Rocafort. *La Constitución Norteamericana y Su Influencia en Latinoamérica (200 Años 1787–1987).* San José, C.R.: Cuadernos de CAPEL, 1987.

Burgin, Miron. *The Economic Aspects of Argentine Federalism, 1820–1852.* Cambridge: Harvard University Press, 1946.

Burgoa, Ignacio. *Diccionario de Derecho Constitucional, Garantías y Amparo.* Mexico, D.F.: Editorial Porrúa, 1984.

———. *Las Garantías Individuales.* Mexico, D.F.: Editorial Porrúa, 1965.

Burkholder, Mark, and Lyman L. Johnson. *Colonial Latin America.* New York: Oxford University Press, 1990.

Burns, E. Bradford. *The Poverty of Progress: Latin America in the Nineteenth Century.* Berkeley: University of California Press, 1980.

Bushnell, David. *The Santander Regime in Gran Colombia.* Newark: University of Delaware Press, 1954.

———. *Reform and Reaction in the Platine Provinces, 1810–1852.* No. 69, University of Florida Monograph. Gainesville: University Presses of Florida, 1983.

———. "The Independence of Spanish South America." In *The Cambridge History of Latin America,* ed. Leslie Bethell. Cambridge: Cambridge University Press, 1985, 3:95–156.

Bushnell, David, and Neil Macaulay, *The Emergence of Latin America in the Nineteenth Century.* New York: Oxford University Press, 1988.

Caffarena de Jiles, Elena. *El Recurso de Amparo Frente a los Regímenes de Emergencia.* Santiago, 1957.

Calder, Bruce J. *The Impact of Intervention.* Austin: University of Texas Press, 1984.

Cambo, Francisco. *Las Dictaduras.* 3d ed. Madrid, Espasa-Calpe, 1929.

Campbell, Leon G. *The Military and Society in Colonial Peru, 1750–1810.* Philadelphia: American Philosophical Society, 1978.

Campos Harriet, Fernando. *Historia Constitucional de Chile.* 3d ed. Santiago: Editorial Jurídica de Chile, 1963.

Capdevielle, B., and C. Oxibar. *Historia del Paraguay.* Asunción: Colegio de San José, n.d.

Cardenas Acosta, Pablo E. *La Restauración Constitucional de 1867. Historia de un Contragolpe de Estado.* Tunja, Colombia: Departamento de Extensión Cultural de Boyacá, 1966.

Cardoso, Ciro, and Héctor Pérez. *Centroamérica y la Economía Occidental (1520–1930).* San José, C.R., EDUCA 1977.

Carr, Raymond. *Spain 1808–1975.* 2d ed. Oxford: Clarendon, 1982.

Carret, Joseph. *L'Organisation de l'Etat de Siège. Politique d'apres Loi du 3 Avril du 1878.* Dijon, 1916.

Carrión Benjamín. *García Moreno. El Santo del Patíbulo.* Mexico and Buenos Aires: Fondo de Cultura Económica, 1959.

Castellanos, Alfredo. *La Cisplatina, la Independencia, y la República Caudillesca 1820–1838.* 3 vols. Montevideo: Ediciones de la Banda Oriental, 1974.

Castro Morán, Mariano. *Función Política del Ejército Salvadoreño en el Presente Siglo.* San Salvador: UCA/Editores, 1984.

Chafee, Zechariah. *Free Speech in the United States.* Cambridge, Harvard University Press, 1948.

Chirinos Soto, Enrique. *La Nueva Constitución al Alcance de Todos.* Lima: Editorial Andina, 1979.

———. *Historia de la República (1821–1930).* 2 vols. Lima: Editores Importadores S.A., 1985.

Christiansen, E. *The Origins of Military Power in Spain, 1800–1854.* London: Oxford University Press, 1967.

Clapham, Christopher, and George Philip, eds. *The Political Dilemmas of Military Regimes.* London: Croom Helm, 1985.

Clusellas, Gregorini. *Estado de Sitio y la Armonía en la Relación Individuo-Estado.* Buenos Aires: Ediciones DePalma, 1987.

Cobban, Alfred. *Dictatorship: Its History and Theory.* New York: Haskell House, 1971.

Colindres, O., Ramiro. ed. Análisis Comparativo de las Constituciones Políticas de Honduras. Honduras: Graficentro Editores, 1988.

Collier, Simon. *Ideas and Politics of Chilean Independence, 1808–1833.* Cambridge: Cambridge University Press, 1967.

———. "Chile from Independence to the War of the Pacific." In *The Cambridge History of Latin America,* ed. Leslie Bethell. Cambridge: Cambridge University Press, 1985, 3:583–613.

Colón de Larriátegui, Félix. *Juzgados Militares de España y Sus Indias.* 5 vols. Paris: Emprenta de C. Farcy, 1828.

Comellas, J. L. *Los Primeros Pronunciamientos en Espanã, 1814–1820.* Madrid: Consejo Superior de Investigaciones Científicas, Escuela de Historia Moderna, 1958.

La Constitución del Perú de 1860 con Sus Reformas Hasta 1915. 2d ed. Lima: Librería y Imprenta Gil, 1916.

Constitución Política de Bolivia. 1826.

Constitución Política para la República Peruana (Constitución Vitalícia de Bolívar). 1826.

Constituciones Políticas del Estado Ecuatoriano. 2 vols. (Vol. 1, 1812–1851; Vol. 2, 1852–1906). San Diego State University Library KHK 2910, 1812.

Constituciones Políticas del Perú, 1821–1919. Lima: Imprenta Torres Aguirre, 1922.

Cornejo Bouroncle, Jorge. *Túpac Amaru. La Revolución Precursora de la Emancipación Continental.* 2d ed. Cuzco, Editorial H. G. Rozas, 1963.

Cortinas Peláez, León. *Poder Ejecutivo y Función Jurisdiccional.* Mexico, D.F.: Universidad Autónoma de Mexico, 1982.
Cosío Villegas, Daniel, ed. *Historia Moderna de Mexico.* 9 vols. Mexico, D.F.: Editorial Hermes, 1955–1974.
Craig, Gordon. *The Politics of the Prussian Army, 1640–1945.* New York: Oxford University Press, 1964.
Cruz Villalón, Pedro. *El Estado de Sitio y la Constitución. La Constitucionalización de la Protección Extraordinaria del Estado (1789–1878).* Madrid: Centro de Estudios Constitucionales, 1980.
Cueva, Agustín. *The Process of Political Domination in Ecuador.* Trans. Danielle Salti. New Brunswick: Transaction, 1982.
Daireaux, Max. *Melgarejo.* Buenos Aires: Andina, 1966.
Darvall, F. O. *Popular Disturbances and Public Disorder in Regency England.* New York: A. M. Kelley, 1969.
Davies, Thomas M., Jr. *Indian Integration in Peru.* Lincoln: University of Nebraska Press, 1970.
Dealy, Glen. *The Public Man: An Interpretation of Latin America and Other Catholic Countries.* Amherst, University of Massachusetts Press, 1977.
Deas, Malcolm. "Venezuela, Colombia and Ecuador, The First Half Century of Independence." In *The Cambridge History of Latin America,* ed. Leslie Bethell. Cambridge: Cambridge University Press, 1985, 3:507–38.
Delpar, Helen. *Red Against Blue: The Liberal Party in Colombian Politics 1863–1899.* University: University of Alabama Press, 1981.
DeShazo, Peter. *Urban Workers and Labor Unions in Chile, 1902–1927.* Madison: University of Wisconsin Press, 1983.
Díaz Cardona, Francia Elena. *Fuerzas Armadas, Militarismo y Constitución Nacional en América Latina.* Mexico, D.F.: UNAM, 1988.
Dicey, A. V. *Introduction to the Study of the Law of the Constitution.* London: Macmillan, 1924.
Diez de Medina, Federico. *Breves Reflexiones Acerca del Principio Federativo y Sobre el Orígen de Nuestras Guerras Civiles.* La Paz: Imprenta de la Unión Americana, 1871.
Diffie, Bailey W., and George D. Winius. *Foundations of the Portuguese Empire, 1415–1580.* Vol. 1. Minneapolis: University of Minnesota Press, 1977.
Dix, Robert H. *The Politics of Colombia.* New York: Praeger, 1987.
———. *Documentos Relativos a la Organización Constitucional de la República Argentina.* 2 vols. Buenos Aires: Facultad de Filosofía y Letras, 1911.
Domínguez, Jorge I. *Insurrection or Loyalty: The Breakdown of the Spanish American Empire.* Cambridge: Harvard University Press, 1980.
Donoso, Ricardo. *Las Ideas Políticas en Chile.* Mexico: Fondo de Cultura Económica, 1946.
Donoso Cortés, Juan. *Obras Completas.* Madrid: Editorial Católica, 1970.
Dunkerley, James. *Orígenes del Poder Militar en Bolivia. Historia del Ejército, 1879–1935.* La Paz, Bolivia: Quipus, 1978.
Durón y Gomero, Rómulo. *Bosquejo Histórico de Honduras.* 2d ed. Tegucigalpa: Ministerio de Educación, 1956.

Efrén Reyes, Oscar. *Breve Historia General del Ecuador.* 4th ed. 2 vols. Quito: Editorial Fray Jodocko Ricky, 1950.

Elliot, J. H. *Imperial Spain.* New York: New American Library, 1964.

Encina, Francisco. *Historia de Chile.* 20 vols. Santiago: Editorial Nascimento, 1949.

Estado Mayor General del Ejército. *Historia del Ejército de Chile.* Vols. 7–9. Santiago: Talleres Morgan Marinetti, 1985.

Eyzaguirre, Jaime. *Historia de Chile.* 2 vols. Santiago: Zig Zag, 1973.

Ferns, H. S. *Britain and Argentina in the Nineteenth Century.* London: Clarendon, 1960.

Fisher, John R., Allan Kuethe, and Anthony McFarlane, eds. *Reform and Insurrection in Bourbon New Granada and Peru.* Baton Rouge: Louisiana State University Press, 1990.

Fisher, Lillian E. *The Background of the Revolution for Mexican Independence.* Gainesville: University of Florida Press, 1966.

Fitzgibbon, Russell H. *Uruguay: Portrait of a Democracy.* New Brunswick: Rutgers University Press, 1954.

Fluharty, Vernon Lee. *Dance of the Millions: Military Rule and Social Revolution in Colombia, 1930–1956.* Pittsburgh: University of Pittsburgh Press, 1966.

Fontana Lázaro, J. *La Quiebra de la Monarquía Absoluta, 1814–1820 (La Crisis del Antiguo Régimen en España).* Barcelona: Ediciones Ariel, 1971.

Friedrich, Carl. *Constitutional Government and Democracy.* Rev. ed. Boston: Ginn and Co., 1950.

———. *Constitutional Reason of State: The Survival of the Constitutional Order.* Englewood Cliffs, N.J.: Prentice-Hall, 1957.

———. *Limited Government, a Comparison.* Englewood Cliffs, N.J.: Prentice-Hall, 1974.

Frühling, Hugo, Carlos Portales, and Augusto Varas. *Estado y Fuerzas Armadas.* Santiago: FLACSO, 1982.

Fuentes, Carlos. *The Buried Mirror: Reflections on Spain and the New World.* Boston: Houghton Mifflin, 1992.

Fuentes, Gloria. *El Ejército Mexicano.* Mexico, D.F.: Grijalbo, 1983.

Galdames, Luis. *Historia de Chile.* 9th ed. Santiago: Zig Zag, 1944.

Galíndez, Jesús de. *The Era of Trujillo.* Ed. Russell H. Fitzgibbon. Tucson: University of Arizona Press, 1973.

Gallardo, Ricardo. *Las Constituciones de la República Federal de Centro-América.* 2 vols. Madrid: Instituto de Estudios Políticos, 1958.

———. *Las Constituciones de El Salvador.* 2 vols. Madrid: Ediciones de Cultura Hispánica, 1961.

Galletti, Alfredo. *Historia Constitucional Argentina.* 2 vols. La Plata: Editora Platense, 1972, 1974.

Gallón Giraldo, Gustavo. *Quince Años de Estado de Sitio en Colombia 1958–1978.* Bogotá: Editorial América Latina, 1979.

Gálvez, Manuel. *Vida de Don Gabriel García Moreno.* 2d ed. Buenos Aires: Editorial Difusión, 1942.

García Calderón, Francisco. *Dicccionario de la Legislación Peruana.* 2d ed. 2 vols. Lima: Libreria Laroque, 1879.

————. *Latin America: Its Rise and Progress.* London: Unwin, 1913.

Garretón Merino, Roberto. "Los Estados de Excepción al Servicio de la Doctrina de la Seguridad Nacional, la Experiencia Chilena." In *Estados de Emergencia en la Región Andina,* ed. Diego García-Sayán. Lima: Comisión Andina de Juristas, 1987; 127–57.

Garro, Alejandro M. "The Role of the Argentine Judiciary in Controlling Governmental Action Under a State of Siege." *Human Rights Law Journal* 4, no. 3 (1983): 311–37.

Gibson, Charles. *Spain in America.* New York: Harper and Row, 1966.

Gibson, William Marion. *The Constitutions of Colombia.* Durham: Duke University Press, 1948.

Gil Fortoul, José. *Historia Constitucional de Venezuela.* 5th ed. 3 vols. Caracas: Ediciones Sales, 1964.

Gillespie, Charles G. *Negotiating Democracy: Politicians and Generals in Uruguay.* Cambridge: Cambridge University Press, 1991.

Gil Novales, Alberto. *Las Sociedades Patrióticas (1820–1823). Las Libertades de Expresión y de Reunión en el Orígen de los Partidos Políticos.* 2 vols. Madrid: Tecnos, 1975.

Glade, William. *The Latin American Economies: A Study of Their Institutional Evolution.* New York: Van Nostrand, 1969.

Gómez Hurtado, Alvaro. *La Reforma del Artículo 121 de la Constitucíon. El Estado de Sitio, Debate en el Senado de la República.* Vol 1. Comp. Héctor C. Samper. Bogotá: Imprenta Nacional, 1962.

González Morales, Felipe, Jorge Mera Figueroa, and Juan Enrique Vargas Viancos. *Protección Democrática de la Seguridad del Estado.* Santiago: Programa de Derechos Humanos, Universidad Academia de Humanismo Cristiano, 1991.

Gootenberg, Paul. *Between Silver and Guano: Commercial Policy and the State in Post Independence Peru.* Princeton: Princeton University Press, 1989.

————. "North-South: Trade Policy, Regionalism and *Caudillismo* in Post-Independence Peru." *Journal of Latin American Studies* 23 (May): 273–308.

Graham, Richard. *Independence in Latin America.* New York: Knopf, 1972.

Grases, Pedro, comp. *Los Proyectos Constitucionales del Libertador.* Caracas: Ediciones Conmemorativas del Bicentenario del Natalicio del Libertador Simón Bolívar, Congreso de la República, 1983.

Greishaber, Erwin P. "Survival of Indian Communities in Nineteenth-Century Bolivia: A Regional Comparison." *Journal of Latin American Studies* 8, no. 2 (1980): 233–69.

————. "Survival of Indian Communities in Nineteenth Century Bolivia." Ph.D. diss., University of North Carolina, 1977.

Grew, Raymond, ed. *Crises of Political Development in Europe and the United States.* Princeton: Princeton University Press, 1978.

Gros Espiell, Héctor. *La Formación del Ideario Artiguista*. Montevideo, 1951.

———. *Las Constituciones Del Uruguay.* Madrid: Ediciones Cultura Hispánica, 1956.

———. *Las Constituciones Del Uruguay.* 2d ed. Madrid: Ediciones Culturas Hispánicas del Centro Ibero Americano de Cooperación, 1978.

Grossman, Claudio. "States of Emergency: Latin America and the United States." In *Constitutionalism and Rights: The Influence of the United States Constitution Abroad*, ed. Louis Henkin and Albert J. Rosenthal. New York: Columbia University Press, 1990: 175–196.

Guier, Jorge. *Historia del Derecho*. 2 vols. San José, C.R.: Editorial Costa Rica, 1968.

Gutiérrez, Alberto. *El Melgarejismo. Antes y Después de Melgarejo*. 2d ed. La Paz: Ediciones Populares Camarlinghi, 1975.

Guzmán, Augusto. *Historia de Bolivia*. 2d ed. La Paz-Cochabamba: Ediciones los Amigos del Libro, 1973.

Guzmán, Germán. *La Violencia en Colombia*. Cali, Colombia: Ediciones Progreso, 1968.

Hale, Charles A. *Mexican Liberalism in the Age of Mora, 1821–1853*. New Haven: Yale University Press, 1968.

———. *The Tranformation of Liberalism in Late Nineteenth-Century Mexico*. Princeton: Princeton University Press, 1989.

Halperín-Donghi, Tulio. *Politics, Economics, and Society in Argentina in the Revolutionary Period*. Trans. Richard Southern. Cambridge: Cambridge University Press, 1975.

Hamill, Hugh. *The Hidalgo Revolt: Prelude to Mexican Independence*. Gainesville: University of Florida Press, 1966.

———, ed. *Caudillos: Dictators in Spanish America*. Norman: University of Oklahoma Press, 1992.

Hamnett, Brian R., "Royalist Counterinsurgency and the Continuity of Rebellion: Guanajuato and Michoacán, 1813–1820." *Hispanic American Historical Review* 62 (Feb. 1982): 19–48.

———. *Roots of Insurgency: Mexican Regions, 1750–1824*. Cambridge: Cambridge University Press, 1986.

Hargreaves-Mawdsely, W. N. *Spain Under the Bourbons, 1700–1833, A Collection of Documents*. London: Macmillan, 1973.

Haring, C. H. *The Spanish Empire in America*. New York: Oxford University Press, 1947.

Haskins, Ralph. "Juan José Flores and the Proposed Expedition Against Ecuador, 1845–1847." *Hispanic American Historical Review* 27 (Aug. 1947): 467–95.

Hassaurek, Friederich. *Four Years Among Spanish Americans*. New York: Hurd and Houghton, 1867.

Hayek, F. A. *Law, Legislation, and Liberty.* Chicago: University of Chicago Press, 1979.

Heise González, Julio. *150 Años de Evolución Institucional*. Santiago: Editorial Andrés Bello, 1960.

————. *Historia de Chile, El Período Parlamentario 1861–1925.* 2 vols. Santiago: Editorial Andrés Bello, 1974.

Henríquez Ureña, Pedro. *Historia de la Cultura en América Hispánica.* 7th ed. Mexico, D.F.: Fondo de Cultura Económica, 1947.

Hernández, Salvador. *El PRI Y El Movimiento Estudiantil de 1968.* Mexico, D.F.: El Caballito, 1971.

Herr, Richard. *Spain.* Englewood Cliffs, N.J.: Prentice-Hall, 1971.

————. *An Historical Essay on Modern Spain.* Berkeley: University of California Press, 1974.

Herrera, Bartolomé. *Escritos y Discursos.* Lima: Librería Francesca Científica, 1929.

Herring, Hubert. *A History of Latin America.* New York: Knopf, 1961.

Hobbes, Thomas. *The English Works of Thomas Hobbes of Malmesbury.* Comp. and ed. Sir William Molesworth. Aalen, Ger.: Scientia, 1966.

Hobsbawm, E. J. *Primitive Rebels: Studies in Archaic Forms of Social Movements in the Nineteenth and Twentieth Centuries.* New York: Praeger, 1959.

Hodges, Donald C. *Argentina's 'Dirty War.'* Austin: University of Texas Press, 1991.

Humphreys, R. A., and John Lynch, eds. *The Origins of the Latin American Revolutions, 1808–1826.* New York: Knopf, 1965.

Huneeus, Jorge. *La Constitución ante el Congreso.* 2d ed. Santiago: Imprenta Cervantes, 1891.

Huneeus Gana, Antonio. *La Constitución de 1833.* Santiago: Editorial Splendid, 1933.

Irizarry y Puente, J. "The Nature and Powers of 'De Facto' Government in Latin America." *Tulane Law Review* 30 (1955): 15–72.

Izard, Miguel. *El Miedo a la Revolución. Lucha por la Libertad en Venezuela, 1777–1830.* Madrid: Editorial Tecnos, 1979.

Izquierdo Muñoz, Homero. *Derecho Constitucional Ecuatoriano.* Quito: Editorial Universitaria, 1980.

Jacome Moscoso, Rodrigo. *Derecho Constitucional Ecuatoriano.* Quito: Imprenta de la Universidad Central, 1931.

Jaksić, Iván. "Sarmiento's Role in the Chilean Press, 1841–1851." In *Sarmiento: Author of a Nation,* ed. Tulio Halperín, Iván Jaksić, and Francine Masiello. Berkeley: University of California Press, forthcoming.

Jane, Cecil. *Liberty and Despotism in Latin America.* Oxford: Clarendon, 1929.

Jiménez de Arechaga, Justino E. *El Poder Ejecutivo y Sus Ministros.* 2 vols. Montevideo: A. Barreiro y Ramos, 1913.

Jiménez de Asúa, Luis. *Códigos Penales Iberoamericanos, Estudios de Legislación Comparada.* Caracas: Editorial Andrés Bello, 1946.

Johnson, John J. *The Military and Society in Latin America.* Stanford: Stanford University Press, 1964.

————. *Jurisdicción Civil y Militar.* Montevideo: Fundación de Cultura Universitaria, 1971.

Karnes, T. L. *The Failure of Union: Central America, 1824–1975.* Rev. ed. Tempe: Center for Latin American Studies, Arizona State University, 1976.

Klein, Herbert S. *Parties and Political Change in Bolivia, 1880–1952*. Cambridge: Cambridge University Press, 1969.

———. *Bolivia: The Evolution of a Multi-ethnic Society*. New York: Oxford University Press, 1982.

Knight, Franklin. *The Caribbean*. 2d ed. New York: Oxford University Press, 1990.

Kolinski, Charles. *Independence or Death! The Story of the Paraguayan War*. Gainesville: University of Florida Press, 1965.

Kuethe, Allan J. *Military Reform and Society in New Granada,1773–1808*. Gainesville: University Presses of Florida, 1978.

———. *Cuba, 1753–1815: Crown, Military, and Society*. Knoxville: University of Tennessee Press, 1986.

Labastida Martín del Campo, Julio. ed. *Dictaduras y Dictadores*. Mexico: Siglo Veintiuno, 1986.

Lanning, John Tate. *The Eighteenth Century Enlightenment in the University of San Carlos de Guatemala*. Ithaca: Cornell University Press, 1956.

Larrea Holguín, Juan Ignacio. *La Iglesia y el Estado en el Ecuador. La Personalidad de la Iglesia en el Modus Vivendi Entre la Santa Sede y el Ecuador*. Seville: Escuela de Estudios Hispanoamericanos, 1954.

Laso, Benito. *El Poder de la Fuerza y el Poder de la Ley*. Lima: Ediciones Hora del Hombre, 1947.

Lastarria, José Victorino. *Proyectos de Lei i Discursos Parlamentarios*. Santiago: Imprenta de la Libertad, 1870.

Latin American Bureau. *Uruguay, Generals Rule*. London, 1980.

———. *Honduras: State for Sale*. London, 1985.

Levene, Ricardo. *A History of Argentina*, trans. William Spence Robertson. Chapel Hill: University of North Carolina Press, 1937.

Lewin, Boleslao. *La Rebelión de Túpac Amaru y los Orígenes de la Emancipación Americana*. Buenos Aires: Hachette, 1957.

———. *Mariano Moreno. Su Ideología y Su Pasión*. Buenos Aires: Ediciones Libera, 1971.

Lieuwen, Edwin. *Arms and Politics in Latin America*. New York: Praeger, 1961.

Lockhart, James. *Spanish Peru, 1532–1560*. Madison: University of Wisconsin Press, 1968.

Lockhart, James, and Stuart Schwartz. *Early Latin America: A History of Colonial Spanish America and Brazil*. New York: Cambridge University Press, 1983.

Lombardi, John. *Venezuela: The Search for Order, The Dream of Progress*. New York: Oxford University Press, 1982.

López Pineda, Julián. *La Reforma Constitucional de Honduras*. Paris: Ediciones Estrella, 1936.

Loveman, Brian. *Chile: The Legacy of Hispanic Capitalism*. 2d ed. New York: Oxford University Press, 1988.

Loveman, Brian, and Thomas M. Davies, Jr., eds. *The Politics of Antipolitics: The Military in Latin America*. 2d ed. Lincoln: University of Nebraska Press, 1989.

Lovett, Gabriel. *Napoleon and the Birth of Modern Spain.* 2 vols. New York: New York University Press, 1965.

Lozada, Salvador María. *Las Fuerzas Armadas en la Política Hispanoaméricana.* Buenos Aires: Colección Esquemas, Editorial Columba, 1967.

Lynch, John. *Spanish Colonial Administration, 1782–1810: The Intendant System in the Viceroyalty of the Río de la Plata.* London: Athlone, 1958.

———. *The Spanish-American Revolutions, 1808–1826.* New York: W. W. Norton, 1973.

———. *Argentine Dictator: Juan Manuel de Rosas, 1829–1852.* Oxford: Clarendon, 1981.

———. "The Origins of Spanish American Independence." In *The Cambridge History of Latin America,* ed. Leslie Bethell. Cambridge: Cambridge University Press, 1985, 3:3–50.

———. "The River Plate Republics from Independence to the Paraguayan War." In *The Cambridge History of Latin America,* ed. Leslie Bethell. Cambridge: Cambridge University Press, 1985, 3:615–76.

———. *Bourbon Spain, 1700–1808.* Cambridge, Mass.: Blackwell, 1989.

———. "The Institutional Framework of Colonial Spanish America." *Journal of Latin American Studies* 24, quincentenary supplement (1992): 69–81.

McAlister, Lyle N. *The "Fuero Militar" in New Spain, 1764–1800.* Gainesville: University of Florida Press, 1957.

———. *Spain and Portugal in the New World, 1492–1700.* Minneapolis: University of Minnesota Press, 1984.

McClintock, Cynthia. "Sendero Luminoso: Peru's Maoist Guerrillas." *Problems of Communism* 32 (Sept.–Oct. 1983): 19–34.

———. "Peru's Sendero Luminoso Rebellion, Origins and Trajectory." In *Power and Popular Protests: Latin American Social Movements,* ed. Susan Eckstein. Berkeley: University of California Press, 1989, 61–101.

McFarlane, Anthony. "Civil Disorders and Popular Protests in Late Colonial New Granada," *Hispanic American Historical Review* 64 (1) (Feb. 1984): 737–65.

Madariaga, Salvador de. *Spain.* New York: Scribner's, 1930.

———. *The Fall of the Spanish American Empire.* Rev. ed. New York: Collier, 1963.

Maingot, A. P. "Colombia." In *The Military in Latin American Socio-Political Evolution: Four Case Studies.* ed. L. N. McAlister. Washington, D.C.: Center for Research in Social Systems, 1970, 127–95.

Mansfield, C., Jr. *Taming the Prince, The Ambivalence of Modern Executive Power.* New York: Free Press, 1989.

Mariñas Otero, Luis. *Las Constituciones de Guatemala.* Madrid: Instituto De Estudios Políticos, 1958.

———. *Las Constituciones de Venezuela.* Madrid: Ediciones Cultura Hispánica, 1965.

Marure, Alejandro. *Bosquejo Histórico de las Revoluciones de Centroamérica, Desde 1811 Hasta 1834.* 2 vols. Guatemala City: Ministerio de Educación Pública, 1960.

Marx, Karl, and Friedrich Engels. *Revolution in Spain.* New York: International Publishers, 1939.

Masterson, Daniel M. *Militarism and Politics in Latin America: Peru from Sánchez Cerro to Sendero Luminoso.* New York: Greenwood, 1991.

Maullin, R. *Soldiers, Guerrillas, and Politics in Colombia.* Lexington, Mass.: Lexington Books, 1973.

Mecham, J. Lloyd. *Church and State in Latin America: A History of Politico-Ecclesiastical Relations.* Chapel Hill: University of North Carolina Press, 1934.

Meinecke, Friedrich. *Machiavellism: The Doctrine of Raison d'Etat and Its Place in Modern History,* Trans. D. Scott. New York: Praeger, 1965.

Mejía, Medardo. *Historia de Honduras.* 6 vols. Tegucigalpa: Editorial Universitaria 1983–1990.

Meyer, Michael C., and William L. Sherman. *The Course of Mexican History.* 2d ed. New York: Oxford University Press, 1983.

Mijares, Augusto. *La Evolución Política de Venezuela, 1810–1960.* Buenos Aires: Editorial Universitaria de Buenos Aires, 1967.

Miller, John C. *Crisis in Freedom: The Alien and Sedition Laws.* Boston, Little Brown, 1951.

Mitre, A. "The Economic and Social Structure of Silver Mining in Nineteenth Century Bolivia." Ph.D. diss., Columbia University, 1977.

Mitre, Bartolomé. *Historia de Belgrano y de la Independencia Argentina.* Buenos Aires: Ediciones Anaconda, 1950.

Molina, Gonzalo. "El Estado de Sitio en Bolivia." In *Estados de Emergencia en la Región Andina,* ed. Diego Garcia-Sayán. Lima: Comisión Andina de Juristas, 1987, 159–81.

Moncayo, Pedro. *El Ecuador de 1825 a 1875. Sus Hombres, Sus Instituciones y Sus Leyes.* Santiago: R. Jover, 1885.

Moneta, C. J., and E. López. *La Reforma Militar.* Buenos Aires: Editorial Legasa, 1985.

Monge Alfaro, Carlos. *Historia de Costa Rica.* 17th ed. San José, C.R.: Librería Trejos, 1982.

Montalvo, Juan. *Las Catilinarias, El Cosmopolita, El Regenerador.* Ed. Benjamín Carrión. Caracas: Biblioteca Ayacucho, 1977.

Moreno Yáñez, Segundo. *Sublevaciones Indígenas en la Audiencia de Quito desde Comienzos del Siglo XVIII hasta Finales de la Colonia.* Quito: Ediciones de la Universidad Católica, 1978.

Morris, James O. *Elites, Intellectuals, and Consensus: A Study of the Social Question and the Industrial Relations System in Chile.* Ithaca: New York State School of Industrial and Labor Relations, 1966.

Moya Pons, Frank. "Haiti and Santo Domingo: 1790–c. 1870." In *The Cambridge History of Latin America,* ed. Leslie Bethell. Cambridge: Cambridge University Press, 1985, 3:237–75.

Muñoz Guillén, Mercedes. *El Estado y la Abolición del Ejército, 1914–1949.* San José, C.R.: Editorial Porvenir, 1990.

Munro, Dana Gardner. *The Latin American Republics: A History.* 3d ed. New York: Appleton-Century Crofts, 1960.

Núñez, Rafael. *La Reforma Política en Colombia,* vol. 1. Bogotá: Editorial Antena, 1945 (essays from 1881–1884).

Nunn, Frederick. *Chilean Politics, 1920–1931: The Honorable Mission of the Armed Forces.* Albuquerque: University of New Mexico Press, 1970.

———. *The Military in Chilean History.* Albuquerque: University of New Mexico Press, 1976.

———. *Yesterday's Soldiers: European Military Professionalism in South America, 1890–1940.* Lincoln: University of Nebraska Press, 1983.

Nwabueze, B. O. *Constitutionalism in the Emergent States.* Rutherford: Fairleigh Dickinson University Press, 1973.

Obregón, Rafael L. *Hechos Militares y Políticos.* Alajuela, C.R.: Museo Histórico Juan Santamaría, 1981.

O'Connor d'Arlach, Tomás. *Dichos y Hechos del General Melgarejo.* La Paz: Ediciones Puerta del Sol, n.d.

Ordenanza Jeneral del Ejército. Santiago: Imprenta de la Opinión, 1840.

Ornes, Germán E. *Trujillo: Little Caesar of the Caribbean.* New York: Nelson, 1958.

Ortega Peña, Rodolfo, and Eduardo L. Duhalde. *Mariscal Francisco Solano López. Pensamiento Político.* Buenos Aires: Editorial Sudestada, 1969.

Osterling, Jorge P. *Democracy in Colombia: Clientelist Politics and Guerrilla Warfare.* New Brunswick: Transaction, 1989.

Ostrom, Vincent. "Cryptoimperialism, Predatory States, and Self-Governance." In *Rethinking Institutional Analysis and Development,* ed. Vincent Ostrom, David Feeny, and Harmut Picht. San Francisco: International Center for Economic Growth, 1988: 43–68.

———. *The Intellectual Crisis in American Public Administration.* 2d ed. Tuscaloosa: University of Alabama Press, 1989.

Ott, T. O. *The Haitian Revolution, 1789–1804.* Knoxville: University of Tennessee Press, 1973.

Otto Pardo, Ignacio de. *Defensa de la Constitución y Partidos Políticos.* Madrid: Centro de Estudios Constitucionales, 1985.

Pagden, Anthony, and Jeremy Lawrance. *Francisco de Vitoria: Political Writings.* Cambridge: Cambridge University Press, 1991.

Palacio, Ernesto. *Historia de la Argentina.* 5th ed. 2 vols. Buenos Aires: A. Pēna Lillo, 1968.

Palacio Atard, Vicente. *La España del Siglo XIX, 1808–1898.* Madrid: ESPASA-CALPE, S.A., 1978.

Pareja Paz-Soldán, José. "Comentarios a la Constitución Nacional." Ph.D. diss., Universidad Católica del Peru, 1939.

———. *Las Constituciones del Perú.* Madrid: Ediciones Cultura Hispánica, 1954.

———. *Derecho Constitucional Peruano.* 4th ed. Lima: Ediciones Libreria Studium, 1966.

Pastor Benítez, Justo. *Carlos Antonio López, Estructuración del Estado Paraguayo.* Buenos Aires, Editorial Ayacucho, 1949.

Pattee, Richard. *García Moreno y el Ecuador de Su Tiempo.* 3d ed. Mexico, D.F.: Editorial Jus, 1962.

———. *La República Dominicana.* Madrid: Ediciones Cultura Hispánica, 1967.

Payne, Stanley G. *Politics and the Military in Modern Spain.* Stanford: Stanford University Press, 1967.

Paz-Soldán, Mariano Felipe. *Historia del Perú Independiente.* 4 vols. Lima: Imprenta El Havre, 1868–1870.

Pegenaute, Pedro. *Represión Política en el Reinado de Fernando VII: Las Comisiones Militares (1824–1825).* Cuadernos de Trabajos de Historia, No. 3 Pamplona: Universidad de Navarra, 1974.

Peguero, Valentina, and Danilo de los Santos. *Visión General de la Historia Dominicana.* Santo Domingo: Universidad Católica Madre y Maestro, 1981.

Peláez, Carlos. *Estado de Derecho y Estado de Sitio.* Bogotá: Editorial Tamís, 1955.

Peña Batlle, Manuel Arturo. *Constitución Política y Reformas Constitucionales, 1844–1942.* 2d ed. 2 vols. Santo Domingo: Publicaciones ONAP, 1981.

Peñagos, Gustavo. *Interpretación y Desarrollo de la Reforma Constitucional. Conferencias de Clase,* Bogotá, 1972.

Peralta, Hernán G. *Las Constituciones de Costa Rica.* Madrid: Instituto de Estudios Políticos, 1962.

Pérez-Brignoli, Héctor. *A Brief History of Central America.* Trans. Ricardo B. Sawrey and Susana Stettri de Sawrey. Berkeley: University of California Press, 1989.

Perry, L. B. "El Modelo Liberal y la Política Práctica en la República Restaurada, 1867–1876." *Historia Mexicana* 23 (1974): 646–94.

Phelan, John Leddy. *The People and the King: The Comunero Revolution in Colombia, 1781.* Madison: University of Wisconsin Press, 1978.

Pike, Frederick. *The Modern History of Peru.* New York: Praeger, 1967.

———. *The Politics of the Miraculous in Peru.* Lincoln: University of Nebraska Press, 1986.

Pivel Devoto, José E. *Historia de los Partidos Políticos.* 2 vols. Montevideo, Garcia & Cia., 1942.

Pombo, Manuel, and José Joaquín Guerra. *Constituciones de Colombia.* 4 vols. Bogotá: Ministerio de Educación Nacional, Biblioteca Popular de Cultura Colombiana, 1951.

Puentes, Milton. *Historia del Partido Liberal Colombiano.* 2d ed. Bogotá: Editorial PRAG, 1961.

Quintana, Linares. "Comparison of United States and Argentine Constitutional Systems." *University of Pennsylvania Latin American Review* 97 (1948–1949): 641–64.

Quiroga, Patricio, and Carlos Maldonado. *El Prusianismo en las Fuerzas Armadas Chilenas.* Santiago: Ediciones Documentas, 1988.

Rabasa, Emilio. *La Constitución y la Dictadura.* 3d ed. Mexico, D.F.: Editorial Porrúa, 1956.

Ralston, David B. *The Army of the Republic: The Place of the Military in the Political Evolution of France, 1871–1914.* Cambridge: MIT Press, 1967.

Rama, Germán W. *La Democracia en Uruguay.* Buenos Aires: Cuadernos de Rial, 1987.

Ramos, Juan P. *El Derecho Público de las Provincias Argentinas.* 3 vols. Buenos Aires, Facultad de Derecho y Ciencias Sociales, Universidad de Buenos Aires, 1914–1916.

Ravignani, Emilio. *Historia Constitucional de la República Argentina.* 3 vols. Buenos Aires: Casa Jacobo Peuser, 1926.

———. *La Participación de Artigas en la Génesis del Federalismo Rioplatense.* Buenos Aires, 1939.

Rebora, Juan C. *El Estado de Sitio y la Ley Histórica del Desborde Institucional.* La Plata: Facultad de Ciencias Jurídicas y Sociales, 1935.

Recopilación de Leyes de los Reynos de las Indias. 3 vols. Madrid: Gráficas Ultra S.A., 1943.

Reglamento Provisional Político del Imperio Mexicano, 1822.

República Oriental del Uruguay, Ministerio del Interior. *Ley de Orden Público. Suspensión de la Seguridad Individual y Estado de Guerra Interna,* Montevideo, 1972.

Reyes, Oscar Efrén. *Breve Historia del Ecuador.* 4th ed. 2 vols. Quito: Editorial Fray Jodocko Ricky, 1950.

Reyes Abadie, Washington. *Crónica General del Uruguay.* 3 vols. Montevideo: Ediciones de la Banda Oriental, n.d.

Rial, Juan. "Los Militares en Tanto 'Partido Politico Sustituto' Frente a la Re-democratización en Uruguay." In *La Autonomía Militar en América Latina,* ed. Augusto Varas. Caracas: Nueva Sociedad, 1988, 197–229.

Rivadeneira Vargas, Antonio José. *Historia Constitucional de Colombia.* Bogotá: Editorial El Voto Nacional, 1962.

Rivas Vicuña, Manuel. *Historia Política y Parlamentaria de Chile.* 3 vols. Santiago: Ediciones de la Biblioteca Nacional, 1964.

Robalino Dávila, Luis. *Orígenes del Ecuador de Hoy,* vol. 1. Quito: Editorial Casa de la Cultura Ecuatoriana, 1966.

Robertson, William Spence. *The Rise of the Spanish-American Republics: As Told in the Lives of Their Liberators.* New York: Appleton, 1918.

———. *France and Latin American Independence.* New York: Octagon, 1967.

Rock, David. *Argentina, 1516–1987.* Berkeley: University of California Press, 1987.

Rodman, Selden. *Quisqueya: A History of the Dominican Republic.* Seattle: University of Washington Press, 1964.

Rodríguez, Jaime. *The Emergence of Spanish America: Vicente Rocafuerte and Spanish Americanism, 1808–1832.* Berkeley: University of California Press, 1975.

Rodríguez, Laura. "The Spanish Riots of 1766." *Past and Present* 59 (May 1973): 117–46.

Rodríguez, Linda. *Ecuador 1830–1940: The Search for Public Policy.* Los Angeles: University of California Press, 1985.

Rodríguez, Mario. *The Cádiz Experiment in Central America, 1808–1826.* Berkeley: University of California Press, 1978.

Roldán, Alcibiades. *Elementos de Derecho Constitucional de Chile.* 2d ed., rev. Santiago-Valparaíso: Imprenta-Litografía Barcelona, 1917.

Romero, José Luis. *A History of Argentine Political Thought.* Stanford: Stanford University Press, 1963.

Romero, Luis Alberto. *Los Golpes Militares, 1812–1955.* Buenos Aires: Carlos Pérez, Editor S.A., 1969.

Romero Carranza, Ambrosio, Alberto Rodríguez Varela, and Eduardo Ventura Flores Pirán. *Historia Política de la Argentina.* 3 vols. Buenos Aires: Ediciones Pannedille, 1975.

Roquie, Alan. *El Estado Militar en América Latina.* Mexico: Siglo XXI, 1984.

Rossiter, Clinton L. *Constitutional Dictatorship: Crisis Government in the Modern Democracies.* Princeton: Princeton University Press, 1948.

Rousseau, J. J. *The Social Contract.* New York: Dutton, 1935.

Rudé, George. *The Crowd in History.* New York: John Wiley and Sons, 1964.

Ruhl, J. Mark. *Colombia: Armed Forces and Society.* Syracuse: Maxwell School of Citizenship and Public Affairs, Syracuse University, 1980.

Sáenz Carbonell, Jorge. *El Despertar Constitucional de Costa Rica.* San José, C.R.: Libro Libre, 1985.

Safford, Frank. "Politics, Ideology, and Society in Post-Independence Spanish America." In *The Cambridge History of Latin America,* ed. Leslie Bethell. Cambridge: Cambridge University Press, 1985, 3:347–421.

———. "The Problem of Political Order in Early Republican Spanish America." *Journal of Latin American Studies* 24, quincentenary supplement (1992): 83–97.

Salcedo-Bastardo, J. L. *Historia Fundamental de Venezuela.* 9th ed., rev. Caracas: Universidad Central de Venezuela, 1982.

Sampay, Arturo E. *Las Constituciones de la Argentina (1810/1972).* 2 vols. Buenos Aires: Editorial Universitaria de Bueno Aires, 1975.

Sánchez Agesta, Luis. *Historia del Constitucionalismo Español.* 2d ed., Madrid: Centro de Estudios Constitucionales, 1964.

Sánchez Viamonte, Carlos. *Ley Marcial y Estado de Sitio en el Derecho Argentino.* Buenos Aires: Ed. Perrot, 1957.

Sanín Greiffenstein, Jaime. *La Defensa Judicial de la Constitución.* Bototá: Editorial Temis, 1971.

Sanz Cid, Carlos. *La Constitución de Bayona.* Madrid, 1922.

Schmitt, Carl. *Political Theology: Four Chapters on the Concept of Sovereignty.* Trans. George Schwab. Cambridge: MIT Press, 1985.

Schodt, David W. *Ecuador: An Andean Enigma.* Boulder: Westview, 1987.

Scholes, Walter W. *Mexican Politics During the Juárez Regime, 1855–1872.* Columbia: University of Missouri Press, 1957.

Scobie, James R. *La Lucha por la Consolidación de la Nacionalidad Argentina, 1852–1862.* Buenos Aires: Hachette, 1964.

———. *Argentina: A City and a Nation.* 2d ed. New York: Oxford University Press, 1974.

Secretaría Jurídica de la Presidencia. *Historia de la Reforma Constitucional de 1968.* Bogotá: Imprenta Nacional, 1968.

Sharpe, R. J. *The Law of Habeas Corpus.* Oxford: Oxford University Press, 1976.
Shumway, Nicolas. *The Invention of Argentina.* Berkeley: University of California Press, 1991.
Sierra, Justo. *Juárez. Su Obra y Su Tiempo.* Mexico, D.F.: Universidad Autónoma de México, 1948.
Sigmund, Paul, ed. *Models of Political Change in Latin America.* New York: Praeger, 1970.
Silva Herzog, Jesús. *El Pensamiento Económico, Social, y Político de México, 1810–1964.* Mexico, D.F.: Fondo de Cultura Económica, 1967.
Simpson, Lesley Byrd. *Many Mexicos.* Berkeley: University of California Press, 1964.
Sinkin, Richard. "The Mexican Constitutional Congress, 1856–1857, A Statistical Analysis." *Hispanic American Historical Review* 53, no. 1 (Feb. 1973): 1–26.
———. *The Mexican Reform, 1855–1876: A Study in Liberal Nation Building.* Austin, Tex: Institute of Latin American Studies, 1979.
Siso Martínez, J. M. *Historia de Venezuela.* 9th ed. Venezuela: Editorial Yocoima, 1967.
Slatta, Richard, ed. *Bandidos: The Varieties of Latin American Banditry.* New York: Greenwood, 1987.
Smith, James Morton. *Freedom's Fetters: The Alien and Sedition Laws and American Civil Liberties.* Ithaca: Cornell University Press, 1956.
Smith, R. March. *Spain: A Modern History.* Ann Arbor: University of Michigan Press, 1965.
Snyder, Frederick E. "State of Siege and Rule of Law in Argentina: The Politics and Rhetoric of Vindication." *Lawyer of the Americas* 15, no. 3 (1984): 503–20.
Solnick, Bruce B. *The West Indies and Central America to 1898.* New York: Knopf, 1970.
Sowell, David. "The 1893 *bogotazo:* Artisans and Public Violence in Late Nineteenth-Century Bogotá." *Journal of Latin American Studies* 21, pt. 2 (May 1989): 267–82.
Spindler, Frank Macdonald. "The Political Thought of Juan Montalvo." Ph.D. diss., American University, 1966.
———. *Nineteenth Century Ecuador: An Historical Introduction.* Fairfax: George Mason University Press, 1987.
Stein, Stanley J., and Barbara H. Stein. *The Colonial Heritage of Latin America.* New York: Oxford University Press, 1970.
Stepan, Alfred. *Rethinking Military Politics: Brazil and the Southern Cone.* Princeton: Princeton University Press, 1988.
Stevens, Donald F. *Origins of Instability in Early Republican Mexico.* Durham: Duke University Press, 1991.
Stoan, Stephen K. *Pablo Morillo and Venezuela, 1815–1820.* Columbus: Ohio State University Press, 1974.
Stokes, William S. *Honduras.* Madison: University of Wisconsin Press, 1950.
———. *Latin American Politics.* New York: Crowell, 1959.

Street, John. *Artigas and the Emancipation of Uruguay.* Cambridge: Cambridge University Press, 1959.

Tau Anzoátegui, Víctor. "Las Facultades Extraordinarias y la Suma del Poder Público en el Derecho Provincial Argentino (1820–1853)." *Revista del Instituto de Historia de Derecho* 12 (1961): 66–105.

Tauro, Alberto, ed. *Ramon Castilla, Ideología.* Lima: Ediciones Hora del Hombre, 1948.

Taylor, Lewis. *Bandits and Politics in Peru: Landlord and Peasant Violence in Hualgayoc, 1870–1900.* Cambridge: Cambridge University Press, 1986.

Taylor, Paul. *Socialism, Liberalism, and Dictatorship in Paraguay.* New York: Praeger, 1982.

Taylor, William B. *Drinking, Homicide, and Rebellion in Colonial Mexican Villages.* Stanford: Stanford University Press, 1979.

Tena Ramírez, Felipe. *Leyes Fundamentales de México (1808–1983).* 12th ed. Mexico, D.F.: Editorial Porrúa, S. A., 1983.

Tilly, Charles. *Coercion, Capital, and European States, AD 990–1990.* Cambridge, Mass.: Blackwell, 1990.

Tilly, Charles, Louise Tilly, and Richard Tilly. *The Rebellious Century, 1830–1930.* Cambridge: Harvard University Press, 1975.

Tobar Donoso, Julio. *La Iglesia Ecuatoriana en el Siglo XIX.* Quito: Editorial Ecuatoriana, 1934.

Tocqueville, Alexis de. *Democracy in America,* vol. 1. Ed. Philip Bradley. New York: Knopf, 1945.

Trigo, Ciro Félix. *Las Constituciones de Bolivia.* Madrid: Instituto de Estudios Políticos, 1958.

———. *Constitución de la Nación Argentina.* Buenos Aires: Ediciones DePalma, 1971.

Tuñón de Lara, Manuel. *La España del Siglo XIX (1808–1914).* Paris: Librería Española, 1971.

Universidad Nacional Autónoma de Honduras. *Recopilación de las Constituciones de Honduras (1825–1965).* Tegucigalpa, 1977.

Uruguay. *Actas de la Asamblea General Constituyente y Legislativa del Estado.* 3 vols. Montevideo, 1896.

Uruguay. *Actas de la H. Cámara de Representantes.* 6 vols. Montevideo, 1905–1908.

Valadés, Diego. *La Dictadura Constitucional en América Latina.* Mexico: Instituto de Investigaciones Jurídicas, UNAM, 1974.

Valcárcel, Carlos Daniel. *Túpac Amaru. Precursor de la Independencia.* Lima: Universidad Nacional Mayor de San Marcos, 1977.

Valdivieso Ariztia, Rafael. *Crónica de un Rescate (Chile 1973–1988).* Santiago: Editorial Andrés Bello, 1988.

Valencia Avaria, Luis. *Anales de la República.* 2 vols. Santiago: Editorial Andrés Bello, 1986.

Valle-Riestra, Javier. *La Responsabilidad Constitucional del Jefe de Estado.* Lima: Benítez-Rivas and Montejo, 1987.

Van Aken, Mark J. *Pan-Hispanism.* Berkeley: University of California Press, 1959.

———. *King of the Night: Juan José Flores and Ecuador, 1824–1864.* Berkeley: University of California Press, 1989.

Vanderwood, Paul. "Genesis of the Rurales, Mexico's Early Struggle for Public Security." *Hispanic American Historical Review* 50, no. 2 (May 1970): 323–44.

———. *Disorder and Progress: Bandits, Police and Mexican Development.* Lincoln: University of Nebraska Press, 1981.

Vanger, Milton I. *The Model Country: José Batlle y Ordóñez of Uruguay, 1907–1915.* Hanover: University Press of New England, 1980.

Vanossi, J. R. *La Influencia de la Constitución de los Estados Unidos de Norteamérica en la Constitución de la República Argentina.* 1976.

Van Young, Eric. *Hacienda and Market in Eighteenth-Century Mexico.* Berkeley: University of California Press, 1981.

Varas, Augusto, ed. *La Autonomía Militar en America Latina.* Caracas: Nueva Sociedad, 1988.

Verduin, R., ed. and trans. *Manual of Spanish Constitutions, 1808–1931.* Ypsilanti, Mich.: University Lithoprinters, 1941.

Vial Correa, Gonzalo. *Historia de Chile, 1891–1973.* 4 vols. Santiago: Santillana, 1981–1988.

Vicuña Mackenna, Benjamín. *Historia de los Diez Años de la Administración Montt.* Santiago, Imprenta Chilena, 1862.

Villanueva, Carlos A. *Fernando VII y los Nuevos Estados.* Paris, 1912.

Walker, Charles. "Montoneros, Bandoleros, Malhechores, Criminalidad y Política en las Primeras Décadas Republicanas." In *Bandoleros, Abigeos y Montoneros, Criminalidad, y Violencia en el Peru, Siglos XVIII–XX,* ed. Carlos Aguirre and Charles Walker. Lima: Instituto de Apoyo Agrario, 1990: 105–36.

Walker, William. *The War in Nicaragua.* New York: Goetzel, 1860.

Warren, Harris Gaylord. *Rebirth of the Paraguayan Republic: The First Colorado Era, 1878–1904.* Pittsburgh: University of Pittsburgh Press, 1985.

Watkins, Frederick M. *The Failure of Constitutional Emergency Powers Under the German Republic.* Cambridge: Harvard University Press, 1939.

———. "The Problem of Constitutional Dictatorship." *Public Policy* 1 (1940): 324–79.

Welles, Sumner. *Naboth's Vineyard: The Dominican Republic, 1844–1924.* 2 vols. New York: Payson and Clark, 1928.

Whitaker, Arthur P., ed. *Latin America and the Enlightenment.* 2d ed. Ithaca, N.Y.: Great Seal Books, 1961.

White, Richard Alan. *Paraguay's Autonomous Revolution, 1810–1840.* Albuquerque: University of New Mexico Press, 1978.

Whittam, John. *The Politics of the Italian Army, 1861–1918.* London: Croom Helm, 1977.

Wiarda, Howard. *The Dominican Republic.* New York: Praeger, 1969.

Wilgus, Curtis A., ed. *South American Dictators During the First Century of Independence.* New York: Russell and Russell, 1963.

Williams, John Hoyt. *The Rise and Fall of the Paraguayan Republic.* Austin, Tex.: Institute of Latin American Studies, 1979.

Woodward, Margaret L. "The Spanish Army and the Loss of America, 1810–1824." *Hispanic American Historical Review* 48 no. 4 (Nov. 1968): 586–606.

Woodward, Ralph L., Jr. *Central America: A Nation Divided.* 2d ed. New York: Oxford University Press, 1985.

————. "Central America from Independence to c. 1870." In *The Cambridge History of Latin America,* ed. Leslie Bethell. Cambridge: Cambridge University Press, 1985, 3:471–506.

Wortman, Miles. *Government and Society in Central America, 1680–1840.* New York: Columbia University Press, 1982.

Zondag, Cornelius H. "Bolivia's 1952 Revolution, Initial Impact and U.S. Involvement." In *Modern Day Bolivia: Legacy of the Revolution and Prospects for the Future,* ed. Jerry R. Ladman. Tempe, Ariz.: Center for Latin American Studies, 1982, 27–40.

Zorraquín Becu, Ricardo. *El Federalismo Argentino.* 2d ed. Buenos Aires: La Facultad, 1953.

Zum Felde, Alberto. *Proceso Histórico del Uruguay.* 5th ed. Montevideo: Arca, 1967.

Zuniga San Martín, Ana María. *Legislación Sobre Seguridad del Estado, Control de Armas y Terrorismo.* Santiago: Editorial Jurídica de Chile, 1985.

Index

Pitt Latin American Series

James M. Malloy, Editor

ARGENTINA

Argentina Between the Great Powers, 1936–1946
Guido di Tella and D. Cameron Watt, Editors

Argentina in the Twentieth Century
David Rock, Editor

Argentina: Political Culture and Instability
Susan Calvert and Peter Calvert

Argentine Workers: Peronism and Contemporary Class
Consciousness
Peter Ranis

Discreet Partners: Argentina and the USSR Since 1917
Aldo César Vacs

The Franco-Perón Alliance: Relations Between Spain and
Argentina, 1946–1955
Raanan Rein

The Life, Music, and Times of Carlos Gardel
Simon Collier

Institutions, Parties, and Coalitions in Argentine Politics
Luigi Manzetti

The Political Economy of Argentina, 1946–1983
Guido di Tella and Rudiger Dornbusch, Editors

BRAZIL

Capital Markets in the Development Process: The Case of Brazil
John H. Welch

External Constraints on Economic Policy in Brazil, 1899–1930
Winston Fritsch

The Film Industry in Brazil: Culture and the State
Randal Johnson

Kingdoms Come: Religion and Politics in Brazil
Rowan Ireland

The Manipulation of Consent: The State and Working-Class
Consciousness in Brazil
Youssef Cohen

The Politics of Social Security in Brazil
James M. Malloy

Politics Within the State: Elite Bureaucrats and Industrial Policy in Authoritarian Brazil
Ben Ross Schneider

Unequal Giants: Diplomatic Relations Between the United States and Brazil, 1889–1930
Joseph Smith

COLOMBIA
Economic Management and Economic Development in Peru and Colombia
Rosemary Thorp

Gaitán of Colombia: A Political Biography
Richard E. Sharpless

Roads to Reason: Transportation, Administration, and Rationality in Colombia
Richard E. Hartwig

CUBA
Cuba After the Cold War
Carmelo Mesa-Lago, Editor

Cuba Between Empires, 1878–1902
Louis A. Pérez, Jr.

Cuba Under the Platt Amendment, 1902–1934
Louis A. Pérez, Jr.

Cuban Studies, Vols. 16–21
Carmelo Mesa-Lago, Louis A. Pérez, Jr., Editors

Cuban Studies, Vol. 22
Jorge I. Domínguez, Editor

Cuban Studies, Vol. 23
Jorge Peréz-López, Editor

The Economics of Cuban Sugar
Jorge F. Pérez-López

Intervention, Revolution, and Politics in Cuba, 1913–1921
Louis A. Pérez, Jr.

Lords of the Mountain: Social Banditry and Peasant Protest in Cuba, 1878–1918
Louis A. Pérez, Jr.

MEXICO
The Expulsion of Mexico's Spaniards, 1821–1836
Harold Dana Sims

The Mexican Republic: The First Decade, 1823–1832
Stanley C. Green

Mexico Through Russian Eyes, 1806–1940
William Harrison Richardson

Oil and Mexican Foreign Policy
George W. Grayson

The Politics of Mexican Oil
George W. Grayson

Voices, Visions, and a New Reality: Mexican Fiction Since 1970

J. Ann Duncan

PERU
Domestic and Foreign Finance in Modern Peru, 1850–1950: Financing Visions of Development
Alfonso W. Quiroz

Economic Management and Economic Development in Peru and Colombia
Rosemary Throp

The Origins of the Peruvian Labor Movement, 1883–1919
Peter Blanchard

Peru and the International Monetary Fund
Thomas Scheetz

Peru Under García: An Opportunity Lost
John Crabtree

CARIBBEAN
The Last Cacique: Leadership and Politics in a Puerto Rican City
Jorge Heine

A Revolution Aborted: The Lessons of Grenada
Jorge Heine, Editor

To Hell with Paradise: A History of the Jamaican Tourist Industry
Frank Fonda Taylor

The Meaning of Freedom: Economics, Politics and Culture After Slavery
Frank McGlynn and Seymour Drescher, Editors

CENTRAL AMERICA
At the Fall of Somoza
Lawrence Pezzullo and Ralph Pezzullo

Mexico Through Russian Eyes, 1806–1940
William Harrison Richardson

SOCIAL SECURITY

Ascent to Bankruptcy: Financing Social Security in Latin America
Carmelo Mesa-Lago

The Politics of Social Security in Brazil
James M. Malloy

OTHER STUDIES

Adventurers and Proletarians: The Story of Migrants in Latin America
Magnus Mörner, with the collaboration of Harold Sims

Authoritarianism and Corporatism in Latin America
James M. Malloy, Editor

Authoritarians and Democrats: Regime Transition in Latin America
James M. Malloy and Mitchell A. Seligson, Editors

The Catholic Church and Politics in Nicaragua and Costa Rica
Philip J. Williams

Chile: The Political Economy of Development and Democracy in the
1990s
David E. Hojman

The Constitution of Tyranny: Regimes of Exception in Spanish
America
Brian Loveman

Female and Male in Latin America: Essays
Ann Pescatello, Editor

Latin American Debt and the Adjustment Crisis
Rosemary Thorp and Laurence Whitehead, Editors

Public Policy in Latin America: A Comparative Survey
John W. Sloan

Selected Latin American One-Act Plays
Francesca Colecchia and Julio Matas, Editors and Translators

The Social Documentary in Latin America
Julianne Burton, Editor

The State and Capital Accumulation in Latin America. Vol. 1: Brazil,
Chile, Mexico. Vol. 2: Argentina, Bolivia, Colombia, Ecuador, Peru,
Uruguay, Venezuela
Christian Anglade and Carlos Fortin, Editors

Transnational Corporations and the Latin American Automobile
Industry
Rhys Jenkins